"In the United States at any one time, there are tens of thousands of police chiefs, and hundreds of thousands have served since American police departments were created. Among them all, the seven chiefs, plus the two scholars, featured in this book, individually and collectively, have had an outsized influence on what American policing is today. August Vollmer personally influenced O.W. Wilson, who personally influenced Herman Goldstein, who personally influenced George Kelling, who personally influenced Bill Bratton. I can attest to this intellectual inheritance because I, too, was personally influenced by Goldstein, and thus my own work as a police chief was, in attenuated but real ways, influenced by all these remarkable chiefs and scholars who preceded me and my contemporaries. For all who are interested in how our society is policed, their stories are very much worth knowing."

Michael S. Scott, *Clinical Professor and Director, Center for Problem-Oriented Policing, Arizona State University*

"Professor Kooi uses the biographies of seven past and present police leaders to weave his way through the history of American policing and many of the key issues we continue to face today. His magnificent seven might or might not be the greatest police chiefs of all time (that can be debated, endlessly), but their lives and accomplishments deserve to be known far and wide."

Gary Cordner, *Former Commissioner of CALEA (Commission on Accreditation for Law Enforcement Agencies), Professor Emeritus, Kutztown University of Pennsylvania and Eastern Kentucky University, Past President Academy of Criminal Justice Sciences (ACJS)*

About the Cover

The book cover is symbolic of opening leadership remarks from Philadelphia Police Commissioner Charles Ramsey at the 2013 IACP Conference at the Philadelphia Convention Center. Ramsey concluded his remarks by challenging the metaphor of the "Thin Blue Line" on the police flag that represents separating good citizens from dangerous criminals. Ramsey stated: "The Problem with being a line is that you're separate and apart from those two things. You're really not a part of either side. I like to think – and as I've gotten older and more mature in this job, I've come to see – a more accurate metaphor, in my opinion. It is one in which we are seen as a thread woven through the communities we serve – a thread which helps hold those communities together, creating a tapestry that reinforces the very fabric of democracy.

Seven Highly Effective Police Leaders

This book provides a valuable addition to the policing literature by detailing the backgrounds and histories of seven important police leaders: Teddy Roosevelt, August Vollmer, O.W. Wilson, Penny Harrington, Bill Bratton, Chuck Ramsey, and Chris Magnus.

Seven Highly Effective Police Leaders teaches important history, highlighting the impact on the evolution of American policing by academia and social science. Each historical biography demonstrates the importance of each leader's decision-making and how it continues to shape the future of U.S. law enforcement. Readers are informed about each police leader's background and how their leadership was shaped by the political and historical environments in which they led.

The book is useful for educational courses in policing, American history, leadership, and strategic planning. Additionally, the general public will find this book insightful regarding contemporary mass social justice protests linked to the unique history of the United States.

Brandon Kooi, Ph.D., is a professor in the Criminal Justice program at Aurora University in Aurora, Illinois. He received his Ph.D. degree from the School of Criminal Justice at Michigan State University in 2004. Before his academic career, Dr. Kooi was a private security consultant/executive, criminal investigator, law clerk, and youth crisis interventionist. He assisted in training police administrators through the Center for Problem-Oriented Policing and the Wisconsin-based Problem-Oriented Leadership Institute for Chief Executives (POLICE). Dr. Kooi's consulting work included the Aurora, Illinois Police Department's anti-gang initiative (*Finding Typhoid Mary*) and Sheboygan, Wisconsin Police Department's community policing (*Neighbors Against Drugs*) unit. Both initiatives were finalists for the Herman Goldstein Award at the Center for Problem-Oriented Policing international conferences. Dr. Kooi also presented his research at the Stockholm Criminology Symposium in 2018.

Seven Highly Effective Police Leaders

1895–Modern Times

Brandon Kooi

Routledge
Taylor & Francis Group
NEW YORK AND LONDON

First published 2022
by Routledge
605 Third Avenue, New York, NY 10158

and by Routledge
2 Park Square, Milton Park, Abingdon, Oxon OX14 4RN

Routledge is an imprint of the Taylor & Francis Group, an informa business

Library of Congress Cataloging-in-Publication Data
Names: Kooi, Brandon R., 1973– author.
Title: Seven highly effective police leaders : 1895–modern times / Brandon Kooi.
Description: 1 Edition. | New York: Routledge, 2021. |
Includes bibliographical references and index.
Identifiers: LCCN 2021013098 (print) | LCCN 2021013099 (ebook) |
ISBN 9781498768924 (hardback) | ISBN 9781032003788 (paperback) |
ISBN 9780429272226 (ebook)
Subjects: LCSH: Police chiefs–United States. |
Police administration–United States. | Police–United States–History.
Classification: LCC HV8141 .K66 2021 (print) |
LCC HV8141 (ebook) | DDC 363.2/20973–dc23
LC record available at https://lccn.loc.gov/2021013098
LC ebook record available at https://lccn.loc.gov/2021013099

ISBN: 978-1-4987-6892-4 (hbk)
ISBN: 978-1-03-200378-8 (pbk)
ISBN: 978-0-429-27222-6 (ebk)

DOI: 10.4324/9780429272226

Typeset in Bembo
by Newgen Publishing UK

Contents

Acknowledgments

Research for the *Seven Highly Effective Police Chiefs* began in earnest five years ago, during a time of enormous transformation for the world of policing and for myself. Personally, the parallels are noteworthy, and I hope the final product will be helpful and perhaps uplifting for the reader. During the past five years, policing in America has been challenged to historical depths. That history continues to shackle how we relate to the communities we are entrusted to serve.

In reflecting on these sentences, the reader may ask, was the author a police officer? The answer is no, but I continue to utilize the term "we" in hopes that "we" can successfully move policing into an era of improved legitimacy and one that better reflects our democratic principles. I continue to draw upon the inspiration of many police leaders and academic scholars who have inspired my thirst for improving the incredible responsibility of policing our beloved country. I recognize that credibility is frequently lost among police officers when the word "we" is used by those who lack personal experience of being a sworn officer. I apologize to those I may offend with the accumulation of research throughout this book. I trust that the proceeding chapters will add some knowledge through the historical lessons that inspire future police leaders and the need for collaborative governing and policing our democracy outside of political partisanship.

The vast majority of officers across the country courageously perform exemplary services and are disheartened by the events that have transpired in the aftermath of George Floyd's death in Minneapolis on May 25, 2020, and January 6, 2021 attack on our nation's Capitol. The public is disheartened and often confused about the destructive acts that evolved out of peaceful protests. I am thankful for the opportunity to clarify the confusion in hopes that readers may understand the depth of our history in policing America and the type of inclusive strategic planning that we must forge to address the root causes of the unrest.

I have been fortunate to teach criminal justice classes for the past two decades and earned my Ph.D. degree from the School of Criminal Justice at Michigan State University in 2004. It is ironic that two of the chiefs, Penny Harrington and Chris Magnus, who made the final seven grew up in Lansing, Michigan, and earned degrees from MSU. These individuals are also, deservingly, part of the MSU School of Criminal Justice Hall of Fame. I did not know their backgrounds before they were selected. I am thankful for the academic support I received at MSU from various professors and graduate school colleagues, many of whom I consider close friends so many years later. I also want to thank several criminal justice faculty from Illinois State University who long since retired. I worked for Professor Frank Morn as a graduate student. His research on the history of criminal justice academia appears throughout this book, which influenced my passion for history 25 years later. I am thankful for his review of this book.

My educational background has led to various opportunities to work with police agencies and help solve multiple problems that frequently overwhelm their service calls. This type of applied research is why the Center for Problem-Oriented Policing exists, as detailed in the appendix to the chapter on O.W. Wilson. I have been fortunate to work with the Center for Problem-Oriented Policing since 2006 and befriend the visionaries – Herman Goldstein and Mike Scott. Mike continued to be my friendly editor and correct my many errors. I am eternally indebted to the lessons of everyone who contributes to the Center for Problem-Oriented Policing and allowing my education to continue well beyond the classroom.

Ultimately, this book's inspiration came in the aftermath of the 2015 protests following the fatal shooting of Michael Brown. In full disclosure, my personal life was also in shambles during this time, and this book publication was delayed not months but years as a consequence. I am fortunate for all of these events because of the critical lessons and the growth of gratitude. Reflecting on the events of 2020, nationally and personally, makes the book delay that much more worthwhile. My family changed dramatically during this time, and I want to thank those who have been so enormously patient for the effort I put into this endeavor. Thank you, Jennifer, Taylor, Jacob, and Brooklyn, for all the love, support, and energy you have brought to our bonus family. Thank you to my children Drew, Ella, and CarliAnn, for continuing to educate and inspire my worthiness as your father. You are all a gift from God, and I am beyond blessed for all that you continue to do to make me so proud of who you are today and who you are destined to become.

Thank you to my mom, and my brother Jami, for raising me with the type of self-assurance necessary to survive life's obstacles. Thank you to my niece Brittany for setting such a great example for all of us. It was a pleasure to also have you as an AU student. Thank you to my nephew Elliott for your service in the United States Marine Corps.

Thank you to my third and fifth grade teacher, Mary Moreno, whom I also acknowledge in my Ph.D. dissertation. The notes you sent home challenging my academic laziness and subsequent high expectations provided the roots for the work that follows. Thank you also to Pastor Jennifer Wilson for your inspiration, curiosity in my career, and desire to know each of our family members. You continue to be a blessing to each one of us. Your ability to quickly see through people and touch their souls is an inspirational gift I wish upon anyone fortunate to be in public service.

I would also like to thank my colleagues and students at Aurora University for the constant encouragement and questioning if the book is ready. I am thankful for English writing specialist Dr. Anthony DiSanto for providing editing assistance and President Rebecca Sherrick and Vice President of Academic Affairs Frank Buscher for the sabbatical support needed for the time and energy to complete this work. Thank you to our criminal justice program's past chair and retired Naperville, Illinois police chief David Dial for your encouragement and interest in police history. All good things must come to an end, and I hope the work that follows meets the expectations so many held for this endeavor.

Getting to the top seven historic police leaders is not an easy task, and many worthy leaders' exclusion was inevitable. With that said, I am eternally grateful for the police leaders selected for this book – Teddy Roosevelt, Gus Vollmer, O.W. Wilson, Bill Bratton, Penny Harrington, Chuck Ramsey, Chris Magnus. Each made their departments and communities better due to their presence, and their impact lasts well beyond their absence.

I want to thank the surviving police leaders that spent time correcting my errors and telling me their story. Their trust in me to tell their story and allow my interpretation is humbling and noteworthy. Their feedback was especially appreciated, given the amateur writing abilities of the given author. In particular, I want to thank the Roosevelt family for allowing me to write about the early police reform efforts of Teddy Roosevelt in the New York City.

Additional appreciation goes to Professor Will Oliver for his feedback on Berkeley's Chief August Vollmer. O.W. Wilson is a protégé to Vollmer, and I extend my gratitude to his family for allowing me to tell his story.

Additionally, I dedicated the appendix to the chapter on Wilson to the life of Herman Goldstein. A couple of months before passing away in January 2020, Herman Goldstein provided feedback to this book. In truth, Herman was the main reason I wanted to write this book, and I am not only a better academic because of his inspiration but also a better father because of his kindness and words of wisdom. Anyone fortunate to be in the company of Herman knows what is meant by the appreciation one expresses for being in the presence of this humble, gracious, and titan of policing intellect. Thank you for being the inspiration, Herman, and I know Heaven is a more organized place with your spiritual presence.

Chief Penny Harrington has become an honored friend who spent countless phone calls, emails, and zoom sessions answering my questions and jumped in to help guest lecture my classes and meet several university students via zoom. Her presence was the one, and perhaps only, useful aspects of teaching through the pandemic. Penny also shared several stories about her personal life and made a concerted effort to mail photos to the author for inclusion in the book. Her attorney, Richard Botteri, was also very gracious with his time and had a keen eye for proofreading the given chapter and providing historical accuracy for the given time of Chief Harrington's leadership in Portland.

Commissioner Bill Bratton provided lengthy phone calls with the author. He went through the chapter written about his career line-by-line correcting many errors while allowing me the academic freedom to interpret the given history. It is humbling to now share the occasional text messages with Bill. Thank you also to Professor David Kennedy from John Jay College for providing the contact and introduction with Commissioner Bratton. The appendix to the chapter on Bratton includes a discussion of the academic career of George Kelling. Enormous appreciation goes to George's wife, Catherine Coles, who provided feedback and input on her beloved and late husband. Thank you, Catherine, for your gracious input.

Commissioner Chuck Ramsey was incredibly considerate in doing a lengthy zoom interview with the author, addressing countless email questions, and sharing personal photos from his stellar career. Appreciation also goes to Assistant Professor and Director of the Institute of Crime Science Cory Haberman at the University of Cincinnati for his friendship and input on Commissioner Ramsey during his leadership with the Philadelphia Police Department (PPD). Dr. Haberman's dissertation from Temple University focused on assessing the PPD strategies in hot spot locations.

Lastly, Chief Chris Magnus showed that he is not only an extremely conscientious reform-leader, but also a prolific writer and provided a lot of detail and corrections through a series of written responses. Undoubtedly, errors remain, and the fault rests with the author. I thank each reader for spending the time to analyze the seven police leaders and the history of the communities they were fortunate to serve. That history should never be forgotten and necessitates the constant challenges of leading through political controversy and varying beliefs of the expectations and needs for policing in a democratic society.

Introduction

Understanding what makes a good leader is one of the most critical topics facing American policing today. However, the populous is more likely to admire celebrities from pop culture, athletic competitions, politicians, highly paid corporate executives, or military commanders. Seldom do we read about police leaders, even though their occupation offers the face of a democratic nation and the type of government that citizens are most likely to have some daily interaction or negative encounter. The importance of "getting this right" became apparent to the world in 2020 amid a pandemic and mass social justice protests directed primarily at perceptions of biased policing.

The men and women who have led, or are leading, our nation's police departments frequently become the center of conversation related to the flaws within our criminal justice system. Indeed, their leadership with the community is essential to provide perceived justice throughout the streets of America. Police officers operate as street-level bureaucrats, and for most Americans, they are the only forms of government they will meet. Police administrators represent symbols of promise and failure about how our government serves its citizens. As one of the most visible aspects of the government-citizen encounter, the police represent potent institutions that can significantly impact the public's lives. The significance of the police impact involves agencies and officers in rural, suburban, and urban environments. Moreover, the challenges for police leadership in the modern era require a skill set and emotional intelligence level that frequently conflicts with the traditional focus of law enforcement academies or in-service training that symbolizes their power. The next generation of police leaders, especially in light of the 2020 mass police protests, will increasingly be expected to bring reform leadership to their communities that do not currently exist within traditional police training or the quasi-militaristic warrior culture.

Challenges in policing America in a post-pandemic era will continue to be among the most critical issues facing our nation. The public expects police leaders to prevent disorder and also effectively solve crime. They also hope that police resources allocated toward criminal offending do not create additional injustices and tragedies such as misuse of force, racial profiling, and questionable shootings. The conflict between enforcing laws and protecting Constitutional rights within our long history of racial tension is at the heart of our national discourse. The historical and modern challenges often create a "short shelf life" for police leaders when they face pressure from police unions, community leaders, or other political entities. Government leaders frequently scapegoat police leaders through the media and their community. When controversy arises, elected officials are, hypothetically, voted out of office. However, they can remedy their political situations by asking their local police leader to resign. Historically, these resignations are frequent and found in each of the seven police leaders discussed in this book. The multitude of police leaders who sought early resignation throughout 2020 amid mass social justice protests represents contemporary political scapegoating.

DOI: 10.4324/9780429272226-1

Seven Highly Effective Police Chiefs creates a list of historical police leaders who avoided becoming political scapegoats, for the most part. They have been able to increase their shelf life long enough to be considered somewhat effective and relevant within their profession. They were successful because of their leadership styles and their persistent focus on challenging existing police subcultures with alternative models that frequently pushed for improvement in collaboration, transparency, and proactively solving problems instead of waiting and reacting to crime.

Within each police leader's biographical sketches, a history of the communities they served informs the reader about the challenges they faced. These historical lessons are critical for understanding the modern struggle. The seven leaders were not successful because of easy problems to solve. Their success came from being asked to lead their department and community out of significant conflict and government dysfunction. When this dysfunction continues without adequate reform, tension builds and eventually erupts, as seen throughout the pandemic of 2020 and at the end of the Trump presidency amid the Capitol insurrection.

Each of the seven leaders discussed provides historical lessons linked to contemporary challenges. Below are sporadic comments that stem from the unique leadership of each individual.

1. Theodore "Teddy" Roosevelt: *Our experience with the police department taught one or two lessons that are applicable to the whole question of municipal reform. Very many men put their faith in some special device, some special bit of legislation or some official scheme for getting good government. In reality, good government can come only through good administration, and good administration only as a consequence of a sustained not spasmodic and earnest effort by good citizens to secure honesty, courage, and common sense among civic administrators. If they demand the impossible, they will fail; and, on the other hand, if they do not demand a good deal, they will get nothing. But though they should demand much in the way of legislation, they should make their special effort for good administration* (Roosevelt, 1897).
2. August "Gus" Vollmer:
   - Legislative and judiciary government: *Laws, as a rule, are hastily read, poorly digested, and occasionally misinterpreted, even by the judiciary.*
   - Crime prevention: *Merely arresting the offender and sending him to jail is like pouring water into a sieve.*
   - Police: *The policeman is denounced by the public, criticized by preachers, ridiculed in the movies, berated by the newspapers and unsupported by prosecuting officers and judges* (Vollmer, 1949).
3. Orlando Winfield "OW" Wilson: *Controls must be provided so that those who exercise authority will be held responsible for the consequences of their actions … Every delegation of authority should be accompanied by a commensurate placing of responsibility. The patrol officer is the ultimate in the decentralization of municipal services and should serve as a roving city-hall information and complaint counter for the distressed citizen. Officers need to know their beats and community geography while they cultivate personal relationships with residents, business owners, and employees. The active interest and participation of individual citizens and groups is so vital to the success of most police programs that the police should deliberately seek to arouse, promote, and maintain an active public concern in their affairs. Public cooperation is without the scrupulous courtesy and fairness on the part of the police. Police agencies should critically examine their own conduct in all public contacts and remodel it to avoid situations unnecessarily unpleasant to citizens. They cannot hope to retain the friendship of the public if their conduct is unfair and unreasonable and if they unnecessarily embarrass, humiliate, annoy, and inconvenience the public* (Wilson, 1950).
4. Penny Harrington: *Once they're in, anything that a woman does wrong is talked about by everybody. Women get labeled early on in their careers … Women are held to a higher standard of*

performance in practically anything. You have to do more than [men] do and you have to do it better to be considered as good as they are. It's that old-boy attitude toward women. In 1964, I started … I was in it for 24 years. I was seeing some small progress. When I started in 1964, there were 12 women in my department; in 1986, there were 85 in my department out of 1000. Any [metric] you want to measure, women do just as well as men, but still, the men don't consider them equal partners. We need to weed out the men [in law enforcement] who are obviously anti-women. How do you think they're going to treat the women victims? Women don't want to complain because they have no support; they suffer retaliation. It's not changing, and that's the sad part (Bello, 2013). *If we really want to change the attitudes of law enforcement officials, we need many more women at all levels. Women receive fewer citizen complaints and do not use excessive force as much as males, thereby saving money on lawsuits. Cost savings and better treatment of the community is needed.*[1]

5 Charles "Chuck" Ramsey: *We got away from some of the basic things we were doing in the 1990s and 2000s, community policing primarily, we got very focused on data-driven policing. You have to be able to maintain close contacts with certain people, but also understand how fragile those relationships really are. Why wouldn't there be an issue of race and policing when there's a problem with race in America? We can't tell officers to treat people with fairness and respect and expect them to listen if officers themselves don't feel treated with respect* (Buntin, 2015).

6 Bill Bratton: *I have been an advocate that the police, rather than being the catalyst for racial tension, racial violence, can, in fact, be a catalyst for the resolution – if not necessarily the solution – of that historical and longstanding problem … I have been supportive of the efforts to reduce the amount of broken windows policing because it's not necessary to the same extent it was in the '90s when the City was totally out of control. You take away the criminal aspect of broken windows enforcement in this city and watch how quickly things change, how ineffective police will become, if they don't have the power of arrest, the power of criminal law. Very quickly you start seeing these hot spots, or clusters, something that Herman Goldstein wrote about in the '80s, Problem-Oriented Policing. Timely accurate information, rapid response to what that intelligence is telling you, effective tactics to deal with it, and then relentless follow up.* (Bratton & Anderson, 2018). *Right now, American policing is an island unto itself. It has no support by and large from a large part of the political leadership in this country. It has no support, ironically, from large segments of the population, minorities, black, Latino, and a huge outpouring, which is very surprising, among whites, particularly younger whites … It's as if the last 30 years didn't exist. It didn't happen. And that's because the memories of so many of these people, they weren't here in 1990* (Bratton & Anderson, 2020).

7 Chris Magnus: There'*s not one simple thing like, "Add this set of ingredients, stir and voilà, you've got a successful policing program … You have to hire people who are really invested in this kind of work, who want to be a police officer and who want to serve their community for the right reasons, and see their job more broadly than just doing enforcement*" (McKenzie, 2017). *Going forward, in order to meet the public's need for immediate transparency, if there is an in-custody death we will release information about these deaths even though it may be preliminary and incomplete. Barring exceptional circumstances involving constitutional rights, statutory prohibitions, or other legal requirements, we will also release body-worn camera footage within 72 hours. This new approach is not without possible negative consequences. Releasing information before an investigation is complete can compromise both criminal and administrative investigations, potentially invalidating disciplinary actions and improperly influencing criminal charging decisions by prosecuting authorities* (Magnus, 2020).

This book aims to provide a unique addition to the policing literature by detailing these seven crucial police leaders' historical backgrounds and legacy. There is a lack of literature available that details American police chiefs' biographical leadership in the context of American history.

1 Author's interview with Harrington on October 22, 2020.

Moreover, in the aftermath of the 2020 mass protests, there is an increased international appetite for understanding how influential police leaders, with varying personalities, are able to navigate historical and contemporary challenges for policing democratic nations effectively. The audience includes the general public, policing professionals, college students, politicians, and academics. Each will reach a fuller understanding of the historical challenges that are unique to American policing and how these leaders were able to, for a time, offer effective leadership through these challenges.

Policing America represents one of the most significant challenges for our democracy. Through the pandemic and social justice protests, we are living during a time when we can reimagine the social purpose of the police within the social fabric of democracy. In doing so, political tension inevitably rises. Through this tension, protesters have demanded reform and improved police leadership. Like critiquing professional athletes through effective coaches, we can increasingly offer critical judgment toward police performance to make improvements. Academics reference these improvements as evidence-based practices. However, evidence-based considerations have not historically been readily accepted within traditional law enforcement and the subculture of policing. Through the protest movements, police agencies appear to be more open implementing change than in the past. These changes have included generalized acceptance of community policing, some aspects of problem-oriented and hotspot policing, and varying versions of broken windows policing. Specific evidence-based research regarding what works to avoid perceived misuse of force is lacking but likely forthcoming and discussed throughout this book.

An analysis of each of the seven leaders offers evidence of how they approached police reform and improved oversight that benefited officer morale and police efficiency. Their leadership examples help us understand modern policing challenges. Specifically, new technology such as body cameras and early warning systems built into the police subculture appears promising. Moreover, crisis intervention training (CIT), policies to govern the behavior of in-custody officer expectations, and varying incentives directed toward avoiding the use of force measures all serve to advance police professionalism. These evolving reform dimensions built into modern police agencies can significantly improve legitimacy and quality of police services to better match our democratic ideals.

References

Bello, Grace (2013). The gals in blue: Where are the real-life Olivia Bensons? *BitchMedia*. March 12.

Bratton, William and Brian Anderson (2018). William Bratton on "Precision Policing." *City Journal*. August 1.

Bratton, William and Brian Anderson (2020). Police on the brink: A conversation with William Bratton. *City Journal*. July 22.

Buntin, John (2015). Charles Ramsey: The man supposed to fix America's relationship with cops. *Governing: The Future of States and Localities*. November.

Magnus, Chris (2020). Changing how we handle deaths in custody: TPD remains a progressive, community-based police force. *The Arizona Daily Star*. July 9.

McKenzie, Lesley (2017). Chris Magnus. *Citizens of Humanity*. June 20.

Roosevelt, Theodore (1897). Municipal administration: The New York police force. *The Atlantic*. September.

Vollmer, August (1949). *The criminal*. Brooklyn, NY: The Foundation Press, Inc.

Wilson, Orlando W. (1950). *Police administration*. New York, NY: McGraw-Hill.

Chapter 1

Teddy Roosevelt – New York Police Reformer

The Man in the Arena

Before he became the 26th President of the United States (1901–1909), Teddy Roosevelt was the Vice President for William McKinley (1901), the 33rd Governor of New York (1899–1900), the Assistant Secretary of the Navy (1897–1898), and the President of the New York Board of Police Commissioners (1895–1897). In all of these positions, Roosevelt was a consummate reformist who fought against government corruption. Theodore Roosevelt Jr. was born on October 27, 1858, in New York City. He died at the age of 60 on January 6, 1919, while sleeping at his home on Oyster Bay, Long Island, New York. Thomas Marshall, Governor of Indiana, was quoted as stating, "death had to take him in his sleep, for if Roosevelt had been awake, there would have been a fight" (Roosevelt, 1947, p. 447). Although Roosevelt was the President of the New York Police Commission for only two years, his leadership in fighting police corruption had a ripple effect across the nation that began a historical challenge against the political status quo. For New York City, the status quo consisted of embedded corruption led by Tammany Hall[1] and the city police department through its patronage system. That system consisted of political favoritism and graft connected primarily to Irish Catholics who worked to help immigrants and local businesses. Police leaders also helped immigrants and their political business interactions as long as they paid their extortion share. Additionally, if those businesses involved illegal gambling and vice crime, police would serve as protection as long as they received their cut of the profits.

History of Police in America and New York City

The police are historically new to the criminal justice system and not mentioned nor conceived of during the writing of the Constitution or state governments' formation. The rise of cities created the need to invent the police, beginning first with loosely organized night watches and constables who worked on behalf of the judiciary. The constable system originally supplemented private civil matters directed toward offenders through the court system (Steinberg, 1989). In 1635, Boston instituted its first semi-organized night watch that operated on a communal volunteer basis. New York created its watch system in 1658, and Philadelphia did the same in 1700. Often these volunteers showed up for their posts drunk or not at all. Many watch volunteers did so to evade military service, while others did so out of punishment for prior

1 Tammany Hall was the democratic political machine in New York City that operated from 1789 until 1967 and exercised a great deal of patronage, mainly with Irish immigrants, to build loyalty while controlling government and commerce in New York City.

DOI: 10.4324/9780429272226-2

criminal activity. Philadelphia created a day watch in 1833, and New York did the same in 1844 to supplement its new bureaucratic police force (Gaines, Kappeler, & Vaughn, 1999).

Influence of the British 1829 Metropolitan Police Act

Reconsideration for the night watch system came in the aftermath of the 1829 Metropolitan Police Act in London. British Home Office Secretary Robert Peel introduced legislation to Parliament that created the world's first modern police department out of Scotland Yard. Based on Peel's prior military experience in Ireland and his governmental experience as the Home Office secretary, a quasi-militaristic and civil social control organization arose (Palmer, 1988). London's full-time officers became known as "Bobbies" or "Peelers." This new police force was cheaper than using the military for populous control and was eventually legitimized by citizens while also being more responsive to voters. The British police system of the 1830s served as an organizational precedent for an evolving urban American police movement. Several historians contend that the creation of the police in the United States was not as a response to increased crime as much as it was for the suppression of riots throughout the nineteenth century.

Consequently, American police development was sporadic and unprofessional compared to the careful strategic planning that occurred with the London police (Miller, 1999). Moreover, the uniqueness of policing American riots frequently had to do with conflicts between abolitionists and proponents of slavery. In 1838, in response to several mob riots, Boston organized the first municipal police department, and Philadelphia formed a police force by state law in 1854 (Lundman, 1980).

New York City Municipal Police before Roosevelt

On May 7, 1844, New York passed the Municipal Police Act, which created a formalized bureaucratic police force at the New York City Common Council's request. The act called for 1,200 quasi-militaristic officers. However, a debate between the common council and the mayor lasted another year over who would be responsible for hiring officers. Mayor William Havemeyer[2] appointed George Washington Matsell as the first police chief after the Municipal Police Act, which passed on May 23, 1845, repealed the watch system. Similar to Peel's London officers, there was an expectation that newly hired New York officers lived in their police precincts. However, that policy was frequently ignored and officially abolished in 1857.

By 1853, New York issued navy blue uniforms to police officers, which was no easy transition. Previously, only soldiers and servants of the wealthy had uniforms. Not only was the public initially resistant to uniformed social control, but the officers were also reluctant due to public ridicule (Lane, 1967). However, the uniforms allowed for easy public access to visible patrol officers and improved communication with the community (Monkkonen, 1992). In 1853, legislators also placed the police under the Mayor, Recorder, and City Judge's control, allowing these officials the authority to hire and fire police officials. In 1854 Fernando Wood[3] was elected as the 73rd Mayor of New York City and re-elected in 1859 as the 75th mayor.

2 Havemeyer was a Tammany Hall Democrat and served three times as the 66th, 69th, and 80th Mayor of New York City. He was elected in 1845, 1848, and 1873 and died while serving his third term as mayor in 1874 at the age of 70.

3 Wood was part of the Copperheads, sympathetic to the Southern Confederacy. Wood was an opponent of the Thirteenth Amendment, which abolished slavery, and was critical of Lincoln and the Civil War. Wood suggested New York City secede and continue its profitable cotton trade with the South.

Political opponents accused Wood of only hiring Democrats and replacing fired officers with Democrats. During the election, Wood had his officers and the street gang Dead Rabbits make sure voters who opposed him did not make it to the polls. Through political corruption, Wood, and other Tammany Hall politicians, had the support of the lower-class Irish[4] voters who felt protected from the patronizing anti-immigrant Republican elitists. Immigrants also supported Wood because he refused to enforce temperance laws on working-class saloons. Consequently, a municipal civil war began with influence from the state legislature in Albany and created predictable tension for New Yorkers.[5]

Municipals vs. Metropolitans

In April 1857, Republican politicians in Albany rewrote the city charter and stripped the mayor of most of his powers. Moreover, the legislatures abolished the corrupt New York City Municipal police. In its place, they created a Metropolitan police force governed by a board of commissioners, Superintendent Fredrick Tallmadge,[6] and ultimately Governor John King. This political power grab from the Republicans in the state capital was a direct attack on the Democratic Party (i.e. Tammany Hall) that controlled the New York City government, Mayor Wood, and the Municipal police force. Wood resisted and claimed the state government's creation of a Metropolitan Police force was unconstitutional (Lankevich, 2002). Chaos soon consumed the city as both the Metropolitans and the Municipals provided police services. Two separate police headquarters operated and lead to physical encounters between officers who represented the opposing departments.

The state law required the city to pay officers for both agencies. Wood argued that the state of New York lacked the authority to remove the Municipal Police. However, the state Supreme Court ruled against the mayor and called the law that created the Metropolitan Police constitutional. The court ruling led to a few hundred Municipal officers, out of the 1,100 man force, replaced by a Metropolitan police force (Williams, 2018). About 800 officers remained with the Municipals. The conflict came to a head when the state attempted to issue an arrest warrant against Wood for inciting riots. On June 16, 1857, only a couple of months after their creation, the Metropolitan officers arrived at City Hall to execute the warrant on Mayor Wood. However, Municipal Chief Matsell and his officers stopped them. A physical confrontation occurred, resulting in several injured officers and a call to the National Guard and Seventh Regiment military to put down the police riot (Williams, 2018).

Wood and King called a truce, and the mayor reluctantly gave up control of the police to the state, but the transition remained contentious. Over the July 4th weekend of 1857, the city suffered one of its most notorious riots, the "Dead Rabbits Riot," in the Five Points district of lower Manhattan (Anbinder, 2002). In 1859, Chief Matsell was forced to resign and moved to an Iowa farm but later returned to New York and became the National Police Gazette magazine publisher. The growing conflicts became a precursor to the New York City "Draft Riots" of 1863, the largest riot in American history at the Civil War's height (Bernstein, 2010).

4 The Irish immigrants grabbed additional political power through the July 11–16, 1863 draft riots, the most violent in American history.

5 American Poet Walt Whitman was living with his mother in Brooklyn and published the first version of *Leaves of Grass* on July 4, 1855, which contained the first 12 poems related to his life in New York City. The book sold in Manhattan book stores and was written in a manner that was not yet seen during the city's turbulent years of growth.

6 Tallmadge graduated from Yale College in 1811 and became a lawyer. He was a member of the U.S. Congress as a Whig from 1847 to 1849 and the Superintendent of the Metropolitan Police from 1857 to 1862. From 1863 to 1865 he was the Clerk of the New York Court of Appeals on the Democratic/Constitutional Union ticket.

In 1873, William Havemeyer returned as the 80th mayor of the city; he was also the 66th (1845–1846) and 69th mayor (1848–1849). Once again, Matsell became the superintendent of the city police and the President of the police commission. However, Havemeyer lost his subsequent reelection, and Matsell was ousted a second time. These changes further cemented the link between politics and police leadership.

Boss Tweed and the Gilded Age

Political corruption in New York had long made national news before Roosevelt's arrival as a police commissioner. The Municipal Police Act of 1844 placed control of the police under local politicians. These elected officials naturally took advantage of this practice and used the police to their advantage. Untrained officers received their jobs based upon political connections and kept these jobs by appeasing those same connections. This political era in policing lasted into the 1930s.

Famous political cartoons from *Harpers Weekly* reporter Thomas Nash exposed William "Boss" Tweed[7] as the most corrupt and influential figure in New York from 1861 to 1871. Nash helped the illiterate population understand the extent of Tweed's corruption as the leader of Tammany Hall that was involved with profits from high price government contracting and kickbacks. Jimmy O'Brien, a former sheriff, and associate of Tweed, turned whistleblower and revealed accounting ledgers to the *New York Times* that showed the extent of Tweed's corruption. In one extreme example, Tweed orchestrated the construction of the county courthouse building at a cost of nearly $13 million when it should have cost $300,000 to build (Ackerman, 2005). The extreme overcharging included kickbacks to Tweed and Tammany Hall. Tweed and his followers embezzled millions while they kept the voters, mainly Irish Catholic immigrants, happy by providing charitable acts and financial support for the poor at a cost far lower than their corrupt profits. By 1878, at the age of 58, Tweed was arrested, convicted, and died in a New York Jail; but the Tammany Hall machine remained entrenched with corruption.

Tweed and Tammany's corruption was followed by what Mark Twain called the Gilded Age of America when the extreme wealth of post-Civil War America met crushing poverty. This period lasted through the 1890s. Twain used the term "gilded" to mean glittering on the surface but corrupt underneath to describe how unabashed capitalism combined with unscrupulous consumption and mass corruption (Stiles, 2010). Invariably, the Gilded Era also led to reform efforts to challenge the heavy political influence of policing across the country.

Politicians had enormous control over the first police agencies that evolved out of the American industrialization movement and the Gilded Era. Payments for hiring and promotions found their way to local politicians, who also influenced choosing police chiefs who ran the police departments. From the beginning, police leaders were heavily influenced or outright controlled by local politicians, and when they resisted, they were easily replaced. Between 1879 and 1894, Buffalo, New York, went through eight chiefs. Chicago saw nine police chiefs through the same era. Los Angeles had 13 police chiefs between 1879 and 1889. New York City went through five police commissioners before Teddy Roosevelt arrived as part of a reform movement that came after early progressive challenges on vice offenses throughout the city.

7 William Magear Tweed was a fourth-generation Scottish immigrant and former firefighter who became Commissioner of Public Works, which helped him understand where to invest in real estate. Tweed eventually became the third-largest landowner in New York City. He was also the Erie Railroad director, the director of the Tenth National Bank, the director of the New York Printing Company, a major stockholder in iron mines and gas companies, an elected Congress member, and a board member on numerous other companies and banks (Ackerman, 2005).

Dr. Reverend Charles Parkhurst

In 1891, Dr. Reverend Charles Parkhurst[8] was elected the President of the New York Society for the Prevention of Crime. He utilized that position and his leadership as the Madison Avenue Presbyterian Church pastor to connect organized crime, Tammany Hall politicians, and police corruption. Public exposure reached a tipping point from Reverend Parkhurst's pulpit, which challenged New Yorkers' policing. Parishioners engaged in rehabilitating criminals, and their reverend provided a momentous crusade to expose political corruption throughout the city. Before Parkhurst, politicians and the police tied into Tammany Hall remained relatively untouched by Grand Jury investigations. However, Parkhurst and his congregation called on a broader inquiry that aimed to purify the police.

> *Virtue is at the bottom and knavery on the top. The rascals are out of jail and standing guard; statesmanship has very largely degenerated into small and dirty politics; something has to be done in New York.*
>
> (Parkhurst, 1895, p. 2)

In response to the reverend's allegations, District Attorney (DA) DeLancey Nicholl called for a Grand Jury presentment against Parkhurst. The presentment led to a reprimand for making unsupported statements within his church (Sante, 1991). However, rather than shutting down his crusade, the charges brought against Parkhurst emboldened him. One week after his legal reprimand, he returned to DA Nicholl's office with evidence he gathered on nine East side saloons that were illegally serving alcohol on Sunday. When the DA refused to investigate the matter, Parkhurst began to solicit support from the city newspapers and personally paid private investigator Charles Gardner $6 a night to help him acquire further police corruption evidence (Sante, 1991, p. 284).

Gardner (1894) reported he helped Parkhurst dress in uncover attire so he could go into the saloons undetected as part of their investigation. Gardner then hired a squad of detectives to gather evidence with Parkhurst on hundreds of establishments serving alcohol on Sundays, engaging in open prostitution often with teenagers, and participating in games inside the saloons such as naked leapfrog that the police protected. In almost every establishment Parkhurst frequented, he was propositioned by some of the estimated 40,000 prostitutes active in the city. The prostitutes also reported they paid police officers through cash or sexual favors to avoid arrest and receive protection. The media published numerous sensational stories related to these arrangements and awakened the public to extensive police corruption. Parkhurst used the information he gathered from his investigations for his sermons, which shocked and outraged his congregation (Todd, 1993). His political movement sought to eradicate gambling and prostitution and the police corruption that continually enabled these vice crimes.

As the media reported on this evidence, police raids came quickly, but officers told the bar owners and the prostitutes Parkhurst was to blame. Despite attempts by the police and Tammany politicians to rally the community against Parkhurst supporters, their investigative work catalyzed progressive reform, albeit not through the city but in upstate Albany with anti-Tammany forces of the tempered conservative Republican-controlled state legislature.

8 Parkhurst died in 1933 at the age of 91 at his New Jersey home in what was believed to be a sleepwalking accident from his roof balcony.

Satan's Circus – New York's Trial of the Century

The most appalling evidence the investigators acquired came from what was known as the Tenderloin District, a description of a square mile in midtown Manhattan with a series of saloons and brothels known as "Satan's Circus" (Dash, 2007). Captain Alexander "Clubber" Williams[9] gave this area of Manhattan its "tenderloin" nickname by referencing the number of bribes he received for protecting brothels. The term tenderloin came when Williams said, "I've been having chuck steak ever since I've been on the force, and now I'm going to have a bit of tenderloin" (Whalen, Messing, & Mladinich, 2016, p. 40). Williams was the Nineteenth Precinct command captain, which covered the Tenderloin District after paying a $15,000 bribe for the choice assignment (Dash, 2007). In one tenderloin establishment, The Golden Rule Pleasure Club, Parkhurst, witnessed young boys dressed in women's clothing sexually exploited by older men.

In 1894, former bar owner turned police officer Charles Becker was in charge of patrolling Satan's Circus, and he extorted monthly payments from each business permitted to operate in his beat. His story and horrific death inside a prison, through the use of an electric chair, demonstrates the depth of police corruption in New York City. After being promoted to lieutenant, with links to Big Tim Sullivan's political patronage, a state senator, Becker was in charge of a unit that kept street gangs in check and protected area businesses after they paid their monthly fee. Becker acquired a fortune from Satan's Circus. He was also a silent partner at the Hesper Club, located in Times Square at 104 W. 45th Street, that Sullivan permitted Herman "Beansie" Rosenthal to operate as a gambling house. In 1912, Becker notified Rosenthal that he would raid the Hesper Club on orders from DA Charles Whitman[10] to "make it look good." However, the chronic graft would continue afterward (Cohen, 2006). In the aftermath, there was a dispute over profits within the casino, and subsequently, Rosenthal refused to pay Becker. This disagreement caused Becker to instigate additional raids on their casino, causing much damage. Rosenthal, upset by the damage, met with the media and explained how Becker received 20 percent of his profits, and these bribes also went directly to Tammany Hall politicians. Becker then placed officers inside and outside of the casino to scare away customers. Rosenthal unsuccessfully petitioned a judge to have the officers removed. On July 15, 1912, Rosenthal, upset at Becker, met with DA Whitman to expose the police bribery. They agreed he would return the next morning with his wife as a second witness and meet at Whitman's home before calling for a Grand Jury. Early the following morning, Rosenthal was shot and killed in a drive-by by the Lenox Avenue Gang, around 2 AM, outside the Metropole Hotel[11] in Times Square on Broadway and 42nd Street (Cohen, 2006).

On July 29, 1912, members of Whitman's DA office arrested Becker. He was found guilty of ordering Rosenthal's murder at his trial, successfully appealed, and was then found guilty a second time in 1914 and sentenced to death, the only police officer ever to receive capital punishment (Roberts, 2012). By this time, DA Whitman had become the 41st Governor of New York (1915–1918), signed Becker's death warrant, and attended Sing Sing Prison's execution on July 30, 1915. To make matters worse, Becker's death by the electric chair was botched,

9 Commissioner Roosevelt forced Clubber Williams to retire on May 24, 1895, with a yearly pension of $1,750, and all of his illicit wealth still intact.

10 Whitman's grandson, John, married Christy Todd Whitman, who became the 50th Governor of New Jersey (1994–2001) and the first female Governor. John and Christy's first date was at the 1973 inaugural ball of Richard Nixon (Bumiller, 1995).

11 The Metropole Hotel was owned by Big Tim Sullivan and boasted a 24-hour liquor license and casino that mobster Arnold Rothstein managed. It is now the location of the Casablanca Hotel.

his head set on fire, and lasted much longer than planned (Cohen, 2006). Several historians subsequently challenged Becker's direct murder culpability (Root, 1961; Roberts, 2012).

Lexow Committee

In January 1894, in the aftermath of the Parkhurst investigation, New York state senator Clarence Lexow became chairman of a select investigative committee that took his namesake and probed into police corruption. The seven senator committee probe, partially funded by business reformers in the New York Chamber of Commerce, lasted a year and produced the most exhaustive and detailed accounts of governmental malfeasance in U.S. history. More than 3,000 witnesses received subpoenas, and 678 testified. The final committee report was over 10,000 pages (Berman, 1987, p. 26). The Senate probe found ample evidence of police administrators involved in numerous counts of extortion, voter intimidation, election fraud, police brutality, and other political scams. The Lexow Committee offered the first glimpse for those outside of the city on how police officers were promoted based upon payments made to supervisors and Tammany Hall, along with determining how payoffs from area businesses were extorted by those assigned to protect and enforce the law. One of the chief witnesses who cooperated with the Lexow Commission was German-born Police Captain Max Schmittberger.[12] He provided evidence of his inclusion into the nearly two-decade-long bribery system, referred to as "the graft," throughout the Tenderloin District (Berman, 1981). Schmittberger informed the committee that he routinely paid "Clubber" Williams $50 a month as part of their payment agreement and several others. His testimony, covered by famed Muckraker journalist Lincoln Steffens,[13] directly implicated past police commissioners and several other police commanders while exposing the daily routine of extortion, blackmail, and bribery (Steffens, 1931).

The media drew upon the testimony of witnesses who described numerous acts of voter intimidation and police brutality. Undoubtedly, the attention directed toward police corruption through the Lexow Committee led to the 1894 Tammany mayoral defeat, and 68-year-old Republican Mayor William Lafayette Strong, a former bank president, sought a robust political reformer to challenge police corruption. A fusion of voters – Democrats fighting against corrupt Tammany Hall and Republican supporters – elected Republican Mayor Strong. He handpicked Roosevelt to assist in the cleanup of rampant corruption throughout the government and the police department. The extensiveness of the Lexow report on municipal malfeasance paved the way for Roosevelt's style of reform leadership and his return from Washington, DC, to his home state.

12 Schmittberger's testimony to the Lexow Commission and his subsequent policing career is complicated. He stands as one of the most critical whistleblowers in American police history, albeit through his own corruption. Seventy-five years later, Frank Serpico became the second historic whistleblower in New York City when he testified in front of the 1970–1972 Knapp Commission, as described in the chapter on Bratton. Like Serpico, Schmittberger became a pariah to the force. However, unlike Serpico, he survived his critics and eventually served as a chief inspector (chief of the department) until he died in 1917. Muckraking reporter Steffens had a change of heart and ultimately discouraged Roosevelt from removing Schmittberger and saved his policing career (Fourman, 2018). In turn, Roosevelt transferred Schmittberger to precincts known for corruption. He found his Captain was eager to help reform not only corrupt officers but also illegal brothels and gambling halls within his precinct's targeted community. Schmittberger's reformation was politically beneficial to Roosevelt for years to come.

13 Steffens was 27 years old during the Lexow hearings and had just started to make a name for himself writing for the *New York Evening Post*. He grew up in California and graduated from the University of California Berkeley in 1889, 15 years before August Vollmer was elected Town Marshall.

Convincing Roosevelt to Become New York City Police Commissioner

Before his position as a police commissioner, Roosevelt lived in Washington, DC, and held an appointed position as the Civil Service Commission under President Benjamin Harrison and President Grover Cleveland. A devastating economic recession hit the country in 1893 and led to widespread poverty and unemployment. Despite being a member of the upper-class establishment, Roosevelt saw poverty connected to political corruption. During his six years in Washington with the Civil Service Commission and the backing of the Pendleton Act of 1883, Roosevelt worked to fight against federal employment nepotism and corruption, earning him the admiration of other reform-minded leaders. One such leader was Henry Cabot Lodge,[14] who is credited with convincing Roosevelt to accept the New York Police Commission position, despite Roosevelt admittedly reporting he knew nothing about police management. Lodge saw the Police Commission position as politically advantageous for Roosevelt's future if he could make a difference in fighting the corruption that plagued the New York Police Department (NYPD).

Police Commissioner Roosevelt (1895–1897)

In 1895, Roosevelt moved his family from Washington, DC, back to New York to be sworn in as police commissioner – a two-year position seen as politically advantageous. During this era, a board of four to six commissioners led the city police. On May 6, 1895, 38-year-old Roosevelt was sworn in by Mayor Strong as one of the four police commissioners in a brief 10 AM ceremony at City Hall and given a $5,000 a year salary.

During his swearing-in ceremony, Roosevelt joined three other new police commissioners: Colonel Frederick Dent Grant (44-year-old Republican and son of President Ulysses Grant), Andrew D. Parker (36-year-old Democratic lawyer), and Avery D. Andrews (31-year-old Democratic lawyer and graduate from West Point). According to the legislation passed during this era, which served as a means to guarantee future Republican representation in police leadership, the city police commission was supposed to consist of a bipartisan police board. While Mayor Strong reportedly requested the commission to ignore their political influences and operate with nonpartisan leadership working toward the city's betterment, the reality of politics in policing was inescapable. It would hamper Commissioner Roosevelt's impact during his short two-year leadership position with the NYPD. For the next few years, Roosevelt would advocate for a single police commissioner to replace a four-man police board until the system changed in 1901 (Photo 1.1).

New York City in 1895

Commissioner Roosevelt inherited a city with two million mainly mixed immigrants and the nation's largest and most corrupt police department. Calling the largest city in New York a melting pot in 1895 may not provide the most accurate picture of how diverse it had become. Roosevelt was in charge of policing a city that was a cauldron of heterogeneity. Some were privy to an extended Gilded Age on the backdrop of a Supreme Court decision that struck down federal income tax laws as unconstitutional. Consequently, the wealthy were allowed

14 Lodge was an heir to a shipping fortune and son of two wealthy Boston families, the Cabots and the Lodges. He was also a Republican U.S. Senator (1893–1924) from Massachusetts who worked toward government reform. Ironically, 90 years later, Massachusetts Governor Michael Dukakis would be involved in bringing Bill Bratton to the Massachusetts Bay Transportation Authority for his first position as Chief of Police in 1983 before becoming the Commissioner of the NYPD.

Photo 1.1 Left to Right: Avery Andrews, Andrew Parker, Theodore Roosevelt, Colonel Frederick Grant in New York City in 1895.

to amass extreme wealth when little to no social service assistance existed for the immigrant poor. Roosevelt was in charge of a police department that included the country's largest port city with over a 100 active piers, four above-ground train lines, an estimated 60,000 horse and carriages, and 1.8 million pounds of daily manure (Jeffers, 1994). The city was also the country's vice capital, with immense leadership challenges placed upon the police commission in the aftermath of the Lexow senate hearings and the political damage to Tammany Hall.

Despite the election of Republican Mayor Strong, Tammany Hall Democrats remained entrenched in local wards. They continued to provide new immigrants with needed services as long as they supported the customary bribery and corruption of politicians and police officers. Many immigrants were police officers, mainly Irish Catholics, who supported Tammany politicians and were anxious about new reform ideas that would hinder their lucrative extortion practices. Roosevelt's reform agenda stood as a progressive cog in the wheel of the powerful Tammany political machine. Police Board President Roosevelt made it apparent that he intended to utilize his Harvard education to reform an infamous city known for its Tenderloin District and Satan's Circus. As a police commissioner (1895–1897), Roosevelt's leadership style was similar to his Presidency (1901–1909), flamboyant, headstrong, energetic, and ultimately, a reformist.

Challenges for the New Police Board

Grant and Roosevelt were given third-floor offices near the boardroom at police headquarters located at 300 Mulberry Street. Parker and Andrews had offices on the second floor. When they arrived, the new commissioners found a recently installed telephone service that connected most of the 38 precinct station houses. The department was also able to receive occasional calls from wealthy private Manhattan residents. Most of the service calls arrived from written notes or in-person through the telegraph office and concerned dead animals and loud saloons.

On the morning of the swearing-in ceremony, the commissioners were escorted to their offices and held their first meeting. Andrews nominated Roosevelt to lead their commission. Grant and Parker agreed, which also meant his single vote would count equal to the other three's combined votes. Ironically, the other commissioners often referred to him as President Roosevelt. The commission was given a $5 million budget and decided to hold three board meetings a week while taking turns presiding over once-a-week police misconduct trials. The new commission was met with a demoralized police force where half of the 38 police precincts lacked a managerial captain due to retirements or suspensions in the aftermath of the Lexow hearings. Roosevelt assigned Parker the task of reorganizing the detective bureau and the department's supervision of elections. Grant led infrastructure repairs and supply inventory in addition to revising departmental regulations. Roosevelt focused on media coverage and officer accountability (Jeffers, 1994).

The new President of the Police Board made it apparent that he would lead through a reform agenda. As a flamboyant leader, Roosevelt commonly wore pink shirts with a broad silk sash under his frock coat in place of a vest (Kaplan, 1974). After Roosevelt was nominated to be the President of the new Police Board, he made the following public statement:

> *The public may rest assured that so far as I am concerned, there will be no politics in the department, and I know that I voice the sentiment of my colleagues in that respect. We are all activated by the desire to so regulate this department that it will earn the respect and confidence of the community. Every man in the force will have to stand on his merits and all appointments and promotions will be made for merit only and without regard to political or religious considerations.*
>
> (Andrews, 1958)

On day three, Commissioner Andrews was first to lead the once-a-week police misconduct trials. These trials were historically used against officers who fell out of favor of Tammany Hall. Now, a new era of reform had begun. The other commissioners joined Andrews, and nearly 100 officers were given trials due to misconduct accusations by police supervisors, referred to as roundsmen. Commissioners also provided trials for officers who received citizen complaints. The commissioners utilized their discretion to levy small fines or exonerate. Other punishments, such as termination,[15] required a majority vote. Predictably, the commission's reform agenda and Roosevelt's leadership as board president threatened the corrupt status quo that permeated the police department. To further the reform movement, the Republican-dominated Senate attempted to increase the police commission's legal authority to cleanse the department. The Police Reorganization Bill sought to remove the right to appeal from officers terminated by the police commission.

In the Police Board Minutes, Roosevelt states

> *If this power is given to the board, we can guarantee a thorough reform of the force, and a clean and efficient police service; without this power, the board will do all it can to produce these results, but will necessarily be cramped and embarrassed by its action.*

15 The commission terminated 88 officers within the first year compared to 41 the year prior and only 11 dismissals two years earlier. Officers dismissed were drunk on duty, lived in or assisted in operating brothels, and seduced women for promiscuity with marriage promises while the officer was married.

However, because of the police officers' lobbying power, assuredly backed by Tammany Hall, the bill failed to pass, maintaining the appellate system. Roosevelt reported the defeat of the Police Reorganization Bill severely slowed his reform efforts. However, he still focused on the termination of corrupt officers, specifically the police superintendent.

Superintendent Thomas Byrnes

Police Superintendent Thomas Byrnes was the most politically powerful individual in the police department, and he epitomized all that was wrong with corruption. Roosevelt knew he had to terminate or force his police superintendent's resignation if he would have any chance of addressing the corruption issues that plagued the city and the police. The removal was not an easy task as Byrnes had several powerful political allies inside the Tammany Hall. He was also very popular in the community and had written a book titled *Professional Criminals of America* detailing his time as the chief of detectives from 1880 to 1895, when he was in charge of the 40-man detective bureau. In his book, Byrnes famously created the rogue's gallery and showed a compilation of criminal photographs along with hundreds of biographical profiles of con artists, forgers, and thieves (Byrnes, 1895). The book also gave details on third-degree interrogation techniques of opium addicts, fugitives, and unsolved murders (Schlesigner, 1969).

Despite his popularity and position as the Police Superintendent, Byrnes was also wealthy because of his entrenchment in political corruption. On the last day of the Senate Lexow hearing, Dr. Parkhurst ordered Byrnes to testify. To their surprise, he dramatically described how he accumulated numerous real estate holdings and a small fortune through his political contacts. Frequently, Byrnes was privately paid to provide police details during labor disputes and workers' strikes. He was also infamous for making a lot of money from Wall Street tips and frequently shared his insider information with many high-ranking politicians. He bragged about his relationships with Gilded Age families such as the Vanderbilts, the Carnegies and using Jay Gould as a personal banker. Formal legislation against insider trading did not exist until the 1930s, and those with the right connections profited.

The appointment of Commissioner Roosevelt provided some challenges for these corrupt practices. To meet the Roosevelt threat, Byrne's supporters successfully lobbied for the passage of legislation that gave equal authority to the police superintendent as wielded by the newly appointed Police Board. However, Mayor Strong vetoed the legislation, and this signaled an end to Byrne's reign. On May 27, 1895, Byrnes submitted his letter of resignation to the Police Board, three weeks after they took office. In doing so, Byrnes was granted a yearly pension of $3,000 for early retirement and thus escaped further prosecution. The resignation was a win for Roosevelt, who felt he had increased his reform authority with the police superintendent's removal. After his resignation, Byrnes became an insurance investigator and operated a detective agency on Wall Street.

Batman and Roosevelt

Paul Levitz, an editor for DC Comics, explained that the Batman comic series foundation came from the story of Commissioner Roosevelt's time in New York City (Springer, 2019). Others wrote about the psychology of Batman with comparisons to Roosevelt (Langley, 2012). In 2013, the *History Channel* did a show titled: *The Psychology of the Dark Knight: Batman Unmasked.* Similarities between the comic character Bruce Wayne and Roosevelt included:

1 Both are considered to be children of New York City, referred to as Gotham City in Batman.

2 Both stem from wealthy families active in philanthropy. Both were young world travelers and often had private tutors.

3 Both had strong fathers they admired.

In his autobiography, Roosevelt writes: *"My father, Theodore Roosevelt, was the best man I ever knew. He combined strength and courage with gentleness, tenderness, and great unselfishness. He would not tolerate in us children selfishness or cruelty, idleness, cowardice, or untruthfulness"* (Roosevelt, 1913, p. 13).

4 Both suffered a tragic loss on a single day. Wayne's parents were murdered by Joe Chill, a corrupt mobster and trucking company owner. Roosevelt lost his wife Alice Lee to sudden kidney failure on February 14, 1884, and his mother, Martha Stewart "Mittie" Bulloch, to typhoid fever 11 hours earlier. Alice Lee had given birth to their daughter and their first child, Alice, two days before her death. Bruce Wayne's love interest was actress Anne Hathaway (similar to Alice), who later became Catwoman.

5 Roosevelt was grief-stricken and left newborn Alice with his sister Anna, known as "Bamie." He then went to the Dakota territories to live as a rancher and work as a sheriff deputy in Billings County for the next two years. Similarly, Bruce Wayne went into exile after his parents' murder and learned martial arts.

6 Both turned their loss into a passion for reform and cleaning up corruption. Roosevelt remarried his childhood and family friend Edith Kermit Carow on December 2, 1886, and the couple had five additional children.

7 Roosevelt had four sons, and they all served in the military. Wayne had four young men who served as his partner under the mantle of "Robin." Roosevelt's son Quentin was killed in World War I, and his namesake son, Theodore III, died of heart failure a month after being one of the first soldiers (and a Brigadier General) to land on Utah Beach during the June 6, 1944, D-Day Invasion. Batman referred to his "Robin's" as good soldiers, and one, Jason Todd, was killed in battle.

8 In April 1895, Roosevelt and Henry Cabot Lodge published *Hero Tales from American History*. In their book, they wrote biographies on several American heroes from Washington to Lincoln. Their book was aimed at young readers to inspire them toward heroism (Lodge & Roosevelt, 1903). Bruce Wayne used Batman as a symbol of heroism and demonstrated that someone could always take on the mantle to symbolize redemption.

Midnight Rambles

Roosevelt spent his time patrolling the streets with city journalists. As a consummate politician, Roosevelt knew the importance of grabbing headlines as a police reformist leader. His walking tours failed to include his fellow commissioners, as indicative of his individualistic leadership style. The tours showed how Roosevelt became a master at utilizing the press and encouraged them to write about his progressive agenda. Roosevelt's cultivation of media relations led to mostly favorable coverage of his leadership. He led the media to believe he needed their advice and reacted to their concerns in a way few police leaders had previously done. One of Roosevelt's first journalistic partners was muckraking journalist Jacob Riis.

Riis became famous for being one of the first American journalists to use flash photography in his reporting of the NY City poor and children working in factories that allowed for a more authentic story to be told. This reporting was the first time photography was able to light up the dark confines of the inner-city poor and demonstrate the world's wealthiest city's dichotomy. In his noteworthy article on the city's poor lives, 19 of his photographs led to an invitation to publish a book. As a 41-year-old photojournalist, Riis attempted to draw attention, for his middle- and upper-class readers, to the city's impoverished living conditions. The eventual book was subtitled *Studies Among the Tenements of New York* and published in October 1890. After reading *How the Other Half Lives*, the main title, and seeing the photos of the poor conditions within the public housing tenements, Roosevelt famously sent Riis a card that stated, "I have read your book, and I have come to help" (Lewis, 1919, p. 106). Roosevelt specifically sought Riis out to conduct walking tours with him and provide media coverage on city crime and lack of officer professionalism. The Parkhurst investigation into the city taverns and the subsequent Lexow Committee Report on police corruption undoubtedly influenced Roosevelt as well.

Riis and Roosevelt discovered a city terrorized by gangs and children working from daybreak well into the evening. Riis (1890) described a child's arm burnt with a hot iron, and then acid poured on it so he could earn more from begging. Disease such as tuberculosis, smallpox, and typhus was rampant and frequently incurable. A frequent scene was small coffins for the children stacked high each day on boats sent to the city cemetery. People often abandoned their babies, dead or alive, because they had no money to feed them or bury them. Children also frequently died of suffocation as hundreds of people crowded into municipal tenements without adequate ventilation.

The media[16] referenced Roosevelt's walking tours as "midnight rambles," and Riis became a reliable guest. Riis, age 46, and Roosevelt, ten years younger, looked similar, wearing wire-rimmed glasses and with the same short and stocky profiles. Riis came from Danish ancestry, grew up in the New York City public housing tenements' horrific conditions, and covered the police as a beat reporter for the *Tribune* and *Evening Sun* for nearly 20 years. Riis was widely known for his 18-page article, *How the Other Half Lives*, which appeared in the Christmas 1889 edition of *Scribner's Magazine*. The article garnered international acclaim for its focus on the conditions of tenement poverty throughout New York City.

Although Roosevelt was born in the city of New York, his reality of growing up with affluence in Oyster Bay, New York, was in sharp contrast to Riis. As a Harvard-educated aristocrat, Roosevelt's midnight rambles through the slums of the city with Riis's journalistic reporting kept national audiences riveted for a time. They found crowded housing tenements with unsanitary conditions, homelessness, unsafe factories, and exploited immigrant populations. The authentic New York visualization would stick with Roosevelt, allowing him to understand unchecked corruption and inadequate healthcare.

During the police accountability walking tours, Riis and Roosevelt would frequently conceal their identities and find officers sleeping, drinking in taverns, or otherwise behaving unprofessionally with members of the community. Riis reported that officers would threaten to "fan" Roosevelt with their nightsticks until he revealed his identity and subsequently filed a report with the precinct captain and ordered the officer to a disciplinary meeting the following day. One political cartoon from this period showed a caricature drawing of Roosevelt as a cowboy lassoing sleeping cops. Another showed police officers hitting the shoes of sleeping vagrants, followed by cartoons with Commissioner Roosevelt hitting the napping police officers' shoes who neglected their patrol assignments. Riis and his editors praised Roosevelt for his honesty, character, and active leadership that differed from his predecessors.

16 In September 1901, shortly after returning from President William McKinley's funeral, Roosevelt extended an invite to the White House to the major media outlets (Juergens, 1982). He then became the first President to have a permanent media presence in the White House.

One journalist described an exhilarated Roosevelt as having great fun in conducting street patrol, not for crooks but corrupt officers. The experiences of these midnight rambles were described as follows:

> *When he asks a question, Mr. Roosevelt shoots it at the poor trembling policeman as he would shoot a bullet at a coyote ... he shows a set of teeth calculated to unnerve the bravest of the Finest. His teeth are very white and almost as big as a colt's teeth. They are broad teeth, they form a perfectly straight line. The lower teeth look like a row of dominoes. They do not lap over or under each other, as most teeth do, but come together evenly ... They seem to say: "Tell the truth to your Commissioner, or he'll bit your head off. Generally speaking, this interesting Commissioner's face is red. He had lived a great deal out of doors, and that accounts for it. His hair is thick and short ... Under his right ear, he has a long scar. It is the opinion of all the policemen who have talked with him that he got that scar fighting an Indian out West. It is also their opinion that the Indian is dead. But Mr. Roosevelt's voice is the policeman's hardest trial. It is an exasperating voice, a sharp voice, a rasping voice. It is a voice that comes from the tips of the teeth and seems to say in its tones, What do you amount to, anyway? One thing our noble force may make up its mind to atone—it must do as Roosevelt says, for it is not likely that it will succeed in beating him."*
>
> (Morris, 1979)

Roosevelt's walking tours influenced his later independent reform movements as President and pointed out the dangers of unregulated monopolies on vulnerable poor immigrant labor pools. The concentrated poverty and an unregulated market structure connected with the high crime rates, which infested the city and the minority immigrants. In a later speech, Roosevelt quipped, "The best test of true love of liberty in any country is how minorities are treated." This speech was entitled "Citizenship in a Republic" and delivered at La Sorbonne, Paris, France, on April 23, 1910. This speech perhaps is the most famous and is worth partially quoting as it reflects his leadership beliefs.

> *It is not the critic who counts; not the man who points out how the strong man stumbles, or where the doer of deeds could have done them better. The credit belongs to the man who is actually in the arena, whose face is marred by dust and sweat and blood; who strives valiantly; who errs, and comes short again and again, because there is no effort without error and shortcoming; but who does actually strive to do the deeds; who knows the great enthusiasms, the great devotions; who spends himself in a worthy cause; who at the best knows in the end the triumph of high achievement, and who at the worst, if he fails, at least fails while daring greatly, so that his place shall never be with those cold and timid souls who know neither victory nor defeat.*

As police commissioner, Roosevelt spoke of the challenges modern police leaders would continue to face in policing urban concentrated poor minority neighborhoods. After becoming President, Riis wrote that Roosevelt was the most useful citizen of New York. In return, Roosevelt wrote that Riis was one of the best Americans he ever knew.

Hiring Reforms

Employment records from nearly 4,000 police officers indicated about two-thirds of the police force were first-generation Irish Americans linked to Tammany Hall (Zacks, 2012). These officers' ancestors had suffered through centuries of British Protestant discrimination, and they certainly did not associate with wealthy reform activists such as Roosevelt. The department was about 400 officers down in the Lexow investigative probe's aftermath, so hiring was a necessity, and Roosevelt promised to do so based upon merit-based civil service standards and not political connections. He successfully opened up an unprecedented statewide public campaign to recruit police officers.

From his previous work in Washington, DC, with the Civil Service Commission, Roosevelt learned about federal employment initiatives that required open examinations and mental, physical, and moral standards not based on political connections. Consequently, he pushed merit-based hiring of police officers to replace the prior employment system of recommendations or political payoffs. Roosevelt also directed the Police Civil Service Board, which was in charge of hiring and promotion policies, to remove the box that asked applicants to self-report political affiliation. Roosevelt's insistence on hiring standards and entrance exam procedures was groundbreaking and quintessential for future police reform leaders.

As a reformer, Roosevelt also hired many women[17] into clerical positions at police headquarters. Roosevelt's critics admonished him for hiring Minnie Gertrude Kelly for $1,700 a year, making her the first woman appointed to an administrative position at a police department (Berman, 1987, p. 77). He also hired several female police matrons, and for the first time, they provided 24-hour coverage within the precincts. The matrons' official duties were to escort detainees, conduct searches of female suspects, and assist in the processing of arrestees and runaway children. Roosevelt's hiring of matrons was a reversal from ten years prior when the city deemed them unnecessary. In 1886, the city detained 14,000 women prisoners at the precincts and 42,000 lodgers for overnight shelter (Schulz, 1992, p. 16). In 1896, Roosevelt appointed a record number of 32 matrons, the most for a single year. The appointment and expansion of female matrons aligned with Roosevelt's affiliation with affluent college-educated Republicans who were part of the Northeastern established Protestants. These economically privileged groups supported women's suffrage and progressive reforms that linked anticorruption with pending prohibition movements. Despite these strides in gender equality, it was not until 1921 that the NYPD would allow for fully sworn female police officers (Schulz, 2004).

Sunday Liquor Laws

Nine months before becoming Police Commissioner, Roosevelt lost his beloved younger brother Elliott after a long battle with alcoholism. The Roosevelt family had high expectations for Elliott, who was academically and athletically superior to Teddy. At the age of 34, suffering from alcoholism and confined to a sanitarium, Elliott jumped out a window and succumbed to his injuries after having seizures a few days later, on August 14, 1894. It is unclear if he jumped out of suicide or suffered from delirium tremens (i.e., delusions from alcohol withdrawal). Elliott also lost his wife, Anna, to diphtheria on December 7, 1892. They left behind a son and daughter,[18] Gracie Hall (they called him "Hall") and Anna Eleanor (they called her "Eleanor"). At 20 years of age, Eleanor married her distant cousin, 22-year-old Harvard University student Franklin D. Roosevelt, who would become the 32nd President of the United States. Eleanor was escorted down the aisle by her uncle Teddy, who was President at

17 Roosevelt was way ahead of his time on gender equality. His progressivism was linked to his earlier Harvard University senior thesis titled "The Practicality of Equalizing Men and Women Before the Law." His paper called for women's right to vote, equal inheritance rights, and women's right to attend law school. He also wrote that we should not assume that women should be forced to take their husband's last name upon marriage (White, 2003, p. 130).

18 Elliott and Anna also had a son, Elliott Jr. (they called him "Ellie"), who died at the age of four of scarlet fever. Elliott was also suspected of having an illegitimate son, Elliott Roosevelt Mann, with a servant (Pottker, 2005).

the time (Roosevelt & Roosevelt, 1946). Eleanor was eight when her mother died and only ten when she lost her father but reported that Elliott was a loving dad while her mother was judgmental over her shortcomings (Hawkins, 2017).

The death of Elliott devastated Teddy, who reportedly felt shamed by his brother's lack of self-control. This event inevitably impacted Commissioner Roosevelt's view on enforcing Sunday liquor laws in the city. As Commissioner, Roosevelt was well aware of Sunday laws that mandated liquor establishments be closed by midnight on Saturday and stayed closed until midnight the following Sunday. For decades saloon owners paid police officers bribes not to enforce the law. Roosevelt's attempt to change this dynamic was one of his significant legacies and downfalls as Commissioner. His enforcement policy began on Sunday, June 16, 1895, when he ordered several uniformed and undercover officers to enforce Sunday drinking laws, leading to violations of 213 saloonkeepers (Berman, 1987, p. 108). The reform-minded Commissioner's attempt to enforce the Sunday liquor sales laws created enormous division with Tammany and his fellow Republicans. At the time, Roosevelt's unpopular quote was he would "enforce the law to the hilt," and he expected to see more family picnics on holy Sunday. His prognosis was a drop in disorderly arrests, a decline in Monday morning hospital stays, and families that would pay their rent and feed their families instead of wasting their money in saloons. The one-day stoppage impacted the poor and immigrant populations more than any other demographic. The laborers worked six days a week and were angry with legal expectations that they avoid being in a tavern on their day off, which happened to be the Sabbath.

The immigrant populous perceived their Commissioner as hypocritical and bullheaded since affluent New Yorkers frequented private clubs, and they were allowed to serve alcohol seven days a week. Moreover, saloon owners catered to the working class and had more sales on Sunday than any other day of the week. Roosevelt's enforcement policies devastated them financially. Enforcement of the Sunday liquor laws polarized the city by pitting the Tammany machine against temperance, women's rights, and church groups who staunchly supported Commissioner Roosevelt. While Roosevelt was not a supporter of Prohibition, he did feel it was his duty as Commissioner to ensure the enforcement of all existing laws, including the Sunday drinking laws. Several of his Irish Catholic officers refused to work on Sundays because of religious purposes but more likely because they did not want to enforce drinking laws. In response, Roosevelt hired additional Jewish officers. The increases in Jewish officers caused consternation in Irish and German communities who rushed to the Democratic Party and the Tammany political machine.

In the aftermath of Roosevelt's enforcement policy, Democratic Tammany politicians painted a picture of men being forced to be drunk in their homes on Sundays and abusing their wives and children instead of being in the taverns. A month after Roosevelt's first enforcement of Sunday liquor laws, the city's drinking population left for open bars on Long Island and New Jersey at an enormous cost to the city saloon owners. Roosevelt attempted to declare victory for the Sunday shutdowns through media and clergy. However, the media determined New Yorkers and tourists alike could still easily find alcohol in most of the city's 8,000+ saloons on Sundays. While Roosevelt was very popular for his first few months as Commissioner, his uncompromising perceptions of the Sunday liquor laws created a lot of political damage for Republican boss Thomas Platt. Republicans wanted a law and order leader, but they did not want the type of leadership that took away the working class's fusion votes. Media outlets began to show Roosevelt as too preoccupied with enforcing liquor laws and not doing enough about serious crime and corruption. The narrative was an elitist Puritan who allowed wealthy private club owners to bypass the law he was hypocritically enforcing onto the working class. These narratives directly challenged Roosevelt's political future.

In response to Roosevelt's attempt at uniformly enforcing Sunday closing laws, German bar owners held a large protest parade to show their disapproval. To their shock, Roosevelt showed up at the parade and supported their right to public protest. His sister described the scene as follows:

> *They were parading to show their disapproval of him, but at the last moment, as a wonderful piece of sarcasm, they decided to invite him to review the parade, hardly thinking that he would accept the invitation. However, Roosevelt accepted the invitation. At the parade, he leaned over the platform, where he had been invited to sit, and saw the mass of marching men carrying banners with "Down with Teddy," and various other unpleasant expletives. One company, as it passed the reviewing-stand, called out "Wo ist Teddy?" "Hier bin ich," called out the police commissioner, leaning over the railing and flashing his white teeth good-humoredly at the protesting crowd, who, unable to resist the sunshine of his personality, suddenly turned and, putting aside the disapproving banners, cheered him to the echo.*
>
> (Robinson, 1921)

By November 1895, the Sunday liquor law enforcement policy had impacted local elections, and Tammany politicians easily defeated their Republican foes. Undeterred, in 1896, Roosevelt got the Republican legislature in upstate New York to pass the Raines Law, an even harsher liquor law requiring saloons to shut down on Saturdays from midnight to Mondays at 5 AM. They were also required to keep their blinds open so officers could observe the inside, and saloon owners were required to provide a nominal liquor tax to curb consumption. Additionally, the law provided an exception to Sunday drinking for hotels with at least ten rooms. The unintended consequence of this law meant tavern owners' entrepreneurial spirit took over. They all began to put up cheap walls and cots to create the minimal ten rooms inside their tavern "hotels" to avoid the Sunday liquor law restrictions. The Raines Law created a legislative botchery of the original intent. It only served to encourage excessive drinking while it benefitted the prostitution trade and gave the image of the city that never sleeps since the "hotels" could now serve alcohol all night. Roosevelt would forever lose the voters of New York City in subsequent state and federal elections, but he did demonstrate other forms of leadership that future police reformers would emulate.

Technological Advances

Bertillon System of Criminal Identification

Roosevelt read about the Bertillon system out of Paris used to track criminal recidivists. The invention stemmed from Alphonse Bertillon, the chief of the Paris Prefecture of Police identification bureau (Wang, 2016). In February 1896, Roosevelt and his Police Board adopted the system to help identify recidivists based on keeping records of measurements taken on a suspect's head, length of fingers, feet, and notations of scars or other physical deformities. Before this system, the police relied on photographs or newspaper descriptions to identify criminal suspects. Bertillon also invented the mug shot with criminals photographed as early as the 1840s in France. Roosevelt installed a photography studio at police headquarters to replace the old system, which required arresting officers to escort criminal suspects to private commercial photographers. Subsequently, a "rogue's gallery" of photographed wanted criminals was displayed based on prior arrest photos. The Bertillon measurement was flawed based on the officer's arbitrariness doing the measurement, and by the early 1920s, fingerprints replaced the Bertillon system.

Patrol

New York did not have call boxes when Roosevelt was police commissioner, and there was no way the precincts or headquarters could communicate with patrol officers other than sending messengers on foot to find them. Roosevelt's Police Board attempted to acquire a bond through the city to fund a communication system upgrade. However, Tammany politicians stalled the bill and favored funds spent on patronage and salaries instead of technology. The Police Board pushed ahead a plan within their existing budget to connect telephone lines underground between headquarters and all 35 precincts, but that plan was financially delayed.

In 1896, the Police Board used its budget to purchase 16 horse-drawn patrol wagons to help answer more than 30,000 annual calls for service (Berman, 1987, pp. 87–88). It was the first time the department used wagons to transport arrestees and bring large numbers of officers to accidents and fires. Additionally, the media helped publicize the bicycle patrol formation, which Roosevelt was initially skeptical of, though he later became a staunch supporter and a cyclist himself. Evidence suggests that New York officers used bicycles as early as 1885 (Richardson, 1970). In 1895 the bike patrol, known as the "Scorcher Squad," grew from four officers to 29 and was responsible for 1,366 arrests in their first year (Jeffers, 1994, p. 209). The bike squad evolved to over 100 elite members and they had their own station house and unique uniforms (Berman, 1987, p. 88). The New York bike squad became a model for other cities and other police forces, including Berkeley, California, as described in Vollmer's chapter. By the end of 1917, the NYPD had 276 motorcycles, 1,025 bikes, 327 horses, and 87 motorized vehicles (Berman, 1987).

Firearms

A Police Board study of officer service revolvers found that uniform weapon requirements went unenforced. Officers were untrained in marksmanship, and they carried a variety of firearms, many of which were dangerous. On December 30, 1895, Roosevelt opened the NYPD School of Pistol Practice, and he authorized the purchase of newly developed Colt .32 caliber double-action revolvers with four-inch barrels (Berman, 1987, p. 89). However, officers were required to purchase the new service revolver for $10 out of their funds. The training and qualification system marked the first organized and mandated training in police history and would become a tradition for American law enforcement. Through his inquiry into firearms accidents, Roosevelt became convinced of the necessity for regular training, and he stipulated bi-annual officer qualifications at the range.[19] Roosevelt's training consisted of non-firing "dry-fire" practice, followed by officers using approximately ten cartridges fired at targets (Berman, 1987). Researchers have questioned the practicality of past and present firearm qualification measures (Morrison & Vila, 1998). By 1909, Roosevelt's pistol practice school evolved into the New York City Police Academy.

Roosevelt's Progressive Reform Leadership

The statutory responsibilities of past Police Boards focused on writing policy and providing civilian oversight. Roosevelt's direct involvement with operational matters was unprecedented and demonstrated his leadership instincts. In the past, formal operational leadership rested

19 The bi-annual requalification is discussed in the chapter on Ramsey. Investigative reporters from the *Washington Post* looked into the sharp increase in officer-involved shootings (OIS) throughout the 1990s in the aftermath of a hiring binge that lacked proper background checks and the issuance of new Glock handguns. Reporters found that the vast majority of officers were not requalifying at a shooting range.

Photo 1.2 New York Police Commissioner Theodore Roosevelt, 1895–1897.
Photo courtesy of the Library of Congress.

with the police superintendent. However, in reality, power was decentralized to the precinct captains, and political ward bosses controlled them. Once Roosevelt had his superintendent removed, he attempted to centralize command from police headquarters. While Chief Peter Conlin replaced Byrnes, Mayor Strong often bypassed Conlin and asked Roosevelt to speak directly to precinct commanders. Roosevelt obliged and closely monitored his officers' activities in a manner that was far different from past commissioners. Roosevelt was ahead of his time as a police reformer.[20] He recognized that limitations had to be placed on officer discretion to minimize the corruption and political favoritism which influenced that discretion (Photo 1.2).

Police Lodging Houses

Roosevelt's active leadership style allowed him to gain a firsthand education on the type of conditions the New York poor were living and working in throughout the city. During his time as a police commissioner, several private charities helped provide beds and shelter for the homeless populations. These charities mainly stemmed from churches. Despite these efforts, no stable government-supported social service providers were setup, and homeless vagrants were common. Homelessness became especially concerning when wealthy homeowners would find vagrants in their neighborhoods and call on the police to solve the problem. One of the last resorts was police lodging homes' operation, which consisted of bunkrooms inside police precincts throughout the city.[21] In theory, these facilities were supposed to assist the

20 Historians report real police reform began during the Professional Era in the 1930s following the Wickersham Commission Report as detailed in the chapter on August Vollmer.

21 Roosevelt's journalist friend Riis resided in the five-point slum and police lodging houses for a time after he arrived in the city as an immigrant in the 1870s, before he became a police reporter for the *New York Tribune*. During his struggles, he contemplated suicide numerous times and would later provide Roosevelt a firsthand account of how difficult the poor had it.

undeserving immigrant poor, but too often, police reformers found their stations filled with thieves, unemployable citizens, and the mentally ill. These stations could house a couple of thousand homeless people who slept on bunks or the floors.

Roosevelt's journalist friend, Riis, complained about his and his dog's mistreatment inside police station tenements in the 1870s when he arrived in the United States (Riis, 1908). Roosevelt understood Riis, saw the police tenements as unprofessional, and subjected officers to contagious disease (Berman, 1987). Roosevelt did not believe police departments should house the homeless and did not buy into the social work paradigm for police agencies. On February 15, 1886, the lodging houses inside police departments were permanently closed (Berman, 1987, p. 92) as part of his police professionalization movement. Like the Sunday liquor law enforcement, Roosevelt's decision to close police lodging houses was unpopular with many working-class families throughout the city. By the 1920s, the police nationally were out of the lodging business (Katz, 1986).

Prostitution

Within his progressive purity campaign, Roosevelt took a different approach toward prostitutes, who were also part of the immigrant working class. The Commissioner saw the prostitute as the exploited victim of male lust and targeted enforcement policies toward the consumer. He also wanted to see brothel owners arrested and their names published in the media for owning properties used for immoral purposes. Traditionally, the patrons of prostitution were ignored or extorted by the police, but Roosevelt ordered them arrested and prosecuted. Several undercover operations through the Central Office Detective Bureau took place during Roosevelt's tenure but at a high cost to the department's contingency fund and personal expenses for undercover vice officers. Eventually, a private anti-vice organization provided funds to underwrite the expense of prostitution investigations (Berman, 1987, p. 105).

Anti-Semitic Freedom of Speech Quandary

A German anti-Semitic preacher requested a permit and police protection to speak out publicly against Jews in Cooper Union. Roosevelt realized he had to protect the individual's constitutional First Amendment, but he wanted to send a message that he did not support the anti-Semitism rhetoric.[22] In response, Roosevelt assigned a Jewish Lieutenant and over 40 Jewish policemen (Miller, 1914). While under Jewish police officers' protection, the ridiculed speaker left town (Miller, 1992).

Professional Model through a Quasi-Militaristic Structure

As the President of the Police Board, Roosevelt took charge of meetings, even though his position was primarily ceremonial and carried no statutory power. Mayor Strong's centralized executive control was consistent with Roosevelt's leadership philosophy. While past police boards were largely advisory, Roosevelt pushed a professional reform model of policing that included reduced autonomy for police precincts and restructuring the department toward a quasi-militaristic structure. This structure redefined the mission of the police toward a narrower legalistic crime control structure. Within his reform agenda, Roosevelt attempted

22 Roosevelt opposed "paranoid nativism" that stemmed from the American Protective Association (APA) and their suggestions that a Jewish conspiracy threatened the nation (White, 2003, p. 132). The APA membership skyrocketed during the financial collapse of the mid-1890s, and Roosevelt consistently made his views about religious tolerance known.

to limit police functions that previously included having officers operate ambulances, supervise elections, censor theatrical performances, and conduct building inspections (Berman, 1987). Roosevelt followed other reform leaders who argued that these extraneous patrol tasks invited political interference, wasted resources, and impacted the police's public image (Czitrom, 2016). For reformers like Roosevelt, the police role had to be better defined. From the turn of the twentieth century through the 1990s, that role would entail a legalistic policing style focusing on enforcing morality and controlling crime. The redefined mission on crime control called for a militaristic structural redesign of the police function.

Roosevelt's push to create a quasi-militaristic structure within the department was supposed to improve discipline through greater efficiency and order. Before his arrival, the fabric of officer allegiance and performance tied in with the Tammany political machine tapestry. Police leaders had little impact on hiring and promotions, and they were not likely to be incentivized through their command. This symbolic leadership excused officers' regard for following policies and procedures. Roosevelt changed this dynamic and introduced a militaristic structure to include procedures that mimicked court-martial, increased use of fines and suspensions, and strengthened disciplinary control. It was critical that precinct supervisors, known as roundsmen, would be allowed to discipline without fear of the political reprisals that often occurred if an officer was politically connected.

In furthering his professional model, Roosevelt frequently used militaristic terminology like "war on crime and corruption" and encouraged officers to act with bravery, valor, and discipline. Officers who served with heroism received promotional opportunities, much the way a military soldier would be awarded a ribbon or medal for exemplifying courage in the field.

Centralized Control

Increased clerical staff hired at police headquarters reduced precinct workload (Berman, 1987) and solidified centralized executive control. Tighter controls reduced operational expenditures, and the budget ran directly through centralized headquarters to counter connections that precinct command staff had with favored suppliers. These new accountability measures combined with a fairer bidding process and stringent audits completed on precinct purchases.

Roosevelt also reduced precinct power by providing more resources to the Central Detective Bureau inside headquarters. He demoted 16 detectives and forced nine to retire, who previously worked for Superintendent Byrnes (Berman, 1987, p. 64). Restructuring the investigative power to headquarters would, in theory, allow for centralized detectives to challenge past investigations run by precinct detectives who too often protected certain criminals based on their political connections or orders from precinct captains. Roosevelt also expanded specialized units, which provided a centralized focus on liquor laws, narcotics, and gambling. A year after the restructuring, the Central Detective Bureau's arrests nearly doubled to 2,527 from the previous year's 1,384 (Berman, 1987, p. 65) (Photo 1.3).

During Roosevelt's tenure, he also had the departmental policy manual updated. He did so by appointing a committee of high-ranking officers and clerical staff to revise policies that gave direction and coordination to the entire department. In doing so, Roosevelt demonstrated a participative management style long before Douglas McGregor's writings or Rensis Likert's advocated consulting with employees (McGregor, 1960; Likert, 1967).

Roosevelt declared in his autobiography that he reformed the NYPD (Roosevelt, 1897). However, long-term changes did not evolve from his short stint as a police commissioner (Zacks, 2012). The media and historians saw his term as the President of the Police Board as uncompromising and too elitist. Many argue that Roosevelt had only a short-term impact

Photo 1.3 Photo courtesy of the NYPD.

on vice and corruption. On January 1, 1898, state legislatures took the lead from Roosevelt's reform efforts of centralized police control. They merged the five boroughs – Manhattan, Brooklyn, Queens, the Bronx, and Staten Island – into New York City and 18 separate police agencies into the NYPD, which would become the largest department in the country.

Assassins

Roosevelt's lessons as police commissioner positively impacted his future political leadership as Governor of New York (1899–1901), Vice President (1901), and the 26th President (1901–1909) following McKinley's assassination. (McKinley's assassination is discussed further in the chapter on Ramsey as it relates to the Metropolitan Police Department.) An officer from the Washington, DC Metropolitan Police Department arrested McKinley's assassin after his escape attempt.

In a similar event, the Milwaukee Police arrested John Flammang Schrank, a saloonkeeper from New York City, after he attempted to assassinate Ex-President Roosevelt on October 14, 1912.

Roosevelt was campaigning for an unprecedented third Presidential term as a Progressive through the "Bull Moose" Party since his ex-friend William Taft was re-nominated at the 1912 Republican convention. After he came out of the Gilpatrick Hotel, now the Hyatt Regency (located at West Kilbourn Avenue and North Old World 3rd Street), Schrank[23] shot

23 Schrank was found legally insane and institutionalized at the Central State Mental Hospital in Waupun, Wisconsin, until his death in 1943 at the age of 67.

Roosevelt as he attempted to enter a vehicle taking him to his campaign speech. The assassin's bullet passed through Roosevelt's overcoat, tore through his 50-page speech inside his coat, and pierced through his steel eyeglass case before lodging in his chest where it remained the rest of his life. Stubbornly, Roosevelt told the mob to leave the assassin be until the Milwaukee Police arrived to arrest him. The former President then refused medical attention, went to the Milwaukee Auditorium, and delivered an 84-minute speech before being taken to a hospital where doctors saw the bullet just missed piercing his lung. The bullet-riddled, blood-stained paper speech and pierced eyeglass case is on display at Roosevelt's boyhood home in Oyster Bay, New York.

Leaving the Police Commission and Becoming President

In two short years, Roosevelt led sweeping reforms that rippled across the nation's municipal police agencies. The concepts and practices Roosevelt fostered in 1895 continue to serve as measuring rods for modern police administration reform efforts. These include better training and unbiased standards for promotion, morale improvement linked to commendations for bravery, and reform leadership directed toward reduced bribery. However, Roosevelt's reform efforts led to enormous political pushback from Tammany Hall and his political party. By 1897, the Republicans asked Roosevelt to move back to Washington, DC, and help campaign for Republican William McKinley's Presidential election. After the election, McKinley appointed Roosevelt to be an assistant to the Secretary of Navy, and he left the police board. A year into this position, Roosevelt pushed for war against Spain, which had empires in Cuba and the Philippines. Upon President McKinley's orders to intervene in Cuba, Roosevelt assembled a volunteer cavalry regiment from New York called the Rough Riders. On June 22, 1898, Roosevelt's regiment came to Cuba and charged up Kettle Hill. The combat ended ten days later. Roosevelt returned to his New York home as a war hero, and with support from the Republican Party, he was elected New York Governor.

As Governor of New York (1899–1900), Roosevelt revisited his police reform agenda, and he signed a law replacing the bipartisan police commission with a single police commissioner. He also used his lessons from Washington, DC, and New York to target unregulated monopolies and push for crime control, economic regulation, and increased sanitation, threatening both Democratic and Republican political bosses. To circumvent Governor Roosevelt's progressive reform efforts, Senator Platt, the boss of the Republican Party, influenced his vice-presidential candidacy (a position seen as not being politically powerful) on the McKinley reelection presidential ticket in 1900. McKinley's first Vice President, Garret Hobart, died in office of heart disease in November 1899 at 55 years of age. On September 6, 1901, President McKinley was shot and died eight days later,[24] allowing Roosevelt to become the nation's youngest President at age 42. President Roosevelt was thrust into a powerful position to further his progressive reform leadership based on lessons he garnered as the President of the New York Police Board. His views of the arrogant, wealthy elitists in New York, from which Roosevelt came, were viewed through a different lens. He would challenge them as being malefactors of great wealth that needed compromise through various acts of reform.

24 McKinley was the 25th President and the last to have served in the Civil War. On September 6, 1901, he was assassinated by Leon Czolgosz, a polish anarchist, during a public event in Buffalo, New York. McKinley died eight days later of his wounds at the age of 58. He is one of four Presidents who have been assassinated, along with Lincoln (1865), age 56; Garfield (1881), age 49; and Kennedy (1963), age 46. Four other Presidents died in office: Harrison (1841) age 68 (pneumonia); Taylor (1850) age 65 (stomach disease); Harding (1923) age 57 (heart attack); and Franklin Roosevelt (1945) age 63 (stroke).

Roosevelt's Federal Bureau of Investigation (FBI)

Amid his reform movements, two events pushed President Roosevelt to create the Federal Bureau of Investigation (FBI) – President McKinley's assassination and the Portland Land Scandal that implicated several members of Oregon's congressional delegation. The assassination of President McKinley shocked the nation and created a perception that anarchists threatened our democratic foundation. The Secret Service was created in 1865 to suppress counterfeiting, and Congress authorized the agency to provide Presidential protection after 1901. However, the gaps in federal investigations and Roosevelt's personal experiences with local law enforcement limitations were apparent. Roosevelt pushed the Department of Justice (DOJ) and his Attorney General (AG) Charles Bonaparte[25] to develop a separate autonomous federal investigative service, to the dismay of many in Congress.

The DOJ was formalized in 1870 during Reconstruction to protect the constitutional rights of freed slaves and battle the Ku Klux Klan (KKK). However, the agency lacked full-time criminal investigators. When early investigations were needed, the DOJ contracted with private detectives. By the 1880s, the DOJ regulated interstate commerce. In 1907, *Looters of the Public Domain: Embracing a Complete Exposure of the Fraudulent System of Acquiring Titles to the Public Lands of the United States* provided details about an Oregon land fraud scandal that dated back to the 1870s (Blumm & Wigington, 2013). Most of Oregon's congressional delegation was indicted for schemes to resell land around railroads at higher prices than what was granted by the Federal Government.

For Roosevelt, the scandal made it clear that the DOJ needed federal investigators. On July 26, 1908, after Congress had adjourned for summer break, AG Bonaparte hired 34 men to lead a new investigative agency and work directly for chief examiner Stanley Finch.[26] In December 1908, Roosevelt's administration informed Congress about the new law enforcement agency. In 1909, Bonaparte's successor, George Wickersham,[27] officially named it the Bureau of Investigation (BOI) (Weiner, 2012).

In 1924, J. Edgar Hoover was appointed the fifth director of the BOI. In 1935, the BOI became the FBI. Hoover was the FBI director for 48 years through the President Nixon administration until he died in his sleep on May 2, 1972, at 77 years of age. He is the only FBI director to die while serving and not retire, resign, or be fired by the President. Although Hoover was personal friends with Nixon, the President attempted to replace him with Bill Sullivan.[28] Hoover responded by forcing Sullivan to retire and replaced him with Associate Director Mark Felt. In 2005, 31 years after Nixon resigned his Presidency and 11 years after his death, Bob Woodward revealed that Felt was the informant known as "deep throat." Felt helped *Washington Post* reporters Carl Bernstein and Bob Woodward expose the Watergate Scandal (Woodward, 2005) that led to President Nixon's resignation. After Hoover died, the director's position became a single ten-year term after appointment by the President and confirmation by the Senate.

25 Bonaparte was one of the founders and Presidents of the *National Municipal League* and served as an activist for advancing Black Baltimore residents' civil rights.

26 Finch started his career in 1893 as a clerk in the DOJ. Between 1893 and 1908, he was the chief examiner, and he advocated for an investigative squad. AG Bonaparte assigned him to oversee the investigators, which were named the Bureau of Investigation (BOI). Four years later, Finch left the DOJ and became a special assistant to AG Wickersham and worked for various private companies.

27 Wickersham was the 47th United States AG (1909–1913). He is also discussed in the chapter on Vollmer for directing the National Commission on Law Observance and Enforcement (otherwise known as the Wickersham Commission) that showed widespread police brutality and corruption in the wake of the Eighteenth Amendment (which made alcohol use illegal and fueled organized crime).

28 Rather than becoming Hoover's successor, Hoover forced Sullivan to retire after serving as the director of domestic intelligence operations from 1961 to 1971. In 1977, Sullivan was killed in a deer hunting accident in New Hampshire (Smith, 1977).

Two proceeding tables include New York City police leaders before 1901, which includes Roosevelt. Since there were multiple commissioners during this time, only one Commissioner is listed each year in Table 1.1. Table 1.2 includes New York Commissioners after 1901 when a single commissioner was appointed.

Table 1.1 New York City Police Leaders Pre-1901

Years	*Name*
1857–1857	Simeon Draper[i]
1860–1863	John Kennedy[ii]
1873–1874	Abram Duryee[iii]
1874–1874	Hugh Gardner
1873–1875	George Matsell[iv]
1877–1879	William Smith
1880–1889	Stephen French
1890–1891	Charles McLean
1892–1894	James Martin
1895–1897	**Theodore Roosevelt**
1897–1897	Frank Moss
1898–1900	Bernard York
1898–1901	William Devery[v]
1900–1902	Michael Murphy

Notes: Before 1901 the NYPD was run by a police board of four to six commissioners. Also, they had police superintendents that managed the day-to-day operations, and this position was relabeled to Chief of Police after 1898.

Table 1.2 New York Police Commissioners (1901–1966)

Years	*Name*
1901–1902	Michael Murphy
1902–1903	John Partridge
1903–1904	Francis Greene
1904–1906	William McAdoo
1906–1909	Theodore Bingham

i In 1856, Draper was a Republican candidate for governor but lost the primary to John King. He then became one of the original Police Commissioners by the New York Metropolitan Police District and was asked to serve as the Police Board's President when it was established on April 16, 1857. However, he resigned as commissioner after only six months due to allegations that his fellow commissioners made police appointments based on political considerations without proper consultation.

ii Kennedy led the police response to the New York City Civil War Irish-led draft riots in 1863. He was badly beaten by mobs of protesters and stabbed numerous times (Brandt, 1999). This was one of the largest civil unrest episodes in American history. Orphanages for Black children were attacked along with media outlets, homes of the affluent, and political buildings. Blacks and interracial couples were brutally and publicly maimed and killed in a house-to-house massacre during the riots before the federal military was called (Bernstein, 2010). The draft in New York City was then suspended.

iii Duryee was a Civil War Union General and led the force of 1,600 policemen to beat labor protesters in January 1874 in Tompkins Square Park, which required the National Guard to quell riots.

iv Matsell was previously the first police chief of the Municipal Police in 1845 and was removed by the Metropolitan Police in 1859 and brought back in first as Superintendent in 1871 and then as the President of the Police Commission in 1873.

v In 1898, the Superintendent title was changed to the Chief of Police. Devery was the last Superintendent and the first Chief of Police. He was enormously corrupt and covered by fame Muckraker Lincoln Steffens (Snow, 1982).

Table 1.2 Cont.

Years	*Name*
1909–1910	William Baker[i]
1910–1911	James Cropsey[ii]
1911–1913	Rhinelander Waldo[iii]
1913–1914	Douglas McKay[iv]
1914–1917	Arthur Woods
1918–1918	Frederick Bugher[v]
1918–1925	Richard Enright[vi]
1926–1927	George McLaughlin
1927–1928	Joseph Warren[vii]
1928–1930	Grover Whalen
1930–1933	Edward Mulrooney
1933–1933	James Bolan
1934–1934	John O'Ryan
1934–1945	Lewis Valentine[viii]
1945–1949	Arthur Wallander
1949–1950	William O'Brien
1950–1951	Thomas Murphy[ix]
1951–1953	George Monaghan[x]
1954–1955	Francis Adams[xi]
1955–1961	Stephen Kennedy
1961–1965	Michael Murphy
1965–1966	Vincent Broderick[xii]

i Baker owned the Philadelphia Phillies from 1913 to 1930. As a police commissioner, he was accused of interfering in gambling investigations.

ii Cropsey also became a New York State Supreme Court Judge.

iii Waldo hired Sam Battle as New York's first African-American police officer in 1911. Battle also became the first Black sergeant in 1926, the first Black lieutenant in 1935, and became the commissioner of the parole board in 1941. Battle died in 1966 at the age of 83. In 2009, the intersection of 135th and Lenox Avenue in NYC was named after him. See Browne, 2015. Moses Cobb is also listed as one of the first Black officers hired in 1892 with the Brooklyn Police Department before its merger into the NYPD. He was not promoted to patrol until 1912 and became the first to serve a full 25 years until his retirement. Cobb inspired his brother-in-law, Sam Battle, to join the NYPD.

iv Waldo hired Sam Battle as New York's first African-American police officer in 1911. Battle also became the first Black sergeant in 1926, the first Black lieutenant in 1935, and commissioner of the parole board in 1941. Battle died in 1966 at the age of 83. In 2009, the intersection of 135th and Lenox Avenue in NYC was named after him. See Browne, 2015. Moses Cobb is also listed as one of the first Black officers hired in 1892 with the Brooklyn Police Department before its merger into the NYPD. He was not promoted to patrol until 1912 and became the first to serve a full 25 years until his retirement. Cobb inspired his brother-in-law, Sam Battle, to join the NYPD.

v Bugher lasted only 23 days as commissioner and was asked to resign for being negatively honest.

vi Enright was the first officer to rise from the rank-and-file to commissioner. He was also the longest-serving commissioner to date until Lewis Valentine (1934–1945).

vii Warren resigned after 20 months after he failed to solve the murder of Arnold Rothstein, which occurred on November 4, 1928. A few years prior, Rothstein was one of the largest organized crime leaders in the country with links to paying off players with the Chicago White Sox to lose the 1919 World Series intentionally. Rothstein was killed for a poker debt from a fixed game organized by Alvin Thomas (AKA Titanic Thompson) (Cook, 2011).

viii See Valentine and La Guardia (2019).

ix Murphy became a federal judge (1951–1970) after being nominated by President Truman.

x Monaghan also served as the NYC Fire Commissioner before being appointed to be police commissioner.

xi Before becoming police commissioner, Adams was a federal prosecutor for the Southern District of New York. After he was commissioner, he served as an assistant counsel in the 1963–1964 Warren Commission that investigated President Kennedy's assassination.

xii Broderick was also a prosecutor and became a federal District Court Judge (1976–1988) appointed by President Ford (see Ginsburg, 1996).

Epilogue

Mass social protests of 2020 provided challenges for numerous demarcations of subjugated Americans. There was a removal of several symbols of this subjugation, and Roosevelt was no exception. Three years prior, New York City Mayor Bill de Blasio established a commission to evaluate monuments in the city that were controversial (Tracy, 2017). A bronze sculpture of Roosevelt on top of a horse, with two indigenous men (American Indian and African-American) walking beside him, remained in front of the Museum of Natural History located at the west entrance from Central Park. The sculpture was supposed to symbolize Roosevelt's paternalistic approach to both indigenous cultures and racial unification. For others, the statue glorified white power and dominance and had been a target of protesters. In the wake of the 2020 protests, the museum asked city officials for permission to remove the statue, which had been on display since Roosevelt's widow, Edith Kermit Roosevelt, unveiled the 16-foot-tall tribute to her husband on October 27, 1940. The mayor once again pushed for the removal of the statue, and this time he was joined by Roosevelt's great-grandson, Theodore Roosevelt IV, and great-great-grandson Kermit Roosevelt III.

Nearly 20 years before the New York statue's unveiling, Roosevelt's equestrian style statue, depicting his time with the Rough Riders during the Spanish-American War, was completed in 1922 and unveiled in Portland. A discussion of the Portland Roosevelt statue appears in the epilogue chapter of Penny Harrington, who was the first woman to be a major city police chief in 1985. Protesters toppled the Portland statue in October 2020 during one of the numerous riots that occurred in the aftermath of George Floyd's death while he was in the custody of the Minneapolis Police Department on May 25, 2020.

For his part, Roosevelt appeared to be a progressive presence throughout his various leadership positions. On October 16, 1901, as one of his first acts in the Presidential House, which he eventually dubbed the "White House," Roosevelt invited Booker T. Washington[29] to dinner. With segregation laws in full effect, condemnation from the Southern media and politicians led to a 30-year absence of any future Black dinner guests to the White House (Davis, 2012). For Roosevelt, it was not unusual to invite African-Americans to dinner or even have them spend the night, as he did when he was Governor of New York (Lusane, 2013, p. 251).

Roosevelt and his wife Edith resided in the White House with their rambunctious six children, and reportedly, he dined with Washington, Edith and their daughter Alice. Dining with one's family took on a different connotation than having a state visit with Black leaders, as past Presidents had done. The dining issue, especially with one's wife and daughter, was seen as a statement of equality and became contentious for Southern politicians and the media. For his part, Washington also faced criticism from some Black community members who felt he was hypocritical by demonstrating support for segregation by attending a White House dinner. Moreover, Blacks feared a violent backlash throughout the South. African-American newspapers suspected Roosevelt's invitation was geared toward Black delegate support for the 1904 Republican Convention, especially from the Democratic South, rather than sincere support for addressing civil rights issues (Norell, 2009).

References

Ackerman, Kenneth (2005). *Boss Tweed: The rise and fall of the corrupt politician who conceived the soul of modern New York.* New York, NY: Da Capo Press, Inc.

29 Booker Taliaferro Washington was an African-American author and community leader for Black elitists who became the voice for former slaves and oppressed Blacks in the post-Reconstruction South. He helped establish the Tuskegee Institute as a historical Black college in Alabama, which Roosevelt visited in 1905 (Washington, 2013) three days before his 47th birthday.

Anbinder, Tyler (2002). *Five points: The 19th-century New York City neighborhood that invented tap dance, stole elections, and became the world's most notorious slum*. New York, NY: Penguin Group.

Andrews, Avery (1958). Theodore Roosevelt as police commissioner. *New York Historical Society Quarterly 42*: 117–141.

Berman, Jay (1987). *Police administration and progressive reform: Theodore Roosevelt as police commissioner of New York*. Westport, CT: Greenwood Press.

Berman, Jay (1981). The taming of the tiger: The Lexow Committee investigation of Tammany Hall and the police department of the City of New York. *Police Studies 3*: 55.

Bernstein, Iver (2010). *The New York City draft riots: Their significance for American society and politics in the age of the Civil War*. New York, NY: Oxford University Press.

Blumm, Michael C. and Tim Wigington (2013). The Oregon & California Railroad Grant Lands' sordid past, contentious present, and uncertain future: A century of conflict. *Boston College Environmental Affairs Law Review 40*(1): 1–77.

Brandt, Nat (1999). *The man who tried to burn New York*. Lincoln, NE: Excel Press.

Browne, Arthur (2015). *One righteous man: Samuel Battle and the shattering of the color line in New York*. Boston, MA: Beacon Press.

Bumiller, Elisabeth (1995). Christine Whitman, sharpshooter. *Washington Post*. January 24.

Byrnes, Thomas (1895). *Professional criminals of America*. New York, NY: Cassell & Company (Digitized by Cornell University Library).

Cohen, Stanley (2006). *The execution of Officer Becker: The murder of a gambler, the trial of a cop, and the birth of organized crime*. New York, NY: Carol and Graf Publishers, Ltd.

Cook, Kevin (2011). *Titanic Thompson: The man who bet on everything*. New York, NY: W.W. Norton & Company.

Czitrom, Daniel (2016). *New York exposed: The Gilded Age police scandal that launched the Progressive Era (1st ed.)*. Oxford, UK: Oxford University Press.

Dash, Mike (2007). *Satan's Circus: Murder, vice, police corruption and New York's trial of the century*. New York, NY: Three Rivers Press.

Davis, Deborah (2012). *Guest of honor: Booker T. Washington, Theodore Roosevelt, the White House dinner that shocked a nation*. New York, NY: Atria Simon Schuster.

Fourman, Victoria (2018). Educating TR: Lincoln Steffens, the Schmittberger case, and the politics of police reform, 1895–1987. Master's thesis: Barnard College, Department of History.

Gaines, Larry. Victor Kappeler, and Joseph Vaughn (1999). *Policing in America (3rd ed.)*. Cincinnati, OH: Anderson Publishing Company.

Gardner, Chas (1894). *The doctor and the devil, or midnight adventures of Dr. Parkurst*. New York, NY: Gardner & Company.

Ginsburg, Ruth (1996). In celebration of the life of Vincent L. Broderick. *Pace Law Review 16*(2): 191–192.

Hawkins, Geraldine (2017). *Elliott and Eleanor Roosevelt: The story of a father and his daughter in the Gilded Age*. Delmar, NY: Black Dome Press

Jeffers, H. Paul (1994). *Commissioner Roosevelt: The story of Theodore Roosevelt and the New York City Police, 1895–1897*. New York, NY: John Wiley & Sons, Inc.

Juergens, George (1982). Theodore Roosevelt and the press. *Print Culture and Video Culture 111*(4): 113–133.

Kaplan, Justin (1974). *Lincoln Steffens: A biography*. New York, NY: Simon and Schuster.

Katz, Michael (1986). *In the shadow of the poorhouse: A social history of welfare in America*. New York, NY: Basic Books.

Lane, Roger (1967). *Policing the city: Boston 1822–1885*. Cambridge, MA: Harvard University Press.

Langley, Travis (2012). *Batman and psychology: A dark and stormy knight*. Hoboken, NJ: Wiley Publishing.

Lankevich, George (2002). *New York City: A short history*. New York, NY: New York University Press.

Lewis, William (1919). *The life of Theodore Roosevelt*. New York, NY: Creative Media Partners, LLC.

Likert, Rensis (1967). *The human organization: Its management and value*. New York, NY: McGraw-Hill.

Lodge, Henry C. and Theodore Roosevelt (1903). *Hero tales from American history, or the story of some Americans who showed that they knew how to live and how to die*. Philadelphia, PA: Gebbie and Company.

Lundman, Robert J. (1980). *Police and policing: An introduction*, New York, NY: Holt, Rinehart & Winston.

Lusane, Clarence (2013). *The black history of the White House.* San Francisco, CA: City Lights Books.
McGregor, Douglas (1960). *The human side of enterprise.* New York, NY: McGraw-Hill.
Miller, Herbert A. (1914). The rise of national individualism. Publications of the American Sociological Society (Volume VIII). *Problems of social assimilation*: Papers and Proceedings at the Eighth Annual Meeting. Minneapolis, MN: University of Chicago Press.
Miller, Nathan (1992). *Theodore Roosevelt: A life.* New York, NY: William Morrow and Company, Inc.
Miller, Wilbur (1999). *Cops and Bobbies: Police authority in New York and London, 1830–1870.* Columbus, OH: Ohio State University Press.
Monkkonen, Eric (1992). History of urban police. *Crime and Justice, 15*: 547–580.
Morris, Edmund (1979). *The rise of Theodore Roosevelt.* New York, NY: Coward, McCann & Geoghegan, Inc.
Morrison, Gregory and Bryan Vila (1998). Police handgun qualification: Practical measure or aimless activity. *Policing: An International Journal of Police Strategies & Management. 21*(3): 510–533.
Norrell, Robert (2009). When Teddy Roosevelt invited Booker T. Washington to dine at the White House. *The Journal of Blacks in Higher Education 63*: 70–74.
Palmer, Stanley (1988). *Police and protest in England and Ireland, 1780–1850.* Cambridge, UK: Cambridge University Press.
Parkhurst, Charles (1895). *Our fight with Tammany.* New York, NY: Charles Scribner's Sons (reprint ed., Freeport, NY: Books for Libraries Press, 1970).
Pottker, Jan (2005). *Sara and Eleanor: The story of Sara Delano Roosevelt and her Daughter-in-Law, Eleanor Roosevelt.* New York, NY: St. Martin's Press.
Richardson, James (1970). *The New York Police: Colonial times to 1901.* New York: Oxford University Press.
Riis, Jacob (1908). *The children of the poor.* New York, NY: Charles Scribner's Sons
Riis, Jacob (1970). *How the other half lives.* New York, NY: Garrett Press. (reprinted for the 1890 edition).
Roberts, Sam (2012). 100 years after a murder, questions about a police officer's guilt. *New York Times.* July 17.
Robinson, Corinne Roosevelt (1921). *Theodore Roosevelt: The man as I knew him.* New York, NY: Charles Scribner's Sons.
Roosevelt, Elliott (1947). *F.D.R. his personal letters early years and 1905–1928.* New York, NY: Duell, Sloan & Pearce.
Roosevelt, Franklin D. and Elliott Roosevelt (1946). *F.D.R.: His personal letters: Early years.* New York, NY: Duell, Sloan and Pearce Publishing.
Roosevelt, Theodore (1897). Municipal administration: The New York police force. *The Atlantic.* September.
Roosevelt, Theodore (1913). *Theodore Roosevelt: An autobiography.* New York, NY: De Capo Press, Inc.
Root, Jonathan (1961). *One night in July the true story of the Rosenthal-Becker murder case.* Albany, CA: Coward-McCann.
Sante, Luc (1991). *Low life: Lures and snares of old New York.* New York, NY: Farrar Straus Giroux.
Schlesinger, Arthur (1969). *The business of crime, in introduction of 1886 professional criminals in America* (by Thomas Byrnes, xiii-xxvi). New York, NY: Chelsea House Publishers.
Schulz, Dorothy M. (1992). *From social workers to crime fighter: A history of women in United States Policing.* Dissertation. New York, NY: Praeger Publishers.
Schulz, Dorothy M. (2004). *Breaking the brass ceiling: Women police chiefs & their paths to the top.* Westport, CT: Praeger Publishers.
Smith, J.Y. (1977). William C. Sullivan, once high FBI aide, killed by hunter. *The Washington Post.* November 10.
Snow, Richard (1982). American characters: Lincoln Steffens. *American Heritage 33*(2): 5.
Springer, Patrick (2019). From the badlands to Batman: How Teddy Roosevelt inspired the caped crusader's creation. *InForum.* March 4.
Steffens, Lincoln (1931). *The autobiography of Lincoln Steffens.* New York, NY: Harcourt, Brace, and Company.
Steinberg, Allen (1989). *The tranformation of criminal justice: Philadelphia 1800–1880.* Chapel Hill, NC: University of North Carolina Press.
Stiles, T.J. (2010). *The first tycoon: The epic life of Cornelius Vanderbilt.* New York, NY: Random House Publishing.

Todd, Jesse (1993). Battling Satan in the city: Charles Henry Parkhurst and municipal redemption in Gilded Age New York. *American Presbyterians 71*: 244.

Tracy, Thomas (2017). Vandals splash red paint on Theodore Roosevelt statue on Museum of Natural History steps. *New York Daily News*. October 27.

Valentine, Lewis and Fiorello La Guardia (2019). *Night stick: The autobiography of Lewis J. Valentine, former Police Commissioner of New York*. Montreal, Canada: Phocion Publishing.

Wang, Hansi (2016). Meet Alphonse Bertillon, the man behind the modern mug shot. *NPR: All Things Considered*. March 8.

Washington, Booker T. (2013). *My larger education: Being chapters from my experience (Dover Thrift ed.)*. Garden City, NY: Dover Publications, Inc.

Weiner, Tim (2012). *Enemies: A history of the FBI*. New York, NY: Random House.

Whalen, Bernard, Philip Messing and Robert Mladinich (2016). *Undisclosed files of the police: Cases from the archives of the NYPD from 1831 to the present*. New York, NY: Black Dog & Leventhal Publishers.

White, Richard (2003). *Roosevelt the reformer: Theodore Roosevelt as civil service commissioner, 1889–1895*. Tuscaloosa, AL: The University of Alabama Press.

Williams, Joseph (2018). In 1857, NYC police didn't keep the peace – they caused a riot: Two separate police forces – state and city – came head to head in a bloody brawl. *History Stories*. September 1.

Woodward, Bob (2005). *The secret man: The story of Watergate's deep throat*. New York, NY: Simon & Schuster.

Zacks, Richard (2012). *Island of vice: Theodore Roosevelt's doomed quest to clean up sin-loving New York*. New York, NY: First Anchor Books.

Chapter 2

August Vollmer – Berkeley's Father of Police Professionalism

The Father of American Police Professionalism

August "Gus" Vollmer (1876–1955) was the most innovative chief and academic police leader in American history. His positions included Marshal of Berkeley (1905–1909); first Police Chief of Berkeley (1909–1932); Los Angeles (LA) Police Chief (1923–1924); University of Chicago Professor of Police Administration (1929–1931); and University of California (UC) Berkeley Professor of Police Administration (1932–1937).

Vollmer presented an imposing presence, standing 6′4″ and weighing a slim 190 pounds. He stumbled into the field of policing with only a grade-school education, and his family initially attempted to dissuade his decision. Despite this inauspicious start, Vollmer worked tirelessly throughout his career and retirement to professionalize American policing. He would end his life with the revolver he carried as chief while suffering from Parkinson's and cancer so he would not be a burden to others. Vollmer's lifelong dedication to reforming American policing should not be lost in the face of the contemporary struggles facing police leaders. His reform efforts at the beginning of the twentieth century are just as critical to the modern challenges facing today's officers and police administrators. His leadership approach is just as relevant in the aftermath of the 2020 mass protests as it was during his era with perceptions of police corruption and brutality.

Main Research Sources – Parker, Carte, Robinson, and Oliver

Four primary researchers have written about the life and leadership of Vollmer. The first came from a biographical sketch by his friend Alfred Parker in 1961 in a book written for school children (Parker, 1961). The second came from Jane Robinson, who conducted audio-recorded interviews in 1971 with several colleagues of Vollmer. The third came from Gene Carte, who wrote his dissertation on Vollmer and a subsequent monograph with Elaine Carte in 1975. Lastly, Will Oliver, Professor at Sam Houston University, has written extensively on August Vollmer. Each of these individual research efforts is described more fully as a means for understanding Vollmer's leadership.

One of the first biographical attempts to capture August Vollmer's history came from Alfred Parker, who wrote *Crime Fighter: August Vollmer* in 1961, with a price tag of $3, for school children. Parker was a personal friend to Vollmer and a counselor at a junior high school in Berkeley. However, Vollmer and Parker's initial meeting produced a 1935 publication, *Crime and the State Police*, published by the University of California Press. In this article, Vollmer proscribed a single state police system and the elimination of town, village, municipal, and county agencies (Parker & Vollmer, 1935). This type of centralized command idea was idealistic

DOI: 10.4324/9780429272226-3

with the reform-minded police leaders of the professionalization era.[1] Later, Parker also wrote a mainstream book on his friend Vollmer (see Parker, 1972).

The second researcher came in the spring of 1971 when Jane Howard Robinson conducted an oral history dissertation on police professionalism funded by the Law Enforcement Assistance Administration (LEAA) in conjunction with the Bancroft Library at the UC Berkeley. Her project included interviews with 12 individuals who worked closely with Vollmer. The board of regents subsequently published transcripts of these interviews at the University of California in 1972.[2]

A third study came from Gene Carte, who attended UC Berkeley and wrote his dissertation on Vollmer. Carte also conducted several interviews with individuals close to Vollmer (Carte, 1973) and completed a subsequent monograph with his wife, Elaine Carte (Carte & Carte, 1975). Gene later became the Chair of the Criminal Justice Department at the University of Cincinnati. Unfortunately, any subsequent research on Vollmer's life, from the Cartes, was cut short on November 30, 1977, when, at the age of 39, Gene was fatally shot while intervening in an armed robbery at the Women's Service Center on East McMillan Street. At the time, he was retrieving research materials from a former student who was the director of the women's center. Ironically, Carte was teaching a course entitled "analysis of robbery," and some of his former students, employed as police officers, were involved in his murder investigation (Kramer, 1977). After his death, the American Society of Criminology (ASC), which began in Vollmer's living room (as later described), named the student paper award competition after Gene Carte and award three prizes at the annual ASC conference.

Lastly, much of our understanding of August Vollmer comes from the extensive research supplied by Professor Will Oliver at Sam Houston State University. Oliver's research on Vollmer's leadership culminated in a 785-page book, *August Vollmer: The Father of American Policing*, in 2017, with Carolina Academic Press. Each of these researchers has supplied a unique and balanced account of Vollmer's life, leadership, and ultimately, his legacy as the father of American police professionalization. That legacy began with his 1876 birth in "The Big Easy."[3]

New Orleans

Vollmer was born in New Orleans on March 7, 1876, to John and Philippine Vollmer. His friends referred to him as "Gus." His sister Josie was adopted five years before his birth, and his brother Edward was born two years after. The Vollmer parents emigrated from Germany as children, met and were married in New Orleans, and owned a prospering grocery store. John Vollmer passed away from a heart attack in 1884 when Gus was only eight years old. Philippine Vollmer operated the grocery store on her own for two years. However, the anxiety eventually forced her to sell the store and take her sons and adopted daughter back to her home village in Germany when Gus was ten years old. Two years later, the Vollmer family moved back to

1 The centralized consolidation approach to policing, which had new momentum during Prohibition, was later challenged by community policing advocates (see Ostrom, Parks, & Whitaker, 1973; Goldstein, 1979). The consolidation momentum occurred again in the aftermath of 9/11 and the National Defense Authorization Act of 1997 that created the Law Enforcement Support Office (LESO) and allowed the transfer of excess Department of Defense equipment to law enforcement agencies through the 1033 program.

2 Documentation of Robinson's oral interview project can be found at- http://digitalassets.lib.berkeley.edu/rohoia/ucb/text/augustvollmer01vollrich.pdf and audio versions can be found at https://archive.org/details/cabeuroh_000191/cabeuroh_000191_t06_access.mp3

3 New Orleans did not get the label "The Big Easy" until the 1960s when gossip columnist Betty Guillaud compared the laid-back lifestyle to the "Big Apple" moniker of New York City. The "Big Apple" came from a horseracing reporter, John Fitz Gerald, who heard the phrase used by African-American stable hands to convey important races the city hosted (LaBianca, 2019).

New Orleans but found the city more crime-ridden than when they left. These concerns culminated when New Orleans Police Chief David Hennessey[4] was murdered by gunfire while walking home after a police board meeting on October 15, 1890 (Gambino, 1998).

The chief was likely murdered in retaliation for recent arrests and possible upcoming testimony at a trial linked to feuds between the Italian Provenzano and Matranga families. Following Chief Hennessey's assassination there were 21 members of the Matranga family arrested, and 19 of them indicted for his murder (Botein, 1979). A couple of months later, Hennessey's widow fled by train to San Francisco along with the Vollmer family. The trial against the defendants was unsuccessful, and the public immediately assumed the jury was fixed through threats or bribery. Local politicians ran an ad in the city newspaper calling for justice against the Italian suspects and coordinated a public meeting.[5] On Saturday, March 14, 1891, after their meeting, a mob of protesters stormed the Parish Prison, shot and killed two prisoners, dragged seven more to a courtyard where they were shot and killed, and then hanged two others from a lamppost and a tree[6] (Botein, 1979). In the aftermath of the New Orleans's lynchings, public hysteria over the country's first impression of "The Mafia" encouraged anti-Italian sentiment across the country[7] (Wood, 2009). This type of lawless mob justice certainly was not lost on the young Gus Vollmer. On April 12, 2019, the city of New Orleans officially apologized for its role in the lynchings and murders of the detainees. Descendants of Hennessey and the Matranga families were present for the apology.

Berkeley

At the age of 12, Gus's life was again in flux as they moved across the country to start a new life, first in San Francisco and then Berkeley. Unfortunately, his adopted sister Josie rebelled against the move across the country and ran away from their home. Reportedly, the family never heard from her again (Oliver, 2008). Mother Vollmer resided in her home on Bonita Street in North Berkeley from 1891 until her death in 1938. The move to California also marked the end of Gus's formal education as he never formally progressed past the seventh grade. Vollmer kept himself busy working as a shipping clerk and messenger in San Francisco and eventually as a Berkeley stenographer. In 1895, he opened up a coal/fuel and hay/oats feed store at Shattuck Avenue and Vine Street in North Berkeley with his friend Ted Patterson. Vollmer was 19 years of age when he helped create the North Berkeley Volunteer Fire Department. He was awarded the town's Fireman Medal in 1897 (Carte & Carte, 1975). The Spanish-American War broke out in 1898, causing Vollmer to liquidate his share of the store and enlist in the army. He arrived in Manila Bay in July 1898 as part of the Eighth Army Corps, where he was responsible for police duties and conducting patrols to fight off Filipino General Aguinaldo's[8] insurgent

4 Hennessey became a police detective at age 20 and made national headlines in 1881 when he captured a notorious Italian criminal, Giuseppe Esposito. He became chief in 1888 and was murdered two years later.

5 Politically inspired vigilante justice was repeated on January 6, 2021, from President Trump supporters when they stormed the Capitol to protest the election of Joe Biden. Capitol police officer Brian Sicknick died of injuries from the mob that broke into the Capitol. On February 2, 2021, his cremated remains were laid in state in the Capitol, and he was buried in Arlington Cemetery. Inside the Capitol, officers fatally shot protester and Air Force veteran Ashli Babbitt.

6 The lynchings were detailed in the book *Vendetta* (Gambino, 1998) and then turned into an *HBO* movie that starred Christopher Walken. *Vendetta* demonstrated the prejudice and political power over Italian immigrants in New Orleans.

7 Between 1860 and 1920, an estimated 64,000 Italian immigrants came to Louisiana, more than any other state, to replace African-Americans in the field, and faced similar discrimination as Southerners attempted to enforce segregation in the aftermath of Reconstruction (Giordano & Giordano, 1979).

8 Aguinaldo is recognized as the first and the youngest President of the Philippines at the age of 29. He served as President from 1899 to 1901, before American forces captured him and Aguinaldo subsequently swore allegiance to the United States (Skillin, 2006).

rebel forces who had revolted against Spanish rule and targeted American troops. Vollmer was selected to run the Laguna de Bay gunboat, help protect soldiers' convoys, and capture river towns held by General Aguinaldo's men. This experience helped shape his thinking when he pushed for professionalizing future police operations through militarized discipline and merit-based testing (Go, 2020). However, the amount of intensity Vollmer pushed for a para-militaristic police force versus balancing social work and community relations is debatable. He left the Philippines on August 17, 1899, and returned to Berkeley.

Marshal – Chief Vollmer

The city of Berkeley was incorporated in 1878 and policed by an elected town Marshal assisted by constables. Through the next couple of decades, the Marshal and Constables mostly served papers and seldom arrested individuals. However, crime increased during the turn of the century, about the time when Vollmer returned home from the war. Upon returning, Vollmer found work delivering groceries and eventually with the U.S. Postal Service as a letter carrier. This position helped him establish essential contacts and friendships throughout Berkeley that would be helpful for his future. Vollmer became a local celebrity while working on his mail route when he jumped aboard a runaway train and prevented a significant wreck with an oncoming commuter train on Shattuck Avenue. On January 18, 1904, the *Berkeley Daily Gazette* detailed the story but spelled his first name "August" incorrectly, from his nickname "Gus." The headline read "Letter Carrier Gustave Vollmer Leaps Aboard Moving Car and Applies Brakes Just as Passenger Train Pulls Into Station." The media account made Vollmer a local hero, and Berkeley was seeking hero leaders to help the growing city battle increases in crime and corruption.

At the turn of the twentieth century, Berkeley was a small town but had issues with prostitution, Chinese gambling operations, and facilities for smoking opium. Citizen leaders were disgruntled that this type of criminal activity took place in their quiet university town, and police officials were bribed to look the other way. Newspaper publisher and future California governor (1923–1927) Friend "William" Richardson convinced Vollmer to run for city marshal. Vollmer's family did not want him to be elected as the city marshal, believing his service within the corrupt police department would bring social disgrace. However, Vollmer's friends had other ideas and persuaded him to run for election and replace the corrupt Marshal Charles Kearns. Kearns had allowed illegal opium dens to flourish and refused to enforce liquor laws claiming his force of three deputies was too small (Oliver, 2008). Richardson owned the *Berkeley Daily Gazette* and was a leader in the Progressive (later the Republican) Party. With his help and media endorsements, Berkeley elected Vollmer their city marshal on April 10, 1905. His lifelong career as a police leader began with an office inside the fire department.

Vollmer immediately let his reform strategy be known when he fired the chief deputy and two deputy marshals. He also persuaded the town trustees to approve nine additional full-time police deputies to be paid $70 a month (Oliver, 2008). Vollmer added police uniforms that consisted of a black coat, tie, and fedora. Deputies also wore a seven-point star badge with the title "Deputy Marshal." Vollmer then established a night patrol to help clean up vice and staged raids on Chinese opium-gambling establishments. These raids were mildly successful with some cases dismissed for insufficient evidence. Operators of the opium dens attempted to bribe Vollmer to avoid future raids. These were bribes former Marshal Kerns had previously accepted. Chinese crime leaders would quickly learn they could not bribe Vollmer, and the raids continued on their gambling-drug establishments.

Marshal Vollmer led his department with a high degree of professionalism and demands for ethical behavior, referred to as the golden rule of policing. He made it clear he would not tolerate forced confessions, referred to as the third degree, or any type of officer brutality. Vollmer also fought for his officer's well-being. In the summer of 1906, Vollmer met with town trustees and demanded an increase in pay beyond the $70 a month his deputies were receiving.[9] Each member of his staff had prewritten resignation letters, including Vollmer, and demanded additional income. A year later, the trustees approved the additional pay.

As a token of their appreciation, Vollmer's deputies threw a Christmas party and presented Vollmer with a Smith and Wesson .38 Special with his name engraved on it. Vollmer carried and used the handgun throughout his policing career. On November 4, 1955, in his Berkeley home at 923 Euclid Avenue, after battling numerous heart attacks, throat cancer, and Parkinson's disease, Vollmer turned his beloved handgun on himself (Oliver, 2017). As the last act of his leadership, he made sure his body went to the University of California for research. The revolver changed hands numerous times over the years and today is located inside the Berkeley Police Department (BPD) but not on public display.

San Francisco Earthquake – Chief Vollmer

Less than a year after Vollmer's election, on April 18, 1906, an estimated 7.9 magnitude earthquake struck San Francisco, causing a significant population shift to Berkeley. The aftershocks were felt throughout Berkeley in more ways than one, and Vollmer led the crowd control strategies. Berkeley opened up its university, several city buildings, and its ice skating rink for the thousands who fled San Francisco's destruction. Vollmer immediately put out a call to deputize fellow Spanish-American War veterans to help police the crowds while preventing riots, looting, and other criminal behavior. His quick, coordinated response gained him positive attention throughout the city, state, and nation. The same year, police leaders across the state created the California Police Chiefs Association to share best practices and active investigations. At age 30, Vollmer was elected as the president.

In 1907, an ordinance prohibited alcohol sales in Berkeley, and much like New York Police Commissioner Teddy Roosevelt, the ordinance put Vollmer in the spotlight of having to enforce violations. Eight years earlier, the city had passed a similar ordinance, but saloon owners successfully repealed it. Unlike Roosevelt, Vollmer's subsequent raids on social clubs and businesses endeared him to the community and the Republican establishment. He was unopposed for his second term as Marshal and easily re-elected to another two-year term.

By 1909, the Berkeley City Council voted for various governmental structural changes that allowed for the election of a mayor and an appointed police chief. The San Francisco population shift brought about the restructuring of government services and an additional 25,000 residents bringing Berkeley's population to 45,000. Berkeley's new police chief position followed national attempts to eliminate political influence over law enforcement leadership. As the elected city marshal, Vollmer's leadership style was well received. Consequently, he was issued a Police Chief badge[10] and appointed to be Berkeley's first police chief on August 13, 1909 (Douthit, 1975). Within his new position, Vollmer was moved from the fire department to the basement of a new city hall[11] building and would remain the chief of Berkeley until his retirement on July 1, 1932 (Photo 2.1).

9 In 1919, as Police Chief, Vollmer was given a raise and paid $250 a month, but this did not keep pace with the inflation that came after WWI. Vollmer persuaded the city council to give his officers $170 a month and $30 extra for their personal cars as patrol vehicles.

10 Vollmer's 1909 14-karat chief of police badge, with a diamond in the center, was accidentally rediscovered in August 2015 by a couple in Austin, Texas. The badge, with Vollmer's name on it, was discovered as the couple was going through boxes of more than 200 books they purchased for $5 from an estate sale. The couple routinely bought old books to sell online through Amazon to help pay for their children to go to college. Vollmer's badge was amongst books from University of Texas at Austin Anthropology professor Brian Stross, a native of Berkeley and UC alum, who died in 2014 and was divorced with no children. The couple mailed the badge to the BPD where it is now on display (Raguso, 2017).

11 The old Berkeley Town Hall burned down in September 1904. A month later, the first paid fire department was created and volunteer James Kenney was named the city's first fire chief.

Photo 2.1 August Vollmer's original badge.
Photo Credit: Michael Meehan with the Berkeley Police Department.

Berkeley was able to isolate itself from much of the high crime and vice that permeated San Francisco and Oakland, becoming an island of progressive liberalism and intellectual respectability (Morn, 1995). Hence, Berkeley absorbed the San Francisco population shift, became the breeding ground for a national police professionalization movement, and successfully collaborated with community expectations. Those expectations became influenced by UC Berkeley and a catalyst for Chief Vollmer's innovative reforms.

As the father of police professionalization, Vollmer sought to reinvent policing in the early twentieth century and free it from the corruption of political influence that had plagued agencies across the country from their inception. His leadership goals strived to define the police's role in a democratic society more clearly while utilizing the most modern technology to improve efficiency. During Vollmer's leadership tenure, his creative and inquisitive mind led him to become our nation's most influential police reformer. His patriarchal leadership in the police professionalization movement demonstrated how critically important innovation was during this reform era and how vital it remains today (Photo 2.2).

Vollmer Innovations

Patrol

Bicycles

In the summer of 1905, after several instances of community frustration with delayed officer response, Marshal Vollmer put his officers on bicycles to make them more mobile and efficient. In doing so, Vollmer faced ridicule from the public and the police. However, according

Photo 2.2 August Vollmer.
Photo courtesy of the Berkeley Police Department.

to his later assessment, through timed checks, bike patrol officers responded more quickly for needed service while covering more extensive patrol areas, which helped address the critics. Consequently, Vollmer became the first police leader to purchase bicycles for his entire force, though he's not the first to use bike patrols. The bike patrol strategy was utilized 20 years prior in New York City, phased out for a short time due to safety concerns, and then brought back by Commissioner Roosevelt, as discussed in the previous chapter, for a limited number of officers.

Emergency Signal Lights

In an effort to become more responsive to community demands, Vollmer took a trip to a wealthy neighborhood in LA patrolled by the Foster Private Patrol Service owned by a married couple. Vollmer met with Jim Foster toward the end of 1905 to acquire more information about his call box invention. Foster had placed boxes on telephone poles throughout his neighborhood, and these boxes contained phones that connected to his house phone. When his wife received a call for service at their home, she would flip a switch, and lights would go off near the call boxes, alerting her husband to pick up the nearest phone to get details about the call and where to respond. Upon returning to Berkeley, Vollmer immediately began attending city council meetings and advocated for a police signal system. The city council reluctantly allowed his request to be voted on. Much like his election as Marshal, Vollmer successfully convinced the community to help fund a $25,000 bond to install a system of flashing red recall lights throughout the city. These lights allowed officers to rush to one of 20 call boxes to get further instructions (e.g. descriptions of suspects). Eventually, they also utilized Morse code through the lights. Signal Alarm Company from Milwaukee received the bid for installing the nation's first signal system for a government police agency and put Berkeley in the national spotlight for police innovation. Vollmer was also able to get phones installed in the homes of each deputy marshal for free. Over the next few months, several criminals were arrested due to Berkeley deputies' faster response times. The media wrote stories about the signal system that further enhanced Vollmer's national reputation.

Motorcycles

In 1909, four years after he put cops on bikes, Vollmer conducted a beat analysis to determine police mobility more scientifically. In his detailed analysis, Vollmer had his patrolmen record each of their tasks during their shift, providing a timeline for understanding completion and how these tasks impacted response. The bikes had improved response time, task completion, and Vollmer had answered his critics despite the initial ridicule he faced from the media and the public. In 1910, Vollmer looked to further his patrol strategies when he lobbied the Berkeley City Council to purchase police motorcycles for a select number of officers. Again, Vollmer was not the first to advocate for motorized patrol as the Detroit Police Department purchased police motorcycles from Harley-Davidson as early as 1908. Evanston, Illinois, bought a belt drive cycle for an officer the same year. Ultimately, motorcycle patrol was short-lived in Berkeley, and by 1913, Vollmer got rid of motorcycle patrol after several officers were injured, including Vollmer himself. In November 1910, Vollmer chased a robber on a motorcycle and reached speeds of 40 miles per hour before he crashed and hurt his knee (Oliver, 2017).

Motor Vehicles

In 1913, Vollmer again defied critics by asking the Berkeley City Council to purchase a Model T Ford for patrol purposes, one of the first in the nation.[12] The belief was that only the very rich drove motor vehicles, and the police would be ridiculed. After receiving permission for one vehicle, Vollmer convinced the city council to provide officers an extra allowance to purchase personnel vehicles that could be used for patrol purposes and to provide them supplemental pay for maintenance. By the end of 1914, each officer had a personal patrol car, and Berkeley became the first city with the entire police force being mobile in patrol functions. Officers were given extra pay for the use of their vehicle and given free fuel and oil. However, Vollmer also expected his officers to be on duty 24/7, whether in uniform or not, if they witnessed criminal acts or disorder. Ironically, Vollmer never wanted to drive a police vehicle and his protégé, O.W. Wilson (as described in the proceeding chapter), became a driver for his chief. Vollmer had no interest in learning to drive (Robinson, 1972).

Criminal Investigations

In 1953, the editorial board for the *Journal of Criminal Law, Criminology and Police Science* asked O.W. Wilson to write an article on the life of his mentor, August Vollmer (Wilson, 1953). Wilson introduced his essay by describing Vollmer's passion for crime scene investigations. One case in particular occurred in 1916 and helped push the police leader toward the growth of criminalistics. Tony Carcopa sold vegetables on the street corners of Berkeley and was extorted by the Mafia through a letter written in Italian postmarked from San Francisco. Going against the advice detailed in the letter not to contact the police, Carcopa reached Vollmer, who subsequently setup surveillance on his home after learning there was a hit placed on Carcopa. Vollmer was likely reflective of his early childhood move across the country that followed New Orleans Chief Hennessey's assassination, in which the Mafia was the primary

12 In 1899, Akron, Ohio is credited with using the first electric police wagon. Akron's Collins Buggy Company designed the vehicle to be powered by two electric motors that would reach speeds of 18 mph for approximately 30 minutes before it needed to be recharged. The 2½ ton wagon had electric lights, a bell, and could seat up to 12 officers or arrestees. In August 1900, a mob rioted in Akron and pushed the police wagon into the Ohio Canal.

suspect. Investigating officers found sticks of dynamite wrapped in a burlap sack next to Carcopa's home.

Birth of the Crime Lab

Vollmer took the dynamite to colleague Dr. Albert Schneider, a UC Berkeley professor of pharmacognosy[13] and bacteriology. After his investigation of the non-exploded dynamite, Dr. Schneider pinpointed the merchant who sold it and the farm where it was created. The farm owner reported two Italians stole the dynamite, and they were later found and arrested. As in the past, Berkeley residents initially ridiculed Vollmer's attempt to merge science with criminal investigations until officers successfully made these arrests. Vollmer subsequently made Dr. Schneider BPD's first criminalist, and forensic science was born. Vollmer and Dr. Schneider began using forensics with blood, fiber, and soil analysis to solve crimes, and crime laboratories began to evolve throughout the country. The Carcopa investigation was the first time criminal forensics made use of science. However, a crime lab was not exclusive for investigative purposes and existed at the university rather than a police department. When Vollmer was Police Chief in LA in 1923, he encouraged establishing the nation's first crime lab within a police department dedicated exclusively to analyzing criminal evidence. Word spread, and large city departments followed, creating additional crime labs throughout the 1920s and 1930s; the FBI lab was built in 1932, under J. Edgar Hoover's direction.

Fingerprinting – Modus Operandi (MO)

Chief Vollmer was an avid police detective who could feel bogged down by leadership. He was continually looking for new ways to identify criminals. In 1909, he introduced the Bertillon[14] method to the BPD, which he borrowed from the French Police, who were focused on better understanding recidivism and banishing repeat criminal offenders. In the days before departmental photography, the Bertillon method called for the police to do a series of arrestees' measurements and descriptions. The measures would help identify recidivists. As the president of the California Police Chiefs Association, Vollmer helped craft a bill to mandate recording details of every California prisoner and have those details on file in every police department. However, Governor James Gillett vetoed the bill, and it would be another ten years before the bill reached congress again and made it successfully into law as a means to track recidivism. Vollmer also pushed the Henry[15] system of fingerprinting[16] and, in 1922, began a single fingerprint classification system. The influx of data cards led to large filing cabinets used for files on criminal identification.

13 Pharmacognosy is the study of medicinal drugs obtained from plants and other natural sources.

14 Vollmer read a report published in 1889, entitled *Alphonse Bertillon's Instructions for Taking Descriptions for the Identification of Criminals and Others*, leading to a system where officers would systematically record precise descriptions of the criminal suspect.

15 Sir Edward Richard Henry helped organize a system of classifying fingerprint data into various categories following Francis Galton's book *Finger Prints* (1892). Henry was the Commissioner of the Metropolitan Police of London from 1903 to 1918.

16 In 1936, Vollmer worked with Berkeley Police Chief John Greening and the Citizens' Committee on Universal Registration to voluntarily fingerprint everyone in Berkeley. The committee distributed 20,000 copies of a pamphlet to educate the Berkeley citizens on the history of fingerprinting and convince them it was necessary to get everyone on file, including children. Fingerprint stations were set up throughout the community and each person was given their own identification card with copies sent to the FBI in Washington, DC. Objectors stopped the campaign after approximately half the city's population was fingerprinted (Aronovici, 2011).

Vollmer also pushed to acquire additional data for detailed descriptions of criminal operations. He read Major General Llewellyn Atcherley's handbook (published in 1913) on a "mode of operating" (MO) system for criminal investigation and detection developed out of England's Yorkshire Constabulary (Fosdick, 1916). Vollmer worked with his Berkeley officers to revise Atcherley's system, and in 1919 he wrote an academic article that detailed the use of MO data. Vollmer wrote, "there is a clew to every crime," and "that clew is the method employed by the criminal in securing his ill-gotten loot" (Vollmer, 1919, p. 229). In 1920, Vollmer provided further detail of his evolving Bureau of Criminal Records system (Vollmer, 1920), including all the existing contemporary models for identifying criminals, recidivists, and modus operandi. Within this effort, there was a significant number of departmental records that needed to be continually classified. Officer Clarence Morrill served as a business secretary and is credited with reforming the Berkeley record-keeping system (Morn, 1995; Carte & Carte, 1975) that allowed for ways to conduct better investigations, police needs assessments, and improved evaluation on overall efficiency. Organized record keeping allowed Vollmer to demonstrate his vision to measure the cost-benefit of police services, an analysis foreshadowed in contemporary challenges levied against the police. Vollmer worked to institutionalize the organization of crime data throughout the state while pushing for a federal database. In 1907, as the President of the California Police Chiefs Association, Vollmer promoted the need for state legislatures to vote in the creation of a state bureau of criminal identification. By 1917, the database launched, followed by a national fingerprint database. The Berkeley criminal record system was widely copied by other departments across the country and eventually by FBI Director J. Edgar Hoover.

The "Lie Detector" Machine (Marston to Larson to Keeler)

Vollmer had long opposed the questioning of criminal suspects that used the third-degree method or other forms of brutality. He saw this method as a violation of constitutional rights and an unreliable strategy for obtaining quality evidence. In 1913, he read about Harvard psychologist William Moulton Marston's[17] work in creating a machine that would intermittently monitor a subject's blood pressure. Marston was unsuccessful in having the use of his device admitted into courts as evidence. He saw other benefits of the machine in psychotherapy and getting subjects to realize and admit to their true feelings regarding love and sexual desires. With his wives' assistance, Marston created the comic book hero *Wonder Woman* during World War II (WWII), with the feature of the magic lasso that operated like his lie detector machine (Lepore, 2015).

Vollmer longed to find an improved method for getting confessions from suspects, and he found a solution with a recently hired college officer John Augustus Larson.[18] In 1915, before arriving in Berkeley, Larson received his master's degree from Boston University with a thesis on fingerprint identification. In 1916, he was attracted to UC Berkeley's newly created criminology program and began work on his Ph.D. degree. On December 1, 1919, Larson was hired

17 Marston created the comic book hero *Wonder Woman*, first published in October 1941 with *All-Star Comics* (later merged with *Detective Comics* [DC]), with the assistance of his wife Elizabeth Holloway and his former research assistant Olive Byrne. Marston, Holloway, and Byrne became polyamorous life partners (see Lepore, 2015). Byrne was the daughter of Ethel Byrne and niece of Margaret Sanger, who started Planned Parenthood in Brooklyn, New York, in October 1916.

18 Larson married Margaret Taylor, the first person he interrogated on his machine. That machine is located at the Smithsonian Institute in Washington, DC. Larson felt some law enforcement officials abused his machine and expressed regret for having invented it later in life. He died in 1965 of a heart attack at the age of 72 in Nashville, Tennessee.

as a patrol officer by Vollmer. However, upon learning about his graduate school education, Vollmer shifted Larson's assignments toward working full-time to see if a lie detector machine could be built to determine if a suspect's blood pressure and respiration changed during questioning. Vollmer and Larson theorized that they might detect changes in respiration and blood pressure to determine signals of stress, as an indication of dishonesty during criminal investigations. Larson's reassignment away from patrol was made easier when his supervisors found out that he was blind in one eye, had the worst marksmanship on the department, and reportedly wrecked two police cars on the same day because he could not drive (Oliver, 2017, p. 342). It took Larson only a month to create a machine that took continual lung capacity readings and pulse readings. After several tests on police officers and Vollmer himself, the device was dubbed a success and began its use in several investigations. Larson completed his Ph.D. degree in physiology in 1920 from UC Berkeley while he still worked for Vollmer. He became the nation's first police officer with a doctorate degree.

The machine's official use came in the summer of 1921 when media representatives from the *San Francisco Call and Post* were invited to be present as Larson hooked the device up to William Hightower and questioned him about the kidnapping murder of priest Patrick Heslin. Hightower, accused of sending a letter to Archbishop Edward Hanna, demanded $6,500 in ransom after Heslin went missing. After the ransom went unpaid, he attempted to visit the Archbishop. Hightower then met a newspaper reporter and told a story about hearing where the priest's buried body could be found. He led several newspaper reporters and the police to a beach location, which led to the recovery of the priest's body. The police then arrested Hightower, and Larson was allowed to question the suspect with his new lie detector. Following the interrogation, on August 17, 1921, the *San Francisco Call and Post* brought national fame to Larson by showing a graph with arrows pointing to each lie and a headline that read "Science Indicates Hightower's Guilt." While Vollmer and Larson heralded the new "cardio-pneumo psychogram" machine, the press labeled it the first lie detector. Although there was a public outcry for Hightower's execution, he ultimately received a life sentence and served his time in San Quentin, where he became a master chef. In 1965, after serving 44 years, Hightower was paroled at 86 years of age, ironically the same year of Larson's death.

In 1922, Larson demonstrated his machine at the International Association of Chiefs of Police (IACP) conference. Vollmer was the president of the association that year and had managed to land the conference in San Francisco to show off his use of scientific advancements in police investigations. In addition to the conference, Larson and his machine helped in the investigation of Henry Wilkens. He was accused of arranging the murder of his wife in a fake car-jacking, while his children, Henry Jr. (age 8) and Helen (age 6), were in the back seat. According to Henry, his wife Anna was shot by bandits in their family car at 19th and Moraga on May 30, 1922, while heading to the Santa Cruz Mountains.

The murder occurred a few days before the 1922 IACP conference, and this time Larson interrogated Henry Wilkens with his lie detector machine and cleared the suspect. The defense would use the results at his jury trial. After the interrogation, Larson privately said he was unsure of his determination as there was some agitation from Henry. Vollmer disagreed with Larson's judgment. A jury deadlocked, and Wilkins went free. Later, investigators found Mrs. Wilken's killer was Walter Castor and his brothers Arthur and Robert. The Castor's, knew Henry for years. Arthur was arrested and confessed that Henry paid them to kill his wife. Robert told the police that Walter was driving a car paid for by Henry's payment to kill his wife, Anna. Walter was at his mother's home on August 3, 1922, when the police arrived to arrest him. Walter shot and killed Detective Sergeant Timothy Baily and Robert's wife, whom he suspected of "squealing" on him. He then turned the gun on himself and committed suicide. The San Francisco Police Department vowed they did not want to use Larson's "lie detector" machine ever again (South Bend News, 1922). After the San Francisco fiasco, Larson worked for Vollmer and the BPD until 1923,[19] before starting medical school in Chicago and taking a position at the Illinois Department of Public Welfare/Institute of Juvenile Research. He also worked as a chief psychiatrist within the Illinois Department of Corrections. Larson regretted inventing his "lie detector" machine, but his protégé would choose to market and utilize the device throughout his career.

Larson's protégé, and co-inventor of the polygraph, was Leonarde Keeler.[20] Keeler began working with Larson while he was still in high school after being introduced by Vollmer. Vollmer was friends with Leonarde's father, Charles, whom he knew from his days as a letter carrier (Alder, 2007). Charles was a famous Berkeley poet. After Keeler graduated high school in 1923, he attended UC Berkeley. However, he transferred to the "southern campus" (now UCLA) to follow Vollmer after he took the chief position with the Los Angeles Police Department (LAPD). Keeler expanded on Larson's work and created a device that ran on an alternating current and was better able to register pulse rates to a recorder. Vollmer thought the machine looked crazy with a mass of wires, tubes, and old tomato cans. Keeler used the term "polygraph" to describe his machine, which meant "many-writing instrument" or the "Emotograph" (National Research Council, 2003). Unfortunately, his initial machine was destroyed in a fire at his residence (Alder, 2007).

In 1929, Keeler joined Larson in Chicago at Northwestern University's Scientific Crime Detection Laboratory, the nation's first forensic lab.[21] Vollmer joined his students in 1930 to teach police science at the University of Chicago. When Vollmer left to return to Berkeley, their collaboration ended, and Larson continued questioning the lie detector machine's validity. Keeler, however, utilized his notoriety and attempted to patent his version of the lie detector machine.

Keeler's notoriety with the polygraph came when the media glorified stories about violent encounters between federal agents and professional criminals such as John Dillinger and Lester Joseph Gillis (AKA George "Baby Face" Nelson). For example, on April 22, 1933, Dillinger and Nelson were involved in a shootout with federal law enforcement officers at the Little Bohemia Lodge at the Manitowish Waters in northern Wisconsin.[22] The Bohemia incident[23] was an embarrassment for J. Edgar Hoover's new Bureau of Investigation (BOI) federal law

19 In the 1923 Supreme Court ruling *Frye v. United States*, the Court ruled that scientific evidence (e.g. obtained from the polygraphy) should be admissible into court if the scientific community sufficiently accepted it.

20 Keeler preferred to be called by his nickname "Nard." He married a psychology student "Kay" Applegate in 1930 while in Chicago. She became the nation's first female handwriting analyst and established an all-woman detective agency in Chicago specializing in forensic investigations. She eventually left Nard for another man, Rene Dussaq, who was a WWII paratrooper. She died on November 26, 1944, flying a solo plane across the country as part of the Women's Auxiliary Service Pilots (WASPs). Nard was devastated by his ex-wife's betrayal and death. He died in 1949 in Door County, Wisconsin, at the age of 45, after suffering a stroke.

21 One of Keeler's students at Northwestern University was future cartoonist Chester Gould, who based his comic book character *Dick Tracy* on Keeler. The comic first appeared in the *Detroit Mirror* on October 4, 1931, and Gould drew the comic strip for 46 years for the *Chicago Tribune* from his home in Woodstock, Illinois (O'Connell, 2007). One of Gould's assistants, Dick Locher, resided in Naperville, Illinois, and helped write and draw the *Dick Tracy* comic from 1957 to 1961 and then returned as the sole cartoonist in 1983 until 2009 (Goldsborough, 2010).

22 A little more than a year later, Dillinger was killed by Hoover's federal agents in Chicago on July 22, 1934, on his 31st birthday, as he exited the *Biograph Theatre* on Lincoln Avenue after watching *Manhattan Melodrama*, a Clark Gable film (Burrough, 2005). Nelson was shot on November 27, 1935, in Barrington, Illinois and later died at a house in Wilmette, Illinois, at the age of 25 (Nickel & Helmer, 2002). Nelson killed one federal agent in the Little Bohemia (Wisconsin) failed raid and he killed two agents in Barrington, Illinois.

23 Ironically, as described in the O.W. Wilson chapter, FBI Agent Virgil Peterson was present at the Little Bohemia raid. Twenty-five years later, he would be on a blue-ribbon committee, organized by Mayor Richard J. Daley,

enforcement agency.[24] The event ended with an innocent bystander, and a federal agent fatally shot and later became part of the FBI academy training on failed operations (Burrough, 2005). Keeler and his polygraph machine later provided the media with sensational propaganda stories that helped convince the public that good would prevail over the criminal element.

In the aftermath of the northern Wisconsin Bohemia Lodge tragedy, Portage, Wisconsin, contacted Keeler for a couple of cases to redeem law enforcement's public image. One case came after a robbery of the Emery and Mash Pharmacy in Baraboo, Wisconsin, on May 22, 1934. The robbery suspects, four Italian youth from a town just outside of Madison, were pulled over on Highway 33 by the Columbia County Sheriff Robert Roche. The men exited their vehicle and shot Roche, who survived and would later be able to return to duty. Madison officers arrested the suspects, and charged them with attempted murder.

The Baraboo shooting of Sheriff Roche became the first court case with a judge allowing evidence gathered from a lie detector based upon a pretrial agreement between the attorneys that either side could utilize the results. Keeler ultimately became the expert at interpreting the results of his test. Keeler administered his test on February 2, 1935, at District Attorney H.B. Rogers' Portage Law Office, and the results were presented five days later at a trial in Green Lake, Wisconsin. Keeler's interpretation of his machine indicated that the two suspects demonstrated a general consciousness of guilt and deception in the sheriff's attempted murder. The jury found both defendants guilty and sentenced them to eight and six years in prison (Lillie, 2018).

In 1936, Keeler became the director of the Scientific Crime Detection Laboratory at Northwestern University. By 1938, he opened his own private polygraph consultant business, referred to as the *Keeler Institute*. Over the next 25 years, Larson lashed out at Keeler and questioned his scientific credentials along with his marketing pursuits. Larson wrote letters to Vollmer and indicated that the machine was no more than a psychological third degree. Despite Larson's warnings, the lie detector machine has continued to evolve and has been controversially used in numerous court cases, employment screenings, civil lawsuits, divorce settlements, and utilized by military/intelligence agencies.

Further Innovation

Radios

In 1925, UC Berkeley College student turned police officer Vivian Anderson (VA) Leonard[25] approached Chief Vollmer with the idea of putting radios into police cars to maintain audio communication with headquarters and assist in criminal investigations. Critics contended that radio signals would not be able to keep up with speeding patrol cars. Through Vollmer's encouragement, Officer Leonard contacted the College of Engineering at the University of California. He collaborated with a student named Reginald Tibbetts who created a one-way radio transmission from the police department to the patrol vehicle. By 1929, after several months of improvements, the BPD installed radios in most BPD police cars and the rest of the nation's police agencies followed.[26]

with Wilson to select a reform leader for the Chicago Police Department (CPD). Peterson would be influential with other committee members in convincing Wilson to take on the task of reforming the CPD.

24 The BOI was renamed to the FBI after 1935.

25 Leonard is described more fully later in the chapter and is credited with initiating the ACJS as a forerunner of the ASC that began during a meeting in Vollmer's living room. For additional history on Leonard, see ACJS Historian Will Oliver https://cdn.ymaws.com/www.acjs.org/resource/resmgr/Historian/ACJS_VA_Leonard.pdf

26 Historians credit the Detroit Police Department with being the first city to utilize one-way patrol communication in 1928 with one police car (Poli, 1942). The patrolling officer would need to use a call box to call the

Juveniles

As the country shifted from a predominantly farming nation to an industrial society, mandatory education was still not a priority. Since children worked on family farms, it also made sense to have them working in plants and factories at an early age. However, many were left to the streets and became truants without jobs or an education. Vollmer was part of the progressive movement that looked for solutions to these burgeoning problems as juvenile crime took up considerable investigative resources. He encouraged his officers to treat juvenile offenders with a certain level of empathy. He had an open-door policy for neighborhood children to visit his office, where they would find "Uncle Gus," a listening ear, and a bowl of candy (Oliver, 2017, p. 290). Vollmer firmly believed that juvenile crime was preventable and that doing so would save a considerable amount of investigative resources. As a progressive reformer, Vollmer favored defining the police within a social work paradigm, unlike other police reform leaders who wanted to more narrowly portray the police as law enforcement crime fighters.

In late 1915, Vollmer became aware of America's Boy Scouts (BSA),[27] which was initially founded in England by British Military Officer Robert Baden-Powell.[28] Vollmer was in favor of creating a troop in Berkeley and worked with Mayor Sam Irving and the University of California to provide a location for their meetings. Vollmer helped train Perry Jenkins as the first Scoutmaster for Troop 1. The BSA combined their efforts with the Young Men's Christian Association (YMCA),[29] which was also founded in England and brought to Berkeley in 1903.

Following the first Boy Scout troop's establishment, Vollmer pushed his officers to consider alternatives to arresting juvenile offenders. Vollmer proposed one such option to bring offending juveniles into the police department as Junior Police officers. Vollmer's deputies hated this idea, but he persisted, ordering two dozen badges and organizing Friday evening meetings that would take place after his weekly Friday afternoon "crab sessions" with his officers (detailed later in the chapter). Borrowing from the BSA, Vollmer created a motto for his junior police officers: to "be honest, polite, helpful, loyal, brave, trustworthy and obedient" (Oliver, 2017, p. 293). Ironically, these were the same qualities Vollmer required from his adult officers. By the fourth meeting, over 200 children had joined, and they had to order a lot more badges, each coded with a unique number for each child. Vollmer utilized the volunteers to form the "School Boy Patrol," and they were actively involved in numerous community service projects. Subsequent juvenile delinquency[30] plummeted (Oliver, 2017).

Vollmer the Social Worker

Juvenile intervention matched Vollmer's goal of using social work as a core mission for policing. His views on individual offenders and his interest in the mental hygiene movement

department back after receiving the radio transmission. The first two-way radio was used by the Bayonne, New Jersey Police Department in 1933.

27 BSA was established by General Robert Baden-Powell in Britain in 1908 and in the United States in 1910 by W.D. Boyce.

28 Baden-Powell founded the first scouts through his 1908 book "Scouting for Boys" and 1915 book "Aids to Scouting" (Baden-Powell, 1915). His sister Agnes founded the Girl Scout Movement.

29 The YMCA was founded in London on June 6, 1844, to help young men who were often homeless and far from family during the industrial revolution. George Williams was the founder and aimed to create a housing environment where all social classes were invited for Bible study and prayer.

30 As early as 1906, Vollmer gave notice to his deputies that juvenile offenders were not to be placed behind bars, and by 1915 crime statistics were separately tracked for juvenile and adult offenders (Oliver, 2008). Vollmer was a proponent of the "child savers" movement and placing juvenile offenders into parental schools where they could be reformed when their own families failed to provide adequate rearing (Douthit, 1975).

demonstrated his unique leadership. Liss and Schlossman (1984) distinguish between law enforcement management and Vollmer's leadership emphasis on "police" social work. In doing so, Vollmer did not directly counter traditional law enforcement functions. He also did not advocate for a return to the police's multiservice role in the nineteenth century, when they allowed the New York City homeless to sleep inside police precincts until Commissioner Roosevelt ended the practice. Instead, Vollmer's social work orientation rests on a genuine sympathy for those in distress, and he believes that stern guidance of troubled people could prevent future criminality. Vollmer perceived the problems of vice crime such as drug addiction, prostitution, and alcoholism were not problems the police could solve. He saw these vice offenses as medical problems, and he advocated for the establishment of federal control and dispensation of addictive narcotics (Vollmer, 1936). Today, this problem-solving justice can be found in therapeutic drug courts (Berman & Feinblatt, 2005) and progressive police leaders who support community and problem-oriented policing strategies (Harris, 2005). However, as was the case at the beginning of the twentieth century, finding police leaders with Vollmer's vision of "police" social work is rare.

Leadership and Training Improvement

Crab "bitch" Sessions

As Town Marshal, Vollmer wanted to instill education into his deputies. In doing so, he also knew the importance of having them become stakeholders in the educational process. Vollmer's participatory management version began with mandatory Friday afternoon open forum discussions at his office inside the fire department. He invited his deputies to meet with him to hear about issues they ran into with community members, politicians, or fellow officers. Disputes with fellow officers, or Vollmer himself, often resulted in boxing matches as part of the resolution. Vollmer would also invite several diverse guest speakers to the Friday afternoon crab sessions, including professors, ex-convicts, and drug addicts. At these meetings, Vollmer would attempt to provide some training on departmental procedures, properly filing paperwork or any other topic that would be considered timely. Many of the questions deputies raised during these sessions drove Vollmer to research criminology readings to find the answers.

Nation's First Police Academy

In 1908, Vollmer started the Berkeley Police School with a friend from the Oakland Police Department, Captain of Inspectors Walter Peterson. The school represented the first formal training for American police officers (Carte & Carte, 1975) and served as a future state police academy model. Despite his vocational New Orleans education that did not surpass junior high school, Vollmer taught classes at his police school with Peterson. Peterson taught because of his expertise in detective work and his reputation throughout the Bay area. Vollmer recognized that departments across the country could only do so much to train new officers and wanted future police leaders to seek recruits who had undergone higher levels of academic training. Vollmer's police school came one year before Philadelphia offered a School of Instruction for police officers; therefore, Vollmer received credit for being the father of the police academy movement (Morn, 1995).

After getting support from Peterson, Vollmer met with biology professor Dr. Jacques Loeb. Dr. Loeb had a long history with Vollmer and the BPD as he had previously persuaded him to run for Town Marshal and assisted the department in a prior murder/suicide case. Loeb lectured to deputies on the effects of poison and how biology can impact psychology. Next,

Vollmer sought Professor William Herms's support, who studied how the Bubonic Plague transmitted from rats to humans. Vollmer had Herms teach his officers sanitation law to impress upon them the importance of public hygiene.

Vollmer's report, in 1911,[31] to Berkeley's first mayor, Beverly Hodghead,[32] and the city council, listed six courses taught at his police academy. The course topics included first aid, criminal evidence and procedures, photography, psychiatry, law, anthropometry, public health, fingerprinting, anthropology, and criminology. By 1916, Vollmer collaborated with university law professor Alexander Marsden Kidd to develop a summer program in criminology. The connection with the police school and the university evolved into police-focused criminology summer sessions that merged training and university education. Vollmer took many of the courses as an eager student, impressing upon his officers the value of diversified education (Shaw, 1938). He believed that officers needed a well-rounded education that included criminology with liberal arts so they could better deal with the complexities and the unpredictability of policing. Vollmer proposed that police officers be trained for their profession the same way physicians, attorneys, and other professionals prepare for their life work (Vollmer & Schneider, 1917). During the summer sessions, Vollmer coordinated experiential learning experiences for his officers, such as taking tours of mental institutions and attending guest lectures at UC Berkeley, where officers were encouraged to enroll in classes.

Dr. Schneider, who helped Vollmer solve the Carcopa case, assisted in forming a more detailed police school in the summer of 1916. The program added hard science courses to the curriculum, allowing for a three-year summer criminology program for existing police officers. Program details included the following:

Year One: Physics, chemistry, biology, criminal anthropology, and toxicology
Year Two: Criminological Psychology, Psychiatry, Criminology (theory and applied), Police Organization and Administration, Police Methods and Procedures
Year Three: Microbiology and Parasitology, Police Micro-Analysis, Public Health, First Aid, Criminal Law

This program was formally accepted by UC Berkeley in 1916 and inaugurated the birth of police higher education (Johnson, 1980). University administrators were likely encouraged and eager to play a large role in teaching traditional courses to police officers while assisting in Vollmer's vision of an educated police profession (Morn, 1995).

The *Journal of Criminal Law and Criminology* published a paper from Vollmer and Schneider (1917) in which they detailed their criminology degree for police officers. They introduced their manuscript by indicating that officers traditionally only need brute strength and political connections to be hired and promoted in policing (Vollmer & Schneider, 1917), but the BPD was reforming these standards. Professor Kidd was a member of the American Institute of Criminal Law and Criminology and invariably influenced Vollmer and Schneider's journal publication. The article was the first of many articles and books published by Vollmer, who would also become an associate editor for the *Journal of Criminal Law and Criminology*.

Media Relations

In addition to improved recruitment and training, Vollmer knew he had to help the media tell the story about how policing was changing and becoming more professional. In doing

31 On May 31, 1911, Vollmer married former operatic star, Lydia Sturtevant. However, due to Vollmer's hectic work schedule, the marriage did not last. They lived apart for five years and divorced on October 8, 1920.

32 Not only was Hodghead the first mayor elected in Berkeley, he was also the first socialist elected Berkeley mayor.

so, he consistently showed the same level of respect to the media as he did toward everyone he led. Vollmer encouraged his officers to be transparent and cooperative with departmental public relations. Today's chiefs might take a cue from the Vollmer playbook by working more closely with members of the media. In 1917, Vollmer supplied *Oakland Tribune* reporter Rose Glavinovich[33] with a desk inside the BPD. Her father was a police chief in Albany, California, hence her attraction to reporting on Vollmer. Vollmer's officers, all male, were not in favor of having females inside their department, let alone a reporter. The officers felt the news stories were not always favorable to the department and the work they did. However, Vollmer assured them the reporting was fair since he allowed broad accessibility. The most important stories for Vollmer's leadership – departmental working conditions, salaries, technology, college education, and ethical decision-making – were all reported on by Glavinovich. Occasionally, the national media would reprint her articles furthering Vollmer's national appeal. Glavinovich was allowed full access to any departmental reports based upon the mutual trust and admiration she developed with Vollmer (Robinson, 1972). Eventually, she was accepted into the Berkeley police culture and became instrumental in furthering the Vollmer leadership legacy.

Improving the Hiring of Berkeley Officers

College Cops

In 1917, the same year Vollmer hired female reporter Glavinovich, Woodrow Wilson[34] took the oath for his second term as the President of the United States. Former President Teddy Roosevelt continued to make speeches arguing for war to counter German aggression, and Wilson used this same language during his campaign speeches. World War I (WWI) would invariably slow Vollmer's Police School's progress by draining resources and attention away from further curriculum experimentation. Moreover, many of his officers were drafted into military service. To counter the loss of officers to the war, Vollmer began hiring students from UC Berkeley as policemen, and the press ridiculed them as "college cops" (Oliver, 2017, p. 306). Now, instead of making cops into college students, Vollmer was making college students into cops. Many of the nation's police agencies scoffed at this idea since most officers were hired in their mid to late 1920s and did not have a high school education, let alone a college degree.

Better Pay – During the Pandemic of 1918

In addition to advocating for college-educated officers, Vollmer continued to support increased officer pay, as he had done when he was the town marshal. In the fall of 1918, during a second wave of the Spanish flu pandemic, Berkeley officers threatened to quit if they didn't receive a pay increase. On October 12, 1918, officers reportedly made $110 a month and demanded $125 a month (Finacom, 2020). The city council met privately with Vollmer, noted his college students' recruitment, and agreed to provide officers with a raise. In the year 2021, controlling for inflation and a comparison with modern police salaries, the officers made a little over $26,000 a year.

33 Glavinovich worked for the *Oakland Tribune* and covered Berkeley news for 42 years. She died in 1992 at the age of 101. She was part of the immigration wave following the 1906 San Francisco earthquake that destroyed her family home. While Glavinovich aspired to take on other journalistic positions, Vollmer reminded her that you take yourself with you no matter where you go, meaning if you're not happy now, you will not be happy somewhere else (Robinson, 1972).

34 President Wilson is also discussed in the Ramsey chapter in reference to his push to segregate workers along racial lines within the Federal Government.

During that same time, in October 1918, America suffered 195,000 fatalities from a pandemic, one of the nation's deadliest months. In Berkeley, on October 12, 1918, a brief mention in an article appeared on page 11 of the *Gazette*, with University Physician Dr. Robert Legge ordering that dancing in university buildings should be banned to prevent further spread of Spanish influenza (Finacom, 2020). By the end of the month, most Berkeley churches canceled indoor services, all indoor meetings were prohibited, and libraries and public schools were closed. However, the UC Berkeley campus remained open, and classes resumed, though they did have a two-week delay in starting the Spring 1919 semester (Adams, 1998). On October 25, 1918, the city council handed Vollmer the challenge of enforcing a city ordinance that required the community to wear masks in public or face a fine of not more than $500 or imprisonment for not more than ten days in jail, or both (Finacom, 2020). Two days after the ordinance, the BPD arrested 171 men and four women as "mask slackers" (Adams, 1998). Female university students produced an estimated 24,000 masks, and signs around Berkeley read "Obey the Law and wear the Gauze. Protect Your Jaw from Septic Paws" (Orenstein, 2020). Between 1918 and 1920, 675,000 Americans, and an estimated 50 million worldwide, perished from the misnomer Spanish flu (Spinney, 2017).

Intelligence Testing – College Recruitment

By the end of 1919, the pandemic had passed, and Vollmer began to utilize intelligence and psychological testing for police recruits. He used the Army Alpha test to screen candidates for intelligence with psychology professor Dr. Jau Don Ball and continued to recruit college students. In the modern era, approximately 25 percent of police officers across the nation have a bachelor's degree or higher (Reeves, 2010). The BPD, under Vollmer, had even fewer officers with college degrees. However, the image of Vollmer recruiting college-educated officers helped shape the police professionalization movement over the next several decades. After 1919, application numbers escalated, with the starting pay increased to $150 a month, with $30 a month for the use of the officer's car with free fuel and oil. These perks provided tremendous incentives for police applicants, especially college students.

Seven noteworthy "college cops" hired by Vollmer include the following:

1. Orlando Winfield (OW) Wilson became one of the nation's leading police reformists (as detailed in the following chapter).
2. William Wiltberger was the Police Chief in Evanston, Illinois, from 1925 to 1927 and was the director of the Police Training School for San Jose State College in 1934. In WWII, he became a Lt. Colonel in the Air Force and then a visiting lecturer in criminal justice at Michigan State University.
3. Vivian Anderson (VA) Leonard was credited with convincing Vollmer to put radio communication into patrol cars while assigned to the BPD records division from 1925 to 1933. In 1941, on Vollmer's recommendation, Leonard became the Chair of the Police Science and Administration Department at Washington State College and helped establish the Academy of Criminal Justice Sciences (ACJS).
4. George Brereton became the Deputy Director for the Department of Justice in California after he was the director of the Police Training School at San Jose (California) State College. He was the first state supervisor for the California State Department of Education Peace Officers' Training and the Chief of the California Bureau of Criminal Identification and Investigation.
5. John Holstrom was the Berkeley Chief in 1944 until 1960 and the president of the International Association of Chiefs of Police (1957–1958).

6 William Dean became an Army General and war hero in WWII and Korea.
7 Walter Gordon was an African-American[35] who played football for UC Berkeley and earned his undergraduate and Juris Doctorate. He became the chairman of the California Parole Board and the 18th Governor of the United States Virgin Islands.

International Association of Chiefs of Police (IACP)

The IACP began in Chicago in 1893 and was initially called the National Chiefs of Police Union. The goal of the initial meeting of chiefs was to share information related to the country's most wanted fugitives and develop a National Bureau of Criminal Identification to share criminal records with their organization members. Vollmer joined the IACP in 1912 and attended his first conference in Washington, DC, the following year (Oliver, 2017, p. 328). In 1914, Vollmer was asked to chair the conference in Grand Rapids, Michigan. By 1920, Vollmer was elected unanimously as the first Vice President of the IACP and would become the association's ninth president at the end of the 1921 St. Louis conference. As IACP President, Vollmer successfully persuaded members to have the conference on the west coast for the first time in 1922. San Francisco became the site for the IACP's 29th Annual Convention. Consequently, the California venue, and Vollmer's professionalization reputation within the progressive era and the IACP, was further cast onto the national spotlight.

LA Police Chief (1923–1924)

The following year, 1923, Vollmer was approached by the Citizen's Anti-Crime Commission of LA and asked to serve as their police chief due to widespread political corruption. Vollmer declined their offer but was then approached a couple of weeks later by some clergy from LA led by Bob Shuler (Shuler, 2011). Additionally, Henry Chandler[36] with the *Los Angeles Times* and Mayor Edward Cryer's[37] chief of staff Kent Parrot[38] came to visit Vollmer in Berkeley. Each worked to persuade Vollmer to take the LA Chief position so he could further test his theories and clean up the vice crime – fueled by prostitution, gambling, and corruption – that permeated the police department as well as city politicians. Vollmer had previously taken a short leave of absence to conduct a survey assessing the San Diego Police Department.[39] Based on this experience, he requested a one-year leave from the BPD to become the chief of the LAPD. He negotiated a salary much higher than his Berkeley pay and higher than the previous LAPD chief, Louis Oaks.[40] At the age of 47, this small town professor and Berkeley chief

35 Gordon was Berkeley's first Black officer in 1919, hired by Vollmer during a time when racial segregation permeated the country (Browne, 2015).
36 Chandler was a publisher for the *LA Times* and became one of the country's largest real estate investors.
37 Cryer was 32nd Mayor of LA (1921–1929). Reverend Robert "Bob" Shuler pushed an unsuccessful libel lawsuit against Cryer, alleging that he used his office for enormous financial gain. Shuler is likely the main reason Vollmer came to LA, and he continued to push reform within the LAPD after Vollmer returned to Berkeley.
38 Parrot was known as the de-facto Mayor in LA and controlled city politics (Hodel, 2018).
39 Vollmer's first police survey occurred from a 1915 invitation from San Diego in the aftermath of publicized police scandals. Vollmer was especially critical of the San Diego Mayor and pushed police officials to be separated from city politics (Carte & Carte, 1975, p. 29). Vollmer would go on to complete more than a dozen other police surveys for various communities and several more that were completed by students or junior officers under his supervision.
40 Chief Oaks was suspected to be a member of the Ku Klux Klan (KKK) (see Turner, 1971) and was arrested in San Bernardino with a prostitute and illegal alcohol during the Prohibition era. Members of the community clergy pressured Mayor Edward Cryer to terminate Oaks and seek his replacement with the reform-minded Berkeley Police Chief August Vollmer.

became the chief of LA, one of the country's largest cities, with 3,000 officers, from August 1, 1923, until August 1, 1924. LA had gone through 15 police chiefs during Vollmer's tenure in Berkeley, and it was clear he had his reform work cut out for him.

Trust the Criminals More than the Politicians

In preparation for his time as the LAPD chief, Vollmer took an untraditional approach and sought the advice of criminals he befriended rather than fellow police administrators. Due to years of treating criminals with civility, Vollmer used his numerous connections with the underworld to tap their knowledge about corruption in LA. He learned that vice crime throughout the city was sanctioned, protected, and lucrative for numerous government officials, including Mayor Cryer and his powerful chief of staff Parrot. Instead of fighting crime, officers were expected to protect it and be part of the systemic graft system.

Predictably, Vollmer made several political enemies during his short time as the LA Police Chief. He found that not only were the officers and executive staff generally incompetent, as measured by IQ exams he had them take, but the infrastructure to run the department was also inept. Vollmer found the LA jail was overcrowded with offenders placed in deplorable conditions. Consequently, he pushed the mayor and city council to fund the construction of a new jail. To Vollmer's surprise, this led to a Grand Jury investigation and allegations that the new chief had instigated mass arrests to further his case for a new jail. After Vollmer appeared in front of the Grand Jury to dispel the lies, they investigated the jail's conditions and reached the same conclusions as Vollmer. Within a month, a new jail was built. The Grand Jury's backing also allowed Vollmer the political steam to request funding from the city council to build 11 new police substations, which was agreed upon but delayed until further budgeting decisions were concluded. Vollmer also asked to hire an additional 500 officers. He was ultimately given 250 but told the hiring would need to come from his existing budget.

Despite his leadership victories, Vollmer made additional political enemies when he challenged the system of corruption that had been built into LA politics. These enemies turned to career extortionist Charlotte Lex, who subsequently filed a breach of promise lawsuit against Vollmer. Lex alleged that she had an ongoing affair with Chief Vollmer, and on May 10, 1924, Vollmer had asked her to marry him. However, at the time of her lawsuit, Vollmer had already remarried Pat Millicent on July 23, 1924, his girlfriend 30 years prior. Vollmer and Pat organized a press conference in Berkeley, vehemently denied the charges, asked to take a lie detector test, and refused any out-of-court settlements. Lex subsequently hired several high priced attorneys. In response, Vollmer hired Pinkerton's[41] International Detective Agency to look into her background. Lex told stories about being driven around by Chief Vollmer in LA and that she was pregnant with his baby. The problem with her allegations was that Vollmer had never learned to drive an automobile, and he had discovered that he was infertile when married to his first wife, Lydia. Eventually, Lex stopped showing up for court dates, and the judge dropped the case.

Before the Lex case dissipated, Vollmer had already announced his plans to resign as LA Chief at a June 30, 1924, luncheon with the LA Crime Commission (Oliver, 2017, p. 391). During his brief leadership attempt in LA the following occurred: a drop in crime, rigorous hiring procedures that included intelligence tests, a new jail. Police substations funded, and the creation of the nation's first crime lab. Vollmer also left behind a final report of recommendations

41 Alan Pinkerton, the founder of the detective agency, is mentioned in the Ramsey chapter. Pinkerton was friends with President Lincoln when he was an Illinois Senator and helped thwart an assassination attempt when he was on a train heading to his inauguration. Pinkerton also became useful as a Union spy during the Civil War.

that was several hundred pages long. The Vollmer Report was formally presented to the LA City Council on July 24, 1924, shortly before his departure back to Berkeley, and he received one month's paid leave. In his recommendations report, Vollmer called for a crime prevention unit that combined the LA mother's bureau, juvenile bureau, parole boards, and female probation units (Schulz, 1993, p. 140). Vollmer's vision for the interdependent collaborative bureau was directed toward mentoring at-risk youth and preventing adult tragedies. The report remained buried until William Parker became chief in 1950 and began implementing several of Vollmer's recommendations. Parker had an unprecedented 16-year tenure as police chief and is discussed more fully in the chapter on Bill Bratton.

Berkeley's Woman Cop – Crime Prevention Division

When Vollmer returned to Berkeley in 1924, he organized a crime prevention division[42] based on his ideas for the LAPD that never materialized. He furthered his prevention agenda in 1925 by hiring the department's first female officer, Elizabeth Gurnell Anderson Lossing, as the crime prevention division supervisor. Lossing was a psychiatric social worker, and she emphasized the intervention into the personal affairs of offenders to prevent future criminality (Myers, 2019). She became the first woman police officer in the country with a college degree. Her focus was on boys under the age of 12 and girls under 21 (Carte & Carte, 1975). As he had done in 1917 when he hired reporter Rose Glavinovich, Vollmer wanted Lossing to become a spokeswoman for the department. In 1926, Lossing gave 90 speeches and four radio addresses (Schulz, 1993, p. 143).

Lossing's social work approach to her job fit what Vollmer envisioned as American policing's primary purpose. Throughout 1927, Lossing met weekly with her chief, and they both had the goal of finding the best solutions for dealing with at-risk youth that moved away from traditional approaches that merely tried to scare delinquents (Pigeon, 1927). Vollmer and Lossing formed a community alliance, which became the genesis of a Berkeley coordinating council through schools, health, welfare, labor, and police officials to combine efforts to deal with youth problems. The coordinating council operated as a social welfare agency within the police department and represented the first national attempt to bring social workers into policing (Carte & Carte, 1975).

Professor Vollmer

University of Chicago (1929–1931)

In February 1928, Vollmer was invited to analyze the Chicago Police Department. He found the same systemic corruption issues and obsolete equipment in the nation's second-largest city that he had seen with the LAPD. During this trip, he met with several faculty members from the University of Chicago. Vollmer would later learn these same faculty members worked behind the scenes to hire him to become the country's first full-time police science professor. While Vollmer had his supporters within the Chicago faculty, the university President Max Mason,[43] an outside hire from the University of Wisconsin, was not inclined to

42 In President Johnson's 1967 Task Force Report, Vollmer is quoted as saying "I have spent my life enforcing the laws. It is a stupid procedure and has not, nor will it ever solve the problem unless it is supplemented by preventative measures" (President's Commission on Law Enforcement and Administration, p. 2) as quoted in Leonard (1964, p. 246).

43 Mason grew up in Madison and was a mathematical physicist at the University of Wisconsin. He was the first faculty member at the University of Wisconsin to receive an appointment as a research professor. Mason

offer a professorial position to a police chief that did not have a college degree, let alone a Ph.D. However, in June 1928, Mason was offered an appointment with the Rockefeller Foundation and abruptly resigned. Robert Hutchins,[44] age 29 and Dean of the Yale Law School, was hired to replace Mason and approved the new police faculty position and Vollmer's hire within the Department of Political Science as head of a special police administration division.

Vollmer, again, was granted a temporary leave from the BPD. For the fall semester of 1929, he received $7,000 for a six-month contract to teach at the University of Chicago. His contract also included an additional stipend to conduct research (Oliver, 2017, p. 423). The following year, in November 1930, President Hutchins and Vollmer utilized the University of Chicago for a coordinated day-long meeting of law enforcement agencies in the Chicago Metropolitan Area with 50 miles surrounding the Loop. At this meeting, speakers included J. Edgar Hoover, Director of the BOI, Vollmer, and representatives from agencies that stretched from Racine, Wisconsin to Michigan City. Vollmer advocated for a metropolitan police agency that would encompass the entire Chicagoland area and its suburbs. The system would include a centralized dispatch service to encompass all the communities represented at their meeting. Traction for this type of broad centralization never materialized.

Vollmer enjoyed his academic life at the University of Chicago but he was pulled in various directions with demands from the BPD, Chicago Police Department, and Washington, DC with the Wickersham Commission (discussed more fully in the proceeding paragraphs). Moreover, he continued to suffer health issues that included a heart attack. During his Chicago stay, Vollmer exchanged multiple letters with the UC Berkeley, and he sought a similar position in his hometown as a police professor.

The Irony of the Rockefeller Foundation – Back to Berkeley

Fate was on Vollmer's side when UC Berkeley President Robert Gordon Sproul secured a grant from the Rockefeller Foundation to create a police professor position similar to the University of Chicago's. Ironically, the Rockefeller Foundation paved the way for Vollmer's hire as the nation's first police professor when it removed Vollmer's detractor, University of Chicago President Mason. That same foundation now paved the way for his return to Berkeley as a police professor. Upon receiving Vollmer's resignation letter, the University of Chicago President Hutchins provided lip service that they would find his replacement, but the funds for advancing the police program were eventually withdrawn, and subsequent police research halted. The legacy of Vollmer would never materialize in Chicago. On March 22, 1931, Vollmer left Chicago and returned to Berkeley to continue his academic career.

Wickersham Commission (1929–1931)

During the time Vollmer had been approached about teaching at the University of Chicago, President Hoover's administration also contacted him for his assistance on a federal study that

received national acclaim when he managed a research team during WWI that developed submarine detectors using a raft and equipment at Lake Mendota. He had little university administration experience when he became the first external President hired by the University of Chicago, where he served from 1925 to 1928 (Weaver, 1964).

44 Hutchins became the youngest President at the University of Chicago and served from 1929 to 1951 before he left to head the Ford Foundation. Ford automotive was extremely lucrative in the 1950s and needed to funnel some of its profits toward education and research. Note: In the appendix to the O.W. Wilson chapter, Herman Goldstein's research is discussed and his funding through the Ford Foundation's grant with the American Bar Foundation (ABF). Problem-oriented policing evolved out of the ABF research.

targeted justice in America. Hoover attempted to position himself as a Roosevelt reformist and campaigned on problems with lawlessness in government. In May 1929, President William Taft's former Attorney General, George Wickersham, was appointed to chair a committee as part of a National Commission on Law Observance and Enforcement. The Wickersham Commission was tasked to study a range of topics such as Prohibition, the causes of crime, and law enforcement corruption. Along with the propaganda from J. Edgar Hoover and the BOI, the national commission further cemented the image that the primary mission of the police should be directed toward crime control.

The one-year study from the Wickersham Commission concluded in May 1931, with 14 separate reports and a series of recommendations to reform justice in America. Vollmer wrote the first two chapters that detailed the challenges of being a police chief. He had two research assistants write other chapters, with his guidance, based on past surveys he did on police agencies throughout the country. Later chapters also called for a repeal of the Eighteenth Amendment that established Prohibition. Vollmer's protégé O.W. Wilson reported his chief was against Prohibition because he felt that it damaged law enforcement by encouraging corruption (Robinson, 1972). Two years after the report, Prohibition was repealed by the Twenty-first Amendment.

The Wickersham Report further cast Vollmer as a national leader in police reform. Although the report would not have any immediate policy impact, it advocated for a professionalization era that would gear the future toward centralized bureaucratic management, focusing on reactive crime control. At the time of the national report, the country was heading into the Great Depression, having felt the impact of Prohibition's failed policies. There was a perceived need for the police to engage in more effective crime-fighting. Outside of the narrowed role advocated for law enforcement, Vollmer recommended a civil service system for hiring and promoting police officers as a means for de-politicizing agencies. He also advocated for police training programs, college education, more reliable records, and better use of technology to improve efficiency.

University of California Berkeley

As previously stated, Vollmer coordinated with law professor Alexander Marsden Kidd to offer summer session courses for training police officers in police science at UC Berkeley. These sessions lasted from 1916 to 1931, and in 1928, Kidd and Vollmer formally proposed establishing the School of Criminology. However, an isolated degree in criminology would not come to fruition until years later, making UC Berkeley the second university to do so, following Michigan State University.[45] In January 1931, Vollmer reached an agreement with the University of California President Sproul to teach courses for $2,000 a year and a supplement of $5,000 a year from the Rockefeller grant (Oliver, 2017). The following fall, UC Berkeley offered the first full session criminology program. The interdisciplinary curriculum included biology, psychiatry, and toxicology courses.

By the summer of 1932, Vollmer realized he could not maintain his hectic schedule of dual positions and officially retired from the BPD. He remained busy with several consulting opportunities, including advising the Motion Picture Producers and Distributors of America (MPPDA) on various Hollywood films.[46] The film industry asked Vollmer to recommend if certain movies were likely to entice juveniles to commit crimes or if the police's portrayal was

45 The School of Criminal Justice at Michigan State University was founded in 1935 and is the country's longest degree granting institution. These efforts were led by LeMoyne Snyder, son of Jonathan Snyder, who was the President of the Michigan's State Agriculture College (now Michigan State University) from 1896 to 1915.

46 Vollmer made cameo appearances, playing himself, in two films *My Lady's Lips* (1925) and *Officer '444'* (1926).

disrespectful. In the end, Vollmer submitted his written responses stating there was no evidence to suggest the film industry impacted criminal offenders or negatively impacted police work.

In addition to being a movie consultant, Vollmer had many consulting opportunities with police departments and colleges. In the spring of 1931, San Jose State College requested Vollmer to review their police training program, the first in the nation. The program's structure was controversial, with some wanting to mirror a vocational training orientation while others pushed for a more well-rounded liberal arts and interdisciplinary degree. San Jose State President Thomas MacQuarrie hired George Brereton, one of Vollmer's "college cops" from Berkeley, to direct the program but was not pleased with his progress. President MacQuarrie envisioned a police vocation degree that was similar to educating teachers. Vollmer supported an interdisciplinary education for police officers, and his subsequent report ran counter to President MacQuarrie's wishes. By 1934,[47] William Wiltberger, another Vollmer Berkeley college officer, replaced Brereton and supported the president's vision of operating a police school that separated itself from the traditional academic programs. The conflicts with idealistic visions of police training at the university level between Wiltberger and Vollmer would materialize seven years later in Vollmer's living room in a meeting that birthed the ASC and eventually the ACJS.

Birth of the American Society of Criminology (ASC) and the Academy of Criminal Justice Sciences (ACJS)

Vollmer's students from UC Berkeley referred to themselves as V-Men, a pun on FBI Director Hoover's G-Men, throughout the 1930s and would frequently meet to discuss the future of police education. They even had lapels made with a "V" etched in the center (Adler, 1997). Several had ongoing discussions about formalizing their meetings into a professional association, and the V-Men respected Vollmer's leadership with his desire to establish a school of criminology. Near the end of 1941, their plans would be delayed.

On December 7, 1941, the Japanese attack on Pearl Harbor thrust America into WWII. The war efforts essentially delayed Vollmer's push for UC Berkeley to establish a school of criminology. However, Vollmer continued to encourage police education onto the national consciousness. On December 30, 1941, Vollmer hosted seven individuals at his home located at 923 Euclid Avenue in Berkeley, which Oliver references[48] as the most renowned address for police education in the world. That home had been purchased by Vollmer and his second wife Pat in 1925, in the aftermath of Vollmer's stint as LA Police Chief. O.W. Wilson sent out invites to Pacific Coast school directors who all taught police science and administration courses. According to minutes from the meeting, they began at 10:15 AM, did not adjourn until 1 AM the next day, and named themselves the National Association of College Police Training Officials (Morn, 1995). Individuals at this initial meeting included the following:

1 August Vollmer: Berkeley Police Chief (retired), University of California Professor Police Administration (retired) *Honorary post of President Emeritus
2 Orlando (OW) Wilson[49]: University of California Berkeley Professor of Police Administration and Director of the Bureau of Criminology *President

47 January 1934 also marks the year Vollmer learned his brother was killed in a car accident in Detroit.

48 See *The History of the Academy of Criminal Justice Sciences (ACJS) V.A. Leonard: The Focal Point in the Creation of the ASC, APS, and ACJS* at https://cdn.ymaws.com/www.acjs.org/resource/resmgr/Historian/ACJS_VA_Leonard.pdf

49 In 1961, the ASC awarded O.W. Wilson with its Edwin Sutherland Award at the annual conference. The award began a year prior.

3 Vivian (VA) Leonard: Washington State College Professor and Head of Police Science and Administration *Second Vice President and Committee chair responsible for preparing a constitution and by-laws
4 Willard Schmidt: Sacramento Junior College Director of Police Training *First Vice President
5 William Wiltberger: San Jose State College Director of Police School *Third Vice President
6 Robert Drexel: San Jose District Attorney's Office chief investigator who occasionally taught courses for Wiltberger
7 Benjamin Pavone: San Francisco Junior College Peace Officers Training Division *Secretary-Treasurer
8 Frank Lee: Former Director of the National Police Academy in China *International Vice President

Disagreements over who should be members of their organization and the general philosophy were controversial and likely took up much of their time. Wiltberger wanted to cater to existing police officers as part of their in-service training. In contrast, others, led by Vollmer and Leonard, wanted membership directed toward university faculty who were involved in degree programs in police science and administration. Morn (1995) contests that Wiltberger was likely delegated to the third Vice President and left the initial meeting early because of this conflict.

Leonard attempted to host the second meeting in December 1942 in Pullman, Washington, but several guests could not attend. Not to be deterred, Leonard utilized his lackluster academic meeting to establish Alpha Phi Sigma, the national criminal justice student honor's society, in 1942, with 17 police science majors at Washington State College. Glenn Hill was elected the first student president, and like his professor before him, Leonard tasked him with formulating a committee to draft the first constitution and by-laws.

The following year, on February 21, 1943, Vollmer's letter to Leonard provided much-needed encouragement

> *Regardless of the opinion of the many police executives today, the college level police training is on its way and nothing that they or any other group might do can stop it from rolling along. Give this no thought but continue to peddle your wares and someday you will wake to find that college trained police officials will be the rule rather than the exception.*
>
> (Oliver, 2013, p. 5)

In its initial years, Alpha Phi Sigma experienced only limited growth. However, on March 24, 1976, in Dallas, Texas, the Executive Board of the ACJS voted unanimously to designate Alpha Phi Sigma the National Criminal Justice Honor Society. At this time, Alpha Phi Sigma had only 14 chapters; however, since then, Alpha Phi Sigma has continued to grow and prosper rapidly, and there are now over 360 chapters (Photo 2.3).

WWII delayed subsequent meetings, and the third conference for the National Association of College Police Officials took place at the Durant Hotel in Berkeley on December 29, 1948. President O.W. Wilson called the meeting to order with Vollmer and 16 other men. On this day, they formulated the organizational constitution, by-laws, and model of curriculums they wanted to see in police science programs. They also took a more academic name and called themselves the *Society for the Advancement of Criminology.* All subsequent meetings took place in Berkeley until 1956. The conference took place in Fresno following Vollmer's suicide. During the March 1957 meeting at the University of Southern California, LA, the

Photo 2.3 August Vollmer and V.A. Leonard.
Photo courtesy of University California Berkeley, Bancroft Library.

executive committee told their 64 male members that they changed their name to the *ASC*[50] (Adler, 1997). In 1959, Donald MacNamara (ASC President from 1960 to 1963 and an east coast criminologist) established the August Vollmer Award to recognize outstanding criminology research. Marvin Wolfgang[51] became the first award recipient. Subsequent awards went primarily to academic researchers engaged in theoretical testing and corrections rather than Vollmer's original intent to bring together academics who were primarily involved in teaching future criminal justice practitioners. Moreover, the ASC conferences were usually held on the east coast, attracting sociology academics that were far different from the Vollmer followers on the west coast (Morn, 1995).

In 1963, Leonard retired from Washington State University. Several police professors organized a party to honor Leonard. They began discussions related to how the ASC organization had morphed into an east coast theory-focused entity consumed by sociologists that drifted from Vollmer's legacy. These displaced police professors created a new organization that matched the eight founders' original intent and started the International Association of Police Professors (IAPP). Six years later, in 1970, they changed their name to the ACJS.[52] Leonard

50 Today, the ASC is an international organization that encourages academic, student, and practitioner membership. Members pursue scholarly, scientific, and professional knowledge directed toward the measurement, etiology, consequences, prevention, control, and treatment of crime and delinquency. See www.asc41.com/

51 Marvin Eugene Wolfgang became a professor at the University of Pennsylvania after completing his graduate degree at the same institution. He published over 30 books and 150 articles, the most famous being the 1972 *Delinquency in a Birth Cohort*. He died in 1998 at 73 years of age.

52 Today, ACJS is an international association with the purpose of fostering professional and scholarly activities in criminal justice. ACJS promotes criminal justice education, research, and policy analysis while catering to both educators and practitioners. See www.acjs.org

spent the next couple of decades of retirement writing books. At the 1976 ACJS conference, the executive board subsumed Alpha Phi Sigma into its organization and designated it as the National Criminal Justice Honor Society. At the 1982 ACJS conference, the board established the V.A. Leonard annual scholarship in his honor. Leonard died in 1984 at the age of 86 and has been called the father of law enforcement education due to his work in furthering the legacy of his mentor, August Vollmer.

Retirement – End of Life

Shortly after WWII ended, Vollmer lost his beloved wife, Pat. Her death certainly took a toll on him, but as he had always done, he threw himself into his work. His final book, *The Criminal* (Vollmer, 1949), supplemented his most renowned book, *Police and Modern Society* (Vollmer, 1936). By 1951, he saw his legacy come to fruition when UC Berkeley established the School of Criminology and his protégé O.W. Wilson was appointed dean (Photo 2.4).

While in his mid-70s, Vollmer had Parkinson's disease and cancer. As he began to lose his ability to take care of himself, Vollmer shared with some of his closest companions that when the time was right, he would end his own life so he would not become a burden to others. Vollmer was a member of the California chapter of the Euthanasia Society and believed that suicide was his right. In preparing for his death, Vollmer destroyed much of the letter correspondence he received from past criminal offenders and anyone else he wanted to keep confidential. Vollmer had the rest of his work and correspondence donated to the Bancroft Historical Society at UC Berkeley. On Friday morning, November 4, 1955, at the age of 79, after breakfast, Vollmer told his housemaid, Mrs. Lyda Miller, he would end his life and told her to call the Berkeley police. He then stepped away from his kitchen and fatally shot himself with the .38 caliber service revolver gifted to him in 1906 by his deputies when he was the town marshal. Miller asked responding Police Chief John Holstrom to take possession of

Photo 2.4 August Vollmer inside his home office, 1950.
Photo courtesy of the University of California Berkeley, Bancroft Library.

the firearm, which he did, and eventually, the gun made its way to the BPD, where it remains today. Vollmer gave his body to science at UC Berkeley. In doing so, there was no funeral, no services, and there is no grave (Kell, 2017).

Conclusion

Vollmer's Leadership Legacy

From its inception, policing has been plagued with racial tension, questionable use of force, and legitimacy concerns. It is interesting to speculate what kind of leadership August Vollmer would have given policing in the twenty-first century. More than most police leaders, Vollmer's leadership was directed toward humanitarianism and treating arrestees with kindness. He made personal connections with everyone he met, including offenders who had been arrested and jailed. Vollmer often shared breakfast or drinks with the offenders upon their release. To the consternation of some officers, Vollmer would visit with offenders in his office upon their release from jail or San Quentin prison to signal their mutual respect. Vollmer even provided some with financial loans with no repayment expectations; however, most paid him back. To understand the criminal mind better, Vollmer frequently visited the jail and conversed with prisoners. He continued written correspondence with many men after they were released.

Vollmer perceived stringent laws and vigorous prosecution of addicts and the mentally ill as counterproductive. As a war veteran, he supported a citizen's right to protest. He pushed policing to become more scientific and driven toward evidence-based practices long before the term was in vogue. Throughout his lifetime, Vollmer became the most articulate and outspoken of practical criminologists in the country (Morn, 1980). His push for police professionalism and increased education is a woven tapestry throughout his work. As Vollmer's career transformed into teaching courses at the university, he looked upon a lack of education as one of the most glaring challenges for policing. In the 1930s, 67 percent of officers had only an eighth-grade education (Folgelson, 1977), and Vollmer's second career met that challenge.

Vollmer had a contagious enthusiasm for his work. He enjoyed promoting his departmental achievements in academic journals, trade magazines, lectures to college classrooms, and speeches to various community groups and media outlets. While the FBI Director J. Edgar Hoover became master of public relations at the federal level, Vollmer's authentic leadership was ripe with a certain level of morality that was not condescending. Unlike Hoover, Vollmer was at ease with academics and held them in high regard.

O.W. Wilson described his mentor with candor in his 1971 interview with Berkeley student Jane Robinson (Robinson, 1972). Wilson said Vollmer inspired a great deal of loyalty from his subordinates and also the ideals of the police service he continually strived to professionalize. Vollmer saw the ups and downs of life as constant learning experiences that were always for pushing improvement. He carried a leadership rule that stated that if you cannot say anything good about someone, don't say anything (Robinson, 1972). However, he was opinionated when he saw the overstretch of law enforcement, as detailed in his portion of the Wickersham Commission Report that questioned Prohibition's usefulness and connection to police corruption. Although the Progressive Era's aftermath narrowed the police role toward crime control, it did not start that way. Vollmer's vision of policing looked to encompass a multitude of responses to crime problems and included social services as a vital connection to justice rather than distinct bureaucratic agencies. Despite Vollmer's vision, the field of policing shifted and became more law enforcement oriented, a shift that his protégé O.W. Wilson would support and lead without the subsequent research evaluations that challenged the strict law and order reactive strategies.

Vollmer epitomized a transformational leader driven toward collaboration with all educational systems, public healthcare facilities, recreation and civic organizations, and anyone else interested in preventing crime. His transformational leadership during the Progressive Era at the turn of the twentieth century was critical for our nation's future and is just as essential as we progress through the twenty-first century, especially in light of the 2020 mass protests. Today's police officer are frequently stressed about being vilified by the public, especially in the aftermath of the #BlackLivesMatter movement. The complexities of policing in America were just as relevant during Vollmer's era. In 1926, Vollmer wrote about the complexity of policing:

> *There is so much dissatisfaction with police methods and policemen in the United States that one might be pardoned for rushing to their defense with a few words of commendation. The policeman is denounced by the public, criticized by preachers, ridiculed in the movies, berated by the newspapers, and unsupported by prosecuting officers and judges. He is shunned by the respectable, hated by criminals, deceived by everyone, kicked around like a football by brainless or crooked politicians, exposed to countless dangers and temptations, condemned when he enforces the law and dismissed if he doesn't. His home life is made unhappy by long hours of duty; he is forced to endure every conceivable form of hardship.... But, despite these obstacles, he has achieved a fair measure of success in protecting the lives and property of citizens and preserving the integrity of the nation.*
>
> (Vollmer, 1926, p. 148)

Vollmer's leadership involved a stubborn insistence that any problem could be solved if it was analyzed long enough and given the proper ingenuity and resourcefulness. He maintained a clear vision and critical mindset, which enabled him to quickly probe into problems and develop solutions often ridiculed by the public, the press, and his fellow officers. However, history has become a better judge of the Vollmer leadership legacy and the creative problem-solving he brought to police administration, and American policing is better because of it. His approach to ethics, accountability, problem-solving, and a police culture driven by social work was needed in 2020 and beyond.

Despite Vollmer's transformational leadership, even the Father of Police Professionalism was not immune to the defunding movement of 2020. In the fall of 2020, City councilmember Cheryl Davila reported that the criminology school Vollmer helped start used curricula that dealt with eugenics, criminal tendencies, and race degeneration (Ruggiero, 2020). Accordingly, Vollmer was suspected of being an advocate of selective breeding to improve the human race's genetic composition. Penn (2020) is critical of Oliver's (2017) heroic portrayal of Vollmer and taking 500 pages of his book before mentioning his 1924 membership in the American Eugenics Society. Vollmer was not immune to the science of the day.

In spite of his eugenics scientific inquiry, Vollmer was also passionate about how social work influences policing, treating drug addicts rather than criminalizing them, and crime prevention directed toward predelinquency youth programs. His work appears to lean more toward understanding the nurture causes of crime rather than on eugenics' nature aspects. However, contemporary criticism led the Berkeley City Council to send a letter to the East Bay Regional Park District and request they rename Vollmer Peak.[53] In 1955, following his death, Bald Peak was renamed Vollmer Peak because Vollmer was an advocate for recreational activities to deter criminal behavior. He was also a founder of the East Bay Regional Park District. Dave Mason, a spokesperson for the East Bay Regional Park District, responded that the park district used Vollmer's name because he was a founding member and served the board

53 Vollmer Peak is the highest point of the Berkeley Hills that overlooks the northeast side of a valley that encompasses the San Francisco Bay.

of directors for 15 years, not because of his status as Berkeley's police chief (Souza, 2020). The possible removal of Vollmer's name from the peak would be unfortunate given his reputation for progressive leadership. Vollmer pushed to end the third degree in police interrogations. He was against capital punishment, and he hired Berkeley's first woman and first African-American police officers while he instructed male white officers who objected to resign. This type of leadership opposes the notion that Vollmer sought a superior race.

The two concluding tables, 2.1 and 2.2, include Berkeley Town Marshals from 1880 to 1909 and Berkeley Police Chiefs from 1909 to 2021.

Table 2.1 Berkeley, California Town Marshals

Years	*Name*
1878–1880	Marvin Gilman[i]
1880–1884	Thomas Knox
1901–1902	Richard Lloyd
1902–1904	Three Marshals (names unknown) followed
1905–1905	Charles Kerns (three months)
1905–1909	**August Vollmer**

Table 2.2 Berkeley, California Police Chiefs

Years	*Name*
1909–1932	**August Vollmer**
1932–1944	John Greening[i]
1944–1960	John Holstrom[ii]
1960–1966	Addison Fording
1966–1969	William Beall[iii]
1969–1974	Bruce Baker[iv]
1974–1977	Wesley Pomeroy[v]

i Gilman was elected marshal in Berkeley's first town election on May 13, 1878 at Union Hall. A total of 304 votes were casted. Gillman was the president of the town's anti-Chinese club, which later became the People's Party when Berkeley was incorporated (Schwartz, 2009).

i Each time Vollmer took leavesfrom Berkeley, he made Greening acting chief but still maintained active control over departmental affairs through various letter writing.

ii Holstrom was a UC Berkeley recruit of Vollmer and the first Berkeley chief with a college degree. To counter rising crime and student riots, Holstrom established an emergency unit of community volunteers who worked in 4-hour shifts to assist the existing sworn officers. He joined the University of California faculty in 1945 and was elected as the President of the IACP in 1957 (Parker, 1972).

iii In May 1969, Beall retired and became the first university-wide coordinator for the nine-campus police agencies covering the University of California system. In 1990, Victoria Harrison became the first female police chief for the University of California system.

iv After he was Berkeley chief, Baker was the chief of Portland Police Bureau from 1974 to 1981 and was boss to Penny Harrington. Portland Mayor Neil Goldschmidt hired Baker after Captain Leo Miller (Harrington's then boyfriend) turned down Goldschmidt's request to be chief because the mayor would not relent in giving up hiring and firing authority.

v Pomeroy began his law enforcement career with the California Highway Patrol. During WWII, he served in the Marine Corps and then rose through the ranks to become an undersheriff in San Manteo County. He received national exposure by leading security around the 1964 Republican convention. During the 1968 Democratic Convention in Chicago, as detailed in the chapter on O.W. Wilson, Pomeroy directed the Illinois National Guard to assist the CPD amid the protests, often while conflicted with Mayor Daley. Through this experience,

Table 2.2 Cont.

Years	*Name*
1977–1980	Odell Sylvester[vi]
1982–1990	Ronald Nelson[vii]
1990–2002	Dashiel "Dash" Butler[viii]
2002–2005	Roy Meisner
2005–2009	Douglas Hambleton
2009–2016	Michael Meehan[ix]
2017-	Andrew Greenwood

Notes:
A table for LAPD chiefs appears at the end of the chapter on Bill Bratton.

References

Adams, Rex (1998). The 1918 Spanish influenza, Berkeley's "Quinta Columna". *Chronicle of the University of California*. Berkeley: CA: The Center for Studies in Higher Education, University of California.

Adler, Freda. (1997). The ASC and women: One generation without, one generation with. *The Criminologist, May/June 22*(3): 1–35.

Alder, Ken (2007). *Lie detectors: The history of an American obsession*. Lincoln, NE: University of Nebraska Press.

Aronovici, John (2011). Fingerprint everyone in Berkeley? *The Newsletter of the Berkeley Historical Society 29*(4): 1–3.

Baden-Powell, Robert (1915). *Aids to scouting: For N.C.O.s and men*. London, UK: Gale & Polden, Ltd.

Berman, Greg and John Feinblatt (2005). *Good courts: The case for problem-solving justice*. New York, NY: The New Press.

Botein, Barbara (1979). The Hennessy case: An episode in anti-Italian nativism. *Louisiana History: The Journal of the Louisiana Historical Association 20*(3): 261–279.

Browne, Arthur (2015). *One righteous man: Samuel Battle and the shattering of the color line in New York*. Boston, MA: Beacon Press.

Burrough, Bryan (2005). *Public enemies: America's greatest crime wave and the birth of the FBI, 1933–34*. London, UK: Penguin Publishing Group.

Carte, Gene (1973). August Vollmer and the origins of police professionalism. *Journal of Police Science and Administration 1*: 274–361.

Carte, Gene and Elaine Carte (1975). *Police reform in the United States: The era of August Vollmer, 1905–1933*. Berkeley, CA: University of California Press.

Pomeroy was also asked to serve as an assistant attorney general, assistant to the DEA Director, and coordinator for the LEAA with Pat Murphy. Pomeroy also ran security at the original Woodstock concert (August 15–18, 1969) and directed security for Led Zeppelin.

vi Sylvester became Berkeley's first Black police chief, 58 years after Vollmer hired the first Black police officer. Sylvester was the first Black officer with the Oakland Police Department to obtain the rank of sergeant, lieutenant, captain, and deputy chief.

vii Nelson also served an additional 12 years as the chief for the University of California, San Francisco.

viii Butler was promoted from lieutenant to Berkeley chief. In 2009, he was asked to come out of retirement to be the interim chief for the Bay Area Rapid Transit (BART) Police, in Oakland, following the controversial fatal shooting of Oscar Grant III in the early morning hours New Year's Day at the Fruitvale train station. In 2010, the documentary film *Operation Small Axe* was released detailing the event. In 2013, the movie *Fruitvale Station*, starring Michael B. Jordan, detailed the last 24 hours of Grant's life.

ix Under Meehan's leadership, Berkeley became the second agency in California to adopt Fair and Impartial Policing. The BPD also developed double-blind lineup procedures to reduce false criminal identification.

Douthit, Nathan (1975). August Vollmer, Berkeley's first chief of police and the emergence of police professionalism. *California Historical Quarterly 54*: 101–124.

Finacom, Steven (2020). Berkeley and the 1918 influenza (second installment). *The Berkeley Daily Planet*. March 22.

Fogelson, Robert. (1977). *Big-city police*. Cambridge, MA: Harvard University Press.

Fosdick, Raymond B. (1916), Modus operandi system in the detection of criminals. *Journal of Criminal Law & Criminology*. 6(4): 560–570.

Gambino, Richard (1998). *Vendetta*. New York, NY: Doubleday Books.

Giordano, Paola and Paul Giordano (1979). Italian immigration in the state of Louisiana: Its causes, effects, and results. *Italian Americana*. *5*(2): 160–177.

Go, Julian (2020). The imperial origins of American policing: Militarization and imperial feedback in the early 20th century. *American Journal of Sociology 125*(5): 1193–1254.

Goldsborough, Bob (2010). Dick Tracy sculpture to keep an eye on Naperville Riverwalk. *Chicago Tribune*. April 5.

Goldstein, Herman (1979). Improving policing: A problem-oriented approach. *Crime & Delinquency 25*(2): 236–258.

Harris, David (2005). *Good cops*. New York, NY: The New Press.

Hodel, Steve (2018). *Black Dahlia Avenger III*. Los Angeles, CA: Rare Bird Books.

Johnson, Carolyn (1980). *The literature of higher education in criminology and criminal justice: An annotated bibliography*. Chicago, IL: The Joint Commission on Criminology and Criminal Justice Standards and the University of Illinois at Chicago.

Kell, Gretchen (2017). August Vollmer biography explores famous police chief's UC Berkeley ties. *Berkeley News*. April 19.

Kramer, Terry (1977). UC Prof slain in attempted robbery. University of Cincinnati: *The News Record, 65*(16): 1.

LaBianca, Juliana (2019). How 8 American cities got their quirky nicknames. *Reader's Digest*. February 19.

Leonard, Vivian (1964). *Police organization and management (2nd ed.)*. Brooklyn, NY: The Foundation Press, Inc.

Lepore, Jill (2015). *The secret history of wonder woman*. New York, NY: First Vintage Books Edition.

Lillie, Richard (2018). First use of lie detector helps convict man who shot sheriff. *Portage Historical Society*. September 26.

Liss, Julia, and Steven Schlossman. (1984). The contours of crime prevention in August Vollmer's Berkeley. *Research in Law, Deviance, and Social Control 16:* 79–107.

Morn, Frank (1980). Academic disciplines and debates: An essay on criminal justice and criminology as professions of higher education. Report to the Joint Commission on Criminology and Criminal Justice Education and Standards. Chicago, IL: University of Illinois at Chicago.

Morn, Frank (1995). *Academic politics and the history of criminal justice Education*. Westport, CT: Greenwood Publishing Group.

Myers, Tamara Gene (2019). *Youth squad: Policing children in the twentieth century*. Chicago, IL: McGill-Queen's University Press.

National Research Council (2003). *The polygraph and lie detection*. Washington, DC: The National Academies Press.

Nickel, Steven and William Helmer (2002). *William J. Baby face Nelson*. Nashville, TN: Cumberland House Publishing.

O'Connell, Jean (2007). *Chester Gould: A daughter's biography of the creator of Dick Tracy*. Jefferson, NC: McFarland & Company.

Oliver, Willard (2008). "August Vollmer". In Jeff Bumgarner, (Ed.). *Icons of crime fighting: Relentless pursuers of justice: Volume 1*. Westport, CT: Greenwood Press.

Oliver, Willard (2013). The history of the Academy of Criminal Justice Sciences (ACJS): Celebrating 50 years, 1963–2013. ACJS Historian. https://cdn.ymaws.com/www.acjs.org/resource/resmgr/Historian/ACJS50thAnniversaryHistoryBo.pdf

Oliver, Willard (2017). *August Vollmer: The father of American policing*. Durham, NC: Carolina Academic Press.Orenstein, Natalie (2020). Berkeley shut schools, required masks in 1918. *Berkeleyside*. April 6.

Ostrom, Elinor, Roger Parks, and Gordon Whitaker (1973). Do we really want to consolidate urban police forces? A reappraisal of some old assertions. *Public Administration Review 33*(5): 423–432.
Parker, Alfred (1961). *Crime fighter: August Vollmer.* New York, NY: The Macmillan Company
Parker, Alfred (1972). *The Berkeley Police Story.* Springfield, IL: Charles C. Thomas Publishing.
Parker, Alfred and August Vollmer (1935). *Crime and the state police.* Berkeley, CA: The University of California Press.
Penn, Nicole (2020). August Vollmer and the sins of the father. *The American Interest 16*(1): July 18.
Pigeon, Helen D. (1927). How Berkeley helps its policewoman. *The Police Journal 14*(10): 5–6.
Poli, Joseph (1942). Development and present trend of police radio communications. *Journal of Criminal Law and Criminology 33*(2): 193–197.
President's Commission on Law Enforcement and Administration of Justice (1967). The challenge of crime in a free society. U.S. Department of Justice, National Institute of Justice. February, 340 pages.
Raguso, Emilie (2017). Berkeley police treasure found in Texas 'mystery box'. *Berkeleyside.* April 22.
Reaves, Brian (2010). Local police departments, 2007. U.S. Department of Justice, Bureau of Justice Statistics – Office of Justice Programs. December.
Robinson, Jane (1972). August Vollmer: Pioneer in police professionalism. Berkeley: Regional Oral History Office. The Bancroft Library, University of California.
Ruggiero, Angela (2020). Berkeley wants Vollmer Peak renamed because of namesake's eugenics views. *The Mercury News.* September 18.
Schulz, Dorothy (1993). *From social worker to crime fighter: Women in United States Municipal Policing.* Westport, CT: Praeger Publishers.
Schwartz, Richard (2009). *Berkeley 1900: Daily life at the turn of the century (10th Anniversary Edition).* Berkeley, CA: Heyday.
Shaw, Robert (1938). Forty fighting years: The story of August Vollmer. *The Oakland Post Enquirer.* The Bancroft Library, University of California, Berkeley.
Shuler, Robert (2011). *"Fighting Bob" of Los Angeles.* Indianapolis, IN: Dog Ear Publishing.
Skillin, Don (2006). *Magdalo: The story of Emilio Aguinaldo; revolutionary hero of the Philippines.* Milton Keynes, UK: America Star Books.
South Bend News (1922). Has the "lie detector" lied? *Times 39*(300): 27. October 27.
Souza, Jacob (2020). Berkeley City Council calls for renaming of Vollmer Peak. *The Daily Californian.* October 20.
Spinney, Laura (2017). *Pale rider: The Spanish Flu of 1918 and how it changed the world.* New York, NY: Public Affairs.
Turner, William (1971). *Power on the right.* Berkeley, CA: Ramparts Press.
Vollmer, August (1919). Revision of the Atcherley Modus Operandi System. *Journal of Criminal Law and Criminology 10*(2): 229–274.
Vollmer, August (1920). Bureau of Criminal Records. *Journal of Criminal Law and Criminology 11*(2): 171–180.
Vollmer, August (1926). The prevention and detection of crime as viewed by a police officer. *The Annals of the American Academy of Political and Social Science 125*(1): 148–153.
Vollmer, August (1936). *The police and modern society: Plain talk based on practical experience.* Oakland, CA: University of California Press.
Vollmer, August (1949). *The criminal.* Brooklyn, NY: The Foundation Press, Inc.
Vollmer, August and Albert Schneider (1917). School for police as planned at Berkeley. *Journal of Criminal Law and Criminology* 7(6): 877–898.
Weaver, Warren (1964). Max Mason (1877–1961): A biographical memoir. Washington, DC: National Academy of Sciences.
Wilson, O.W. (1953). August Vollmer. *Journal of Criminal Law and Criminology 41*(4): 91–103.
Wood, Amy (2009). *Rough justice: Lynching and American society, 1874–1947.* Chapel Hill, NC: North Carolina Press.

Chapter 3

O.W. Wilson – Chief, Professor, Dean, Superintendent with Appendix on Herman Goldstein – Father of Problem-Oriented Policing

Vollmer's Protégé

Orlando Winfield (O.W.) Wilson was active in law enforcement from 1921 to 1967. His career began as a college cop in Berkeley, California, under Chief August Vollmer in 1921. In 1925, at the age of 25, Wilson went from patrol officer to chief of the Fullerton, California Police Department, but that position lasted less than a year. From 1928 to 1939 Wilson was the chief of the Wichita, Kansas Police Department. From 1939 to 1960 Wilson was a professor and Dean of criminology at the University of California (UC) Berkeley. From 1960 to 1967 he served as the Superintendent of the Chicago Police Department (CPD).

Wilson was also the author of several law enforcement textbooks and a national leader in the police professionalization movement. He was a student and eventual leader of the early twentieth-century police reform movement. He became a national leader that pushed for the removal of political influence from policing in America in the professionalization era. The primary function of the police was law enforcement within the professionalization reform era. For Wilson, professionalism meant urban police leaders should be more than figureheads, and he combined academic scholarship with military discipline and sympathy for his officers and the community's needs. He did so through demonstrative efficiency and reform while rewarding officer honesty with promotions based upon merit and not politics.

Much of what we know about the life of Wilson comes from the doctorate dissertation of William Bopp. Before earning his doctorate at FSU, Bopp was a graduate student at the UC Berkeley, 50 years after Wilson attended the same university. He submitted his dissertation research to the College of Education at Florida State University in March 1975. Professor Bopp revised his research and published *O. W. Wilson and the Search for a Police Profession* in 1977 with National University Publications. Bopp later became the first chairman of the Florida Atlantic University criminology program and eventually professor emeritus.

Roots of O.W.

Orlando Winfield (O.W.) Wilson was born on May 15, 1900, as the eldest son of seven children born to Knute "Ole" and Olava Vraalson. His father, Ole, was born in Norway in 1869 and immigrated to the United States when he was a child. Ole grew up on a family farm in Sedan, Minnesota, with a strict Scandinavian work ethic and uncompromising morals. His parents sent him to the University of Minnesota, where he received his bachelor's degree in 1890 and a law degree in 1893.

Ole only practiced law for a short time and became frustrated with his profession. He purchased a large farm in Veblen, South Dakota, where he met Olava, a schoolteacher, whom he would marry. Ole decided to enter local politics and changed his name to "Wilson" as he

DOI: 10.4324/9780429272226-4

believed the name would be more acceptable to voters and community leaders. Ole served as county treasurer and one term as a Populist state legislator (Bopp, 1977). In 1905, they sold their farm and moved to Saskatchewan, Canada. The family was successful with the farm and by 1911 again sold and relocated to Pacific Beach, a suburb of San Diego, California. Wilson's father purchased a gold mine, and Orlando spent time with several miners who sought gold. Based on these experiences, Orlando wanted to become an engineer in the mines.

The Wilson home was patriarchal with a tight-knit family dynamic despite multiple moves. O.W. Wilson was called "Winfield" or "Win" by his close friends and was motivated by his father to be academically successful. He grew up during progressivism and prohibition experimentation. Wilson's ethical foundation came from his father, who believed the difference between right and wrong was clear, and the gray area of questionable behavior existed only in the imagination of those concerned with excuses for their failures and faults. In his adolescence, Winfield feverously read articles from muckraking journalists and became appalled with stories detailing government corruption.

In 1918, Winfield graduated from San Diego High School as valedictorian and, in the fall of 1919, attended the UC Berkeley, majoring in civil engineering. His father approved his engineering major and paid for his son's education through the family savings. Ole had raised Winfield to always be a gentleman and academically successful through frugality, courtesy to others, soft-spoken, independent, scholarly and well-disciplined. This grounding allowed Winfield to have a clear sense of right and wrong that would later drive him to be a "black letter guy" as a police administrator by pushing strict adherence to the law and departmental policies.

Berkeley's College Cop Program

While attending the UC Berkeley, it became clear to Wilson that he was an introvert and exhibited considerable shyness. While he found temporary housing in student dorms, he elected to rent a studio apartment inside a private home located at 1119 Laurel Street in Berkeley to isolate himself and focus on his studies (Bopp, 1977). Wilson took note of what he considered a debilitating part of his personality and made a conscious effort to attend numerous social gatherings to assist him in his education and self-therapy. He used these events as an experiment for his development rather than as a pursuit of pleasure. Wilson saw parties and social gatherings as counterproductive but also as challenges for his introverted personality. Wilson's goal was to meet his father's expectations and not disappoint his family's investment in his education.

Ole Wilson was holding onto a large parcel of land he had purchased during World War I, believing he would net a future profit. Unfortunately, the post-WWI recession was economically disastrous for the Wilson family, and O.W. had to determine a new strategy for financing his education at Berkeley. None of his brothers or sisters attended college, and Wilson invariably felt the pressure to succeed. During his third semester, he came across a solicitation in the university newspaper for college cops. The ad read,

> *College Men wanted for police force. Interesting experience. Learn a new profession. Serve on the Berkeley Police Force while you go to college. Contact August Vollmer, Chief of Police.*
>
> (Parker, 1961, p. 100)

Most students did not perceive policing as a career choice for those with college degrees, but the temporary pay was enticing. In his 1971 interview with Jane Howard Robinson,[1]

1 See http://digitalassets.lib.berkeley.edu/rohoia/ucb/text/augustvollmer01vollrich.pdf p. 155.

Wilson reported he received good marks from an intelligence test that UC Berkeley gave to incoming freshmen and he figured he would also do well on the policing intelligence exam, which would be an easy job to get.

Wilson arrived at the Berkeley High School to test for a police job in the spring of 1921 and met Chief August Vollmer[2] for the first time. The Berkeley Police Department (BPD) tested applicants by using the Army Alpha Test for intelligence. Wilson ranked high among those tested, and his results allowed him to go onto the physical and psychological examinations conducted by Dr. John Rowell. The last stage of the hiring process was his interview in Chief Vollmer's office at the BPD located in City Hall's basement. The interview went well, and in May 1921, Wilson was hired and told he would need to purchase a car for his patrol duties. Additionally, he would need to go to the local hardware store and buy a .38 caliber Smith and Wesson revolver and a billy club[3] (Bopp, 1977, p. 21). Lastly, he would also need to purchase a police uniform.

The BPD was fertile ground for a movement toward police professionalization. The rest of the country's police agencies suffered from embedded corruption, ill-equipped officers, lack of hiring and promotional standards, and low pay (Lane, 1992; Uchida, 1993). Vollmer's officers policed a community of 25,000 residents with low crime and were offered excellent training, education, pay, and detachment from politics. Like many of his college-recruit officers, Vollmer's influence on Wilson's future endeavors was monumental for the future of policing in America. Despite his remedial education, Vollmer provided enormous support for secondary education for police officers. Vollmer became a police science professor at the University of Chicago and the UC Berkeley and provided further incentive for his officers to earn their university degrees.

As one of Vollmer's earliest college cops, Wilson attended his college courses in the daytime and was given the 4 PM to midnight shift, six days a week, to patrol north Berkeley in his newly purchased Model T Ford car. He was paid $140 monthly and an extra $30 for auto maintenance. Overtime was frequent, unpaid, and came primarily from court time. Two important contacts came out of Wilson's earliest patrol and court time. During his court time, he met Earl Warren, a prosecutor for the Alameda County District Attorney's Office. Wilson maintained his connection with Warren later in life as he became a three-term California Governor (1942–1953) and a United States Supreme Court Justice (1953–1969). The second contact came in 1921 when he uncharacteristically gave a warning ticket for speeding to Vernis Haddon, a swimming/diving athlete at Berkeley who transferred from the University of Texas. Six weeks later, they eloped and married in Sacramento (Ward, 2000).

In 1923, Wilson suffered academic set-backs due to his work at the police department and his new marriage. Low grades caused him to switch his major to economics and refocus his efforts in the classroom. Vollmer was particularly impressed by Wilson's ability to write clear police reports and often used his young protégé as his driver since he never learned how to drive himself. During these occasions, they discussed their ideas about police professionalism that later became engrained into Wilson's future reform efforts.

In 1924, Wilson earned his baccalaureate degree in economics and was ready to put his policing job behind him as he never seriously considered law enforcement a viable career.

2 Wilson described Vollmer as always immaculately dressed and an imposing figure who would never smoke in his office because he thought it might offend women or someone who might be allergic to tobacco smoke (Howard, 1972).

3 The term "billy club" likely evolved from a slang term burglars used to describe a crowbar. Another explanation reports that students from Yale University in the early 1800s gave a ceremonial stick called a "bully club" to those in the position of authority.

However, his mentor Chief Vollmer had different plans for his protégé. In 1925, town trustees from Fullerton, California, had contacted Vollmer to recommend their next police chief after terminating Arthur Eells. Vollmer recommended Wilson for the position despite his mentee's limited four years of experience in policing. Despite his reluctance, Vollmer convinced Wilson to relocate to Fullerton with Vernis and take the chief position. On April 1, 1925, Wilson became the nation's youngest chief at the age of 24.

Failure in Fullerton (Chief for Eight Months)

In 1905 Fullerton incorporated, and by April 1925 had close to 10,000 residents. The city paid Wilson $250 a month to lead seven officers on a $27,500 budget. Like most departments outside of Berkeley, the Fullerton police lacked any scientific crime detection methodology, did not have a way to track criminal offenders, did not have any communication system between police headquarters and patrol officers, and lacked any pre-service or in-service training. Wilson had Vollmer mail him police reports from Berkeley and then developed a modified check box form for his officers to keep track of criminal offenses and offenders.

Increased Mobile Patrol

Wilson took over a department of seven officers, two of whom did motorcycle patrol. As the new chief he convinced the town trustees to fund a lighting system on top of three city buildings to signal his patrolling officers that they should call headquarters to receive timely direction. With only two police cars for seven officers, Wilson also convinced the city to provide a $45 vehicle allowance for officers to drive their personal vehicles as a means of supplementing their patrol duties (Bopp, 1977, p. 32). Wilson recommended discontinuing motorcycle patrols in an unpopular directive, which he saw as too expensive and a liability. Increased mobile patrol became a cornerstone of Wilson's reform movements throughout his leadership career. The police themselves frequently backed this institutional-level change to regain confidence in the aftermath of corruption and perceived police ineffectiveness. However, a drawback was the police increasingly became more detached from the public as mobile patrol increased.

Increased Training

Like Vollmer, Wilson also began to teach training sessions and seminars to both his officers and the public on scientific crime scene investigations and the latest sociological research on crime causation. Wilson was a consummate student of the latest theories in criminology. One theory he discussed with Fullerton's citizens was the emergence of social disorganization theory from sociology researchers at the University of Chicago. Wilson explained the concentric zone approach, demonstrating that crime is concentrated in neighborhoods with high transition and population density. However, Wilson's interpretation of the criminological policy implications became directed toward population control and even the study of eugenics.[4] This theoretical discussion led to a series of complaints from prominent and religious Fullerton citizens, and Wilson would discover that, unlike Berkeley, Fullerton's small-town politics greatly impeded departmental leadership.

4 Eugenics is the study of human populations and solutions for increasing desirable genetics while weeding out undesirable genes such as retardation. Eugenics was developed by Sir Francis Galton and discredited by subsequent researchers. Its indoctrination was controversially done in Nazi Germany to justify extermination of Jews, the disabled, and other minority groups.

A committee of five citizens governed the Fullerton Police Department, and that committee reported to the city trustees. Wilson's ambitious departmental reorganization and discussion of contemporary criminology caused the police committee to recommend his dismissal. Wilson's youthful naiveté collided with the town's puritan political leaders and created valuable lessons for his future in police leadership. While he had several allies and could have fought the recommendation, this was not Wilson's leadership style. On December 1, 1925, he submitted his letter of resignation to the board of trustees, did not make any public statements, left town the same day with Vernis, and moved to Los Angeles (LA) by his wife's family. Once there, Wilson reported that Vollmer contacted Lee Phillips, President of the Pacific Finance Corporation, who helped him get hired as an investigator to do backgrounds on credit applicants and conduct repossessions (Robinson, 1972). Vernis was ecstatic to be in LA and registered with the Motion Picture Casting Service with the hopes of becoming a movie star. She did some stunt work connected to her swimming and diving talents (Ward, 2000).

Wichita, Kansas (Chief: 1928–1939)

After two and a half years of low pay and unsatisfied work, Wilson decided to apply to be a patrol officer with the Los Angeles Police Department (LAPD). However, Vollmer once again intervened and influenced Wilson's destiny. The chief of police in Wichita, Kansas, I.B. Walston,[5] had been terminated because of a booze protection scandal, which resulted in several federal indictments and criminal charges filed against officers and administrators as part of the prohibition Volstead Act.[6] City manager Bert Wells[7] sought Vollmer's recommendation for a strong and honest leader, high moral character, and no connection with the historically corrupt Wichita department. In March 1928, Vollmer's letter arrived at the Wilson home, and he encouraged his protégé to meet with Wells. Wilson was again reluctant, as was his wife Vernis, to follow his mentor's advice to interview for the Wichita chief's position. Wilson was concerned about the city's reputation for being a strict Puritan community with intolerance for vice, yet plagued with stories of police brutality and corruption. Indeed, the challenges of policing Wichita were quite different than what Chief Wilson experienced in Fullerton.

Wichita Police History

Wichita's law enforcement held a rogue and brutal reputation. The town was incorporated in 1870 and given city status the following year. In 1871 Will Smith and Mike Meagher[8] became Wichita's first town marshals. On April 21, 1875, Wyatt Earp[9] was appointed deputy

5 Walston appears on a February 23, 1934, FBI report while he worked as a house detective for the Phillips Hotel in Kansas City, Missouri. Walston had contacted the KC FBI Division Office with a letter related to the whereabouts of Charles "Pretty Boy" Floyd. His contact with the FBI came in the aftermath of a June 17, 1933, shootout that killed four law enforcement officers in front of the Union Station railroad depot in Kansas City. One of the gunmen was suspected to be Floyd but this was never proven (Wallis, 1992).

6 The Volstead Act was named after Andrew Volstead, chair of the House Judiciary Committee, which established legislation to carry out the 18th Amendment prohibiting intoxicating beverages in the United States. The law went into effect in January 1920 and lasted until the end of 1933 when the Twenty-first Amendment repealed the Eighteenth Amendment, voiding the Volstead Act.

7 Wells was the fifth city manager and served three terms (1927–1939). He was known as an extremely honest and effective city manager who worked well with Chief Wilson. His retirement led to Wilson's departure.

8 Meagher was born in Ireland and became Wichita's first Town Marshal at age 28. He was elected mayor of Caldwell, Kansas, in 1880 and was killed in a shootout in 1881.

9 Earp moved to Tombstone in 1881 with his brothers due to a silver boom. Clashes with a cowboy gang culminated in a shootout at the O.K. Corral on October 26, 1881, where Earp and Doc Holliday famously killed three of the cowboys.

under Marshal Meagher, Assistant Marshal John Behrens, and James Cairns,[10] the only other policeman. The marshal's salary was $91.66 a month, while the town paid Earp and Cairns $60 a month (Williamson, 2001, p. 15). In May 1876, Earp was fined $30 and terminated by the city council, but the reasons for this are not clear. One report states the following-

> *Mike Meagher and William Smith alternated as marshal of Wichita through most of the seventies, and Earp's demise came during a close election in 1876. As a campaign tactic Smith charged that Meagher had offered Earp's brothers jobs as policemen at a time when extra officers were not needed in Wichita. Earp was furious; he attacked and would have beaten Smith severely had not Meagher intervened and fired Earp for conduct unbecoming to an officer.*
>
> (Miner, 1982, p. 133)

Other reports indicated that Earp's sister-in-law was a prostitute, and Earp did not turn fines over to the city, which he was supposed to collect from his brother's wife. The mayor, James Hope (elected 1873–1874 and again from 1876 to 1874), also owned a saloon and ordered an internal investigation on Earp. Regardless of the reasons, voters re-elected Meagher over Smith, and the Wichita Commission decided Earp's violent behavior as a deputy was detrimental and did not rehire him.

The arrival of Reform Chief Wilson

On March 27, 1928, less than 50 years after Earp policed Wichita, city manager Wells announced 27-year-old O.W. Wilson would be their next chief with a monthly salary of $335, later reduced to help pay for Wilson's proposed one-way police car radios. Wilson found an archaic department plagued with dysfunction. There were no standards in place for hiring officers other than a recommendation by another officer, and there were no written policies to govern on-duty conduct, training, or promotion. Consequently, crime flourished, officers were bribed for non-enforcement, and excessive force was the norm when officers did make arrests.

One of Vollmer's most famous college cops led a reform movement within the Wichita Police for the next 11 years, and his leadership success rippled throughout the nation. His ability to last more than a decade in Wichita was due to his perceived obligation to the citizens, their eventual public approval of his reform efforts, and his passion for advancing the field of policing into an honorable profession. Like most reformists, however, Wilson's ideals ran counter to local politicians' political whims, but not before his work had a lasting impact on Wichita.

Patrol

Wilson and Vollmer exchanged numerous letters, referred to as administration by correspondence, during his time as chief. Vollmer attempted to persuade Wilson early on to be patient and cautious with his reform agenda. However, the new chief ignored his advice and plunged into the immediacy of modernizing his department and cleansing it of corruption. Wilson was in charge of 100 officers, and only 35 initially assigned to mobile patrol. Through an immediate organizational redesign, Wilson shifted foot patrol and clerical staff to mobile patrol. He also ordered one-man patrol even during evening shifts, going against what was a prior custom. Officers argued one-officer patrol was more dangerous, but their new chief

10 Cairns became town marshal through most of the 1880s. His famous brother-in-law was Bat Masterson who became a national celebrity in the 1880s into the early 1900s as a professional gambler, gun fighter, and journalist.

argued the opposite. Moreover, Wilson believed two officers were nonproductive, and subsequent research demonstrated his argument's validity (see Boydstun, Sherry, & Moelter, 1977; Kaplan, 1979).

Wilson utilized a daily activity sheet and required officers to turn in daily reports to demonstrate their shift productivity. To further professionalize the department's look, the new chief changed the standard blue law enforcement uniforms to a khaki[11] color, giving his officers a quasi-militaristic look. Wilson had the blue police cars painted white to a make his mobile patrol more visible. As a means for communicating with his mobile patrol officers, Wilson convinced the city council to fund the implementation of 20 call boxes and 42 warning lights to be installed throughout Wichita so officers could more efficiently respond to police headquarters. On March 17, 1929, the *Wichita Eagle* reported,

> *Police Use Call Boxes First Time Saturday Night- Desk Sergeant can Notify All Patrolmen of Big Crime at Same Time... More modernization in law enforcement occurred when 20 call boxes for police were activated... The desk sergeant has a means of immediate communication with all officers as each box is equipped with a bell that rings loud enough to be heard two or three blocks away. Should a major crime occur the patrolmen would be called to the call box rather than the sergeant waiting for them to call individually during their tour of duty.*
>
> (as cited in Williamson, 2001, p. 58)

In 1931, he also argued for installing radios in the police cars to allow one-way communication with patrol officers, but he ran into budget conflicts due to the crashing economy. To circumvent the city's funding opposition, Wilson asked his officers to take a pay cut of $5 a month. To help with the costs, he reduced his chief's annual salary from $4,800 to $3,956, and he relinquished his city vehicle (Bopp, 1977, p. 48). The departmental sacrifice resulted in police cars equipped with one-way radios, but Wilson was stuck with the reduced salary for the rest of his time as chief.

Traffic enforcement and safety became a key focus for Wilson after attending a conference in Kansas City in 1929, which showed the number of traffic accidents with injuries increased from 103 in 1927 to 181 by 1929. To draw the public's attention to safety conditions, Wilson bought a truck and placed a loudspeaker on the vehicle to inform traffic violators of their violations. This public address system led to Wichita being named the "safety city," among those with similar population size, in the National Traffic Safety Contest of 1932. Wilson also organized the nation's first Junior Traffic Patrol program that evolved into school crossing guards.

This initial success with traffic safety led Wilson to develop a mobile crime laboratory equipped with various investigative equipment. By 1934, Wilson instigated the development of a crime lab inside police headquarters and purchased the Keeler Polygraph machine to improve investigations. The polygraph was utilized on more criminal suspects than in any other department in the nation over the next several years.

Recruitment

Following Vollmer's Berkeley lead, Wilson administered the Army Alpha Test to recruits, did psychological exams with existing officers, and conducted intensive background investigations.

11 The Wichita Police wore khaki-colored uniforms for the next century. In 1990, outside Chief Rick Stone from Dallas attempted to change the uniform to blue, but officers overwhelmingly voted to keep their traditional khaki militaristic uniforms citing tradition. It was not until the spring of 2019 the department transitioned to dark blue uniforms citing a Midwest study on how citizens react to uniform colors (Johnson, 2005).

The media openly reported on which officers tested highest on the exams. On April 11, 1928, the Wichita Eagle reported,

> *To Charles Giles, a Negro patrolman on North Main goes the credit of having the most ability of members of the police department, to recall lists of numbers and write them down several minutes afterward. Giles was the only member of the department to make a perfect score in this part of the mental test given Tuesday by Chief O.W. Wilson. Ability to remember numbers is important in police work, as automobile license numbers must be taken in cases of accidents, and when speeding cars pass. Patrolman D.J. Finney, only three years in the service, placed highest in the entire examination. Finney also walks a North Main beat. The purpose of the examination is to develop the men's ability to think quickly.*
>
> (as cited in Williamson, 2001, p. 56)

Several veteran officers were less enthused about the intelligence tests administered by their youthful college-educated police chief. On April 14, 1928, the Wichita Eagle reported,

> *Mental Tricks and Tests Have Cops Bothered – New Chief's "Psychology" is Viewed With Doubt by Old Timers – The boys at police headquarters are frankly nervous. It was usual and the expected thing when the new chief took over Ike Walston's swivel chair that the ax should swing and a few faces turn up missing. That caused anxiety among those whose conscience was clear. But this thing of psychology tests is a fast one on 'the boys'. The chief has gone too far this time, some of the old-timers say, shaking their gray heads dubiously. Chief Wilson has administered two psychological tests to each member of the department. He has announced another examination, competitive, to 110 applicants for positions on the force to be held at the Winter Garden Monday night. 'How do I know how many wives Henry VIII had and how is that going to show whether I can clean up a burglary job!' snorted another greybeard. The tests cover the usual methods of intelligence examinations and are aimed at determining native common sense and ability to think quickly. The college-bred police chief believes seriously in the efficacy of his tests, but he asserts that there are many other qualities in making of an officer than those brought out by such tests and that his estimate of any man is not based primarily on his grades. Wilson grades the papers himself and has kept secret the results.*
>
> (as cited in Williamson, 2001, p. 56)

Chief Wilson personally interviewed recruits who passed the intelligence exams. If Wilson hired the recruits, they went through three weeks of in-house training, with a later intensive six-week training, before they could work patrol. Officers were paid $150 a month, and applicants dramatically increased in 1929 following the stock market collapse and the beginning of the Great Depression. Wilson further advanced his recruitment efforts by openly promoting his reform agenda to several professional associations, church groups, and civic organizations. He encouraged all his officers to do the same networking throughout the community, leading to more legitimacy through transparency. In 1928, Wilson hired Mrs. Jessie Lewis, Wichita's first policewoman, but she resigned on November 15, 1929. Lewis was replaced by Wanda Lee Resnick, a college graduate and experienced social worker (Williamson, 2001).

Criminal Investigations

Wilson set up a vice squad with his most trusted officers, who were expected to enforce laws related to gambling, prostitution, and bootlegging[12] as liquor was constitutionally prohibited

12 The term bootlegging is believed to have started in the 1880s when settlers concealed flasks of illicit whiskey in boot tops when going to trade with Indians.

throughout the country from 1920 to 1933. Wilson continually sought out officers he referred to as producers so he could promote them to be detectives, and he looked to eliminate officers who were non-producers. In this manner, Wilson reformed the department by becoming statistically driven while narrowing the police's role to crime-fighting with intensive follow-up investigations.

As he did in Fullerton, Wilson devised a record-keeping system to keep track of police reports and aid in criminal investigations. The reports were also used to create documented accountability to show what the officers did during their patrol time. He revised the system to track the modus operandi (MO) for robberies and burglaries and extended the Berkeley knowledge of the MO system by conducting a reliability study on its usefulness. He found that most criminals are not nearly as predictive as prior assumptions indicated and concluded that a significant amount of criminality was random and opportunistic. Wilson saw the record keeping of most MO patterns were a waste of resources.

Father of the Police Code of Ethics "A Square Deal"

Wilson borrowed from the nineteenth-century "square deal" language of New York City Police Commissioner Teddy Roosevelt's Progressive Era reform, telling the Wichita community he was leading a "Square Deal Department." His officers had to operate with a "square deal code" that consisted of high morals and ethical behavior. He created the Commandments for law enforcement, which became a forerunner for the Law Enforcement Code of Ethics, later adopted by the International Association of Chiefs of Police (IACP) in 1957. Consequently, Bopp (1977) contends that Wilson is the originator and the father of the police code of ethics. Wilson's Square Deal Code was printed in the *Wichita Eagle* on July 23, 1929:

To Serve on the Square:

1. *To be a friend to MAN*
2. *To protect citizens and guests, safeguard lives, guarantee liberty and assist in the peaceful pursuit of happiness*
3. *To be honest, kind, strong, and true, always proud of our department and city*
4. *To give friendly aid in distress*
5. *To be gentlemen, practicing courtesy and weaving a daily thread in the habit of politeness, always thoughtful of the comfort and welfare of others*
6. *To keep our private lives unsullied, an example for all*
7. *To be honorable that our character may be strengthened*
8. *To bear malice or ill will toward none*
9. *To guard our tongues lest they speak evil*
10. *To act with caution lest our motives are questioned*
11. *To be courageous and calm in the face of danger, scorn, or ridicule*
12. *To ignore unjust criticism and profit by good*
13. *To be alert in mind, sound in body, courteous in demeanor, and soldierly in bearing, a comfort to the distressed, a protector of the weak, and a pride to our city*
14. *To practice self-restraint, using no unnecessary force or violence*
15. *To intimidate no one, nor permit it to be done*
16. *To take appropriate action whenever an offense is committed*
17. *To have the moral courage to enforce the law*
18. *To be unofficiously, firm but mindful of the rights of others*
19. *Never to permit personal feelings, animosities nor friendships to influence decisions*

20 *Never to act in the heat of passion*
21 *To assist the public in their compliance with regulations*
22 *To save unfortunate offenders from unnecessary humiliation, inconvenience, and distress*
23 *With no compromise for crime, to be relentless toward the criminal, our judgment charitable toward the minor offender*
24 *Never to arrest if a summons will suffice*
25 *Never to summons if a warning would be better, never to scold or reprimand but inform and request.*

Wilson received national recognition from *Reader's Digest* for reforming the department and creating the square deal with Wichita's citizens (Williamson, 2001). Within his square deal, Wilson also focused on eliminating police misuse of force. On June 12, 1928, the *Wichita Eagle* reported,

> *Lawyers Boost Wichita's New Chief of Police- Protection League Disbanded as No Longer a Necessity. Chief Wilson received good reviews from the local attorneys who stated there had not been one case of police brutality since he took over the position from Chief Walston. Chief Wilson instituted new, mandatory reporting procedures which gave him the opportunity to review individual cases and officers' actions to make sure they were operating within the law when making arrests. This was met, initially with resistance, but greatly improved the department.*
>
> (as cited in Williamson, 2001, p. 58)

On May 28, 1928, the *Wichita Eagle* reported that all officers had to submit to fingerprinting and have a photograph filed with the national Department of Justice:

> *File Photographs and Fingerprints of all Policemen: New Order of Wichita Chief Doesn't Set Well with Members of Force for Record Purposes- An order, effective immediately, calls for the fingerprinting and photographing of every officer on the Wichita police force for record purposes. No other order issued recently has resulted in as much objection on the part of the men, who contend the taking of the Bertillon measurements places them in the same category as the ordinary criminal. The original record will remain on file in the record office of the local department. Duplicates will be sent to the department of justice in Washington, to Columbus, OH., and to other places where pictures and records of all criminals are kept. While few officers object to the measurements being on file so long as they are members of the departments, most of them object on the grounds that the records will remain on file after they leave the force. This is considered unfair. It was recalled Sunday that all soldiers who entered the service for the World war had their Bertillon measurements taking although they were not photographed. These measurements are still on file in Washington. Officials declare the order will ensure perfect identification of any officer in case of accident or death and is a benefit rather than a liability.*
>
> (as cited in Williamson, 2001, p. 57)

Later, in the fall of 1928, Wilson trained 40 officers in fingerprint methods, including lifting latent prints and creating a classification system. This training followed with a new departmental policy that prohibited gratuities from area businesses. Officers were expected to refuse any discounts or free goods. Several veteran officers objected but were told to follow the orders or resign. Wilson let officers know the days of fixing tickets for privileged Wichita citizens were over. To educate the community on this policy change, Wilson encouraged the newspapers to attend role call meetings and openly access their departmental files. Like Vollmer, Wilson also urged his officers to cooperate with the media and create a culture of open accountability and a focus on community trust.

Another means for improving community relations came from the departmental newsletter Wilson put out called *The Buzzer* aimed primarily at community business owners. A second publication called the *Hue and Cry* focused on providing crime data and updates on the department to the public. The newsletters delivered transparency in a department that was previously plagued by the corruption that infested city businesses and politics. Ironically, Wilson orchestrated the essence of community-oriented policing in Wichita decades before academics pushed against his reform movements that were connected to quasi-militaristic law enforcement. Wilson received media coverage when beat officers were required to meet with new residents and inform them about local church services, schools, and businesses. Officers also met with residents to explain how they could report violations of sanitary regulations and file police or fire reports. Beat officers were expected to serve residents and produce well-managed neighborhoods.

"West Point" Police Cadet Program – Recruitment of University Students

An educated police force became a priority for Wilson, noting his career in Berkeley began through the city police recruitment at his university. He favored part-time police employment with reduced course loads for college students to ensure success for both. Wilson was able to hire many financially stressed college students due to the 1930s depression. Wilson's program had university police science students working four-hour days as police officers while carrying a 12-hour course load. Bopp (1977, p. 57) referred to this setup as the nation's first police cadet program, but the cadets had to be at least 21 years of age. Wilson marketed his cadet program to students from the University of Wichita (today Wichita State University) and Friends University. Hired cadets made $50 a month, and Wilson led a six-week training session twice a year during university semester-breaks. Several college students were subsequently placed in other agencies throughout Kansas, including the state police, and Wilson's training program inside the Wichita Police earned the title "the West Point of Law Enforcement" (Bopp, 1977, p. 58).

In 1931, Wilson's tenacity for education further materialized when he created a Training School through support from the Kansas League of Municipalities, which named him the director of the board. Various instructors taught in the interdisciplinary school from agencies such as the federal Department of Justice, Cook County Juvenile Detention, and the National Safety Council. Wilson's Wichita Police Headquarters served as a host agency, and officers from throughout Kansas sent their personnel for training. This national outreach further solidified Wilson as a premier reformer in American policing and created additional lifetime networks that served to advance his career status.

Juveniles

Wilson was preoccupied with a national rise in juvenile delinquency during the 1930s. He believed juvenile courts should operate differently than adult courts with goals directed to adjusting future behavior. He partnered with social science professors from Friends University and the University of Wichita to help develop an instrument to predict criminality. While academics failed to create a prediction instrument, several sociologists consulted with the police department to advocate for improving delinquent lifestyles. Wilson encouraged his officers to creatively mentor and engage juvenile delinquents rather than rely on reactive arrests and traditional court processes. In rather dramatic language, Wilson called his initiative "human engineering" (Bopp, 1977, p. 53) to describe his experimental plan to redirect juveniles instead of merely focusing on punishment and labeling. Initially, the juvenile court judge favored this collaboration, but politics would later create a wedge between the courts and the reformist police chief.

In 1930, Wilson required his officers to show up a half-hour before their shift to attend his training programs. He may have been the first chief to implement these roll call training sessions, and the rest of the country would soon follow his lead. As chief, Wilson often worked seven days a week to shape ethical standards within the Wichita police. Similar to New York Police Department (NYPD) Commissioner Teddy Roosevelt near the turn of the twentieth century, Wilson was not immune to arriving at a crime scene during the midnight shift or conducting unannounced inspections of officer patrols anytime during the day or night. Wilson went beyond surveilling his officers to also wanting to hear from them. Like Vollmer, Wilson set up Saturday "crab meetings" to listen to their feedback. These sessions also included in-service training opportunities. The media and community were often invited to these sessions to better understand their police department's efforts to professionalize its ranks. For Wilson, the days of the blue curtain of secrecy were over, and his leadership offered the square deal of transparency.

National Recognition – FBI Fracture

Through reforms and progressive innovations, Wilson's leadership attracted the attention of *Readers Digest* and *True Detective Mysteries*, giving him the same type of national exposure Vollmer received in Berkeley. Vollmer continued to encourage and influence his student's evolving prominence. This prominence included Wilson's five-month position as a visiting lecturer at Harvard University. He was assigned to the Bureau for Street Traffic Research under Miller McClintock's supervision, who later went to Germany and assisted Adolph Hitler in constructing the autobahn. Wilson directed the New England Traffic Officers' Training School and coordinated a two-week course for police officers on traffic safety and enforcement policies. In addition to teaching courses for Harvard, Wilson spent two months traveling Europe and learning about various police agencies. Lastly, Wilson consulted with several departments across the United States, recommending various reorganization and innovation strategies. These experiences gave Wilson national exposure as a premier police leader while still serving as chief in Wichita.

However, Wilson's national recognition created a disconnect with J. Edgar Hoover and the FBI, and federal law enforcement support of Wilson evaporated. There are a few possible explanations as to why the FBI director withdrew his support from Wilson. First, some speculated there was animosity from Hoover, who envisioned himself as the patriarch of law enforcement reform. Second, Wilson wrote an article for the Kansas Bar Association. He questioned the rise of federal law enforcement authority and advocated for more local police cooperation with criminal investigations (Wilson, 1934). Wilson saw the Federal Government as a clearinghouse for information rather than leading criminal investigations or setting local law enforcement standards. Lastly, Hoover may have been troubled with a participant observation research project Wilson assisted in with renowned criminologist Edwin Sutherland, chair of the Indiana University sociology program. In 1936 Wilson helped Sutherland's University of Chicago graduate student, Hans Riemer, with an ethnographic study inside the Kansas State Prison (Haynes, 1949). Riemer served two weeks in the county jail and three months inside the prison as an inmate (Bowker, 1977). Neither the court officials that convicted Riemer of a forged check nor the correctional staff or inmates knew Riemer was a covert researcher. After the project was completed, Hoover was contacted to make sure Riemer's record and fingerprints were withdrawn from their database, and the director was not amused. The aftermath of these events resulted in FBI agents removed from Wilson's police training in Wichita, and other prior pledges of assistance went unanswered. There was no known or documented reason the FBI gave for why it withdrew support from Wilson.

Wichita Politics

By 1931, Wilson and Vernis had a son named Henry Haddon Wilson,[13] but the hectic schedule O.W. placed upon himself created havoc for his marriage. Over the next eight years, there was not much improvement. In addition to his personal life, professionally Wilson faced several disgruntled yet influential Wichita community members, mainly connected to the enforcement of vice crime. Similar to Teddy Roosevelt's enforcement of Sunday drinking laws in New York City, Wilson's desire to enforce vice laws did not come from a place of omnipotence but instead an obligation to the policing profession. Interestingly, Wilson believed prostitution should be legalized and monitored by the government (Bopp, 1977, p. 59), but he still had leadership responsibility for legal enforcement. Like many cities and towns of the Great Depression, Wichita had many vacant buildings. Prostitutes were reliable tenants, and as the police cracked down on their trade, area businessmen lost many of their dependable renters.

City commissioners were eventually influenced to rally against Wilson and began to call for his resignation. Wilson's detractors found further susceptibility through juvenile judge Clyde Hudson and the chief's human engineering program. Judge Hudson felt he was not receiving enough credit for the program, and Wilson lacked the legal authority to be involved with the judiciary. Since judges are politically elected, pushing Wilson out of the spotlight was advantageous. To counter Wilson's juvenile diversion initiative, the judge asked for a legal opinion from the state attorney general, who predictably ruled the police department had no legal authority to be involved with the juvenile court. Wilson was ordered to disband any police strategies with the court. The city council followed up the attorney general's opinion by blaming Wilson for frivolous use of tax dollars and unnecessary progressive programs. Wilson recognized the political forces operating against his leadership. On May 15, 1939, he privately met with the city council, took a leave of absence, and later formally resigned as Wichita's chief. He left his position as chief convinced that politics provided the most significant barrier for national police reform.

Chicago

Wilson and Vernis left Wichita and headed straight for Chicago to meet with the non-profit Public Administration Service (PAS) to survey municipal police agencies and make reorganization recommendations. Donald Stone, Director of the PAS, encouraged Wilson to write reports on his experiences as the country's premier police scholar. Stone and the PAS sought to provide professional service support for those engaged in the study of government policy and public administrative leadership. In 1941, through Stone's encouragement and support, Wilson published the *Distribution of Police Patrol Force* that indicated strategies for distributing patrol in medium-sized cities based on an analysis of serious crime and predictions of subsequent crime. The report's data came from a 1939 patrol distribution in both Wichita and San Antonio and his success with traffic safety improvement. Eliot Ness, famous for his work as a prohibition agent that targeted Al Capone, was Director of Public Safety in Cleveland when Wilson wrote his report. He provided praise in the forward section of the manuscript, stating

13 At the age of 21, Henry joined the BPD while he was a junior in the UC criminology program while his father was dean. Before joining the police department, Henry worked as a correctional guard at San Quentin Prison. His wife, one year younger, was also a criminology student, and both graduated with their bachelor's degrees in 1954. Henry later became an Episcopal minister in Wiesbaden, Germany.

that, for the first time, police leaders had a reliable standard to assess the effectiveness of their resources.

University of California Berkeley (1939–1960)

Not that he needed it, but Vollmer again provided Wilson the safety of a second career following his successful leadership of the Wichita Police Department. Vollmer's failing health and his desire to see Wilson remain an active national leader in police reform led to his protégé replacing him as the police administration professor at UC Berkeley. Wilson remained a UC Berkeley professor for the next 20 years, except for his three years of service in the Army during World War II. Like Wichita, Wilson was initially hesitant to accept Vollmer's request to teach police administration courses. However, Vollmer's persuasiveness with the university administration and President Robert Sproul was evident when they offered Wilson a full-tenured professor position with an annual salary of $6,000 and moving expenses of $500. He also received summers off and a reduced teaching load of two courses a semester. Wilson accepted the faculty position on July 24, 1939, becoming America's first full-time police administration professor (Bopp, 1977, p. 65). In doing so, his goal was to create a pragmatic program that was acceptable to both practitioners and academic colleagues. The university gave Wilson the autonomy to develop the Bureau of Police Administration within the political science department. However, his main goal, along with Vollmer, was to create an independent School of Criminology.

Textbooks

During his academic time, Wilson authored several textbooks on policing. The first publication came from a request from the International City Manager's Association. *Municipal Police Administration* was published as a manual in 1938 and *Distribution of Police Patrol Force* in 1941 (Wilson, 1941). In 1942 Wilson published *Police Records: Their Installation and Use.* His most famous text was *Police Administration,* published by McGraw-Hill in 1950, and four editions followed over nearly 50 years. The book became a staple textbook across the nation for police academies and university classrooms, with a broad international publication rewritten in several different languages. In his 1971 interview with the Bancroft Library at UC Berkeley, Wilson indicated that he went through each chapter line-by-line with his mentor August Vollmer. The text demonstrated Vollmer's foundational views on police administration (Robinson, 1972). Notably, Wilson's writings on police administration did not discuss police discretion, use of force, or issues related to discriminatory arrest (Walker & Katz, 2018). These gaps necessitated research opportunities for Wilson's proteges, such as Herman Goldstein, as detailed in the proceeding appendix.

Co-authors continued to revise *Police Administration* long after Wilson's death in an effort to change and update materials in a manner Wilson would have done himself. These revisions were a testament to Wilson's lifelong belief in education and furthering our knowledge of how best to administer the police in a democratic society.

Co-authors of *Police Administration* included the following:

1st Edition 1950 (Wilson, 1950)
2nd Edition 1963[14] (Wilson, 1963)

14 Much of the 2nd edition revision came from Wilson's second wife, Ruth, a former criminology student from the UC Berkeley, while they resided in Chicago. Wilson spent very little time reviewing his wife's revisions for McGraw-Hill. While she did successfully capture her husband's philosophy toward police administration and his professional values, she was not listed as a co-author (Bopp, 1977).

3rd Edition 1972 with Roy Clinton McLaren[15] (Wilson & McLaren, 1972)
4th Edition 1977 with Roy Clinton McLaren (Chief of Police Arlington, Virginia) (Wilson & McLaren, 1977)
5th Edition 1997 with James Fyfe & Jack Greene (Temple University) and William Walsh (University of Louisville) (Fyfe et al., 1997)

American Society for Criminology (ASC)

In 1941, Vollmer asked Wilson to extend a meeting invite to all Pacific Coast school directors involved in teaching courses related to police administration. The intent of the meeting was to develop a national model for university police education. On December 30, 1941, seven men that Wilson invited met with Vollmer in his Berkeley living room and established the National Association of College Police Training Officials (NACPTO). Vollmer nominated Wilson to be the President of the new association. The men met from 10 AM to 1 AM the next day, discussing the future of national higher education for police officers (Morn, 1995). Disagreement over the philosophy of who should be the members of their association likely took up much of their time. Some members wanted to cater to existing police officers and have the association serve as their in-service training. However, Vollmer, Wilson, and V.A. Leonard favored membership directed toward university faculty who were involved with research in police science programs (see Chapter 2 for a more thorough discussion on Vollmer). For Wilson, his efforts to create the NACPTO set the academic structure for studying the police and advocated for professionalism through university education.

Wilson's Divorce

Teaching and curriculum development at his alma mater assuredly gave Wilson a great deal of pride and respect, but his personal family life continued to be stressed. In the summer of 1939, Wilson, Vernis, and their son Henry relocated to Berkeley. On January 7, 1940, their daughter Sally Jo was born. By 1941 they lived apart, and in November 1942, they filed for divorce, which was finalized in 1943. Vernis moved to LA to live with her mother and committed suicide in 1948 from an overdose of sleeping pills (Bopp, 1977, p. 66).

World War II – United States Army

When World War II broke out, Wilson was 41 years old and estranged from Vernis with a pending divorce. He petitioned his department chair, Retired General David Barrows, to assist him in being commissioned into the Army. He also received assistance from Joe Harris, former Berkeley Political Science Professor, an Army colonel. Wilson was encouraged to contact the newly established School of Military Government in Charlottesville, Virginia, developed to assist liberated countries with the reestablishment of their government. With the assistance of Barrows and Harris, Wilson applied for an officer's position within the school, and in January 1943, he became a lieutenant colonel. After graduating from the school with honors four months later, Wilson went to Italy to set up law enforcement agencies. He then went to England as the Director of the Public Safety Division and rebuilt Germany's police force in a post-Nazi world. Wilson worked to assure that high-ranking Nazi sympathizers were not a part of the new German police. Wilson attempted to have Vollmer appointed his aide, but the

15 McLaren was a Berkeley criminology graduate and the director of the Field Services Division with the IACP. Later he became police chief in Arlington, Virginia.

Army turned down this request. Wilson served an additional year in Germany as a civilian after the war ended and continued to work with German police agencies. He left with the rank of full colonel along with a Bronze Star and Legion of Merit. Lessons from his war service transferred to his police reform belief that law enforcement agencies should be managed through a centralized authority and be structured under a militaristic model led by highly ethical leaders whom politicians did not influence.

Back to Berkeley

In the summer of 1947, Wilson returned to UC Berkeley and again joined Vollmer to establish a new autonomous school of criminology. In 1950, Wilson and Vollmer met their goal when the Bureau of Police Administration became the School of Criminology, and the UC Berkeley promoted Wilson to be Dean. Wilson continued to expand the program throughout the decade despite his academic colleagues' contempt. At one point, they attempted to relegate criminology to minor academic status. Several professors outside of criminology did not feel Wilson should be a dean since he did not hold a Ph.D. degree,[16] and they did not see the major as a proper academic discipline. Moreover, Wilson did not have the best teaching evaluations, and some students felt he was a poor lecturer and generally detached. However, Wilson stayed active throughout the country as a police consultant, and these trips helped provide refuge from the faculty in-fighting at Berkeley.

In the fall of 1950, Wilson married his second wife, Ruth Elinor, a former criminology student. Ruth was an older divorcee. Wilson admired Ruth for her intelligence, her social grace, and her ability to nurture him while she provided the independence he needed in his career. In 1953, Wilson's third child, Patricia Anne, was born; his previous two children, Henry and Sally, were with his first wife, Vernis. In 1954, Wilson was asked by city leaders in Portland, Maine, to help organize their police department because of internal administrative issues and low officer morale. Wilson's consulting funds came from Donald Stone and the Chicago-based Public Administrative Service that had hired him after leaving Wichita. Once in Portland, Maine, Wilson met Herman Goldstein,[17] working as an assistant to the city manager, initially on an internship. Wilson and Goldstein developed a close bond. They worked on additional projects, including the newly created American Bar Foundation (ABF) study that analyzed the administration of justice across the nation (American Bar Foundation Report, 1955–1956). Six years after they met, Wilson brought Goldstein to Chicago to serve as his civilian executive assistant, as detailed in the appendix.

By 1957, the School of Criminology at UC Berkeley became a target for incoming President Clark Kerr.[18] Kerr had been the chancellor under the Sproul administration, and his followers had reputations as academic elites. The new president saw Berkeley as a premier research institution that should produce a large number of scholarly graduate students from its undergraduate programs. Wilson had hired several non-Ph.D. faculty members to teach in the criminology program, and they were not looked favorably upon by the new university administration. By

16 Wilson was the Superintendent of the Chicago Police Department from 1960 to 1967 and received honorary doctorate degrees from Carthage College in 1962 and Northwestern University in 1965. The Chicago Press Club named Wilson "Chicagoan of the Year" in 1964.

17 An appendix on Herman Goldstein is attached to this chapter, given his enormous contribution to the field of policing and the lessons he garnered while assisting Wilson.

18 Kerr was a professor of economics and the first chancellor for the University of California, Berkeley (1952–1957) in addition to being the 12th president for the University of California (1958–1967). Governor Ronald Reagan and Board of Regents Edwin Pauley worked with J. Edgar Hoover to have Kerr removed from the university presidency by casting him as a radical liberal who failed to contain student protests.

the summer of 1959, after several investigations, a committee recommended the School of Criminology at Berkeley was a training school and did not belong in academic universities. Wilson responded and rallied numerous supporters that included Governor Pat Brown,[19] Attorney General Stanley Mosk,[20] law enforcement executives, correctional administrators, and several state legislatures to save the School of Criminology at Berkeley. Consequently, Kerr faced an abundance of political pressure to protect the Berkeley criminology program. A subsequent committee reversed the course and recommended only curricular changes.[21]

Back to Chicago – CPD Scandals

In the aftermath of battling Kerr and saving the criminology program, Wilson took a one-year sabbatical. He planned to take Ruth and Pat to Hawaii for an extended vacation and revise his *Police Administration* textbook. This trip was interrupted by an emergency telegram received from Mayor Richard J. Daley[22] from Chicago, who requested his assistance in chairing a committee to find and select a new police commissioner. At the time, Wilson was unaware that several city leaders had discussed strategies to convince him to take over the CPD, which he would eventually do from 1960 to 1967.

In 1959, the year before Wilson's arrival, Anthony Joseph "Big Tuna" Accardo[23] turned over the Chicago crime syndicate to Sam Giancana.[24] Accardo left to tour Europe and was accompanied by CPD Lieutenant Anthony DeGrazio, demonstrating the extent of police corruption Wilson would face. DeGrazio, suspended by Commissioner Timothy O'Connor, was subsequently terminated following a Civil Service Commission hearing (Flood, 2012). Accardo avoided other mob bosses' publicity and became a consulting consigliere after turning over operations to Giancana. Retired FBI agent Bill Roemer wrote a book on Accardo, whom he

19 Brown was the 32nd Governor (1959–1967) of California and he defeated Richard Nixon in his second term reelection but lost to Ronald Reagan for his third term. Brown's son Jerry was the 34th (1975–1983) and 39th (2011–2019) Governor of California.

20 Mosk later became a justice on the California Supreme Court and served longer than any other justice (1964–2001). The Los Angeles County Courthouse is named in his honor.

21 After Wilson's departure, the academic critics pushed the Berkeley criminology program to hire more Ph.D. faculty and eliminate coursework that was considered vocational. Retired officers began to leave the faculty to find more hospitable academic programs. Throughout the 1960s the faculty became more sociological and outspoken critics of law enforcement. By 1976, the School of Criminology at Berkeley was closed and other police science professors throughout the country were under attack. Gradually, criminal justice programs grew to include an expanded focus on the courts and correctional aspects of the system. Today, criminal justice programs are nonexistent in the vast majority of campuses under the University of California. One exception is California State University in Sacramento that launched a Law Enforcement Candidate Scholars Program in 2016 that prepares students from all majors to become police officers through workshops and internships.

22 Richard Joseph Daley was Chicago mayor from 1955 until his death in 1976. His son, Richard Michael Daley, was the longest-serving Chicago mayor from 1989 to 2011, surpassing his dad by one year. Richard M. Daley called Wilson the best police leader Chicago ever had (Kaas & Recktenwald, 1991).

23 Accardo's grandson Eric Kumerow and great-grandsons Joey and Nick Bosa all played pro football in the NFL. They were the second family to hold this distinction, after the Mannings: Archie, Peyton, and Eli.

24 Giancana, who worked for Al Capone in his youth, lived a high-profile lifestyle and had unconfirmed links to President Kennedy's election and assassination. He was also linked to the Bay of Pigs invasion and the attempted assassination of Fidel Castro through CIA funds. Giancana was fatally shot seven times in the head and neck inside his Oak Park, Illinois home on June 19, 1975 (Giancana & Giancana, 1992), shortly before he was supposed to testify before the Church Committee, a Senate select committee that looked into abuses by the CIA. Giancana's friend Tony Spilotro was the suspected gunman. Spilotro was killed by blunt force trauma to the head and discovered in a shallow grave near a cornfield in Enos, Indiana on June 22, 1986, after the mob disapproved of his management of their Las Vegas rackets. Martin Scorsese's (1995) film *Casino*, starring Joe Pesci and Robert De Niro, is based on Spilotro's time and demise in Las Vegas.

suspected of being Al Capone's bodyguard and trigger man in the St. Valentine's Day Massacre on February 14, 1929, inside a parking lot warehouse in Lincoln Park (Roemer, 1996).[25] In 1978, burglars hit Accardo's home, leading to ten retaliatory murders. Brashler (1984) reported the gruesome details of the retaliation. Each burglar had their throats cut, one was castrated and disemboweled. The Italian had his face removed with a blowtorch as a sign that he should have known better. Subsequent convictions of the assassins occurred through the FBI's Family Secrets Trial (Calabrese, Zimmerman, Zimmerman, & Pompian, 2012). Accardo died of natural causes in 1992 at 86 years of age, having never spent more than one night inside a prison cell.

Other Chicago police scandals in 1959 included detectives indicted in a federal grand jury, patrol officers caught in possession of $95,000 worth of marijuana, and an officer killed when he crashed a stolen car into a building (Ward, 2000, p. 66). These events were precursors to the media sensation that encompassed organized burglaries that involved numerous CPD officers.

Corruption in Summerdale[26] (Chicago's Northside) – Babbling Burglar

In January 1960, the CPD was rocked by the Summerdale Scandal when *Sun-Times* reporter Walter Spirko[27] broke a one-page exclusive that Chicago police officers were involved in organized burglaries. The prior summer, Richard "Richie" Morrison was arrested and boasted that he was the most extraordinary burglar that Chicago had ever seen; yet reporters initially ignored his story. Morrison later became known as the "Babbling Burglar" and implicated various officers as his co-conspirators. Eventually, the *Sun-Times* and the *Chicago Tribune* ran stories detailing how eight Chicago police officers assisted Morrison in a series of burglaries throughout the Summerdale District on the city's North Side.

Morrison's connection with the police began in 1957, at the age of 21, while working at Wesley's Restaurant at 1116 Bryn Mawr Avenue delivering pizza, often for free, to police officers in a nearby police district. The owner of Wesley's also invited officers to eat for free and allow his delivery workers to double park. Morrison's past burglary reputation from LA and Las Vegas was well known, and eventually, officers began asking him to engage in various retail theft and safecracking. The officers also helped him haul away proceeds from his burglaries in their squad cars and, after some time, were emboldened to conduct their own burglaries. The burglary partnership between Morrison and the Chicago officers lasted a year and three months, throughout 1958 and 1959. Insurance companies, such as West Bend Mutual, had served the needs of small businesses throughout north Chicago for nearly 45 years. They reported a 288 percent loss in ratio to premiums received and announced they would stop writing policies for open stock burglary insurance to retailers along Clark, Sheridan Broadway, and Ashland business corridors (Lindberg, 1991, p. 305). The 40th District indicated a 48 percent burglary increase in 1959 compared to the previous year. According to Morrison's testimony, eight officers and Captain Herman Dorf from the Summerdale District split burglary profits. Dorf refused to take a polygraph, turned in his resignation, and moved to California.

25 The history of Capone is also detailed in the chapter on Ramsey.

26 Infamous serial killer John Wayne Gacy also resided in the Summerdale area; his home is located at 8213 W. Summerdale Avenue. Twenty-six of his 33 murder victims (killed between 1972 and 1978) were found in the crawl space under his house. He was executed by lethal injection at Stateville Correctional Center on May 10, 1994.

27 Spirko also broke the news from St. Valentine's Day Massacre in 1929 (described in more detail in the chapter on Chuck Ramsey) but was initially not trusted by the City News Bureau (CNB) of Chicago, which released a bulletin that six men are reported to have been seriously injured (Dornfeld, 1983).

The extent of the connection between Morrison and the CPD officers was more than alarming, as indicated with Richard Lindberg's final chapter: *To Serve and Collect: Chicago Politics and Corruption from the Lager Beer Riot to the Summerdale Scandal.*

> *Anyways, we were running around [in the store] when we were getting the stuff. I happened to think, "Who was listening to the radio calls in the squad car?" I said I would. So I went to the car, and I was sitting there. They were counting out the bacon and hams and everything you could think of in the store. Real expensive foods! They kept filling the back seat of the squad car. So that's how rotten these cops were. They did just anything to get a dollar. (Richard Morrison, cat burglar, 1960).*
>
> Lindberg (1991, p. 263)

However, the partnership between cops and crook was disingenuous. Officers from Summerdale tipped off detectives from the Northside detective bureau, letting them know where they sent Morrison to conduct burglaries. They were then bribed unknowingly from Morrison so he could avoid arrest. It was their way of cutting in others on their arrangement and keeping their cooperative relationship with Morrison.

Morrison was arrested on March 3, 1959, by the Secret Service in a counterfeiting ring. The CPD officers chastised him for making $100 bills and not $20 bills (Lindberg, 1991, p. 300). Despite the arrest, Morrison and the officers continued their burglary sprees, but this ended on July 30, 1959, with another arrest. Rather than becoming a martyr, Morrison provided a 77-page confession that implicated several CPD officers in numerous burglaries. In the aftermath of Morrison's admission, truckloads of stolen goods were retrieved by investigators from the homes of Chicago officers during a predawn raid on January 15, 1960.

The criminal case building against the CPD quickly politicized. Cook County State's Attorney Ben Adamowski, not a Daley supporter,[28] ordered out-of-state polygraph tests for 130 officers at the Summerdale CPD station. On January 23, 1960, Commissioner O'Connor resigned under the cloak of poor health. Illinois Republican Governor William Stratton demanded that Daley resign his chairmanship from the Cook County Democratic Committee and help reform the CPD without distraction. He also called for creating a state-run police board to monitor the CPD's future reform efforts. Predictably, Daley bucked these political challenges.

Julius Lucius Echeles[29] served as one of the defense attorneys for the officers. Echeles also defended several individuals connected to the mob and spent time in federal prison himself after being convicted of selling jobs and promotions at the Chicago Post Office. Judge James Parsons,[30] the first Black to receive a lifetime appointment as a federal trial judge, supervised the proceedings in front of an all-female jury. In the summer of 1961, seven of the eight officers in the Summerdale Scandal received convictions. As Judge Parsons mediated, since the female jurors refused to provide a sentence, their sentences ranged from one to five years, with two officers fined $500. While the media ran headlines on the corrupt eight, several other officers from outlying districts escaped punishment.

28 Adamowski, leader of the northwest side Polish community, lost to Daley in the 1955 mayoral Democratic primary. He served as State's Attorney for Cook County from 1957 to 1960 and ran against Daley as a Republican in 1963 after he renounced the Democratic Party.

29 Julius Lucius "Lucky" Echeles died at the age of 83 in September 1998 in south Florida of heart failure. He never obtained a college or law degree yet became one of Chicago's top-ranked attorneys for nearly 60 years. He passed the bar exam in 1936 after taking a few night classes at John Marshall Law School (Mendell, 1998).

30 Judge Parsons was appointed by President Kennedy in 1961 and became the nation's first Black U.S. District judge. He died in Chicago in June 1993 at the age of 81 (Thornton, 1993).

Morrison moved to Florida after prosecutors dropped charges against him in exchange for his return to testify against the CPD. Morrison made his way back to Chicago a few years later. On March 20, 1963, prosecutors scheduled Morrison to testify in a mob case that involved Dr. Leonard Macaluso,[31] who reportedly treated him for a bullet wound he received during one of his burglaries. Prosecutors accused Macaluso of treating other members of the mob that were wounded. As he was outside the Cook County Courthouse prepared to testify, Morrison was struck in the arm by a shotgun blast from a drive-by assassin (Benzkofer, 2013). His attorney escorted him in the ambulance, and Morrison begged not to be left alone with the police. His later testimony on the witness stand indicated that he did not know Dr. Macaluso, and Morrison was successfully scared into silence by the mob (Lindberg, 1991, p. 316).

The Summerdale Scandal, on the heels of Mayor Richard J. Daley's superhighway and the White Sox American League Championship, required long-term solutions and reform, or it would cost him his career. The scandal led to the resignation of Police Commissioner Timothy O'Conner and created a rip in the nation's public confidence in police services and morale among officers nationwide. While the public customarily heard stories about Cook County politics and police bribery, they were unaware of officers who were active partners in felony crime or police leaders who actively covered up these crimes. The scandal led some to believe that thousands of officers across the nation were on the take because of low wages, unprofessional working conditions, and lack of accountability.

Few Americans viewed police work as an honorable profession leading into 1960, and the aftermath of the Summerdale Scandal did further damage. Despite Vollmer and Wilson's efforts, very few officers nationwide attended college, and there was little attempt to train or properly educate new officers on ethics or effective police work. In the pre-professionalization era, reports from Chicago officers indicated their assigned field training officer often disappeared. The rookie officers were put on the street and left to figure out the job on their own. The Summerdale Scandal provided the catalyst for the needed reform movement toward police professionalization.

Superintendent Wilson (1960–1967)

It should not be understated how far morale had fallen in the CPD in 1960 after the Summerdale Scandal broke. The arrest and conviction of seasoned Chicago police investigators, who facilitated their organized burglary ring, confirmed the public perception of rampant corruption in policing and made officers the brunt of many jokes. The lack of leadership shown throughout the scandal was enormously damaging for policing everywhere. Mayor Daley recognized the unprecedented challenge toward professionalism in the CPD, along with his political fallout. Consequently, he ordered a blue-ribbon screening committee to conduct a national search to replace Commissioner O'Connor. Based on a recommendation from Fred Hoehler, the superintendent of the Chicago House of Correction and Daley's civil service adviser, the mayor reached out to Wilson.

Daley requested Wilson chair a five-person search committee and assist the city in finding a top-rate police administrator to lead them out of the Summerdale Scandal. Other committee members included Virgil Peterson from the Chicago Crime Commission; Paul Goodrich, the President of the Chicago Association of Commerce; Frank Kreml,[32] the head of the

31 Dr. Macaluso died at the age of 83 in Chicago in August 1988.

32 In 1972, following Wilson's death, as the President of the Chicago Police Board, Kreml thanked the former Superintendent and said he gave the CPD back its self-respect. Kreml was the Northwestern University Traffic Institute's founding director in 1936 and university administrator for over 35 years. He died in 1998 at the age of 91.

Photo 3.1 Photo of O.W. Wilson in 1967 courtesy of the Chicago Police Department.

Northwestern University Transportation Center; and William McFetridge,[33] the Vice President of the Chicago Federation of Labor. The screening committee met for 28 days behind closed doors at the University Club in downtown Chicago and considered 53 applicants, 24 from within the CPD (Lindberg, 1991, p. 308). The committee interviewed any member of the CPD who applied out of courtesy. Five finalists were selected and submitted to Daley for consideration.

McFetridge, personal friends with Daley, had likely been primed to insist on getting an outside reformer. He pushed for either Kreml or Wilson to be hired. Kreml declined the offer because of obligations to Northwestern University. Wilson also initially refused, citing family obligations, but the committee and Kreml were persistent. Through their persistence, Wilson took the job as CPD's first civilian Superintendent and resigned as Dean at UC Berkeley, where he was subsequently honored with the title professor emeritus.

Reform as a Superintendent – not a Commissioner

By March 1960, Wilson successfully negotiated a three-year contract at $30,000 a year, more than twice his salary at UC Berkeley and $7,500 more than past Commissioner O'Connor. His contract was guaranteed by the Lloyd's of London, and he was given assurance from Mayor Daley that he could function as a reformist without political interference. The one snag to this arrangement came from a city attorney who pointed out the police commissioner position could only be filled by an Illinois resident. Daley did some political maneuvering, worked with the Illinois legislature, and established a police board to have Wilson technically serve under. Wilson was also given the title Police Superintendent rather than Commissioner as a way around the residential requirement. A charade of having the police board sign off on paperwork occurred throughout the first year Wilson was Superintendent (Reeves, 2016). Wilson knew that the department he inherited was archaic, in need of a significant modern overhaul, and hostile to expert outsiders that carried academic notions of criminology. However, Wilson was a seasoned police leader, and he knew that any reform efforts would need the mayor and dedicated officers' support (Photo 3.1).

33 McFetridge became one of the most critical behind-the-scenes political operatives during Daley's mayoral reign (Cohen & Taylor, 2000).

Following his appointment by Daley, Wilson outlined his plans with two speeches given at the Amphitheatre in the Union Stock Yards in the morning and evening, telling his officers that he would be instituting higher standards and accountability to professionalize the CPD. With that in mind, he was supported by both officers and the mayor when he pushed for better pay, allowing officers to supplement their income by moonlighting, improving education and training opportunities, and modernizing their equipment and vehicles. Wilson hired former FBI employee Everett Leonard to create a new comprehensive computerized record-keeping system. To further separate politics and be closer to his police department, Wilson moved his office away from City Hall to the fourth floor of police headquarters at 1121 S. State Street, which Chicagoans would describe as Eleventh and State. He also had the building renovated and doubled the number of civilian employees. The CPD headquarters was remodeled for $39,801 and dedicated on March 5, 1963 (Lindberg, 1991, p. 310). The remodel provided a robust command and control center and improved recruitment, standards for hiring, training, promoting, and termination.

Wilson's one-year progress report came during the IACP conference in 1961 in Montreal, Canada. His speech to the convention of 26 nations discussed a clean breeze blowing through the CPD. He outlined 35 changes that would provide the nation's second-largest police department integrity and respectability. The enormous political capacity that Mayor Daley afforded Wilson allowed for real reform to occur within the first year.

Two Goals: Infrastructure Investment and Eliminating Corruption

When he was named CPD Superintendent, Wilson's goals were to eliminate corruption/political influence from the CPD and reorganize the department through infrastructure investment. Mayor Daley opened up seemingly unlimited funds to refurbish police buildings and communication systems. The operating budget in 1960 was approximately $73 million (Ward, 2000, p. 84). Wilson successfully raised the budget to $86 million by the end of 1961[34] (Lindberg, 1991, p. 313), mainly to update the CPD's archaic equipment and renovate police headquarters. There were only two radio frequencies that served Chicago's three million residents. Eventually, Wilson had this split into eight radio zones. Blue-and-white squads replaced old black-and-white police cars. Thousands of officers who patrolled neighborhoods on foot were, through LAPD Deputy Chief Arthur Hohman's consulting advice, transitioned into a fleet of 500 additional automobiles (Ward, 2000, p. 85). Officers were also required to wear brass name tags. However, in contrast, the additional mobile patrol increased anonymity and often distanced the officers from the community.

Wilson's departmental reorganization created three bureaus that reported directly to him: Bureau of Staff Services; Bureau of Inspectional Services; and Bureau of Field Services

1. Pierce Fleming was appointed Deputy Superintendent within staff services and led a revamped crime lab, enhanced training, and automotive/radio maintenance. Goldstein, Wilson's executive assistant, also urged creating a new planning division to evaluate police effectiveness with specific disorder and crime problems (Scott, 2016).
2. Within inspectional services, Captain Joseph Morris, an internal applicant to replace O'Connor, was appointed to collaborate with the FBI's organized crime squad and target Sam Giancana and the Chicago mob. They also investigated police corruption through

34 On December 29, 1961 the ASC gave OW Wilson a metal plaque. They also awarded the August Vollmer Award to Harvard University researchers Sheldon and Elanor Glueck. Wilson thanked the ASC for the award, noting that he was present in 1941 when their organization was created in August Vollmer's living room.

the Internal Investigation Division (IID), led by Captain William Szarat. On Wilson's orders, the IID investigated officer links to the mob (Wiedrich, 1964). Officers also worked undercover in the IID, and their tactics included committing traffic violations to determine if officers would accept bribes.[35] Others faked being intoxicated to determine if officers would attempt to take money or valuables from their pockets and determine if regulations were followed in booking and lockup facilities. In Ben Ward's dissertation, he described his time as an officer in the CPD in the 1960s when he unknowingly arrested an undercover officer who posed as an intoxicated homeless man with cash and later told him he did everything appropriately (Ward, 2000). To determine if booking procedures were followed correctly, Morris also had his undercover officers processed at the Cook County Jail.

3 Within field services, Captain James Conlisk was in charge of the largest bureau with patrol, traffic, detectives, criminal intelligence, and youth divisions. This appointment was likely a concession to Daley, close friends with Conlisk's father, who served as administrative assistant to the prior five police commissioners. Wilson took Goldstein as his executive assistant instead of keeping Conlisk but promoted his son, who would also become his successor and Daley operative.

Captains, such as Morris, Szarat, and Conlisk, held ranks exempt from Civil Service protection. The exemption meant Wilson exercised direct control over their daily activities and could terminate or demote them. All three divisions were new to the CPD and very useful in reforming and modernizing the department. Within the first year of the restructuring, over a thousand officers resigned or received terminations from the CPD, and Wilsonian reform was underway.

From 1948 to 1960, the CPD blocked numerous promotions due to lawsuits filed against the Civil Service Commission. Wilson requested that the commission reinstitute promotional exams but did not receive a response. Noting there was a shortage of supervisory sergeants, Wilson temporarily promoted 125 patrol officers (Ward, 2000, p. 88). Wilson's strong stance led to the commission relenting. They provided promotional exams while allowing Wilson to tweak some categories such as the weight of seniority or years of job experience.[36] This tweak in the promotional exam assessment meant that talented officers could rise through the CPD ranks more quickly than was done in the past. For the first time in over a decade, on September 29, 1960, an exam was offered, leading to 137 patrolmen promoted to sergeant, including 50 Black men[37] (Lindberg, 1991, p. 312). After achieving his goal of adequately creating proper supervision, Wilson focused on consolidating and restructuring police district departments.

To facilitate centralized control, Wilson shut down 17 police districts, going from 38 to 21, and redrew the lines to eliminate political control between the district captains and the local aldermen. The redistricting plan took a year to materialize based on tactical considerations that added additional patrol to high-crime communities. Wilson had his Director of

35 In December 1960, Wilson appealed to the Chicago business community to help support his policy that forbid officers from accepting gratuities, especially at Christmas time.

36 From 1960 to 1964, 873 officers were promoted to sergeant, 226 to lieutenant, and 94 to captain (Lindberg, 1991, p. 323). Young officers received morale-boosting incentives to be promoted based upon competitive merit tests and not political connections. Wilson was in charge of the detective promotions and not the Civil Service Commission.

37 Wilson discovered that the Civil Service Commission had been denying Black officers promotion based upon doctors indicating that they had flat feet. Wilson encouraged that this rule was changed and by 1962, there were an additional 500 Black officers hired, bringing the total to 1,200 in the CPD (Lindberg, 1991, p. 312).

Personnel, Richard McDonnell, provide extensive messages to the media to explain the consolidation process. They did not want the community perceiving that the CPD was sacrificing police services through the consolidation. There was little political fallout from this change as aldermen[38] worried that their complaints would lead Wilson to report their indiscretions to the media. As was the case with his mentor Vollmer, Wilson was successful in his public relations campaigns. Moreover, the move toward centralized managerial control had occurred under the prior policing reform movements in Chicago (see Haller, 1970, 1976). Wilson spoke to the media to justify the consolidation.

> *The police districts the stations serve will be consolidated with other districts. In some cases, two districts will be combined, and in others, the abandoned district will be divided between two more districts. This will leave Chicago with twenty police stations in addition to central headquarters. Previously the city had thirty-seven police districts, numbered one to forty-one, with blanks in the list where old stations had not been replaced.*[39]

The redistricting dramatically increased the number of officers on mobile patrol, and Wilson utilized one-man patrol as the dominant method, as he had done in Wichita. Early studies on the benefits of one-officer patrols also helped counter union critics (see Day, 1956). Wilson's professionalization model centered on taking officers off other street assignments and putting them in cars to fulfill a preventative patrol strategy. However, this reactive stance evolved into more tension between the public and the police, especially after Wilson departed in 1967. The rise of the reform "law and order" politics was useful for initial reform but persisted in less valuable ways with future CPD leaders.

In December 1961, editors from *Law & Order* covered each of the 35 strategies Wilson outlined to reform the CPD. These changes had internal critics, but Wilson's leadership style and support from Mayor Daley insulated him from political damage. Daley continued to maintain a hands-off approach with his new police superintendent and consequently was able to shake off the Summerdale Scandal and ride the good press that Wilson continued to receive due to his transparency with the media. New district commanders were chosen based on psychological profiles and new testing procedures. When the promotions were complete, only two of the previous 38 district captains remained (Bopp, 1977, p. 103). The commander ranks did not receive civil service protection, meaning Wilson could have them demoted anytime he wanted without dealing with an appeal system. Several of the police captains Wilson ousted were part of the old-line Irish power brokers, including long-time executive assistant James Conlisk, Sr., whom Wilson replaced with Goldstein (described more fully in the appendix). Conlisk's son, James Conlisk, Jr., took for Wilson upon his retirement in 1967 and gave power back to Mayor Daley.

Reforming CPD Training

Like other influential police leaders brought in to reform police departments, Wilson brought many outsiders with him. As a mentee to Vollmer, Wilson made training and education a foundation for changing the CPD culture from the ground up. He brought in George O'Connor, one of his criminology graduate students from UC Berkeley. Like most outsiders, O'Connor

38 "Aldermen" is the appropriate term in this context. Anna Langford became the first African-American woman elected to the Chicago City Council in February 1971, and she served three nonconsecutive terms. However, the gender-specific term is still used in Chicago politics (Sato, 2019).

39 *Chicago Tribune* – "Six police stations to be closed December 18th," November 22, 1961 (sec. 1, p. 13).

was not initially well-received by the CPD training staff in the Bureau of Staff Services. During this time, the CPD police academy was located at 720 W. O'Brien Street in a three-story building constructed in 1856 and served as a Union hospital during the Civil War. The Chicago Public School attempted to utilize the building until deemed unfit for school children (Ward, 2000). The building conditions were inadequate for police training, but a new academy was not budgeted for during Wilson's reform era, so they had to make do.

As he did in Wichita, Wilson launched a Chicago Police Cadet program[40] for young men aged 17–19 on July 1, 1963. Wilson wanted the morale of the department to improve and for his officers to look professional and proud. He allowed officers to have short-sleeved summer uniform shirts and established a new motto: "We Serve and Protect." He held ceremonies for each police district for the best-dressed officer of the month. As Wilson's executive assistant, Goldstein was concerned that real reform needed to move beyond ceremonial image and spent many hours in the field observing the officers on patrol and at roll calls (Reeves, 2016). Officers were initially very hostile to the reform efforts, but eventually, relations and morale improved.

Chicago Crime Rates

Wilson knew there were enormous ethical problems with reporting crime statistics in the CPD. The year before Wilson came to the CPD, Virgil Peterson,[41] the Operating Director of the Chicago Crime Commission, said residents reported 57,511 major crimes to the CPD (Peterson, 1960). This report indicated a 13.8% increase from 1958 (Ward, 2000, p. 101). However, Wilson soon learned there was a dramatic underreporting of these numbers, and they would need to establish new accountability mechanisms. On July 17, 1960, Wilson met with the *Chicago Press* in an attempt to discuss how improvements in reporting crime would be beneficial:

> *I don't think we know what the crime situation was a year ago and I am quite certain that we do not know what it is today. I do know, however, that in the course of time we will have accurate crime statistics and that we will know where we stand at any period of time and where we are going. On July 5th we instituted a new form for the Chicago Police Department, which requires a report on the assignment by every officer who is dispatched dealing with an incident. One of the purposes of this report on assignment is to get a more accurate appraisal of the actual amount of crime and as a consequence of the institution of this new form and reporting procedure, I anticipate that July 1960 as compared with July 1959 will produce a crime increase that is greater than one hundred percent.*[42]

Wilson's prediction of a one percent increase in crime was understated. In 1960, the new reporting system indicated nearly 130,000 major crimes and over 175,000 in 1961, a 305% increase from the misreports of 1959 (Ward, 2000, p. 103). Like all good police leaders, Wilson continued to communicate with the media to explain the long-term strategic plans. From 1962 to 1965, Chicago experienced reductions in crime while most of the nation reported continual increases. In 1965, New York Mayor John Lindsay reportedly reached out to Wilson

40 Ramsey, described in a later chapter, received his start at the CPD through Wilson's cadet program in 1968, a year after he left Chicago for his California retirement.

41 Peterson was an FBI agent in the 1930s and was present during the raid at the Little Bohemia Lodge in Wisconsin when John Dillinger and Baby Face Nelson escaped. Peterson moved to the Village of Riverside, Illinois in 1942, where he lived with his wife until his death in 1989.

42 July 17, 1960 address of O.W. Wilson to the Chicago Press Corps. The Orlando W. Wilson Papers, Special Collections, Bancroft Library, University of California, Berkeley.

to take over the NYPD, stating Chicago was winning the war on crime while New York was losing. Wilson told reporters he was happy in Chicago and had no plans to leave (Ward, 2000, p. 103).

Interestingly, Wilson advocated for tighter gun control laws and helped push through stop-and-frisk legislation in the Illinois General Assembly, which Governor Otto Kerner vetoed[43] (Lindberg, 1991, p. 312). In 1968, the United States Supreme Court ruled in *Terry v. Ohio* that the use of stop-and-frisk was constitutional and did not violate the Fourth Amendment. As described in the chapter on Bratton, broken windows policing, as linked to stop-and-frisk, would be the primary strategy for lowering New York crime. This strategy came 30 years after Wilson advocated for it.

Departmental and Community Admiration (and frustration)

Wilson earned the admiration of many officers, especially the younger recruits. Except for some veteran officers, most saw their Superintendent throw off the political shackles that impeded past CPD leaders. Wilson allowed qualified officers to be promoted more fairly by instituting competitive exams, so officers advanced based on merit and not political connections. A revamped communication Center improved responses to emergency calls for service. A massive purchase of new squad cars and two-way radios moved foot patrol officers to mobile patrol. Wilson believed that increased mobile patrol prevented crime through a sense of omnipresence that deterred criminal behavior. Wilson also carried the belief that increased mobile patrol would improve response time and clearance rates. These assumptions, challenged through subsequent research, were unknown to Wilson at the time he was Superintendent.

The new Superintendent frustrated the Chicago Catholic community. Chicago's Catholic churches frequently used bingo as a fundraiser and traditionally asked for support from the CPD when they scheduled the events. Wilson, noting that bingo was a form of illegal gambling, refused to permit the tradition. The controversy resulted in protests from the Catholic community, but Cardinal Albert Meyer publicly supported Wilson. In addition to pushing back on Catholic bingo events, Wilson diversified the CPD chaplains and added a Protestant minister and a Jewish rabbi.

Wilson also created an intelligence unit that targeted organized crime, reorganized the detective division, and created a canine unit. He provided officers the opportunity to do the job and be the police without the political interference of the past. By 1965, Chicago showed a decline of Part I Crimes by three percent while the rest of the country indicated a 13 percent increase, and Wilson was quick to give his officers credit. According to surveys in the aftermath of the Summerdale Scandal, police sergeants were not favorable toward CPD

43 Kerner was a two-term Democratic Illinois Governor from 1961 to 1968 and ally of Daley, who defeated incumbent Stratton. Kerner was elected in 1960 and helped Illinois elect President Kennedy that same year. In 1967, Kerner chaired a commission on behalf of President Johnson as part of the National Advisory Commission on Civil Disorders to determine why so many race riots occurred throughout the 1960s. It was one of the most in-depth studies of policing in America. Ultimately the 1968 report – which became infamous for "our nation is moving toward two societies, one Black, one white, separate and unequal"– blamed societal problems on white privilege and failed to include the police in the solution equation. The report caused the police to be in a reactive stance for the next several decades, negating partnerships, problem-solving, and place-based criminology. In February 1968, 9-1-1 dispatch was introduced dramatically increasing officer workload and reactive strategies. Kerner was also an appointed federal prosecutor and judge before being found guilty in a 1973 trial that stemmed from a 1969 bribery case that involved Arlington Park horseracing manager Marje Lindheimer. Future Illinois Governor James Thompson successfully prosecuted Kerner, and he was sentenced to federal prison in July 1974 but released early based upon a terminal cancer diagnosis. He died in May 1976 at the age of 67.

executive leadership. Five years into Wilson's administration, sergeants reported the department was respected and professional. However, these same sergeants also noted the move to create a centralized authority for the CPD weakening of community relations. While they believed Wilson's leadership improved efficiency, it frequently isolated the police from civilians (Weistart, 1974).

To improve community relations and quell the historic racial tensions in Chicago, Wilson provided public-relations workshops in each of the 21 districts. He also pushed his version of desegregation within the CPD by ordering white officers to partner with minority officers. Wilson promoted a record number of Black sergeants to become supervisors while insisting on police restraint in racially charged conflicts.

Dr. Martin Luther King, Jr.

On January 26, 1966, Dr. Martin Luther King Jr. moved into an apartment on the west side of Chicago at 1550 S. Hamlin Avenue, by Douglas Park, as part of a coordinated effort to draw attention to northern cities' discriminatory housing practices. The landlord quickly renovated the apartment before the King family arrived to avoid the bad publicity. However, as typical of the housing discrimination during that era, King was charged $90 a month for rent in the slum while white families typically paid $70 a month for better housing in the north of Chicago (Calkhoven, 2019, p. 87).

The Chicago Freedom Movement targeted their protest marches throughout white neighborhoods that included the Bridgeport neighborhood where Mayor Daley lived. Daley was incensed by the publicity King and his supporters received. He also felt the city and the Democratic Party looked terrible as a consequence. In one of the few instances that the mayor circumvented Wilson's authority, Daley called the district station within his neighborhood and ordered the arrest of protesters (Ward, 2000, p. 105). However, Wilson directed the CPD to protect the protesters rather than hinder and harass as southern police leaders had previously done.

Daley seethed at Wilson's law and order views that did not hold for civil disobedience from African-American protesters. However, Wilson and his mostly civilian executive staff did not relent and continued to protect civil rights demonstrators. Civil rights leader Whitney M. Young, Jr.'s[44] reflection on Wilson showed when asked what he thought about NYPD Commissioner Michael Murphy. Young responded

> *He had his heart in the right place; however, he does not possess the socially perceptive and understanding manner in working with Negro leaders demonstrated by Orlando W. Wilson. If Chicago is spared a riot this summer, it may be because of the concern of Wilson. Wilson has done outstanding police work.*
>
> (Bopp, 1977, p. 220)

While Mayor Daley fretted about the scope of the pending demonstrations, Wilson enthusiastically responded to the challenge by inviting Dr. King and his wife for a meeting at police headquarters, where both leaders posed for a photo on January 27, 1966, with coffee. Wilson educated Dr. King on his views of diversity in the CPD, showing the civil rights leader statistics

44 Young was a major leader in the civil rights movement throughout the 1960s. At the age of 40, in 1961, he became the director of the National Urban League. Within four years, membership grew from 38 to 1,600 employees. He also became an advisor to Presidents Johnson and Nixon and helped write the "Marshall Plan" as a strategy for combatting the wealth gap between Black and white citizens. In 1975, Whitney Young High School was opened in Chicago as the city's first public magnet school.

Photo 3.2 Martin Luther King Jr. and Chicago Police Superintendent O.W. Wilson in Wilson's office at 11th and State streets in Chicago on January 27, 1966.
Photo courtesy of the Chicago Tribune.

on more than 20 percent of the rank-and-file represented by Black officers, ten Black captains, and three Black district commanders (Bopp, 1977, p. 118). They also discussed ambitious programs the CPD was implementing to improve relations with Black citizens (Photo 3.2).

Wilson invited King and his wife Coretta Scott to tour the CPD and to address high-ranking officers in the departmental gymnasium to explain the reasons behind their pending nonviolent civil disobedience marches. After his speech, King answered questions from the command staff. King said that Chicago was moving too slowly to end housing discrimination and school desegregation and that protesters planned to conduct rent strikes and school boycotts along with the marches. He told the officers that this was the first time a police agency afforded him any hospitality. King told the officers that his followers had received training not to fight with the police, and they knew arrests could occur. He stated he wanted to avoid the next Watts[45] riots. King closed his speech by saying, "This is the first meeting I've had with any police department in the Nation. The only other time I faced groups of policemen, I was thrown in jail[46]" (Ward, 2000, p. 105). He assured his police audience that

45 Watts is a neighborhood in Los Angeles where riots broke out from August 11 to16, 1965. The National Guard was called to help end the riots that caused millions of dollars in damage and 34 deaths. Reasons cited for the riots included unfair housing practices, politics, and years of police brutality despite LA Chief Parker's attempts to depoliticize and professionalize the LAPD.

46 See "King Sees Police, Warns of Possible Watts Here," *Chicago American*, 27 January 1966, sec 1, p. 6.

he did not promote violence in protests and congratulated them for not using excessive force against demonstrators. King also stated he would take personal responsibility to ensure his staff properly notified the CPD of pending protests.

Wilson's earlier released directive to the CPD regarding race relations, circulated to other police leaders, and adopted across the nation was timely. The directive read:

> At all times, the departmental personnel will:
> 1. *Never show any bias or prejudice against race, religion, or any other group or individual*
> 2. *Act, speak, and conduct themselves in a such a manner as to treat all persons with complete courtesy and with that respect due to every person as a human being*
> 3. *Never talk down to any group or individual or engage in the use of derogatory terms such as "Nigger," "boy," "Wop," "Kike," "Chink," "Shine," "burrhead," "Dago," "Polack," "Bohunk," and the like.*
>
> (President's Commission on Law Enforcement, 1967, p. 181)

The Chicago civil rights movement culminated on July 10, 1966.[47] King gave an impassioned speech in 98-degree heat to more than 30,000 attendees in Soldier Field.[48] After his speech, attendees continued their demonstrations throughout the city and marched to City Hall to demand an end to slum housing. The following day, King personally presented his demand to Mayor Daley.

Despite Wilson's best efforts, the CPD could not always maintain the safety of the demonstrators. On August 5, 1966, King led protesters into white neighborhoods surrounding Marquette Park, southeast of Midway Airport. Approximately 4,000 counterprotesters showed up at Marquette Park and threw rocks and bottles at King and his supporters. The counterprotesters waved Confederate flags and carried signs of white power. King was struck in the head by a rock and famously shielded by his supporters. When the demonstrators returned to their cars, they found several burned and pushed into Marquette Park's lagoon.[49]

In the aftermath, King and his followers planned to march in Cicero. On September 2, 1966, Governor Kerner issued an executive order mobilizing 2,000 National Guard troops after pleas from Christy Berkos,[50] Cicero town attorney, and Cook County Sheriff Richard Ogilvie.[51] They noted that Cicero rioted in 1951 when a Negro attempted to move into a Cicero apartment (Halvorsen, 1966). Ogilvie also worked with King to cancel the Cicero march.

Before the Cicero demonstrations, Mayor Daley made it known that the Chicago Housing Authority worked with the Mortgage Bankers Association to build public housing in

47 Three days after King's speech in Soldier Field, Richard Benjamin Speck broke into a Chicago townhouse located at 2319 E. 100th Street, raped, tortured, and fatally stabbed eight student nurses. A ninth nursing student, Corazon Amurao, hid under a bed while her classmates were raped and murdered. She later identified Speck. Wilson held a press conference asking for the public's help to capture Speck. Two days later, a desk clerk at the skid row Starr Hotel, located at 617 W. Madison Street, called for emergency help after Speck attempted suicide by cutting his wrists. A doctor at the Cook County Hospital recognized Speck and contact the CPD. In 1996, a videotape surfaced from 1988 inside Stateville Prison, showing Speck using illegal narcotics, dressed in women's underwear, and engaging in sexual contact with other inmates (Johnson, 1996). In 1991, Speck died inside Stateville from a heart attack, one day shy of his 50th birthday (Green, 2019).

48 King previously spoke at Soldier Field on June 21, 1964, at the Illinois Rally for Civil Rights.

49 In 2016, a memorial to MLK was erected in Marquette Park.

50 Berkos was a WWII Navy Veteran and Criminal Court Judge in Cook County. He passed away in 2011 at the age of 85.

51 Ogilvie made a name for himself by investigating the Chicago mob, and he became the 35th Governor of Illinois (1969–1973) as a Republican. His Democratic lieutenant Governor was Paul Simon, future U.S. Illinois Senator (1985–1997). Ogilvie died in 1988 at the age of 65.

predominantly white neighborhoods. They did so to cut a deal with King so he would cancel a planned march through Cicero. This solution became known as the Summit Agreement, and the Chicago Freedom Movement, led by King, called off the Cicero march. The open-housing agreement signed by Daley became a precursor template for President Johnson's Fair Housing Act, signed as part of the Civil Rights Act on April 11, 1968. Despite these victories, some of King's supporters felt that canceling Cicero's march was a mistake that led to Daley's false promises. These false promises have caused Chicago to remain one of America's most segregated cities.

President Johnson's 1968 Civil Rights Act came a week after King's assassination (Kotz, 2005). On April 4, 1968, a fatal shot struck King, only 39 years old, in the face at 6 PM while he stood on the balcony at the Lorraine Motel in Memphis, Tennessee. King was in Memphis to support Black sanitation workers who were on strike for equal pay. He was speaking to Jesse Jackson at the time of the shooting. James Earl Ray had rented a room in a boarding house across from the motel. Police found a rifle and binoculars with Ray's fingerprints after the fatal shooting. Ray later pleaded guilty to firing the fatal shot and received a life sentence. At the time, Ray was a fugitive from the Missouri State Prison and was arrested in London's Heathrow Airport, almost a month after he assassinated King (Posner, 2013). King's son Dexter visited Ray in prison in 1997. He publicly supported a retrial believing that a broader conspiracy within the government existed, and Ray was a scapegoat for his father's assassination. Unfortunately, Ray died in prison on April 23, 1998, at the age of 70, from kidney and liver failure caused by hepatitis C from an earlier blood transfusion after being stabbed in prison (Pepper, 2016).

Wilson's Retirement

Wilson announced his retirement from the CPD on May 16, 1967, his 67th birthday. A hereditary tremor in his writing hand was cause for concern. Wilson recommended Daley's close political ally James Conlisk, Jr. as the next superintendent, overstepping the police board's authority. Through Conlisk, Daley reclaimed political control of the department in the aftermath of his reelection. Less than a year after Wilson left, the CPD clashed with Vietnam War protesters and those angered by King's April 4, 1968 assassination. From August 26 to 29, the Democratic National Convention took place at the International Amphitheatre[52] in Chicago, where Wilson had given his first speeches after being named the new police superintendent. The convention, held on the heels of the June 5, 1968 assassination of Robert Kennedy and mass protests throughout the country, led to numerous clashes between protesters and the CPD and Mayor Daley's orders to shoot looters (Johnson, 2020). These clashes resulted in over 190 injured officers and over 660 arrests (Kusch, 2008). Since Wilson left, no mayor has given a police superintendent the kind of independence Daley did, mainly due to the Summerdale Scandal and fear for his political future. Undoubtedly, police use of force during the 1968 Democratic Convention would not have had the same results under Wilson's apolitical leadership.[53] In the short decade from 1968 to 1979, the three James's led the CPD – Conlisk, Rochford, and O'Grady, as seen in Table 3.9.

52 The International Amphitheatre was located at Halsted and 42nd Street across from the Union Stock Yards. It was the home of the NBA's Chicago Packers from 1961 to 1962, later named the Chicago Zephyrs, and the Chicago Bulls from 1966 to 1967. Before 1968, the Amphitheatre hosted both the 1952 Republican and Democratic Conventions, the 1956 Democratic Convention, and the 1960 Republican Convention. After the construction of the McCormick Center on the lakefront, the profitability of the amphitheater declined and the building was destroyed in 1999.

53 In September 2020, Netflix released *The Trial of the Chicago 7* as a historical legal drama from the 1968 Democratic Convention that dealt with a 1969 federal trial against various individuals for conspiracy to incite

In the more than 60 years since Mayor Richard J. Daley was elected, Chicago has gone through seven mayors and 14 police chiefs. Mayors continue to go through significant scandals, and police chiefs get sacrificed through either termination or resignation. Real reform within the CPD has not occurred since Wilson left the CPD for his final retirement. After seven years serving Chicago as police superintendent, Wilson moved to Poway, California, a small unincorporated town about 60 miles northeast of San Diego, to be close to his brother and sister. Wilson remained an avid reader in his retirement but also appreciated his privacy. He did allow two recorded interviews on July 2, 1971, as part of an oral history dissertation conducted by Jane Howard Robinson through the University of California and the Bancroft Library at Berkeley at his home in Poway, California (Robinson, 1972). Robinson conducted the interviews as part of a dissertation on the life of August Vollmer. She conducted one interview with Wilson, and John Holstrom completed the other.[54] Wilson resided in Poway until his death from a stroke at 72 years old on October 18, 1972. His co-author, Roy McLaren, referred to Wilson as the most significant authority in police administration history (McLaren, 1973).

Unintended Consequences of the Wilson Professionalization Movement

Wilson's most significant contribution to the policing profession was directed toward administration and integrity. His leadership experiences, the need to detach policing from politics, and the lack of social science research on effective policing led Wilson to believe, like Vollmer, in centralized police managerial structures. In doing so, he was part of a reform movement that narrowed the police's role to crime fighters with strategies that pushed patrol distribution toward prioritizing rapid response to calls for service. When Wilson originally wrote *Police Administration* and took over the CPD, bureaucratic centralized control of police agencies and narrowing the mission to law enforcement appeared to be the best solution to counter the corrupt and politically influenced police departments that had evolved across the country.

Wilson followed other reform-minded chiefs in adhering to the popularity of Frederick Taylor's Scientific Management Principles.[55] Reform theorists believed they could train police officers to be semiautomatic and controlled the same way a skilled musician plays an instrument or a secretary learns to type. Taylor thought workplace efficiency came when laborers (i.e. patrol officers) became directed, controlled, coerced, and even threatened to achieve organizational goals (Copley, 1923; Taylor, 1911). Police agencies sought to routinize police work in the same manner that assembly lines became efficient in the automobile industry. Centralized control centers are then used with additional administrators to stabilize the workforce (Harring, 1981).

As such, patrol labor was perceived as an easily replaceable commodity, allowing reform chiefs, like Wilson, to dismiss officers perceived to be corrupt or resistors of reform efforts. Expectations were for managers to tightly control officers and limit some of their functionality when it came to nondiscretionary law enforcement (Kelling & Stewart, 1991). In essence, the

a riot. Counter-arguments centered on how poor leadership in the CPD incited violent confrontations that began when officers rushed the protesters in Lincoln Park and used tear gas and clubs in their attack. See Kusch (2008).

54 Holstrom was a student of Vollmer's, Berkeley Police Chief (1944–1960), and the President of the IACP (1957–1958). Like Vollmer, he also taught policing courses at the UC Berkeley.

55 Taylor was a mechanical engineer and managerial theorist during the Progressive Reform Era. His work centered on scientific management and finding the best method to increase industry efficiency. Wilson and other law enforcement reformers looked to utilize his managerial approach by quantifying the effectiveness of policing.

rank-and-file officer became the "forgotten person" of reform (Walker & Katz, 2018: p. 14). Reform goals became quantifiable whenever possible and included efforts to decrease UCR crime data, improve response time, and increase clearance rates. Advancements in technology coincided so superiors could keep track of officers more closely through two-way radios. Telephone advancements also meant the public could, and were encouraged to, call the police more frequently. These advancements caused police reformists to refocus the police on reactive responses to meet the increased community demands for service. During the professionalization era, the reinvention of the police helped reformers address problems with political corruption. However, officers' increased isolation via mobile patrol and reactive law enforcement created decades of questionable legitimacy, especially among minority communities.

While the legacy of scientific management and reactive law enforcement was part of policing from the turn of the twentieth century until the 1970s, we should not negate reform leaders' significance. Wilson was a pioneer in that leadership in the aftermath of August Vollmer's reform impact. The aftermath of these reform movements led to further development of rules and regulations regarding discipline and routinizing tasks related to preventative patrol and rapid response to calls for service. However, while these reform efforts were necessary, they did little to shape police behaviors toward the real challenges officers face when dealing with neighborhood conflicts, mental health problems, substance use, and disorder. Wilson restructured the CPD to emphasize preventative patrol and rapid response without the luxury of having subsequent research that would challenge these strategies. Crank and Langworth (1992) point out that police structures built during the professionalization era further enabled institutional expectations that focused primarily on law enforcement as the main activity without considering perceptions of legitimacy and problem-solving capabilities.

A more narrow view of law enforcement came out of the professionalization era. The police themselves often constructed this institutional-level change to gain public confidence when crime and disorder continually worsened through urban America (Klockars, 1985; Manning, 1997). As calls for service and crime reporting increased throughout the 1950s into the 1990s, it further reinforced the public perception about the need for law enforcement as the primary purpose for the police. The heavy reliance on mobile patrol and quick response coincided with growing calls for service and advanced scientific principles in police investigations. However, the so-called professionalization movement also equated to professional aloofness by separating the patrol officer from the community. As this separation grew throughout the 1970s, the paradox of increased mobile patrol undermined efforts to control and prevent crime due to increased police isolation and the growth of an "us versus them" subculture.

Reform efforts pushed police agencies to become more quasi-militaristic, with rank-and-file command structure and expectations that officers follow the chain of command. Police organizations continued to mimic the military in a post 9/11 America. From its inception in 1997 through 2020, the program has issued billions in excessive military hardware transferred through the Department of Defense's 1033 program to local law enforcement agencies. These federal grant programs provide law enforcement with military equipment directed toward a warrior mindset that targets drugs and terrorism, frequently with increased use of Special Weapons and Tactics (SWAT) teams equipped with armored vehicles and drones, and other advanced equipment. In the wake of the 2015 riots in Ferguson, Missouri, following Michael Brown's death, President Obama's executive order restricted some military equipment from being transferred to police agencies (e.g. grenade launchers, bayonets, ammo higher than .50 caliber). By 2017, President Trump's executive order deregulated Obama's order. This militarization movement followed Wilson's early reform efforts that monitored discretionary decision-making with higher expectations that officers follow increased rules and regulations.

This professionalism movement advocated for a less corruptible and more disciplined militaristic police force.

Today, the professional model of policing is the dominant strategy for most communities. Although subsequent research has routinely challenged underlying assumptions, as detailed throughout this book, features such as rapid response, attempts at fair and efficient handling of reported incidents, and thorough investigations of crimes persist as the main strategies for law enforcement agencies. Other models of policing have evolved that attempt to offer alternatives to the professional era. Seven prominent examples include the following:

1. <u>Broken Windows</u> emphasizes negotiating or enforcing the law on disorderly and minor offenses to demonstrate that the community cares and will keep in check more serious criminal activity (see Kelling & Wilson, 1982; Sousa & Kelling, 2006).
2. <u>CompStat</u> is closely connected to broken windows policing. This police management tool originated out of the NYPD in the 1990s and is detailed in the chapter on Bratton. This strategy utilizes computer crime data to map, analyze, and provide rapid deployment to hot spots while holding police supervisors accountable for understanding and responding to targeted problem areas (see Silverman, 2006; Willis, Mastrofski, & Kochel, 2010).
3. <u>Hot Spots</u> directs intensive patrols toward small geographic areas identified as the primary source of repeated police calls (see Weisburd & Braga, 2006).
4. <u>Evidence-based Policing</u> contends that policing should be based on what works best according to scientific evidence (see Sherman, 1998).
5. <u>Reassurance Policing</u> popularized in the United Kingdom following the original principles of Sir Robert Peel in 1829. The focus is on reducing public insecurity, focusing on crime and disorder that indicates red flags for more serious criminal activity. The approach connects to broken windows concerns and incorporates a closer connection to problem-oriented and community-oriented policing (see Millie & Herrington, 2005).
6. <u>Community Policing</u> directly challenged problems with the professional model and promoted organizational strategies that support the use of systematic partnerships to proactively address the fear of crime and social disorder (see Trojanowicz, 1994).
7. <u>Intelligence-led Policing</u> uses data and crime intelligence to help make decisions on how criminal activity should be disrupted or prevented through strategic enforcement strategies, focusing on prolific and serious offenders (see Ratcliffe, 2016; Kirby & McPherson, 2004).

Policing leaders may feel a sense of frustration with the abundance of management strategies that have evolved out of Wilson's professional reform era. It may also be tempting to combine each management technique's best strategy and deflect criticism by endorsing one strategy (Scott & Kirby 2012). However, Goldstein offered an alternate comprehensive approach to the professional model that went beyond operational tactics while demonstrating a firm grasp of the challenges officers face in democratic policing. That strategy, problem-oriented policing (POP), is presented in the appendix to this chapter as a practical alternative to what many officers previously perceived as the "strategy of the day" that changes when the next chief takes over. These strategies often come and go every few years, depending on the given police leader's philosophy. The appendix chapter on Goldstein offers a long-term paradigm shift in police leadership that differentiates from parts of Wilson's reform model. If adequately implemented, POP should resist innovation fatigue and provide lasting change with a focus on the end results rather than on the means of how we police.

The concluding nine tables include police leaders from Fullerton, Wichita, and Chicago. Each of these cities was represented by the influence of O.W. Wilson, starting in 1925 and ending in 1967 (Tables 3.1–3.9).

Table 3.1 Fullerton, California Constables and Marshals

Title	*Years*	*Name*
Constable	1887–1900	A.A. Pendergrast
Constable	1900–1900	James Gardiner[i]
Constable	1900–1904	Oliver Schumacher
Marshal	1904–1904	W.A. Barnes[ii]
Marshal	1904–1910	Charles Ruddock[iii]
Marshal	1910–1912	Roderick Stone
Marshal	1912–1918	William French[iv]

Table 3.2 Fullerton, California Police Chiefs

Years	*Name*
1918–1921	Vernon Myers
1921–1925	Arthur Eeles
1925–1927	**O.W. Wilson**
1927–1940	James Pearson
1940–1951	John Gregory
1951–1957	Ernest Garner
1957–1977	Wayne Bornhoft[i]
1977–1987	Martin Hairabedian[ii]
1987–1993	Philip Goehring
1993–2009	Patrick McKinley[iii]
2009–2012	Michael Sellers[iv]

i Gardiner died of pneumonia he contracted while rescuing people in the Great Flood of 1900.

ii Under the newly incorporated city, Fullerton voters elected Barnes Town Marshall. His duties were to make sure residents had proper licenses, supervise all road work, and be on duty from 7AM until midnight. He resigned shortly after his election.

iii When Ruddock was re-elected in April 1906, Fullerton also passed a referendum to go "dry," more than a decade before the Volstead Act, otherwise known as federal Prohibition.

iv Under French, in 1914, the Fullerton Police received their first official uniforms. In 1916, on a cold January night, inmates locked in the town's jail broke out of the wood planked building, stole some coal from a nearby neighbor, and then went back inside the jail to burn the coal so they could stay warm.

i Bornhoft was a lieutenant of the Pasadena Police Department when he received a lateral transfer to be the Fullerton Chief. He reformed the department by providing merit-based examinations for hiring and promotion purposes. Duties were divided into uniform, investigative, and service divisions. Bornhoft also established bureaus for juveniles, training, and professional standards. Under his leadership, in 1959, Geraldine Gregory was hired as the first female officer, coming from the PPD as a lieutenant with 13 years of experience. Gregory was tasked with juvenile crime investigations and handling female arrestees.

ii Hairabedian was a lateral transfer from the LAPD, where he was a captain. As Fullerton Chief, he initiated the status-quo programs of the era – Neighborhood Watch, Drug Abuse Resistance Education (DARE), and a K-9 program. In 1987, he was appointed to be a judge.

iii McKinley also came to Fullerton from the LAPD with two decades of law enforcement experience. McKinley initiated the Special Problems Unit and pushed officers to become more analytical. He also brought back foot patrol in the downtown area.

iv Sellers came to Fullerton from the LAPD. He also taught at Fullerton College and was chief for the Seal Beach and Laguna Beach Police Departments. His base salary as the Fullerton chief was $192,000.

Table 3.2 Cont.

Years	*Name*
2012–2017	Dan Hughes[v]
2017–2018	David Hendricks
2018–	Robert Dunn

Table 3.3 Wichita, Kansas City Marshalls

Years	*Name*
1871–1874 & 1875–1877	Michael Meager
1871–1871 & 1874–1875	William Smith
1877–1878	Richard Cogdell
1878–1879	Daniel Parks
1879–1887 & 1889–1890	James Cairns
1887–1888	William Haines
1888–1889	Tom McNamara
1889–1889	Lewis Aspey

Table 3.4 Wichita, Kansas Police Chiefs

Years	*Name*
1890–1893 & 1895	Charles Burrows
1893–1895	Rufus Cone[i]
1895–1897 & 1902–1905	O. Park Massey
1897–1899	William Campbell
1899–1902 & 1905–1907	Charles Jones
1902–1905 & 1909–1910	Frank Burt
1907–1908	Bedford Wood
1911–1913 & 1919–1923	G.T. (George) Cubborn
1915–1919	G.C. (Jack) Hay
1924–1926	T.J. Thompson
1926–1928	I.B. Walston
1928–1939	**O.W. Wilson**
1939–1941	Leroy Bowery
1941–1941	Clyde Wilder
1941–1946	Thomas Jaycox
1957–1968	Eugene Pond[ii]
1968–1972	Merrill Kirkpatrick
1972–1976	Floyd Hannon, Jr.[iii]

v Hughes started his career in law enforcement as a cadet in Fullerton two weeks after graduating high school. Under his leadership, they became the first agency in Orange County to have patrol officers equipped with body-worn cameras.

i Cone was also elected and re-elected Sheriff.

ii Pond inadvertently started the department's K-9 unit. Chief Pond mentioned to reporters that he was interested in starting a K-9 program, which led a 17-year-old to donate his two-year-old German Shepherd "Rinni" to the department.

iii Hannon served in the Marine Corps during World War II in the Pacific campaign against Japan. He was the lead investigator on the first murder from the BTK serial killer (Smith, 2007), committed by Dennis Rader. Between 1974 and 1978, ten individuals were murdered by Rader. He was arrested and convicted in 2005.

Table 3.4 Cont.

Years	*Name*
1976–1988	Richard LaMunyon[iv]
1988–1989	Kerry Crisp
1989–1989	Floyd Powell[v]
1989–1995	Rick Stone[vi]
1995–1999	William Watson
1999–2000	John Hershberger
2000–2015	Norman Williams
2015–	Gordon Ramsay[vii]

Table 3.5 Chicago Police High Constables

Years	*Name*
1835–1837	Orsemus Morrison[i]
1837–1839	John Shrigley
1839–1842	Samuel Lowe[ii]

Table 3.6 Chicago Police Marshals

Years	*Name*
1842–1844	Orson Smith[i]
1844–1847	Philip Dean
1848–1852	Ambrose Burnham
1852–1854	James Howe
1854–1856	Darius Knights[ii]

iv In 1981, LaMunyon created the Law Enforcement Special Olympics Torch Run.

v Powell became Wichita's first African-American police chief.

vi Stone became chief at 37 years of age through a lateral transfer from the Dallas Police Department. In 1991, he was named the Law Enforcement Officer of the Year by the Department of Justice Marshal's Service. Stone went on to be the chief of the Hollywood, Florida Police Department and served on the Wichita State University faculty (see Stone, 2000).

vii Ramsay was police chief for the Duluth, Minnesota Police Department for ten years from 2006 to 2016. At 43 years of age, he received a salary of $170,000 as a lateral transfer to Wichita. In January 2020, Ramsay was selected to be commissioner for the President's Commission on Law Enforcement and Administration of Justice 2020.

i Morrison was the first elected Town Constable or High Constable on August 15, 1835. The population was approximately 3,200 for the incorporated Town of Chicago. The constable police predates the City of Chicago that was incorporated in 1837. Chicago celebrates 185 years in 2022.

ii Lowe also served two terms as Cook County Sheriff starting in 1842. Lowe Park is named in his honor, located at 5203 S. Lowe Avenue.

i In May 1842, Smith was elected as Chicago's first City Marshal.

ii A year into Knights's term as City Marshal, Chicago legislatures decided to appoint a police chief. For the next six years, the department was headed by two individuals, the appointed chief, and the elected city marshal. Eventually, in 1876, the elected city marshal would be phased out.

Table 3.7 Chicago Police General Superintendents

Years	*Name*
1855–1856	Cyrus Bradley[i]
1863–1863, 1866–1867, 1873–1875	Jacob Rehm
1863–1865	William Turtle
1871–1872	William Wallace Kennedy
1872–1873	Elmer Washburn[ii]
1875–1875	George Dunlap[iii]
1875–1878	Michael Hickey
1875–1876	Roswell Goodell[iv]
1875–1878	Michael Hickey
1878–1879	Valerius Seavey
1879–1880	Simon O'Donnell
1880–1882	William McGarigle
1882–1885	Austin Doyle
1885–1888	Frederick Ebersold
1888–1889	George Hubbard
1890–1891	Frederick Marsh
1891–1893	Robert McClaughry[v]
1893–1895	Michael Brennan
1895–1897	John Badenoch
1897–1901	Joseph Kipley
1901–1905	Francis O'Neil
1905–1907	John Collins
1907–1909	George Shippy
1909–1911	LeRoy Stewart
1911–1913	John McWeeny
1913–1915	James Gleason
1915–1917	Charles Healy
1917–1918	Herman Schuettler
1918–1920	John Garrity
1920–1923	Charles Fitzmorris
1923–1927	Morgan Collins

i Bradley became the first politically appointed head of the police department and he served co-currently with elected Marshal Knights. They both submitted reports to the mayor's office. Bradley also served as the secretary of the police board.

ii Washburn was formerly the Warden of the Illinois State Penitentiary, later called the Joliet Correctional Center. That prison was open from 1858 to 2002 and is featured in the movie, *The Blues Brothers* released in 1980.

iii Dunlap was appointed as City Marshall as was Goodell. In 1875, the Board of Police Commissioners was disbanded by the city council. Dunlap was the first city Marshal to be appointed by the Mayor under a new law.

iv On May 31, 1876, the city council abolished the City Marshal position. Mayor-elect Thomas Hoyne removed Goodell and the Chicago police would be run by one individual.

v McClaughry employed Mary Owens, the nation's first female policewoman.

Table 3.8 Chicago Police Commissioners

Years	*Name*
1927–1928	Michael Hughes[i]
1928–1930	William Russell
1931–1946	James Allman[ii]
1946–1950	John Prendergast
1950–1964	Timothy O'Connor

Table 3.9 Chicago Police Superintendents

Years	*Name*
1960–1967	**O.W. Wilson**
1967–1973	James Conlisk, Jr.[i]
1974–1977	James Rochford[ii]
1978–1979	James O'Grady[iii]
1980–1983	Richard Brzeczek[iv]
1983–1987	Fred Rice, Jr.[v]
1987–1992	LeRoy Martin[vi]
1992–1997	Matt Rodriguez[vii]
1998–2003	Philip Cline[viii]
2008–2011	Jody Peter "JP" Weis[ix]

i Hughes, an Irish immigrant, was known as "Iron Mike" and is credited with running Capone out of Chicago. Hughes was admittedly opposed to hiring "dagos" or Italian-Americans into the CPD.

ii Allman became known as "Iron Man" because of his work ethic and his long run as police commissioner.

i Conlisk passed away in 1985 at the age of 85. He was criticized by Mayor Richard J. Daley when he failed to order his officers to shoot rioters in 1968.

ii Rochford died in 2004 at the age of 84. In 1968, he was a Deputy Superintendent during the Democratic Convention riots. He testified in *The Trial of Chicago 7* stating that he regretted 60 people and 190 police officers were injured. On April 14, 1969, Frank Kulak, a Marine Corps veteran of World War II and Korea, killed two police officers (Detective Jerome A. Stubig and Sergeant James Schaffer) and wounded six others in a six-hour firefight in which Kulak threw homemade bombs. Later that evening, Rochford walked into Kulak's apartment (located at 9251 S. Exchange Avenue), unarmed, and got him to surrender. Rochford appealed to their shared military experience serving in the Pacific campaign. Two weeks before the apartment raid, Kulak placed a bomb inside a department store that killed a woman and injured several shoppers. A week later, he placed a bomb in a railroad yard that killed a man. In 1986, after 15 years of serving time at the Chester Mental Health Center in Chester, Illinois (adjacent to the Menard Correctional Center), an appellate court ruled Kulak should be released. Cook County State's Attorney Richard M. Daley argued against Kulak's release.

iii O'Grady also served as Cook County Sheriff from 1986 to 1990. He lost his 1990 reelection amid corruption allegations.

iv Brzeczek was brought up on charges of dereliction of duty following the Jon Burge torture revelations. He was later acquitted of those charges, which included using city funds to carry out an extra-marital affair. Brzeczek unsuccessfully ran as a Republican for Cook County State's Attorney against Richard M. Daley. He later published a book with his wife titled *Addicted to Adultery: How We Saved Our Marriage/How You Can Save Yours* (Brzeczek, Brzeczek, & De Vita, 1989).

v Rice, Jr. became Chicago's first Black Police Superintendent.

vi After Martin's law enforcement career, he served as Director of Public Safety for the Chicago Housing Authority from 1992 to 1994. He unsuccessfully ran as a Republican against Michael Sheahan for Cook County Sheriff in 1998. Martin died of a heart attack in Dyer, Indiana in August 2013 at the age of 84.

vii Rodriguez was the first Hispanic appointed to lead the CPD.

viii Cline has been the long-time Director of the Chicago Police Memorial Foundation to honor CPD officers killed in the line of duty.

ix Weis brought two decades of experience with the FBI before coming to the CPD.

Table 3.9 Cont.

Years	*Name*
2006–2011	Garry McCarthy[x]
2016–2019	Eddie Johnson[xi]
2019–2020	Charlie Beck (interim for five months)
2020–	David Brown[xii]

Appendix: Herman Goldstein

Herman Goldstein became one of our nation's premier police leaders without wearing a uniform and a leading law professor without a law degree or a Ph.D. Goldstein's prolific writing, teaching, and consultation with police leaders throughout the world have impacted policing in a manner like few leaders before or after him. Goldstein served most of his career as a professor within the University of Wisconsin (UW)-Madison Law School, beginning in 1964 and earning emeritus status 30 years later. He remained very active throughout his retirement, engaged in international conferences, and consulting with police agencies worldwide. He was most recently honored with the 2018 Stockholm Prize in Criminology,[56] often referred to as the "Noble Prize" for criminology research.

A description of Goldstein's life and experiences that led to POP came from five primary sources. First, the author's personal conversations with Goldstein throughout 2005–2018 at several POP conferences and serving on a Madison, Wisconsin committee geared toward institutionalizing his policing approach into departments throughout Wisconsin. Second, an extensive video interview[57] with Goldstein in 2005 by criminology historian Samuel Walker.[58] Third, a series of audio-recorded oral history interviews[59] occurred throughout 2016 and 2017 in Goldstein's Madison apartment with Troy Reeves, the Director of the Oral History Program at the UW Law School Library. Fourth, a video interview[60] with Goldstein in 2017 done by criminologist Lawrence Sherman[61] through the Cambridge Centre of Evidence-Based Policing. The interview came after a jury from the Stockholm Criminology Symposium announced that Herman would receive their 2018 prize in criminology. Lastly, on May 10, 2018, William Clune, Emeritus Professor of Law at UW Madison, the Director of the Policy

x McCarthy rose through the ranks of the NYPD and became a Deputy Commissioner in 2000. In 2006, he was asked by Newark Mayor Cory Booker to lead their police department. When Mayor Emanuel brought McCarthy to Chicago, he became the highest-paid city official with a salary over $260,000. McCarthy and the fatal shooting of Laquan McDonald are discussed more fully in the Ramsey chapter.

xi In 2017, Johnson was remarried to CPD lieutenant Nakia Fenner. That same year, he also received a kidney from his son, Daniel Johnson, also a CPD officer. In 2019, Mayor Lori Lightfoot terminated Johnson for ethical lapses.

xii See Brown & Buford (2017).

56 The Stockholm Prize in Criminology has been awarded at a ceremony in Sweden since 2006. Each summer the conference culminates with an honorary recipient who has achieved extraordinary success in the study and application of research directed at the reduction of crime and the advancement of human rights. Goldstein was the 12th American to win the award out of the 21 previous winners. Recipients receive a monetary prize of one million Swedish krona, about $119,000. The author of this book was privileged to present at the 2018 Stockholm Criminology conference and personally congratulate Herman on his prestigious award.

57 See- https://popcenter.asu.edu/content/herman-goldstein-interview

58 Walker is a professor emeritus with the School of Criminology and Criminal Justice at the University of Nebraska, Omaha.

59 See https://repository.law.wisc.edu/s/uwlaw/item/27562

60 See www.youtube.com/watch?v=Dra6EM3N4XE&t=20s

61 Professor Sherman holds a joint appointment with the University of Maryland and the University of Cambridge Institute of Criminology as the Director of the Jerry Lee Centre of Experimental Criminology and Wolfson Professor of Criminology Emeritus.

Photo 3.3 Photo was taken at the June 2018 Stockholm Prize in Criminology with the author's daughters, Ella and Taylor, posing with Herman.

Group of the National Institute of Science Education and Senior Research of the Consortium Policy Research in Education (CPRE), interviewed Herman (Photo 3.3).

New London, Connecticut

This unassuming police leader was born on December 8, 1931, in New London, Connecticut, as the youngest of three children. His parents were both immigrants from Eastern Europe, and they met in America. His mother, Bella Howscha, was from Lithuania, lost her parents during the Holocaust, and worked in the garment industry in New York City before meeting his father. Herman's father, Max Goldstein, was from an area north of Poland and moved to the United States with his parents. Max was a tobacco farmer in Connecticut and used his product to process high-quality cigars. He also attempted to run a dairy manufacturing plant with his father, but they lost their business during the Great Depression. Max delivered milk for the rest of his working career.

Max's parents lived near their family home in New London. Herman described his family home on Grand Street as a three-level flat with an Italian family, the Piscatella's, living on the top floor, and an Irish family, the O'Sullivan's, residing on the bottom floor (Reeves, 2016). The Goldstein's were the only Jewish family on a very heterogeneous block of immigrants. The neighbors all got along, were curious about each other's traditions, shared meals, and demonstrated how a diversified neighborhood could be involved with high levels of informal social control. Herman's grandparents owned an Army Navy Surplus store that catered mainly to Navy personnel during World War II. Owning this store turned out to be a savvy decision since New London was a port city. At the age of 12, Herman worked in his family's store, selling and merchandising product. At the age of 16, he worked as a cashier at Ocean Beach Park on the southern end of New London, an operation he described as highly developed. Herman would eventually become a cashier supervisor. This experience was Goldstein's first experience with the operation of local government. His interest grew further from a research paper he wrote related to Ocean Beach Park's development in the aftermath of the 1938 Hurricane in New London.[62]

Herman attended the Bulkeley School[63] in New London. In the New England tradition, the high schools were divided by gender and academic rigor. While others attended a technical high school, Herman and his brother attended the college prep school due to their mother's strict academic expectations. Herman's brother Sidney, four years older, was the Valedictorian of his graduating class. Herman's high school extra-curricular activities included being a stage manager for the drama club, and he also worked on the yearbook.

Herman's parents did their best to expose him, along with his half-sister and brother, to experiential educational trips to New York City and Washington, DC. However, his family never traveled west of the Hudson River due to their meager incomes. He followed in Sidney's footsteps as the first in their family to attend college. Sidney went on to become a prestigious demography professor[64] at Brown University from 1955 to 1993. Sid became known as the "dean" of Jewish demographers, and numerous leading Jewish sociologists were at one time his students. He studied rural to urban migration patterns within several countries, which included surveying the American Jewish culture. Sid authored more than 100 books, monographs, and scholarly articles, several co-authored with his wife, Alice. Sid passed away in August 2019, the day after his 92nd birthday. Herman passed away five months later at the age of 88.

Both Goldstein brothers earned degrees from the University of Connecticut. Sidney received his undergraduate and graduate sociology degrees in 1949 and 1951. After Herman received his undergraduate degree, he was uncertain what professions or law schools he could get into because of his Jewish background, so he followed his brother to graduate school at the University of Pennsylvania. Herman began graduate school in 1953, the same year his brother completed his Ph.D. in sociology. At that time, Sid had a house on campus with his wife. After he was given a scholarship for free tuition and $150 a month through the Warton School, Herman attended graduate school. As part of his graduate program, Herman worked in various city departments in the mornings and attended public administration classes in the afternoons. The class would often go into the evening hours and on Saturdays, depending on the guest presenters' schedules.

One of his morning field experiences included research on the Philadelphia Police Department (PPD). Herman described this experience as a culture shock when he witnessed a high degree of conflict between the officers and citizens. This culture shock was unique compared to his diverse New London neighborhood experiences where everyone got along. Herman's assignment was to research a police precinct in Philadelphia that happened to be controlled by Captain Frank Rizzo.[65] Herman observed that Rizzo's management style

62 The hurricane struck on September 21, 1938, and is the most powerful and deadliest hurricanes on record in New England.

63 The Bulkeley School was founded in 1873 as a private all-boys secondary school. After 1951 it was merged into the public school system, a few years after Herman graduated.

64 Ironically, Sidney Goldstein founded Brown University's Center for Population Studies & Training (POP Center) and Herman Goldstein co-founded University of Wisconsin's Center for Problem-Oriented Policing (POP Center). The former website is www.popcenters.org and the latter website is www.popcenter.org (Scott, 2016).

65 Rizzo became PPD commissioner (1968–1971) and 93rd mayor of Philadelphia (1972–1980).

seemed to cause increased hostility toward the community and negatively impact the police culture. Rizzo went down in Philadelphia's history as a very popular Italian political leader who became police commissioner and then mayor. Rizzo also exemplified problems with racial tension and political control (Daughen & Binzen, 1977). In front of the Philadelphia City Hall, his statue was a target for 2020 mass police protests (Wilson, 2020) and eventually removed. Rizzo's legacy is described more fully in the chapter on Ramsey.

Herman finished his graduate degree in 1955 in governmental administration from the Fels Institute of Government,[66] which focused on improving state and local government management. As part of his graduate degree completion, he secured an internship in Portland, Maine, and worked as an assistant to the city manager. Herman was eventually hired as an administrative assistant to the city manager for $3,600 a year and discovered mismanagement problems with the city's police department. During this same time, O.W. Wilson worked at a fevered pace consulting with police departments across the country, primarily during his summer breaks from teaching at UC Berkeley. The city manager hired Wilson as a consultant. He worked closely with Herman for several months in Portland, surveying the department and conducting site visits to solve various police dysfunction problems. Several recommendations were made by both Herman and O.W., which eventually led to the resignation of Chief Clarence Hofacker and the hiring of Chief Leon Webber.[67] Webber implemented many of the Wilson and Goldstein recommendations and served longer than any other chief until that time (1956–1968).

American Bar Foundation (ABF) Study

Throughout the mid-1950s, there was a national concern about increased crime and how effective the justice system was in addressing these concerns. Academics spent little time studying the system at the ground level. In 1952 this knowledge gap caused Federal Supreme Court Justice Robert Jackson[68] to call for an ambitious study of the criminal justice system through the ABF, founded in that same year. The ABF study was sanctioned because of the gap between what statutes called for and what was occurring at the system's ground level (Morn, 1995). The unique and ambitious research, to study the legal system's practical actions from the police through the court system, was funded by the Ford Foundation[69] and directed

66 Samuel Simeon Fels started Fels-Naptha Soap Company. The Fels Institute of Government was founded after his Southside Philadelphia mansion was converted and given to the University of Pennsylvania in 1937. The institute was founded in response to corruption and mismanagement of government that was connected to the Great Depression. Goldstein used his ivy graduate education as a springboard for the next 60+ years to advocate for accountable and ethical uses of government services.

67 Webber retired in 1968, two months shy of serving 12 years as the longest Portland chief until being surpassed by Chief Michael Chitwood who served 17 years (1988–2005).

68 Like Goldstein, Jackson did not have a law degree as this is not a requirement to be a Supreme Court Justice; however, he is the last one to lack a law degree. He served the Supreme Court from 1941 to 1954 and was the only justice to also serve as U.S. Solicitor General (1938–1940) and U.S. Attorney General (1940–1941) under President Franklin Roosevelt. In 1945, he was granted a leave of absence from the Court and served as U.S. Chief of Counsel to prosecute Nazi war criminals in Nuremberg Trials.

69 As the founder of the Ford Motor Company, Henry Ford attempted a series of social engineering strategies for his diverse workforce to create a prototypical American family. This social engineering included owning his hometown Dearborn *Independent* weekly news so he could publish a series of anti-Semitic articles and directly publicize his political opinions, which were then distributed to over 7,000 car dealerships throughout the country (Baldwin, 2002). In an effort to make amends for his father, Edsel Ford initiated the Ford Foundation in 1936, which provided funds that were directed toward the benefit of scientific and educational public welfare. From 1953 to 1956, Foundation President H. Rowan Gaither expanded the foundation grants toward higher education research. It was not likely lost on Wilson when he asked his young Jewish protégé, Goldstein, to be part of the seminal Ford Foundation ABF research noting the historical anti-Semitic attitudes of Henry Ford.

by Professor Frank Remington[70] from the UW-Madison Law School. Wilson was named one of the law enforcement consultants on the project and asked to create a survey to better understand how the police operated, collaborated, and impacted the community during their day-to-day work. Other researchers would conduct similar surveys on prosecutors, defense attorneys, and judges. Wilson recommended Goldstein to assist in the first wave of observational field research on the police.[71] The research's original intent was to study the system in 48 states but quickly got bogged down in three states (Wisconsin, Michigan, and Kansas) because there was so much to observe.

In 1956, Goldstein was on a team of five researchers sent by Remington to Milwaukee because of the law school's familiarity with the state justice system's personnel. The observational research conducted by Goldstein and his team was groundbreaking since very little observational research had been conducted behind the blue curtain of policing. Similar to Roosevelt's work during his midnight rambles as police commissioner (described in the first chapter), Goldstein took a front seat to peer into the secretive world of policing and better understand the challenges and faults of a system that had yet to receive adequate academic attention. His team carried a Dictaphone and recorded conversations with officers that were later transcribed. To his surprise, police unions and several department leaders let Goldstein know they supported the groundbreaking research project. Notably, the individual researchers were respected by leaders within law enforcement.

Goldstein and the field researchers conducted observational tours throughout Wisconsin in Milwaukee, Ashland, Eau Claire, Superior, Madison, and Detroit, Michigan. In each of these departments, researchers shadowed officers on mobile and foot patrol, surveillance, investigations, and arrests. The ABF study shed light on a previously obscured justice decision-making process. Conventional assumptions of the justice system were exposed, and this highlighted the value of understanding how discretion is exercised throughout policing and the courts. Prior assumptions stood that officers operated similarly to workers in the Ford assembly line process and mechanically made arrests based on deciding if someone violated a statute. It was assumed that courts routinely processed those arrests. However, the field researchers found this was an inaccurate portrayal of the informalities that the researchers discovered. Goldstein and other ethnographic researchers exposed the realities of street-level bureaucrats: the lack of coordination throughout the criminal justice system; robust discretionary decision-making from individual officers that often differed from police executive planning; and firmly established practices that involved processing a large number of suspected offenders through a court system that would dispose of the cases in informal ways. For example, Goldstein was introduced to units that policed prostitution that were informally called "whore squads," and he discovered the officers were very lackadaisical at handling cases, that these cases often led to arrests for disorderly conduct, and cases did not go through a formal court process. Policing was seen as sloppy, used for personal or political harassment, and not focused on addressing crime problems.

After two years of intense observational ethnography, Goldstein and his team produced an interim report with copies distributed to a limited number of people who had to agree not to make copies or distribute the pioneering research. The ABF headquarters, located in Chicago, eventually had their funding cut. Goldstein was one of the last researchers to leave.

70 Remington died in 1996 the day before his 73rd birthday. The Frank Remington Center was dedicated at the UW-Madison Law School and provides a number of clinical programs that include legal assistance to Wisconsin inmates. Michael Scott, Goldstein's protégé, taught at the UW as a clinical faculty member within the Frank Remington Center.

71 Goldstein was part of the first ABF field research team that included Robert Cassidy, William Hungate, and Louis Trent (ABF, 1956).

Law professors at the UW-Madison were shocked at what the data revealed and used it to develop a legal seminar course. Remington partnered with Lloyd Ohlin,[72] headquartered within the University of Chicago's sociology department and then Columbia University, to write a multivolume report and five books with several other law professors. The text on policing, entitled *Arrest: The Decision to Take a Suspect into Custody*, was written by Wayne LaFave. LaFave received his law degree from UW-Madison in June 1959 and continued to work with Remington afterward on his book, using notes from the ABF-sponsored ethnographic research on the police.[73] In September 1960, LaFave was hired as a law professor at Villanova University, and one year later, he was hired at the University of Illinois. His book on arrest decisions, with assistance from Remington, Ohlin, and Goldstein, was published in 1965. The book demonstrated the value of observational research and how it can influence judicial reasoning. LaFave would later become a national expert on the Fourth Amendment and one of the country's most cited law professors.

The ABF research offered alternatives to the standard model of law enforcement for police leaders and academics. Findings from their ethnography called for a deeper understanding of how low-level decision making contributed to crime control and, if properly led, problem-solving capacities that did not always need to include court processes. Before the ABF survey research, academics did not use the term discretion. Prior to their research, assumptions were made that the police did not use a lot of their own decision-making skills. The ABF revealed the police did far more than simplistically enforce the law, and they used discretion regularly. The reality that police agencies were critical administrative policymaking organizations, operating as street-level bureaucrats (Lipskey, 1969),[74] did not sit well with political leaders.

Consequently, the ABF research led to a significant movement to structure discretion through enhanced administrative rulemaking. Before the ABF, police manuals offered nothing in terms of citizen interactions or managing discretion. Indeed, the greatest failure of the professionalization era of police reform, led by O.W. Wilson, was the inattention placed on police discretion, especially as linked to the misuse of force and biased policing. Wilson's first four editions of *Police Administration* failed to discuss police discretion (Walker & Katz, 2018), and the first book to address the concept was not published until 1975 (Davis, 1975).

The ABF research demonstrated that criminal behavior was enormously complex and not easily understood nor deterred through criminal statutes. Therefore, merely training practitioners to memorize or enforce statutes did little for their understanding of how they could reduce crime and disorderly behavior. Once recognition of policing complexities existed, a validation for improved standards for recruitment, training, and promotion could occur (Goldstein, 1987).

After Goldstein's formative ABF field research concluded, he left Chicago and returned to Connecticut to be close to his father after his mother's death. He found work in Hartford

72 Ohlin and Cloward wrote *Delinquency and Opportunity: A Theory of Delinquent Gangs* in 1960 arguing juvenile crime was a symptom of poverty and could be countered with local social programs (Ohlin & Cloward, 1960). They argued if we simply process juvenile offenders through the criminal justice system, we may be encouraging future criminal behavior. In 1967 Ohlin joined Harvard University as one of the few faculty members without a law degree and retired in 1982. He died in 2008 at the age of 90.

73 Author's interview with LaFave on February 6, 2020.

74 Professor Lipskey coined the term "street-level bureaucrat" and was colleagues with Goldstein in 1969 when he wrote his original paper on the concept (see Lipskey, 2010). His manuscript was supported by the Institute for Research on Poverty at the University of Wisconsin as part of the Economic Opportunity Act of 1964. Dr. Lipskey went on to become a political science professor at MIT, program officer for the Ford Foundation, and Distinguished Senior Fellow at Demos, a non-partisan public policy research institution and advocacy organization based in New York.

with a local government watchdog institution but did not find that career path rewarding. After a year, he left Connecticut again to work for the PAS, which, ironically, had hired Wilson as a consultant after he left Wichita. Like Wilson, Goldstein traveled around the country to research governmental administration and attended seminars in Madison sponsored by Remington as they worked through their analysis of the ABF data. Several researchers used the ABF data for academic studies, including Joe Goldstein from Yale University. His academic research was often confused with Herman's writings, even though Herman rejected Joe's conclusions from the ABF study. Joe argued that police officer discretion should be limited and simplified (Goldstein, 1960), while Herman would write seminal manuscripts that argued the contrary (Goldstein, 1977, 1990).

Chicago Police Department

In April 1960, while working as a consultant with the PAS, Goldstein read in a newspaper that Wilson had accepted the Chicago Police Superintendent position. The following day, he received a call from Wilson asking him to be his civilian executive assistant. Similar to Wilson's hesitation to follow Vollmer's offers, Goldstein was reluctant to accept Wilson's request. He felt Wilson was naïve for taking the challenging position to lead the CPD. Goldstein saw the CPD as the laughingstock of the criminal justice world, and with a police force of 12,000 officers, he considered if Wilson was over his head in terms of reform potential. With the same persistence he learned from Vollmer, Wilson eventually got Goldstein to agree to assist him with the needed reform efforts in Chicago, as long as he could remain on the payroll with the PAS and be paid as a contract employee. After six months of being in Chicago, he was convinced of Wilson's ability to reform the CPD based upon his strong support from Mayor Daley that excluded political meddling and a three-year guaranteed contract. Goldstein spent the next four years living in Chicago, working in the field, and fully supporting Wilson's reform efforts. Goldstein was hired as Wilson's civilian executive assistant and paid $11,000 a year (Woltman, 1960) (Photo 3.4).

Goldstein was on the frontlines of America's turbulent 1960s to determine what role the police should play in our communities. Chicago, like other urban cities, became an epicenter for the civil rights movement. Goldstein had several meetings with Mayor Daley. He was impressed with his commitment to the city and his ability to persuade others. However, he also found the CPD was in shambles. The past police commissioner, Timothy O'Connor, brought back many retired captains who were all dismissed by Wilson. Within the first year of Wilson's leadership, over 1,000 officers resigned, and Daley mostly kept his promise to not interfere with Wilson's reform efforts. As part of the reform effort, Goldstein was assigned to find officers on the payroll but not reporting to work. Once he found these officers (often employed in other jobs), many resigned rather than face corruption charges. Like Roosevelt's midnight rambles in New York City 70 years prior, Goldstein would frequently show up at the CPD during the evening hours and on weekends and conduct field observations as he learned to do from the Ford-funded ABF research. Goldstein enthusiastically attended many of Wilson's roll call meetings and found officers were initially hostile toward him as an outsider civilian assistant to Wilson. However, Goldstein described the CPD union as weak, and while they tried to undercut their reform goals, they still made enormous progress during a relatively short period of time.

Reform changes in the CPD were both structural and substantive. In the preceding chapter on Wilson, the CPD structural changes are detailed. Examples included closing down police districts, modernizing police buildings, and adding undercover internal affairs units. Structural changes also included ordering 500 new police vehicles based on Goldstein's discovery that

New Police Department Bosses

Police Superintendent Orlando W. Wilson (seated, second from right) with his new aids. They are (seated, left to right) Capt. John D. Madl, Lt. Terrence Doherty, James B. Conlisk Jr., Wilson, and Maurice Begner. Civilian aids (standing, left to right) are Richard E. McDonell, Frank J. Leahy, Jacque K. Boyer, George W. O'Connor, Herman Goldstein, and Col. Minor K. Wilson. [TRIBUNE Photo]

Photo 3.4 Photo courtesy of the *Chicago Tribune*, January 1, 1961.

CPD officers were using their personal cars to patrol or conduct police business since there were not enough operable squad cars. Substantive changes included reassignment of patrol officers to low income, minority neighborhoods, and increasing Black police applicants. Goldstein discovered that Black citizens applying to become CPD officers had been disproportionally dismissed from the pool for subjective reasons such as flat feet. He convinced Wilson to remove the physical exam criteria and redesigned the selection process, so applicants immediately knew if they passed their exam.

Other substantive reform came when Wilson and Goldstein decided to help protect protesters attempting to integrate Chicago public beaches. While Jim Crow was not formally in existence as it was in the south, informal segregation nevertheless existed, especially at public beaches. In 1960, Blacks were highly unwelcome at Rainbow Beach Park, on the South Shore. Although they could legally be there, Black residents who dared to integrate faced heavy ridicule and could expect to have rocks thrown at them. The history of such violence was common. In 1919, a Black teen was killed when his raft drifted toward the whites-only beach near 29th Street, leading to a riot that claimed 38 lives and hundreds of injuries (William & Wambsgans, 2019). (This incident is discussed more fully in the Ramsey chapter.) On August 28, 1960, organizers for a youth council and white students from the University of Chicago intentionally tried to integrate Rainbow Beach. After facing ridicule, the group attempted to pack up and leave but had to go through a gauntlet of angry whites to get off the beach. Rocks were thrown, and injuries occurred. On July 8, 1961, nearly 100 activists repeated the protest, but this time Wilson and Goldstein ensured they would have protection from 200 police officers. The police presence led to a limited number of young white males arrested for harassing the demonstrators. For several weeks the demonstrations continued with police protection, and gradually the mistreatment and violence dissipated.

When Dr. Reverend Martin Luther King, Jr. (MLK) was formally invited to meet with Wilson in 1966, there was much to discuss. The success of an increased number of Black police applicants, mixing Black and white patrol officers, and integrating public beaches with police protection were discussed with pride with MLK and his wife as they became primed for organizing their demonstrations on housing discrimination. (The MLK meeting is covered more fully in the chapter on Wilson.) By the time of their formal meeting, MLK had been visiting Chicago for years and, like other civil rights protesters, had been provided CPD escorts for his protection.

Martin Luther King, Jr. and John F. Kennedy

As early as January 1958, under the auspices of the Sunday Evening Club,[75] southern civil rights leaders were invited to speak in Chicago. MLK began doing speeches at the Orchestra Hall Symphony Center, located at 220 S. Michigan Avenue. However, when MLK and other southern leaders arrived in Chicago, white limousine drivers refused to escort them from the airport. Consequently, Black funeral homes were contacted to drive famous African-Americans that came to Chicago. The Reverend A.R. Leak volunteered his son Spencer, 25 years old at the time, to escort MLK as his chauffeured limousine driver (Drennan, 2014). As MLK's notoriety increased, Wilson arranged for CPD escorts to be placed in Spencer's limousine during his visits. Goldstein met with MLK and described him as approachable and very interested in their efforts to reform the CPD.

Civil rights protests throughout Chicago occurred throughout Goldstein's time at the CPD and tested their reform efforts. From January 23 to February 5, 1962, students at the University of Chicago organized a sit-in to protest the university's off-campus residential properties. One of the student leaders was 21-year-old Bernie Sanders,[76] and their protests became part of the Chicago Freedom Movement (Frizell, 2016). This movement also referred to as the Chicago open housing movement served as the most extensive civil rights campaign in the North and included several race-based quality of life demands. On April 19, 1962, King spoke for a fifth time at the Orchestra Hall Symphony Center,[77] again escorted by the Leak Funeral home and Wilson and Goldstein's protection. His sermon was called "staying awake through the revolution," and one audience member that evening included Hillary Clinton,[78] who was brought to

75 The Chicago Sunday Evening Club was created in February 1908 through the insistence of clergyman Clifford Barnes as a means to fill a void after so many churches left following the Great Chicago Fire of 1871. The club exists today as an innovative, faith-centered outlet that hosts meetings, speakers and artists that work to improve common civic life.

76 Sanders served in the U.S. House of Representatives from 1991 to 2007 and has been a U.S. Senator from Vermont since 2007. He is considered the Progressive leader of the Democratic Party and ran for President in 2016 and 2020.

77 The Chicago Symphony Orchestra Hall, located at 220 S. Michigan Avenue, was founded in 1891 and hailed as one of the best orchestras in the world.

78 Clinton served as First Lady to Arkansas Governor Bill Clinton (1979–1981; 1983–1991) and First Lady to President Clinton (1993–2001). She was then elected as U.S. Senator from New York (2001–2009) and became President Obama's Secretary of State (2009–2013). She ran against Donald Trump as the Presidential Democratic nominee in 2016.

the speech by her youth Methodist minister Don Jones and their suburban Park Ridge church group (DNAinfo, 2016).

Another notable Chicago event for Goldstein occurred on November 2, 1963. Mayor Daley had arranged for President Kennedy and Vice President Johnson to attend an Army-Air Force game at Soldier Field. It was the first time these teams would meet at Soldier Field since 1926, and the event was supposed to serve as a venue for the President's reelection campaign. President Kennedy was supposed to walk across the field during halftime to switch fan bases. Newspapers reported the exact time of the President's arrival from O'Hare airport to Soldier Field, 13 minutes before kickoff (Ford, 2009, p. 72). The inadequate planning for the President's security terrified both Wilson and Goldstein.

Additionally, federal agents notified Wilson that plans were underway to assassinate Kennedy in his motorcade from O'Hare Airport to Soldier Field. The first notification involved Thomas Vallee, a vocal right-wing Kennedy critic and expert marksman. The CPD arrested Vallee after a traffic stop for possession of an M-1 rifle, a handgun, and 3,000 rounds of ammunition. The second tip came from a housekeeper who reported seeing rifles with scopes inside a rooming house rented by two Hispanic looking men along the route that Kennedy was supposed to take from O'Hare to Soldier Field. Secret Service agents were dispatched to investigate but lost the suspects (Otto, 2017).

Goldstein was relieved when the CPD received communication from the White House that a last-minute travel change meant only Vice President Lyndon Johnson would arrive in Chicago. It's unknown if the President's travel was changed because of the assassination threats or events that unfolded from South Vietnam.[79] For Goldstein and Wilson, there was still a logistical nightmare to provide the Vice President with adequate security, which did not go well. A traffic officer accidentally misdirected the Vice President motorcade and sent them down streets that were not part of the security detail. Twenty days later, in Dallas, President Kennedy was assassinated (Bojczuk, 2014).

> Abraham Bolden,[80] the first African-American Secret Service agent[81] to serve on White House Presidential protection, attempted to publicize the precursor Chicago assassination threat.[82] He was later arrested and convicted of accepting a bribe in a counterfeiting case he worked in all-White Villa Park, Illinois (Bolden, 2009). According to Bolden, he was set-up. Later, he was denied transcripts of his case, despite filing a freedom of information request, after serving three years in prison at the Springfield, Illinois Medical Center for Federal Prisoners.

79 On November 1, 1963 the president of South Vietnam was arrested and assassinated through a successful military coup.

80 Before he became a secret service agent, Bolden was the first African-American detective to work with Pinkerton National Detective Agency and was later hired as a patrol officer with the Illinois State Police. Kennedy referred to him as the "Jackie Robinson of the Secret Service" (Kelly, 2009).

81 Charles Gittens joined the Secret Service in 1956 and is noted as the first Black agent. Prior to doing Presidential protection, Gittens was part of an elite special detail that targeted counterfeiting operations throughout the country. He was one of the 16 founding members of the National Organization of Black Law Enforcement Executives (NOBLE) in 1976. Gittens retired in 1979, joined the Department of Justice's (DOJ) Nazi-hunting Office of Special Investigations, and became a deputy director of the criminal division. He died in July 2011 at the age of 82 (Wilber, 2011).

82 In January 1978, Bolden testified to the House Select Committee on Assassinations regarding the discrimination he faced within the Secret Service and the lapse of security provided to President Kennedy (Bolden, 2009; Cheever, 2014). The Committee's report released in March 1979 concluded the Secret Service was deficient in their duties in Dallas when Kennedy was assassinated.

University of Wisconsin-Madison Law School

In 1963, amongst the civil rights events, Goldstein managed to publish his first two articles: (1) "Police Discretion: The Ideal versus the Real" in the *Public Administration Review*; and (2) "Guidelines for Effective Use of Police Manpower" in *Public Management*. In the first article, he lamented about the lack of research that existed to understand how officers utilize discretion (Goldstein, 1963a). In the second article, he described the conflict regarding adding additional officers to communities with surging crime and providing adequate training, education, and salaries (Goldstein, 1963b). That same year, the Ford Foundation provided funds to the UW-Madison Law School to develop an academic research program to improve justice teaching and research. The funding initially directed law students to be placed in state and federal prisons to help inmates with legal services. During this same year, Frank Allen,[83] at the University of Chicago Law School, invited Goldstein to speak about his articles and his understanding of police discretion. In December 1963, Goldstein received a letter from Willard Hurst[84] that discussed Remington's plans to hire him at UW-Madison in an effort to expand the law school's research into policing. Encouragement from both Allen and Hurst influenced Goldstein's career in academia.

The UW Law School's goal was to bridge the understanding of police operations with the administration of the law as a topic for future research and expansion. After serving four years as Wilson's executive assistant, in 1964,[85] Goldstein was encouraged by Remington to leave the CPD and work for the UW Law School, without a law degree, on the Ford Foundation grant. In doing so, he was allowed the latitude to teach and study the law, not just through statutory and judicial language, but as it was exercised and experienced in the field. His first teaching assignments was with Remington, Ed Kimball, and Don Newman in their newly developed experimental courses. He also monitored summer student interns that were placed in prisons and police departments across the country. Students were expected to propose legal policies while also observing prison and police administration.

Goldstein's addition to the Madison Law School faculty caused a paradigm shift in the pedagogy of teaching law. Traditional law classes called for students to recite case law precedent, and the paradigm shift required students to understand the law in action at the ground level. Goldstein was afforded academic partners that allowed a commitment to interdisciplinary study and an understanding of how society influences the exercise of the law. In his first year, he team-taught a new course titled Criminal Justice Administration. By year two, he established his policing course. Goldstein's law students were given several experiential educational opportunities to see the law in action. In particular, they spent a weekend taking a train from Madison to the CPD where they met with Wilson and conducted observational ride-alongs. On Saturday morning, they would observe criminal court calls and then return to observe officers on Saturday evening. The field experiences helped shape these students throughout their legal careers; many went into policing, research, or government employment. Goldstein was able to transfer his lessons from the ABF study to his students and provide them the street experiences necessary for their critical understanding of how discretion impacts justice.

83 In 1961, Allen chaired a joint committee that helped Illinois become the first state to decriminalize sodomy by consenting adults in private. Prior to the legal change, police corruption and blackmail were prevalent with homosexual populations.

84 Hurst was an emeritus law professor at the University of Wisconsin and internationally recognized as the dean of American legal historians. He died in 1997 at his home in Madison at the age of 86.

85 Goldstein also married Shulamit Elkayam in May 1964. He had two sons, Mark and David, and one daughter, Rahel.

Four changes in the way criminal procedure classes were taught stemmed from Goldstein's ABF study. First, the idea of the interconnected system from first police contact through probation or parole was challenged. Second, the pervasive role of low-visibility discretion at every stage of the system was revealed. Third, the differential impact of police interventions on those with the least power (e.g. homosexuals and minorities). Lastly, the important connections between behavioral problems (e.g. street prostitution, public intoxication) and how these problems are handled informally by the justice system. Law schools around the country also began to change how their courses were taught as the Wisconsin School of Law evolved.

The 1967 President's Commission on Law Enforcement and the Administration of Justice

In the summer of 1965, President Johnson created an executive order and appointed 19 individuals to a Commission tasked with the study of law enforcement and the administration of justice in America, followed by their recommendations. These commission members were joined by 63 staff members, 175 consultants, and hundreds of additional advisers, including several ABF Survey researchers. Ohlin became an associate director of the commission, and Remington, along with Goldstein, worked with the commission's executive director James Vorenbert, a Harvard Law School professor.

The final report, titled *The Challenge of Crime in a Free Society*,[86] was released in 1967. The commission recommended that Congress creates a new office in the Justice Department devoted to assisting local and state law enforcement. The recommendation led to the creation of the Office of Law Enforcement Assistance (OLEA), which evolved into the Law Enforcement Assistance Administration (LEAA). LEAA existed until 1981 and pumped billions of federal tax dollars into justice agencies; however, conservative politicians ensured the federal money flowed through state planning councils rather than through direct grants, carrying an assumption that these councils existed or did any planning (Kelling, 1992). The reality of our decentralized policing structure meant chiefs would not realistically be held accountable to state planning boards. Additionally, federal money for improving police agencies became the prerogative of individual police leaders. The unaccountable federal funds meant police administrators could use the grants on items such as weapons or anti-riot gear rather than on training and education.

Chapter 2: "Law Enforcement: The Police Role," written by Remington and Goldstein, advocated for the development of police policies to guide discretionary decision-making for sensitive topics such as when citizens should be stopped and questioned, when the police should engage in high-speed pursuit, and when the police should use of force. Herman also indicated that the police should turn over arrestees to a different entity because of the systemic problems with interrogation (President's Commission on Law Enforcement and the Administration of Justice, 1967, p. 89). Before this report, we knew little about policing in America. On page 91, in the first line of the policing chapter, it states 420,000 people work in approximately 40,000 separate agencies. These numbers turned out to be a typo but spoke to the lack of knowledge regarding American policing's basic facts.

The Johnson Crime Commission provided expectations for criminal justice reform at a scale not done before 1967 or since that time. The study included several recommendations. Notably, the commission called for more funding for research and accumulated data that surpassed any previous initiative. For example, the commission sponsored Albert Reiss and

86 See https://assets.documentcloud.org/documents/3932081/Crimecommishreport.pdf

Donald Black's study on police patrol, which discussed use of force and discretionary decision-making (Walker & Katz, 2018, p. 50). The Johnson Crime Commission's push for reform led to the national crime victimization survey (NCVS) that collects unreported crime data. Another lasting legacy was the emergence of criminal justice as a university academic field worthy of further scientific study (Newman, 1993).

According to the police chapter, the commission recommended that all policing supervisors have bachelor's degrees, and colleges should create criminal justice programs. It's interesting to see the full circle advocation of higher education advancements related to both criminology and the police. August Vollmer pressed higher education as a critical component for professionalizing the police. In the winter of 1941, in Vollmer's Berkeley living room, his student, O.W. Wilson, was selected as the inaugural President of the *National Association of College Police Training Officials*. This organization birthed the *American Society for Criminology (ASC)* and ostensibly the *Academy of Criminal Justice Sciences (ACJS)*. Wilson became Goldstein's protégé in Chicago, and Goldstein, along with Remington, pressed recommendations onto Johnson's crime commission to increase education for the police. LEAA became a federal funding source for several universities and college programs to develop criminal justice majors in the 1970s. The creation of LEAA links back to recommendations from the ABF ethnographic researchers. LEAA was also supposed to monitor the hiring and promotion of officers to ensure civil rights equality.

Wrong Conclusions from the Traditionalists of the President's Commission on Law Enforcement

The traditionalists of the President's Commission wanted to divest the police of non-law enforcement functions and reduce their workload. The belief was that if the police focused on fewer tasks and became more focused on law enforcement, they would be more effective and less likely to be corrupted. However, these conclusions contradicted earlier ABF ethnography, which demonstrated that the police spend a considerable amount of time dealing with broad social issues that include mental health, social justice, and poverty. The notion that the police can simply state, "I don't make the law, I just enforce it" wrongfully encourages officers to abuse their authority in democratic nations.

Additionally, the traditionalists from the President's Commission on Law Enforcement continued to push the *Great Society Program* with the Democratically controlled Congress of 1965. Based on President Johnson's *Great Society Program* and the underpinnings of the 1967 *Challenge of Crime in a Free Society* report, poverty and social injustice sociologically caused criminal behavior. The commission's report backed this theoretical foundation, which appeared to argue that the police could do little more than react and arrest law violators. Academic leaders relegated this simplistic view of law enforcement to lower-level "cop shop" training programs. Moreover, academics distinguished the simplicity of law enforcement from more academically rigorous undergraduate criminology programs. This narrowed definition of reactive standard law enforcement, instead of a broader view of POP, was fed into traditional reform agendas, led by LAPD Chief Parker. *The Challenge of Crime in a Free Society*, and police leaders that followed, called for controlling discretion, and corruption, through additional administrative rulemaking, which ultimately stifled creative decision-making.

As discussed more fully in the Vollmer chapter, the east coast criminology programs that sprang up in the 1970s were dominated by theory-focused researchers. These sociologists created the nation's core criminology curriculum, starting in SUNY-Albany. The SUNY research advocacy steered away from the 1940s *National Association of College Police Training Officials* (Morn, 1995). This departure would have significant ramifications for how academics and police leaders related to one another for several decades. Ironically, police executive reformists pushed for autonomous urban police agencies through the foundational support of progressive scholars. During this era, Goldstein described urban police as the least accountable branch of urban government (Goldstein, 1977). Standard law enforcement paradigms would remain until Goldstein unassumingly provided the necessary challenges he received from his time as an ABF researcher and executive assistant in the Chicago PD.

Knapp and NYPD Commissioner Patrick Murphy

The 1960s–1970s were chaotic times in American history. NYC Mayor John Lindsey[87] reached out to Goldstein, likely with the memory of his failed attempt to recruit O.W. Wilson away from Chicago, to be part of a task force to address police issues in the NYPD. Mayor Lindsey wanted Goldstein to work specifically with his new police commissioner, Patrick Murphy,[88] who was tapped in 1970 to lead the nation's largest police department in the Knapp Commission's aftermath. The Knapp Commission formed after whistleblower Frank Serpico revealed pervasive corruption and misuse of force that permeated the NYPD (Fyfe & Skolnick, 1993). The commission's investigation and solicitation of witness testimony demonstrated the extent of police corruption throughout the NYPD. The culture forced good officers to become part of a bribery system, with payments made to supervisors and information sold to organized crime. (The commission is discussed more fully in the chapter on Bratton.) Like Wilson, Murphy planted field associates throughout the department to uncover corrupt officers and established performance expectations that previously did not exist. Goldstein encouraged Murphy to openly discuss corruption issues and protect honest officers who come forward to report unethical police behavior. By being transparent about the problem of police corruption, reform efforts were more successful.

In 1972, the UW Law School hosted a seminar on managing the use of force for 15 police chiefs from the largest cities. Murphy was in attendance, and when he returned to NYC, he adopted many of the seminar's policies. These policies narrowed police authority in virtue of statutes that allowed officers to shoot fleeing felons. Murphy's reform efforts on the use of force and not shooting fleeing suspects were controversial due to the enormous opposition from entrenched law enforcement traditionalists and local politicians.

Today, these policies vary considerably across the country. However, the 1985 civil case out of Memphis, *Tennessee v. Garner* generally guides departmental policies. That decision ruled that the police cannot use deadly force to stop a fleeing suspect unless the officer has probable cause to believe the suspect poses a significant threat of death or serious physical injury to others. Sherman and Langworthy (1979) documented the dramatic decrease in NYC shootings after Murphy enacted his use of force policy changes and established an equivalence to the National Transportation Safety Board's formal inquiry into every single officer firearm discharge. Rather than solely focusing on firearm marksmanship, Murphy introduced simulations to train officers to de-escalate and avoid shooting suspects. At the time Murphy led the NYPD, they fatally shot about 90 civilians per year. Today, the NYPD shoots and kills about ten people per year. Murphy stepped down as police commissioner in 1973 and became nationally recognized as a police reform leader in a short three-year time span.

87 Lindsey was two-term mayor during 1966–1973. Prior to being mayor, he served Congress as a U.S. Representative from New York during 1959–1965. In 1971, Lindsey announced he was no longer a Republican and became a Democratic Presidential candidate. He died in 2000 at the age of 79.

88 Murphy served as a Navy pilot in World War II and was hired to do foot patrol for the NYPD in 1945. His father and brother also worked in the NYPD (Murphy & Plate, 1977). He died in 2011 at the age of 91.

Murphy left the NYPD to become the President of the Police Foundation, which began in 1970 with a $30 million grant from the Ford Foundation. The Chairman of the Board of Directors for the Police Foundation was James Q. Wilson, and he was also a Professor of Government at Harvard University. Wilson sought out Murphy after having priority differences with the first President, Charles Rogovin.[89] Wilson pushed for the Police Foundation to have more of a research emphasis rather than police leadership training.[90] Goldstein's ABF research and employment at the UW Law School were funded by the Ford Foundation as was the Police Foundation, which took its name from their Police Development Fund. To avoid the connotation that the Ford funds were relegated to improve policing in a manner similar to underdeveloped countries, they avoided the title "Police Development Foundation" and stuck with the Police Foundation. (The foundation's research is explained more fully under the appendix of the chapter on Bratton under George Kelling, a graduate student to Goldstein.) By 1976, Murphy helped form the Police Executive Research Forum (PERF)[91] with Gary Hayes[92] (a Goldstein student) and began to advocate for Goldstein's more effective policing approach. The founding principles of PERF[93] stated the following:

1. *Research, experimentation, and exchange of ideas through public discussion and debate are paths for the development of a professional body of knowledge about policing;*
2. *Substantial and purposeful academic study is a prerequisite for acquiring, understanding, and adding to the body of knowledge of professional police management;*
3. *Maintenance of the highest standards of ethics and integrity is imperative to the improvement of policing;*
4. *The police must, within the limits of the law, be responsible and accountable to citizens as the ultimate source of police authority; and*
5. *The principles embodied in the Constitution are the foundation of policing.*

Evolution of Problem-Oriented Policing (POP)

The 1970s

Throughout the 1970s, law professors updated coursework at the UW-Madison Law School. Goldstein and his students continued to do several field research projects with the Madison Police Department (MPD). He also created his own course in policing for law students. He utilized a binder of lecture material, academic articles, and police reports that were updated

89 Before coming to the Police Foundation, Rogovin worked as an Assistant Public Defender in Philadelphia and Chief Assistant District Attorney. Under President Johnson, he was Assistant Director for the President's Commission on Law Enforcement and the Administration of Justice. He then became Assistant Attorney General for Massachusetts and the Administrator for the LEAA under the DOJ. He died in 2016 at the age of 84.

90 A similar argument occurred in August Vollmer's living room in 1941 between supporters of Vollmer's views on police research and William Wiltberger's views on police training. As described in the earlier chapter, Vollmer hosted seven individuals at his home in Berkeley and they created the *National Association of College Police Training Officials*, which would later become the *American Society of Criminology (ASC)*.

91 PERF was established in 1976 and is located in Washington, DC operating on tuition payments for educational programs, grants from private or nonprofit organizations and membership dues. Members include police leaders, primarily from large city, county, and state law enforcement agencies. See www.policeforum.org/.

92 Gary Hayes passed away in September 1985 of cancer at the age of 40. During his short time, Hayes championed the development and impact of PERF onto the policing field by pushing reform efforts that were directed toward the business of leading police departments along with more adequately measuring the effectiveness and fairness of responses to crime problems. He is also discussed in the chapter on William Bratton, who won the second annual Gary Hayes Award at the 1987 PERF conference.

93 See www.policeforum.org/principles

each semester to stay current with the field. This course binder culminated into Goldstein's first book, *Policing A Free Society*, in 1977. He purported the quality of one's life in a democracy is primarily impacted by the quality of services the police provide. Throughout the book, Goldstein pointed out the vast majority of the tasks the police are asked to accomplish has little to do with crime. The job's complexity requires the police to help those who have difficulties caring for themselves such as the elderly, mentally ill, and addicted populations. Police should resolve conflicts between groups that are often fueled by these obstacles while also protecting citizens' constitutional rights and providing a sense of safety throughout the community. Many of the challenges placed on the police stem from a lack of resources or leadership provided by other non-justice entities to deal with non-criminal problems. Goldstein demonstrated how this setup causes the police to become dependent on the rest of the justice system to process the large caseloads they have created, with results that often have negative consequences (Goldstein, 1977).

Goldstein's field research led him to conclude that police work was driven by complex discretionary decisions, and guidelines should be created to manage the discretion but not impede it. Unlike Wilson and other professional reformists, Goldstein departed from the view that policing could be directed more narrowly to enforcing the law and creating expert crime fighters. Reformists believed these narrowed roles would reduce corruption (Rumbaut & Bittner, 1979). Goldstein argued substantive leadership in policing had to move beyond the professionalization era of simplistically telling officers what not to do. This "telling them what not to do" is how standard operating policies and procedural (SOP) manuals evolved during this same era. Instead, officers should be encouraged to utilize their discretion to understand criminal behavior causes and seek solutions to prevent or change those behaviors.

Goldstein discovered that the police had simplistic and generic responses for everything they did (Goldstein, 1977). The police chose to enforce the law, not always knowing if the enforcement was appropriate or effective or ignored offenders. Goldstein's revelation introduced a third alternative, which required the police to look for more effective solutions that could be less intrusive than arrest. While both academics and police leaders often looked at the means for doing police work, Goldstein argued we needed to look at the end results. Those results may change if we think critically about alternative responses. However, these creative responses, often outside the formal criminal justice system, should be implemented after a thorough analysis of the given problem.

Improving Policing: A Problem-Oriented Approach (Goldstein, 1979)

Goldstein's views on POP, initially taught to his Wisconsin law students, were given to the rest of the world in April 1979 with an article in *Crime & Delinquency*, a publication of the National Council on Crime and Delinquency, titled "Improving Policing: A Problem-Oriented Approach." Kelling[94] (1992) points out a journal directed toward juvenile counselors on delinquency was not high on the reading list for police leaders. Police officers likely never heard of the journal, and Goldstein's article was not the lead in the journal that month (pp. 236–258); it was last. Without a J.D. or Ph.D. degree, the law professor did not have much impact, initially, on academics or criminal justice professionals. Gradually, his manuscript gained traction in policing due to stature from his previous work with the ABF and his direct contact with the police in Chicago. Both police leaders and police unions respected Goldstein as a thoughtful and sympathetic friend of policing (Kelling, 1992).

94 George Kelling received his graduate degree in social work from UW-Madison in 1973 where he also had contact with Goldstein as a student.

Goldstein's (1979) "Improving Policing" eventually became a seminal article in criminal justice academia and served as one of the rare publications that created a paradigm shift in policing. The unassuming manuscript swept through the policing field mainly because of the advocacy of PERF and Goldstein's former UW-Madison student Gary Hayes's leadership. Hayes made copies of Goldstein's 1979 manuscript for each PERF member and mailed the article to chiefs of all major cities. A typewritten letter, enclosed with the manuscript, declared it would revolutionize policing across the democratic world.[95] Under Hayes's leadership, PERF encouraged the experimentation of problem-solving as the primary long-term strategy for reengineering policing across the country. Goldstein's quiet revolution contrasted law enforcement's two dominant images during the 1950s–1970s reform era. The first imagery came from Wilson's Chicago view that saw officers as crime fighters and Parker's LA view of the police as a "thin blue line" that separated good people from evil. The second imagery saw the police as the front end of a system that controls crime by feeding the courts and correctional agencies with offenders. This latter imagery allowed for the possibility that the police could creatively prevent crime and collaboratively challenge disorderly behavior through a multitude of responses, which could include law enforcement, but did not have to.

Repairing Race Relations – Diverging from Crime Control Assumptions

Up until Goldstein's time, we assumed that arresting and processing offenders equated to crime control. For example, people in prison can no longer victimize, and deterrence naturally occurs because criminals learn not to repeat their mistakes. Moreover, the larger community will stop committing crimes based on seeing others get punished. In this sense, citizens should respect their police as local heroes who provide a thin blue line against the bad guys, as advocated by Chief Parker's LA television talk show, "The Thin Blue Line" created by his department's press office in 1956. Parker became a darling to the media despite the high crime rates in LA during his 16-year tenure as police chief, longer than any other chief. Along with FBI Director J. Edgar Hoover, Parker established enormous influence on molding American policing's national perspective – an influence simplified through a series of dichotomized metaphors – good vs. evil; citizen vs. lawbreakers; white vs. Black; and those people vs. us. Interestingly, like Wilson, Parker also had a long-strained relationship with FBI Director Hoover (see Donovan, 2005).

Parker and Wilson diverged in the 1960s with their views on race. Wilson, and Goldstein, focused on repairing race relations in Chicago, while Parker provided his community with apocalyptic opinions of citizens, criminals, and the police. However, police professionalism was seen for both reform leaders through management strategies that limited discretion and provided militaristic discipline. These models see citizens as passive witnesses and reporters of crime rather than active participants. The simplistic views of crime allowed for propaganda metaphors to justify law enforcement reactions to crime. The propaganda included labels such as stranger rape, random violence, and predatory criminals, despite the realities that friends and family commit most criminal victimization.

Other metaphors flourished, such as the war on crime and the war on drugs, each producing a warrior mindset into policing. Bittner (1990) lamented that the warrior mindset fails to value or recognize police work directed toward prevention, order maintenance, dispute resolution, and social services. These alternative policing models were improvements for meeting

95 Remarks made by Professor Lawrence Sherman at the Stockholm Criminology Symposium awarding Herman Goldstein on June 13, 2018. See www.youtube.com/watch?v=mVnQP-eieq0&list=PLm1L7U7MTrmAftj5H4tH-Q7XQGj_kzD4I&index=4

the challenges of racial conflict throughout America and were seized upon by Goldstein as he advocated for these alternative models. The alternative model helped provide the early framework for POP in the 1970s, which needed further empirical evidence. Several academics and police leaders would help provide the building blocks for POP into the 1980s.

Establishing Problem-Oriented Policing

The 1980s

As the POP concept evolved throughout the 1980s, police agencies were encouraged to select specific problems in their communities and conduct an intensive analysis of the root causes of those problems. Data gathered from the analysis is used to devise tailor-made responses that attempt to prevent further damage. Several followers of Goldstein took up his proposals through either research or police administration. Very few were uniquely positioned to attempt both, except Michael Scott. Scott made a career in advocating for POP as both a practitioner and an academic researcher.

Michael Scott

Michael Scott was a protégé to Goldstein, and Goldstein was a protégé to Wilson, albeit one that deviated from a reform agenda that attempted to narrow the role of the police to strictly law enforcement. From Vollmer and Wilson's lessons, Goldstein encouraged police education, and Scott became one of the most notable Goldstein's legal studies, undergraduate students. Scott's father was an English professor at UW-Madison and knew of his son's interest in law enforcement. He encouraged him to explore the new Behavioral Science and Law and Sociology major, where Scott would earn his Bachelor of Arts degree in 1980. The program would later be named the Center for Law, Society and Justice. Scott's first practical experience with the police came with a 1980 internship with the Middleton, Wisconsin Police Department. That same year, Goldstein hosted the first gathering in Madison of about two dozen researchers and practitioners to discuss POP. Ten years later, Scott would launch the international POP conference with hundreds in attendance. Before doing so, he would make his career as both a practitioner and researcher, and he started with an application to the MPD after graduation.

During Scott's application process to the MPD, he helped Goldstein test POP theories through a grant from the National Institute of Justice (NIJ) and MPD Chief David Couper.[96] Like Goldstein's experiences in Chicago, Couper (who was in the Marine Corps before becoming a police officer in Edina, Minnesota) helped protect Vietnam War protesters, despite critics who claimed he coddled criminal offenders. He also hired several women, minority, and openly gay officers.

The early POP experiments in Madison focused on reducing drunk driving and repeat sex offenders. By 1981, the MPD hired Scott as a patrol officer, where he worked through 1984. His academic preparation continued when he decided to leave the MPD and attend Harvard University. Scott received his Juris doctorate in 1987. (Ironically, as described earlier, Wilson taught as a visiting lecturer at Harvard University in the 1930s while he was a chief in Wichita.) Scott continued to work for several police agencies after he received his Harvard University law degree.

96 Couper served as Madison chief from 1973 to 1993, the longest tenure of any chief. He was 35 years old when he became chief. After retirement, he attended a seminary and became an ordained Episcopal priest (see Couper, 2017).

From 1987 to 1988, Scott worked as a legal assistant to NYPD Commissioner Ben Ward, the city's first African-American commissioner. From 1988 to 1990, he worked as a senior researcher for PERF and trained police executives on POP. Scott's position at PERF came at a critical time following the death of PERF founder and Director Gary Hayes a few years prior. Under PERF's second Director, Chief Darryl Stephens,[97] the agency continued to be an epicenter for pushing POP as a paradigm shift into policing. Federal funds supported PERF and allowed the POP approach to be further tested and taught to national police leaders. From 1990 to 1992, Scott became the Director of Administration for the Fort Pierce, Florida Police Department. From 1992 to 1994, he was a special assistant to Commissioner Clarence Harmon[98] at the St. Louis Metropolitan Police Department (SLMPD).

From 1994 to 1996, Scott had a unique opportunity to lead a new municipal police department in Lauderhill, Florida, with over 100 employees that policed a multicultural community of 50,000 residents. His work as a police leader culminated in 1996 when he received PERF's 11th Annual Gary Hayes Award for innovation and leadership in policing.

From 1997 to 2003, Scott transitioned his work and became an independent consultant in Savannah, Georgia. During this period, he helped launch and establish the Center for Problem-Oriented Policing, described more fully later. In 2003, the Scott Goldstein connection would mimic the Wilson Vollmer connection. In 1939, Vollmer convinced Wilson to return to his alma mater and teach as a Professor of Police Administration at UC Berkeley. In 2003, the retiring Goldstein convinced Scott to return to his alma mater and teach as a clinical professor. Ironically, Scott's academic career began through the Frank Remington Center, one of the prominent individuals credited with bringing Goldstein to Madison. Scott would teach in the Madison Law School for the next 12 years. In 2015, he became a clinical professor at the Arizona State University School of Criminology and Criminal Justice.

It is interesting to note that Vollmer influenced Wilson in Berkeley; Wilson influenced Goldstein in Chicago, and Scott was influenced by Goldstein in Madison. Each of these cities provided laboratories for testing emerging policing reform. The research efforts throughout the 1980s would eventually lead to the seminal book *Problem-Oriented Policing* (Goldstein, 1990) and the creation of the Center for Problem-Oriented Policing. The POP concept resonated with all levels of police agencies since street-level officers up through command staff could all work creatively toward addressing problems without an over-reliance on the criminal justice system. This approach to strategic planning would emerge as a leading model to improve democratic policing throughout the world.

Newport News, Virginia (The Birth of SARA)

In 1987, the same year Scott graduated from Harvard University, John Eck and William "Bill" Spelman published a 161-page report through the NIJ and the PERF that tested POP in Newport News, Virginia. Their research began a couple of years before the first significant POP experiment, with the assistance of Hayes and Goldstein. Goldstein believed the foundational concepts of POP, as developed through the 1960s and 1970s, needed to be applied

97 Stephens has been a long-time supporter of POP. His police career began in 1968 in Kansas City, Missouri where he became assistant chief in 1976 and then chief in Largo, Florida in 1979. He became chief in Newport News, Virginia in 1982 and ran the first departmental test of POP, as described later in this appendix. Stephens was director of PERF from 1986 to 1992. He was also chief in St. Petersburg, Florida beginning in 1992 and Charlotte-Mecklenburg, North Carolina beginning in 1999 before retiring in 2008 with 40 years of policing experience. Stephens has remained active in retirement working for John Hopkins as director of state and local problems beginning in 2008 and as the executive director of the Major Cities Chiefs Association in 2010.

98 Harmon was the first African-American to lead the SLMPD from 1991 to 1995. From 1997 to 2001 he became the 44th Mayor of St. Louis and the city's second African-American mayor.

to officers involved in routine patrol assignments. He was fortunate to find a willing partner when Chief Stephens took over the Newport News Police Department (NNPD) and funding through the NIJ. Research on Newport News evaluated the impact of the following criteria as defined by Goldstein and the NIJ:

- Officer of all ranks and from all units should be able to use the POP system as part of their daily routine.
- The POP system must encourage the use of a broad range of information, including but not limited to conventional police data.
- The POP system should encourage a broad range of solutions, including but not limited to the criminal justice process.
- The POP system should require no additional resources and no special units.
- Any large agency must be able to apply the POP system.

Past findings indicated that increased patrol at New Briarfield reduced burglaries by 60 percent. However, sustaining the burglary reductions did not occur once the POP process stopped and the officers received transfer orders out of the apartment complex. By 1984, when Eck and Spelman began the POP initiative, New Briarfield was the main hot spot for the city's calls for service. The research project implementation occurred through a task force of 12 officers from all ranks. The group selected burglaries from the New Briarfield apartment complex and larceny from vehicles as targeted problems. This task force developed a four-stage problem-solving process known as SARA (scanning, analysis, response, assessment). In the *scanning* stage, officers identified issues that repeated and defined as problems. They conducted an opinion survey with apartment residents to understand repeated concerns. In the *analysis* stage, officers collected information from inside and outside the police department to determine who the stakeholders were and the extent of the burglary/larceny problem. The opinion survey revealed that residents historically complained about dilapidation throughout their complex, but the city failed to respond. In the *response* stage, officers used their analytical data to instigate creative solutions. These solutions included collaboration from stakeholders in both the public and private sectors to develop a coordinated strategy for improving the complex. Officers helped residents organize a tenants' association to pressure local politicians to fund repairs throughout New Briarfield. In the last stage, officers *assessed* the impact of their responses and were open to redefining the problem or conducting more analysis, depending on overall effectiveness. The city eventually decided to demolish the apartment complex and relocate the residents. However, before the demolition, reported burglaries did decrease (Eck & Spelman, 1987). More importantly, the POP experiment represented a new social purpose for the police to become community organizers and brokers of government services.

The SARA process model gave agencies a structure for conducting their individualized POP initiatives. Additionally, a kinship with POP developed with England's situational crime prevention (SCP) (Clarke, 1997) and environmental criminological theories (Brantingham & Brantingham, 1991; Jeffrey, 1977; Newman, 1973). These additions to Goldstein's work have allowed his concepts to remain relevant beyond any other historic police reform models.

San Diego Police Department (SDPD)

The San Diego Police Department (SDPD) historically became the leader in using POP concepts and served as the host city for the first several international conferences. Gary Cordner[99]

99 Professor Emeritus Cordner received his Ph.D. from Michigan State University and commanded the St. Michaels, Maryland Police Department for three years. Dr. Cordner taught at Eastern Kentucky University for 21 years and Kutztown University in Pennsylvania for five years. He was a senior research advisor for the NIJ

conducted one of the most extensive POP implementation evaluations into the SDPD when he interviewed 320 officers throughout the city's eight police districts. He also conducted surveys on approximately 25 percent of patrol officers and their immediate supervisors. The SDPD institutionalized POP approaches more than any other urban department. Close to 70 percent of officers in Cordner's research indicated they used POP elements, and almost half of the respondents stated POP was an essential part of policing. However, the POP initiatives at the SDPD were determined to be non-sophisticated with small-scale problems officers chose to focus on such as low-level drug dealing, public disorder, or transient populations. Cordner concluded that POP continued to evolve very slowly and not as a true paradigm shift previously idealized by academics (Cordner & Biebel, 2005).

Advancing Problem-Oriented Policing

Twenty-First Century

The Office of Community-Oriented Policing Services (COPS Office), a branch of the Department of Justice, provided funding for POP initiatives from 1999 to 2012. The Clinton Administration created the COPS Office through the 1994 Violent Crime Control and Law Enforcement Act. At the time, $8.8 billion was allocated over six years to assist with the campaign promise for putting 100,000 new police officers on the streets of America. The COPS Office was created to distribute and monitor national funds given to local agencies to implement the community policing philosophy.

In 2002, Goldstein's academic followers got together and created a private non-profit center dedicated to POP. The founders included Michael Scott, along with professors Ronald Clarke[100] and Graeme Newman.[101] Other instrumental academics that assisted in developing the POP Center included Herman Goldstein, John Eck, Deborah Lamm Weisel, Rana Sampson, and Karin Schmerler. The center's purpose was to provide a clearinghouse for research directed toward advancing the POP concept. In 2003, the POP Center website was established, fulfilling the mission.[102]

Since then, the POP Center has provided millions of copied research guides and downloadable material on specific problems and strategies, free of charge, to any entity seeking knowledge for implementing a POP approach. Materials from the POP Center are utilized throughout police academies and college classrooms, certainly to the appreciation of police reformer leaders like Vollmer, Wilson, and Goldstein. Over the past two decades, the POP Center has issued 74 problem-specific research guides. Michael Scott and Kelly Dedel wrote the first, *Assaults in and Around Bars*. The second edition of that guide appeared in 2006, and many other guides have received updates. The latest guide, *Exploitation of Trafficked Women*,

and served on the Commission on Accreditation for Law Enforcement Agencies (CALEA) from 2007 to 2016. He is a past President of the ACJS and has been a judge for the Herman Goldstein Award for Outstanding POP since 1996.

100 Ronald Victor Gemuseus Clarke is a British criminologist and Professor at Rutgers University in Newark. Clarke is known for his research on rational choice, the development of SCP, and the associate director of the Center for Problem-Oriented Policing. In 2015, he was awarded the Stockholm Prize in Criminology (see Scott & Goldstein, 2012).

101 Graeme Newman is a distinguished teaching professor emeritus, retired from the University of Albany who established the United Nations Crime and Justice Information Network. His research is geared toward crime prevention and he is an associate director of the Center for Problem-Oriented Policing.

102 The mission of the POP Center is to advance the concept and practice of problem-oriented policing in open and democratic societies and allow for the accessibility of literature related to POP to assist in efforts to address specific crime and disorder problems.

2nd Edition, was published in 2020 by Graeme Newman and James Corey. Other first guides starting in 2001 included *Robbery at Automated Teller Machines*, *Drug Dealing in Privately Owned Apartment Complexes*, *Disorderly Youth in Public Places*, and *Loud Car Stereos*. These research-focused guides are available free of charge to the general public, academics, and police executives through the POP Center. Each peer-reviewed problem-focused guide includes a thorough review of existing research literature and reported police practices. Leading scholars independently manage the peer-review process.

In addition to the 74 problem-specific guides, there have also been 13 response guides and 14 tool guides. These guides explain how to apply analytical methods and techniques to improve our understanding of crime and disorder problems. Design and programming work for the POP Center website, from its inception through 2017, was done by staff at the Professional Development Program at the State University of New York at Albany. In 2013, the POP Center faced budget cuts from the COPS Office. In 2015, Michael Scott relocated to Arizona State University's Watts College of Public Service and Community Solutions.

Problem-Oriented Policing Conference – Herman Goldstein Award

The year 2020 marked 30 years since the first formal POP conference took place. Unfortunately, 2020 also marked the year of Herman Goldstein's passing on January 24 at 88 years of age. The 30th annual POP conference did not occur in Ann Arbor, Michigan, in September 2020. Like most events in 2020, the Covid-19 pandemic caused a cancellation of the conference. The rescheduled conference, the first without Herman, took place in September 2021. The purpose of the annual meeting is to bring together police agencies, academic researchers, and vested stakeholders worldwide in an American host city to discuss the success and failure of their POP initiatives openly. Throughout the 1990s, the conference drew more than 1,000 annual international attendees. The 1990s was during a period of consistent funding from PERF and the COPS Office. However, as other policing models gained popularity, the attendance at POP conferences over the past couple of decades drew an average of 300–600 attendees.

Since 1993, a panel of judges vote on the best POP project at the conference, and the winner receives the Herman Goldstein Award. Judges include a mix of experienced research academics and police executives who select projects based upon the following: development of clear and realistic response goals; a thorough and demonstrable analysis; relevant measures of effectiveness; and the involvement of citizens and other community resources to help resolve the given problem. In the months leading up to the conference, judges select five to ten projects to present at the annual international conference. Nearly every submission since 1993 is available for public view online through the Center for POP,[103] as are the finalists and the Goldstein Award winners.[104] Each finalist receives a certificate of recognition for their innovative and effective problem-solving efforts to achieve measurable success in reducing crime, disorder, and public safety problems. The number of submissions for the Goldstein Award has ranged from the high teens to over 100, reflecting the varied interest in POP practice across the profession. Conference coordinators announce the winner of the Goldstein Award at the culmination of the conference. Starting in 2006, attending audience members were also allowed to vote on the best POP projects at the conference, and their votes were weighted with the panel of judges to determine the Goldstein Award (Photo 3.5).

103 See https://popcenter.asu.edu/content/pop-projects

104 See https://popcenter.asu.edu/content/2011-goldstein-awards-winner-finalists

Photo 3.5 Photo taken at the October 2005 Problem-Oriented Policing Conference in Charlotte, North Carolina for the Herman Goldstein finalist project from Sheboygan, Wisconsin "Neighbors Against Drugs" (Left to Right: Michael Scott, Herman Goldstein, the author Brandon Kooi, Sheboygan Police Chief David Kirk, Officer Todd Priebe, Lt. Jeff Johnston, and Ron Clarke).

Since 1999, the United Kingdom has also hosted a POP conference, and they provide a Tilley[105] Award for the best POP project. Historically, the British Home Office funds the award and the Reducing Crime Unit, now called the Crime and Policing Group. Winners of the Tilley Award receive funds to attend the POP conference in the United States. The Tilley Award is open to all UK police forces. In 2010 the awards ceased but were relaunched in 2018 by the Problem Solving and Demand Reduction Programme, led by the South Yorkshire Police.

At the 2001 POP conference in San Diego, and reiterated by Scott (2010), POP was summarized by Goldstein as follows:

> *Problem-oriented policing is an approach to policing in which discrete pieces of police business (each consisting of a cluster of similar incidents, whether crime or acts of disorder, that the police are expected to handle) are subject to microscopic examination (drawing on the personnel) in hopes that what is freshly learned about each problem will lead to discovering a new and more effective strategy for dealing with it. Problem-oriented policing places a high value on new responses that are preventive in nature, that are not dependent on the use of the criminal justice system, and that engage other public agencies, the community and the private sector when their involvement has the potential for significantly contributing to the reduction of the problem. Problem-oriented policing carries a commitment to implementing the new strategy, rigorously evaluating its effectiveness, and, subsequently, reporting the*

105 Nick Tilley is a sociology professor at Nottingham Trent University (120 miles north of London) and visiting professor at the Jill Dando Institute of Crime Science at University College London. He has written extensively on POP and brought Goldstein's vision of policing to the UK.

results in ways that will benefit other police agencies and that will ultimately contribute to building a body of knowledge that supports the further professionalization of the police.

The POP conferences encourage academics and police practitioners to fully understand the pragmatic challenges the police face in their daily operations while also encouraging them to be more transparent with their activities, so effectiveness is easier to measure. The need to be transparent was a historical lesson from both Vollmer and Wilson, and in doing so, policing became more effective. These lessons appear lost on many police leaders post 9/11 as agencies became more militaristic (Balko, 2014). As such, Goldstein lamented: "unless one maintains certain pressures and pushes for change, it's easy for things to revert all the way back to where they were a long time ago" (Rosen, 1997, p. 9).

Research Evidence Supporting POP

Evaluations of POP have been more promising than research directed toward community policing. Goldstein's prescription toward improving the police was profoundly sensible and spawned numerous experiments to put his ideas into practice. His concepts also triggered decades of debate over what the POP prescription meant and how it might be realized (Klockars & Mastrofski, 1991). In 2004, the National Academy of Sciences conducted a comprehensive report on police research and described POP as a major paradigm shift.[106] The academy submitted that POP provided an avenue away from generic, reactive responses and offered a proactive, often customized, and multi-faceted approach to some of society's most pressing problems (Skogan & Frydl, 2004). POP emerged as one of the most widely accepted and used strategies in progressive law enforcement agencies (Weisburd, Telep, Hinkle, & Eck, 2010).

Weisburd and colleagues (2008) conducted a systematic review of studies published using POP via the Norwegian government-supported Campbell Collaboration (Littell & White, 2018). Studies had to meet four criteria: (1) Use of the SARA model (Scanning, Analysis, Response, and Assessment); (2) a comparison group had to be included; (3) at least one crime or disorder outcome had to be reported with sufficient data to calculate effect size; and (4) the unit of analysis had to include people or places. Only ten studies were selected from over 5,500 research projects that took place in eight cities: Jersey City, New Jersey (Weisburd & Green, 1995; Braga et al., 1999); Knoxville, Tennessee; Oakland, California (Mazerolle, Price, & Roehl, 2000); Minneapolis, Minnesota (Sherman, Buerger, & Gartin, 1989); Atlanta, Georgia (Stone, 1993); San Diego, California (Thomas, 1998); Philadelphia, Pennsylvania (Stokes, Donahue, Caron, & Greene, 1996), a small town in Pennsylvania (Baker & Wolfer, 2003); and six wards (neighborhoods) in the United Kingdom (Tuffin, Morris, & Poole, 2006). Four of these studies were from peer-reviewed journals, two from government reports, three were from unpublished reports, and one was a doctoral dissertation. The studies focused on various problems: probationer/parolee recidivism; drug markets; vandalism and drinking in a public park; hot spot violence; school vandalism; problem addresses; and overall crime. Conclusions from the meta-analysis found support for POP and determined it was most effective with police departments that are fully committed to the tenants of POP. Moreover, expectations for the POP initiatives must be realistic with the adequate time given to officers engaged in analytical skillsets and creative responses. Larger effect size was found when agencies focused

106 An annotated bibliography of studies conducted on POP can be seen at https://popcenter.asu.edu/sites/default/files/library/reading/PDFs/Annotated-Bibliography-of-Studies-of-Implementing-Problem-Oriented-Policing.pdf

on specific problems as opposed to general crime. The more detailed the problem and place locations are defined, the more likely Goldstein's POP concepts will be effective.

Hinkle and colleagues (2020) conducted the most recent systematic analysis of POP, again with support from the Campbell Collaboration. They reviewed thirty-four studies between 1989 and 2018. Most of these came from the United States (28), five from the United Kingdom, and one from Canada. The updated review indicated that POP is associated with a statistically significant overall reduction in crime and disorder by 34 percent. Tailor-made responses were found to be more effective than standard reactive strategies and specifically, place-based interventions diffused crime-reduction benefits more than offender-focused strategies (Hinkle et al., 2020).

Conclusions: The Politics of Policing

Reform eras under Roosevelt, Vollmer, and Wilson pushed against the political influence within police decision-making. America has a long history of political corruption, and the police consistently fall prey to this history and its links to misuse of force. Goldstein's vision of the police, as it evolved from his experiences with the ABF research and as Wilson's executive assistant, foresaw a future with a profession that was held accountable by a political process that preserves democratic input and safeguards against corruption (Goldstein, 1975). To reach this vision, communities would need to be re-educated away from the simplistic view that the police can enforce the law equally through legal decisions without political influence. Reform movements from Roosevelt, Vollmer, and Wilson assumed procedural decisions are in check through the judiciary, represented by attorneys and judges who would ensure unbiased law enforcement. However, the police offer the most visible representation of the government. By that nature, they are always political, and any decision they make is influenced by wealth and power distribution throughout society (Scott, 2016). Goldstein advocated that the police should not hide behind the false promise of political neutrality and instead be transparent with the public. There is a deeper understanding of the inevitable political decisions made and how these decisions can become more effective when done collaboratively. Collaboration and open dialogue with the public directly relate to procedural justice (i.e. discretionary procedural decisions widely supported by the public) and attempts to understand criminal behavior analytically.

The causes of criminality are complicated and immense. Abstract jurisprudence and traditional criminological theories often fail to illuminate practical policy implications in addition to missing the realities of policing at the ground level. Goldstein demonstrated that policing can be effective when we understand street-level realities outside of strict adherence to enforcing laws. Unfortunately, when we fail to confront this reality, the police are given primary and exclusive responsibility to do something about complex crime problems, and they will naturally be left with immediate negative responses that include: misuse of force; community distrust; ineffective and mixed messages; and challenges to the very democratic nature of their profession. Goldstein's vision of policing stemmed from these challenges and the intellectual curiosity of creating effective policing within democratic nations without an over-reliance on heavy-handed law enforcers that once persecuted his ancestors in Nazi Germany.

Neither law enforcement nor scientific analysis will suffice in offering a complete understanding of how particular criminal behaviors begin and repeat. The conditions and causes of crime and disorder are politically driven and cannot be answered solely by statutory language. As much as past reformers wanted to rid the police of political influence, Goldstein begins with the premise that this is not realistic in democratic nations. Instead, suppose the police were to engage in a consistent and transparent conversation with their citizenry, neighborhood leaders, and local politicians. In that case, they could share a clear understanding of the extent of crime and disorder and negotiate an appropriate response to those problems. Goldstein premised that this engagement is best accomplished by shifting and sharing responsibilities, especially with those linked to the given problems (Scott & Goldstein, 2005). In this manner, the police not only become more effective at their job; they also become more equitable in how they service targeted neighborhoods. Goldstein's development of his vision for impartial and effective policing would begin after he left Chicago.

Goldstein demonstrated how the Wilson/Chicago model of reform inadvertently placed most police resources on responses to residential and businesses' calls for service and left little time for strategies geared toward crime prevention and problem-solving. Police officers would naturally hurry calls along, especially in situations where it was evident that no arrest would take place, in order to be "in-service" for the next call. If they were dealing with a response to a caller, ironically, they were "out of service" and often felt pressured to be back "in-service" to take the next call. Within the standard model of law enforcement, they are held hostage to the calls for service. Moreover, communities are frequently untapped and left out of police strategies that may otherwise be used to reduce the problem with repeat calls for service. Under this standard model, chosen responses are overly reliant on the punitive justice system. Instead, Goldstein advocated for the police to seek partners with targeted stakeholders throughout the community who can help prevent the given problem (Goldstein, 1990). These entities are further encouraged to assess the results of their efforts and share their conclusions with other practitioners in an unbiased and transparent way. The assessment component was a departure from standard law enforcement that was preoccupied with management and discipline (the means of doing the job) while ignoring the evaluative effectiveness of these efforts (the end results). Assuredly, the criminological researcher in Wilson would have greatly appreciated Goldstein's evolved wisdom and other academic/practitioner advocates of the POP approach.

A Personal Note

Like many fortunate individuals to have befriended or conversed with Herman Goldstein, my life became forever altered by his wisdom and love for solving personal and communal problems. I have been fortunate to engage in problem-oriented training with police leaders in several contexts and present at several POP conferences, twice as a finalist for the Herman Goldstein Award with the Sheboygan, Wisconsin and Aurora, Illinois Police Departments. Based on Herman's vision for policing, the training and conference experiences provide an unusual outlet for bringing together practitioners, police leaders from all ranks, and vested stakeholders in one forum to share the best solutions to society's most pressing problems. The setting is as unique as Herman was and continually challenges the status quo or what Herman often referred to as the generic law enforcement model (Photo 3.6).

I was also fortunate to attend Herman's Madison funeral service. With great appreciation to Mike Scott, Director for the Center for Problem-Oriented Policing, he provided permission for me to include a copy of his eulogy that eloquently captured who Herman Goldstein was for so many of his followers.

Eulogy for Herman Goldstein

By Mike Scott

January 26, 2020
Beth Israel Center, Madison, Wisconsin

I'm Mike Scott. I became a student of Herman's in 1980 and remained one for the next 40 years, not so much because I'm a slow learner; I prefer to think of myself as a lifelong

Photo 3.6 Herman Goldstein and the author.

learner. Each of us knew Herman in our own way and in accordance with his role in our life: as a father, a grandfather, an academic colleague, a teacher, a member of this religious community. I want to speak today from the perspective of the police world to share with you what Herman meant to it.

At the core of Herman's work was reconciling coercive government authority with freedom. Coincidentally, at this time of Herman's passing I am reading the English philosopher John Stuart Mill's "On Liberty" essays in which he is addressing this very same issue in 1859, not long after the creation of both British and American police forces. So I think of Herman as a modern-day political philosopher, though he would never have identified himself as such.

This concern about the conflict between coercive government authority and freedom lies at the core of many contemporary concerns about the police: the excessive use of force, mass incarceration, and the disparate treatment of minority citizens. While these particular issues were not Herman's specialty – he focused more on police effectiveness, Herman understood that all facets of policing are inter-related and that policing democracies is inherently complex and yet critical to their success or failure. He opened his seminal book, "Policing a Free Society" by writing, "The police by the very nature of their function, are an anomaly in a free society." Not only did Herman understand that everything in policing is inter-related, but also that what other sectors in society do or don't do affects policing.

When announcing Herman's death to my Arizona State University colleagues on Friday, some of whom would not have known of Herman's work, I said that if there were a Mount Rushmore of police scholarship, Herman would be one of the four faces on it. Indeed, the Stockholm Prize and other prizes awarded to Herman over the years have put him there virtually. But upon further reflection, I think that Mount Rushmore is a decidedly inappropriate metaphor for Herman: Mount Rushmore is inaccessible, rigid, permanent, imposing, intimidating, and inviting of reverence, all characteristics that Herman was not. Herman aspired to be accessible and familiar, and to make people comfortable – in his writing and in person. I learned to try to be like him in this regard – in relating to students, police and non-police scholars, journalists, and, especially, police officers. I learned from Herman to always be available to sincere and eager learners.

Also on Friday, when sending out notifications of Herman's death selectively to people in the police world whom I knew felt close to Herman, and he to them, I noted that half the people I was notifying were scholars and half were police and criminal justice practitioners, a near perfect reflection of what Herman tried to build: bridges between these historically separate worlds.

One scholar wrote back to me saying that he once heard Herman described as the "pope of policing." This also, on reflection, is an inapt metaphor, not merely because it's hard to imagine a Pope Goldstein, but because what we often associate with popes is their infallibility and dogmatic authority. Herman aspired to neither trait; rather, he aspired to teach people how to think about policing and to use his ideas as only a framework from which to expand, to apply, and, yes, to improve. He wanted us to think for ourselves, not merely to understand what he thought.

So, rather than being the "pope," to my mind, Herman has been, in a secular sense, the "rabbi" to the police: a teacher, scholar, counselor, and moral guide. Some police departments have a term for a high-ranking member of the department who helps selected younger members succeed in the department and protects them from various threats to their career. In St. Louis, it was called an "ace"; in the New York City Police Department, it was called a "rabbi." Not in the crass politically opportunistic sense, but in the truer sense, Herman was my rabbi.

When another colleague of mine offered condolences on Herman's death, I found myself saying, "If one lives to 88 years of age, one can't really complain." I quickly rethought that sentiment: If one is 88 and everything on one's body hurts and nothing works as it used to or should, as was the case for Herman in recent years, then there is very much to complain about. Indeed, in recent years, many of my conversations with Herman were consumed by our bemoaning the state of modern medicine, him from his personal experiences and me from my experiences helping my own similar-age parents through this phase of their lives. But even from what might seem a digression from discussing our common interest in policing, Herman used the failures of the modern medical system – to attend to patient needs by emphasizing medical procedures and profits – to illuminate similar distortions in policing where police can fail to attend to true community needs by emphasizing criminal justice system procedures and narrowly focusing on arresting offenders.

Whatever Herman's vision of an afterlife, mine envisions Herman getting the afterlife better organized, solving the problems of the afterlife (such as they might be), and generally improving it for us, if and when we get there.

I thank Rabbi Forester for allowing me the opportunity to speak here today. And I thank my rabbi – Herman – for giving me something worthwhile to say. On behalf of all my colleagues in the police world who knew and worked with Herman, thank you, Herman: We loved and respected you as much as you loved and respected us. Also published in Mazerolle (2020).

References

American Bar Foundation Annual Report (1955–1956). Retrieved from www.americanbarfoundation.org/uploads/cms/documents/1955_-_1956_abf_annual_report.pdf

Baker, Thomas and Loreen Wolfer (2003). The crime triangle: alcohol, drug use, and vandalism. Police Practice and Research: An International Journal *4*(1): 47–61.

Baldwin, Neil (2002). *Henry Ford and the Jews: The mass production of hate.* New York, NY: Perseus Books Group.

Balko, Radley (2014). *Rise of the warrior cop: The militarization of America's police forces.* New York, NY: PublicAffairs.

Benzkofer, Stephan (2013). The Summerdale Scandal and the case of the babbling burglar. *Chicago Tribune.* July 7.

Bittner, Egon (1990). *Aspects of police work.* Boston, MA: Northeastern University Press.

Bojczuk, Jeremy (2014). *22 November 1963: A brief guide to the JFK assassination.* West Sussex, UK: Boxgrove Publishing.

Bolden, Abraham (2009). *The echo from Dealey Plaza: The true story of the first African-American on the White House Secret Service detail and his quest for justice after the assassination of JFK.* New York, NY: Three Rivers Press.

Bopp, William (1977). "O.W.": O.W. Wilson and the search for a police profession (Interdisciplinary Urban Series). Port Washington, NY: Kennikat Press.

Bowker, Lee H. (1977). *Prisoner subculture.* Lexington, MA: Washington, D.C. Heath & Co. U.S. Government Printing Office.

Boydstun, J., M. Sherry, and N. Moelter (1977). Patrol staffings in San Diego: One-or-two-officer units. Washington, DC: Police Foundation.

Braga, Anthony A., David Weisburd, Elin J. Waring, Lorraine Green Mazerolle, William Spelman, and Francis Gajewski. (1999). Problem-oriented policing in violent crime places: A randomized controlled experiment. *Criminology, 37*(3): 541–580.

Brantingham, Paul L. and Patricia Brantinham J. (1991). *Environmental criminology (reissue).* Prospect Heights, IL: Waveland Press.

Brashler, William (1984). Big tuna: The 40-year reign of Chicago Mafia Kingpin Tony Accardo nears an end. *Chicago Tribune,* November 18.

Brown, David and Michelle Burford (2017). *Called to rise: A life in faithful service to the community that made me.* New York, NY: Ballantine Books.

Brzeczek, Richard, Elizabeth Brzeczek, and Sharon DeVita (1989). *Addicted to adultery: How we saved our marriage and how you can save yours.* Clear Spring, MD: Dorley House Books, Inc.

Calabrese, Frank, Kent Zimmerman, Keith Zimmerman, and Paul Pompian (2012). *Operation family secrets: How a mobster's son and the FBI brought down Chicago's murderous crime family.* New York, NY: Broadway Books.

Calkhoven, Laurie (2019). *Life stories: Martin Luther King, Jr.* New York, NY: Penguin House.

Cheever, Susan (2014). Could the secret service have saved J.F.K.? *VanityFair.* October 17.

Clarke, Ronald (1997). *Situational crime prevention: Successful case studies* (2nd ed.). Guilderland, NY: Harrow & Heston.

Cohen, Adam and Elizabeth Taylor (2000). *American pharaoh: Mayor Richard J. Daley- His battle for Chicago and the nation.* New York, NY: Back Bay Books.

Copley, Frank (1923). *Frederick W. Taylor: Father of scientific management.* New York, NY: Harper and Brothers.

Cordner, Gary and Elizabeth Perkins Biebel (2005). Problem-oriented policing in practice. *Criminology and Public Policy, 4*(2): 155–180.

Couper, David (2017). *Arrested development: A veteran police chief sounds off about protest, racism, corruption and seven steps necessary to improve our nation's police* (2nd ed.). Scotts Valley, CA: CreateSpace Independent Publishing Platform.

Crank, John P. and Robert Langworthy (1992). Institutional perspective on policing. *Journal of Criminal Law and Criminology, 83*(2): 338–363.

Daughen, Joseph and Binzen, Peter (1977). *The cop who would be king: Mayor Frank Rizzo.* Boston: Little Brown.

Davis, Kenneth (1975). *Police discretion.* St. Paul, MN: West Publishing.

Day, Frank D. (1956). The issue of one-man vs. two-man patrol cars. *Journal of Criminal Law and Criminology, 46*(5): 698–706.

DNAinfo Staff (2016). How seeing Rev. King speak in Chicago changed Hillary Clinton's life. *DNAinfo.* July 28.

Donovan, John (2005). I have no use for this fellow Parker: William H. Parker of the LAPD and his feud with J. Edgar Hoover and the FBI. *Southern California Quarterly, 87*(2): 171–198.

Dornfeld, A.A. (1983). *Behind the front page: The story of the City News Bureau of Chicago.* Chicago, IL: Academy Chicago Publishers.

Drennan, Patrick (2014). TCR talks: A chauffeur and admirer remembers his times with Martin Luther King. *The Chicago Reporter.* January 20.

Eck, John E. and Spelman, William (1987). *Problem solving: Problem oriented policing in Newport news.* Washington, D.C.: Police Executive Research Forum.

Flood, Dawn (2012). *Rape in Chicago: Rape, myth, and the courts.* Champaign, IL: University of Illinois Press.

Ford, Liam T. (2009). *Soldier field: A stadium and its city.* Chicago, IL: University of Chicago Press.

Frizell, Sam (2016). Photographer says disputed 1962 photo really does show Bernie Sanders. *Time.* February 13.

Fyfe, James and Jerome Skolnick (1993). *Above the law: Police and the excessive use of force.* New York, NY: The Free Press.

Fyfe, James, Jack Greene, William Walsh, O.W. Wilson, and Roy McLaren (1997). Police administration (5th Edition). New York, NY: McGraw-Hill Publishing.

Giancana, Bettina and Chuck Gianacana. (1992). *Double cross: The explosive, inside story of the mobster who controlled America.* New York, NY: Grand Central Publishing.

Goldstein, Herman (1963a). Police discretion: The ideal versus the real. *Public Administration Review 140.* University of Wisconsin Legal Studies Research Paper No. 1335.

Goldstein, Herman (1963b). Guidelines for effective use of police manpower. *Police Management 45*: 218–222.

Goldstein, Herman (1975). *Police corruption: A perspective on its nature and control.* Washington, DC: National Police Foundation.

Goldstein, Herman (1977). *Policing a free society.* Cambridge, MA: Ballinger Publishing Company.

Goldstein, Herman (1979). Improving policing: A problem-oriented approach. *Crime & Delinquency, 25*(2): 236–258.

Goldstein, Herman (1987). Toward community-oriented policing: Potential basic recruitment and threshold questions. *Crime and Delinquency, 33*(1): 1–21.

Goldstein, Herman (1990). *Problem-oriented policing.* Philadelphia, PA: Temple University Press.

Goldstein, Joseph (1960). Police discretion not to invoke the criminal process: Low-visibility decisions in the administration of justice. *The Yale Law Journal, 69*(4): 543–594.

Green, Ryan (2019). *The townhouse massacre: The unforgettable crimes of Richard Speck.* Herefordshire, England: Ryan Green Books.

Haller, Mark (1970). Civic reformers and police leadership: Chicago 1905–1935. In Harlan Hahn (Ed.), *Police in urban society.* Beverly Hills, California: Sage.

Haller, Mark (1976). Historical roots of police behavior: Chicago, 1890–1925. *Law and Society Review, 10*: 303–323.

Halvorsen, David (1966). Kerner heeds pleas of suburb officials: Order soldiers to shoot if fired upon. *Chicago Tribune.* September 3.

Harring, Sidney (1981). The taylorization of police work: Policing in the 1980s. *The Insurgent Sociologist, 10*(4): 25–32.

Haynes, F.E. (1949). The sociological study of the prison community. *Journal of Criminal Law and Criminology, 39*(4): 432–440.

Hinkle, Joshua, David Weisburd, Cody Telep, and Kevin Peterson (2020). Problem-oriented policing for reducing crime and disorder. Oslo, Norway: Campbell Collaboration Systematic Review Final Report.

Howard, Jane Robinson (1972). *August Vollmer: Pioneer in police professionalism.* University of California. Bancroft Library Berkeley Regional Oral History Office. The Regents of the University of California. Berkeley, CA.

Jeffrey, C. Ray (1977). *Crime prevention through environmental design.* Beverley Hill, CA: Sage Publication.

Johnson, Dirk (1996). Killer's prison video sparks Illinois lawmakers' outrage. *New York Times.* May 16.

Johnson, Richard R. (2005). Police uniform color and citizen impression formation. *Journal of Police and Criminal Psychology, 20*(2): 58–66.

Johnson, Ted (2020). Fox news anchor Harris Faulkner presses Donald Trump on use of phrase "When the looting starts, the shooting starts." *Deadline*. June 11.

Kaplan, E. H. (1979) Evaluating the effectiveness of one-officer versus two-officer patrol units. *Journal of Criminal Justice, 7*: 325–355.

Kass, John and William Recktenwald (1991). Daley says top cop search open: Mayor denies administration pursued Southern chief. *Chicago Tribune*. October 29.

Kelling, George L. (1992). Toward new images of policing: Herman Goldstein's Problem-Oriented Policing. Law & Social Inquiry *17*(3): 539–559.

Kelling, George L. and James K. Stewart (1991). The evolution of contemporary policing. In William A. Geller (Ed.), *Local government police management* (pp. 5–6). Washington, D.C.: International City Management Association.

Kelling, George L. and James Q. Wilson (1982). Broken windows: The police and neighborhood safety. *Atlantic Monthly 249*(3): 29–38.

Kelly, Joyce (2009). First African-American secret service agent to speak in Franklin. *The Milford Daily News*. February 25.

Kirby, Stuart and Ian McPherson (2004). Integrating the National Intelligence Model with a 'problem solving' approach. Safer Communities 3(2): 36–46.

Klockars, Carl. (1985). The idea of police. *Volume 3 of law and criminal justice series*. University of Michigan: Sage Publications.

Klockars, Carl. and Stephen Mastrofski (1991). *Thinking about crime: contemporary readings* (2nd ed.). New York, NY: McGraw-Hill.

Kotz, Nick (2005). *Judgment days: Lyndon Baines Johnson, Martin Luther King, Jr., and the laws that changed America*. New York, NY: Houghton Mifflin Company.

Kusch, Frank (2008). *Battleground Chicago: The police and the 1968 democratic national convention*. Chicago, IL: The University of Chicago Press.

Lane, Roger (1992). Urban police and crime in the nineteenth-century America. *Crime and Justice, 15*: 1–50.

Lindberg, Richard (1991). *To serve and collect: Chicago politics and police corruption from the Lager Beer riot to Summerdale scandal*. New York, NY: Praeger.

Lipskey, Michael (1969). Toward a theory of street-level bureaucracy. *Paper presented at the 1969 Annual Meeting of the American Political Science Association*.

Lipskey, Michael (2010). *Street-level bureaucracy: Dilemmas of the individual in public serves, 30th anniversary expanded edition*. New York, NY: Russell Sage Foundation.

Littell, Julia and Howard White (2018). The Campbell collaboration: Providing better evidence for a better world. *Research on Social Work Practice, 28*(1): 6–12.

Manning, Peter (1997). *Police work: The social organization of policing* (2nd ed.). Prospect Heights, IL: Waveland Press.

McLaren, Roy (1973). In memoriam: Orlando W. Wilson. *Police Chief Magazine, 107*: 12.

Murphy, Patrick and Thomas Plate (1977). *Commissioner: A view from the top of American law enforcement*. New York, NY: Simon and Schuster.

Newman, Donald J. (1993). The American Bar Foundation survey and the development of criminal justice higher education. In Lloyd Ohlin and Frank Remington (Eds.), *Discretion in criminal justice: The tension between individualization and uniformity*. Albany, NY: State University of New York Press.

Newman, Oscar (1973). *Defensible space through urban design*. New York, NY: Collier Publishing.

Mazerolle, Lorraine Green, James F. Price, and Jan Roehl. (2000). Civil remedies and drug control: A randomized field trial in Oakland, California. *Evaluation Review, 24*(2): 212–241.

Mazerolle, Lorraine (2020). Herman Goldstein (1931–2020). A tribute. *Policing and Society, 30*(3): 349–354.

Mendell, David (1998). Julius Lucius 'Lucky' Echeles 83, high-rolling defense lawyer. *Chicago Tribune*. September 6.

Millie, Andrew and Victoria Herrington (2005). Bridging the Gap: Understanding Reassurance policing. Howard Journal of Criminal Justice *44*(1) 41–56.

Miner, Craig (1982). *Wichita, the early years, 1865–1880*. Lincoln, NE: University of Nebraska Press.

Morn, Frank (1995). *Academic politics and the history of criminal justice education*. Westport, CT: Greenwood Publishing Group.

Ohlin, Lloyd E. and Richard A. Cloward (1960). *Delinquency and opportunity: A theory of delinquent gangs.* Glencoe, IL: Free Press.

Otto, Richard (2017). *The paradox of our national security complex: How secrecy and security diminish our liberty and threaten our democratic republic.* Alresford, Hants, UK: Chronos Books, John Hunt Publishing.

Parker, Alfred (1961). *Crime fighter: August Vollmer.* New York, NY: The Macmillan Company.

Pepper, William (2016). *The plot to kill King: The truth behind the assassination of Martin Luther King, Jr.* New York, NY: Skyhorse Publishing.

Peterson, Virgil W. (1960). A report on Chicago crime for 1959. *A report on Chicago crime for 1959.* Chicago, IL: Chicago Crime Commission. July 26.

Posner, Gerald (2013). *Killing the dream: James Earl Ray and the assassination of Martin Luther King, Jr.* New York, NY: Open Road.

President's Commission on Law Enforcement and Administration of Justice (1967). *The challenge of crime in a free society.* U.S. Department of Justice: National Institute of Justice. February, 340 pages.

Ratcliffe, Jerry (2016). Intelligence-*led* policing (2nd Edition). Abingdon, UK: Routledge Publishing.

Reeves, Troy (2016). Interview with Herman Goldstein. University of Wisconsin Law School library. Oral History Project. October 26 and November 2.

Roemer, William F. (1996). *Accardo: The genuine godfather.* New York, NY: Ivy Books

Robinson, Jane (1972). *August Vollmer: Pioneer in police professionalism.* Berkeley: Regional Oral History Office. The Bancroft Library, University of California.

Rosen, Marie (1997). Professor Herman Goldstein, the "father" of problem-oriented policing. *Law Enforcement News*, 8–14. https://media.law.wisc.edu/m/jfhyt/law_enforcement_news_feb_14_1997_volxxiii_no461.pdf.

Rumbaut, Ruben and Egon Bittner (1979). Changing conceptions of the police role: A sociological review. *Crime and Justice, 1*: 239–288.

Sato, Mia (2019). What the Gov: Why is she called 'Alderman'? Better Government Association. *Better Government Agency.* April 18.

Scott, Michael (2010). Policing and police research: Learning to listen, with a Wisconsin case study. *Police Practice and Research, 11*(2): 95–104.

Scott, Michael and Stuart Kirby (2012). *Implementing POP: Leading, structuring, and managing a problem-oriented police agency.* Washington, DC: US Department of Justice, Office of Community-Oriented Police, Center for Problem-Oriented Policing.

Scott, Michael (2016). Pioneers in policing: Herman Goldstein. *Police Practice and Research: An International Journal, 17*(6): 582–595.

Scott, Michael and Herman Goldstein (2005). *Shifting and sharing responsibility for public safety problems.* Washington, DC: US Department of Justice, Problem-Oriented Response Guide Series No. 3, Center for Problem-Oriented Policing. University of Wisconsin Legal Studies Research Paper, No. 1340.

Scott, Michael and Herman Goldstein (2012). Ron Clarke's contribution to improving policing: A diffusion of benefits. In Nick Tilley and Graham Farrell (Eds.), *The reasoning criminologist: Essays in honour of Ronald V. Clarke* . New York, NY: Routledge.

Sherman, Lawrence (1998). *Evidence-based policing: Ideas in American policing series.* Washington, DC: Police Foundation. www.policefoundation.org.

Sherman, Lawrence, Michael Buerger, and Patrick Gartin. (1989) *Repeat call address policing: The Minneapolis RECAP experiment.* Washington, DC: Crime Control Institute.

Sherman, Lawrence and Robert Langworthy (1979). "Measuring homicide by police officers." *The Journal of Criminal Law and Criminology, 70*(4): 546–560.

Silverman, Eli (2006). Compstat innovation. In David Weisburd and Anthony Braga (Eds.), Police Innovation: Contrasting perspectives (pp. 267–300). Cambridge, UK: Cambridge University Press.

Skogan, Wesley and Kathleen Frydl (2004). *Fairness and effectiveness in policing: The evidence.* Washington, DC: National Research Council. National Academies Press.

Smith, Carlton (2007). *The BTK murders: Inside the "Bind Torture Kill" case that Terrified America's Heartland.* New York, NY: St. Martin's Press.

Stokes, Robert, Neil Donahue, Dawn Caron, and Jack R. Greene. (1996). *Safe travel to and from school: A problem-oriented policing approach.* Washington, DC: National Institute of Justice, Office of Justice Programs, U.S. Department of Justice.

Stone, Rick (2000). *Behind the gold star*. Lincoln, NE: Writers Showcase.

Stone, Sandra S. (1993). *Problem-oriented policing approach to drug enforcement: Atlanta as a case study*. Atlanta, GA: Dissertation submitted to Emory University.

Sousa, William and George Kelling (2006). Of "Broken Windows," criminology and criminal justice. In David Weisburd and Anthony Braga (Eds.), Police innovation: Contrasting perspectives. New York, NY: Cambridge University Press.

Taylor, Frederick Winslow (1911). *The principles of scientific management*. New York: Harper & Brothers.

Thomas III, George R. (1998). *Coordinated Agency Network (C.A.N.)*. San Diego Police Department. Madison, WI: Herman Goldstein Award Submission for the Center for Problem-Oriented Policing.

Thornton, Jerry (1993). James B. Parsons, 1st Black U.S. judge. *Chicago Tribune*. June 21.

Trojanowicz, Robert (1994). *Understanding community policing: A framework for action*. Washington, DC: U.S. Bureau of Justice Monograph Series. U.S. Department of Justice.

Tuffin, Rachel, Julia Morris and Alexis Poole. (2006). *An evaluation of the impact of the National Reassurance Policing Programme. Home Office Research Study 296*. London: Home Office Research, Development and Statistics Directorate.

Uchida, Craig (1993). The development of American police: An historical overview. In Robert Dunham and Geoff Alpert (Eds.), *Critical Issues in Policing: Contemporary Readings*. Prospect Heights, IL: Waveland Press.

Wallis, Michael (1992). *Pretty boy: The life and times of Charles Arthur Floyd*. New York, NY: W.W. Norton & Company, Inc.

Ward, Bernard J. (2000). Orlando W. Wilson and the development of his education and training policies while superintendent of the Chicago Police Department, 1960–1967. *Dissertation in Educational leadership and policy studies, Loyola University Chicago*. Ann Arbor, MI: UMI Dissertation Services.

Walker, Samuel and Charles Katz (2018). *The police in America: An introduction* (10th ed.). New York, NY: McGraw-Hill.

Weisburd, David, Cody Telep, Joshua Hinkle, and John Eck (2008). *Effects of problem-oriented policing on crime and disorder*. Oslo, Norway: Campbell Collaboration Systematic Review Final Report.

Weisburd, David, Cody Telep, Joshua Hinkle, and John Eck (2010). Is problem-oriented policing effective in reducing crime and disorder? *Criminology & Public Policy, 9*(1): 139–172.

Weisburd, David and Anthony Braga (2006). Hot spots policing as a model for police innovation. In David Weisburd and Anthony Braga (Eds.), Police innovation: Contrasting perspectives. New York, NY: Cambridge University Press.

Weisburd, David and Lorraine Green (1995). Policing drug hotspots: The Jersey City drug market analysis experiment. *Justice Quarterly, 12*(4): 711–735.

Weistart, John C. (1974). *President's commission on law enforcement, task force report: The police*. Dobbs Ferry, NY: Oceana Publications.

Wiedrich, Robert (1964). Wilson admits mob tie probe of city police. *Chicago Tribune*. February 27.

Wilber, Del Quentin (2011). Charles Gittens, secret service agent, 82. *Washington Post*. August 11.

William, Lee and Jason Wambsgans (2019). 'Ready to explode': How a black teen's drifting raft triggered a deadly week of riots 100 years ago in Chicago. *Chicago Tribune*. July 21.

Williamson, Roger E. (2001). *Wichita police department, 1871–2000*. Wichita, KS: Wichita Police Benefit Fund Association.

Willis, James, Stephen Mastrofski, and Tammy Kochel (2010). *Maximizing the benefits of reform: Integrating Compstat and community policing in America*. Washington, DC: U.S. Department of Justice, Office of Community-Oriented Policing Services.

Wilson, Orlando W. (1934). What can be done about crime? *Journal of the Kansas Bar Association*, 3(1): 177–185.

Wilson, Orlando W. (1941). *Distribution of police patrol force*. Chicago, IL: Public Administration Service.

Wilson, Orlando W. (1950). *Police administration*. New York, NY: McGraw-Hill.

Wilson, Orlando W. (1963). *Police administration* (2nd ed.). New York, NY: McGraw-Hill.

Wilson, Orlando W. and Roy C. McLaren (1972). *Police administration* (3rd ed.). New York, NY: McGraw-Hill.

Wilson, Orlando W. and Roy C. McLaren (1977). *Police administration* (4th ed.). New York, NY: McGraw-Hill.

Wilson, Reid (2020). Philadelphia removes statue of ex-mayor seen as 'deplorable monument to racism, bigotry, and police brutality. *The Hill*. June 3.

Woltman, George (1960). Top cop posts now in hands of outsiders: Wilson brings in his own team. *Chicago Tribune*. October 2.

Chapter 4

Penny Harrington – Portland Feminism and the Nation's First Female Chief

America's First Female Police Chief

Penny Eileen Ledyard Orazetti Harrington, and the city of Portland, was the catalyst of many firsts for women in American policing. Female police matrons have existed since the mid-1800s. However, with some controversy explained below, Portland appointed the nation's first official policewoman in 1908, when Lola Baldwin became the Superintendent of the Women's Protective Division. Penny[1] became Portland's first police sergeant, first lieutenant, first captain, and finally first chief in 1985, making her the first woman to lead a major urban police department.

Women in Policing Today

The number of women police officers has not changed much in the past couple of decades, especially within higher ranks. Women comprise slightly more than 12 percent, or 58,000, sworn law enforcement officers across the United States (Hyland & Davis, 2019), about the same number of African-American officers. This percent is smaller than the 15 percent of females that make up branches of the United States Military. The 12 percent of female sworn officers is about a 4 percent increase over the past 25 years when the inception of the Law Enforcement Management and Administrative Statistics (LEMAS) Survey was completed in 1987. In urban departments (over 1 million residents), female officers represent 18 percent of sworn compared to only 7 percent of sworn officers in departments servicing fewer than 10,000 residents. While there has historically been over 200 female police chiefs, almost all of these have been in command of departments with less than 1,000 officers. Table 4.1 lists female police chiefs from large city departments that followed Penny Harrington.

Table 4.1 Women Municipal Police Leaders for Large Cities (Black Leaders in Italics)

Name	*City*	*Years*
Penny Harrington	Portland	*1985–1986*
Elizabeth Watson	Houston	*1990–1992*
	Austin	*1992–1997*

1 Throughout the chapter, "Penny" will be referenced by her first name, unlike other chapters that use the police leader's last name. This is done to avoid confusion for the reader as she did not take the "Harrington" name until 1982 from her second husband, Gary, who was also a PPB officer. Penny's maiden name was Ledyard, and Orazetti was her first husband's last name.

DOI: 10.4324/9780429272226-5

Table 4.1 Cont.

Name	*City*	*Years*
Beverley Harvard[i]	Atlanta	1994–2002
Mary Bounds	Cleveland	2001–2002
Shirlene Anderson	Jackson, MS	2002–2005
Ella Bully-Cummings[ii]	Detroit	2003–2008
Annetta Watts Nunn[iii]	Birmingham	2003–2008
Heather Fong[iv]	San Francisco	2004–2009
Kathleen O'Toole	Boston	2004–2006
	Seattle	2014–2017
Rosie Sizer	Portland	2006–2010
Cathy Lanier[v]	Washington, DC	2007–2016
Rebecca Coleman	Jackson, MS	2009–2013
Jane Castor[vi]	Tampa	2009–2015
Michelle Freeman	Las Vegas Public Safety	2011–2020
Sheilah Coley	Newark	2011–2014
	Trenton	2019–
Janee Harteau	Minneapolis[vii]	2012–2017
Kim Jacobs	Columbus	2012–2019
Carmen Best[viii]	Seattle	2013–2020
Cassandra Deck-Brown	Raleigh	2013–2021
Shelley Zimmerman	San Diego	2014–2018
Ivonne Roman[ix]	Newark	2014–2014
Deborah Black	Glendale, AZ	2014–2016
	Prescott, AZ	2016–2021

i After taking a bet from her husband and his friend, Harvard entered the Atlanta Police Academy in 1973 to prove that she could make it through. She went on to become the first Black Female Chief in America. In 2002, she was named Security Director for the U.S. Transportation Administration, and in 2010 President Obama named her U.S. Marshal for the Northern District of Georgia.

ii Bully-Cummings completed her law degree from MSU and has a legal firm in Detroit.

iii Nunn is a life-long member of the Twenty-Third Street Baptist Church and serves as a Sunday school teacher and Christian education director.

iv Fong was San Francisco's first female chief and the first Asian-American big city chief.

v After her retirement, Lanier became Senior Vice President, Chief Security Officer for the National Football League (NFL).

vi Castor was a Republican until 2015 when she retired from law enforcement. She then became a member of the Democratic Party and in 2019, she was elected 59th Mayor of Tampa, Florida. Note: The first female mayor of a major American city was Bertha Ethel Knight in Seattle from 1926 to 1928.

vii Harteau's resignation followed the accidental fatal shooting of Justine Ruszczyk Damond, a white female from Australia, by Black police officer Mohammed Noor from Somalia. (This incident occurred shortly after the acquittal of Latino officer Jeronimo Yanez in Philando Castile's shooting in 2016 in Falcon Heights, Minnesota.) Officer Noor was convicted of third-degree murder and sentenced to 12 years in prison. The city settled a lawsuit with the Damond family for $20 million, one of the largest wrongly death lawsuits involving a police officer (Lartey & Weichselbaum, 2020). George Floyd's family settled their civil suit for $27 million after the city council voted 13-0 to approve the funds including $500,000 to build a George Floyd Memorial at the intersection of 38th and Chicago Avenue. Noor and Chauvin were the first officers in Minnesota to be convicted of murder.

viii Best blamed her resignation on the city council, who cut her salary and her command staff salary. As part of the 2020 defunding movement, $4 million was cut from the SPD budget and they needed to reduce as many as 100 officers. In October 2020, it was announced that Best was hired as a law enforcement analyst for NBC's Seattle news affiliate, *KING5*.

ix Roman served as the first Latino police chief for five months before Ras Baraka was elected Newark Mayor and replaced her. Roman held a fellowship with the NIJ and the Police Foundation.

Table 4.1 Cont.

Name	*City*	*Years*
Erika Shields	Atlanta	2016–2020
	Louiseville	2021–
Sylvia Moir	Tempe	2016–2020
Roxana Kennedy	Chula Vista	2016–
Kristen Ziman[x]	Aurora, IL	2016–2021
Cerelyn "C.J." Davis	Durham	2016–
Jeri Williams	Phoenix	2016–
Susan Ballard	Honolulu	2017–
Gina Hawkins[xi]	Fayetteville	2017–
Anne Kirkpatrick	Oakland	2017–2020
Renee Hall	Dallas	2017–2020
Catrina Thompson	Winston-Salem	2017–
Danielle Outlaw	Portland	2017–2019
	Philadelphia	2019–
Pamela Ojeda	North Las Vegas	2018–
Jami Resch	Portland	2019–2020
Maris Herold[xii]	Boulder, CO	2020–
Vanessa Wilson	Aurora, CO	2020–
Mary Barton	St. Louis County	2020–
Bisa French	Richmond, CA	2020–
Yvette Gentry (interim)[xiii]	Louisville	2020–2021
Cynthia Herriott-Sullivan[xiv]	Rochester	2020–
Sheryl Victorian[xv]	Waco, TX	2021–
Tawana Moody[xvi]	Jersey City, NJ	2021–
Elaine Bryant	Columbus, OH	2021–
Estella Patterson	Raleigh	2021–

Noteworthy is the seven women chiefs that have resigned in 2020 amid the mass police protests: Best (Seattle), Shields (Atlanta), Moir (Tempe), Kirkpatrick (Oakland), Hall (Dallas), Freeman (Las Vegas Public Safety), and Resch (Portland).[2]

Females constitute approximately 10 percent of first-line supervisors and 3 percent of local police chiefs, arguing that gender discrimination through a "brass ceiling" (instead of a glass ceiling) continues to plague female officers. Table 4.2 provides a summarized total.

x Ziman received her undergraduate degree from Aurora University and two subsequent graduate degrees. She was a finalist for both the Chicago Police Department's Superintendent position and the Nashville Police Department's chief position.

xi Hawkins became the first woman and first Black police chief in Fayetteville. At the same time, five other Black women were police chiefs in smaller agencies in North Carolina.

xii Herold was previously the Chief for the University of Cincinnati Police Division (UCPD). Her work was recognized for the Herman Goldstein Award at the 2017 Problem-Oriented Policing conference.

xiii Gentry became the first Black woman to lead the Louisville Metro Police Department. She came out of retirement to become the interim chief on October 1, 2020, in the aftermath of the fatal police shooting of 26-year-old EMT Breonna Taylor (March 13, 2020) during a no-knock warrant execution at her apartment. For the first time in 20 years, the September 2020 edition of *The Oprah "O"* magazine did not feature Oprah Winfrey on its cover, but instead a photo of Breonna Taylor.

xiv Herriott-Sullivan became Rochester's first female chief after the in-custody hospitalization and subsequent death of Daniel Prude (also footnoted in the Ramsey chapter).

xv Victorian came through the ranks of the Houston Police Department rising to deputy chief.

xvi Moody is also the first non-sworn civilian to lead the Jersey City Police Department.

2 See Schulz (2020).

Table 4.2 Percentage of Females in Law Enforcement

Population Residents	*% Female Sworn*	*% Female First-Line Supervisor*
Combined total	12.3	9.5
Over 1 million	17.8	15
Less than 10,000	7.3	6

Female officers have been referred to as tokens in some jurisdictions, especially in smaller agencies, and no community has reached Kanter's (1977) balanced ratio of 60:40. In the National Center for Women & Policing study, Pittsburgh and Washington, DC had the highest number of female officers, with approximately 25 percent of sworn officers being female. Both departments had been under consent decrees, and Pittsburgh had over 37 percent of their command staff positions held by females. However, these command positions declined after the consent decree was lifted (Martin & Jurik, 2007). Despite these challenges, women in policing have made strides since their earliest inception into the criminal justice system.

Policewomen Pioneers – Laying the Groundwork

Because of the non-standard historical methods used to appoint females to police functions and the questions on their legal authority, determining who was the country's first official policewoman is difficult. Women have always worked in various capacities within American law enforcement but, in the past, exclusively relegated to corrections and social work positions dealing primarily with juveniles and family disputes (Cordner, 2019). Females were encouraged to play a rehabilitative role within the criminal justice system by many religious organizations such as the National Woman's Christian Temperance Association who gave the following report in 1845:

> *During the last half of the nineteenth century, women's organizations manifested an interest in securing the appointment of women for the special handling of women and girls held in custody by law enforcing agencies – police, sheriffs, superintendents of jails, detention homes, institutions for the insane, and any publically controlled institutions. The records show that in 1845 two such appointments were made, through the interest of the American Female Society, and two matrons were appointed in New York City at the City Prison (The Tombs) and four on Blackwell's Island – the first prison matrons in this country. Particularly active in the field of organizations to secure women in the service was the Women's Christian Temperance Union. Their early records report that in the 1870s prominent members of that group in Portland, Maine, visited the women prisoners and attended court, and in 1877 they employed a paid visitor. Soon after, one-half of her salary was paid by the city. The next year the city paid her salary in full, and she became a police matron.*[3]

Female matrons were encouraged to work inside jails to help correct situations where female inmates were being housed with male inmates or were being sexually exploited by male guards. Most of the female inmates were mentally ill, homeless, or alcoholics and easily manipulated. The male-dominated justice agencies did not welcome the female matrons believing their work with the vile offending population was no place for respectable pure-minded women.

3 The report came from minutes of the National Woman's Christian Temperance Union's annual meeting from Mrs. J.K. Barney, Department Secretary for work in Prisons, Jails, Police, and Alms Homes out of Providence, Rhode Island.

They also worried the matrons were spies for the media, and they would publish stories that would make the correctional system look bad to the public. Attempts to hold off hiring matrons began with claims that budgets did not exist to pay them. However, lobbying groups began funding the matrons directly, and eventually, state laws mandated the presence of matrons (Mishkin, 1981), and they continued to receive support from various temperance leaders. In 1845, Flora Foster worked in the New York City (NYC) Prison, known as the Tombs, and became one of the first documented matrons.

The police, and firefighters, have historically been one of the most masculine occupations in America. Dorothy Schulz, a professor of law, police studies, and criminal justice administration at John Jay College of Criminal Justice in NYC, has done a considerable amount of research looking at how women have broken into male-dominated policing. She was also the first captain to serve with the Metro-North Commuter Railroad Police Department (formerly the Conrail Police Department) before completing her Ph.D. from New York University in 1992. Schulz details how the women's matron history focused on using their unique female role and how this evolved into attempts at a unisex role with male colleagues (Schultz, 1995, 2003). Further, she writes about how the policewomen movement's roots came through force and an abundance of conflict with unwilling political establishments and police hierarchy. While the initial demands on women's entry into the police were limited and specialized based upon gender stereotypes, demands for equality by frontline leaders such as Penny Harrington pushed against the limitations that these stereotypes provided. The courageous demands ultimately pushed women to be involved in uniform patrol and then leadership positions with male subordinates.

Who's the "First" Policewoman? (Chicago, Los Angeles, or Portland)

American cities were organizing their first police departments during the same period women reformists were advocating for larger public roles through the Temperance Movement, voting rights, and protecting child welfare. Before the formation of police departments, policing was dependent on volunteers and private security for those who could pay for protection. It is not until the Progressive Era and the passage of Prohibition that policing became a career option for both men and women. However, the police professionalization movement was still in its infancy stages with reform advocates like August Vollmer and O.W. Wilson. For almost the first century of policing, departments mainly hired under-educated and lower-class male immigrants. High school diplomas only became mandatory for most police department hiring in the 1950s (Schulz, 1995).

In contrast, the first policewomen who appeared on the urban landscape were overwhelmingly upper-middle-class, native-born, and college-educated social workers. Despite their higher education levels, the pioneers of women in policing receive significantly less pay than male policemen. Also, women were relegated to social work positions that dealt exclusively with crimes perpetrated against other women and their children.

Chicago

In 1889, Chicago passed an ordinance forbidding the employment of children under the age of 14. This ordinance led Marie Owens and five other women to be hired by the Commissioner of Health for $50 a month to investigate factories and stores for child labor violations. They also investigated absentee fathers and turned the cases over to the police. A year before being hired by the Commissioner of Health, Owens lost her husband, who was also the father to her five children, from typhoid fever. In 1891, General Superintendent of Police Robert McClaughry[4] hired Owens as a detective sergeant. As a reform leader within the Chicago Police Department (CPD), McClaughry had a deep concern for rehabilitating juvenile offenders and sought out Owens to assist the detective bureau. Owens retired in 1923, at the age of 70, after 32 years of service, and moved to New York to live with her daughter until her death in 1927.[5] Her obituary did not mention her police service. Her work faded into history until Rick Barrett, a retired DEA agent with multiple family connections in the CPD, discovered and alleged he corrected the first American policewoman's historical accuracy (Mastony, 2010). Marie Owens's story appears to have been confused with the 1893 CPD hiring of Mary Owens, a Chicago policeman's widow.

The hiring of widows followed a national pattern as an alternative to pensions or death benefits that were nonexistent. However, Mary Owens was given the title and pay of a "policeman" rather than a matron and assisted detectives on cases involving women and children (Schulz, 1995, p. 30). In either case, historians believe Marie and/or Mary Owens were the first policewomen that differed from early matrons. Criminologist Lois Higgins[6] pointed out the importance of policewomen as distinguished from matrons (Higgins, 1950). However, it would not be until 1974 the CPD used females for regular patrol and provided them with standardized police uniforms.[7]

Los Angeles

The Los Angeles Police Department (LAPD) also claims they hired the first American-born policewoman on September 10, 1910. The 350-member LAPD hired 37-year-old former Kansas minister Alice Stebbins Wells and gave her full arrest authority (Schulz, 1995; Segrave, 1995). In actuality, Wells practically hired herself after she presented the mayor and police chief with a petition signed by more than 100 influential citizens who advocated for hiring a policewoman to protect and prevent victimization of women and children. *The Herald* ran the following article:

> *NEW POLICE OFFICER ASSUMES HER DUTIES – 'PATROLMAN' WELLS GIVEN STAR. If you happen to be prowling around the streets late at night in a suspicious manner and are arrested by a woman who informs you in a gentle voice she is an officer of the law and then flashes a star on you to make you believe it don't be alarmed or ask any questions, but give an explanation, for it will be Alice Stebbins Wells, the only woman on the department of Los Angeles.*
>
> (Bultema, 2013)

4 McClaughry graduated from Monmouth College in Illinois in 1860. He was the Illinois State Reformatory warden in Pontiac and Joliet before leading the CPD from 1891 to 1893. He also led the federal prison in Leavenworth, Kansas, and was an early advocate for penal reform to replace retributive punishment with work to save young inmates. McClaughry was one of the founding members of the National Association of Chiefs of Police (today the IACP) and the National Prison Association (today the American Corrections Association) (Morn, 2010).

5 See Chicagology – https://chicagology.com/chicagopolice/marieowens/.

6 Higgins was the Director of the Chicago Crime Prevention Bureau for 14 years. She was hired as a policewoman in Chicago in 1937 and later became an instructor at Loyola University in the Institute of Social Administration.

7 In a proceeding chapter, Chuck Ramsey commented that the first female patrol officers at the CPD in the 1970s helped create a bond between Black and white officers who were often in conflict when working in what was referred to as "salt and pepper" police cars. The new women patrol officers created somewhat of a common enemy for the male officers – author's interview with Ramsey on August 20, 2020.

Wells was a Puritan-raised New Englander who actively lobbied for her position in the LAPD as a means for applying her Christianity. After being hired, she took on the role of the social worker and the prevention of crime. Although she had full arrest authority, she did not wear a standard uniform, did not carry a weapon, and worked the streets with no more than a rule book and call box key. A little over five-feet tall, some community members accused Wells of using her husband's badge to get free rides on the streetcars. In response, the LAPD created a badge that read "Police Woman's Badge No. 1" signifying she was the woman hired into the LAPD (Feinman, 1986). During her immorality crusades on foot patrol, Wells made 13 arrests during her first year on the job (Eisenberg, 2009). By 1913, the LAPD swore in two more female officers along with 16 other cities. From 1912 to 1914, Wells gave 136 speeches (an uncommon activity for women) in 23 cities across the United States and Canada (Schulz, 1995, p. 37) supporting women police officers. She also spoke at the 1914 annual meeting for the International Association of Chiefs of Police (IACP). August Vollmer, detailed in a previous chapter and an advocate for women officers and the social work aspect of police reform, reflected on Wells's 1914 IACP speech:

> *There was an acid comment (by) the men ... They couldn't see why any woman should want to work around a police station; ... They all but put Mrs. Wells out of the meeting. So forcefully, however, did she present her argument that women and children, and especially wayward girls, were best served by women officers that many of those who arrived scoffing remained – convinced.*
>
> (Vollmer, 1930)

It is interesting to note that 1914 marked the first use of radio communications between officers in Berkeley. That year Vollmer also created the first juvenile officers. He saw the need to hire women officers to support advances in technology and crime prevention aimed at juvenile offenders. In 1925, Vollmer hired the first college-trained woman officer, Elizabeth Gurnell Anderson Lossing, to supervise a crime prevention unit. Vollmer advocated for a criminological understanding of criminal behavior, emphasizing crime prevention rather than an exclusive reaction that had become dominated by cues of masculinity.

In 1923, the LA Crime Commission invited Vollmer to reorganize the LAPD as their chief. His plan called for a crime prevention unit that pushed for interdependent collaboration with the city's mother's bureau, juvenile bureau, parole boards, and the female probation unit to focus on early juvenile delinquency (Schulz, 1995, p. 140). Wells and the other female LAPD officers would have played a key role in Vollmer's reorganization plans, which never materialized since he chose to return to Berkeley. In the aftermath of the 1992 LA riots, the city council unanimously voted to require their police department to dramatically increase the hiring of female officers. The hiring of additional female officers was also suggested by the Christopher Commission, as described in the chapter on Bratton. A goal of 44 percent of women on the force by 1999 may have been unrealistic (Eisenberg, 2009). Today, women account for approximately 18 percent of the 10,000 LAPD officers.

In 1915, Wells organized the International Association of Women Police (IAWP),[8] originally called the International Association of Policewomen,[9] and became its first president. Three years later, she persuaded the University of California Southern Division (now UCLA) Criminology Department to offer a course on the specialty work done by women police officers. In 1915, Wells founded the International Association of Police Women (Bultema, 2013). This international association later became the Women's Peace Officers Association

8 Today, the IAWP includes members from 73 countries and holds annual conferences throughout the world.

9 See IAWP website – www.iawp.org/history.

of California, with Wells being the President. In 1934, Wells was named curator and LAPD historian until her retirement in 1945. She was 72 years old when she retired after 35 years of service. She passed away at the age of 84 in 1957 (Appier, 1998). Six years after they hired Wells, the LAPD also hired the first Black female, Georgia Robinson, in 1916, as a matron and then in 1919, as a policewoman (Schulz, 1995, p. 52).

Portland

Portland, Oregon has claimed that they hired the first female police detective sworn in specifically to do regular law enforcement. On February 12, 1908, the city passed an ordinance allowing the hiring of women police detectives. The Police Commission was responsible for all hiring and termination during this time, and they hired 48-year-old Aurora "Lola" Green Baldwin on April 1, 1908 (Myers, 1995). She was the first woman to be employed under civil service rules as a full-time paid non-uniformed police detective. Mayor Harry Lane[10] administered the official oath, and Baldwin reported directly to Chief Charles Critzmaucher. Baldwin was hired based upon her experience protecting young women who were part of the Lewis and Clark Centennial Exposition brought to Portland three years prior. Before being hired by the Portland police, she was the secretary of the Travelers Aid Society[11] and the Director of the Department of Public Safety for the Protection of Young Girls and Women. Portland relegated Baldwin's duties to social work and crime prevention rather than law enforcement, and she did not carry a weapon or wear a police uniform.

Baldwin's office was set up at the YMCA rather than in the exclusively male police headquarters. In 1922, she resigned at 62 years of age after 17 years of service, 14 of those years being a paid police officer. Baldwin passed away in 1957, at the age of 97 (Myers, 1995). She paved the way for creating the Women's Protective Division and hiring Penny in 1964. Portland appointed the country's first female police chief 77 years after they hired Baldwin.

Foundational Leadership – Lansing, Michigan

Penny Ledyard was born on March 2, 1942, in Lansing, Michigan. She was the first of four children born to Ed and Mary Ledyard and the first grandchild on both sides of the family. Penny became the first female to head a large city department when newly elected Mayor Bud Clark gave her the oath as the chief of the Portland Police Bureau (PPB) on January 24, 1985. Her position as chief only lasted a year and a half, and she resigned in June 1986. As detailed in her book, a *Triumph of Spirit* (Harrington, 1999), the ascent to this leadership position involved numerous challenges

Penny Ledyard grew up in Lansing, Michigan, within a lower-middle-class neighborhood. The neighborhood was diverse and little awareness of racial discrimination. Her father was

10 Lane, a physician by training, was appointed the superintendent of the Oregon Insane Asylum before becoming a two-time mayor (1905–1910) in a non-partisan reform campaign. Within his first year as mayor, he hosted the National American Woman Suffrage Association convention and brought the Rose Festival Parade to Portland in 1907. He was elected U.S. Senator (1913–1917) and advocated for Women's Suffrage. Germany granted national suffrage in 1918, and the United States did so in 1920. Lane was joined by five other senators who voted against declaring war against Germany in 1917. He battled Bright's disease and died shortly after his anti-war stance on his way back to Portland at the age of 61.

11 The Travelers Aid Society began in St. Louis in the 1850s to assist American pioneers and immigrants who became stranded, especially women and children who were susceptible to abuse and human trafficking. The society represents the oldest non-religious social welfare organization in the United States (Cimino, 2012).

a plant supervisor at a steel company that manufactured automobile wheels and a frequent union strife target. Due to her father's conflict with organized labor, Penny grew up being anti-union. Her mother was a secretary for a utility company but terminated when she got pregnant with Penny. Penny described her upbringing as genderless, with household workload divided amongst her siblings (Harrington, 1999). She was the oldest of four children.

Penny's brother Michael was two years younger and a graduate of Michigan State University (MSU). Michael was in Officer Candidate School (OSC) with the Army before going to Vietnam as a Lieutenant after college. Upon returning, Penny's brother worked for the Michigan Department of Transportation (MDOT) in the planning section. He died in 2015 with health issues he contracted in Vietnam linked to Agent Orange, a tactical herbicide our military utilized to clear vegetation with the goal of improving military operations.

Penny's sister Roberta is five years younger and followed her siblings' path earning an MSU degree. After visiting Penny in Portland, she became enamored with policing and eventually joined her sister at the PPB. Roberta retired from the PPB in 1997 as a deputy chief and also married a police captain.

Penny's youngest sibling, Russell, was ten years younger. Russel attended Olivet College in Olivet, Michigan, and graduated with a degree in hospitality management. He died at the age of 40 of liver failure.[12] Penny's parents encouraged her to attend college, work hard, and become a role model for her siblings. However, for Penny, women role models in professional positions were pragmatically nonexistent. There were no female lawyers, doctors, or dentists, and women were much more likely to be nurses, teachers, salesclerks, or homemakers.

Michigan State University – Police Administration

Penny attended Lansing Eastern High School from 1956 to 1960. During a career day, she met Lansing policewoman Sergeant Clarissa Young and was inspired to learn more about the police administration degree at MSU. Young told Penny she should complete her undergraduate degree before she attempted to gain employment in policing. At MSU, Penny would step into a university with an established history in training the country's future police leaders within its police administration program. Today, the program is referred to more generally as the School of Criminal Justice.

The roots of police education at MSU began when the Michigan State Police Commissioner, Oscar Olander,[13] proposed developing a police school at Michigan State College in the 1920s. Olander closely followed August Vollmer's ideas, chief in Berkeley, California (as detailed in chapter 2), who dedicated his career advocating for police higher education. In 1930, the university created a police school, but it only lasted a few years before being canceled due to the Great Depression (Morn, 1995). Olander was a colleague of LeMoyne Snyder, whose father Jonathan Snyder[14] was the former President of Michigan State Agricultural College from 1896 to 1915, 40 years after the college began. LeMoyne Snyder worked as a surgeon in New York and with the Army before returning home to study law in Lansing, Michigan. In 1933, he became the Medicolegal Director of the Michigan State Police and helped facilitate a state crime laboratory while proposing a forensic science police program at Michigan State College (Beal, 1989). Donald Bremer, the chief of the Michigan State College police

12 Author's interview with Penny on April 11, 2020.

13 Olander was the youngest and the longest serving commissioner of the Michigan State Police (1926–1947).

14 Jonathan Snyder was the seventh President of Michigan State Agricultural College, formerly renamed Michigan State College of Agriculture and Applied Science in 1925. Enrollment under Snyder's leadership increased from 300 to 2,000 students, and he advocated for training women at the college in domestic sciences.

department, assisted Snyder and Olander in a proposal to President Robert Shaw[15] to restart a police administration program.

In the fall of 1935, eight years into Shaw's presidency, the police administration program was officially launched at Michigan State College with 39 students (Morn, 1995). Instructors included a lawyer, a medical doctor, and various state police employees. It is worth noting the new dean's description of the new police science administration program. His description pushed for a militaristic program that mimicked the reform in the given era. The dean specified that

> *The graduates of the course be, first of all, well-trained college men with fundamental training in English and the sciences – both physical and social. That over-specialization be avoided in the first three years of training. That students be given instruction in criminal law and evidence. That the third year of training be given to a general survey in police science and administration. That after approximately three years of training at the college, intensive training at the State Police – along special lines for which his earlier training has fitted him. That four years of military science be required so the student may become trained in military discipline.*
>
> (Brandstetter, 1989)

After the students completed their academic curriculum, they went onto an 18-month field training program, expanding on O.W. Wilson's training program inside the Wichita Police, referred to as "the West Point of Law Enforcement" (Bopp, 1977, p. 58). From 1935 until World War II, the Police Administration Program at Michigan State College served as the West Point for the country's future police leaders (Morn, 1995) and is the longest continuous degree-granting higher education institution in criminal justice.

Penny entered MSU's police administration program 25 years after its inception.[16] During that time, only a few females majored in police administration out of several hundred male students. Despite the apparent gender imbalance, Penny did not perceive discrimination, even though her academic advisor directed her to take courses primarily in juvenile justice and child psychology. In contrast, the men took courses in criminal investigations and crime scene analysis. Penny did well in high school, earning mainly "A" grades, but she struggled initially in college courses while also working full-time. After she struggled academically, Penny decided to drop out of college, which quickly ended when she got a phone call from Sergeant Clarissa Young from the Lansing Police Department, who originally inspired her during her high school career day.[17] Sgt. Young told Penny she was disappointed and encouraged her to finish her degree, clearly not knowing that Penny's destiny called for far more than merely finishing her police administration degree.

In her junior year, Penny married Richard "Rick" Orazetti, whom she met while she was an MSU student from 1960 to 1964. Rick and Penny planned to have policing careers for five to ten years, get their Ph.D. degrees, teach college courses, and write books. One of their former professors, Dr. Sam Chapman (who taught at MSU from 1959 to 1963), was hired as the undersheriff at the Multnomah County Sheriff's Department, headquartered in Portland.

15 Shaw was married in Portland, Oregon, on January 2, 1900, and was the 11th President of Michigan State College from 1928 to 1941. He created several new programs and two dean positions, one for men and one for women. When Shaw retired in 1941, staff doubled to 680, and enrollment nearly tripled to almost 7,000.

16 In 1947, Michigan State College created its own police force separate from the East Lansing Police Department. In 2019, Kelly Roudebush became the university's first female police chief, and historically, only its fifth police chief. In the summer of 2020, she was forced to take leave to fight breast cancer.

17 Author's interview with Penny on September 15, 2020.

Chapman convinced Rick and Penny to look into law enforcement careers out West where it was less corrupt and offered them both employment after they graduated. Also, Penny's grandmother lived in Portland.[18] Rick successfully tested for the sheriff's office. The county told Penny she could only work in the jail, but then recanted and said they could not hire a married couple, so she had to look elsewhere. In order to stay close to her husband, the PPB[19] became an obvious alternative, especially since they had a history of hiring female officers dating back to Lola Baldwin in 1908.

History of the Portland Police Bureau

Portland officially formalized its law enforcement in 1851, when the town elected its first marshal. The system of selecting the town marshal occurred informally every couple of years through both elections and appointments until 1870 when a council ordinance established the Portland Metropolitan Police Force. In 1915, the department changed its name to the PPB.

James Lappeus became the first police chief of the new department in 1870 and put in charge of six patrol officers who policed a town of fewer than 9,000 residents (Finn, 2012). Lappeus had previously been the town marshal from 1859 to 1861 and from 1868 to 1869. Typical of early police leaders, Lappeus was co-owner of a gambling/prostitution parlor linked to corruption and bribery. By 1872, Lappeus's officers had standardized police uniforms that consisted of dark blue coats with velvet collars and brass buttons. Officers also wore black hats with a cord and tassel. A new three-story police headquarter was placed at S.W. 2nd and Oak Street and included offices, a men's jail, and a detention area for women and children (Lansing, 2003). As chief, Lappeus worked under the supervision of the city council but was still elected. He served two terms as chief (1870–1877) and (1879–1883). Civil reforms eventually depoliticized the chief's position and allowed for a mayoral appointment. The mayor also historically retained the position as police commissioner with the ability to terminate the chief.

Lewis and Clark Centennial and American Pacific Exposition Fair (1905)

From May 1804 to September 1806, a select group from the U.S. Army conducted the first westward exploration under Captain Meriwether Lewis's command and Second Lieutenant William Clark. President Thomas Jefferson commissioned Lewis and Clark's expedition shortly after the Louisiana Purchase to determine practical routes into the West before British and European countries attempted to claim it. In 1845, Francis Pettygrove purchased land from William Overton and named it Portland after his hometown Portland, Maine. On April 27, 1846, Portland's first law enforcement officer, William Johnson, was indicted for "retailing ardent spirits," meaning he was involved with liquor sales.

In 1905, Portland became the host city for a centennial celebration of the Lewis and Clark expedition (Baumgardner, 2000). The city built an extensive exposition in celebration. The centennial was informally referred to as a world's fair due to the exhibits and the international tourists. The exposition ran from June 1, 1905, until October 15, 1905, and included exhibitions from 21 nations and 16 states. In preparation for the fair, in late 1904, the National Travelers

18 Author's interview with Penny on November 30, 2020.

19 Dr. Chapman wrote a recommendation letter to the PPB, which stated that Penny was a brilliant student and would likely only stay with the police department for a few years before going onto something better. After a long delay, she went directly to Mayor Terry Schrunk and spoke passionately about her desire to be a woman police officer and promised she would not leave if she was hired. Mayor Schrunk told the PPB to hire her (Painter, 1985).

Aid Association asked Portland's Young Women's Christian Association (YWCA) to help protect young women who filled temporary jobs associated with the exposition. Numerous travelers came to see the exhibitions and subsequently settled in Portland. From 1905 to 1910, the city grew from 161,000 to 270,000 residents due to the centennial exposition's attraction.

Baldwin and Plumlee

Baldwin had previous experience through temperance movements to conduct social work outreach and served on a committee that organized Portland's Juvenile Court. Judge Arthur Frazer led the court who appointed Baldwin as an unpaid probation officer for girls. In 1905, the YWCA hired her to supervise its Travelers Aid program, formally organized in New York. That same year, Portland was changing police chiefs. In 1905, according to the Portland Police Museum,[20] Charles Gritzmacher was convinced to forego retirement and was appointed to be police chief in charge of three Captains, three Sergeants, 110 patrol officers, three patrol wagon drivers, three jailors, and eight detectives.

When the Lewis and Clark Exposition closed in October 1905, Baldwin recognized the importance of her work. She persuaded the YWCA to continue its welfare outreach to at-risk women and girls. Financial support dissipated by 1907, leading Baldwin to ask for assistance from Mayor Harry Lane and the Portland City Council. They agreed to an appropriation of city funds to assist her with the stipulation that she pass the civil service exam for police work. Gritzmacher opposed hiring women police detectives, but he was not in charge of those decisions as the Police Commission was responsible for all officers' hiring and termination. In 1908, the commission approved Baldwin's hiring to assist male officers in dealing with women and children's increased victimization. Baldwin was given the rank of detective and sworn in as the Superintendent of the Women's Auxiliary to the Police Department for the Protection of Girls. The auxiliary post was later renamed the Women's Protective Division (Schulz, 1995). The detective position led Baldwin to initiate a Domestic Relations Court, and by 1912, she helped create an industrial school for girls and a venereal detention facility. Baldwin's popularity as an investigator grew nationally, and the Immigration Bureau utilized her to assist with cases that involved interstate prostitution and vice control on military facilities. She gave several public lectures through the Oregon Social Hygiene Society and the state parole board on the necessity for women's protection. After her retirement in 1922, Baldwin served numerous terms on the Oregon Parole Board and the National Board of Prisons and Prison Labor. Until her death in 1957, at 97 years old, she remained a passionate advocate for women in police service (Myers, 1995).

In 1947, the Women's Protective Division hired female officer Sybil Plumlee who would also go on to have a commendable policing career. She originally applied to be a police officer out of financial necessity for her family and not to become a pioneer during her 20-year career in policing. She wrote an unpublished memoir titled *Badge 357* about her time as a non-uniformed female officer and the specialty investigations she conducted, often dealing with rape and child victimization. Plumlee ran undercover investigations on homosexuals through Portland Mayor Dorothy McCullough Lee[21] (Boag, 2004). The goal of the investigations was to solicit men or women for homosexual relations and then arrest them. Plumlee did several educational campaigns on behalf of the Women's Protective Division to educate women

20 See http://portlandpolicemuseum.com/charles-gritzmacher.html.

21 Lee was the first female member of the Portland City Council. She became the first female mayor, 42nd overall, of Portland (1949–1953). Lee also served on the U.S. Parole Commission after being appointed by President Eisenhower.

on not to become victims of crime. She lived past the age of 100, passing away in 2012 (Hallman, 2012).

In the 1940s, Portland had an infamous reputation for gambling halls, strip clubs, and brothels. In 1907, Mayor Lane made Portland the city of roses, and a few decades later, it offered every addiction known to man. The mafia controlled an illegal abortion racket that brought women in from all over the West, and venereal disease was so rampant that the Navy refused liberty time in Portland. Mayor Earl Riley, linked to police corruption, netted an estimated $60,000 a month that he hid in a vault next to his office desk in City Hall (Lipman, 2017). Lee defeated Riley in the primary and was elected the first woman mayor in Portland.

Interestingly, August Vollmer (detailed in a previous chapter) was hired as a reorganization consultant and completed a survey on the Portland Police Department in 1947, which was the same year the department hired Plumlee. Vollmer wrote about Portland's rapid increase in population and a dramatic increase in crime. He determined that Portland police salaries were below acceptable levels, the pension system was disgraceful, and the traffic division was overstaffed since it included 26 percent of the patrol officers.[22] The 1947 Vollmer Report spoke of the archaic organizational structure that allowed too much political interference into managing the PPB. Vollmer encouraged creating a Department of Public Safety that would include law enforcement, fire protection, and civil defense. He urged this agency to be free from direct mayoral supervision, something that other cities had done but continued to be resisted by the commission system of government in Portland, even in the year 2020 amidst the worst public protests and riots in the country.

Policing the 1960s

Before the PPB hired Penny, there were movements nationally to create gender equality in policing. Gertrude "Gertie" Schimmel[23] joined the New York City Police Department (NYPD) on June 5, 1940, and she was assigned to the Bureau of Policewomen. Female officers did not patrol, and the NYPD banned their promotions above their entry-level job. Schimmel worked undercover to break up gambling operations and worked in the Youth Aid Division to help youth find temporary shelter if their parents could not take care of them. In 1943, female officers were issued a black shoulder bag with space for a holster and a makeup kit. Mayor Fiorello La Guardia[24] remarked, "use the gun as you would your lipstick; don't overdo either one" (Jeffers, 2002). After 20 years of police service, Schimmel convinced fellow officer Felicia Shpritzer[25] to file a lawsuit, with her, against the NYC Department of Personnel after being denied a request to test to be police sergeants with four other female applicants. Police Commissioner Michael Murphy (1965–1961) argued that women lacked the physical strength to be sergeants. In 1963, the Equal Pay Act was passed, which prohibited unequal pay between genders for the same occupation. The law's language had little initial impact on police agencies across the country since departments categorized policewomen under

22 See History of Portland Police – www.portlandoregon.gov/police/40004.

23 Schimmel joined the NYPD on June 5, 1940, with a historic class of 18 women and 300 men. She is credited with becoming the first female sergeant, lieutenant, captain, deputy inspector, inspector, and deputy chief in the NYPD. Schimmel retired in 1981 and died in 2015 at the age of 96.

24 La Guardia was the 99th mayor of NYC and served three terms as a Republican from 1934 to 1945. He stood five feet and two inches tall and was rated as the best mayor in American history (see Holli, 1999).

25 Shpritzer spoke at the Fifth Biennial IAWP in Portland in August 1966. She spoke about the problems of only 1.1 percent of the police being women. At the time of her speech, the international president was Captain Elizabeth Mumford, the commander of the PPB Women's Protective Division and Penny was the secretary. Shpritzer retired as a lieutenant in 1976 and died in 2000 at the age of 87.

different civil service titles and gave them different duties than male officers. Since the job was considered unequal based on the varying descriptions, politicians argued the pay and employment qualifications could also be unequal. However, the state judiciary stepped in the same year, 1963, and the New York State Court of Appeals ruled in the female officers' favor and opened the door for policewomen promotions. In 1964, both Schimmel and Shpritzer passed their promotional exams and became the first female officers to become sergeants in an urban department (Schulz, 1995), 25 years after being hired.

In 1968, the Indianapolis Police Department (IPD) employed Betty Blankenship and Elizabeth Robinson as the first women to do street patrol in a squad car with a two-way radio. Both officers worked the first year in secretarial duties and convinced their chief to put them on patrol. Robinson's husband was also a veteran in the IPD. Officially, the department announced the move would free up male officers for crime-fighting. The female partners were assigned to mobile patrol without field training and had the disadvantage of wearing a skirt and high heels as their initial police uniform. Moreover, a female officer had to carry their firearm in their accompanied purse. These women police officers' advancements accompanied the 1964 Civil Rights Act, followed by President Nixon's 1969 executive order that prohibited federal employment discrimination (Martin, 1980). The legal buildup would factor into Penny's career advancements within the PPB.

Portland Police Bureau – Women's Protective Division

Penny's policing career began in September 1964, when she was one of four women hired into the PPB's Women's Protective Division, with Jacqueline Jeppe, Ruth Dunafon, and Mrs. Janet Helzer, by Chief Donald McNamara. The four new hires started their academy training on October 1, 1964, and brought the total to 15 women employed in the Women's Protective Division. As was the case in other departments, Portland avoided equal pay arguing male and female officers had a different job description and exclusive divisions. McNamara had been chief from 1951 to 1953. He returned a decade later for a reappointed to a second term leading the department from 1964 to 1974. When McNamara hired Penny, out of the 700 officers within the PPB, there were only five men of color – and four came from her academy class of 36 recruits. Chief McNamara let Penny know she was the first officer – male or female – hired with a police administration degree. Women officers were required to have college degrees, and their degrees were customarily in social work or education. Male officers were only required to have a minimal GED degree. Despite the gender and educational disparities, male officers received higher pay than the college-educated female officers relegated to the Women's Protective Division (Photo 4.1).

Female officers in the Women's Protective Division wore white gloves, a hat, tailored suits, silk blouses, and sling-back pumps. They did not openly carry firearms and did not participate in any type of patrol. Neither the public nor their male officer counterparts considered them to be the real police. Instead, women became support staff for male officers, and by state law, they were present anytime the police questioned a woman or child about sex crimes and abuse. Male officers did not mind women officers' presence when the cases dealt with discussing sex crimes and decisions to remove abused children since they typically did not want to investigate these types of offenses. Outside of these specific cases, female and male officers remained segregated. Despite this separation, Penny was not initially bothered by the apparent discrimination based on today's standards.

For Penny, her role in the Women's Protective Division was a dream job. She immediately applied what she learned from her child psychology and juvenile justice course at MSU. Moreover, female officers were highly supportive of one another within their division. Male officers were also very supportive of the women since there was no threat to their employment or promotions. A challenge to the supportive cooperation came in the aftermath of the

Photo 4.1 Left to right: Ruth Dunafon, Jacqueline Jeppe, Janet Helzer, Penny Orazetti.
Photo provided to the author by Penny Harrington.

1964 Civil Rights Act that President Johnson signed into law. The act prohibited any labor rules that discriminated based on race, color, religion, national origin, or gender. The first state sex discrimination lawsuit filed against the PPB centered on pay disparity, the department's 18-women quota, and the ban on women taking promotional exams delegated for policemen. Federal congresswoman Edith Green[26] aided the women officers' lawsuits from Oregon.

Unsuccessful Promotions

On June 18, 1968, the PPB provided an internal notification that any police patrolmen, radio dispatchers, or identification officers were eligible to test for a police detective position. The 60 existing detectives were all male and earned more money than any of the female officers. Sergeant Jaye Merrill was attending law school during her off-duty time and encouraged Penny to sign up for the detective exam citing the Civil Rights Act of 1964. A couple of weeks after her initial application, the PPB Civil Service Division told Penny she did not meet the requirements for testing to be a detective despite her four years of investigative experience within the Women's Protective Division. After pushing the Civil Service Division to allow her to test, they relented and said it was approved, pending the chief's approval. However, the deputy chief denied the request and told Penny there was no avenue for an appeal. In the aftermath, Penny's assignment changed, and she was demoted to secretarial duties and told not to leave the Women's Protective Division's offices.

26 Green was the second Oregonian woman elected to the U.S. House of Representatives. She remained very popular with voters and served a total of ten terms.

After Merrill completed her law degree, she resigned from her sergeant position, and Penny immediately put in to test for the promotion. At the time, her husband Rick Orazetti took a leave of absence from his job and worked toward a graduate degree. Their son Brian was born in 1967, and their family became supported on Penny Orazetti's meager Women's Protective Division pay. Penny studied, tested, and came in number one for the sergeant exam with a motivation for higher pay and advancement. However, the department promoted the woman who tested second on the exam based on differences in years of experience. Police administrators told Penny she was young and could get the next one; however, with only three police sergeants in their isolated division and a severely limited opportunity for future promotion, it was clear to Penny that she was being punished for her "detective stunt" when she attempted to leave the Women's Protective Division through a promotion. The PPB transferred Penny to afternoon shifts after she complained about being passed up for both promotions, and she was put back on secretarial duties. The message from the bureau was clear – "don't rock the boat." This message would perpetuate throughout the rest of her policing career.[27]

The Union – Portland Police Officers' Association

In 1942, a police union came to the PPB. Initially, the union was associated with the American Federation of State, County, and Municipal Employees, but eventually, they became independent and were called the Portland Police Officers' Association. In 1969, based upon her father's history as a plant supervisor, Penny refused to be part of the Portland Police Officers' Association. Leo Miller, the youngest captain in the police bureau, was sent to change her mind. At the time, Penny made $350 a month, and the union was asking for $50 from each officer and $100 from everyone in command staff to hire a labor lawyer to advocate for better pay, college/career counseling, and the establishment of a planning and research unit. Also, Miller and Penny met with Lee Brown,[28] then an instructor at Portland State University. Brown helped them strategize how to run a fact-finding process to establish goals for the union. Brown would go on to become Houston's Police Chief (1982–1990), NYC Police Commissioner (1990–1992), Director of the Office of National Drug Control Policy (1993–1996) under President Clinton, and the 59th Mayor of Houston (1998–2004). Penny's contact with Brown would occur again after she became chief, and a year later, Brown testified on her behalf to a commission that ultimately worked to force her resignation.[29]

Friedan – The Feminine Mystique

Miller continued to visit Penny to encourage her input on causes advocated by the union. He also brought her a copy of *The Feminine Mystique*. This best-selling book became influential in focusing Penny's drive for gender equality in law enforcement. The book was written

27 Frequently women officers found out about promotions after the positions had been filled. It was not until 1978 that Penny was able to get the rules changed so the PPB had to officially post promotion and training opportunities to all officers (Jenning, 1978).

28 Brown became one of the premier leaders in community policing or what was originally labeled Neighborhood-Oriented Policing (NOP). Academically, he completed a master's degree in sociology at San Jose State University in 1964, and served as an assistant professor there until 1968. His graduate criminology degree came in 1970 from UC Berkeley where he learned about the legacy of Vollmer. Penny met him after he moved to Portland to, serve as the chair of the Department of Administration of Justice at Portland State University until 1972. He became an associate director at the Institute of Public Administration at Howard University until he returned to Oregon in 1976 as the Sheriff of Multnomah County.

29 Author's interview with Penny on April 9, 2020.

by Betty Friedan[30] and published in 1963, based on her survey of fellow Smith College alumni at their 15th reunion. Despite popular assumptions, Friedan identified that a large percentage of women were not content with the limitations of being housewives and raising children. Friedan's writing inspired Penny to realize that a meaningful life for women has to challenge and rethink the traditional feminine mystique projected onto them by patriarchal male dominance. The book transformed public awareness of gender inequality and propelled many women to advocate for their autonomy and leadership opportunities. In 1966, Friedan helped start the National Organization for Women (NOW), which called for equality for all women in economic and positional advancement. The organization demanded that the Equal Employment Opportunity Commission (EEOC) enforce Title VII guarantees for employment equality under the Civil Rights Act of 1964. Between the influence of Miller and reading Friedan, Penny's support for the union was now unquestionable. She told Miller *The Feminine Mystique* spoke about all the emotions she felt toward the bureau but could not articulate. She agreed to support the union if they included gender equality. Miller agreed.

The legislation directed toward equality, and the female voter in the 1960s and 1970s, created a second wave of feminism. The first occurred during the Progressive Era and Temperance Movements. This second wave of women's rights impacted the number of women challenging the traditional male-dominated roles in society, including law enforcement. The rules that governed law enforcement employment entry and promotion would be increasingly challenged in the years following the Civil Rights Act of 1964. Moreover, the Johnson Administration's Commission on Law Enforcement (described more fully in the chapter on Wilson/Goldstein and Bratton/Kelling) proscribed the hiring of more minorities and women.

In continuance of the commission goals for creating diversity in policing agencies, the administration passed the 1968 Omnibus Crime Control and Safe Streets Act. The Crime Control Act called for creating the Law Enforcement Assistance Administration (LEAA) within the Department of Justice (DOJ). LEAA administered federal funds to state and local law enforcement educational programs, research, training, and local crime initiatives. Agencies that received federal funds were mandated to avoid any practices that may be deemed discriminatory on the basis of gender, race, or other protected categories. For example, in March 1973, any agency receiving federal funds through LEAA had to end the gender-biased minimum height requirements. This order increased opportunities for education and police hiring more women. Additionally, political support for "get tough on crime" legislative acts created an even greater demand for police services.

Policing the 1970s

A Police Foundation Report *Women in Policing* (Milton et al., 1974) stated in 1971 that there were fewer than a dozen policewomen patrolling municipalities in the United States. A 1971 Supreme decision, *Griggs v. Duke Power Company*, would help change this disparity. The court decision mandated that job descriptions had to include essential expectations and should not discriminate based upon arbitrary physical requirements such as height and weight that worked against female applicants. In just a few short years, several hundred female police leaders were in charge of both males and females. Subsequent research on the Washington, DC and NYPD departmental use of female uniformed patrol determined no significant

30 Betty Friedan (1921–2006) was born Bettye Goldstein in Peoria, Illinois, to Jewish parents from Hungary and Russia. She attended the all-female Smith College from 1938 to 1942, graduating with a degree in psychology. The following year she attended UC Berkeley on a graduate fellowship. Friedan is credited with creating a second wave of feminism in the 1960s.

gender differences in performance. However, there was considerable prejudice against women from within the departments (Bloch & Anderson, 1974). In response, the Police Foundation created a National Information and Research Center geared toward understanding women in policing and published research[31] advising the departmental use of female officers and leaders (Milton et al., 1974).

In Portland, Miller and the police union president moved to capitalize on the gains women were making in hiring practices. Penny became part of the union's strategic planning meetings. In addition to rewriting the union contract, Penny helped develop a career counseling unit and a research/planning unit. Penny also advocated that female officers should transfer out of the Women's Protective Division and into the traditional rank through promotional exams. The ad hoc team successfully got new union members, organized large meetings, planted questions in the audience during the union meetings, and advanced their causes.

Transferring Out of the Women's Protection Division – Again

Once they created the Planning and Research Division, Miller became the natural command fit. He asked that Penny be allowed to transfer out of the Women's Protection Division to join him, but Chief McNamara refused to approve the transfer. Upon hearing about the chief's refusal from Miller, Penny walked ten blocks to Mayor Terry Schrunk's[32] office, entered unannounced, and received an impromptu meeting. She told the mayor about all the existing problems: women confined to one division; women paid less than men; mandatory college degrees for women and not men; and women passed up for promotions. The mayor explained to Penny there was nothing he could do and suggested that she discuss her malcontent with Chief McNamara. Penny then blurted out, "transfer me, or I'll sue you," and walked out (Harrington, 1999). She believed the PPB would terminate her by the time she walked back to the Women's Protection Division. However, to Penny's surprise, Miller contacted her, stating Chief McNamara told him to transfer her to the research and planning unit to supervise her. Her persistence had paid off, and on January 29, 1970, there were four desks and chairs crammed into a small office, and the work of planning and research for the PPB began.

Police officers were called patrolmen specialists who worked in the planning and research division, while Penny was called a policewoman. She made less money than the other specialists doing the same work. She pushed Miller to rectify the pay disparity through the union, but Chief McNamara refused to offer Penny more money. Penny then called Mayor Schrunk and was given a raise and the title policewoman specialist since the term police officer did not exist.

Penny recognized that policewomen's classification interfered with promotion eligibility and transfers away from the Women's Protective Division. She filed a complaint with the Civil Service Office of the City of Portland. The Oregon State Civil Rights Division requested everyone's classification in the police bureau falls under a generic term – police officer.[33] No one objected to this simple change, but it became critical for women police officers' ability to be promoted out of the Women's Protective Division. In May 1971, the PPB announced

31 See www.policefoundation.org/publication/women-in-policing-a-manual/.

32 Schrunk was the longest-serving Portland mayor for 16 years (1957–1973), tied with George Baker, who also served 16 years (1917–1933). Schrunk was also elected Sheriff of Multnomah County in 1949. Within months of being elected Sheriff, prosecutors accused him of taking a $500 bribe from a gambler and lying about it. A jury acquitted Schrunk of the charges in that same year (Griffin & Sulzberger, 2009). His son, Michael, carried this lesson with him when he became the Multnomah District Attorney for 32 years, from 1981 to 2012, the longest-serving district attorney in Oregon's history (Green, 2019).

33 Author's interview with Penny on April 11, 2020.

exams for police detectives for all officers, and this would include four women from the Women's Protective Division. Afterward, Penny was listed fourth on the list behind three men.

Because she never wore a traditional police uniform, she had difficulty convincing her 4-year-old son Brian that she would be a police detective since he believed only men could do this job (Wohler, 1971). Critics contended the male officers would not be able to rely on female detectives; women could not handle the work required to be a detective, and the wives of male officers would object to their husbands paired with female partners. During Penny's interview to be a detective, they asked if she thought men would resent her. The male interviewers also asked how she would deal with policemen's jealous wives, what she would do if she couldn't handle a dangerous situation, and if she was a women's libber. Male officers frequently let Penny know she wasn't qualified to be a detective, and her efforts were taking jobs away from men who have to support a family. When Penny retorted that she was a single mom supporting her family, they suggested that she go back to her ex-husband or find another husband.

Successful Promotion – Detective Orazetti (1972)

Nearly ten months passed from the testing date because of a reluctance to promote Penny to detective. However, by February 1972, the department could not delay any further, and the PPB promoted Penny as their first female police detective, along with four additional male officers. This promotion came a decade after the NYPD had promoted Officers Schimmel and Shpritzer to become sergeants. The press covered Penny's promotion (Wohler, 1971), and this brought on further scrutiny. The male detectives did not associate with Penny and made it clear that they did not welcome her into their ranks. When she asked for assistance from any of her sergeants or other detectives, they gave her the runaround. Penny began to receive lewd phone calls and hate mail. One letter called her a "fat homely double chin humpback cow" (Harrington, 1999, p. 70). This resistance was the first time Penny reported that she experienced open hostility from patrolmen, who yelled, "You aren't qualified to be a detective!" "You're taking the job away from the man that has to support a family!" Eventually, the departmental secretaries recognized what was happening and began to teach Penny how to do the job. Penny's valuable leadership lesson was always to make friends with the secretaries who can teach the newbies how to navigate office politics and do their job (Photo 4.2).

Promotion Announcement

Successful (but Unsuccessful) Promotion – Sergeant Orazetti (1972)

A few months later, Penny tested for the sergeant promotional exam. During her oral board interview, the interviewers asked what she would do for a baby-sitter if she had to work nights, if her menstrual cycle would affect her performance, and if she really thought women could discipline male officers without them being resentful (Pintarich, 1975). Despite the discriminatory tone of the questions, Penny was still placed second on the list of fifty who applied for promotion. She received a promotion to become a sergeant but was transferred back to the Women's Protective Division to her dismay. On July 13, 1972, Penny was sent back to where she started in 1964 and put on the midnight shift supervising only her sister Roberta, whom the PPB recently hired after a two-year delay.

Fortunately, the promotional assignment back to the Women's Protective Division would not last long after Miller received a multi-million dollar grant for the Columbia Region Information Sharing System (CRISS). The smitten Miller asked Penny to take the sergeant position and help supervise the project. For the next two years, Penny worked on the CRISS

Photo 4.2 Left to right: Penny Orazetti (Detective), Bill Richardson (Captain), Dave Simpson (Detective), John McNabb (Sergeant), with Chief Donald McNamara.
Photo provided to the author by Penny Harrington.

project, with the impossible goal of designing a single computer system to link 42 law enforcement agencies, five prosecutor's offices, and judges from five counties and two states in more than 60 courtrooms.

While leading the CRISS project, Penny's work on filing civil rights and gender equality complaints persisted during her off-duty time. By the end of 1972, the women activists from the Women's Protective Division hired attorney Jane Edwards. Penny used her personal savings to pay for Edwards's legal assistance. At the beginning of 1973, the policewomen filed their first grievances with the union alleging discrimination in pay and unequal promotional transfers. Over the next three years, 42 additional complaints alleged discrimination practices violated federal and state laws (Harrington, 1999). Negotiators responded to pay disparity complaints with the retort to lower everyone's pay to create equality rather than providing raises for policewomen. This response led to increased animosity between male and female officers.

Challenging Height Requirements (Hint: It's Not Really about Height)

Another essential matter that involved hours of negotiations concerned the so-called height requirements for hiring and promotion. Studies indicated such requirements were discriminatory and pragmatically unnecessary. The height restrictions discriminated against women and certain ethnicities such as Mexicans, Puerto Ricans, and Asians. In 1973, approximately 97 percent of a large sample of police agencies had a height requirement with a minimum of 68 inches, as reported from the Police Foundation in *Police Officer Height and Selected Aspects of*

Performance (White & Bloch, 1975). Guidelines from the DOJ permitted height restrictions if recipients of federal funding were able to convincingly demonstrate, through supportive data and professionally validated studies, that the requirements were an operational necessity for designated job categories (Department of Justice, 1973).

The reasons for excluding shorter applicants (typically under 68 inches) cited research that linked body build to strength, and strength correlated to height and weight (Hoobler & McQueeny, 1963). Moreover, limited studies indicated that taller officers could see better in crowds and control public disorder more efficiently (Verducci, 1974). The Police Foundation Report also discussed an internal and unpublished study from the Bureau of Police in Portland that concluded shorter officers were more likely to be assaulted than taller officers (White & Bloch, 1975). However, the reanalysis of the data indicated statistical flaws that did not control for seniority variables.

In Portland, to counter the height requirement's discriminatory nature, Miller utilized the planning division to run his study. Miller had one officer study fences and first-floor windows throughout Portland and countered the argument that tall officers were needed to climb or look over fences to observe suspicious activity. Penny's research on height restrictions from 30 police agencies nationwide indicated that the policies varied tremendously from agency to agency without sound rationale. For example, the San Diego Police Department lowered its height requirement from 5'9" to 5'7 ½" in July 1968, and by September 1971, the department again lowered the minimum standard to 5'6 ½ " (White & Bloch, 1975). Many of these departments had already discontinued height requirements and archaic language, indicating that shorter officers were more likely to get assaulted.

Mayor Neil Goldschmidt

In January 1973, Neil Goldschmidt[34] became mayor while the civil service hearing regarding the height restriction was pending. At the age of 32, Goldschmidt was the youngest mayor for any major city in the country. In the month prior, Penny told the press that they expected several changes when the new mayor took office. Four months later, *The Oregonian* (Smith, 1973) asked Penny about progress, and she responded

> *We are disappointed. There have been no changes to speak of at all … The mayor has asked us to do studies and make reports – all of which we have done on our own time. We've spent even more time talking with his staff … but we hear nothing back. They never respond to anything I give them. There's just not action … Now we are taking whatever action is available to us to make the city move.*
>
> (Harrington, 1999, p. 80)

Mayor Goldschmidt and his chief of staff came into the Police Bureau the following day for an impromptu meeting with Penny. The mayor was visibly upset and told Penny that if women were allowed to be patrol officers, they would get hurt and take early pensions ruining the existing system. The mayor felt that women were not strong enough to do traditional law enforcement. Furthermore, women partnered with male officers would upset their wives and lead to increased divorces. Penny told the mayor he was wrong, and if women received the

34 Goldschmidt would later become President Carter's U.S. Secretary of Transportation from 1979 to 1981 and then serve as an executive for Nike before becoming governor of Oregon from 1986 to 1991. In 2004 he was forced to admit to having a sexual relationship with a 13-year-old girl for six months during his first term as Portland mayor.

same training and had the same expectations as the men, they would do the job just as well. She then challenged the mayor to go outside and see if she could handcuff him in less than a minute, and if she failed, she would shut up and go away. The mayor was outraged, accused Penny of threatening him, and stormed into Miller's office, telling him to get her under control. Miller reportedly laughed at the mayor, stating that he could not control her, and Goldschmidt left.[35] The next morning, Penny received a call from the mayor's executive assistant saying that he read the report on why the height restrictions were impractical. He was going to support dropping the restrictions at the upcoming civil service hearing. The hearing took place on June 6, 1973,[36] and multiple media outlets covered the event. Wives of police officers protested with signs stating "we want real cops, not midgets" and "if the height requirement goes, our children will die." The police officer wives also passed out a petition that stated

> *The safety and welfare of the taxpaying citizens of Portland, Multnomah County, and the State of Oregon is being put into probable danger. We recognize that men and women are physically different and we support the concept that men are the protectors of women and children.*
>
> (Harrington, 1999, p. 84)

After hours of testimony at the hearing, the Civil Service Commission all voted to eliminate the height requirement for being a Portland Bureau police officer. By the end of 1973, the PPB had revised the civil service examination regulations and hired three women under the new genderless designation Portland Bureau police officer. Rita Sorenson became the first female PPB patrol officer one year after being hired into the Women's Protective Division. She left the PPB a year later. Other female officers, such as Annette Jolin[37] (Professor Emeritus at Portland State University), reported being "punished" throughout their careers and male officers refusing to work with them and the department refusing to make them (Roman, 2018).

Like Penny, Miller had high expectations for Mayor Goldschmidt in 1973. The newly elected mayor was friends with Miller and offered him the chief's position, but Miller turned him down. Miller insisted that as chief, he should have the authority to hire and terminate police personnel. However, the mayor's office controlled hiring/firing, and Goldschmidt refused to relent. The conflict Miller had was the same one Vollmer and Wilson had with politics penetrating police leadership. Having the mayor's office directly involved in police personnel's hiring/firing naturally created political baggage for police administrators. Miller attempted to break that link by providing Goldschmidt with his terms to be the next chief. Instead, Goldschmidt went external and hired Bruce Baker, chief from Berkeley, California,[38] and graduate from the University of California (UC), Berkeley. Chief Baker and Miller clashed over many subsequent issues, including budget cuts. Miller eventually transferred to be a traffic captain, a perceived demotion.

Nervous Breakdowns – Miller's Tragic Suicide

After two years of working on the CRISS project, it became clear in 1974 that it was a failure with numerous technical, personnel, and accounting problems. Penny began to challenge the

35 Author's interview with Penny on November 30, 2020.

36 In June 1973, the Youth Division officially replaced the Women's Protective Division.

37 Jolin is originally from Germany and served as a long-time chair of the Criminology & Criminal Justice Department at PSU. Her research focuses on international and comparative law enforcement practices, drawing on her experiences as one of Portland's first female police officers.

38 Baker was the sixth chief of Berkeley, California (1969–1974) and served five years as Berkeley's chief, 37 years after the city's first police chief – August Vollmer (1909–1931). Baker served eight years as PPB chief (1974–1981).

Director of Data Processing, not knowing he had already used his political clout with the CRISS Advisory Board to campaign against Penny's oversight. The Advisory Board called an emergency meeting and fired Penny as project director[39] with a vote of 6 to 1, with Beaverton Police Chief Don Newell, interim board chairman, casting the only dissenting vote (Olmos, 1974). A subsequent state audit determined that a quarter-million dollars of the federal grant were missing or misspent, but no investigations occurred after the report (Harrington, 1999). Penny's leadership lesson was that unless you have spent time within office politics to gain necessary support, you should wait to challenge subordinates for not completing their work or misappropriating funds. The PPB reassigned Penny to work on a new 911 dispatch system with the same data processing team and gave her an office in an old bomb shelter basement. Penny worked the next several months without seeing daylight, which added to her stress.

In addition to the stressors of being reassigned, the dangers of police work became evident on August 9, 1974, when Officer Dennis Darden was shot and killed. It had been 33 years since a Portland officer died by gunfire. Five other officers were wounded by gunfire that same year. Toward the end of 1974, Penny had anxiety attacks, fainting, and worried about being seen as too weak to be a real police officer. She knew she needed a leave of absence, but she pushed herself to stay on a strict timeline for promotion. In November 1974, Penny tested to become a lieutenant and placed first. Part of the oral board promotional interview process had to take place at the hospital while doctors were testing her to determine why she fainted. Roman (2018) reported that discriminatory interview questions during this time included if promoted, "Do you think men would respect you? Do you really believe a woman could discipline a man?" Because of her lack of patrol experience, Penny was fourth on the oral board interview list. She subsequently filed a complaint with the Equal Opportunity Commission in Seattle and claimed the interview questions were discriminatory. Penny's written complaint went unanswered, and the stress continued. After seeing several doctors, she was eventually encouraged to see a psychiatrist who put her on antidepressants. Penny took a leave of absence that would last ten months and told Miller to hide her gun at his house while she recuperated. The PPB did not want Penny to return. They had been paying her 60 percent of her pay and claimed her breakdowns were not related to her job. Penny and the union successfully petitioned the PPB, and they had to retroactively pay her 100 percent for her time off, linking her breakdowns to her employment.

Over the next several months, Miller received other disciplinary transfers. On March 19, 1975, at the age of 46, three years and nine months short of his pension, Miller abruptly put in his resignation papers (Erickson, 1975) and refused to take any other job within the department. Instead, he chose to spend time helping Penny recover from her panic attacks. Penny prepared to return to work in July 1975. A few days before her return, she spent time with Miller at his home while her son was in Michigan with her parents. Penny and Miller planned to see each other the weekend after she returned to work. Before that could happen, Penny received a call from Miller's roommate, Detective Eugene Yocum, on July 23rd. He found Miller dead from suicide after he created a toxic mixture of Quaaludes. Before his suicide, Miller deposited his savings into Penny's account and left a note that stated, "my work was my life, and I chose not to seek a second career" (Harrington, 1999).[40]

39 Author's interview with Penny on April 11, 2020.

40 In the epilogue of *Triumph of Spirit*, Penny discussed the adversarial respect she had for Chief Baker. She states that Baker would call and advise her during her time as chief and respected her courageous stands. A few days before Baker's death in March 1996, he called Penny to unburden his guilt over any role he may have played in Miller's suicide. Penny explained to Baker that the suicide was Miller's choice and he should not shoulder any guilt over his death.

Uniformed Supervision – North Precinct

When Penny returned to work in July 1975, it was the first time a uniformed policewoman would be in charge of male officers. Her previous role as a sergeant did not have her in a standard police uniform.[41] The police uniform had to be specially tailored for Penny and was hideously disproportioned. As a new uniformed sergeant, the PPB assigned her to the North Precinct, which had the city's highest crime rate and had become perceived as a dumping ground for misfits. To Penny's surprise, she found that the men she supervised supported her, and they shared a bond as malcontents who would defend one another. The officers rallied around their supervisor following Miller's death and let her know they wanted her to succeed.

An example of Penny's innovative leadership came when she worked to shut down a pool hall on civil code violations that had been contributing to fear and crime in a predominantly Black neighborhood. Prior attempts to infiltrate the business had failed since neighbors did not trust the police and no Black officers worked in the North Precinct. Penny set up a crime analysis section in the precinct and had officers working from a crime map to understand trends. After she cut crime in half in her precinct, she waited to hear about the next promotional opening to become a lieutenant.

Throughout 1975 and 1976, the PPB failed to fill several openings for lieutenant. Between 1975 and 1978, Penny hired an attorney and filed 42 complaints against the PPB for pay disparity. Also, on September 4, 1975, Penny and her sister, Roberta, joined 12 other plaintiffs in a $20 million class-action lawsuit in U.S. District Court in Washington, DC, against the Federal Government for not supporting fair employment practices. The lawsuit, collaboratively brought by the National Black Police Association and the IAWP through the American Civil Liberties Union (ACLU), sought to suspend the LEAA funding for agencies that were noncompliant with civil rights laws when it came to hiring and promoting women and Black officers (Read, 1982). In addition to Portland, plaintiffs included Richmond (California) officers, Oakland, Philadelphia, New Orleans, and Honolulu. Penny supplied the media with the 59-page lawsuit, which showed that only 22 of the 730 PPB officers were women, or 3 percent of their force (Ruble, 1975). Penny described how women police officers were routinely discriminated against and denied promotions. By 1977, in the aftermath of several complaints she filed, Penny was allowed to test and placed first on the written lieutenant's exam. However, the PPB again used discriminatory oral interview questions and lowered her to fourth on the list.

Additionally, Mayor Goldschmidt instituted a freeze on all hiring and promotions to pay for a deficit caused in part by the over-expenditure of the CRISS project. The freeze on promotions allowed for two years to pass, and the promotional list expired. Penny would not get promoted. In response, she filed complaints with the state civil rights office and the EEOC based on the discriminatory interview questions. Penny also sent copies of the complaint to members of the city council and the media. In February 1977, the delays stopped, and Penny received her promotion, but they kept her in the North Precinct. In addition to becoming the first female lieutenant, Penny successfully got many of her North Precinct officers promoted by having them take practice exams and holding study sessions on her off-duty time. The officers respected their new lieutenant for the time she put into their future, and the morale of the North Precinct improved dramatically.

41 Today, a police product line exists unique to women police officers. See www.police1.com/police-products/female-police-officers/.

Retaliation

The job shifted for Penny after she became a lieutenant. She had several hostile encounters with deputy chief Jim Brouillette (22-year veteran) and Captain Vern McCabe (40-year veteran). Both commanders made it apparent to Penny that they did not feel women should be police officers. On one occasion, Penny walked in on McCabe as he pinned a new secretary to a filing cabinet leading both Penny and the secretary to scream, "get away from me and don't do that" (Harrington, 1999, p. 126). Penny wrote a memo to Chief Baker on behalf of the secretary detailing the incident, and Baker said he would investigate. Rather than turning the investigation over to internal affairs, Baker gave the memo to Deputy Chief Brouillette, who interviewed both Penny and the secretary and assured them that he would terminate McCabe. However, after a two-week previously planned vacation, McCabe returned to work and asked to meet with Penny in his office. After asking for a rundown of events that occurred during his vacation, Harrington (1999) (p. 127) reported,

> all of sudden, he reached over, grabbed my hand, and rubbed it down the front of his pants, right across his genitals. I pulled my hand back and punched him square in the jaw. It was an immediate reaction; I didn't even think about it; I was so appalled.

The incident led to a meeting between Penny (shown as Lt. Orazetti below from her first marriage), Brouillette, and McCabe. The meeting was memorialized through Brouillette's interpretation with the following memo to Chief Baker:

> *Date: October 17, 1977*
> *To: Chief B. R. Baker*
> *From: Deputy Chief Brouillette, Patrol Branch*
> *Subj: Interview with Lt. Orazetti and Captain McCabe*
> *At 1:30 PM on October 10, 1977, in my office, I conducted an interview between Lt. Orazetti and Captain McCabe regarding a professional relationship between Captain McCabe and Lt. Orazetti. We discussed Captain McCabe's conduct which we have been made aware of recently involved familiarity attitude towards female persons on his staff and other females entering the precinct on police business.*
>
> *I outlined the events that Lt. Orazetti had made me aware of in front of Lt. Orazetti and Captain McCabe. I explained to each that this was not the conduct that I expected of a captain on the Portland Police Bureau. I explained to both that I expected a professional air space between Captain McCabe and females that he comes in contact with which could not be construed as sexually suggestive or overly familiar. I explained to both Captain McCabe and Lt. Orazetti that the requirements of the job demanded a professional atmosphere between the two. Both expressed at that time a willingness to work with each other. They both expressed an attitude that it was good to air their problems and get it on the surface so that they could deal with it and both offered support of each other in their working relationship. I expressed to Captain McCabe my concern that I would not tolerate any retaliation action against Lt. Orazetti for bringing this problem to my attention so that we could deal with it. I further suggested to both Lt. Orazetti and Captain McCabe that by Lt. Orazetti making us aware of Captain McCabe's actions in no way should be construed as an effort to usurp his command at North Precinct nor should it be looked upon as an effort to undermine the captain, lieutenant relationship that we demand on the bureau. I asked of Lt. Orazetti to make me aware of any future conduct of this nature that she may witness in an effort to correct or to assist Captain McCabe in improving his stature as a Captain. She should make Captain McCabe aware of any expression from each that they would both work toward the betterment of North Precinct. Both expressed a willingness to work with each other and thought the professional demeanor*

between the two would be resolved. I again reaffirmed my earlier statement to Captain McCabe that Lt. Orazetti was to be treated in a manner befitting the rank of lieutenant on the Portland Police Bureau. No more, no less.

It is my intention to meet with Captain McCabe and Lt. Orazetti during the first week in November to discuss the progress being made toward the resolution of this situation, with special reference to their professional relationship and/or any indication of a reoccurrence of the problem. This does not preclude, of course, their meeting with me any time prior to the date of our projected meeting, at their own request.

(Harrington, 1999, pp. 130–132)

Penny denied stating that she was "glad the air was cleared" or that she perceived the professional demeanor would be resolved, but she also knew it was useless to protest further.[42] As she dealt with retaliation from supervisors within the PPB, the department also suffered from a couple of high-profile public legitimacy issues in 1980 and 1981. The first dealt with an officer killed by gunfire, and the second dealt with dead opossums. Both would result in discipline from Penny after the PPB put her in charge of the personnel department.

Police Legitimacy Problems –Death of an Officer and Opossums

Trust between the community and the PPB deteriorated following an officer's shooting death and a subsequent scandal with the narcotics team. On the evening of December 12, 1979, Penny's sister Roberta had just transferred to narcotics, Special Investigations Division (SID), as a sergeant and was on her first night. The SID team executed a search warrant at the *Outsiders* motorcycle gang clubhouse at 9014 North Lombard Street, based on a supposed confidential informant's tip. As the team breached the door, Robert "Pigpen" Christopher fired a 12-gauge shotgun that struck 27-year-old Officer David Crowther in the head. Conflicted testimony disputed if the officers properly identified themselves before they breached the door. Officer Crowther died two weeks later. Ten members of the *Outsiders* were arrested and charged with narcotics violations and murder. A baggie of cocaine found in Officer Crowther's pocket would have been used to plant inside the clubhouse if the narcotics search did not provide any fruitful evidence. Officers at the hospital destroyed the evidence, in violation of departmental policy (Turner, 1981). This finding triggered a large-scale internal investigation and eventually allowed Christopher to go free, and several other drug convictions overturned.

The investigative team consisted of internal affairs, investigators from the District Attorney's (DA) Office, and other criminal investigators. Patrol officer Neil Gearheart filed the affidavit that secured the original search warrant. He was forced to resign and then granted immunity to testify against SID officers. Gearheart also admitted that the confidential informant did not exist. He revealed that narcotics officers had planted amphetamine tablets during their illegal raid on the *Outsiders* clubhouse, which was also the alleged leader's home. The internal investigation determined that SID officers routinely committed perjury, planted drugs, and stole narcotics and money. Ten officers were fired or resigned in the aftermath, and one officer was convicted of drug charges. Newly elected Multnomah County DA Michael Schrunk[43] released

42 Author's interview with Penny on April 21, 2020.

43 Schrunk was DA of Multnomah County for over three decades from 1981 to 2012, longer than any DA in Oregon history. He collaborated with five Portland mayors, eight Multnomah County sheriffs, and 14 PPB chiefs. As a DA, Schrunk was an innovative leader – he pioneered the second drug court after Miami-Dade; he publicly shared memos to explain cases in which his office declined to prosecute; he allowed his deputy prosecutors to freely speak to the media; he automatically sent officer-involved shooting cases to a grand jury

a report citing 94 cases of police misconduct and asked Governor Victor "Vic" Atiyeh[44] for 58 pardons for the wrongly convicted (Roman, 2018). Only two narcotics officers were left unscathed, Penny's sister Roberta and Charles Moose.[45] A new drug unit, reorganized into the Drug and Vice Unit, had similar issues that produced problems with rogue officers. In 1982, Portland voters responded to the scandal and approved the creation of a citizen police-oversight panel.

On March 12, 1981, another scandal hit the PPB when officers Craig Ward, age 28, and Jim Galloway, age 32, tossed four dead opossums in front of the Burger Barn. The Burger Barn was a popular Northeast restaurant owned by George and Geraldine Powe in a predominantly Black neighborhood located at 3962 N.E. Union Avenue. The opossums incident touched off a contentious battle between the police, City Hall, and the public that would last for years. George Powe called the media when he saw the police car driving away after officers tossed the dead opossums at his restaurant's entrance (Pickett, 1981b). The officers responded that they were protesting the frequent calls for service they received from the restaurant and their actions were not racially charged but a way to relieve stress (Pickett, 1981a). The Black United Front (BUF)[46] responded by organizing a protest on March 25, 1981 that called for the officers' termination, the formation of a civilian review board, and improved officer training and supervision. The following day, City Commissioner Charles Jordan,[47] the city's first Black commissioner who was also in charge of the Police Bureau per former Mayor Goldschmidt, fired Ward and Galloway (Serbulo & Gibson, 2013). Penny supported Jordan's termination of the officers. The city council subsequently refused to provide legal defense for Ward and Galloway after they were sued for $3.8 million in the federal court (Williams, 1982). Ward and Galloway then sued the city in circuit court and contended that state law required the city to provide them legal defense since they were on-duty when they put the dead opossums in front of the Burger Barn.

On April 3, 1981, an estimated 1,000 officers staged a counter-protest to support Ward and Galloway (Serbulo & Gibson, 2013). The police union also authorized a no-confidence vote against both Jordan and Chief Baker. The union appealed the officers' termination to Gary Axon, an arbitrator, who reinstated both Ward and Galloway after they served a 30-day unpaid suspension. Eleven months after the police protest, on March 3, 1982, someone threw a dead chicken in front of the Burger Barn with a KKK business card attached and a note that used a racial slur and stated next time it would be a stick of dynamite. The Burger Barn manager then received phone calls asking if they had any chickens and where the restaurant got its chickens (Hallman, 1982).

In the aftermath of the original opossums incident, Chief Baker, who suffered from health concerns, resigned, and Jordan announced he would do a national search for the next chief.

for scrutiny and he supported legislation (that failed) to record the grand jury hearings in police shootings (Green, 2019).

44 Atiyeh served as the 32nd Governor of Oregon (1979–1987), the last elected Republican. He was the nation's first Arab descent governor and established a state-wide food bank, the nation's first (Mapes, 2014).

45 Moose became the chief of the PPB, six years after Penny resigned, in 1993. Moose was also the chief of police for the Montgomery County, Maryland Police and became the spokesman for efforts that led to the apprehension of the D.C. snipers in October 2002. Moose had called Penny Harrington "an American icon." In the forward of her autobiography (Harrington, 1999) Moose states: "Harrington has never understood her place. She has always sought another place, and the scars have become part of her. When we consider how difficult it is to change a law enforcement agency, Penny's efforts really begin to take shape. Her ability to break through so many barriers in less than 25 years is the stuff of legends" (Harrington, 1999, pp. 9–11).

46 The BUF in Portland was a branch of the national organization based in Chicago. The organization facilitated a civil rights agenda in the 1980s that focused on police brutality, desegregation, and apartheid in South Africa.

47 Jordan served as the first Portland Black city commissioner for ten years, from 1974 to 1984.

The newly elected Mayor Frank Ivancie opted to take leadership of the Police Bureau away from Jordan and internally promoted Captain Ronald Roy Still to be the next police chief. The city settled the Burger Barn Owners' civil rights lawsuit, $3.4 million, for $64,000 (Dawdy & Menzies, 2005).

Making Captain – 1980

In November 1977, Penny went to the Civil Service Board to request permission to take the Captain's exam. The department's delay in her lieutenant promotion put her behind in timing out her ability to test for becoming a captain. Moreover, her civil rights complaint from two years prior was related to the delay and still pending in 1977. Despite her pending 1975 complaint and a promise from her superiors to make her last promotion retroactive, the board ruled that Penny had not been a lieutenant long enough to test to be a captain (Zaitz, 1978). Two years of additional complaints led to a compromise, and Penny was allowed to take the captain's test in 1980, but the results would be sealed until there was a ruling from the state on her previous civil rights complaint.

> On May 18, 1980, Mount St. Helens erupted and was the deadliest volcanic event in United States' history. The eruption caused a 5.1 magnitude earthquake, took fifty-seven lives, 250 homes, and miles of highways. The volcano is located fifty miles northeast of Portland in Skamania County, Washington. When it erupted, police officers from surrounding towns, including Penny, were sent to Washington to assist. One of Chief Baker's major concerns was how to keep police vehicles active for response calls as several had engine air filters clogged with volcanic ash. During a brainstorming session, Penny suggested they wrap pantyhose around police cars' air filters, which could be easily changed. This solution, unique to Penny, provided a cheap alternative to a problem that needed an immediate creative response.

Later that spring, the captain list came out, and Penny's name was not on the list. As previously ruled, her test results remained sealed due to the pending 1975 civil rights complaint from her previous lieutenant promotion. Penny wanted to see where she ranked, but the department refused to reveal her score on the captain's exam until she agreed to drop her previous complaint, give up any back pay, and agree the department did not violate her civil rights. The board was surprised when Penny immediately dropped her case, and then asked where she ranked on the list. The board told her she was number one. However, even with this victory, no captains were scheduled to retire, and the list could expire.

Penny noted all existing captains worked daytime shifts and none worked in the evenings. She proposed that the department promoted her to be the only nighttime Captain since supervision was needed when most of the use of force and shooting incidents occurred. Penny used her friend Bill Rhodes in city Commissioner Jordan's office to support her proposal to be night captain and then asked Chief Baker if he could speak to Jordan. Baker promised to talk to Jordan about promoting Penny to a night shift commander, not knowing that she had already connected with the city commissioner. On July 17, 1980, the political maneuvering paid off, and Penny formally became the first female captain in the PPB, one of 12 captains. At the age of 38, Penny was the youngest PPB captain ever promoted. She became the personnel captain tasked with recruitment, addressing community concerns, and any police practices that were deemed discriminatory. Two days later, Chief Baker suffered a massive heart attack.

Mayor Ivancie and Chief Still (1980–1985)

The end of 1980 also brought in changes with Portland's mayor. Goldschmidt left the year prior and began work in President Carter's Administration. His replacement, Connie McCready,[48] did not have the same political backing. Ivancie served on the city council for a decade before becoming the new mayor on November 24, 1980. As previously discussed, the new mayor also made himself Portland's police commissioner taking the position away from Jordan following the opossum debacle. Ivancie carried a conservative "war on crime" perspective, as did his internal replacement for Chief Baker. Chief Still's background allowed him to meet Ivancie's goals. That background included being part of the SID Unit in the 1970s when Officer Crowther was fatally shot during their raid on the *Outsiders* motorcycle gang headquarters. He also led an investigation on the Black Panthers breakfast program and was a strong opponent to Jordan's affirmative action hiring strategies (Serbulo & Gibson, 2013). Retired PPB Officer Don DuPay wrote a retort to the Portland State University professors Serbulo and Gibson's (2013) essay. In his report, he described Still as a horrific choice to be chief due to his brutality of residents and offenders in custody (DuPay, 2019). The Black community said the selection of Chief Still was frightening (Cameron, 1981).

Fortunately, Penny was able to be promoted to Captain before the election of Ivancie and Still being selected as the PPB chief. Only 7 percent of PPB officers at that time were female. Penny openly told the press that she was going to recruit female and minority officers to Portland. She held community meetings in the North Precinct and invited church ministers and other Black community leaders to determine how common ground could be found and policing improved. Like many Black communities, the ministers were vital instruments for improving police relationships. After being invited to speak at Sunday services, Penny recruited parishioners to test for police jobs. PPB recruitment materials included photos of minority officers, and the location for testing moved from downtown to urban league offices in the heart of Black neighborhoods. As she had done as a supervisor in the North Precinct, Penny arranged for classes to teach applicants how to pass the civil service exam and offered practice physical agility tests on the weekends. Potential candidates received several follow-up calls and rapport building to encourage their application.

One particular story demonstrated the extent of Penny's leadership and her recruitment of female officers. She met a female recruit who could not complete the process because she had her driver's license suspended when she could not afford to get auto insurance. Previously, this candidate had been on welfare, been in an abusive relationship, and became a teenage mother. Penny recognized the potential and loaned her money to get her car insurance and license reinstated. Eventually, she was hired as a police officer, became a stellar employee, and created several innovative policing strategies.

By the end of 1980, recruitment efforts doubled the number of minority police officers in the bureau. As the city commissioner and head of the police bureau, Jordan developed a two-tier civil service system that created more minority police candidates opportunities. However, the police union filed a lawsuit that effectively stopped the civil service reforms, claiming that the PPB quality would decline (Serbulo & Gibson, 2013). A judge further ruled that Jordan wrongly instituted reforms and the board lacked the authority to initiate affirmative action strategies. The decision countered efforts to recruit and hire more women police officers.

48 McCready was the 46th mayor of Portland, the second of three female mayors, and the last Republican mayor. McCready was the first, and only, Portland mayor to be appointed under the city's commission form of government.

As she did in the North Precinct, Penny looked to improve morale issues and pushed her personnel staff to socialize in off-work events at least once a month. In 1981, Officer Bruce "Gary" Harrington[49] was transferred in as a specialist in personnel, managing promotions and civilian union contracts. During off-duty socializing events, Gary and Penny got to know each other better and began dating. By February 1982, they were married and bought a home on the Tualatin River.

After their marriage, Chief Still moved Penny out of personnel to be the East Precinct commander, the largest precinct in Portland. With support and pressure from Mayor Ivancie, Chief Still presented a "war on crime" agenda with new ordinances directed toward prostitution, public drunkenness, and loitering (Harrington, 1999, p. 163). Penny openly criticized the chief's stance and called the ordinances illegal. Moreover, problems persisted with jail overcrowding and the lack of planning for locking up additional low-level offenders. Chief Still suggested using "paddy wagons" to keep prostitutes locked up overnight until they went to court the following morning. Penny again questioned the constitutionality of the directives. Her criticism led Chief Still to order a private meeting with Penny, where he accused her of being disloyal and asked for her resignation. Penny refused and told the chief not only would she not resign, but she would also refuse to order her officers to make illegal arrests.

As the East Precinct commander, Penny began working with the various 20 neighborhood associations and set up a citizen advisory council. The council included a diverse group of 40–50 representatives from the neighborhood associations who attended monthly meetings with Penny. The discussions helped the community bond and support the police department and Penny personally. She also found that crime in her precinct was not as low as previously assumed since it often went unreported, especially amongst Asian residents. Often these residents feared the police based upon their immigrant backgrounds and past experiences with brutal militarized police forces. Penny set up tours and open houses of the precinct. She had crime prevention manuals translated into different languages, successfully created community bonds, and recruited minority officers. Her leadership lesson was to find community members who have the least voice because they are often the ones most vulnerable to crime and disorder problems.

Another lesson Penny learned as Captain of the East Precinct dealt with an officer suffering from burnout who also received numerous civilian complaints. After several unsuccessful attempts to get the officer to change his attitude and demeanor, Penny put him in charge of installing locks on the poor and elderly homes. Begrudgingly, the officer obliged his captain. To both of their surprise, the officer's attitude about policing changed as he got to know and respect citizens in need. After his lock initiative, the officer worked in the crime prevention unit rather than going back to patrol. He became a critical component for enhancing police legitimacy in the East Precinct. The lessons on handling officers with morale issues or facing civilian complaints ran deep, and something Penny would bring into her next career phase.

Chief Penny Harrington (1985–1986)

In Dorothy Schulz's (2004) book *Breaking the Brass Ceiling: Women Police Chiefs & Their Paths to the Top*, her chapter on Penny Harrington's ascent to become the country's first urban female police chief was titled *The Women who Broke the Bulletproof Barriers*. Indeed, when a tavern owner, turned Portland mayor, opted to name 42-year-old Penny Harrington as the PPB leader with an official swearing-in on January 24, 1985, it was monumental. However, her 17 months at the top would be as controversial and challenging as her ascent. Her ascent culminated from a political outsider and reform-minded mayor.

49 Gary began his career as a patrol officer with the PPB on May 1, 1969.

Mayor "Bud" Clark (1985–1992)

On October 11, 1984, John Elwood "Bud" Clark, Jr.[50] appeared on the *Tonight Show* with Johnny Carson (Cody, 1984). Talk show host Carson said what made the Portland Mayoral candidate interesting was that the only political office he ever held was being treasurer of his high school class. Clark prepared for his mayoral office by taking a public administration course at Portland State University, which surprised Carson (Hamburg, 1984). Clark made further headlines when he used "This Bud's For You" as his mayoral campaign slogan and stood on street corners to hand out rosebuds,[51] only to be challenged by Anheuser-Busch for copyright infringement. Clark then refused to buy any more Budweiser beer at the Goose Hollow Inn,[52] the tavern he had owned since 1967 at 1927 S.W. Jefferson Street in Portland. Moreover, Clark was offended when Budweiser Columbia Distribution used its employees in California commercials to help defeat a voter-initiated referendum that would have created a bottle and can deposit. Clark supported the extra deposit costs that Oregon had in place since the early 1970s.

The popular tavern owner, and Korean War veteran who served in the Marine Corps, also became a Portland icon. Clark became iconic when he was photographed for a mass marketing poster in 1978, wearing a raincoat that made it look like he was flashing or exposing himself to a nude female public statute in downtown Portland with a caption that read "Expose Yourself to Art." On May 16, 1984, at the age of 52, Clark surprised everyone when he was elected the mayor of Portland, beating incumbent Ivancie in the primary with a vote total over 50 percent, meaning a general election did not have to occur. He did so without the support of the police or the fire union. Clark demonstrated how an everyday neighborhood activist with a grassroots campaign could get elected, bring politics to the citizens, and shake up City Hall. The new mayor arrived for his first post-election press conference in a canoe (Kirchmeier, 2014), frequently commuted to work on his bicycle, and ushered in various Portland changes. Upon officially taking office in January 1985, city council members notified Clark that Ivancie had reduced Portland's reserves of $27 million down to a few thousand dollars due to lucrative pension contracts and giving the police and firefighters a 10 percent wage increase. Ivancie had trashed the city budget to buy votes from the police and fire department. A new budget, and an early lesson in politics, was part of Clark's first month in office.

One of the first actions by Mayor Clark was to fire Chief Still. In an interview, he stated that he wanted to fire the whole department and start all over again because of doubts that he could change the existing culture (Roman, 2018). In a later reflection (see Classen, 2010), after Clark read Seattle Police Chief Norm Stamper's 2005 memoir, conclusions were drawn that police structures built around quasi-militaristic bureaucracies impede reform and encourage a warrior culture (Stamper, 2005). Clark followed the lead of Mayor Ivancie and took over police oversight, despite advice from city commissioner Jordan that he would spend too much time doing so, and it would be a political nightmare. Clark compared his leadership to

50 Clark was a Democratic populist mayor with little political experience when he was elected in 1985. He served until 1992 as one of the city's most popular mayors. During this time period, he went through four police chiefs and three additional interim chiefs.

51 Richard Botteri represented Chief Harrington after her forced resignation as police chief. One of Botteri's specialties was campaign law, and he represented Mayor Clark in a lawsuit filed by Republicans with the Oregon Secretary of State's Election Division, which contended Candidate Clark violated a campaign corruption statute by giving something of value to potential voters when he handed out rose buds and notes that stated "This Bud's for You" as one might do when running for treasurer of their high school class. The case was later dismissed (author's interview with Botteri on August 26, 2020).

52 Clark owned several businesses in town, and his Goose Island Inn (not a hotel) tavern became a popular hangout for the members of the city council, businesspeople, and those who supported the fine arts (Harrington, 1999).

President Truman's statement "the buck stops here" (i.e. he fired General Douglas MacArthur on April 11, 1951, as noted in the chapter on Ramsey and the history of the Madison Police Department (MPD)). The newly elected mayor prepared himself to defend the authority of his office (Classen, 2010). Within this mayoral authority, Clark pushed for a true paradigm shift toward community policing strategies that mimicked what he learned about Japan's centralized policing structure.

Clark befriended Tokyo Governor Shunichi Suzuki after watching a documentary that compared police agencies in Santa Anna, California, Portland, and Tokyo. Suzuki explained that Japanese officers live in the communities they serve as a prerequisite for community policing, but unions in the United States often block officers' residential requirements.[53] The documentary also pointed to the cultural issues with police scandals in Portland.

In September 1984, four months after the election of Clark but a few months before he would officially take mayoral office, Chief Still called meeting for his command staff, his first in two and half years. Twelve members of the PPB command staff gathered at a table. Still walked into the room and announced he was retiring and walked out of the room, blind-siding everyone at the table (Harrington, 1999). The mayor-elect had previously met with Still to let him know that he would be choosing a different chief.

Did You Sleep Your Way to the Top?

A police sergeant who worked for Penny in the East and North Precinct was camping buddies with Clark. He told Penny that he recommended to Clark that he should name her the next police chief (Harrington, 1999). Clark had also received numerous letters from business leaders throughout Portland, and each advocated for Penny to become the next police chief. To her surprise, a community group had paid for a billboard that headlined, "We want Penny Harrington as our next police chief."[54] After panel interviews with community leaders, Clark named Penny his police chief in January 1985. She beat out 14 other applicants and four finalists, leading to a media frenzy. Penny was officially sworn in as chief by city auditor Jewel Lansing (Photo 4.3).[55]

Penny was one of 86 women in the PPB and now in charge of 710 officers. Jane Pauley interviewed Penny on *NBC Today* at 3:45 AM on January 28, 1985, for the morning broadcast and asked if her appointment was a publicity stunt by Clark (Katz, 1985). In September 1985, Penny spoke to more than 400 women police officers at the IAWP conference in Anchorage, Alaska, led by IAWP President Carol Ann Halliday.[56] The vast majority of the attendees were lower-ranked officers, and very few had met many chiefs outside of their department, let alone the first female chief of a major city. In her keynote speech, Penny described how she filed 42 lawsuits, split equally between state and federal courts, against her department to reach the top rank. These statements led the *Alaska Daily News* to describe how the PPB chief "sued her way to the top" (Schulz, 2004, p. 144), causing some consternation amongst the

53 Stamper's memoir indicated that police unions are too often a significant impediment to reform. Some unions fought against equal employment opportunities for women, minorities, and gay/lesbian officers. They also often opposed civilian review initiatives and undermined accountability measures while protecting the due process of brutal and corrupt cops (Stamper, 2005).

54 Author's interview with Penny on November 30, 2020.

55 Lansing was one of the first two women elected to Multnomah County government and the fifth woman elected to the Portland government. She served as Multnomah County Auditor from 1975 to 1982 and Portland City Auditor from 1983 to 1986. In 2018, Mayor Ted Wheeler proclaimed May 23rd was Jewel Lansing Day for Portland.

56 Halliday served 30 years as a police officer in Vancouver, British Columbia and retired in 1999 as a detective. The International Association of Women Policing (IAWP), discussed earlier, was created by LAPD's first female officer, Alice Wells.

Photo 4.3 Swearing-in ceremony on January 24, 1985, with Mayor-elect Bud Clark.
Photo provided to the author by Penny Harrington.

conference attendees. Penny told the conference attendees that she faced other members of the media[57] that asked her if she "slept her way to the top," "will men take orders from her" and if her husband Gary is "having a macho crisis" (Harrington, 1999, p. 185; Schulz, 2004). The questions caused Penny to reflect upon her gender-biased promotional interviews. By mid-February 1985, after only one month as chief, Penny had done nearly 200 media interviews (Harrington, 1999, p. 187).

As police chief, Penny was in charge of a $40 million budget and earned an annual salary of $56,000, which constituted a raise from her previous $43,000 captain salary. In leading nearly 800 officers, she emphasized de-escalation of excessive force, reduced undercover drug and vice squads, and increased uniform patrol. Penny did not want to see a repeat of the narcotics scandal that caused an officer's death. As chief, she chose to dismantle the drug unit and incorporated the narcotics investigations into the detective bureau to increase accountability. In doing so, she emphasized community policing relationships before community policing was a buzzword amongst academics and the media. (In October 1989, three years after Penny had left the PPB, the city council adopted a resolution to implement community policing.) The following month, Mayor Clark announced the hiring of 100 additional officers, 40 filling

57 Hollywood movie producers wanted to tell her life story in a two-hour docudrama (Read, 1985). Harvard Law School named her one of the top ten most influential women in law, and *Ms. Magazine* named her the Woman of the Year (Gillins, 1986).

retirements. Penny wanted to promote her sister, Roberta,[58] to be one of her three deputy chiefs, but Clark was against that idea. Instead, her sister led the personnel division and internal affairs.

The Oregonian coverage of Chief Penny Harrington was peculiar. One article described the color pattern of her office and the following description of the nation's first woman chief:

> *Harrington without the badge looks more like the one most likely to bring brownies to a picnic than someone injured to the ways of crime. Her attractive, friendly face is warmed by auburn coloring, and she is surprisingly small for a policewoman, only 5-feet-6. The blue uniform is reserved for ceremonial occasions, so a typical work outfit is a feminine suit, patterned blouse, and sling-back pumps. Her figure is matronly, her ankles slim. Her favorite exercise is pounding nails and lifting sheetrock, the only "domestic chores" she enjoys. She would rather dine out than cook and divides housework right down the middle with her husband.*
>
> (Rasmussen, 1985)

The media description of the nation's first female chief demonstrated a level of gender bias that is not likely to occur with any chief in the twenty-first century but indicates what readers were likely interested in given the time.

Penny recognized that her coverage from *The Oregonian* might be biased and connected to an earlier prostitution response she created with the East Precinct. Portland has a tradition of utilizing neighborhood associations and giving citizens a say in how their city operates. As captain, Penny set up a citizen advisory council that included elected residents from 20 neighborhood associations. At these meetings, the council expressed concerns about a growing overt prostitution problem. However, Penny refused to be a part of Chief Still's sweeps to conduct mass arrests on female prostitutes. Instead, she targeted Union Avenue and used undercover officers to arrest the "Johns" (the men who were propositioning the prostitutes) and saw the prostitutes as victims. On other evenings, she had residents and business owners armed with instant cameras and lawn chairs. They would photograph the male customers of the prostitutes and keep track of license plates. The license plates were used to mail letters to the vehicle owner alerting them that their vehicle was seen in a high crime location. The letters warned the owners to be careful as the PPB was conducting crime reduction strategies within the given locations. The letters were impactful, and internally, officers knew that those involved in propositioning prostitutes included members of the media, established businessmen, and those with political connections. Consequently, the press felt Penny went too far with the letters and may have later wrote biased news stories against the city's first female chief.

Penny's Descent

Penny faced several immediate and insurmountable challenges when she became chief. First, Clark agreed to take on approximately 32,000 additional calls for service when Portland annexed a large portion of Multnomah County. Penny inherited 56 county deputies into the PPB, but the city council laid off 72 officers the following week because of the budget shortfall left by Ivancie. Second, the city lost a significant arbitration battle with the police

58 Penny's sister, Roberta Webber, retired from the PPB in 1997 after nearly 26 years of service. She served as the first female Commander, Deputy Chief, and Assistant Chief of the PPB. In 1994, she was named one of Ten Outstanding Women in Oregon by the Women's Foundation of Oregon. Roberta's husband, Ronald, retired as a PPB Captain with 27 years of service.

union, and officers received their pay raises, leading to additional budget cuts.[59] Third, crime was surging. Portland ranked eighth in violent crime and sixth in property crime, compared with 183 other cities with more than 100,000 residents (Harrington, 1999, p. 191). Penny felt much of the property crime was linked to truancy and established a juvenile division. Other reports indicated that Portland's rate of burglaries (40.8 per 1,000 residents) ranked the highest in the nation for three consecutive years (Turner, 1986a). Fourth, Penny was faced with a controversial chokehold death of a Black citizen at a white officer's hands. Fifth, a Black grandma and her mentally ill foster grandson were killed by the PPB. And finally, her husband Gary was under investigation for allegedly tipping off a cocaine dealer during an ongoing narcotics investigation. The latter three are discussed more fully in the proceeding sections.

As political pressure mounted, Clark ordered an independent review of Penny and Gary Harrington. A three-member panel, all men, concluded Gary had unknowingly tipped off a drug suspect about an ongoing investigation but not to the level that they would criminally prosecute. However, the panel went further, and on June 2, 1986, released a report that was highly critical of Penny's management decisions as chief. Clark used this report to force Penny's resignation. Penny's challenges as the nation's first major city police chief were insurmountable given the political pressure against her leadership. *Rap Sheet* Editor Sergeant Jeff Baker lamented,

> the resistance may be no more than an angry response to impending budget cuts, but it might also reflect the uncertainty with which certain members of the force still view a female chief in a bureau where male officers outnumber females by seven to one.
>
> (Harrington, 1999, p. 194)

These challenges came from the traditional status quo of law enforcement officers that plotted against their new chief's reform movements. For Penny, the challenges began only a couple of months after she became chief.

Death of Tony Stevenson

On April 20, 1985, Lloyd "Tony" Stevenson died in a chokehold from a PPB officer. He was a 31-year-old off-duty Black security guard honorably discharged from the U.S. Marine Corps and a father of five. At 11:30 PM, Stevenson entered a Northeast 7-Eleven located at 3rd Avenue and Weidler Street as store clerk Robert Wells attempted to detain a shoplifter. Customers Vicki Tyler and Devin Bass reportedly encouraged the shoplifter to run, and an altercation proceeded outside the store with the suspect and store clerks. Two attendants from a Shell gas station across the street came to the 7-Eleven parking lot to help Wells detain the shoplifter. Stevenson told the employees to return to the gas station, which led to a verbal altercation. Four police officers then arrived and witnessed store clerks with the shoplifter and Stevenson arguing with gas station attendants. Officer Gary Barbour came from behind Stevenson, likely with the belief that he was the perpetrator, and put him into a carotid artery sleeper chokehold. The chokehold cut off circulation to Stevenson's brain, causing him to pass out. A witness to the incident would later testify that he tried to tell the police they had the wrong guy, but they didn't pay attention (Hamburg & Rollins, 1985).

According to the subsequent police report, Stevenson hit Officer Bruce Pantley. Officers Barbour and Pantley then brought Stevenson to the ground, and Barbour administered the

59 To accommodate the second wave of budget cuts, 72 positions were eliminated within the PPB, and less than 20 officers were laid off from the 963-member force (Harrington, 1999, p. 194).

Photo 4.4 **Chief Harrington describes carotid hold at community meeting.**
Photo provided to the author by Penny Harrington.

chokehold. Barbour would later testify that he distributed the chokehold after Stevenson was on the ground since he knew that a standing chokehold violated his training and departmental policy. However, witnesses testified that Barbour jumped on Stevenson's back to apply the chokehold. Barbour reported he cuffed Stevenson after he lost consciousness, but he then uncuffed him while officers checked his pulse and attempted to resuscitate him. Again, witnesses challenged the official report, and the emergency medical technicians (EMTs) found Stevenson on his side, still handcuffed and not breathing. Witnesses further said that Stevenson did not touch any officers and did not resist arrest during the police encounter. Stevenson was pronounced dead at the Holladay Park Hospital at 12:15 AM (Rollins, 1985).

In the aftermath of Stevenson's death, Penny put an immediate ban on officers' use of the carotid chokehold[60] and formed a six-member citizen advisory committee to examine the PPB's use of force policies (Photo 4.4).[61]

The union immediately denounced Penny and claimed the chokehold was "the only tool that separates physical restraint from deadly force" (Harrington, 1999, p. 207). The given chokehold had been part of police academy training across the country. However, the situation was heightened for Penny when two white officers, Paul Wickersham, age 31, and Richard Montee, age 46, from the training division, sold T-shirts they had created in the East Precinct parking lot, at 4735 E. Burnside Street. The T-shirts had a stenciled picture of a smoking handgun with the words, "Don't Choke 'Em Smoke 'Em" (Ewens, 2017). The officers also distributed the shirts at the Portland Police Athletic Association club at 618 S.E.

60 Ironically, this same situation would play out on a national stage nearly 30 years later with the asphyxiation death of Eric Garner in NYC as described in the chapter on Bratton. Mass police protests under Black Lives Matter would also use the anthem of "I Can't Breathe" as a result. The world stage would be swept up in mass social justice protests following the May 25, 2020 asphyxiation death of George Floyd in Minneapolis.

61 Penny relieved both officers of street patrol and ordered them into counseling to help them with the stress the incident had caused. She frequently called them to check on their well-being and let them know she realized they were simply following police procedure and how they were trained. Clark announced a public inquest into the incident. Penny attended several roll calls to quash rumors and show that she was supportive of the officers involved and she would testify on their behalf (Harrington, 1999, p. 210).

Alder Street. They did so on April 26, 1985, the day of Stevenson's funeral. The Black community[62] responded and posted signs on telephone poles throughout their neighborhoods that pictured a police car and the words, "smoke them before they smoke you" (Harrington, 1999, p. 208), which led to additional protests (Turner, 1985).

The police union asked Penny to discipline the officers but not terminate them. With support from Mayor Clark, Penny defied the union request and called for the termination of officers Wickersham and Montee. She did not call for Officer Barbour's termination since he was doing what his training may have called for, albeit with the wrong suspect. Other officers and supervisors received suspensions for buying the T-shirts (Painter, 1985b). Most of the PPB officers did not support any of the suspensions or terminations. They believed the shirts were a harmless prank heightened by the media. A later survey showed 95 percent of officers thought the terminations were harmful to officer morale (Barker, 1985).

Attorney Richard Botteri, who would later represent Penny and her husband Gary, wrote a letter to *The Oregonian* editor supporting the chief's decision to ask for Wickersham and Montee's termination. After the newspaper published his letter, he received an obscene and anonymous call at his law office critical of his letter.[63] DA Schrunk and Sidney Lezak, former U.S. Attorney for Oregon, considered the T-shirt incident more serious than the opossum incident. However, Herb Cawthorne, the president of the Portland Urban League, stated the opossum was more insulting to the Black community (Painter, 1985a).

Three months into Penny's position as chief, she feared the entire city would erupt in riots. The community trust in Penny, dating back to her years as an officer, may have prevented the riots. Ronnie Herndon spoke on behalf of the BUF

> *While we still feel the great majority of Portland police officers do their best to perform a very difficult job and are truly concerned with the safety and welfare of Portland's citizens, this ugly and cynical response to events connected with the security guard's death serves to remind us all that there is still an element within the police bureau that is unfit for the serious responsibilities that the public has entrusted to them ... These officers should be subjected to the severest form of appropriate disciplinary actions ... I hope Harrington does her dead-level best to try to root this element out of the force*
>
> (Harrington, 1999, p. 209)

A subsequent inquest found Stevenson's death caused by negligent homicide. However, like most cases dealing with questionable use of force, competing experts testified. Dr. Richard Banner, a cardiologist who assisted the Portland police in training sleeper holds, testified that he doubted Barbour applied the chokehold too long. Neither Barbour nor the officers involved with the T-shirts received criminal charges, and they all kept their jobs.

Penny received a no-confidence vote from the police union. They argued that their chief did not provide enough support to the officers, but Mayor Clark ignored it. A confidential survey conducted by *The Oregonian*, and answered by 220 of the 730 PPB force, reported that 85 percent of officers felt the carotid chokehold on Stevenson was justified, and another 93 percent believed the hold should still be permitted (Hogan, 1985). The union, and their President Stan Peters,[64] regularly worked against Penny and stated that her ban on the carotid

62 During this time period, Blacks represented about 8 percent of Portland's 371,500 residents.

63 Botteri wrote his letter to *The Oregonian* before meeting Penny, and the visceral response intrigued his deeper curiosity. The attorney received his law degree from the University of Chicago and was an experienced litigator in Portland (author's interview with Botteri on October 19, 2020).

64 Penny described Peters as a 6'4" former motorcycle officer who attempted to intimidate perceived enemies. When he ran for union president, he asked her to be his campaign manager when she was a sergeant at the North Precinct. Penny had told him no. When he asked for her support, she again told him no. As union

hold would make officers' jobs more dangerous. Peters referred to Penny and Clark's leadership as "amateur hour" and claimed that city budget shortfalls were made up with money hidden from the union (Mapes, 1985). Penny described how Peters attended roll calls and made statements that she was trying to bust the union and emasculate him (Roman, 2018). Mayor Clark described how Peters would take a pistol from the small of his back and place it on the mayor's desk. Their meetings would begin with a gun between them as structured by Peters.

With a push from Peters, Wickersham and Montee sued Penny and the city for wrongful termination and a violation of their First Amendment rights. Penny's death threats increased, some that were blatantly sexists, "I'm going to cut your breasts off" or "You cunt, what do you think you're doing!" (Harrington, 1999, p. 213). She used a Native-American officer, and her husband Gary, as her constant bodyguards.

By the end of October 1985, an arbitrator ruled the termination of the officers who sold the T-shirts was excessive, but they should be suspended for six months without pay. While the union declared victory and Penny attempted to make sense of it all, City Commissioner Mike Lindberg sounded off on the arbitrator's ruling "a devastating blow to the police chief and city council and our inability to manage the police department … It's almost an unsupervisable (police) force at this point in time" (Harrington, 1999, p. 213). The commissioner's observation points out an ongoing problem with police leadership and their inability to supervise and hold officers accountable for behaviors that impact the entire department and city's they serve. On April 23, 1986, a final challenge to the police leadership authority came when a federal Judge James Redden refused to ban the use of the carotid-artery hold by the PPB and also refused to order the removal of officers Barbour and Pantley from active duty (Laatz, 1986). Before the federal ruling, Pantley left the PPB and filed a disability claim for stress.

Officers Kill Two in Hostage Negotiation – One 37-Year-Old Male and One 85-Year-Old Female

On the evening of July 5, 1985, Thomas Graves, a 37-year-old mentally ill Black man, got into an argument with several Native-American patrons at the Pub Tavern located in northeast Portland at 1526 N.E. Alberta Street. A witness saw two men beating Graves up outside the tavern before they told him to leave. Graves told patrons that he would return with a gun. When officers responded to a subsequent call for service, they knew who Graves was by a witness description.

Additionally, Officer Derrick Foxworth had prior encounters with Graves earlier in the day. Foxworth, a Black officer, responded when a group of white officers were arguing with Graves, who reportedly had a four-inch hunting knife in his possession. After white officers exchanged racially derogatory language with Graves, Foxworth de-escalated the encounter and convinced him to walk away (Hamburg, 1985). Later that evening, after the Pub Tavern incident, officers went to his home, where Graves had resided for more than a decade with Alberta "Berta" Tate, an 86-year-old Black woman who was part of an adult foster care program. Berta's son Luther also lived in the home, located at 5106 N.E. 16th Avenue, and told officers that he asked his mother to clean his room, where he kept his hunting rifles. When the

president, Peters claimed his full-time work dealt with disputes and meetings. However, half his salary was being paid by the city for several years. Penny attempted to move him into taking crime reports at least half the time, and he refused. Instead, he convinced the union to support his full-time pay as their steward and claimed that their new chief attempted to bust prior union agreements (Harrington, 1999, pp. 195–197). Peters was the President of the PPA from 1974 to 1991. He passed away in 2011, and the PPA provides a yearly award to select members in his honor.

officers arrived around 7 PM, they saw Graves in the front yard with one of Luther's hunting rifles. Neighbors Rocky Orr and Tony Washington said Graves had already fired the gun from his front porch. Graves ran back into the home when he saw the police.

A hostage negotiator arrived on the scene and contacted Tate through their house phone, who reported she thought Graves would eventually get tired and go to sleep. Penny was at her home during the standoff and briefed on the situation by her captain. She recommended that the Special Emergency Response Team (SERT) respond, continue negotiations, and wait for Graves to surrender. Penny then fell asleep, not knowing that the phone near her bed was inoperable because the phone company had inadvertently shut it down during a repair (Harrington, 1999, p. 217). Several calls to Penny's home phone went unanswered throughout the evening, and her police radio was on a charger away from her bedroom. Later, the phone company verified they had accidentally disconnected her phone line (Harrington, 1999, p. 221).

After several hours into the evening, Berta Tate, the elderly woman, spoke to the police and said she was scared and Graves was acting more erratic. The police negotiators instructed Tate to lock herself in a room and, following hostage protocol, cut the power to the house. The police then lost contact for several more hours. Graves continually ran out the front door throughout the evening, fire shots in the air, and then did the same out the back door. Police reports indicated Graves fired as many as 30 shots over the next several hours. Luther Tate waited outside his home, helpless and angry, while Graves held his mother hostage and continued to fire off his guns (Wilson, 1985).

As the evening went on, the PPB captain on the scene decided to go home and left a newly promoted lieutenant in charge without any notification given to Penny. The lieutenant, William Osborne, ordered that if the suspect fired his weapon near any of the officers, they should return fire (Danks & Rollins, 1985). When Graves came out the front door to again discharge a firearm in the air, an officer fired his shotgun, and unknowingly, a slug fatally hit Graves in the jaw and neck, severed his carotid artery, struck his spinal cord, and knocked him back into the house. However, no one saw him fall. Instead, they saw a shadow running toward the back door, which appeared to repeat what Graves had been doing throughout the evening. As soon as the back door opened, an officer in the backyard standing behind a tree fired his buck-shot-loaded shotgun into Tate, the elderly female, who had attempted to run out the backdoor to escape. Pellets hit Tate in the left thigh. Officers were reluctant to immediately render aid to the dying elderly victim, not knowing if Graves would ambush them. As Tate lay bleeding to death by her back door, an officer finally decided to run and scoop the woman up into his arms and rush her down the street to an awaiting ambulance, where she was pronounced dead on arrival around 1 AM on July 6th. It was not until 5 AM when officers made entry and found that officers had killed Graves before Tate attempted to run out the back door.

The outrage from the Portland Black community was predictably intense. Ron Herndon, the BUF's co-chair, sponsored a meeting at the King Neighborhood facility, which Penny attended. An estimated 300 people filled the facility on the hot summer day, and the air-conditioner broke. Young Black teens protested with pig heads on stakes, a derogatory statement toward the PPB that everyone understood. Penny provided a 30-minute presentation and attempted to be as transparent as she could about what transpired. She also released a copy of the given police report on the incident, which was unprecedented for a chief to do at that time, and implored the community to trust her leadership.

Mayor Clark initially declined an invitation to attend the King Neighborhood facility and later decided to attend but not speak (Hamburg & Painter, 1985). Penny fielded questions from the angered community for the next three hours. In the end, to her surprise, she was given a standing ovation (Harrington, 1999, p. 223). The DA and Grand Jury inquiry verified that Penny's phone was inoperable the evening fatal police shots killed Graves and Tate. Penny demoted the captain who had left the scene and disciplined the lieutenant but did not hold any other officers accountable. She met again with the community and eased racial tension by being transparent with the facts and her internal leadership. However, an angry union perceived their chief caved into the Black community's demands.[65]

Richard Brown, another co-chair of Portland's BUF, expressed the perceptions of the Black community when he stated, "the police were always viewed … like an occupying force in Black communities … Anytime there was an issue in our community, we were on one side, and they were on the other side" (Thacher, 2000). In July, the BUF requested that the DOJ probe the police shooting. The following month a Grand Jury declined to issue a criminal indictment but was critical of how the Tate/Graves event was handled (Hallman, 1986a). By November, the city council agreed to pay the Tate family more than $625,000 to settle their lawsuit.

Participatory Management – Cracking Down on Truants

Penny demonstrated creativity in moving toward participatory management[66] during her short tenure as chief. She did voluntary ride-along with officers during all shifts and at each precinct to hear about their concerns. She helped officers receive a pay raise, and she developed a ten-year vision for the PPB linked with a value system. The union was vocal in their criticism of Penny, but her leadership success, in a short period, could be seen in other ways. *The Skanner*, a north Portland newspaper, wrote the following:

> *If the police chief has a liability, it is the fact that she is the first woman to head the police bureau here, and perhaps some of the male officers want her to fail. We feel that Harrington represents a new approach, a listen-and-learn, and a what-do-the-citizens-want attitude that is very much overdue. She has our support and the support of many citizens in the city. And that should count as a strong vote of confidence for a police chief who is willing to make tough decisions and stand behind them.*
> (Harrington, 1999, p. 223)

In addition to the positive press from select areas of the city, Penny also launched her truancy strategy that utilized juvenile patrol officers to stop kids who were not at school and inform their parents in addition to bringing them back to school. When truancy occurred, notification went out to the juvenile court, and the impacted family received contact from social services. The immediacy of intervention frequently led to counseling and other services. In return, schools agreed not to suspend the truant while other parts of the city worked to assist the impacted family. In four weeks, about 300 truants were picked up by the juvenile

65 The landmark case *Tennessee v. Garner* also came in 1985. The Court determined that lethal force could no longer be used to stop a fleeing suspect unless the officer had probable cause to believe the suspect poses a significant threat of death or serious injury to the officer or others. Consequently, police departments across the country gradually changed their policies to manage the use of force better. The PPB changed its use of force policy in response to a federal lawsuit filed on December 17, 2012, that alleged Portland's officers engaged in a "pattern and practice" of excessive force against those suffering from mental illness (Berstein, 2012).

66 Participatory management practices evolved out of Harvard University's research at the Hawthorne Western Electrics Plant in Cicero, Illinois, from 1927 to 1932. (The plant opened in 1905 and operated until 1983. The original town name was Hawthorne.) The researchers determined that improved lighting had nothing to do with factory worker's productivity, but merely paying attention to them caused changes in their morale. The revolutionary findings created a human relations movement based on the principle that subordinates should be empowered to participate in organizational decision-making. This management style is at the heart of community policing and problem-solving that both Chief Penny Harrington and Mayor Bud Clark mutually emphasized.

division and referred to services through the courts. The truancy accountability program cut daytime burglaries in half (Harrington, 1999, p. 231). Penny had initial success as the nation's first female big-city chief, but her biggest challenge came from her own department.

Narcotics Investigation – Mr. Robert "Bobby" Lee and Rickashaw Charlie's (PART I)[67]

During the 1960s, Chinatown in Portland thrived along Northwest Fourth Avenue. Bobby Lee opened Rickashaw Charlie's at 331 NW Davis Street in 1966, in Old Town Portland, and the restaurant became a popular night-spot with a live piano player. Lee resided at 631 N. Tomahawk Island Drive. For a couple of years, Gary Harrington lived in a condominium next door to Lee on Hayden Island before getting married to Penny. During this time, Harrington and Lee visited each other's homes a few times. Gary reported that Lee always got to know his customers at his restaurant, and he frequently hung out there with other officers after his police shift was over.

On February 11, 1985, around 1 AM, Lee, 52 years old, shot and wounded 28-year-old transient John Winford Tate, who resided temporarily at the Royal Palms Hotel at 310 NW Flanders Street. Tate had a toy gun, and Lee believed he was about to be robbed. Lee did not have a license for the two handguns he was carrying, shot Tate three times, and then attempted to contact Penny for advice. On March 25, 1985, Tom Hallman, Jr., from *The Oregonian*, interviewed Penny and asked about her contact with Lee. Penny explained that she returned office phone calls from Lee and offered him the opinion that a Grand Jury would not likely indict in the shooting case, advice she would provide any citizen. A subsequent Multnomah County Grand Jury later declined to indict neither Lee nor Tate.

Gary's connection with Lee went back to the late 1970s when he warned him not to associate with Raymond Cook, a known drug dealer who belonged to organized crime, managed a downtown massage parlor and hung around Lee's restaurant. Cook was eventually convicted of federal tax evasion in 1984 and sentenced to three years in prison (Long & Zaitz, 1986a). Additionally, Sgt. Jay Decker[68] testified that he told Penny, sometime in the spring of 1985, that he had heard rumors that Lee was being investigated for being involved with the sale of illicit narcotics and recommended that she avoid going to his restaurant. At the time, Decker served as Penny's public information officer. Later, prosecutors compelled Decker to reveal how he acquired information about Lee being an illicit drug dealing suspect. Decker disclosed that he heard about the drug investigation from Sgt. Robert Clary[69] (Zaitz & Long, 1986b). Subsequent investigations determined that Clary received information from Detective Michael Guinn, a member of the cocaine task force partnered with other federal agents. Penny was under the impression, in the spring of 1985, an arrest of Lee was imminent based upon what Decker had told her, and she was shocked to hear that he was involved with drug activity.

Penny and Gary stayed away from Lee and his restaurant for approximately six months due to the rumor but did not have specific knowledge about any drug investigation. After six months passed, they figured the investigation was indeed a rumor and no longer active. In February 1986, Gary attended a party at Lee's restaurant for a retiring friend from a gas

67 PART II of this section is detailed below as part of the Lezak Commission investigative probe.

68 Decker worked under Penny's command in the East Precinct from May 6, 1982, until she was appointed chief. Penny named Decker to be her public information officer on March 19, 1985. After the Lezak Commission was formed, Decker was transferred back to being a patrol sergeant in the East Precinct.

69 On November 6, 1987, Mayor Clark terminated Sgt. Decker and Sgt. Clary for using cocaine while off-duty. The termination came in the aftermath of an internal investigation (Hallman & Ellis, 1987).

company, unaware that a two-year federal and state investigation into cocaine dealing through out Portland was still ongoing and included Lee and his restaurant. On the evening of the retirement party, Gary asked Lee if any officers had spoken to him about drug dealers being in his restaurant. Lee told him no but asked what he should do if officers questioned him. Gary told Lee to cooperate and tell the truth if any investigators came to question him.

On Tuesday, March 11, 1986, federal officers' joint task force with the PPB and sheriff's department arrived at Rickashaw Charlie's Restaurant and questioned Lee about anything he knew about Portland cocaine trafficking (Harrington, 1999, p. 235). The investigators wanted to use Lee as a witness or confidential informant based on dealers he knew from his restaurant. Lee supposedly told them what he knew, and as the officers were leaving, he commented that he knew the chief and Gary Harrington had told him he should cooperate. Officers returned the following day, on March 12th, but they reported Lee was much more evasive and refused to cooperate further. The investigating officers took this information to federal and county prosecutors (i.e. U.S. Attorney Charles Turner[70] and DA Michael Schrunk). They claimed that Gary Harrington interfered with a two-year drug investigation and tipped off a criminal suspect.

DA Schrunk contacted Penny at home and asked her to meet him alone at a restaurant. When she arrived, he told her that Gary was a suspect in a drug investigation, the police were at her house questioning him, and they would question her next. Both Penny and Gary cooperated with the questions and felt prosecutors would clear them of any wrongdoing. For the next eight days, investigators questioned 14 individuals, including both Penny and Gary and the PPB command staff (Zaitz & Long, 1986b). These investigators reported directly to Mayor Clark and DA Schrunk. After the investigation, Schrunk contacted Penny and told her Gary would be exonerated, and they would send a letter. However, the letter did not fully exonerate Gary. Penny was notified formally by two letters from Turner and Schrunk, which stated they had found "clear and convincing" evidence that Gary had violated departmental policies by "tipping off" Lee. However, there was not sufficient evidence to warrant criminal prosecution. The case was officially closed on March 21st, or so they thought. Subsequently, Penny called a press conference on March 25, 1986, to discuss two investigations against her husband, Gary.

The first investigation concerned allegations that he tipped off Bobby Lee in February 1986 about a drug investigation. Penny stated that federal and state prosecutors informed her that they lacked evidence to prosecute Gary on the allegation that he had disclosed confidential information about a narcotics investigation (Turner, 1986b). However, he would face an internal investigation through a deputy chief that would report directly to the mayor's office. At the time, her sister Roberta was a Captain in charge of the Internal Investigations Unit but would not be part of the internal investigation.

The second investigation of Gary concerned internal reports from 1972 to 1973, leaked to the press, and showed a link between Gary Harrington and convicted heroin dealer Wey Him "Wayne" Fong.[71] During her press conference, Penny passed out a written statement to the media that stated the allegation that a heroin dealer bribed Gary was disproven 13 years

70 Turner was an assistant to Sidney Lezak for 14 years before being appointed to replace him as a U.S. Attorney by President Reagan in 1982. Turner was a close friend to Schrunk (Griffin & Sulzberger, 2009) but not necessarily Lezak. He had several high-profile cases as a prosecutor including the nation's first modern domestic terrorism case that dealt with several ex-convicts and Portland State University French professor Frank Giese who conspired with the Northwest Liberation Front to bomb the U.S. Army Recruiting Center in Portland in 1973. Turner died on January 8, 2018, at the age of 81.

71 Fong was convicted of dealing heroin and died at the McNeil Island Federal Penitentiary in 1976, the final year the Federal Government managed the prison.

prior. Through his attorney Jacob Tanzer, Gary also commented that Captain Leo Miller had cleared him in the aftermath of a 1973 investigation, and the files were supposed to be destroyed. However, part of the files was not destroyed and instead hidden for more than a decade at Captain Wayne Inman's home.[72] Inman was an investigating sergeant in 1972. In the internal investigative reports, allegations from a confidential informant stated Harrington was present with Fong on June 13, 1972, during a drug transaction. Gary received what appeared to be a cash payment from the heroin dealer. Also, the informant claimed Fong bought Gary a new car. However, a subsequent investigation from the Internal Revenue Service (IRS) failed to find irregularities in Gary's finances. Records from the Oregon Motor Division showed he acquired a lien on a new vehicle, a 1972 Pontiac Grand Prix, with his wife, Virginia, on June 8, 1972. On August 1, 1978, Gary sold the Grand Prix, and it still had a lien, which created some doubt in the informant's allegations that Gary was gifted Fong's vehicle (Zaitz, Long, & Hallman, 1986). On May 15, 1986, Gary testified in front of a commission that he met Fong in the 1970s at Dragon's I restaurant and described him as a talkative bar companion. He did not learn until a year after they met that Fong had a criminal record (Long & Zaitz, 1986a).

Mayor Clark publicly supported Penny and her attempt at being transparent with the allegations, but he also opted to form a special review commission based upon continued media scrutiny. This move was unprecedented as no other chief ever had to defend their family or leadership decisions in a public forum. On March 28, 1986, Clark called his press conference at City Hall. He announced former U.S. Attorney Sidney Lezak[73] would be heading a special commission to monitor an internal PPB investigation into allegations that Gary Harrington prematurely disclosed to Bobby Lee that he was a suspect in a narcotics trafficking investigation.

Lezak Commission

Lezak, who retired as federal prosecutor five years earlier, recommended Senior Judge John Beatty, Jr.,[74] of the Multnomah County Circuit Court, be added to the commission. Beatty subsequently became the draftsman for their investigative notes. Beatty was named senior judge a couple of years before forming the special commission and was old friends with Lezak. They were both entrenched with Portland's Democratic politics. Having no actual law enforcement management experience, Lezak and Beatty asked Colonel Doyle Watson, the Deputy Superintendent of the Oregon State Police, to be their third and final commission member. The mayor assured Watson that the committee's investigation would be independent of Portland City Hall. Despite this assurance, Watson still insisted the city made a contract to pay for future defense attorneys if the committee got sued in the aftermath of their recommendations (Beatty, 2010). The commission met with Mayor Clark's press secretary

72 Inman would later be promoted to be assistant chief to Tom Potter, Mayor Clark's last chief appointment. Potter was one of the main witnesses to testify against Chief Harrington. Inman was selected as his assistant chief despite a lawsuit filed against him by Officer Dale Larson, who alleged Inman denied him a promotion after Larson reported being a witness to police brutality. Larson alleged that Inman was out to get him. The lawsuit ended with an undisclosed settlement (Budnick, 2017).

73 Lezak was the longest-serving U.S. Attorney (1961–1982). He served five Presidents from Kennedy to Reagan and has been labeled the father of Alternative Dispute Resolution (ADR) (Hammer, 2006). He died in 2006 at the age of 81.

74 Beatty died in 2016 at the age of 97.

Charles "Chuck" Duffy[75] and City Attorney Jeff Rogers[76] to receive legal assurance for future defense and established perimeters for their investigation.

The commission asked for $50,000 to run the probe and initially began holding secretive interviews with at least 14 individuals as part of their investigation from an office at the First Interstate Bank Tower, located at 1300 S.W. Fifth Avenue (Zaitz & Long, 1986a). Lezak argued the commission was exempt from the Oregon Public Meetings Law. However, as a proponent of government transparency, Mayor Clark opted to have an open hearing broadcasted over public and cable television. This decision to hold a public commission inquiry into Penny's leadership would serve as the precursor for a subsequent lawsuit filed by Penny for wrongful termination. Throughout the commission's probe, Clark continually reassured Penny that he would keep her on as chief and recommended a light cross-examination of any police witnesses so future relationships with the chief did not get negatively impacted. The hearings took place on the second floor of the Portland Building auditorium located at 1120 SW Fifth Avenue, a gloomy architectural setting (Beatty, 2010). Proceedings consisted of two sessions, each two weeks long, with a ten-day recess (April 17–29 and May 13–16). Richard Botteri represented Penny, and he recommended that her husband Gary retain his own attorney. Botteri contacted Jake Tanzer, a retired Oregon Supreme Court justice, who agreed to represent Gary.

On April 6, 1986, Mayor Clark announced the commission was expanding their probe to investigate Chief Harrington (Long & Zaitz, 1986b). The expansion of the commission's role evolved after reporter Tom Hallman's March 26th and April 2nd articles in *The Oregonian* (Hallman, Long, & Zaitz, 1986; Zaitz, Hallman, & Long, 1986) linked Penny to Bobby Lee when she told Hallman that she returned phone calls from Lee. (The interview with Hallman and Penny is discussed more fully below.) Penny was the first to testify and take questions from the commission on April 17th and the last to take commission questions on May 16th.

During her opening testimony, Penny described the department that she inherited as being in crisis with budget cuts, high crime rates, corruption, and in need of reorganization. She presented several charts and statistics while her three deputy chiefs sat in support of her. The charts indicated that the controversial reorganization of a new Narcotics, Vice and Intelligence Section within the Detective Division had increased drug arrests compared to the following year. This retort referenced the commission's probe into whether the reorganization had caused an increase in drug trafficking. After Penny's testimony, Lezak made it clear to the media (Read, 1986a) that he would be calling witnesses that were critical of Penny's policies along with a more thorough probe into allegations that Gary tipped off drug suspect Bobby Lee.

A subsequent evening commission session took place with U.S. Attorney Charles Turner and several deputies. Turner was a former deputy prosecutor who worked for Lezak, distrusted the entire commission process, and made it clear he thought they were engaged in a planned whitewash of Chief Harrington (Beatty, 2010). Houston Police Chief Lee Brown, described earlier in the chapter, testified on behalf of Penny. Brown, who was also the former Multnomah

75 Duffy's father was a well-connected Chicago building commissioner who worked with Mayor Richard J. Daley throughout the 1960s into the 1970s. In 1975, his family moved to Portland to escape Chicago's problems with machine politics, racial strife, and police mismanagement. Duffy recently blamed Portland's problems with community conflict on a political dismantling of neighborhood associations that were historically prevalent throughout the city (Classen, 2019). The importance of neighborhood associations and links with the police were a continued goal of Penny's leadership that was halted by her forced resignation.

76 Portland's City Attorney Jeff Rogers's father was William Rogers, former U.S. Attorney General (1957–1961) under President Eisenhower. When Clark's special commission was formed, William Rogers was heading an investigation into why the Space Shuttle Challenger blew up on January 28, 1986, 73 seconds into its flight. Lezak jokingly commented that he too was now part of a Rogers's investigation.

County Sheriff, told the commission, via speakerphone, that he supported Penny's reform efforts as PPB chief, and the truancy program they both had implemented was based upon the work of Chief Bud Willoughby[77] in Salt Lake City. Brown testified that he admired Penny's leadership in dismantling the stand-alone drug unit and upgrading the narcotics officers to detectives, an organizational change that he had also implemented in Houston.[78] *The Oregonian* initially failed to write an account of Lee Brown's support for Penny within their coverage of the Lezak Commission (Read, 1986d). Chief Willoughby also testified in front of the commission, on behalf of Penny, and argued that the commission was setting a terrible precedent for challenging police chiefs and they should support her leadership (Lloyd, 1986a). Despite Lee and Willoughby's national notoriety and admiration for Penny's leadership, in the end, the commission disregarded their testimony.

In between the April 17–29 and May 13–16 hearings, Penny addressed her 11 captains and deputy chiefs at their weekly command staff meeting. She expressed the importance of the department sticking together, that she had been informed by the mayor that her position as chief was not in jeopardy and that her detractors would not run her out. Despite this plea, her detractors continued to speak anonymously to the press. They provided the opinion that they felt alienated by their chief and that she had lost credibility throughout the PPB (Long, Hallman, & Zaitz, 1986).

After a two-week break, which occurred because one of the commissioners, Beatty, had a preplanned vacation with his wife (Beatty, 2010), Lieutenant Charles Karl, commander of the drug unit that Penny disbanded, testified against his chief and claimed the existing drug unit was inefficient. According to Karl, it would take six months to a year before the unit was as good as before the PPB's reorganization. Union president Peters also took his shots at Penny and claimed that corner drug dealers "are selling heroin like it was candy" (Turner, 1986c) due to her reform leadership. In April 1985, in response to budget cuts, Penny disbanded the Drug and Vice team, which had previously replaced the SID after the scandals in the 1970s. The new Narcotics, Vice and Intelligence Section was aligned in the Detective Division to allow investigations into theft and burglaries to collaborate with narcotics investigations. Lt. Charles Karl headed the smaller section inside the Detective Division and testified they were only half as effective as the prior drug unit that Penny disbanded (Read, 1986b). However, subsequent statistics were presented that indicated drug arrests were up with the new detectives.

In retort to Turner, Brown, and Willoughby's favorable testimony, several of Penny's police detractors followed Lt. Karl and Union President Peters's testimony. Her attorney Botteri requested that the commission put the police witnesses under oath, believing they may be more likely to give truthful answers, but he was denied.[79] Lezak surprised many when he called for secret testimony that would not be part of the public record. The union had persuaded the commission to allow additional officers from the defunct drug unit to testify against Penny. Penny's reorganization of the Drug and Vice team naturally created internal enemies. These enemies claimed that their chief disbanded the undercover narcotics strike team to placate Portland's Black community concerns. The officers, who understandably did not want to appear in front of the mayor's public hearing, were upset about losing their highly sought-after undercover investigative positions and notoriety that such positions carried in the department. However, there was also the historical corruption that plagued such units. Several testified

77 Willoughby was Salt Lake City Chief from 1977 to 1988, the longest in the city's history. He served on the Major City Chiefs (MCC) association and the National Executive Institute, where he continued to serve as a consultant after retirement.

78 Author's interview with Penny on April 9, 2020.

79 Author's interview with Botteri on August 29, 2020.

under threat of subpoena. They blamed rampant drug use in Portland on Penny's departmental reorganization and backed prior testimony from Lt. Karl.

The other pertinent witness that testified critically against Penny, to her surprise, was Tom Potter, 45 years old at the time. Potter's ambitious career trajectory played out for the next couple of decades.

> When Penny became chief, she had three openings to fill for deputy chiefs. She promoted Clell Winters, age 50, to patrol deputy chief and Robert Tobin, age 43, to investigations deputy chief. That left one more slot, and she selected Potter, age 44, as the third deputy chief after a lengthy discussion with Mayor Clark. Clark wanted to see either Jim Davis or Potter promoted. Penny preferred to appoint her sister Roberta Webber as deputy chief to ensure her reform efforts would not lose momentum, but Clark refused. Mayoral press secretary Duffy reminded Clark that President Kennedy had appointed his brother Robert to be Attorney General. However, Clark was adamant and refused to allow Penny to promote her sister as the third deputy chief. Penny did not trust Davis since they were often rivals for promotions and assignments throughout their careers. Penny also discovered that Davis attempted to sabotage her during the chief selection process by telling at least one community member on the selection panel, Annette Jolin, that Penny had said negative things about her. When Jolin contacted Penny to confront her about the allegation, Penny assured her that she did not speak negatively about her and the allegation was contrived by her detractors. At the time, the mayor pressured Penny into promoting Potter to be her deputy chief even though they did not know each other very well. Potter became Mayor Clark's last police chief appointment in 1990 and served in that capacity for three years before he retired at 52 years of age with 25 years of law enforcement experience. Potter enjoyed union support as chief. In 2005–2009 he was also elected as a one-term Portland mayor.

Before his testimony to the Lezak Commission, Potter gave every indication he was supportive of Penny as his chief and for her community policing policies. Potter joined the other deputy chiefs in signing off to support her opening statement to the Lezak Commission. However, after the chief's opening statements on April 17th, Potter stated that he felt Penny misled the commission when she said that there was a long-term plan connected to the department's reorganization (Read, 1986c). Consequently, on April 25th, Potter requested and was granted a demotion. He told *The Oregonian* that he asked for the demotion because he did not want to be critical of his chief from a high-level administrative position (Lloyd, 1986b). Botteri reported he witnessed Potter's meeting with Penny in her office before his April 28th testimony. Potter tearfully told her that he could no longer support her because of the pressure he faced from other department members.[80]

Narcotics Investigation – Mr. Robert "Bobby" Lee and Rickashaw Charlie's (PART II)

The most significant precursor for the Lezak Commission's expanded investigation was Penny and Gary's contacts with Lee and his restaurant's drug investigation. The mayor, and subsequently the special commission, felt forced to react to the investigative media reports from Tom Hallman with *The Oregonian* newspaper. Hallman's account linked a friendship between

80 Author's interview with Botteri on August 29, 2020.

Gary and Lee, in addition to a drug investigation into Lee's Chinese restaurant. Hallman aggressively pursued the story and also attempted to link Penny to Lee. This link came in a pink phone message slip that Penny had received at her office to return a phone call from Bobby Lee after being involved in the February 11th shooting of transient John Tate outside his restaurant. This incident was discussed previously as a precursor to the formation of the Lezak Commission. Penny always returned phone calls from citizens, and at the time of her response to his call, she had no reason to be suspicious that he was under investigation. Lee asked Penny about being interviewed by officers, and she urged him to tell the officers the truth regarding any law enforcement questions. Penny then crumpled up the message and threw it into her wastebasket. A night janitor at the PPB, who had known Penny for many years, told her he saw Potter going through her wastebasket late at night after she had left her office. Attorney Botteri believed Potter passed on the phone message slip to reporter Hallman to support Penny and Lee's link for his newspaper story.[81] Penny later recalled that Hallman interviewed her for a news story and held several pink phone message slips in his hand when he asked about the extent of her relationship with Lee.

The commission elected to subpoena Lee to testify, but his attorney told them that he would plead his Fifth Amendment right to remain silent. Despite this plea, the commission still ordered Lee to testify in front of the media. On Tuesday, May 13th, Lee spent less than five minutes on the witness stand (Zaitz & Long, 1986c). Forcing Lee to plead the Fifth Amendment gave the impression that Penny and Gary had something to hide and further damaged their reputations.[82] On the same May 13th date, Lt. Kenneth Amos and Detective William Law, from the PPB Internal Investigations Unit, testified about their investigation into Gary and Penny, her returned phone calls to Lee after he shot the transient Tate, and Sgt. Decker's warning not to go around Lee because he was a suspect in a drug investigation.

On May 30th, the commission held a closed meeting with Mayor Clark and his administration members to brief them on their report. The city council was disappointed that they were left out of the private meeting. Ultimately, the commission issued a scathing 38-page report that questioned Penny's leadership, stated she lost her command staff's confidence and recommended her removal as police chief (Turner, 1986c). Specifically, the commission challenged Penny's "unyielding" management style that was labeled as a "defect in leadership," making some question if gender bias was involved with the labels placed on the nation's first female police chief for a major city.

The commission recommended a 25-day suspension for Gary. The prosecution cleared Gary of criminal wrongdoing related to his connection with Lee, but internally the PPB found that he violated general orders regarding associations with suspected criminals. The report was delivered in person to Mayor Clark by Lezak, which supposedly blindsided Clark and his assistant Duffy. Clark delivered the report to Gary and Penny at their West Linn home and then released the full report to *The Oregonian* published on June 3, 1986. *The Oregonian* June 4, 1986 editorial was titled "Clark Undercut Chief" and argued that an amateur politician undermined his police chief appointee's authority, which caused Penny to resign. A subsequent editorial was titled "Harrington Judged in Wonderland" and encouraged Clark to resign (Sarasohn, 1986). Another editorial headline read, "Lezak Commission was a hatchet job on Harrington" (Mitchell, 1986).

Clark perceived he had lost control of the situation and informed Penny he would demote her back to Captain. The mayor reported he had no choice but to terminate Penny based

81 Author's interview with Botteri on September 8, 2020.

82 Lee was later found guilty of drug conspiracy and was connected to a multistate drug ring. He received a ten-year federal sentence at a prison camp in Minnesota (Hallman & Ellis, 1987).

upon the Lezak Commission's distinguished reputations. Penny opted to resign, provided her own written response, and asked Clark to distribute her explanation to the media. She stated the commission report left her no choice but to resign. The meeting concluded with Clark (in)famously telling Penny "tits up" to lift her spirits. Clark routinely used the "tits up" phrase when he hoisted a beer at his bar (Crotty, 1997). On June 2, 1986, he formally announced Penny's resignation, which was effectively a termination.

After Penny's resignation, Clark heard demands from Elizabeth Waters, who became a coordinator for a community delegation named *People for Penny*. The delegation formed in the wake of the forced resignation and held a rally with several speakers at the Terry Schrunk Plaza on June 22, 1986 (Severson, 1986). The delegation's main goal was to demonstrate support for Chief Harrington's strategies and implore the mayor to continue these goals (Durbin, 1986).

Behind the formality of the resignation, Clark tried to negotiate an early retirement package with Penny. However, City Attorney Rogers told the mayor that he did not have the authority to do so. The mayor encouraged Penny to apply for stress disability, which allowed her to get paid until her pension became effective in 1992. Penny was 44 years old when she resigned as chief with 22 years of PPB service. According to the city charter, employees must have at least 25 years of service or have reached 50 before drawing on the pension system. On October 22, 1986, *The Oregonian* front-page story headlined "Penny Harrington wins disability payments" on a 6–3 vote from the city's Fire and Police Disability and Retirement Board (Hallman, 1986b). In ruling that Penny suffered stress as chief and should be compensated, the board determined that she should receive a captain's salary for one year, a patrolman's salary for four years, and then 60 percent of a patrolman's salary (Hallman, 1986b). However, their ruling was subject to future review. In the aftermath of the board's ruling, Penny and Gary traveled to Lansing, Michigan, to be by Penny's parents, and then they moved to California.

About six months later, on May 12, 1987, the retirement board ruled that Penny should show cause on why she could not return to work at the PPB. On the board's orders, two separate psychiatrists reexamined Penny, one being her personal psychiatrist. The psychiatrists offered conflicting reports regarding her future well-being if she were to come back to the PPB. Botteri provided legal representation for Penny during the retirement board's closed session meeting and argued that she would not be able to return to work at the PPB without being subjected to enormous stress from the foul-mouthed hatred of Portland officers. In offering evidence, Botteri had resident Daniel Florea testify that in the summer of 1986, he witnessed at least ten officers in Cathedral Park openly celebrate the announcement of her termination (Lane, 1987), with one exclaiming, "We finally got rid of the bitch."[83] On May 27, 1987, *The Oregonian* front-page story headlined "Board ends Penny Harrington's stress pay," and the Fire and Police Disability Retirement Board voted 9–1 to end the disability payments and declared Penny could return to work as a captain (Lane, 1987). Additionally, the Civil Rights Division dismissed Gary and Penny's complaints in February 1988.

Gary continued to feel guilty for his wife's predicament and wanted to move back to Portland to rebuild his name. Penny wanted to put Portland in her rearview mirror, refused to take a demoted position with the PPB, and sought to rebuild her life in California. On July 2, 1986, the Fire and Police Disability and Retirement Board denied Gary's request to be placed on full medical disability with a 6–2 vote. On July 22, 1986, Mayor Clark suspended Gary for ten days without pay based on the Lezak Commission's findings that he had violated PPB general orders (Oliver, 1986). On March 9, 1989, the Oregon Court of Appeals rejected Gary's

83 After his testimony, the resident contacted Botteri because he had received an anonymous, angry, and threatening phone call attacking him for his testimony about the officers' behavior after Penny was terminated (author's interview with Botteri on September 8, 2020).

attempt to further draw on the disability pension. On June 1, 1989, Gary returned to Portland as an officer because his disability pay ran out (Austin, 1989). The divorce of Penny and Gary was inevitable. With her disability canceled, Penny sold her home, lived in an apartment, and then a small camper. She unsuccessfully applied to over 30 police agencies. She was told by one placement agency that she was "too hot" to hire and that no mayor or city manager wanted to hire her and then have to explain the Portland Lezak report (Painter, 1990d).

Penny's Federal Lawsuit – Post-Termination

After the retirement board reversed its prior decision and denied Penny's disability payments, she filed a federal sex discrimination lawsuit against the mayor, the city of Portland, and the three members of the special commission. Lezak wanted to destroy all notes and past drafts of their report in the days leading up to the commission report becoming public. Commission member Judge Beatty decided to save everything. Ultimately, the files were boxed up and sent to the city archives (Read, 1986e). Penny hired Linda Eyerman as her attorney, filed a federal lawsuit in the Portland U.S. District Court, and subpoenaed all Lezak Commission documents. Don Marmaduke, from the Tonkin Torp law firm, led the legal defense for Mayor Clark. Beatty called the defense of their work complicated and discussed their depositions in his autobiography (Beatty, 2010).

The jury trial for the lawsuit began on February 20, 1990, with presiding Judge Helen Frye. The trial lasted 15 days over four weeks. On February 23, 1990, Penny testified that the Lezak Commission ruined her reputation and the mayor's forced resignation made it impossible for her to secure employment in policing (Painter, 1990b). Past attorneys for both Penny and Gary Harrington testified that the Lezak hearing was overly broad and difficult to understand what was precisely investigated. Penny's job was not perceived to ever be at stake from a legal defense. Simultaneously, both Penny and Clark maintained that they had no idea the commission would conclude their investigation with a report that recommended the city replace their police chief (Snell, 1990).

Botteri also testified at the federal trial that he randomly came across Sid Lezak near an intersecting street in Portland. Lezak commented, "We did Penny dirt," meaning they pushed her out.[84] For his part, Lezak testified that he recalled saying to Botteri, "I'm sorry about the amount of dirt that had to be dumped on Penny during the hearing" (Painter, 1990c). Additionally, on March 13, 1990, City Attorney Jeff Rogers testified that Clark was under pressure to remove Penny even before the Lezak Commission formed. Rogers testified that he questioned why the commission carried the dual role of reviewing Chief Penny Harrington's reorganization of the PPB while also looking into the investigation on if Officer Gary Harrington tipped off suspected drug dealer Bobby Lee (Painter, 1990d).

A top aide to Mayor Clark, Christina Tobkin, testified that they (Clark and his mayoral staff) felt it was unfair for the commission to link the Chief's reorganization of the PPB with her husband's friendship with drug suspect Lee. This link only came about because of the March 26, 1986 article in *The Oregonian* by Hallman, Long, and Zaitz. Lezak testified that halfway through the hearings, they discussed a recommendation to remove Penny as chief. However, they did not issue any communication to indicate their stance until completing their final report. Judge Frey eventually dismissed the lawsuit against the commissioners. On March 16, 1990, the jury ruled in favor of the mayor and the city. On July 31, 1990, Penny dropped her appeal for disability payments with the ninth U.S. Circuit Court of Appeals in San Francisco because she ran out of money for her legal expenses and had reached the time she was eligible

84 Author's interview with Botteri on October 21, 2020.

for her pension (Painter, 1990a). During this time, the California Bar Association's Office of Investigation employed Penny. The city also dropped claims for recovering their legal expenses.

Mayor Clark's Firing of a Third Chief

On April 7, 1987, Clark met with Jim Davis, Penny's replacement as PPB chief. They met at Fat City Café on Southwest Capitol Highway in Multnomah Village for breakfast. Today, the booth they sat at has a framed photo of *The Oregonian* newspaper from the following day with the headline "Mayor Fires Police Chief Davis" (Gallagher, 2019). During their meeting, there was a debate about the upcoming budget and an audit of the PPB. Before their meeting, Davis had threatened to resign because of a budget proposal that did not allow additional police hiring.

Davis also expressed his desire to use legal action to get files used in an audit to prepare the PPB budget, the largest general fund budget in Portland. Clark told Davis to stand down on his criticism, and he didn't have any right to the police audit. Davis wanted to see the police audit and lobby the city council for additional funding. He pushed back against Mayor Clark by stating, "Mr. Mayor, read my lips" leading Clark to retort, "Jim, read my lips, you're no longer the police chief, and their breakfast abruptly ended" (Lane & Hallman, 1987). When Clark returned to City Hall, he didn't quite remember what had happened until his assistant Duffy checked with Davis, who verified the mayor fired him (Gallagher, 2019). Former chiefs, Davis and Still, each ran against Clark in future mayoral elections, but both were soundly defeated. Penny Harrington was the only chief to resign through the use of a commission recommendation.

Penny's New Life Post PPB

Penny was an assistant director of investigations for the California Bar Association from 1988 to 1995.[85] In that capacity, she helped train attorneys on ethics, investigations, and the development of policies and procedures. In the aftermath of the 1992 LA Riots, the Christopher Commission, described in the Bratton chapter, created a Women's Advisory Council to recruit and retain female officers. Penny, along with several prominent women leaders, worked on the advisory council. Each became vital to Penny's post-law enforcement career. These individuals included Katherine Spillar[86] of the Feminist Majority Foundation, Jenifer McKenna of the California Women's Law Center (CWLC),[87] and Connie Rice[88] of the NAACP Legal Defense and Education Fund, Inc.

85 Lezak sent copies of their commission report to attorneys that showed any interest in hiring Penny, causing her to lose business. Penny contacted Lezak to inquire about his actions and was told he would continue to send out the report, but eventually, he stopped. There was a belief that Lezak was disgruntled by the federal lawsuit Penny filed that challenged his work. Although her lawsuit was later dismissed, Lezak was never called to conduct another important public investigation (author's interview with Penny on September 15, 2020).

86 The Feminist Majority Foundation began in 1987 with Spillar as its Executive Director. She also became the editor for *Ms. Magazine* in 2005 (Martin, 2018), which previously named Penny Woman of the Year in 1985. Spillar has been a consistent public speaker on domestic and international feminist topics.

87 The CWLC was founded in 1989 by McKenna, along with Shelia Kuehl and Abby Leibman, to address legal needs of women and girls while promoting gender equality. The center assists women with protection orders and comprehensive civil rights. See www.cwlc.org/.

88 The work of Rice is described in the Bratton chapter as well. In 1996, Rice became the co-director of the LA NAACP Legal Defense Fund and a criminal defense litigator that challenged police misconduct, along with race and gender discrimination (Rice, 2012). She has served on several government boards and successfully advocated for housing, education, and quality of life in less affluent neighborhoods.

Through their work with reform movements in the LAPD, the women forged a friendship. They encouraged the National Center for Women & Policing formation as a division of the *Feminist Majority Foundation*. Penny served as the director of the center from 1995 to 2001. As the director, Penny helped build the membership to over 500 women and obtained a grant to write a comprehensive training program aimed at investigations of acquaintance sexual assaults. She was also the principal author of a self-assessment guide for police agencies to recruit and retain female officers (Harrington, 2001). The *National Center for Women & Policing* continued to host an annual conference for women in top leadership positions. Penny has been a regular presenter in leadership, discrimination, harassment, recruitment, hiring, and training policewomen. Penny testified three times before the U.S Civil Rights Commission on bias in law enforcement through this national exposure.

In May 1993, Hallman traveled to Los Angeles (LA) to interview Penny and provide an update on her life for *The Oregonian*. Perhaps, Hallman felt a sense of responsibility to update the story since his past reporting instigated the mayor's formation of the Lezak Commission's investigation of Penny. In this follow-up article, Penny told Hallman that she looked back at her forced resignation with anger, not sadness (Hallman, 1993). Penny Harrington's leadership brought community policing to the PPB, which several successors embraced and created a much-needed reorganization of narcotics investigations.

Penny had many career highlights after leaving Portland. Some of these included being on the editorial board for the journal *Women & Criminal Justice*; presented with a "Lifetime Achievement Award" from the Feminist Majority and the National Center for Women & Policing; induction into the School of Criminal Justice Wall of Fame at MSU; interviewed by Mike Wallace on 60 Minutes about Police Family Violence; participated in a roundtable discussion with President Clinton on issues of police brutality and diversity recruitment; appointed by Attorney General Janet Reno to a national panel on police brutality and diversity recruitment; served as a consultant to the U.S. DOJ Civil Rights Employment Litigation Section; and hired as a consultant by the LA Fire Chief to train fire academy staff on how to treat women equally and to train internal investigators on how to conduct discrimination investigations. Lastly, in 2019, Penny made a video presentation for the U.S. DOJ on how to increase the number of women in policing.

Penny Harrington's Personal Life and Family Tragedy: 2006–2020

Penny Harrington has been very gracious with her time and feedback with the writing of this chapter. Her reflections came through numerous phone calls and emails throughout 2019 and 2020. She was honored to be a part of a book on the nation's most influential police leaders and stated that the stress she went through, and the personal tragedies she faced in her life, appears to be worth it to be remembered in this way.

Penny eventually settled in Morro Bay, California, 200 miles north, up the coast, from LA, and 230 miles south of Berkeley. In 2006, she built a home next door to her beach cottage and invited her son Brian to move into the house with his family. Brian was an attorney with a specialty in civil rights investigations and medical malpractice. His life partner, Siobhan O'Toole, was an associate professor in the School of Professional Psychology at Alliant University, and she commuted to the Fresno campus. Brian and Siobhan's daughter, Aine, was three years old when they moved and Penny helped watch her granddaughter while her parents worked. In 2009, Brian began to experience neurological problems and was diagnosed with anaplastic astrocytoma, a rare malignant brain tumor. The medical staff gave Brian six months to live. They elected to have the tumor removed, and he began aggressive treatments of radiation and chemotherapy. In 2010, Penny opened up the Ruby Dragon Rock Shop, a crystal rock shop, to help others heal from stress and spent time staying with Brian during his treatments. Brian rented a hotel suite in Fresno and received his treatments. He lived for six additional years. He stayed with Penny during his last days and died in her arms on October 11, 2015. A few years into Brian's cancer struggle, Siobhan was diagnosed with stage three colorectal cancer. Siobhan's mother stayed with her daughter during her treatments, but Siobhan lost her battle on April 10, 2016, just months after Brian passed away. Shortly before her death, Siobhan arranged for a secretive adoption of Aine, 12 years old at that time, with her brother Sean and his wife Maureen, in Truckee, California, and Penny's time with her granddaughter was limited.

Conclusion

Penny Harrington shattered the brass ceiling for women police officers. The profession owes her a debt of gratitude for taking on the rigid bureaucratic law enforcement system to her peril. She continues to push for a critical mass of women in policing before a cultural change can occur. In politics, the critical mass is estimated at 20 percent of the female legislatures before meaningful laws can be passed (Newton-Small, 2016). In policing, the critical mass is somewhere between 20 and 30 percent of women officers (Rodriguez, 2020) that are needed to overcome various barriers. Schulz (2003) indicated the uniqueness of the barriers women officers face from internal (driven by the male-dominated police occupation) and external barriers (caused by conflicts between work and family). Research continues to support Penny's push for hiring more women into policing as a means for meaningful reform. The latest came in 2019 from the National Institute of Justice (NIJ), which reported female officers have fewer use of force incidents and fewer citizen complaints. On December 3–4, 2018, NIJ organized a Research Summit on Women in Policing at their Washington, DC headquarters. Nearly 100 attendees participated in the summit to generate a research agenda to assist professional movements toward gender parity in policing (Starheim, 2019).

The Pew Research Center determined that 11 percent of female officers will fire their weapons while on duty compared to 30 percent of male officers. Only 22 percent of females will physically struggle with a suspect who resists arrest compared to 35 percent of male officers (Stepler, 2017). Despite the research, most departments have not shown an increase in hiring women officers unless forced to do so. Once the pressure is off, any increases in hiring female officers tend to disappear. For example, in 1975, Pittsburgh was under a federal consent decree that required the agency to hire a Black female, a Black male, and a white female for every white male they hired. As minority officers grew, the decree was eventually ruled unconstitutional in 1991. The number of female officers has since declined to 15 percent (Worthy, 2019).

Moreover, the testing and training requirements for officers can be influenced by gender bias (Bello, 2013). In New Jersey, between 2009 and 2018, more than 9,800 men applied to their state police academies, compared with 1,460 women. During this period, 91 percent of men graduated from academies compared to only 66 percent of women (Ford, 2020). A new fitness test was instituted in 2015 and caused the rate of failure in females to triple (Ford, 2019; Ford, 2020). Before this test was created, women failed at a similar rate as males. From 2009 to 2014, women failed academy physical tests at a rate of 2 to 4 percent, compared to less than 1 percent for men. However, in 2015, 12 percent of women failed the test, but 99 percent of men continued to pass. In 2017, 31 percent of women failed the physical test, and 18 percent failed in 2018. The male failure rate hovered around 2 percent for both 2017 and 2018 (Ford, 2020). The test consisted of the following: 15-inch vertical jump; one minute to do at least 28 sit-ups; 300 meter run at a minimal 70.1 seconds; one minute to do at least 24 push-ups; 1.5 miles run in 15:55 minutes or less.

In Massachusetts, women completed the same obstacle course as men but failed at a rate of 20 percent compared to only 2 percent of men (Weichselbaum, 2019). The inherent gender bias that is involved in physical tests can become costly. The city commissioners in Colorado Springs recently approved a $2.5 million settlement with 12 female officers who filed a lawsuit that alleged the physical aptitude test was discriminatory. The settlement was done six months after a federal judge ruled that the plaintiff's civil rights were violated when 40 percent of the department's female officers over the age of 40 failed to pass a mandatory physical aptitude test (Benzel & Mulder, 2018). Their failure caused them to lose their existing police duties, and they were reassigned.

Departments that continue to make it difficult for women to be hired repeat the history Penny endured through the PPB. The system intentionally or inadvertently confines females and perpetuates the warrior mindset of law enforcement. This message assumes that women officers are inferior, and their vulnerability will cause increased criminal violence and offending. However, some departments challenge the status quo (Muhlhausen, 2019). For example, the MPD comprises 28 percent female police officers (Maxwell, 2020), more than double the national average. MPD female officers report high morale and male counterpart support. Harassment of female officers is practically nonexistent in the MPD since so many female officers are represented throughout the ranks (Rodriguez, 2020). The organizational context of the MPD is historically credited to the reform efforts of Chief David Couper (see Couper, 2017) (Table 4.3).

Couper advocates that every police academy should have a mandatory 50 percent of candidates being female/minority (Couper, 2017). In a state-to-state comparison, Louisiana has the largest ratio of female officers at 22 percent. The Louisiana State Police recently promoted Treone Larvadain to lead the coveted Protective Services unit as the first African-American female captain in the state agency history (Thomas, 2020). West Virginia has the lowest female police officer representation at 3.82 percent, and at least 13 states have less than 8 percent of women officers (Ford, 2019). A dozen chiefs have passed through the PPB since Penny Harrington. Noteworthy, the last two Portland chiefs have been female, as shown in Table 4.4, until Chuck Lovell became chief in 2020.

Table 4.3 Portland City Marshals (1851–1870)

Years	*Name*
1851	Hiram Wilbur[i]
1851–1853; 1854; & 1856–1857	William Higgins
1853–1854 & 1861–1863	William Grooms
1854	Richard Perkins
1854–1856	Thomas Holms
1857–1859	Samuel Holcomb
1859–1861 & 1868–1869	James Lappeus[ii]
1863–1864	William Clark
1864–1867	Henry Hoyt
1867–1868	David Jacobi
1869–1870	Phillip Saunders

i Portland's first city council meeting took on April 14, 1851. Their first ordinance provided for the appointment of Wilbur to be the city marshal.

ii Lappeus was an influential Democratic leader in Portland who was also the Police Chief from 1870 to 1877 and then again from 1879 to 1883.

Table 4.4 Portland Police Chiefs

Years	*Name*
1870–1877 & 1879–1883	James Lappeus[i]
1877–1879	Lucerne Besser[ii]
1883–1884	William Watkinds[iii]
1884–1892	Samuel Parrish[iv]
1892–1892	Ernest Spence (chief 3 ½ months)
1892–1894 & 1903–1906	Charles Hunt[v]
1894–1896	John Minto[vi]
1896–1897	L.W. "Doc" Robertson[vii]
1897–1897	John Myers (chief four months)
1897–1897	Patrick Barry (chief less than one month)
1897–1898	Michael Clohessy
1898–1903	Daniel McLaughlin[viii]
1906–1909	Charles Critzmaucher
1909–1911	Arthur Cox
1911–1913	Enoch Glover
1913–1917	John Clark
1917–1919	Nelson Johnson
1919–1933 & 1946–1948	Leon Jenkins[ix]
1933–1934	Burton Lawson
1934–1946	Harry Niles
1948–1948	James Fleming

i Lappeus served two terms as city marshal and as police chief. He was part owner of a gambling parlor that featured nude dancing and prostitution. He was plagued with charges of corruption and bribery with links to several criminal gangs. On April 7, 1874, he arrested 15 members of the "Women's Temperance and Prayer League" after they began a protest around the downtown taverns. The following day the women were found guilty by an all-male jury and sentenced to a day in jail.

ii Besser also served in the city council as a Republican and fought to remove Democratic Chief Lappeus.

iii Watkinds admitted to paying Mayor James Chapman a bribe to fire Chief Lappeus so he could become police chief. His wife worked as a matron at the state prison.

iv Parrish, a Republican city council member without any law enforcement experience, brought stability to the police department amid impeachment proceedings of Mayor Chapman.

v Hunt was previously the police chief in Providence, Rhode Island, and the Superintendent of the state prison. He moved to Portland because the climate was supposed to be good for his wife's failing health. He was quickly asked to replace the unpopular Chief Spence. In 1894, Hunt hired the first two Black officers as wagon drivers, and George Hardin eventually became the first Black patrol officer. After his reappointment, he also advocated for Lola Baldwin and the Traveler's Aid Society to help clean up vice crime before the Lewis and Clark Exposition.

vi Minto's brother, Harry, was the Superintendent of the Oregon State Penitentiary until Otto Hooker fatally shot him in a prison break on September 27, 1915. After serving as Portland's Police Chief, John Minto took his brother's position as Superintendent at the state prison in Salem. However, he resigned the following year after a scandal related to harsh prisoner treatment.

vii Robertson was the beginning of Mayor Sylvester Pennoyer's house cleaning. In 1896, the mayor replaced the entire police force and went through four different chiefs in nine months. Mayor Sylvester Pennoyer discharged and replaced entire police force. He appointed four different chiefs within a nine-month period.

viii After he fired the entire 84-member police force, Mayor William Mason appointed McLaughlin and replaced the Police Commission.

ix Jenkins is recognized as one of the most innovative chiefs in Portland, serving two terms for a total of 14 years. Like Vollmer, Jenkins organized the first traffic division, police academy, and made claims of using the country's first police radio. He also assisted in establishing the UCR through a committee he chaired for the International Association of Chiefs.

Table 4.4 Cont.

Years	*Name*
1949–1951	Charles Pray
1951–1953 & 1964–1974	Don McNamara
1953–1956	Jim "Diamond" Purcell[x]
1957–1960	William Hilbruner
1964–1960	David Johnson
1974–1981	Bruce Baker
1981–1985	Ron Still
1985–1985	Gary Haynes (19 days)
1985–1986	**Penny Harrington**
1986–1986	Robert Tobin (interim for three months)
1986–1987	Jim Davis[xi]
1987–1990	Dick Walker[xii]
1990–1993	Tom Potter[xiii]
1993–1999	Charles Moose[xiv]
1999–1999	Lynnae Berg (interim for three months)[xv]
1999–2003	Mark Kroeker[xvi]
2003–2006	Derrick Foxworth[xvii]
2006–2010	Rosie Sizer[xviii]
2010–2015	Michael Reese
2015–2016	Larry O'Dea[xix]
2016–2017	Michael Marshman

x Purcell was linked to Portland mob boss Jim Elkins and protecting vice and the pinball racket. During this time period, pinball machines were illegal to have in drinking establishments.

xi Upon his termination, Davis took a demotion back to Captain and retired in 1992. He passed away in 2012 at the age of 80.

xii Walker was Commissioner Dick Bogle's chief of staff when Mayor Clark asked him to take over as his fourth PPB chief. Walker would later resign after being accused of slapping a female subordinate.

xiii Potter was Mayor Clark's last appointment as chief. Potter was elected Portland Mayor 2005–2009 and continually advocated for community policing and a less militarized police force.

xiv Charles Moose was the first African-American chief of police for Portland on June 29, 1993, and he completed his Ph.D. degree from Portland State University. Moose became nationally known in October 2002 as the chief of the Montgomery County Police Department in Maryland during the manhunt to apprehend two individuals who became known as the D.C. snipers, John Muhammad, aged 41, and Lee Malvo, aged 17. The snipers killed 17 people and wounded 10. Muhammad was put to death by lethal injection while Malvo received a life sentence.

xv Berg joined the PPB in 1981 and was the first female Mounted Patrol Officer from 1984 to 1986. She retired in 2009 and became the Executive Director for Clean and Safe Portland and the Vice President of Downtown Services with Portland Business Alliance.

xvi Mayor Vera Katz brought in Kroeker from LA, Portland's first external police chief in 25 years.

xvii Foxworth was removed by Mayor Potter (former chief) after an inappropriate relationship with a subordinate (Reddin, 2019). His sexually explicit emails to a police desk clerk became public.

xviii Sizer's forced resignation mimics Penny's struggle as the PPB chief. Her early retirement came on the heels of an officer shooting a 12-year-old girl with a beanbag (November 2009), the police union marching in protest against City Hall, and a vote of no confidence in the aftermath of two fatal police shootings. Like many chiefs, Sizer was challenged with balancing support for her officers, the public's often unrealistic expectations on officer performance, and managing those expectations in a very politically liberal city. Sizer criticized the mayor's proposed police budget cuts and claimed he inaccurately stated the police department overspent $5 million. To her surprise, Sizer was asked to resign a couple of days after the criticism (Bernstein, 2010).

xix O'Dea was forced to resign after he violated departmental procedures and did not report that he accidentally shot a friend during a hunting trip (Liedle, 2016).

Table 4.4 Cont.

Years	*Name*
2017–2019	Danielle Outlaw[xx]
2019–2020	Jami Resch[xxi]
2020–	Chuck Lovell[xxii]

Epilogue – Portland's Mass Social Justice Protests

Portland has long been a mass protest city dating back to its first large demonstration in 1857 when Brigham Young and a Mormon missionary defied federal law and President Buchanan. That same year Oregon's territorial constitution, written two years before becoming a state, banned Black people from entering or owning property in their land of white utopia. By 1862, the state could not stop Black emigration, so they passed legislation that provided a tax on people of color and banned interracial marriages (Ortiz, 2020). Interracial marriages were illegal in Oregon until 1951. In 1867, the city school board refused to integrate schools and opened up a "colored school" for African-American residents. In December 1873, the "colored school" closed, and Black students were integrated into the elementary schools. In 1926, the state officially repealed the Black exclusion clause from its constitution (Brooks, 2004).

In 2020, Portland's 655,000 population was more than three quarters white, with roughly the same percentage of residents registered as Democrats. According to the 2019 Census, Portland's Black population was just under 6 percent, and Latinos accounted for just under 10 percent of the total. The state-wide population was 87 percent white and only 2 percent Black. According to 2019 PPB data, Blacks accounted for 18 percent of traffics stops. Blacks' traffic stops rates increased from 2005, when former PPB chief Potter was mayor, with Blacks accounting for 13 percent of traffic stops. In 2019, Blacks were twice as likely to be asked to consent to a search after a traffic stop (Vaughn, 2021). As one of the whitest cities in America, media images of white protesters roughed up by police officers intrigued national commentators and once again caused the PPB chief's position to become a revolving door, as was the case during the Clark administration. In June 2020, Lovell became the city's third chief in less than six months.

Outside of Portland, numerous rural racism symbols created conflict between the anti-Fascist pro-labor union population and right-wing President Trump supporters such as Patriot Prayer and the Proud Boys.[89] On August 29, 2020, 39-year-old Portland native Aaron "Jay" Danielson, a member of the Patriot Prayer, was fatally shot as a caravan of pro-Trump trucks drove through downtown Portland and clashed with protesters. On September 3, 2020, a multi-agency federal task force of officers arrived at an apartment complex in Lacey, Washington, with an arrest warrant for 48-year-old Michael Reinoehl, an Antifa supporter who was suspected of shooting Danielson. Agents cornered Reinoehl and fatally shot over 30 rounds into his Volkswagen.

xx Outlaw was the first Black female to become the chief of the PPB. She was ceremonially sworn in by Carmen Sylvester, the first Black woman patrol officer in the PPB, hired in 1973, and retired in 1999. After 26 months, Outlaw left to become the first Black female and the first permanent female Police Commissioner in Philadelphia.

xxi At the age of 45, Resch became the 49th Chief on December 31, 2019, and the fourth female to lead the PPB. After only six months, amid the start of the 2020 mass police protests, she announced her resignation.

xxii Lovell was promoted from lieutenant to chief amid the 2020 protests. He became the 50th Chief to lead the PPD and the fourth Black chief.

89 On January 21, 2020, Proud Boys Leader Joseph Biggs was arrested in Ormond Beach, Florida, for his role in the January 6, 2020 siege at the Capitol in protest of Joe Biden's election. On February 3, 2021, Proud Boys leader Ethan Nordean (AKA Rufio Panman) was arrested in Seattle on similar charges. In the aftermath of the siege, the Capitol Police named Yogananda Pittman as their first female and first African-American acting chief a day after Chief Steve Sund resigned.

The ongoing conflict between the community and the PPB was on full display, and the city continued to be the epicenter for stagnant mass protest. In the months leading to the 2020 election, Presidential candidate Joe Biden argued that President Trump exacerbated the problem when he blamed Portland Mayor Ted Wheeler for the death of Danielson and encouraged his supporters to move into Portland.

> Counter-protesters were also seen in Kenosha, Wisconsin, following the August 23, 2020, police shooting of 29-year-old African-American Jacob Blake that was caught on cell phone video by a neighbor.[90] After the city erupted in protest and riots, estimated at $2 million in damage, several white vigilantes arrived in the city armed with automatic rifles to protect area businesses. President Trump called rioters domestic terrorists. Kyle Rittenhouse, a 17-year-old police cadet from Illinois, arrived in Kenosha with his AR-15 rifle to help protect property in Kenosha from the protesters. In the chaos, on the evening of August 25, 2020, Rittenhouse fatally shot 26-year-old Anthony Huber[91] and 36-year-old Joseph Rosenbaum. He unsuccessfully attempted to give himself up, after the shooting, to the 19 armored vehicles from various police agencies that were in Kenosha to monitor the protests. Officers thanked several of the armed youth in the streets of Kenosha who were passing out water. Rittenhouse was arrested at his home in Antioch, Illinois, the following morning and charged with two counts of first-degree murder and attempted murder. President Trump commented that Rittenhouse could have been killed, meaning he was likely acting in self-defense.

While outrage over the constitutionality of federal law enforcement intrusion into Portland may have provoked counter-protests or played to presidential politics in the 2020 election year, it's also embedded in the deep history of questionable police legitimacy. This same history, unique to Oregon and Portland, fueled the politics that forced Chief Penny Harrington's resignation. Only a few short years after Penny's termination, President George H. Bush's administration gave Portland the nickname "Little Beirut." Republican politicians have historically avoided Portland due to its history of protest. Stories exasperated the city's protest image such as anarchists gathering near the Hilton Hotel along Southwest Broadway for Republican Presidential visits. When President Reagan or Bush came to town, protesters ate various potatoes dyed red or blue with food coloring. As the Presidential motorcades arrived, they drank Ipecac syrup to puke red, white, or blue barf puddles all over the hotel where the president was staying (Palahniuk, 2003). Often the stomach bile mixed with the food coloring and unintentionally created green protest barf. The name "Little Beirut" stuck and can be found on Portland bumper stickers, T-shirts, and other informal marketing apparatus.

In 2018, JoAnn Hardesty became the first Black woman elected to the Portland City Council. In June 2020, amid the protests in the aftermath of George Floyd's death on May 25, 2020, Hardesty and activists pushed for a $50 million cut to the police budget. The city council settled with a $15 million cut to the PPB. The state legislature passed a bill that banned tear gas use unless the police announce they have declared a riot. During this period, Hardesty

90 Blake was shot seven times in his back by Officer Rusten Sheskey after attempting to get into his vehicle following a domestic violence call for service after arguing with his fiancée Laquisha Booker. Three of Blake's sons were in the back seat, including his oldest son Izreal who was celebrating his eighth birthday. The shooting occurred after a physical altercation with the police, and Blake was reaching for a knife. Blake was paralyzed as a result of being shot. On January 5, 2021, the Kenosha County District Attorney Robert Zapf announced he would not file charges against the officers.

91 While holding his skateboard, Huber tried to grab the rifle out of Rittenhouse's hands before being fatally shot (Maxouris, 2020). Rittenhouse, and other counter-protesters, were referred to as "larpers" based on their experiences with "live-action role-playing" video games, but they were now armed with real guns.

was the fire commissioner but publicly demanded that she should be police commissioner. This position has historically been tasked with the mayor, as detailed earlier in this chapter. In her capacity as fire commissioner, Hardesty banned the fire departments as staging areas for law enforcement preparations to combat protesters.

In early July 2020, President Trump ordered federal law enforcement agents into Portland to manage the protests and protect federal property. They utilized the federal IRS building and the Mark O. Hatfield federal courthouse to stage their forces. Throughout July, Homeland Security Investigations, Border Patrol Tactical Units, and Federal Protective Services all combined to manage the protests. An estimated 100–150 agents were involved. On July 18, 2020, a wall of moms arrived to provide a visible block between the police and the protesters. Many of these moms, mainly white women from neighboring suburbs, put on helmets and gas masks to protect themselves against the tear gas that PPB and federal agents continually launched. That same evening, protesters broke into the Portland Police Association (PPA) building, where the police union meets, and lit a fire inside that was later extinguished. That incident led the police to declare a riot.

Portland Mayor Ted Wheeler demanded that the PPB stop working with federal law enforcement agents sent by the Trump Administration. He called the President's use of federal law enforcement agents an attack on our democracy. Wheeler marched with the protesters on July 22, 2020, outside a fence that protected the federal court building in downtown Portland. The mayor was hit in the face with tear gas from federal agents while he was with the protesters, and this photo op became coupled with a video that surfaced of federal agents using a rental van to snatch and arrest a protester off the street.[92] Agents also cleared out several homeless individuals with a sweep of the park across the street from the federal courthouse. These events appeared to encourage additional protesters to arrive in Portland and maintain the city's reputation for being the epicenter of national mass protests and police legitimacy questions. The demonstrations continued every night into the fall of 2020, leading Penny to send the following unanswered email to Mayor Wheeler:

> *September 19, 2020*
>
> *Mayor Wheeler: You don't know me, but I was the Chief of Police of Portland in 1985–86. My heart is heavy seeing what has happened to that beautiful city. I had to handle protests as chief and I have some suggestions for you to consider.*
>
> *I agree that people have the right to protest. Our country is built on peaceful protests such as throwing the tea into the harbor. (I was not there for that one!)*
>
> *However, you have lost control of the situation and you now have full-scale rioting on your hands. The City Council has established an adversarial relationship against the police bureau holding it responsible for all the problems in Portland. The police are overwhelmed with all the demands placed on them.*
>
> *We have faced these same issues before. I banned the carotid hold in 1985. I established a "use of force" committee to recommend what types of force officers should be allowed to use.*
>
> *But before you can accomplish any of your goals, you have to get the current situation under control. You have given free rein to any group that comes to Portland to carry out any activity they want to do with no consequences. It is going to take a lot of work to turn that around.*
>
> *In addition, you and the City Council are blaming the police for all the problems in the world. Look at all the officers who have retired or quit and more will be leaving.*

92 Video footage of unidentified federal agents taking protesters into custody without a warrant or explanation prompted Oregon Attorney General Ellen Rosenblum to file a federal lawsuit against the Department of Homeland Security and the Marshals Service for constitutional infringement. Rosenblum also sought a temporary restraining order to stop federal agents from allegedly and unlawfully detaining Oregonian citizens.

I can give you some suggestions to get you started. First of all, you need more officers not less. If I were in your shoes, here is what I would do:

1. *Declare a state of emergency and call in whatever help you need from the Governor.*
2. *Put every police officer you have back in uniform … detectives, command staff, everyone.*
3. *Temporarily disband all special units.*
4. *Do not dispatch any police unless it is a serious problem and the likelihood of injury is great.*
5. *Make a plea for officers on disability to come back to work as report takers.*
6. *Call back officers who are on vacation.*
7. *Offer to pay time and a half to any officers who have retired within the last three years.*
8. *Offer officers from other agencies time and a half to come work at Portland on their days off.*
9. *Pay current officers at time and a half to voluntarily work on the protest assignments.*

Once you have done all of this, you can tackle the violence from the protestors because you will have a lot more resources.

Implement a new policy that anyone carrying a weapon or assaulting anyone or committing a crime of violence in the riot area will be arrested. Make deals with other counties to hold these prisoners in jail.

Call for leaders of the various "protesting" groups to meet with you on a regular basis. Meet with them individually to start with.

a. *What are they trying to accomplish? Get them to be specific. If they say something like "get the police to stop killing black people", agree with them that it is a good goal. Ask them how they would accomplish it.*
b. *Either pick an idea that they come up with that can be accomplished in a short time or tell them what you can accomplish on that issue.*
c. *Get an agreement that they will stop using violence against the police and each other so that they can help you accomplish the goal that has been set.*
d. *Bring in a police representative to work specifically with that group on a daily basis.*
e. *Repeat this process with each of the other groups.*
f. *It would be a good idea to contact ministers and other community leaders to be involved also.*
g. *Set a reasonable time for a follow-up meeting. Report your progress to the media being positive about all sides working together.*
h. *You need to rebuild the trust of the people in the police.*

You need to ask the other city council members to tone down the rhetoric while you are trying to reduce the violence. DON'T MAKE THE POLICE THE BAD GUYS. Your long term goal is to get people trusting that things are getting better and that they can always let you know if there is a problem.

DISBANDING THE POLICE IS NOT THE ANSWER. REMOVING DUTIES FROM THEM THAT CAN BETTER BE ACCOMPLISHED BY OTHERS AT A LOWER PAY LEVEL.

I hope you will read this. Feel free to call me if you want to discuss it.

Penny Harrington

On September 24, 2020, the PPB officially declared the protests had become a riot. Three weeks earlier, the police had made a similar declaration. The riots on September 24, which included firebombs thrown toward officers, were a catalyst for other protests going on throughout the country in the aftermath of the failed Grand Jury indictments in the fatal police shooting of Breonna Taylor in Louisville. These were the worst riots since protests started in May after the death of George Floyd. However, no police officer or firefighter was injured, and the police did not use tear gas. On October 11, 2020, police again declared a riot as people marched the day before the federally recognized holiday for Columbus Day in what was labeled "Indigenous Peoples Day of Rage." Protesters vandalized area businesses and toppled statues of Teddy Roosevelt and Abraham Lincoln.

On October 6, 2020, a third quarterly report was issued by the Compliance Office/ Community Liaison (COCL) as required by a settlement agreement between Portland and the DOJ from 2012. This agreement came from a judge ruling that the PPB engaged in a pattern or practice of excessive force, specifically when encountering people with mental illness. The settlement allowed for creating the COCL to synthesize data related to PPB's use of force and issue quarterly reports to the City Council, DOJ, and the media. The October 2020 report shows a department overwhelmed by hundreds of use of force events within the nightly protests, hundreds of untrained officers (training was cut when the Covid-19 pandemic started) on crowd control and use of force certification, and severe funding cuts to their 2020–2021 budget. Out of the 50 largest departments in the country, Portland ranked 49th in proportional budgets (Rosenbaum & Associates, 2020). Lastly, Multnomah County Commissioner Sharon Meieran and Mayor Wheeler considered merging the Sheriff's Department[93] with the PPB (Azar, 2020).

References

Appier, Janis (1998). *Policing women: The sexual politics of law enforcement and the LAPD*. Philadelphia: Temple University Press.

Azar, Kellee (2020). Should Portland Police Bureau, Multnomah County Sheriff's Office merge? *KATU News*. October 21.

Austin, David (1989). Gary Harrington returns to police force. *The Oregonian*. June 2.

Barker, Jeff (1985). Portland Police Association continues to stand behind its members 100%. *The Rap Sheet*, June 1.

Baumgardner, Randy (2000). *Portland's finest: Past and present*. Paducah, KY: Turner Publishing Company.

Beal, W.T. (1989). *History of the Michigan agricultural college and biographical sketches of trustees and professors*. East Lansing, MI: Michigan Agricultural College. 1915. *MSU Alumni Magazine*, 7(1): 519.

Beatty, John (2010). *The politics of public ventures: An Oregon memoir*. Bloomington, IN: Xlibris, Corporation.

Bello, Grace (2013). The gals in blue: Where are the real-life Olivia Bensons? *BitchMedia*. March 12.

Benzel, Lance and Ellie Mulder (2018). Colorado Springs pays $2.5 million to female officers to settle physical fitness test lawsuit. *The Gazette*. January 19.

Bernstein, Maxine (2012). Portland police use of force: Feds formally sue city, submit proposed settlement. *The Oregonian/Oregon Live*. December 17.

Bernstein, Maxine (2010). Day after removal, Rosie Sizer reflects on 4 years as Portland's police chief. *The Oregonian/Oregon Live*. May 14.

Bloch, Peter and Deborah Anderson (1974). *Policewomen on patrol: Final report*. Washington, DC: Police Foundation.

Boag, Peter (2004). Does Portland need a homophile society? Gay culture and activism in the Rose City between World War II and Stonewall. *Oregon Historical Quarterly, Oregon Historic Society, 105*(1): 15–16.

Bopp, William (1977). "O.W.": O.W. Wilson and the search for a police profession (Interdisciplinary Urban Series). Port Washington, NY: Kennikat Press.

Brandstetter, A. (1989). Genesis and early history of criminal justice studies at Michigan State University. *Paper Presented at the Midwestern Criminal Justice Association Annual Meeting*, Chicago, IL.

Brooks, Cheryl (2004). Race, politics, and denial: Why Oregon forgot to ratify the Fourteenth Amendment. *Oregon Law Review 83*: 731–762.

93 Mike Reese was elected Sheriff of Multnomah County in 2016 and was also the PPB chief from 2010 to 2015.

Budnick, Nick (2017). The Potter files: Digging for dirt on Portland's Mr. Clean. *Willamette Week*. January 24.
Bultema, James (2013). *Guardians of Angeles: A history of the Los Angeles Police Department*. West Conshohocken, PA: Infinity Publishing.
Cameron, Diane (1981). Ivancie police actions insult to black community. *Oregon Journal*. June 3.
Cimino, Eric (2012). *On the border line of tragedy: White slavery, moral protection, and the Travelers' Aid Society of New York, 1885–1917* (Ph.D. Thesis). Stony Brook University.
Classen, Allan (2010). Cop shop beyond fixing. *Mental Health PDX*. Mental Health Portland. Retrieved from www.mentalhealthportland.org/cop-shop-beyond-fixing/
Classen, Allan (2019). What's wrong with Portland? Longtime resident traces dysfunction to campaign against neighborhood associations. *NW Examiner 32*(11): 1–6.
Cody, Robin (1984). Mayor Bud. The sunday Oregonian. *Northwest Magazine*: 7–13. November 11.
Cordner, AnnMarie. (2019). Female police officers. *The encyclopedia of women and crime*, 1–6. Hobken, NJ: John Wiley & Sons, Inc.
Couper, David (2017). *Arrested development: A veteran police chief sounds off about protest, racism, corruption and the seven steps necessary to improve our nation's police*, (2nd edition), Blue Mounds, WI: New Journey Press.
Crotty, James (1997). *How to talk American: A guide to our native tongues*. Boston, MA: Mariner Books, Houghton and Mifflin Co.
Danks, Holly and Michael Rollins (1985). Chief says policeman mistook woman for gunman, shot her. *The Oregonian*. July 8.
Dawdy, Philip (2005). Badge of honor. *Willamette Weekly Newsletter*. March 8.
Dawdy, Philip and Grant Menzies (2005). Playing possum. *Willamette Weekly Newsletter*. March 8.Department of Justice (1973). Equal rights guidelines: Minimum height requirements – Minorities and women. *Federal Register 38*(473): No. 46.
DuPay, Don (2019). The black and blue retort report: Police-community relations in Portland's Albina District: 1961–1967 from the perspective of the working PPB police officer and active participant, with commentary on events that occurred in the 1980s. In: Theresa Griffin Kennedy (Ed.). *Public Media*. October. 16.
Durbin, Kathie (1986). Clark urged to continue Penny Harrington police philosophy. *The Oregonian*. August 13.
Eisenberg, Adam (2009). *A different shade of blue: How women changed the face of police work*. Los Angeles, CA: Behler Publications.
Erickson, Steve (1975). Although not unexpected, suicide 'absolute waste'. *The Oregonian*. August 3.
Ewens, Elise (2017). *Don't Choke 'Em, Smoke 'Em': Lloyd "Tony" Stevenson and the long reach of history in "Post-Racial" Portland* (Master's Thesis). Oregon State University Honor's College.
Feinman, Clarice (1986). Women in the criminal justice system. New York, NY: Praeger Publishers.
Finn, John (2012). *Wicked Portland: The wild and lusty underworld of a frontier seaport town*. Charleston, SC: The History Press.
Ford, Andrew (2019). Can American police close the gender gap? *The Crime Report*. August 6.
Ford, Andrew (2020). NJ police tests fail women recruits. Here's how it hurts your safety and your wallet. *Asbury Park Press – USA Today Network*. February 25.
Gallagher, Bill (2019). The day Mayor Bud Clark fired the chief of police over breakfast in Multnomah village. *Southwest Connection: Pamplin Media Group*. April 1.
Gillins, Peter (1986). Portland police chief survives a tough year. *South Florida Sun-Sentinel*. February 5.
Green, Aimee (2019). Mike Schrunk: Multnomah County DA retires with a legacy of firm and fair leadership. *The Oregonian/Oregon Live*. January 10.
Griffin, Anna and Gregg Sulzberger (2009). The case of the discreet DA. *The Oregonian*. March 22.
Hallman, Tom (1982). 'KKK chicken' thrown at Burger Barn's door. *The Oregonian*. March 4.
Hallman, Tom (1986a). Problems plague Harrington. *The Oregonian*. January 19.
Hallman, Tom (1986b). Penny Harrington wins disability payments. *The Oregonian*. October 22.
Hallman, Tom, James Long, and Leslie Zaitz (1986). Harrington says spouse leaked case. *The Oregonian*. March 26.
Hallman, Tom (1993). Harrington: 'I had to start a new life'. *The Oregonian*. May 2.

Hallman, Tom (2012). She was one of kind, family says of Sybil Plumlee, one of Portland's first female police officers. *The Oregonian/Oregon Live.* January 13.

Hallman, Tom, James Long, and Leslie Zaitz (1986). Harrington says spouse leaked case. *The Oregonian.* March 26.

Hallman, Tom and Barnes Ellis (1987). Mayor fires police sergeants. *The Oregonian.* November 7.

Hamburg, Ken (1984). Clark gets Carson to 'whoop' it up. *The Oregonian. October 12.*

Hamburg, Ken (1985). Grave met police twice earlier on day he died. *The Oregonian.* July 11.

Hamburg, Ken and John Painter (1985). Herndon calls for panel to analyze deaths. *The Oregonian.* July 11.

Hamburg, Ken and Michael Rollins (1985). Witnesses tell their versions of fatal events. *The Oregonian,* May 10.

Hammer, Susan (2006). A tribute to Sid Lezak: Oregon's Johnny Appleseed of dispute resolution. *Mediate.com: Mediate Everything.* Retrieved from www.mediate.com/articles/hammerS1.cfm

Harrington, Penny E. (1999). *Triumph of spirit: An autobiography.* Chicago, IL: Brittany Publications.

Harrington, Penny E. (2001). *Recruitment and retaining women: A self-assessment guide for law enforcement.* Washington, DC: U.S. Department of Justice.

Higgins, Lois (1950). Women police service. *Journal of Criminal Law and Criminology 41*(1): 101–106.

Hogan, Dave (1985). Many police say they've changed approach to job. *The Oregonian.* July 28.

Holli, Melvin (1999). *The American mayor: The best and worst big-city leaders.* State College, PA: Penn State University Press.

Hoobler, Raymond and J.A. McQueeny (1963). A question of height. In: Clifford Morgan (Ed.), *Human engineering guide to equipment design.* New York, NY: McGraw-Hill.

Hyland, Shelley and Elizabeth Davis (2019). *Local police departments, 2016.* Washington, DC: U.S. Department of Justice, Office of Justice Programs Bureau of Justice Statistics. Retrieved from www.bjs.gov/content/pub/pdf/lpd16p.pdf

Jeffers, Paul (2002). *The Napoleon of New York: Mayor Fiorello La Guardia.* New Jersey: John Wiley & Sons, Inc.

Jenning, Steve (1978). 5-year-old struggle against sex bias in police bureau drawing to an end. *The Oregonian.* March 18.

Kanter, Rosabeth (1977). *Men and women of the corporation.* New York: Basic Books, Inc.

Katz, Jesse (1985). NBC's lights shine on a new police chief. *The Oregonian.* January 29.

Kirchmeier, Mark (2014). May 16, 1984: A saloon owner shock City Hall … *Willamette Weekly.* November 4.

Lane, Dee (1987). Board ends Penny Harrington's stress pay. *The Oregonian.* May 27.

Lane, Dee and Tom Hallman (1987). Mayor fires Police Chief Davis. *The Oregonian.* April 8.

Lansing, Jewel (2003). *Portland: People, politics and power.* Corvallis, OH: Ohio State University Press.

Lartey, Jamiles and Simone Weichselbaum (2020). Before George Floyd's death, Minneapolis police failed to adopt reforms, remove bad officers: The department allows officers to use choke holds barred in other cities. *The Marshall Project: Nonprofit Journalism about Criminal Justice.*

Laatz, Joan (1986). Judge won't ban police hold. *The Oregonian.* April 24.

Liedle, Chris (2016). Portland police chief accidentally shoots man while hunting in Harney County. *KATU. May 20.*

Lipman, Meryl (2017). Dorothy McCullough Lee (1902–1981). *The Oregon encyclopedia.* Portland, OR: Portland University and Oregon Historical Society: Retrieved from https://oregonencyclopedia.org/articles/lee_dorothy_mccullough_1902_1981_/#.XoIL2WB7nIU

Lloyd, Michael (1986a). Salt Lake City chief: Leave Harrington alone. *The Oregonian.* April 18.

Lloyd, Michael (1986b). Police chief offers rebuttal to previous testimony. *The Oregonian.* April 30.

Long, James and Leslie Zaitz (1986a). Investigation expanded to police chief. *The Oregonian.* April 5.

Long, James and Leslie Zaitz (1986b). Gary Harrington says rumor sparked talks. *The Oregonian.* May 16.

Long, James, John Hallman, Jr., and Leslie Zaitz (1986). Captains alienated by chief. *The Oregonian.* May 2.

Mapes, Jeff (1985). Portland police found critical of mayor and chief. *The Oregonian.* July 28.

Mapes, Jeff (2014). Republican Vic Atiyeh, who guided Oregon through economic upheaval, dies at 91. *The Oregonian/Oregon Live.* July 21.

Martin, Lisa (2018). Katherine Spillar fights for feminism: Activist helps lead the charge for gender equality. *TCU Magazine*. Spring.
Martin, Susan (1980). *Breaking and entering policewomen on patrol. Berkeley and Los Angeles.* Oakland, CA: University of California Press.
Martin, Susan and Nancy Jurik (2007). Doing justice, doing gender: Women in legal and criminal justice occupations. Thousand Oaks, CA: Sage Publishing, Inc.
Mastony, Colleen (2010). Was Chicago home to the country's 1st female cop? Researcher uncovers the story of Sgt. Marie Owens. *Chicago Tribune*. September 1.
Maxouris, Christina (2020). The 26-year-old man killed in Kenosha shooting tried to protest those around him, his girlfriend says. *CNN*. August 28.
Maxwell, Dani (2020). Madison has higher than average number of female police officers. *27 WKOW*. January 1.
Milton, Catherine, Ava Abramowitz, Laura Crites, Margaret Gates, Ellen Mintz, and Georgette Sandler (1974). *Women in policing: A manual.* Police Foundation. Washington, DC.
Mishkin, B. (1981). Female police in the United States. *Police Journal 54*(1): 22–33.
Mitchell, Joyce (1986). Lezak commission was a hatchet job on Harrington. *The Oregonian*. June 18.
Morn, Frank (1995). *Academic politics and the history of criminal justice education*. Westport, CT: Greenwood Publishing Group.
Morn, Frank (2010). *Forgotten reformer: Robert McClaughry and criminal justice reform in nineteenth-century America.* Lanham, MD: University Press of America.
Muhlhausen, David (2019). *Women in police: Breaking barriers and blazing a path.* National Institute of Justice Special Report. Office of Justice Programs. New York, NY: Cambridge University Press.
Myers, Gloria E. (1995). *A municipal mother: Portland's Lola Green Baldwin, America's first policewoman.* Corvallis, OR: Oregon State University Press.
Newton-Small, Jay (2016). *Broad influence: How women are changing the way America works.* New York, NY: Time Books.
Oliver, Gordon (1986). Clark slaps suspension on Gary Harrington: Policeman to appeal 10-day leave without pay. *The Oregonian*. July 23.
Olmos, Robert (1974). CRISS board fires director of project. *The Oregonian*. May 23.
Ortiz, Jorge (2020). A 'very dark history': Oregon's racist past fuels protests against injustice in Portland. *USA Today*. July 21.
Painter, John Jr. (1985a). Police career a rocky road for Harrington: New chief battled sexism to succeed. *The Oregonian*. January 25.
Painter, John Jr. (1985b). Police sale of T-shirts termed 'serious'. *The Oregonian*. August 29.
Painter, John Jr. (1990a). No talks held; trial of Harrington lawsuit resumes. *The Oregonian*. February 27.
Painter, John Jr. (1990b). Lawyer's testimony hits Harrington panel. *The Oregonian*. March 1.
Painter, John, Jr. (1990c). Lezak testifies that Harrington's fate saddened him. *The Oregonian*. March 2.
Painter, John Jr. (1990d). Witness says Clark under pressure to remove Chief Harrington. *The Oregonian*. March 14.
Palahniuk, Chuck (2003). *A walk in Portland, Oregon*. New York, NY: Crown Journeys.
Pickett, Nelson (1981a). Two officers deny racial harassment. *Oregon Journal*. March 23.
Pickett, Nelson (1981b). 150 rally to protest possum incident. *Oregon Journal*. March 26.
Pintarich, Paul (1975). Women have 70-year history of filling police roles in Portland. *The Oregonian*. September 21.
Rasmussen, Randy (1985). Portland chief endowed with open, direct manner, tough core. *The Oregonian*. May 2.
Read, Richard (1982). Captain reflects on 18-year battle. *The Oregonian*. November 14.
Read, Richard (1985). TV movie planned of Harrington's career: Story of chief's rise through ranks could be pilot for series. *The Oregonian*. October 23.
Read, Richard (1986a). Chief testifies on changes to the bureau. *The Oregonian*. April 18.
Read, Richard (1986b). Police say drug unit inadequate. *The Oregonian*. April 19.
Read, Richard (1986c). Harrington misled probe, witness says: Disbanding drug unit planned, ex-deputy chief claims. *The Oregonian*. April 29.

Read, Richard (1986d). Harrington says union, panel, newspaper ran her out of office. *The Oregonian*. June 8.
Read, Richard (1986e). Lezak commission records sent to city archives. *The Oregonian*. June 14.
Reddin, Jim (2019). Portland continues to churn through police chiefs. *Portland Tribune. December 30.*
Rice, Connie (2012). *Power concedes nothing: The unfinished fight for social justice in America*. Los Angeles, CA: Scribner Publisher.
Rodriguez, Isidoro (2020). Predators behind the badge: Confronting police sexual misconduct. *The Crime Report*. March 12.
Rollins, Michael (1985). Police well trained in 'sleeper' chief says. *The Oregonian*. April 23.
Roman, Ivonne (2018). Opinion: A Portland police pioneer on her unfinished business. *The Oregonian*. September 17.
Rosenbaum and Associates, LLP (2020). *Compliance officer and community liaison quarterly report: Quarter 3 updates & analysis for the city of Portland, Oregon*. October 6.
Ruble, Web (1975). $20 million suit charges bias in police agencies. *The Oregonian*. September 5.
Sarasohn, David (1986). Harrington judged in wonderland. *The Oregonian. June 4.*
Schulz, Dorothy (1995). *From social worker to crimefighter: Women in United States municipal policing*. New York, NY: Praeger Press.
Schulz, Dorothy (2003). Women police chiefs: A statistical profile. *Police Quarterly 6*(3): 330–345.
Schultz, Dorothy (2004). Breaking the brass ceiling: Women police chiefs and their paths to the top. Santa Barbara, CA: ABC-CLIO, Inc.
Schulz, Dorothy (2020). Why are America's women police chiefs resigning? *The Crime Report*. August 13.
Segrave, Kerry (1995). *Policewomen: A history*. Jefferson, North Carolina and London, Jefferson, NC: McFarland & Company, Inc.
Serbulo, Leanne and Karen Gibson (2013). Black and blue: Police-community relations in Portland's Albina District, 1964–1985. *Oregon Historical Society 114*(1): 6–37.
Severson, Kim (1986). Harrington supporters plan rally. *The Oregonian*. June 14.
Smith, Judd (1973). Status quo irks women law officers. *The Oregonian*. April 30.
Snell, John (1990). Duffy says Harrington wasn't fired. *The Oregonian*. March 8.
Stamper, Norm (2005). *Breaking rank: A top cop's expose of the dark side of American policing*. New York, NY: Nation Books.
Starheim, Rianna (2019). *Women in policing: Breaking barriers and blazing a path*. Washington, DC: National Institute of Justice Special Report: U.S. Department of Justice – Office of Justice Programs. July.
Stepler, Renee (2017). Female police officers' on-the-job experiences diverge from those of male officers. *Pew Research Center: Fact Tank*. January 17.
Thacher, David (2000). *National COPS evaluation organizational change case study: Portland, Oregon*. Washington, DC: National Institute of Justice.
Thomas, Rachael (2020). Woman becomes first female African-American captain in Louisiana State Police history. *WAFB 9*. January 28.
Turner, Wallace (1981). Police scandal in Portland, Oregon leads to shake-up of narcotics squad and conviction of an ex officer. *New York Times*. May 27.
Turner, Wallace (1985). Blacks protest choke-hold death in Oregon. *New York Times*. May 5.
Turner, Wallace (1986a). Police chief in rift with her officers. *New York Times*. January 31.
Turner, Wallace (1986b). Queries mount for police chief in Oregon city. *New York Times*. April 23.
Turner, Wallace (1986c). Under fire, woman quits as Portland police chief. *New York Times*. June 3.
Vaughn, Courtney (2021). Can faith in police be restored? A former Portland chief thinks so. *Portland Tribune*. February 3.
Verducci, Frank (1974). *Height and weight requirements for police officers*. Submitted to the Civil Service Commission, City and County of San Francisco.
Vollmer, August (1930). Meet the Lady Cop. *The Survey*. March 15.
Weichselbaum, Simone (2019). Desperate for recruits, more police departments looking at non-citizens. *USA Today*. February 15.
White, Thomas and Peter Bloch (1975). *Police officer height and selected aspects of performance*. Police Foundation and International Association of Chiefs of Police in cooperation with the Urban Institute.

Williams, Linda (1982). Council to appeal order to defend police facing suit. *The Oregonian*. March 4.
Wilson, Lerry (1985). Son waits, helpless and angry. *The Oregonian*. July 7.
Wohler, Milly (1971). I'll do the job anywhere, says detective. *The Oregonian*. July 20.
Worthy, Ariel (2019). Recent report shows step back for police force diversity. *National Public Radio Pittsburgh*. July 12.
Zaitz, Leslie (1978). Policewoman says city torpedoed bias accord. *The Oregonian*. October 27.Zaitz, Leslie and James Long (1986a). Panel lays foundation for Harrington Probe. *The Oregonian*. April 10.
Zaitz, Leslie and James Long (1986b). Harrington untruthful, Deputy DA tells Panel. *The Oregonian*. May 15.
Zaitz, Leslie and James Long (1986c). Restaurateur balks at inquiry: Lee refuses to testify about Harringtons. *The Oregonian*. May 14.
Zaitz, Leslie, Tom Hallman, and James Long (1986). Harrington says she gave details to businessman. *The Oregonian*. April 2.
Zaitz, Leslie, James Long, and Tom Hallman, Jr. (1986). Gary Harrington case surfaces: '73 police probe shows link to heroin dealer. *The Oregonian*. April 15.

Chapter 5

Bill Bratton – Commissioner NYPD and Chief of the LAPD with Appendix on George Kelling – Broken Windows Policing

Turnaround Leadership

William Joseph "Bill" Bratton was born on October 6, 1947, in Boston, Massachusetts. He graduated from Boston Technical High School in Roxbury in 1965. In 1966 Bratton enlisted in the Army during the Vietnam War, serving as a Military Police Officer until April 1968. On October 7, 1970, at the age of 23, Bratton's law enforcement career began when he successfully tested onto the Boston Police Department (BPD). As he rose through the ranks, his leadership as a change agent was in high demand in a short period. In ten years, Bratton's unprecedented leadership in five different agencies consisted of the following: Chief Police, Massachusetts Bay Transportation Authority (MBTA) (1983–1986); Superintendent, Metropolitan District (1986–1990); Chief, New York City Transit Police Department (1990–1992); Commission BPD (1992–1993); and Police Commissioner, New York City Police Department (NYPD) (1994–1996). Bratton then spent the next six years as a consultant before he became the Chief of the Los Angeles Police Department (LAPD) (2002–2009), and he returned to the NYPD as Commissioner (2013–2016). Bratton's success as a "turn-around" transformational leader provided several career opportunities across the nation and spoke to the ongoing reform efforts throughout American policing.

Boston – Patrol to Superintendent (1970–1983)

Bratton's 1970 BPD police academy class consisted of 157 recruits, the largest since 1919, with three Black officers and no women. At the time, the BPD consisted of approximately 2,800 sworn officers with 55 minorities (2 percent) and no women to police a population of 641,000 with about 25 percent minority citizens. Their badges read "Policeman" – women officers did not arrive at the BPD until 1973 and the gender neutral badge "Police Officer" would not arrive until 1997 (Bratton & Knobler, 2021, pp. 43). A 1973 federal consent decree[1] ordered the BPD to increase its hiring and promotional diversity. However, it would take nearly three decades to address the decree adequately and withstand court challenges from white officers. Three decades later, Bratton worked on a similar consent decree for the LAPD. Bratton took advantage of a federal grant that most BPD officers ignored and took classes at Boston State University (now University of Massachusetts Boston). His American Government course was taught by Michael Dukakis, who would later be elected Massachusetts Governor and nominated as the Democratic Presidential candidate in 1988. One of Bratton's favorite classes was art appreciation. He learned to look for the message beyond the image and consider how

1 A consent decree is a federal court order forcing police departments to overhaul their practices and policies under judicial supervision.

DOI: 10.4324/9780429272226-6

and why it was created. This helped Bratton look beyond the poverty and crime that exists in urban minority communities and to truly see the residents beyond what his implicit bias indicated. Bratton earned his bachelor's degree in law enforcement in 1975 and became a sergeant the same year. The following year, he became the second recipient of the Schroeder Brothers Memorial Medal, the BPD's highest award for valor after he got an armed bank robber to surrender after he took a hostage. The Schroeder Brothers Memorial Medal was named after Walter Schroeder, killed by a bank robber in 1970 and his brother John Schroeder who was killed in a pawn shop robbery in 1973. During the last six months of 1993, Bratton was the Commissioner of the BPD.

BPD Civilian Influences – Wasserman, Goldstein, Kelling

Robert di Grazia[2] was the commissioner of the BPD from 1972 to 1977. As an outsider reformer, he pushed younger BPD officers to get their degrees through the newly developed Department of Justice grant called the Law Enforcement Education Program (LEEP). Di Grazia was a native of San Francisco, a son of Italian immigrants, and received his bachelor's degree from Boston College. Before becoming the BPD external appointment as commissioner, di Grazia was chief in Novato, California in the 1960s, and then he led the St. Louis County Police Department from 1970 to 1972. The BPD Police Commissioner is a mayoral appointment and serves as a civilian while the Executive Superintendent runs the department's daily activities. The BPD needed an external commissioner to clean up one of the most brutal, racist, and corrupt urban departments in the country. To Commissioner di Grazia's credit, he placed free-thinking civilians from outside the department into power positions. Bratton would later replicate this style of reform leadership. Outside academic perspectives served Bratton and other Executive Superintendents well during their leadership development. The academic attention Bratton received at the BPD would impact his desire to become a change agent for multiple departments in the future.

Neighborhood Policing – Bob Wasserman

Bob Wasserman,[3] director of training and education at the police academy and then assistant to Commissioner di Grazia in charge of operations, pushed decentralized neighborhood-oriented policing into the BPD during the 1970s. Traditionally, the community expected police commanders to host meetings to update the public on crime statistics. As a civilian, Wasserman led the BPD Operations through a different lens and brought the police and neighborhoods together to prioritize their concerns. Wasserman's leadership approach challenged the status quo and put the department in the position to directly ask the community what they perceived as the primary issues their police needed to address. At these neighborhood meetings, the police brought in flip charts and created a series of actionable strategies to address the concerns they

2 Di Grazia helped enforce controversial court rulings related to school desegregation. After Boston, he served as superintendent for the Montgomery County Police Department, and he was one of the founding members of the PERF. Di Grazia died on April 26, 2018, at the age of 90, at his home office in Fort Myers, Florida.

3 Wasserman is a Senior Vice President for Hillard Heintze and served as a consultant and monitor for numerous urban police departments. He received his graduate degree in police administration from Michigan State University. In 1972, Wasserman was a police consultant for the Kansas City Police Department. At that time, three hundred new officers were being added to the KCPD and Wasserman persuaded Chief Clarence Kelley to allow the Police Foundation, and George Kelling, to test how these officers could best be utilized (i.e., the start of the famous Kansas City Preventative Patrol Experiment).

identified through the neighborhood voice. The police and the neighborhood would then sign the flip chart, acknowledging the listed contributions, and they would reconvene every six weeks to assess their progress. These meetings helped establish legitimacy, community relationships where none existed, and trust in ways not previously experienced with the BPD. Commissioner di Grazia's approach to bringing outsiders into police management, along with Wasserman's approach to community policing and repairing race relations, became the main playbook for Bratton's transitional leadership success. Wasserman became directly connected to Bratton throughout his career.

Police Executive Research Forum – Herman Goldstein

In 1977, Bratton was exposed to Herman Goldstein's[4] *Policing a Free Society* (when Bob Wasserman gifted Bratton the book),[5] which provided the initial concepts for problem-oriented policing (POP) strategies. In 1982, Bratton attended a three-day Police Executive Research Forum (PERF) conference, which brought together progressive police leaders and academics from across the nation interested in conducting research and advanced ideas related to police professionalism. At the time, Gary Hayes,[6] who also worked as a civilian liaison in the BPD under Commissioner di Grazia, was PERF's founding executive director. Goldstein's seminal 1979 article, "Problem-Oriented Policing," published in *Crime & Delinquency* (Goldstein, 1979), heavily influenced PERF leadership conferences and received funding from the Department of Justice (DOJ). Hayes's untimely death led to Darryl Stephens,[7] Chief of Newport News Police, becoming the new PERF Director (1986–1992) and continued support for POP. Bratton learned from Wasserman and Goldstein that the police could provide resources to prevent crime rather than simplistically reacting to the aftermath's damage. In 1987, Bratton received the second annual Gary Hayes Award at the PERF conference due to his transformational leadership as the chief of the MBTA and the Superintendent of the Metropolitan Police Department (Mets), discussed more fully below. In 2004, Bratton was elected President of PERF by its members while serving as the Chief of the LAPD.

Broken Windows – George Kelling

In the same year Bratton attended the three-day 1982 PERF conference, he became exposed to an article published in 1982 in the *Atlantic Monthly* by James Q. Wilson and George Kelling entitled "Broken Windows: The Police and Neighborhood Safety." The ten-page paper influenced his leadership for the next several decades. The academics argued that public disorder offenses led to an atmosphere of permissiveness and fear. Kelling and Wilson further hypothesized that more serious crime flourished when these low-level disorderly offenses were unchallenged (Kelling & Wilson, 1982). Therefore, police leaders were encouraged to enforce all ordinances and laws in a manner that signaled or modified behavioral norms within public spaces. Further details on Kelling and broken windows policing appear in the chapter appendix.

4 Details of Goldstein are discussed in the appendix to the O.W. Wilson chapter.

5 Author's interview with Bratton on November 3, 2020.

6 Hayes, a Madison Goldstein student, died at age 40 of cancer; a memorial award through PERF continues to honor his legacy.

7 Stephens is in the Hall of Fame with the Center for Evidence-Based Crime Policy and is widely recognized as one of the most innovative chiefs in modern American policing. He retired as chief for Charlotte Mecklenburg (1999–2008) and also served as chief for St. Petersburg (1992–1999) and Newport News (1983–1986) police departments.

Bratton's BPD Leadership

Two years after becoming a sergeant, the BPD promoted Bratton to the rank of lieutenant. Three years after that, he became the youngest Executive Superintendent, BPD's second-highest rank, in 1980, at 32 years old. However, Bratton's leadership position did not last long after *Boston* magazine ran a profile article on him and quoted his desire to be the next Police Commissioner. In 1982, as a reaction to Bratton's perceived brashness, he was reassigned as Inspector of Bureaus to serve as a liaison with minorities and the lesbian, gay, bisexual, and transgender communities.[8] The department gave Bratton an older marked police car and uniform (a sign of demotion in police leadership) and a fifth-floor corner office (instead of the powerful sixth-floor headquarters office) without a secretary. His lesson was that stating a goal that you want to be the top leader in your police department is not always politically the best move. However, it was clear that Bratton was defining the mold of Bostonian police leaders in a way that differed from past tough Irishmen known more for their brawn than brains.

Bratton's position as Inspector of Bureaus working with minority and LGBTQ communities was short-lived. After four months, he was brought back to the sixth-floor headquarters as superintendent in charge of labor relations. This return also provided all the symbols and trappings of power in traditional policing (i.e. office near the commissioner, plainclothes instead of a uniform, and a nicer unmarked car). As superintendent, Bratton argued for using single-officer patrols,[9] much like O.W. Wilson did in Wichita and Chicago. Bratton supported a proposition that called for a reduction in the number of officers and staff in the BPD. This position did not endear him with the union leadership, and he discovered that the internal politics of promotion could slow down any progressive leader. Bratton opted not to wait his turn patiently and looked outside of his traditional bureaucracy for lateral transfer opportunities external to the BPD's confines. A decade later, he would return to the BPD for the top spot.

Massachusetts Bay Transportation Authority – Chief (1983–1986)

In 1983 Bratton received a call from Jim O'Leary, the MBTA general manager, asking him to be police chief. Governor Michael Dukakis[10] appointed O'Leary to lead the MBTA after O'Leary mistakenly received an envelope with $10,000 cash. Barry Locke,[11] the existing general manager, was supposed to receive the money as a bribe. After a Grand Jury indicted Locke, Dukakis tasked O'Leary with reforming the MBTA since the governor was a frequent subway user. Bratton was sworn in as the chief of the MBTA by Governor Dukakis, who wanted an efficient, clean, and secure commuter rail and subway system to become part of his legacy. The rail system stretched over multiple counties and 79 towns (Photo 5.1).

8 In 1993 BPD Commissioner Bratton made national headlines by openly recruiting gay and lesbian officers. He had done the same as the chief of the New York City Transit Police in 1990 when he was able to separate the testing and hiring away from the NYPD. He also made strides to create partnerships with the police and the LGBTQ community in both NY and LA, which included open officer recruitment. Bratton revealed his sister Pat was gay and consequently he had a better sense of when bias occurred and empathy.

9 Research generally supports one-person patrol over two-person patrol (Wilson & Brewer, 1992).

10 Dukakis was Governor from 1975 to 1979 and again from 1983 to 1991. He won the Democratic Primary for President but lost to George H. Bush in 1992. The Lt. Governor from 1983 to 1985 was John Kerry. Kerry was the U.S. Massachusetts Senator (1985–2013), President Obama's Secretary of State (2013–2017) and the 1st United States Special Presidential Envoy for Climate with the Biden Administration beginning in 2021.

11 Locke became the only Massachusetts Cabinet Secretary to be convicted of a felony while in office since 1970 when the state adopted a cabinet system (Cooper, 1981). After serving two years in prison, he moved to Maryland and served as president for an organization that served the developmentally disabled. Locke died in 2007 at the age of 76.

Photo 5.1 Massachusetts Bay Transportation Authority Police Chief William J. Bratton answers questions at a news conference at the McCormack Building in Boston on Wednesday, July 20, 1983.

Photo credit: Associated Press.

Bratton's leadership style as the chief of the MBTA was hands-on. He began riding the subway system in full uniform, arrived at crime scenes, and asked his officers to brief him on problems that needed to be solved. Bratton recognized how morale is negatively impacted by officers who feel the top leadership is out of touch. By placing himself frequently in the field while in full uniform, Bratton developed trust with his officers and understood what problems existed at the ground level. In his memoir, *Turnaround*, he reports that he wanted to understand his officers' hopes, aspirations, and frustrations (Bratton & Knobler, 1998).[12]

Part of the frustration from MBTA officers came from driving around all day in small Ford Fairlane vehicles, which the department purchased in the 1970s in response to international gas shortages. To prove the extent of this issue, Bratton asked O'Leary to do a ride-along with him in the Ford Fairlane to reach his own conclusions about the patrol vehicle's size and comfort. The comfort and symbolism of a proper police vehicle are essential for the morale of departments. Moreover, Bratton quickly discovered that officers' archaic radios did not work well when in the subway system, creating accountability and safety issues. Over the next three years, the MBTA invested $4 million on a new comprehensive subway radio network system, increased its size to a 110-person department, purchased 55 new vehicles, and reduced crime by a reported 27 percent. Moreover, MBTA became the 13th police agency to receive national accreditation through the Commission on Accreditation for Law Enforcement Agencies (CALEA).

12 Bratton's second memoir, titled *The Profession: A Memoir of Community, Race, and the Arc of Policing America*, was published in June 2021 (Bratton & Knobler, 2021).

Other leadership wins that came from Bratton's time as the chief of the MBTA stemmed from unaccounted revenue. Bratton transferred all revenue from the MBTA into one room in Charlestown. After a year-long investigation with numerous hidden cameras, he had 38 employees out of the 70 that worked in the transit money room arrested for stealing. Bratton recognized the need to market these types of victories and worked intently with the media to ensure proper transparent coverage. An organization reflects its leader, and Bratton worked on selling the MBTA transformation as an agency that tackled both crime and corruption.

Massachusetts Metropolitan District Commission Police Department

Superintendent (1986–1990)

Bratton developed a reputation for turning around dysfunctional police agencies. In 1986, following major corruption scandals in the Mets, Bratton was asked to become superintendent. The Mets were the third-largest police agency in Massachusetts, with 600 officers behind the 2,800 officers of the BPD and the 2,100 officers in the state police. The Mets were responsible for policing highways, the Boston Harbor, reservoirs, parkways, and several beaches. Bratton described the Mets as the worst police department in America when he took over as their superintendent. The department had a fleet of 113 marked squads; yet only 25 were in good condition. Officer morale was abysmal. To improve morale, Bratton asked for input from all department levels and created a new values system. He also sought state money to upgrade the police vehicles and created a more stringent accountability discipline system to incentivize officers to drive safely. State funding was approved to upgrade radios and purchase new police vehicles and a helicopter. By 1987, Bratton was honored through PERF and given the second annual Gary Hayes Award in appreciation of his leadership and reform efforts. By 1990, lawmakers moved to centralize agencies and merged the Mets into the state police functions with the Capitol police and Registry of Motor Vehicles police. Bratton did not have any interest in working for the state police, but he had established a reputation for being a transformational change leader.

Bob Kiley[13] was very familiar with Bratton since he served as deputy mayor in Boston and directed the MBTA. In his new role as the chair of the New York City Metropolitan Transit Authority, Kiley hired Bob Wasserman and George Kelling as consultants to research the subway system in New York and suggest solutions to persistent crime and disorder problems. Based upon his success with the MBTA, Wasserman and Kelling contacted Bratton and encouraged him to bring his leadership skills to New York City (NYC). Kiley had previously pinned the Gary Hayes PERF Award to Bratton's lapel and spoke highly of Wasserman and Kelling.

Brief History of the New York City Police Department

In 1844, NYC modeled its police department after Robert Peel's 1829 Metropolitan Police Act that had created the first modern police department in London. Riots and increased crime from the 1830s through the 1850s led to the formation of police agencies in every major U.S. city (Trojanowicz & Carter, 1998). It is imperative to reflect on the history of policing the

13 Kiley's career experiences included CIA agent, consultant within the Police Foundation, CEO of the MBTA, Deputy Mayor of Boston, CEO of the Metropolitan Transpiration Authority, CEO of New York Partnership, and Commissioner of Transport for London. He died in 2016 at the age of 80.

nation's largest city to understand the various leadership challenges of NYC. Much of what we know about these challenges come from the media's attempt to gain access and crack the blue curtain of silence. Moreover, police leaders needed to allow access while also trusting their command staff and officers to share reform visions with the media. Past police reformers, such as Teddy Roosevelt, August Vollmer, and O.W. Wilson, led their departments with a high degree of transparency and a collegial relationship with the media. They were also leaders who trusted the loyalty of their command staff. In Bratton's first memoir, *Turnaround: How America's Top Cop Reversed the Crime Epidemic*, he alludes to this trust when he opens his book with a quote from New York Police Commissioner Theodore Roosevelt: "The best executive is one who has sense to pick good men to do what he wants done, and self-restraint enough to keep from meddling with them while they do it." Roosevelt's unique connection with the media is described below, followed by scandals that rocked reform efforts of the NYPD and set the stage for Bratton's transformational leadership.

Commissioner Teddy Roosevelt and the Muckrakers

During the 1890s, clergy leaders throughout NYC preached about political corruption and the need for reform leadership. Charles Parkhurst was one of the most outspoken critics of the corrupt democratic Tammany Hall political establishment, and in 1891, the New York Society for the Prevention of Crime elected him as their president. They linked political corruption with the police department, noting that politicians and police leaders protected their illegal profitability by circumventing religious efforts to convert criminals. The Parkhurst campaign was a catalyst for the first commission to investigate police corruption. State Senator Clarence Lexow led the campaign from 1894 to 1895. The extent of the political and police entangled corruption, broadcasted by the Lexow Commission hearings, led to Tammany Hall's defeat and the election of reform Mayor William Strong, who then appointed Roosevelt as Police Commissioner in May 1895.

Commissioner Roosevelt partnered with muckraking journalists Jacob Riis and Lincoln Steffens to expose the police department's problems and the police board's leadership challenges. Roosevelt offered Riis and Steffens unprecedented access to the department, and they worked across the street[14] from the old police headquarters located at 300 Mulberry Street. Steffens wrote for the *Evening Post* and competed with a dozen other city newspapers for stories related to the nation's largest city and police department. However, unlike the NYC media today, these early muckrakers did not fear being isolated from the department if they negatively reported corruption (Levitt, 2009). Indeed, Commissioner Roosevelt encouraged their midnight rambles with him to see for themselves the problems with police corruption and tenement housing. While there are only a few remaining NYC newspapers, Bratton learned from the early police leaders to be transparent with the media regarding the challenges for urban policing and the strategies he utilized to meet those challenges.

For NYC, historical challenges persisted in terms of the sheer size of the population and officers' corruption. By 1898, after Roosevelt left, NYC absorbed the Brooklyn Police Department and 18 other police agencies. This growth required significant structural changes in the department's leadership and how communication within the agency would take place while policing over three million city residents. Decades of corruption followed that plagued the NYPD. Stories of embedded corruption came to a critical conclusion in the late 1960s. There was a revelation that NYPD Detective Frank Serpico worked with the media and the

14 Confines for the muckraking journalists were referred to as "the shack," and reporters today continue to use the term inside One Police Plaza to describe their second-floor office that provides occasional access to the NYPD.

U.S. Attorney's office to uncover widespread corruption throughout the city's criminal justice system and was going to testify in numerous criminal and congressional proceedings.

New York City in the 1960s–1970s: Serpico and the Knapp Commission

As early as 1967, Serpico partnered with Sergeant David Durk and attempted to blow the whistle on widespread corruption throughout the NYPD. He initially met with Jay Kriegel[15] (chief of staff and special counsel to Mayor Lindsay), but the mayor's office failed to take any action. In 1968, the District Attorney's (DA) Office had Serpico break the code of silence and testify before a Bronx Grand Jury on a smaller corruption case. Officers soon found out he was the whistleblower and began to exert enormous pressure on him. Despite his testimony and threats from fellow officers, the NYPD did not pull the eccentric Serpico off the streets and, instead, placed him on undercover narcotics detective work. In 1970, Serpico, Durk, and Paul Delise[16] (a boss of Serpico's) instigated a meeting with David Burnham[17] from the *New York Times* and helped him write articles to expose the depth of the corruption (Burnham, 1970). Burnham gave Mayor Lindsay's press secretary a forewarning that they were investigating corruption in the NYPD. A week later, Lindsay attempted to preempt the media stories about police corruption and called for an internal investigatory commission that included the city attorney, a few DAs, and the police commissioner. After three weeks, the commission received over 1,500 complaints related to police and judicial corruption. The commission passed this information back to Lindsay and said they would not continue their investigation due to conflict of interest concerns and not having adequate staff.

In April 1970, Mayor Lindsay appointed an external five-member committee in what became known as Knapp Commission, named after its Chair Whitman Knapp.[18] In October 1970, Lindsay replaced Commissioner Howard Leary[19] with Patrick Murphy.[20] Predictably, those who were corrupt got nervous. On February 3, 1971, while doing an undercover drug buy in Williamsburg, Brooklyn at 778 Driggs Avenue (apartment 3G), Serpico was shot in the face. When he got out of the hospital, Serpico demanded the incident report from internal affairs from the night he got shot and found out that one sector car responded to a 10–10 citizen call (possible crime) and no 10–13 call (assist patrolman) went out. Serpico believed his fellow officers set him up to be murdered, although no formal investigation took place.

On October 18, 1971, the Knapp Commission began to hear testimony from other whistleblowers (also called lamplighters) who detailed the collection of graft by officers who in

15 Kriegel died in December 2019 at the age of 79. He helped initiate civilian oversight of citizens' complaints against the police and helped draft a lengthy 1968 report for the Kerner Commission on civil disorders, which used the phrase "our nation is moving toward two societies, one black, one white – separate and unequal" (Roberts, 2019). That report put the police into a reactive posture for the next several decades arguing that white supremacy was the cause of crime problems and the police didn't really matter. The same year the Kerner report was issued, 1968, the country was introduced to 9-1-1 dispatch and calls for service increased dramatically.

16 In August 1971, Commissioner Patrick Murphy promoted Delise to Deputy Chief Inspector (Burnham, 1971).

17 After Burnham's articles came out, Serpico received numerous death threats from what he suspected were NYPD officers.

18 On June 15, 1972, President Nixon nominated Knapp to be a federal judge for the Southern District of New York.

19 Leary was the Philadelphia Police Commissioner from 1962 to 1965, where he was initially hired as a foot patrol officer in 1940.

20 Murphy is discussed in the Herman Goldstein appendix to the O.W. Wilson chapter. In addition to being the Commissioner of the NYPD, he also served as chief in Syracuse, Washington, DC, and the Detroit Police Department.

return protected gambling and prostitution, just as they did when Roosevelt was police commissioner. In his December 1971 testimony, with Ramsey Clarke's representation,[21] Serpico spoke for nearly three hours and demonstrated how difficult it was to be an honest cop while corrupt officers operated with impunity and tolerance from upper command. The Knapp Commission confirmed that pervasive and well-organized corruption existed throughout the NYPD and the city's criminal justice system (Armstrong, 2012). The commission issued a series of recommendations in their 1972 report, which lead to a restructuring of the internal affairs units and new anti-corruption policies. According to his biographer (Maas, 1973),[22] Serpico was the first officer in the police department's history to voluntarily blow the whistle on police corruption and was willing to testify in open court.[23] While outsiders revealed past corruption scandals, this was the first time corruption in the NYPD came from an internal source.

In the Knapp Commission's aftermath, crime rates rose throughout the country, and NYC became the epicenter of media and Hollywood attention for crime drama.[24] Clashes between the police and public, which began in the 1960s during various social movements, continued into the 1970s. During these clashes, protesters and the media challenged the police department's legitimacy, which may have stemmed from earlier reform movements of O.W. Wilson and other advocates for professionalization. These reform movements caused the police to increase preventative patrol and narrow their role to fighting only serious crime while effectively decriminalizing low-level offenses. Crime rates reached historic highs over the next few decades, and New York, like other cities, experienced "white flight" during this era from wealthy and middle-class families who could afford to escape the crime-ridden city. Retailers that catered to the affluent social classes also moved to the suburbs. In the 1970s, NYC lost 10 percent of its population due to fear of crime and disorder (Woldoff, 2011). As the demographics shifted, cities were increasingly occupied by poor minorities and immigrants, causing disadvantaged families to be more highly concentrated. Racial fears persisted, and predominantly white police forces feebly attempted to address inner-city violence. Reciprocally, the city experienced a financial crisis, which caused a hiring freeze on the NYPD from 1976 to 1980.

New York City in the 1980s: Goetz and the Central Park Five

By the 1980s, crime worsened again with crack cocaine, and the media introduced Americans to new terminology: drive-by shootings, carjacking, and teenage wilding or wolfpacks. Two famous NYC cases from this era that took on an international media frenzy, Bernhard Goetz and the Central Park Five, are discussed below.

21 Clarke was assistant and Deputy Attorney General from 1961 to 1967 in the Kennedy and Johnson Administrations and Attorney General from 1967 to 1969. He became a staunch anti-war figure throughout his career and represented several controversial clients, including Iraqi dictator Saddam Hussein in front of the Iraq Special Tribunal. His father, Tom Clark, was the Attorney General for President Truman from 1945 to 1949 and a Supreme Court Justice from 1949 to 1967.

22 In 1973, Maas's biography was brought to film in the movie *Serpico* that starred Al Pacino, who was nominated for a Best Actor Academy Award.

23 As described in the chapter on Roosevelt, Captain Max Schmittberger also became a whistleblower in 1894 and testified in front of the Lexow Commission. However, his testimony was initially a forced and led to the admission of deep rooted corruption, bribery, and extortion. Unlike Serpico who left the NYPD in the aftermath of his testimony, Schmittberger remained for an additional 23 years and was promoted to the chief of the department.

24 Examples of the NYPD movies and television shows include: *Car 54, Where Are You?* (1960–1963); *Mean Streets* (1973); *Serpico* (1973); *Kojak* (1973–1978); *Death Wish* (1974); *Barney Miller* (1975–1982); *The Warriors* (1979); *Prince of the City* (1981); *Night Court* (1984–1992); *New Jack City* (1991); *NYPD Blue* (1993–2005); *Blue Bloods* (2010-today); *Brooklyn Nine-Nine* (2013-today) and several *Law & Order* series.

On December 22, 1984, 37-year-old Bernhard Hugo Goetz, Jr.,[25] who had a degree in nuclear engineering, shot and wounded four Black teenagers on the NYC subway because he feared they were going to rob or beat him. The injured Black teenagers were Barry Allen, Troy Canty (who asked Goetz to give him $5), Darrell Cabey, and James Ramseur.[26] They traveled in the subway car from a South Bronx housing project with plans to break into video arcade machines with screwdrivers they carried in their pockets. After the shooting, America split on outrage or sympathy toward Goetz, and this split was divided by race. At a White House news conference, President Reagan stated, "it seems that we got overzealous at protecting the criminals' rights and forgot about the victims." Public fundraising efforts paid for Goetz's bail and defense fund. At his criminal trial for attempted murder, the jury found him not guilty, but he served eight months on Riker's Island for using an unlicensed firearm. One victim, Darryl Cabey, suffered brain damage, is a paraplegic, and successfully sued Goetz and received $43 million in civil court. Goetz subsequently declared bankruptcy.

The media frenzy over the shooting led to the title "subway vigilante" to describe Goetz.[27] His case symbolized the frustration with the high crime rates of the 1980s. The civil suit also strengthened the National Rifle Association's (NRA) push for less restrictive concealed carry laws (Fletcher, 1988). Goetz purchased a .38 Smith and Wesson handgun in Florida and illegally brought the firearm to NYC. He claimed he bought the gun due to owning his own repair business and suffering a prior mugging in 1981 on the NYC subway that left him with a knee injury (Serena, 2018). He was denied a gun permit with the State of New York during a period when Mayor Ed Koch[28] was pushing for mandatory jail time for anyone caught with an illegal firearm.

Consequently, Goetz became a high visibility story for the NRA (Cutner, 2015), who stated in a news conference that "a government that cannot protect its citizens has no right to deny them the means for protecting themselves." Bumper stickers that read "Ride with Bernie – He Goetz 'em!" were sold throughout NYC. The Reverend Al Sharpton[29] held counter-rallies in front of Goetz's home, arguing that vigilante racism soaked his actions. Malcolm Gladwell, the author of *The Tipping Point*, goes further in arguing that Goetz may not have pulled a gun on the subway if he had not been for the influence of the subway dilapidation and the graffiti-covered walls (Gladwell, 2000). Gladwell's argument referenced Bratton's later use of the broken windows theory and his subsequent strategies to significantly reduce crime as the chief of the New York City Transit Police.

On the evening of April 19, 1989, 28-year-old Trisha Meili[30] was attacked and raped in the northern section of Central Park.[31] She was not found until 1:30 AM the next day, naked,

25 Goetz has remained living in the same apartment near Union Square and became an advocate for NYC's squirrel population and marijuana legalization. He was arrested in 2013 for selling marijuana to an uncover officer, but charges were later dropped (Kutner, 2015).

26 In 2011, Ramseur, at the age of 45, was found dead of an overdose in Bronx motel room exactly 27 years to the day that Goetz shot him. Ramseur was sentenced in 1986 for rape and robbery and served 25 years in prison.

27 In 2020, *Netflix* detailed the Goetz case in the series *Trial by Media*.

28 Koch was NYC Democratic Mayor from 1978 to 1989. In later years, he publicly supported Giuliani and Bloomberg for Mayor in addition to George W. Bush for President in 2004.

29 Sharpton appeared next to Mayor Bill de Blasio and Bill Bratton, during his second stint as NYPD Commissioner, in a press conference following the July 2014 death of Eric Garner. The optics of the press conference infuriated many members of the NYPD rank and file. Bratton remained silent not wanting to embarrass the mayor and knowing he had to carefully lead the department out of its latest scandal.

30 Meili married in 1996 and resides in Connecticut, but still suffers physically and emotionally from the attack (Nicolaou, 2019).

31 In May 2012, Ken Burns released a documentary film on the Central Park five case, which helped lead to a 2014 legal settlement with the city. In May 2019, Ava DuVernay released a four-episode miniseries on *Netflix* titled *When They See Us*. Both films received numerous awards.

bound, and gagged in a ravine of a wooded area near 102nd Street, hours after the initial attack. Miraculously, Meili woke up after a 12-day comatose but did not remember anything about her attack (Meili, 2003). Witness accounts reported large groups of young Black and Latino males running through Central Park that evening, and the media dubbed them "wilding" and "wolfpacks." The police questioned several suspects. Ten suspects were indicted and later received plea bargains based on political pressure, while others had their charges dropped.

On May 1, 1989, Donald Trump infamously paid media outlets to publish his letter as a full-page ad imploring the New York state legislatures to bring back the death penalty in response to the Central Park Five case. The title of his letter was "Bring Back the Death Penalty – Bring Back our Police." Five defendants confessed to the rape without legal representation being present but later recanted their confessions. They were eventually convicted and sentenced to prison. Four of the defendants appealed their cases, and the appellate court affirmed the lower court's decision. In 2001, Matias Reyes[32] confessed that he attacked and raped Meili in 1989. A subsequent investigation proved his story accurate, and DNA evidence further corroborated Reyes's confession. A year later, the NYC DA vacated the convictions against the Central Park Five, and they subsequently filed a lawsuit for malicious prosecution. The city refused to settle the case for a decade.

In 2014, Mayor Bill de Blasio settled the case, on behalf of NYC, for $41 million. In 2016, the State of New York settled for $3.9 million. During his Republican presidential campaign in 2016, Trump stated he disagreed prosecutors should vacate the Central Park Five convictions. This statement led, in part, to Senator John McCain's withdraw of support for candidate Trump (Burns, 2012). Bratton viewed Presidential candidate Trump as insensitive and unfit for office.

New York in the 1990s (Mollen Commission)

Following the 1990 Central Park rape case, NYC set a record with 2,262 murders across the five boroughs, represented by 7.3 million residents. In contrast, today, NYC has less than 300 murders a year with 8.4 million residents. (During the 2020 pandemic, murders rose to 462). In 1992, Mayor David Dinkins[33] appointed the Mollen Commission to investigate corruption throughout the NYPD again. The Mayor called for the commission one month after the arrest of ten-year veteran officer Michael Dowd and five other NYPD officers in Suffolk County for drug conspiracy. Dowd had long been investigated internally for bribery, extortion, selling cocaine, robbing drug dealers, and protecting drug dealers, mainly Adam Diaz.[34]

The Mollen Commission would find that drug-related corruption and police brutality were rampant, especially in the 75th Precinct. The command staff was guilty of covering up and allowing the misconduct and corruption to flourish. Worse yet, officers who cooperated with the commission experienced various acts of retaliation through threats and denial of promotions. Red flags arose as early as 1986 when officers were arrested on drug charges from the 77th Precinct. These officers borrowed ladders and axes from an area fire department to break into drug houses to steal cash and drugs. Several officers resigned in the aftermath to avoid investigations, but Dowd and others stayed to commit further crimes until his arrest

32 Ultimately, Matias could not be convicted of the Central Park jogger rape because of the statute of limitations. However, he is still incarcerated because of an earlier murder and several previous rapes he confessed to.

33 Dinkins was the first and the only African-American mayor of NYC. He died on November 23, 2020, in NYC at the age of 93.

34 Diaz spent eight years in prison and was deported to the Dominican Republic. Dowd spent 12 years in prison for racketeering and drug conspiracy. In 2016 he launched a cigar brand from the Dominican Republic with Diaz under the brand name "Seven Five" after the precinct he corrupted.

in 1992. He agreed to testify in front of the Mollen Commission, revealed the extent of his crimes, and demonstrated how he made several thousand dollars a week from corruption. Dowd served 12 years and five months in prison. The Mollen Commission provided over a hundred recommendations to reduce corruption through structural changes, improved training, and reforms with hiring and promotion practices.

Bratton was the chief of the New York City Transit Police during the testimony and sentencing of Dowd. After he was appointed the Commissioner of the NYPD in 1994 by Mayor Giuliani, Bratton took recommendations from the Mollen Commission and reorganized the Internal Affairs Division (IAD), making it more centralized. Bratton elevated the IAD to a Bureau with all new staff and policies for timely rotation. The Internal Affairs Bureau (IAB) took on a proactive focus and aggressively pursued allegations of corruption and looked for emerging patterns and trends to prevent corruption through ongoing investigations. These investigations occurred through an independent and external monitoring entity called the Commission to Combat Police Corruption.

New York City Transit Police – Chief (1990–1992)

Watershed events like Serpico, the Central Park Five, Goetz, the mob, and corruption signaled the need for more robust police protection in NYC. However, Bratton was an outsider to the NYPD status quo and an outsider to traditional police chiefs. Unlike Chiefs such as Daryl Gates in Los Angeles (LA), Bratton reveled in outside academic ideas and saw something different for the NYPD and the transit police he would inherit. After Bratton studied NYC for six months, the New York Transit Police hired him in April 1990 to lead their 3,500 demoralized officers. Like Commissioner Roosevelt's midnight rambles nearly a century earlier, Bratton personally visited transit officers throughout the subway system. He discovered officers with very little pride in their job preferring not to let family/friends know where they were assigned. The officers said they worked for the NYPD rather than saying they were transit cops. Ineffective strategies from the transit police included trying to have 400 of the patrolling officers cover over 700 street-level entrances through an attitude of permissiveness toward disorder and crime. This permissiveness created an image that transit officers were in a no-win situation and worked for an organization that genuinely did not care about them or their effectiveness.

John Linder – Marketing Issues for Transit Policing

Bratton and his leadership team recognized the need to understand the public's perceptions and realities of crime and disorder throughout the subway. John Linder was the director of marketing and corporate communications for the Metropolitan Transportation Authority[35] (MTA), the NYC subway parent organization. The MTA planned a multi-million dollar advertisement campaign to promote the use of the city subway system. However, before instituting this investment, Linder conducted focus group studies to analyze why the community did not use the subway. Community respondents felt 30 to 40 percent of the city's crime occurred in the subway, and 40 to 50 percent of murders probably occurred underground. In reality, only 3 percent of the city's felony crime and 1 to 2 percent of all murders happened in the subway system (Bratton & Knobler, 1998, p. 151).

35 The MTA is responsible for public transportation and serves 14 counties in New York and southern Connecticut.

Although the public's perceptions were inaccurate, they nevertheless impacted the general use of the subway system. The perceptual surveys did not indicate that the subway did not have serious crime issues. Linder found that robberies had increased 48 percent in the two years preceding Bratton's hire and graffiti blanketed the interior of the subway and virtually every subway car. Moreover, an estimated 5,000 homeless people were living underground, and there were an estimated 17,000 fare evaders daily that cost the city an estimated $80 million a year (Bratton & Knobler, 1998, pp. 143–144). Linder's perceptual research with officers concluded they were demoralized and didn't believe they could realistically impact graffiti, crime, or disorder within the subway. The disorderly environment encouraged criminal behavior and demoralized the self-described sewer cops.

Police agencies did not typically have a marketing budget nor the ability to conduct professional focus group studies as a means for analyzing their customer base. Linder's invaluable study indicated that transit users were less concerned with crime and more about the daily disorder they witnessed. Statistically, these perceptions were accurate since there were over three million transit users every day, yet only approximately 60 crime victims a day. While the odds of being a victim of a subway crime were very low, transit users still witnessed subway cars covered in graffiti and the daily disorder of rowdy youth, fare evaders, panhandlers, and homeless people. Even if the transit police were to target and eliminate all crime, transit users would still feel unsafe because of the daily disorder. This perspective is what drove the strategic broken windows policing.[36]

Confronting Moral Problems – Finding Stakeholders

With broken windows policing strategies in mind, Bratton recognized that he had to confront his officers' morale to counter the misconceptions and realities of crime and disorder throughout the NYC subway. His leadership style as the chief of the NYC Transit Police mimicked his past performances within a larger arena. Within the first two months, Bratton divided the Transit Police into operations and administration bureaus. He promoted two deputy chiefs to run the new bureaus, and he also added a director of media services and a director of planning. Bratton expected his new leaders to analyze the persistent problems of graffiti, disorder, and crime and develop new responses to change the subway's notorious reputation.

During the transition period, Bratton's leadership style included holding numerous meetings to establish more effective communication, trust, and transparency. The sessions often included taking command staff out of headquarters and into the district stations and the subway system so they could personally visualize the horrific conditions of public transit throughout NYC. These experiential strategies allowed Bratton to build internal stakeholders to help back his problem-solving objectives. They also served to empirically convince the department's bureaucracy about the realities of the subway crime and disorder crisis.

Like the MBTA, Bratton discovered that the methods and technology used to police the subway system were archaic. Officers were issued outdated radios that did not work underground, and officers were assigned to stand guard at select turnstiles throughout their entire shift to deter fare beaters. Understandably, officers did not feel they were doing real police work, and city leaders did not adequately understand the challenges of policing the transit system. Bratton soon set up tours of the transit system with prominent individuals in business, government, and the media. He expected transit police administrators to frequently tour the stations and respond to crime scenes in what became referred to as "getting the white shirts out." The tours with prominent community members concluded with discussion forums regarding the

36 Author's interview with Bratton on November 3, 2020.

problems with dangerous conditions the transit police worked in, the outdated equipment they used, and the issues that arose from thousands of homeless people living underground. While some police leaders worried about what these prominent individuals might say or write regarding police shortcomings, Bratton's leadership style took the approach that the net result would only be beneficial and that increasing stakeholders was critical for creating change. These stakeholders would come from political leaders, transit officers, supervisors, and the media. The transit tours proved to be very useful.[37]

Jack Maple[38] *– Roots of CompStat*

Maple was a lieutenant in the transit police department in charge of the Central Robbery Squad when Bratton became chief in 1990. Over the next two years, Bratton promoted Maple to detective lieutenant and special assistant to the chief. When Mayor Giuliani appointed Bratton to be the NYPD Police Commissioner in 1994, Bratton named Maple his Deputy Commissioner for crime control strategies. Maple used pin maps within transit, called "Charts of the Future," to track subway crime. He followed subway robberies and categorized the robberies based on guns, knives, wolfpack, bag snatching, booths, or strong-armed. Based on his maps' data, Maple and his squad would conduct undercover operations in areas with the most concentrated robberies. The maps also allowed for rapid response and predictability of future robberies.

For Bratton, the use of analytical maps made sense since he used them when he was a lieutenant with the BPD during the time he attended his first PERF conference. Bratton was intrigued about how the transit police could utilize data analysis more fully. He began to hold accountability meetings with his district commanders to encourage their problem-solving capabilities. Without this data, Bratton realized transit officers were flying blind as they attempted to counter criminal activity, and there was no efficient way to hold their supervisors accountable.

Ten district commanders led the Transit Police. Bratton expected his commanders to provide solutions to problems of fare evasion, crime, and disorder. Transit officers presented creative solutions in a series of competitive problem-solving meetings hosted by command staff. Commanders videoed the presentations so the 3,500 officers could watch. The video presentations and speeches from a chief became a more helpful tool for conversing with the new generation of officers[39] about solutions instead of distributing a bulletin or memo they were not likely to read.

Bratton's leadership goal was to encourage data analysis followed by creative solutions, and he found officers became inspired by these challenges. These problem-solving sessions became part of a transit renaissance. Maple complained that uniformed transit officers were often powerless and not incentivized to investigate crime and make arrests. Detectives worked out of headquarters for the transit police, and patrol officers had to fill out "unusual occurrence" reports if they made a drug arrest. Transit officers gave their drug arrests to NYPD plainclothes detectives (Maple & Mitchell, 1999, p. 24).

37 Author's interview with Bratton on November 3, 2020.

38 Maple died in August 2001 of colon cancer at the age of 49. In September 2015, Bratton helped dedicate "Jack Maple Place" as a street co-name in front of Maple's boyhood home on the corner of Park Lane South and 108th Street in Queens, NY.

39 James "Jimmy" O'Neill was a "new generation" transit police sergeant when Bratton took over as chief. He would later succeed Bratton as the 43rd Commissioner of the NYPD (2016–2019) after Bratton resigned from the NYPD a second time.

Photo 5.2 Left to right: Jack Maple, Bill Bratton, Louie Anemone.
Photo credit: Bill Bratton.

Maple provided Bratton with numerous ideas and made presentations showing that robberies were increasing in the subway, and these increases were highest among Chinese and other Asian victims. Maple showed that transit robberies rose 21 percent in 1988, 26 percent in 1989, and about 25 percent in the first two months of 1990 (Bratton, 1999). The belief was that these crimes were also heavily underreported because many victims were not legal citizens and the robbery offenders specifically chose Asians because they did not pose a viable risk. Maple instigated undercover operations using Asian decoys. He also challenged fare evaders (AKA turnstile jumpers) through arrest and had transit officers run a warrant check on all of them (Photo 5.2).

Arresting Fare Evaders

The NYC Transit Police instituted Kelling's broken windows style of policing through a focused attack on fare evaders and Maple's idea of running warrant checks. Going after subway fare evaders became a problematic cultural shift since most officers did not initially buy into arresting turnstile jumpers as real police work. The officers were also apprehensive about dealing with panhandlers and homeless people who may have AIDS.[40] As the police began to arrest fare evaders, they discovered one in seven had other bench warrants, and one in 21 had

40 The risk of officers contracting AIDS from criminal suspects is almost nonexistent. In one 6-year study of an Ohio police department with 1,000 officers, 13 reports of needlestick injuries occurred out of over a million calls for service during the 6-year study. In 9 of the 11 incidents, the individuals were found to have hepatitis C; none had hepatitis B or HIV (de Pario, 2017).

a weapon (Bratton, 1999, p. 13). To complement the initiative, Bratton had his transit police set up their own warrant squad. They were able to develop an electronic system to track past arrestees who did not show up in court so they could quickly make contact and re-arrest. An old paper version of the court warrants often took a month or longer for the police to be notified and haphazardly track them down. Bratton's transit police were able to follow up warrant checks in a matter of a day or two, achieving the goal of relentless pursuit. The transit police warrant unit started their work at 2 AM when the fugitives were still at home, and the apprehension rate rose to over 60 percent (Bratton, 1999, p. 13).

As predicted in the broken windows theory, the link between disorder and serious crime soon became believable for transit officers. They reduced the underground homeless population in the subway by 80 percent, and intensive truancy sweeps coincided. The establishment of rules and regulations throughout the transit system significantly reduced illicit merchants, smoking, drinking, panhandling, and other disorderly acts. The broken windows policing strategies also had the benefit of an earlier $40 million investment.

Murder of Brian Watkins – $40 Million to Transit

Mayor Dinkins was a fan of tennis and instrumental in keeping the U.S. Open in NYC. Brian Watkins was a 22-year-old college student and Mormon tourist from Utah. He came to see the tennis tournament and was horrifically stabbed at 10:20PM on a Sunday evening, September 2, 1990, on a Manhattan Subway platform at the 53rd Street station in front of his family during a wolfpack robbery while he attempted to protect his family.[41] The murder created international headlines, and Governor Mario Cuomo[42] contributed $40 million of state money to build a turnaround in the city subway system. As he had previously done in Massachusetts, Bratton immediately bought new upgraded equipment for each officer. This upgrade consisted of new uniforms, new recruitment posters to hire qualified officers, and, after a bureaucratic battle, new nine-millimeter semiautomatic Glock firearms[43] for each officer. Transit officers respected Bratton, and he continued to boost their morale by hosting many ceremonial events that gave commendation awards. There was a 40 percent drop in robberies in the New York subway from 1990 to 1992. Due to these efforts, Bratton gained national accreditation through CALEA, becoming the second department in New York to do so and one of only 175 agencies nationwide. Bratton touted this success by feeding several stories to the media and creating commercials letting the public and the transit officers know that the subway system was no longer under the control of criminal offenders. Between 1990

41 Seven individuals were convicted and sentenced to 25 years to life in prison for Watkins's murder and stealing $203 from Watkin's father's wallet. However, one individual, Johnnie Hincapie, was granted a new trial in 2015 by a Manhattan Supreme Court Judge, and prosecutors later dropped the case. Over the years, several media stories reported 18-year-old Hincapie had falsely confessed to being present during the attack and was wrongfully imprisoned. Comparisons of his case were made with the Central Park Five exoneration. Moreover, clemency was sought for others convicted through the controversial use of the felony murder rule.

42 Cuomo was a three-time Governor of New York (1983–1994). He died in 2015 at the age of 82. His son Andrew married and is divorced from Kerry Kennedy, daughter of Robert Kennedy. Andrew was also elected three times as Governor of New York starting in 2010. He resigned in August 2021 amid sexual harassment investigations. Cuomo's younger son Chris is a national news journalist who has anchored numerous networks, including ABC, CNN, and his own prime time show.

43 Note from the chapter on Commissioner Roosevelt: On December 30, 1895, Roosevelt opened the New York Police Department School of Pistol Practice and authorized the purchase of newly developed Colt .32 caliber double-action revolvers with four-inch barrels. Bratton was able to secure the upgraded semiautomatic firearms for his transit officers despite the NYPD officers maintaining the outdated .38 six-shot revolver and opposition from Mayor Dinkins, NYPD Commissioner Lee Brown, and the *New York Times*.

and 1994, felony crime on the subways dropped by 75 percent (Williams, 2016). While the national murder rate declined 5 percent in 1994, NYC declined 17 percent, and robberies fell to 1973 levels (Bennet, DiIulio, & Walters, 1996).

In the summer of 1991, LAPD Chief Daryl Gates announced his intention to retire, and Bratton made it known that he was seeking new leadership challenges. Bratton applied with 11 other candidates for the $175,000 a year salary, the country's highest-paid chief. In the aftermath of the LA Riots (April 29–May 4, 1992), city council members pressured Chief Gates to resign, and he left in the summer of 1992. After Gates departed, it became clear LA would select an African-American chief, and Bratton removed his name from consideration.

Throughout 1991, Bratton also kept track of Boston and the St. Clair Commission Report that found substantial leadership problems in the BPD. These problems culminated with the department's handling of a murder case in October 1989. Charles Stuart reported his pregnant wife, Carol DiMaiti, was shot in the head and killed by a Black man as they left childbirth class. Stuart also claimed the Black assailant shot him in the stomach. The BPD responded and led a massive manhunt in predominantly Black neighborhoods, leading to the wrongful arrest of Willie Bennett[44] and the harassment of many other young Black males. Eventually, Stuart's story fell apart, and it was revealed he fabricated a robbery and shot his wife in the head and himself in the stomach to collect life insurance. He then jumped to his death from the Tobin Bridge.

In 1992, the St. Clair Commission, led by attorney James St. Clair (who had represented President Nixon in the 1970s), reported the BPD was involved in a series of narcotics corruption and civil rights violations.[45] The commission recommended civilian oversight and the resignation of Commissioner Francis "Mickey" Roache, Bratton's former college classmate and patrol partner. Bratton contacted Roache, and the BPD hired him as second in command, a position he had held ten years prior. Bratton believed the mayor would fire Roach in light of the St. Clair Commission Report, and the top job would open up. However, Boston Mayor Ray Flynn was childhood friends with Roache and temporarily defied the St. Clair Commission recommendation to replace the commissioner. Bratton brought in Linder and Kelling as consultants and began to implement the strategic plans that were successful with the New York City Transit Police. In March 1993, Mayor Flynn announced he was going to resign as mayor, and by the summer of 1993, Roache also resigned. The departures meant Bratton was the new BPD Commissioner.

At the BPD, Bratton immediately transformed the sixth floor of police headquarters into an open, accessible office following Douglas McGregor's Theory Y management style (see Lynch, 1978). The BPD had not promoted a captain since 1977. Bratton replaced most of Roach's management staff with new captains tasked with revitalizing neighborhood policing, as Wasserman had previously inspired. Bratton also brought in Maple from the NYPD as an executive assistant in charge of the detective bureau.

Typical of most commission recommendations, St. Clair wrote that the BPD should hire more officers and allotted $2 million. Bratton argued the BPD needed to modernize its

44 A year after his wrongful arrest, Bennett was convicted of armed robbery in Brookline and served 12 years in prison. He was released in 2002 and denied committing the robbery.

45 In November 2020, *Netflix* released an eight-episode documentary titled "Trial 4" that detailed corruption in the BPD and the events surrounding the September 26, 1993, fatal shooting of Boston Detective John Mulligan. Sean Ellis was convicted in a third trial after the first two ended in mistrials, and he spent 22 years in prison. The documentary film leads up to a fourth trial and the eventual dismissal by newly elected DA Rachael Rollins (Lowry, 2020).

departmental technology and opted to use the extra funds to create a planning unit to assess BPD effectiveness over hiring more police. As the new commissioner, Bratton argued for new technology investments, saving time and resources for officers. The plan was to use the savings to hire additional officers eventually.

The timing of the mayoral campaigns also worked to Bratton's advantage. He quickly transformed the BPD without a lot of the political direction that typically occurred from City Hall. Additionally, due to a lack of political oversight, Bratton was able to stand side-by-side with President Clinton at the White House to announce the new 1994 crime bill. Bratton was invited as the only member of law enforcement to give a speech next to President Clinton because Boston had not yet elected its new mayor (Bratton & Knobler, 1998, p. 188). He attended the Rose Garden ceremony on August 11, 1993, with President Clinton and spoke in support of his 1994 crime bill, a political promise to federally fund 100,000 new police officers and create the Department of Justice Office of Community-Oriented Policing. (Note: The 1994 crime bill led to controversial determinate sentencing models that greatly expanded the number of Americans incarcerated.)

While Bratton was commissioner, criminologist David Kennedy[46] made his initial proposal to understand the link between drugs, guns, and youth violence. Bratton and the National Institute of Justice (NIJ) backed Kennedy's research proposal. In 1994, after Bratton had left the BPD, a group of clergy leaders called the Ten-Point Coalition collaborated with Boston anti-gang officers and initiated the Youth Violence Strike Force. Through support from Harvard University, Kennedy partnered with federal law enforcement and the U.S. Attorney's Office to target specific gang members in Boston through a series of call-in meetings. At these call-in meetings, the BPD, DA, and the Federal Government gave the targeted gangs warnings to stop the violence or face federal prison time. The coalition also met with and offered gang members several alternatives to help them exit the gang. By 1996, the initiative was referred to by various names: Boston Miracle, Boston Gun Project, and Operation Ceasefire. Over the 1990s, homicides dropped 75 percent in Boston and 71 percent in NYC (Harris, 2005). Kennedy's call-in initiatives evolved into implementing the *National Network for Safe Communities* in dozens of cities.

During Kennedy's initial 1993 proposal to BPD Commissioner Bratton, NYC was also in a mayoral election year. On November 2, 1993, Rudy Giuliani[47] defeated incumbent David Dinkins, the city's first African-American mayor, and became the first Republican mayor since John Lindsay in 1965. Fear of rising crime, with blame placed on young male minorities, was a significant concern with voters, especially on the heels of the 1992 LA riots in the aftermath of the Rodney King beating and officers' acquittal. Giuliani's campaign promise was to restore order and reduce crime. Giuliani then called on Bratton to return as the 38th Commissioner of the NYPD in February 1994 (Photo 5.3).

46 David M. Kennedy is a criminal justice professor at John Jay College in NYC and the director of the *National Network for Safe Communities*. See https://nnscommunities.org/.

47 Giuliani was NYC Mayor from 1994 to 2001. He unsuccessfully ran for Republican President and, in April 2018, became a personal attorney for President Trump. Giuliani called the 2020 election of Joe Biden a fraud. On the morning of January 6, 2021, Giuliani spoke outside of the White House at President Trump's rally and called for a "trial by warfare" shortly before the Capitol insurrection. Giuliani later claimed he was referencing the *HBO* series *Game of Thrones* (Bradley, 2021). Bratton called for a commission similar to 9/11 to investigate the storming of the Capitol (Moore, 2021), which was formed in the aftermath of President Trump's second failed impeachment. On January 25, 2021, after Giuliani faced a $1.3 billion defamation lawsuit filed by Dominion Voting Systems, he stated that Biden won the presidency (Sheth, 2021).

Photo 5.3 Left to right: Rudy Giuliani, John Timoney, William Bratton, Jack Maple (circa 1993).
Photo credit: New York Daily News.

New York City Police Department – Commissioner (1994–1996)

Bratton accepted Giuliani's appointment and put Bob Wasserman in charge of a 30-day transition team that included Jack Maple and John Linder. They found the NYPD to be very dysfunctional, centralized, para-militaristic, and bureaucratic, with little decision-making power given to precinct commanders or beat officers. Bratton had a strong belief that the NYPD was underperforming and in need of re-engineering to achieve its full potential. He also believed that crime prevention had to be tasked to the precincts and neighborhood level with less centralized oversight. For decades, the NYPD headquarters assumed they could control corruption by burdening precincts with limited discretionary decision-making. This centralized control went back to the reform efforts of Roosevelt. If neighborhood prevention of crime were a realistic goal, its practicality would be decentralized to the precinct level and not through centralized control from police headquarters. The right leaders would need to be in place at the precincts, and within the first week, Bratton forced four of the department's five senior commanders to resign. Within the first year, he replaced a third of the 76 precinct commanders.

Remnants of neighborhood community policing in the NYPD were present from Commissioner Lee Brown (1990–1992). Brown's community policing model's implicit assumption was that more cops walking the beat would form neighborhood partnerships and reduce crime. However, this simplistic approach was not evident in reduced crime statistics. Additional planning on where and when to deploy officers was needed. Perhaps more importantly, officers needed to be given targeted goals through more precise policing strategies that would challenge the past 13th-floor status quo super chiefs that had been in place for years.

Along with Jack Maple, Bratton's main self-selected change agents were Louie Anemone, Mike Julian, and John Timoney. Within this group, the transit cops were Bratton, and they were the outsiders coming in to make changes to the "real" NYPD. The real veterans were Anemone and Timoney. They would eventually win them over.

Louie Anemone

Following the Crown Heights riot[48] of 1991, Governor Mario Cuomo ordered a panel to improve crowd control to avoid future problems. Louie Anemone[49] was promoted to a deputy chief position and revamped the city response to respond to civil disturbances quickly through specialized units equipped with riot gear. Anemone wanted to learn from the LAPD 1992 failures during their riots and developed a different crowd control strategy for the NYPD. Through his leadership, NYC became one of the first cities to implement improved crowd control.

On the day Bratton met Anemone, he promoted him to the chief of patrol, in charge of the precincts' day-to-day operations, based upon his ability to challenge organizational resistance in quelling civil disturbances. Bratton wanted him to conduct the same type of challenges for driving down crime and disorder throughout the NYPD precincts via the CompStat accountability process. Anemone reported that he was surprised when Bratton named him to be his chief of patrol since he had not interviewed for the position, and he jumped over the two-star chiefs and 20 other one-star chiefs. In doing so, Bratton made it known that his leadership style challenged past conventions. Anemone and Maple became the CompStat process architects and were infamous for their critiques and pressure for improving strategic plans. In one noteworthy roundtable exercise, Tony Simonetti, a chief from Brooklyn South, was presenting, and an animation of Pinocchio appeared behind him on a screen with his nose growing (Levitt, 2009, p. 69). While the graphic caused laughter, Bratton was upset about this antic, and Anemone and Maple apologized for embarrassing the chief.

Mike Julian

Julian became known in the NYPD from his undercover work in Crown Heights and his off-duty academic efforts as a law student. After earning his law degree, he legally represented both officers and the city in corruption cases. Under Commissioner Lee Brown, Julian directed community policing efforts. Under Commissioner Ray Kelly, Julian ran advisory groups that invited street officers to help identify departmental policies that interfered with their ability to solve problems. Under Bratton, Julian expanded cops on bikes, an innovation executed by Commissioner Teddy Roosevelt a century earlier and detailed in a previous chapter. Naysayers balked at this idea, indicating that northern cities could not have police bikes and the officers would look silly. Julian pushed forward. Today, the NYPD has one of the most extensive bike programs in the country. Unlike foot patrol, officers on bikes are less likely to get bored or avoid patrolling larger geographic areas.

Bratton named Julian "chief of big ideas" (Bratton & Knobler, 1998, p. 203), but he was more formally called Chief of Personnel. Julian retired in 1994 and later ran security for Madison Square Garden and the Rockefeller Center before being brought back by Bratton in 2014 as Deputy Commissioner of Training in the aftermath of the Eric Garner chokehold

48 The Crown Heights race riot lasted three days from August 19 to 21, 1991 in Brooklyn between Blacks and Orthodox Jewish Chabad residents. The riots began after two Guyanese immigrant children were accidentally hit by a motorcade of cars for a Jewish Rabbi (Shapiro, 2006). Gavin Cato, a 7-year-old boy, died. His 7-year-old cousin Angela was severely injured. When the ambulance arrived, a crowd was attacking the driver of the vehicle that had struck the children. Over the next few days, numerous officers were attacked and injured along with several residents leading to over 100 arrests. The riot became a major political issue in 1993 when Giuliani ran against Mayor Dinkins and blamed him for an ineffective police response.

49 Anemone resigned in June 1999 at the age of 53 after serving four years as the chief of the NYPD, third in command.

death. During Bratton's second stint leading the NYPD, Julian instituted new training to sensitize officers to race relations and de-escalation strategies. A year later, stop-and-frisk incidents plummeted, as did the use of force and reports of officers using foul language.

John Timoney[50]

Timoney was born in Dublin and carried a heavy Irish accent. The Bratton transition team recognized he was very self-confident and bought into Linder's strategic intent, or what they referred to as stretch goals. Most police managers in the NYPD believed Bratton's goals of a 20 percent drop in crime over two years was unrealistic. However, Timoney thought that, through reorganization, significant reductions in crime were possible. Bratton named Timoney the chief of the department in charge of investigations, patrol, and organized crime. At the age of 46, Timoney was younger than any chief in the history of the NYPD. After Howard Safir became Commissioner in 1996, Timoney retired and became a consultant before becoming the Philadelphia Police Department Commissioner (1998–2002). In 2002, he was LA's second choice to be chief before they went with Bratton. Timoney then became the chief of the Miami Police Department (2003–2010). See Timoney (2010).

Elaine's – The Rebirth of Maple's CompStat

Elaine Kaufman operated a bar and restaurant in Manhattan on 2nd Avenue and East 88th Street in upper east Manhattan from 1963 until she died in 2010. Numerous celebrities and acclaimed journalists frequented the restaurant, which closed after Kaufman's death. The location was also a hot spot for Jack Maple, who got to know the owner and several writers that also hung out at Elaine's. In his book, *The Crime Fighter: Putting the Bad Guys Out of Business*, Maple reflected on Roosevelt's muckraking journalist Jacob Riis and their strategies to create police accountability (Maple & Mitchell, 1999). As described in an earlier chapter, Riis and Commissioner Roosevelt would conduct unannounced midnight rambles to check on officers to motivate them to be more efficient. Maple observed that Elaine Kaufman would do the same with her employees by telling them she was going on vacation but then showed up to check on them. She also vigilantly checked the nightly profits and intervened with her wait staff if receipts were down. Maple pondered why the NYPD did not conduct their timely assessment of crime data and why there was so much discomfort in discussing how cops might actually be able to influence crime. This type of thinking was precisely what Bratton's leadership style was looking for when he took over as NYPD Commissioner. As part of Bratton's transition team and Deputy Commissioner, Maple recognized that he had become the "they," and he held heightened expectations to be a creative and effective leader. Maple demonstrated creativity through his attire, often sporting carnations in his lapel, homburg hats, and iconoclastic bow ties (*iconoclasm* being defined as the action of assertively rejecting cherished institutions).

One snowy evening in December 1993, Maple shared a table at Elaine's with Bratton and John Miller. Miller was a local investigative journalist known for his interviews with John Gotti, boss of the Gambino crime family. He shared stories about how his father was a close friend of Frank Costello, boss of the Luciano crime family, and that Costello's wife, Lauretta, was Miller's godmother. Maple reported that he started sipping his third glass of champagne on ice, scribbled on a cocktail napkin the essential components of CompStat (Maple & Mitchell, 1999, p. 31), and the NYPD's new crime-suppression/crime-prevention strategy was born.

50 Timoney passed away of cancer in the summer of 2016 at the age of 68.

The four principles would become the guides for redefining how the NYPD would measure its objectives, proactive methods, and outcomes for decades to come:

1. **Accurate timely intelligence**: crime data mapped daily from every precinct and analyzed to understand emerging hot spots, trends, and root causes.
2. **Rapid deployment**: an easier flow of communication from all ranks to assist one another and counter crime trends with bureaus no longer operating out through their silos
3. **Effective tactics**: proactive innovation encouraged along with best-practice solutions shared and reinforced.
4. **Relentless follow-up and assessment**: gave birth to the weekly Compstat meetings and provided new accountability measures for precinct command staff.

(Maple & Mitchell, 1999, p. 32)

CompStat

CompStat created an accountability feature that Maple only dreamt about as a transit cop previously looked down upon by the NYPD. As crime became quickly mapped, the new leadership team invited precinct commanders to bi-weekly crime meetings at headquarters to discuss strategies for addressing the data. Broken windows policing became statistically assessed through the use of CompStat and the theatre of accountability meetings. The overcrowded meetings took place in the second-floor press room and eventually moved to the eighth floor. Before these meetings, precinct commanders had no expectations of having consistent conversations with police headquarters command staff. Now commanders were expected to discuss arrests and the results of their strategies for preventing crime and disorder.

The city refused to fund a search for geocoding specialists, so taking a page from Vollmer, Bratton's team reached out New York City's colleges and universities for academic assistance. Despite internal resistance, "you can't let them (academics) in the building, they are going to see our crime numbers!" (Bratton & Knobler, 2021, pp. 185), statistics professors and graduate students helped correct some errors and push the CompStat accountability reform movement forward. Crime prevention and reduction began to supplement and even replace reactive arrest data.

Serious crimes such as murders and shootings received most of the attention, and the hot spots for violence predictably occurred in predominantly minority neighborhoods. These neighborhoods would receive increased attention. Crime mapping and place-based strategies were implemented in all the precincts. Police thinking began to change when expectations changed. You expect what you inspect, and through more thorough analysis, expectations began to shift towards crime and disorder prevention.

CompStat[51] meetings evolved into police Darwinism, where only the fittest precinct leaders survived. Over time data was skewed by precinct commanders, so they looked more efficient for headquarters (see Eterno & Silverman, 2010). For Maple, the justification for the accountability sessions and bruised egos was critical. "Reasonable people didn't change the world; the world was changed by unreasonable people because when you are unreasonable, you get reasonable results" (Bratton & Knobler, 1998, p. 235). Eventually, managerial approaches in the

51 On June 23, 2020, NYPD Union President Chris Monahan wrote a letter to Mayor de Blasio and Commissioner Shea requesting an end to Compstat, arguing that the accountability system of the analysis creates tension between minority communities and the police by embarrassing and coercing commanders into proactive policing (Moore & McCarthy, 2020).

accountability meetings would shift to become more collaborative. A commitment to crime prevention, utilization of accurate and timely data, and relentless follow-up led to a massive crime reduction in 1994 and 1995. Long before a popularized hashtag, Bratton and Maple sent the message that Black lives matter. Consequently, patrol and detectives produced a more concerted effort to reduce violence in predominantly minority neighborhoods. Subsequent strategies that directed officers to hot spot locations also became known as cops on the dots and were supported by several academic studies (see Braga, 2005; Braga & Bond, 2008; Rosenfeld, Deckard, & Blackburn, 2014; Weisburd & Green, 1995; Weisburd & Eck, 2004).

Resignation – After 27 Months

The timing of Bratton's role as the NYPD Commissioner was ideal. The year 1994 marked the start of President Clinton's federal money that fueled police departments across the country to pay for new equipment, training, and new officers under the Office of Community-Oriented Policing (COPS). Former NYC Mayor Dinkins and Governor Cuomo had previously invested millions, with the Federal Government's support, to build thousands of single-residency apartments for the homeless (Domanick, 2015). The following year, Bratton merged the transit and housing authority police into the NYPD and the city's transportation department. In December 1994, Mayor Giuliani and his advisors were invited to the NYPD's eighth-floor command center and sat through a two-hour presentation led by Maple and Anemone. The presentation centered on "Operation Juggernaut" and taking back the streets from drug dealers with an all-out police offense and the need to increase the budget for the jail system. Initially, Giuliani gave his support, and his name was in the headlines for this new war on drugs. Subsequent headlines gave credit to Bratton, and the mayor began to question his support for their plan. The new police strategies coincided with the crack cocaine epidemic subsiding and a significant reduction in homeless people. These events correlated with reductions in crime that few predicted. Murders dropped 25 percent from 1,571 in 1994 to 1,182 in 1995, which was a more significant decrease than most cities experienced in a single year.

On the January 15, 1996 cover of *Time* magazine, Bratton's photograph appeared with the title, "Finally, we're winning the war against crime. Here's why," and a story on Bratton titled "One Good Apple." Mayor Giuliani and his deputies soon intervened and erupted on Bratton and Miller for violating the talking-without-authorization media gag rule. Miller served as Bratton's Deputy Commissioner of Public Information (DCPI) and chose to resign, publicly and tearfully in front of the media, after being in position for 14 months. He did so in the aftermath of being confronted by City Hall (i.e. Giuliani) to cut his staff because the mayor wanted to have better control over public information coming out of Miller's office. Bratton and other members of his team threatened to resign with Miller, but they were convinced to stay. Bratton's transparency and positive use of the media were a strength of his leadership in explaining how the NYPD could impact crime and disorder. However, like Miller, this same transparency led to conflict with Giuliani in what Bratton described as driving outside the mayor's headlights. After only 27 months, Bratton resigned from his position as commissioner on March 26, 1996.

NYPD Post-Bratton (1997–1999)

In June 1996, Amnesty International (AI)[52] issued a report on excessive use of force in the NYPD, specifically looking at 90 cases from the late 1980s into 1996. These cases primarily

52 See www.amnesty.org/en/documents/amr51/036/1996/en/.

dealt with racial minority suspects. While the AI Report mentioned recent reform progress, which occurred during Bratton's leadership, they also warned about future problems with indicators of increased misuse of force and civil lawsuits against the NYPD. Despite these warnings, reform efforts did not seem to continue after Bratton resigned. Two high profile cases are noteworthy: Abner Louima (August 9, 1997) and Amadou Diallo (February 4, 1999).

On August 9, 1997, officers arrested 31-year-old Haitian born Louima outside a Brooklyn nightclub following a call for service after patrons were involved in a fight. Officers of the 70th Precinct responded, took Louima into custody, and physically attacked him following a strip search. While in the department bathroom, Officer Justin Volpe[53] forced a broken broomstick into the rectum of Louima. The following day, officers escorted Louima to the hospital and attempted to say that his injuries were from abnormal homosexual activity. Louima required three major surgeries and received an $8.75 million civil settlement four years after his attack. In November 1997, voters re-elected Mayor Giuliani.

On February 4, 1999, 23-year-old West African born Amadou Diallo was fatally shot 19 times outside his apartment at 1157 Wheeler Avenue in the Bronx by four plainclothes NYPD officers who allegedly mistook him for a rape suspect. The officers fired 41 times,[54] striking him 19 times, despite no weapons found on or near Diallo. The four officers were part of a Street Crimes Unit (SCU) and were indicted on March 25, 1999, by a Bronx Grand Jury. However, the subsequent jury trial received a change of venue to upstate Albany, and the officers were acquitted on February 25, 2000. The SCU disbanded in 2002 on account of the Diallo shooting and in the aftermath of a federal investigation. In 2004, the Diallo family accepted a $3 million civil settlement four years after filing a $61 million lawsuit against the city.

Bratton compared these incidents to giving chemotherapy or radiation to a cancer patient after they are cancer-free. He stated that the NYPD should pull back from assertive policing and institute more community-based policing to improve race relations while still impacting crime and disorder, envisioned initially by Kelling.

Private Life/Private Sector – Consulting (1996–2002)

After Bratton resigned from the NYPD, Giuliani appointed Howard Safir, the NYC Fire Commissioner the previous two years, as the next Police Commissioner. Bratton formed his own private consulting company called The Bratton Group, LLC, which provided security and risk assessment consulting throughout the country and four continents. In 1999, he married Rikki Klieman who served as an anchor with Courtroom Television Network and a legal contributor for several other media outlets (see Klieman & Knobler, 2004). In the summer of 2000, Safir retired from the NYPD, and Bernie Kerik was his replacement. The NYPD hired Kerik in 1986. He went on to serve as a driver and bodyguard for Giuliani during his 1993 mayoral campaign. In 1994, Kerik moved to the NYC Department of Corrections, and four years later, he was appointed to be the Commissioner of the same department. In 2000, he was named the Commissioner of the NYPD, and he served in that capacity through 2001 before he joined the board of directors of Taser International. In 2004 President George W. Bush nominated Kerik to lead the Department of Homeland Security (DHS) but withdrew that nomination a week later due to tax evasion investigations and his housekeeper's illegal

53 Volpe pleaded guilty in a 1999 federal trial and was sentenced to 30 years in prison without parole. Two other officers were acquitted of charges that they beat Louima in their patrol car. Officer Charles Schwartz, who allegedly led Louima to the bathroom, was found guilty of perjury, but his case was later overturned after he spent five years in prison.

54 Bruce Springsteen wrote the song *American Skin (41 shots)* in tribute to Diallo. In 2000 he began to sing the song in concert.

immigration status. In 2006, Kerik pleaded guilty to ethics violations for receiving monetary gifts from a construction company that did his home renovations. He failed to declare those gifts for tax purposes while he was Commissioner for the Department of Corrections. In 2009 he pleaded guilty to tax fraud and making false statements to the White House during his vetting process to lead the DHS. In 2013 Kerik was released from federal prison after serving three years of a four-year sentence.[55]

September 11, 2001

Kerik was the NYPD Commissioner on 09/11/01 when four coordinated attacks were launched inside the United States by terrorists who hijacked commercial airlines. Two planes, American Airlines Flight 11 and United Airlines Flight 175, were intentionally flown into the North and South towers of the World Trade Center complex in Manhattan. Less than two hours afterward, both buildings collapsed. A third commercial plane, American Airlines Flight 77, crashed into the Pentagon in Arlington County, Virginia. The last aircraft, United Airlines Flight 93, was suspected of targeting Washington, DC, but passengers forced the plane to crash in a field near Shanksville, Pennsylvania.

Mayor Giuliani provided a public presence immediately following the attacks and in the weeks that followed. In December 2001, he matched Bratton's earlier cover photo when *Time* magazine put Giuliani on its cover as the person of the year. In the weeks and months that followed the terrorist events of 9/11, American pride was contagious, and the public demonstrated a deep level of respect for both law enforcement and firefighters. In the months and years that followed, Americans also began to accept evolving technology that allowed for more effective surveillance. Bratton was able to ride the wave of this evolution and understand that the police's role had shifted to collecting and using data to fight crime and terrorist threats more effectively. His leadership and notoriety in driving down crime in the 1990s[56] pushed the modern era of policing and put him in the spotlight for responding to international terrorism, all of which would benefit his leadership in the private security sector and as a modern police leader.

Los Angeles Police Department – Chief (2002–2009)

After Bratton left the NYPD, he briefly considered a mayoral run against Giuliani, and his name came up as a possible FBI director nomination. His direct exposure to the LAPD came from his contracted consulting work under Michael Cherkasky with New York-based Kroll Security firm and their assistance in monitoring a 2000 Federal Consent Decree. During his consulting trips to LA, Bratton frequently met with Mayor James Hahn to develop strategic plans to meet the federal decree's objectives.

Federal Consent Decree 2000

On November 3, 2000, federal oversight of the LAPD began and was supposed to last five years. The DOJ investigated the LAPD for the previous four years based on misuse of force,

55 On February 18, 2020, President Trump provided Kerik with a full pardon. The same day he commuted the sentence of former Illinois Governor Rod Blagojevich for attempting to sell the vacant Senate seat of Barak Obama.

56 Some NYPD precincts also demonstrated that crime could be reduced along with civilian complaints (Davis, Mateu-Gelabert & Miller, 1999).

false arrests, and a series of cases that violated constitutional rights. These cases were primarily tied to the Rampart Scandal, described later in this chapter. The LAPD agreed to the consent decree to avoid future lawsuits from the DOJ. The consent decree recommended several changes to the LAPD related to training, internal investigations, and officers' disciplinary procedures.

Additionally, the consent decree recommended an improved system to identify officers who demonstrated a pattern of unethical behavior more quickly. Based on the recommendations, the LAPD created an early warning tracking system for the following: all uses of lethal and non-lethal force, uses of officer-involved shooting incidents, complaints filed against officers, and all arrest and stops made by officers, including the race, ethnicity, gender, and age of the suspects. The consent decree further established procedural reforms for the use of force investigations, search and arrest procedures, the use of confidential informants, and limits on the time officers can spend in anti-gang units. Lastly, the consent decree stated that the civilian Police Commission should have proper resources, and the Inspector General given consistent and meaningful oversight of the LAPD. By March 2001, an independent monitor was selected to oversee the implementation of specified reforms within the consent decree. The overseer included consulting work from Bratton, contracted with the Kroll Security Firm.

As chief, and in an effort to demonstrate the importance of the consent decree, Bratton appointed Gerry Chaleff to a position in his command staff and gave him an office next to his at headquarters. Chaleff was a defense attorney and former president of the Board of Police Commissioners who previously oversaw recommendations of the consent decree on behalf of the city. While some police leaders attempt to negate a consent decree, Bratton utilized the federal oversight to help transform LAPD culture. Chaleff served as a decisive internal police appointment and signaled to the city that Bratton and the LAPD were serious and transparent about their strategies to make the department fair and effective. Chaleff continued his leadership in the LAPD after Bratton's departure as Special Assistant for Constitutional Policing (SACP) to the chief. In this role, he facilitated operations from the Legal Affairs Division, Internal Audits and Inspections Division, Fiscal Operations Division, and the Planning and Research Division.

Brief History of LA before Chief Bratton (starting in 1950)

1950–1966: Chief Bill Parker

William Parker III is LAPD's longest-serving chief (16 years) and served the department for a total of 37 years after being hired as a patrol officer in 1929. The old police headquarters was named the Parker Center in 1966, following his death,[57] until the new headquarters opened in October 2009 at the end of Bratton's tenure. The demolition of the Parker Center building began in the summer of 2019. Parker became the chief of the LAPD in 1950, and he faced the same political corruption issues that August Vollmer faced when he took on the chief challenge in 1923.

Parker reformed the LAPD into a professional law enforcement agency that separated itself from ward politics. The city also passed a charter that allowed Parker to separate the police from city government politics. Hence, officers became accountable to police executive leaders rather than politicians. Parker coupled the reform movement with the formation of a professionalized quasi-militaristic police department and the first use of Special Weapons

57 Parker died of a heart attack on July 16, 1966, at the age of 61, after he returned home from a dinner where he received a commendation. He was still the chief of the LAPD.

and Tactics (SWAT) in 1965 by Inspector Daryl Gates.[58] Subsequent discrimination against minority residents led to numerous police brutality complaints, and Parker used the term "thin blue line" to describe policing efforts to control pervasive crime. Like J. Edgar Hoover[59] with the FBI, Parker was a master at marketing the LAPD's polished image, first with his approval of the 1951–1959 television show *Dragnet* and second with his 1956 talk show called *The Thin Blue Line*.

However, a new reality that challenged Parker's self-promotion played out in a series of violent confrontations between the LAPD and residents, culminating on August 11, 1965, when Marquette Frye,[60] a Black motorist, was arrested after he resisted an officer, from the California Highway Patrol (CHP), during a traffic stop. Six days of riots followed throughout the Watts neighborhood in South Central LA. An estimated $40 million ($320 million in the modern era) in property damage occurred from hundreds of burned buildings. Nearly 4,000 members of the National Guard assisted the 16,000 law enforcement personnel mobilized throughout the city. Thirty-four people were killed in the Watts riots, and the police or the National Guard shot 23. Parker compared the riots to insurgencies in Vietnam. The heavy militaristic response appeared to intensify the protests and create further damage.

In response to the Watts Riots, the McCone Commission, headed by former CIA director John McCone, was formed under Governor Pat Brown. The commission identified several root causes of the riots and provided a series of recommendations that included literacy programs, increased job-training, improved police-community relations, and increased low-income housing. Nearly three decades later, the LA Riots of 1992 would surpass the Watts Riots and lead to Chief Gates' forced resignation. However, the Watts Riots did little to damage Parker's reputation and reaffirmed the chief's previous speeches to white Californians about the dangers of minority crime waves.[61] His legacy as a conservative law and order chief who fought for an independent police department detached from politicians lived on a decade after his death through his protégé, Chief Gates.

1978–1992: Chief Daryl Gates

Chief Daryl Gates[62] had the second-longest tenure as LAPD Chief (14 years) after Parker. He began his career in the LAPD in 1949. His time as chief coincided with the nation's war on drugs stance and increased attention on gang violence. Along with SWAT, Gates created "Community Resources Against Street Hoodlums" or CRASH units, later linked to the Rampart Scandal, described in more detail below. By the mid-1980s, as crack cocaine

58 Some point to December 8, 1969, as the first SWAT team raid. The raid was done on the Black Panthers headquarters in LA. The no-warrant SWAT raid by the FBI and the LAPD resulted in 13 arrests and 72 criminal charges against members, but most of those charges were later dropped (Churchill & Vander Wall, 2002, p. 82). A few days prior, as detailed in Ramsey's chapter, Fred Hampton was killed in Chicago in a similar raid. During the six-hour LA raid, Gates was granted permission by the Pentagon to use a grenade launcher from the Marine Corps, but the Panthers surrendered before it was used (Brown & Barganier, 2018, p. 231).

59 Parker and Hoover were similar in terms of trying to keep politicians out of their agencies. However, as mentioned in the chapter on O.W. Wilson, who had a contentious relationship with the FBI Director, the same was true for Parker (see Donovan, 2005).

60 Marquette Frye died of pneumonia on December 20, 1986 at the age of 42.

61 Former LAPD officer Gene Roddenberry was a speechwriter for Parker and also the creator of *Star Trek*. He modeled the *Spock* character after Parker, describing him as intolerant of fools and incorruptible (Buntin, 2009).

62 Gates was despised in the LA Black community over perceived racism and for remarks, such as Blacks were more likely to die when placed in police chokeholds because their arteries did not reopen as quickly as those of "normal people." Gates blamed his command staff for letting the riot get out of control during its early hours. He died of cancer on April 16, 2010, at the age of 83.

arrived in LA, neighborhood gun violence rose dramatically, and Gates launched Operation Hammer. Over the next several years, an estimated 25,000 arrests came from weekend sweeps of minority neighborhoods in South LA. Prosecutors frequently dismissed the arrest charges at a later date. The scarred relationship between the LAPD and communities of color culminated in March 1991, when multiple officers beat motorist Rodney King after resisting a roadside stop.

1991: Rodney King

On March 3, 1991, Tim and Melanie Singer,[63] husband and wife officers with the CHP, observed Rodney King's 1988 Hyundai Excel speeding with two passengers. A high-speed pursuit commenced along highway route 210, with King reaching speeds over 100 mph. King, a 26-year-old African-American, attempted to avoid a DUI arrest that he knew would violate his parole from a November 1989 convenience store robbery, for which he served one year of a two-year sentence. King exited the highway during the pursuit, and the chase continued for eight miles through several residential neighborhoods. LAPD patrol and a police helicopter joined the pursuit and eventually cornered King's Hyundai. After the stop, the police ordered the passengers out of the vehicle. Bryant Allen and Freddie Helms immediately complied with the officers, exited the car, and laid on their stomachs with their hands behind their backs. Both men later reported officers inappropriately struck them, and they subsequently received settlements from the city in 1994: Allen $35,000; Helms (post-mortem)[64] $20,000.

King initially refused to exit his vehicle and defied commands from multiple officers. When he emerged, King slapped the ground, waved at a police helicopter, and then grabbed his buttocks. Fearing he was reaching for a gun, State Patrol Officer Singer pointed her firearm at King and ordered him to lie down. King complied and laid on his back. Singer approached King to make the arrest. LAPD Sergeant Stacy Koon ordered Singer to holster her weapon and back off since their departmental procedures required officers to holster their guns before approaching a suspect. Koon then ordered King to turn over and put his hands behind his back to be handcuffed. When King did not comply, Koon ordered his officers to strike him with their batons to force compliance. In King's biography, he justified his behavior through detailed accounts from his youth of defying his physically abusive father by taking the pain from the beatings. He connected the LAPD baton blows in the same manner (King & Spagnola, 2012).

The commotion awoke George Holliday, a 31-year-old Argentine plumber. He videoed the police and King's encounter from his Lake View Terrace apartment balcony near Foothill Boulevard and Osborne Street. After filming the police beating King, Holliday called the LAPD twice to inform them of the video and asked if they wanted the videotape. Holliday reported that the LAPD told him that they were not interested and hung up on him. The following Monday morning, he contacted a local television station and showed the evening news coverage. In Atlanta, CNN obtained a copy of the film, and on Tuesday morning, the video made international news. Holliday received $500 for the rights to broadcast his footage. The original tape is currently in the federal archives.

Sergeant Koon used his Taser on King twice, and Officer Lawrence Powell struck King with his baton more than 40 times. Koon and Powell were both terminated by the LAPD and were the only officers found guilty at a federal trial. Today, Powell lives in San Diego and

63 Melanie retired in June 2017 as CHP sergeant.

64 On July 1, 1991, Helms was killed when he and fellow passenger Bobbie Dixon were thrown from a 1978 Pontiac Bonneville driven by intoxicated driver Robert Gilliam after the car hit a telephone pole at an estimated speed of 75 mph. Gilliam suffered minor injuries and was charged with vehicular homicide.

works in the computer retail industry. Koon was a 14-year veteran of the LAPD who wrote a 1992 memoir, *Presumed Guilty: The Tragedy of the Rodney King Affair* (Koon & Deitz, 1992). He blamed the riots on the media and city politicians. Today, he works as a chauffeur in LA for the limousine company Music Express. Officer Timothy Wind also followed Sergeant Koon's commands and struck King with his baton in a tactic known as "swarm" in order to restrain the suspect. Wind was in his tenth month as a probationary officer, and despite being acquitted of both state and federal charges, the LAPD still terminated him. He was the only officer not to testify. He eventually went to law school at the University of Indiana, returned to his home state of Kansas, and avoided publicly discussing his time in the LAPD.

Officer Theodore Briseno also stomped on King's back and neck during the beating to keep King from getting back up. At the federal trial, Briseno broke rank and criticized his fellow officers, stating Powell was excessive. Interestingly, among the four indicted officers, only Briseno had been previously suspended for misconduct. In 1982 he was accused of beating a handcuffed man. Briseno, a ten-year veteran of the LAPD, was acquitted of all charges at the state and federal courts but still terminated; he moved to Illinois.

In April 1991, Mayor Tom Bradley[65] appointed a commission to exam the training, recruitment, discipline, and complaint processes at the LAPD. The commission was chaired by Warren Christopher,[66] who later became President Clinton's Secretary of State. The Christopher Commission found accusations of excessive force against a significant number of LAPD officers and that departmental leadership failed to manage or investigate these officers. This lack of follow-up caused repeated incidents of excessive force. The commission further recommended creating a new standard of accountability and holding ranking officers responsible for their officers' actions. This accountability system was not be started until 2007, over 15 years after the initial recommendation and five years into Bratton's tenure as chief. The TEAMS II early warning system is detailed below and created to avoid the next Rodney King misuse of force incident.

King suffered a fractured skull, brain damage, a crushed right eye socket, broken teeth, a fractured ankle, and multiple lacerations. The city did not charge King with any crimes and instead charged LAPD officers Koon, Powell, Wind, and Briseno. Their defense attorneys successfully moved for a change of venue due to pretrial publicity, from LA County to Ventura County in Simi Valley, a more affluent county compromising significantly fewer minorities. Simi Valley had a 1992 population of 103,288, hundreds of law enforcement officials, and Black residents were less than 1.4 percent. A jury of 10 Caucasians,[67] one Filipino, and one Hispanic acquitted the four white LAPD officers on April 29, 1992. Despite some media coverage that stated otherwise, the acquittal did not come from an all-white jury.

A federal court later retried all four officers for violating King's civil rights. In the subsequent federal trial, Koon and Powell were found guilty by a jury and sentenced to 30 months in prison, while Wind and Briseno were acquitted. The federal judge waived all monetary fines against the officers and reduced their sentence, despite prosecutors' appeal to the Supreme Court. To publicly compensate King for the ordeal, Mayor Bradley offered him $200,000 and a four-year college scholarship. Instead, King filed a multi-million dollar lawsuit, and a civil jury awarded him $3.8 million and legal expenses.

King's personal life was tumultuous. He fathered three daughters with three different women and experienced ongoing problems with alcoholism. In 2008, producers from the

65 Bradley was mayor of LA for 20 years (1973–1993). He died in 1998 at the age of 80.

66 Christopher died of cancer at his LA home in 2011 at the age of 85.

67 In 2012, jury no. 8, Henry King (no relation to Rodney King), revealed his mixed racial identity and his Black father that he had previously kept secret. Henry perceived the LAPD officers were wrong in beating King, but they did not violate the law.

Celebrity Rehab with Dr. Drew sitcom made King a cast member, and he appeared in a spin-off show, *Sober House*, where he discussed his struggles with sobriety. In 2010, King was engaged to Cynthia Kelley, who had served as a juror in his $3.8 million civil lawsuit. On June 17, 2012, which was Father's Day, his fiancée found 47-year-old King at the bottom of his swimming pool, where he died 28 years to the day after he discovered his father Ronald King dead in his bathtub in 1984. An autopsy report was released a couple of months later and indicated that alcohol, cocaine, and marijuana were in King's system and likely caused a heart attack. The Reverend Al Sharpton delivered the eulogy at King's funeral. Chief Charlie Beck, chief after Bratton, stated that Rodney King changed LAPD's culture.

1992: Riots

The media announced the four LAPD officers' acquittal in Simi Valley to the nation on Wednesday, April 29, 1992, at 3:11 PM. Within an hour of the verdict, residents began to violently confront unprepared LAPD officers at the intersection of Florence and Normandie, leading officers to retreat, which further incited the crowds. Riots and looting[68] erupted, with non-Black drivers being dragged from their vehicles and beaten, most notably 36-year-old white construction truck driver Reginald Denny. Denny was born in Lansing, Michigan, and was 39 years old when the rioters attacked him in 1992. His skull was fractured in 91 places, causing brain damage that impacted his speech and ability to walk. Denny filed a civil suit against LA but was unsuccessful and moved to Lake Havasu, Arizona, to become an independent boat motor mechanic.

When the riots broke out, Gates was at a fundraiser in affluent Brentwood to defeat Proposition F that sought to place term limits on LAPD police chiefs and put Gates out of a job. Consequently, the LAPD lacked leadership at their command post and did not initially provide officers with any direction in response to the riots. That evening, after rioting had begun, Gates returned to LA and went to the city's Emergency Response Center to meet with African-American Mayor Bradley, whom he had not spoken to in over a year. Bradley had been an officer with the LAPD, but Parker considered him a traitor, and Gates shared that sentiment. In the aftermath of the Rodney King incident, Bradley publicly asked for Gates to resign, which he adamantly refused. This conflict between the chief and the mayor caused a complete breakdown of communication between Bradley and Gates.

King was advised by his attorney, Steve Lerman, to stay away from the media during the riots. By Friday, May 1st, the third day of the riots, Lerman seized on the publicity opportunity and asked his client to give a prepared speech outside his Beverly Hills office. King agreed and was dressed in a bulletproof vest and a fancy suit but was overwhelmed by the international media contingency and did not read from Lerman's prewritten speech. Instead, he spoke from his heart and muttered the famous words "Can we all get along?" that appeared on *Time* magazine's cover.

Rioters also came to the Parker Center Headquarters and threw rocks at the building. Firefighters began to retreat or refused to battle fires after being attacked by rioters.[69] In

68 The author was an undergraduate student at Illinois State University when the LAPD officers were acquitted. Stores in downtown Normal, Illinois, were also looted in the verdict's aftermath, and students protested the campus police department for perceived racial practices. Several other cities reported riots, including San Francisco, Las Vegas, Atlanta, NYC, Seattle, and Toronto.

69 Fred Hampton, Jr. was convicted of aggravated arson after being found guilty of firebombing a Korean grocery store during the 1992 riots. His father is discussed in the chapter on Chuck Ramsey in conjunction with the Black Panthers' Philadelphia Police raid. Fred Hampton was the chair of the Illinois Black Panthers Party (BPP) and was killed in his bed on December 4, 1969, after his apartment was raided by a tactical unit from the Cook

response to the riots, Bradley called for a local state of emergency and summoned assistance from President George H. Bush, who promised the violence would end. Bush activated 6,500 National Guard Troops, 600 Army soldiers, and 1,100 Marines to assist the LAPD. The LAPD arrested nearly 12,000 people during the riots. Chaos in South Central LA lasted six days and led to more than 50 deaths, 2,000 injuries, 5,000 fires, 1,000 businesses damaged, and $1 billion in losses (Cannon, 1999).

1992–1997: Chief Willie Williams

In the aftermath of Gates's resignation, Bradley's choice to appoint former Philadelphia police Commissioner Willie Williams to head the LAPD was shortsighted. He was the first African-American chief in both departments' histories and the first chief appointed from outside the LAPD's ranks since 1949. Williams lacked the educational background needed for a reform chief, having only completed his GED degree without any secondary education. LAPD officers criticized Williams for not returning to LA from his Las Vegas vacation to attend an officer's funeral and not passing the POST exam, which would have allowed him to make felony arrests symbolically. The unique and insular LAPD subculture was not going to accept a Black obese East coast outsider, despite his well-intentioned attempts to move the LAPD towards a community policing philosophy. After his first term, the police commission used its new term limit rule, passed in the wake of Gates's refusal to resign, to unanimously deny Williams a second term. In 2002, Hartsfield Atlanta International Airport appointed him to be federal security director, and in 2016 he died of cancer in Fayetteville, Georgia, at the age of 72.

1994: O.J. Simpson

On the evening of June 12, 1994, Nicole Brown Simpson, age 35, and Ron Goldman, age 25, were murdered at Brown's home located at 875 South Bundy Drive in LA's Brentwood neighborhood. Brown's body was discovered outside her home shortly after midnight on June 13. Autopsy reports indicated that she was stabbed seven times in the neck and scalp and that the gash across her neck nearly decapitated her. She also had defensive wounds on her hands. Five days after, the LAPD asked to question Simpson, Brown's ex-husband, about the murders and issued an arrest warrant on June 17 when he refused. Simpson subsequently led the LAPD on a nearly two-hour low-speed pursuit while seated in the back seat of his friend Al Cowling's 1993 white Ford Bronco,[70] a chase that was covered live by the media. Simpson had a gun and threatened to kill himself during the pursuit. The chase, which ended at Simpson's home, was not shown at his subsequent criminal trial. Simpson also owned a matching white Ford Bronco parked at his Brentwood home. The LAPD, prosecutors, and forensic scientists claimed that Simpson's Bronco had traces of both Brown and Goldman's blood inside, and blood matched Simpson's DNA at the murder scene.

County State's Attorney's Office, the Chicago Police Department, and the FBI. His fiancée, laying in the same bed, was eight months pregnant at the time with Fred Hampton, Jr. Miraculously, she was uninjured during the raid (Haas, 2011).

70 The infamous white Bronco was featured on *Pawn Stars* (season 14), but Rick Harrison, Las Vegas pawnshop owner and host of the show, refused to buy the Bronco from Simpson's former agent Mike Gilbert, who was asking over $1 million. The Bronco is currently on loan and displayed at the Alcatraz East Crime Museum in Pigeon Forge, Tennessee. Gilbert wrote a book claiming Simpson confessed to the murders after his acquittal (see Gilbert, 2008). In a later footnote, *Pawn Stars* (season 15), Harrison passed up on $1.5 million offered for the black BMW Sedan that Tupac Shakur was shot in on September 7, 1996.

Simpson was eventually arrested and put on trial for the murders. The media televised the trial internationally. Simpson's defense team included several attorneys, including Robert Shapiro, Robert Kardashian, and Johnnie Cochran. The defense team heavily scrutinized the LAPD for improperly handling evidence from Simpson and at the crime scene. Detective Mark Fuhrman was the main target for the defense, whom they alleged was racist and planted evidence. On October 3, 1995, after three hours of jury deliberation, a verdict of not guilty was read. The public believed the verdict was vindication for the white police officers' acquittal in the 1992 Rodney King beating case. In 1997 the Brown and Goldman families won a civil trial against Simpson, and he was found liable for their deaths and ordered to pay a judgment of $33.5 million. On October 3, 2008, exactly 13 years after his acquittal, Simpson was found guilty of armed robbery and kidnapping from a Las Vegas hotel incident. Likely because of his past murder trial, the judge sentenced Simpson to 13 years in prison. In his defense, Simpson claimed he, along with his armed security, was attempting to recover his memorabilia that dealers had stolen from him. He served nine years at the Lovelock Correctional Center in Nevada. Simpson was granted parole and released in October 2017 at 70 years of age. He joined Twitter in June 2019.

At the time of Simpson's acquittal of a double homicide, the media discredited LAPD Chief Williams for his police detectives' faulty investigative work. He denounced Simpson's defense attorneys for their claims that the LAPD mishandled evidence. However, the not guilty verdict was a critical blow to the perceived professional efficiency of the LAPD in the end.

1997–2002: Bernard Parks[71]

In 1997, Mayor Richard Riordan replaced Williams with a Black LAPD veteran, Bernard Parks. The LA City Council unanimously approved Parks to be the 52nd LAPD chief. Supporters of Parks carried the belief that he was not only an African-American leader but, unlike Chief Williams, he was a trusted insider. In his opening speech, he commented that he was wearing the same police belt that he wore as an LAPD rookie officer, taking a swipe at Chief Williams. In 1998, he was named one of *People* magazine's "50 Most Beautiful People." However, Chief Parks did not lead the department as a reformist and he did not believe in Chief William's community policing strategies. What many in the Black community did not realize was Park's was a protégé of Chief Gates and did not support Black officers nor strategies to improve community relations. The Rampart Scandal would destroy Park's legacy, cause a federal consent decree, and cause Mayor Hahn to lose his mayoral reelection. Before the loss, he sought out Bratton to lead the LAPD out of its crisis, which Bratton had wanted to do since the 1992 riots.

Rampart Scandal

The term "rampart" refers to a defensive wall or protection around a castle. In LA, "rampart" refers to a division within the police department that targets a densely populated geographic area west of downtown that includes Rampart Boulevard. For the traditional chiefs, Parker and Gates, the police served as the defensive wall to keep criminal gangs away from more affluent neighborhoods and downtown LA. The Rampart Division policed an estimated 165,000 citizens occupying an eight-square mile area. The division was created in 1966 under Chief Parker

71 Parks continued to serve the city as a three-term member of the city council from 2003 to 2015, marking 50 years of public service. In 2006 he was honored in Atlanta with an induction into the International Civil Rights Walk of Fame.

and received notoriety under Chief Gates and his anti-gang program called "Community Resources Against Street Hoodlums" (CRASH). In the late 1990s, stories emerged of significant corruption and misuse of force through the Rampart Division's CRASH unit.

While numerous officers and detectives were involved in misconduct related to the CRASH unit, Rafael Perez[72] and David Mack,[73] former police partners known as Ray and Mack, received most of the attention. The officers set up several suspected gang members with drugs, weapons, and false testimony. While their crimes were numerous, one is noteworthy. On November 6, 1997, 38-year-old Mack conspired with the 27-year-old assistant branch manager Errolyn Romero, his girlfriend for seven years, at a South Central Bank of America near the University of Southern California to commit a staged robbery that netted them $722,000. The police never captured the two accomplices of Mack. The following weekend Ray, Mack, and others went to Las Vegas and spent thousands of dollars partying. Romero, the assistant branch manager, eventually confessed to the bank heist and implicated Mack, who was sentenced to 14 years in federal prison and released in May 2010.

Rampart and LAPD's Investigation on the Murders of Tupac Shakur and Christopher Wallace

The LAPD ran two separate investigations on the murders of Shakur and Wallace, which came up with competing conclusions. The first conclusion came from Detective Russell Poole,[74] who investigated the murders from 1997 to 1999. He resigned after Chief Parks dismissed him from the case after Poole implicated LAPD Officer David Mack. Detective Greg Kading and a federal task force led a second investigation from 2005 to 2009. Both Poole's and Kading's investigations are detailed below in separate sections. No arrests have been made for the fatal shootings of either Shakur or Wallace.

Detective Russell Poole's Investigation (1997–1999)

Detective Poole was part of a team investigating Officer Mack's bank robbery, but Mack refused to cooperate in implicating others. The bank never recovered their money ($722,000) from the heist (Domanick, 2015, p. 393). Poole alleged that Mack and Perez were tied to Marion "Suge" Knight[75] and arranged the drive-by murder of 24-year-old East Coast rapper Christopher Wallace (AKA Biggie Smalls / AKA Notorious B.I.G.) on March 9, 1997. That drive-by murder took place in front of the LA Petersen Automotive Museum at Wilshire

72 Perez inspired Denzel Washington's character in the movie *Training Day*.

73 Mack was a past track star at the University of Oregon, qualified for the 1983 national team, and ran the 800-meter race at the world championships. He holds the seventh-best American time in that race, running 1:43.35. A leg injury kept him out of the 1984 Olympics that took place in LA. Mack grew up in Compton, as did Suge Knight.

74 Poole resigned from the LAPD in 1999 (14 months shy of his 20-year pension) and formed a private detective agency. On August 19, 2015, he died at the age of 58 of a heart attack while discussing Suge Knight with the LA County Sheriff's Department and working on the book *Chaos Merchants* (Carlin & Poole, 2016).

75 Knight started Death Row Records in 1992 with Andre Young (AKA Dr. Dre). They launched several artists' careers, including Calvin Broadus, Jr. (AKA Snoop Dogg), Stanley Burrell (AKA MC Hammer), and Tupac Shakur. At its peak, Death Row Records was making an estimated $100 million a year. In 2006, the record label filed for bankruptcy and was auctioned to WIDEawake Entertainment for $18 million. In September 2018, Knight was sentenced to 28 years in prison for a fatal hit-and-run of Terry Carter from a 2015 brawl. Carter was called in to help mitigate a dispute between Knight and F Gary Gray, who was a producer for the movie *Straight Out of Compton*. Knight felt Gray owed him money and was upset about the derogatory nature of his portrayal in the film. The attempted mediation resulted in a fistfight with Knight running over Carter. Knight is eligible for parole in the year 2037.

Boulevard and South Fairfax Avenue. Detective Poole believed that Bloods street gang member Amir Muhammad (AKA Harry Billups) was paid to kill Wallace, and Mack had affiliations with the Bloods street gang. Billups and Mack both grew up in Compton and were athletes and close friends at the University of Oregon – Mack a track star and Billups a football running back. According to prison informant Ken Boagni, the money from Mack's bank robbery was slated to pay Harry Billups (AKA Amir Muhammed) for Wallace's murder. However, Billups was only paid half of his contract because he failed to murder Sean "Puffy" Combs. Boagni later recanted his story and refused to be part of Wallace's family lawsuit. Another informant from the LA County Jail, Michael Robinson (AKA "Psycho" Mike), also implicated Billups as Wallace's shooter. However, he gave a lot of conflicting names, and like Boagni, Robinson recanted his story.

Wallace sat on the passenger side of a Chevy Suburban driven by Greg "G-Money"Young when someone in a black Chevy Impala Sedan, ironically the same type of vehicle driven by Officer Mack before his bank arrest, shot him four times. Wallace never regained consciousness after he was shot and was pronounced dead on arrival at Cedars-Sinai Medical Center on March 9, 1997. His autopsy was made public in 2012 and indicated only one of the four bullets was fatal. The drive-by shooting[76] occurred after Wallace and his entourage left an after-party[77] for the 11th Annual Soul Train Music Awards. Sean Combs[78] (AKA Puff Daddy) was in another suburban with three bodyguards in front of Wallace. Wallace was likely killed in retaliation to the murder of West Coast rapper and 25-year-old Death Row Records star artist Tupac Shakur six months earlier in Las Vegas.[79]

> On September 7, 1996, Shakur and Knight attended a Mike Tyson boxing match at the MGM Grand Hotel in Las Vegas. (Tyson won with one of the fastest TKO's in a title fight lasting one minute 49 seconds. Two months later, he would lose to Evander Holyfield and again in a subsequent rematch). After the Vegas match, an excited Shakur and his entourage members beat up Orlando Anderson (AKA Baby Lane)[80] inside the MGM Hotel. Anderson was allegedly part of the LA Southside Crips and four months prior had robbed Piru Bloods gang member Travon "Tray" Lane of his Death Row Records gold medallion inside a Foot Locker store at the LA Lakeland Mall. The fight inside the MGM Hotel was started by Shakur and recorded on the MGM CCTV cameras before being broken up by hotel security. Knight was also involved in kicking Anderson, a violation of his previous

76 At the time of his death, Wallace's daughter T'yanna was 3 years old and his son Christopher "CJ" Wallace, Jr. was four months old. Sixteen days after his death, his album *Life After Death* was number one on the Billboard charts. Today CJ is referred to as "Lil Biggie" and is an actor. T'yanna runs a clothing line.

77 Ironically, the LA after-party Wallace and Combs attended was sponsored by Quincy Jones's *Vibe* magazine. The night Shakur was killed in Las Vegas, he left his fiancée in his MGM Hotel room – Quincy Jones's daughter Kidada.

78 Combs started his own record company, Bad Boy Entertainment, in 1993 and launched the career of Wallace. His record company often conflicted with Knight's Death Row Records. Today, Combs is one of the wealthiest and most successful recording artists and music producers in history.

79 Poole helped contribute to the book *Tupac 187: The Red Knight* (Bond & Carlin, 2014).

80 Anderson was killed on May 29, 1998, at the age of 23, after a shootout outside a carwash in Compton after he attempted to collect money from a cocaine debt. In 2009, Anderson's uncle, Duane "Keefe D" Davis faced serious drug charges. As part of a plea agreement, he provided information to LAPD Detective Greg Kading that he helped his nephew, his sister's son, kill Shakur for revenge from the MGM beat down. Davis was also in Vegas to see the Tyson fight on September 7, 1996 and claimed he was given a gun by Eric "Von Zip" Martin, a major Harlem drug dealer who was also godfather to Wallace's son and connected to Sean Combs. Davis and Martin were longtime friends and connected in 1991 to sell narcotics coast to coast. With this connection, Davis provided Combs and Wallace security through the Crips street gang when they came to LA. Martin died of cancer in August 2012 (see Davis & Jah, 2019).

probation. (Six months later, on March 1, 1997, Knight was sentenced to 5 years in prison for this violation and released in August 2001. Anderson, paid by Knight, unsuccessfully testified that Knight did not kick him during the MGM fight. Later, Knight denied his involvement in the Wallace shooting since he was locked up in the LA County Jail a week prior). Three hours after the MGM fight, Shakur was shot four times (by someone in the back seat of a white Cadillac) while riding in the passenger side of a BMW Sedan[81] driven by Knight on their way to Knight's *662 Club*[82] on Flamingo Road. Knight was attempting to secure a gambling and liquor license for his Vegas club, and Shakur was supposed to perform that evening. Shakur died six days later at the University Medical Center in Las Vegas.

Nine days after Wallace was gunned down (with the same number of bullets that hit Shakur), LAPD Officer Kevin Gaines, a Black officer, was fatally shot by undercover LAPD Detective Frank Lyga, a white officer, in a suspected road rage incident. There was no evidence that the officers knew one another. Gaines had been on the force for seven years, assigned to the CRASH unit, and linked to the Rampart Scandal. On March 18, 1997, Gaines was driving a vehicle owned by Sharitha Lee Golden,[83] Suge Knight's estranged wife. Officer Gaines was dating Sharitha and resided in her mansion. A few days after Gaines' fatal shooting, his family retained attorney Johnnie Cochran (mentioned earlier as part of O.J. Simpson's legal team) and filed a $25 million wrongful death lawsuit. LA eventually settled for $250,000. Judge Bill Schoettler, a mediator specialist, sent a letter to Chief Parks stating he would have decided on behalf of the city, meaning the settlement was unnecessary. City Attorney James Hahn likely pushed for the concession to appease the Black population since he was preparing his mayoral campaign.

Poole investigated the Gaines shooting, which led him to conclude that Knight had several connections with corrupt officers. However, Sharitha stated that Gaines never worked for Death Row Records. Because of the links made to the LAPD and Knight, Detective Poole, and later head of the FBI's LA field office Phillip Carson, claimed that Chief Parks and the LAPD command staff hampered subsequent investigations. Additionally, they argued the city and the LAPD hindered their investigative efforts because of a $500 million lawsuit filed by the Wallace family. The cover-up allegations were detailed in two books by journalist Randall Sullivan (see Sullivan, 2002, 2019). His work also became the source for the movie *City of Lies,* starring Johnny Depp, who played Detective Poole. The film was scheduled to be released on May 21, 2018, on Small's 46th birthday. After a delay, the new release date was September 7, 2018, on the 22nd anniversary of Shakur's shooting in Las Vegas. However, ongoing lawsuits between Depp and the filming management halted the movie release.

For his part, on July 6, 2005, Chief Bratton made a statement after Federal Judge Florence-Marie Cooper ordered a mistrial in the Wallace lawsuit against the city.[84] Bratton stated that

81 In a 2018 episode of *Pawn Stars* (season 15), the black BMW Sedan was listed at $1.5 million but did not sell.

82 Knight opened the private Las Vegas *662 Club*, where guests had to be invited, in 1994. The "662" spelled out M-O-B, short for Member of Bloods, their gang affiliation.

83 Sharitha was Knight's first wife, and they dated throughout high school. Sharitha was co-owner of Death Row Records and served as a manager for their artists. In 2017, Suge Knight alleged Sharitha and Reggie White, Jr. (former Compton police officer and Director of Death Row Records security) tried to kill him the night Shakur was fatally shot. Sharitha and White vehemently denied these allegations.

84 A $1.1 million judgment against the city of LA was originally awarded to the Wallace family for their legal expenses but later revoked after Judge Cooper was informed the attorneys for Wallace had the information they told the court they did not have access to. Attorney Perry Sanders also excused David Mack and Harry Billups from their lawsuit after their witnesses began to recant. Judge Cooper passed away in January 2010 from lymphoma. In April 2010, Judge Jacqueline Nguyen dismissed the Wallace lawsuit.

there were corrupt officers in the LAPD who had already been arrested and incarcerated. However, there was no evidence that these same officers were involved with the fatal shooting of Wallace. He also stated he was ordering a comprehensive review of Wallace's murder, and Gerald Chaleff would oversee the investigative process. This new federal task force was called the Rampart Federal Investigation Team (or RamFIT) and included the FBI, LAPD, and LA County Sheriff's Department. Others referred to the task force as *Operation Transparency*.

Detective Greg Kading Investigation (2006–2009)

A ten-episode *USA Network* series titled *Unsolved: The Murders of Tupac and the Notorious B.I.G* chronicled the RamFIT task force investigation, released in 2018, the same year when the movie *City of Lies*, based on Poole's theories, should have been released. Detective Greg Kading served as a co-producer for the network series and self-published his book on the Shakur and Wallace murders (Kading, 2011).[85] Kading's team followed up on Poole's prior investigative theories, the alleged CRASH officers' involvement with Death Row Records, and the development of new leads.[86] Kading concluded that only Inglewood and Compton[87] officers worked directly for Death Row Records and not LAPD officers to the extent Poole assumed.

In the RamFIT investigation, Kading met with Knight's girlfriend.[88] She confessed to visiting Knight in prison after his incarceration on a probation violation for his role in beating up Anderson[89] in the MGM before the fatal shooting of Shakur. His girlfriend disguised herself as a paralegal so she could meet with Knight privately. According to Kading, Knight provided her orders to pay Wardell "Poochie" Fouse (AKA Darnell Bolton)[90] to kill Wallace for the Shakur shooting. Fouse, a 36-year-old member of the Piru Bloods, received two cash payments from Knight's girlfriend – one for $9,000 and one for $4,000 to kill Wallace. Knight's girlfriend reportedly received $1,200 for her part or a total of $25,000 for the hit on Wallace. According to Knight's girlfriend, Fouse killed Wallace in the drive-by shooting and had done similar work on Knight's behalf. In terms of Poole's theories about Billups (AKA Amir Muhammad) killing Wallace Billups had no association with either Compton or the Crips putting into doubt the prison/jail informants' revelations. Kading's investigations also determined that LAPD CRASH officers were not directly involved in Wallace's murder. However, there was little doubt of the Rampart Unit's corruption, albeit not to the extent indicated by Officer Perez's proffers.

85 Random House provided a lucrative offer to publish Kading's account of his investigations into the Shakur and Wallace murders. However, they decided to bypass believing that his account of the events would put Knight's girlfriend in harm's way, and they would be negligent.

86 Similar to Poole, Kading was dismissed from the investigations and quit the LAPD in protest. Both officers made copies of their reports, which later became books: Poole with Sullivan's *LAbyrinth* (Sullivan, 2002) and *Dead Wrong* (Sullivan, 2019) and Kading with his self-published book *Murder Rap* (Kading, 2011).

87 In September 2000, the Compton Police Department was disbanded by their city council due to uncontrolled corruption, and a subsequent contract was made with the LA County Sheriff's Department to police their city.

88 Knight's girlfriend, Tammy Hawkins, sued Knight for child support in 2010. Kading referred to her as Theresa Swann in *Murder Rap* (Kading, 2011). Hawkins also helped Knight hide assets from Death Row Records following their 2006 bankruptcy.

89 Anderson testified on behalf of Knight during his probation revocation hearing and attempted to argue that he was trying to break up the fight rather than kick him. That testimony was paid for by Knight and was not successful.

90 Fouse was fatally shot in the back on July 24, 2003, while riding on a motorcycle in Compton. His death was believed to be ordered because of in-fighting between *Pirus Bloods* and the *Fruit Town Bloods*.

Rampart Scandal: Officer Ray Perez

Within the infamous LAPD CRASH unit, Officer Ray Perez became the most corrupt officer in LAPD history.[91] He was implicated in murder, drug dealing, extortion, and corruption. Among other crimes, Perez admitted to signing out cocaine evidence from the department, often using other officers' signatures, and replacing stolen cocaine with pancake mix. Perez was not immune to also attempting to set up officers. A year after Lyga[92] fatally shot Gaines, he was under investigation for one pound of cocaine missing from the LAPD property room from one of his cases. Perez took the cocaine, likely to set up Lyga for revenge in killing his fellow CRASH Officer Gaines.

Perez admitted to shooting and killing suspects and planting evidence. He chose to cooperate with the DA partially. Perez implicated dozens of officers and provided testimony that would subsequently shut down all CRASH units throughout the LAPD. He testified that officers routinely engaged in brutality, framed suspects with planted evidence, committed perjury, and operated with impunity, protected by the LAPD culture. On September 8, 1999, Perez signed a plea agreement that provided him immunity for most of his charges, and he received a five-year sentence.

By the fall of 2000, Perez implicated 70 LAPD police officers. The administrative board brought 58 officers in and charged 24 with several offenses that included misuse of force, planting evidence, attempted murder, and murder charges. The board suspended 12 officers, forced 7 to resign, and terminated 5 officers. Ultimately, only officers Michael Buchanan, Brian Liddy, and Sergeant Edward Ortiz received convictions. Ortiz, Buchanan, and Liddy were all found guilty by a jury on November 15, 2000, of conspiracy to obstruct justice and filing false police reports. A fourth officer, Paul Harper, was found not guilty. However, on appeal, the court overturned the convictions. On December 22, 2000, Judge Jacqueline Connor overturned the guilty verdicts citing contrary evidence and the rule of law. In 2009, the city agreed to pay the four officers $20.5 million ($5 million each) for malicious prosecution.

Over 140 subsequent civil lawsuits filed against LA related to police misconduct. These lawsuits cost the city approximately $90 million in legal defense and a reported $125 million in settlements. Additionally, the court dismissed over 100 criminal cases and exonerated inmates arrested by corrupt Rampart officers. After serving three years, Perez received parole. A few months later, he plead guilty to federal charges for shooting and framing Javier Ovando[93] and served a couple more years in federal prison. The DOJ subsequently intervened, and the LAPD agreed to court-monitored reforms in addition to a federal consent decree.

The Rampart Scandal has been repeated, to a lesser extent, throughout American policing with its use of undercover drug units. Each police leader in this book has confronted these accountability and ethical dilemmas. Ethical leadership is not merely a matter of how the leader carries her/himself (Johnson & Cox, 2004), but how they ensure subordinates carry out

91 Perez legally changed his name to Ray Lopezz after he served five years in prison for stealing cocaine from an LAPD evidence room and two years in federal prison for shooting Javier Ovando. In 2015, he worked as a limousine driver, which included driving movie producer Harvey Weinstein.

92 Lyga was terminated from the LAPD in 2014 after he was secretly recorded talking to an LAPD academy class and made derogatory comments about the Gaines shooting and several supervisors within the department. In August 2016, the city agreed to pay Lyga $50,000 after he filed a federal lawsuit arguing that he was wrongfully perceived to be racist. As part of the agreement, Lyga was still not allowed to get his job back.

93 Perez and his corrupt partner, Nino Durden, shot and paralyzed Ovando on October 12, 1996, inside his apartment. Perez recanted his perjured testimony and admitted he shot and planted a gun on Ovando after he wrongfully spent more than two years in prison. Ovando received $15 million, the city's largest settlement from police misconduct.

their duties in the desired fashion (Schafer, 2013). Rampart occurred because the CRASH unit operated with minimal oversight based upon its high productivity of arrests (Reese, 2005). In the aftermath, a new leadership was necessary to create a cultural shift toward honesty and integrity that countered noble cause corruption and unchecked undercover operations.

LAPD Chief Bratton: The Most Ambitious Reform Experiment in Police History

LA's prior decade of questionable police practices culminated in the Rampart corruption scandal and the DOJ announcing they had enough evidence to sue the LAPD for ongoing patterns of misconduct. To avoid the lawsuit, the city government opted to enter into a consent decree and be monitored by the Federal Court. A federal monitor of the LAPD began in June 2001. By 2002, after a decade of decline, violent crime was back up in LA. Murders in the city peaked in 1992 at 1,100 and dropped to 419 in 1998 but rose to 648 in 2002. The city was still reeling from the riots a decade earlier and suffering persistent community trust problems and increasing crime.

Mayor Hahn subsequently appointed the outsider Bratton as the city's 54th police chief. He is the only person to ever serve as a top law enforcement executive in NYC and LA. Mayor Hahn swore Bratton in as the Chief of the LAPD on October 25, 2002. As chief, Bratton's goal was to adhere to the recommendations given through the consent decree and reform the department to the point that the decree would be lifted. Under his leadership, the LAPD began one of the most ambitious experimental reforms in police history with a simultaneous focus on reducing crime, fully complying with the consent decree recommendations, and improving officer morale along with community relations. Mayor Hahn's decision not to renew the contract of Chief Parks lost him votes with the Black population and in 2005 Antonio Villaraigosa defeated Hahn for mayor. His political decision to do the right thing predictably cost him the reelection. The new mayor would still benefit with four more years of Bratton's leadership.

In terms of crime, during Bratton's tenure as LAPD Chief, homicides decreased 36 percent, and violent crime was 54 percent lower than Park's final year in 2002, with a reduction in total crime levels not seen since the 1950s. This turnaround is comparable to Bratton's leadership in the NYPD but with fewer officers: NYPD had 40,000 officers or a ratio of 1:209 residents; LAPD had 9,000 officers or a ratio of 1:409 residents.

Bittner (1970) challenged researchers to examine what the police do, rather than merely writing about what they ought to do. At the 2006 American Society of Criminology (ASC) conference, Bratton declared that the police are now focused on crime more than at any time in our history. He invited researchers to assess his leadership efforts and focus their attention on what the police actually do to impact crime. In 2007 the police commission reappointed Bratton to a second five-year contract, the first chief to receive a second term under the new term limits set in 1992 by an amended city charter in the wake of Gates's forced resignation. In July 2009, after six years of crime reduction under Bratton, a federal judge removed the consent decree. Bratton then planned his early resignation, and in October 2009, he returned to NYC to work for Kroll Security firm.

Bratton's Leadership as LAPD Chief

Bratton determined that the events in the 1990s – the LAPD officers' acquittal in the King beating, the 1992 LA Riots, the OJ Simpson verdict, the Rampart Scandal, and the consent decree – had all caused the city to operate under a risk aversion model that created performance barriers in the interest of avoiding future liability. With the help of Kelling, he replicated a broken windows style of policing and CompStat accountability meetings with LAPD command staff. In an effort to enhance transparency, CompStat meetings were frequently open to the public with some being run in halls around Black churches. Bratton targeted the 106 officers with the rank of captain or higher to assist in transforming the LAPD. Over the next seven years, pedestrians' stops increased by nearly 50 percent, and the number of arrests from these stops doubled. Community satisfaction with the police from all demographics improved, and systems were put in place to more quickly identify officers who might be misusing their authority and needed additional training. Bratton's leadership style encouraged officer discretion within broken windows policing and allowed for mistakes to be made, especially for challenging problems such as the homeless population.

LA Homeless – Skid Row

Skid Row consists of a 50-block area east of downtown LA with an estimated 10,000 homeless individuals, the country's largest stable homeless population. This location has been a stopping point for the homeless since the 1880s. Train lines stop at Skid Row. Surrounding areas became crowded with drifters, people running from their past mistakes, and transient laborers. Throughout the twentieth century, single-occupancy hotels[94] emerged along with many saloons and brothels along Skid Row. Several unsuccessful attempts were made to clean up the area through social work organizations and building codes that targeted dilapidated commercial property. Hotel owners found it cheaper to demolish their buildings than bring them up to code, which increased homelessness. Legislation de-institutionalizing mental hospitals exacerbated the problem and filled Skid Row with mentally disturbed homeless people.

Bratton perceived homeless populations as part of a broken windows puzzle. In 2002, he announced a plan to clean up Skid Row by aggressively enforcing anti-camping ordinances ignored by past chiefs. The LAPD issued thousands of tickets to the homeless who violated the ordinances. Others were jailed or hospitalized, and their belongings confiscated. Lawsuits alleged hospitals "dumped" homeless people onto Skid Row, and the LAPD was asked to investigate. A subsequent lawsuit against the hospitals was filed by the city attorney, resulting in several hospitals' settlements. However, since no laws existed that prohibited "dumping," new legislation was needed.

By the fall of 2007, the southern California ACLU filed a lawsuit against the LAPD for violating due process with the homeless. The court reached a compromise and ruled the LAPD could not arrest or confiscate belongings from individuals in Skid Row between 9 PM and 6:30 AM. This ruling allowed the homeless to sleep within ten feet of any commercial or residential entrance between those evening and early morning hours without the fear of being cited or arrested. The city also attempted to limit the total amount of property a homeless person could possess in Skid Row, but the courts ruled against those restrictions.

94 In 2021, *Netflix* released a four-episode series titled *Crime Scene: The Vanishing at the Cecil Hotel,* exploring Elisa Lam's February 2013 disappearance. The Cecil Hotel is located near Skid Row at 640 S. Main Street by the train station and opened on December 20, 1924. The 15-story hotel room with 700 guest rooms is noted for daily police calls for service, numerous drug overdoses, five suicides, 11 deaths from falls or accidental poisoning, and two murders that both ended in acquittals. Lam was suspected of accidentally drowning inside an unlocked water supply tank on the hotel's rooftop after reducing her medication for bipolar disease. Her naked body was found three weeks after she went missing by a maintenance worker who found the tank hatch open and guests complained of low water pressure (Anderson, 2020). Lam's parents' civil suit against the Cecil Hotel was dismissed.

Rogue Cop – Christopher Dorner

Christopher Dorner was a naval reservist who joined the LAPD academy in 2005 and graduated in 2006. On July 28, 2007, he partnered with field training officer (FTO) Teresa Evans, and they responded to a call for service at a hotel. (This same year, Dorner's wife had filed for divorce.) FTO Evans arrested a man suffering from mental health issues. A few weeks later, Evans wrote a report on Dorner stating areas he needed to improve. Dorner retorted his review by alleging that Evans misused force when she arrested the hotel's mentally ill man. After a lengthy seven-month investigation, a review board determined that Dorner lied and made false statements in his testimony against FTO Evans. Consequently, Bratton terminated Dorner. Dorner appealed his termination in court, but a judge withheld the LAPD decision, and an appellate court affirmed the judgment.

On February 1, 2013 (noting Bratton left the LAPD in 2009), Dorner mailed a package to CNN correspondent Anderson Cooper that contained a challenge coin that police recruits received from Bratton. The coin had a bullet hole that Dorner alleged he shot from 100 yards away, and he was now threatening several LAPD officers and their families, including Bratton. Two days later, Dorner fatally shot Monica Quan, daughter of an LAPD Captain, a lawyer who represented him during his dismissal hearing. Keith Lawrence, Quan's fiancée, was also killed. Four days after Quan and Lawrence's murder, Dorner ambushed officers from the Riverside Police Department. Dorner fatally shot Officer Michael Crain and wounded his partner. Five days after Crain's murder, Dorner hid in a cabin in Big Bear Lake, California. Detective Jeremiah MacKay, from the San Bernardino County Sheriff's Department, was fatally shot in a subsequent firefight. Officers surrounded Dorner's cabin and burned it with projectiles. Later, investigators determined Dorner died from a single self-inflicted gunshot (Gascon & Roussell, 2019).

Harvard University Study – May 2009

In January 2008, structured discussions between police leaders and academics took place as part of the Executive Session on Policing and Public Safety with the Harvard Kennedy School and the NIJ. During these discussions, Bratton suggested policing would benefit from thorough and independent studies of departmental effectiveness. Specifically, Bratton wanted to know if an evaluation of the LAPD's decade-long process of becoming compliant with the hundreds of standards set by the consent decree a decade ago also reduced crime/disorder and improved race relations. Such an evaluation needed to be done by unbiased external reviewers and is too often avoided by police leaders.[95] The LA Police Foundation subsequently provided financial support for the research to determine the impact of broken windows policing throughout LA during Bratton's time as chief.

Researchers from Harvard University Kennedy School's Program in Criminal Justice Policy and Management used various mixed research methodologies to produce a 68-page report, essentially measuring Bratton's leadership effectiveness. Their research included hundreds of hours of participant observation of every rank from patrol to command staff. Researchers analyzed data on the following: use of force, civilian complaints, crime, arrests, and stops. They were able to compare surveys conducted on officers and residents over the past decade with their own surveys of officers, community members, and recently arrested detainees. Focus

95 External review is also detailed in the chapter on Ramsey when he asked the DOJ to review the Washington, DC Metropolitan Police Use of Force policies. As Philadelphia Police Commissioner, Ramsey again requested a collaborative review of officer-involved shootings from the DOJ Office for Community Policing.

groups also interviewed residents, public officials, and police officers (Stone, Foglesong, & Cole, 2009).

Predictably, researchers found a steep increase in the use of broken windows policing through the arrests of Part II crimes such as loitering, DUI, and disorderly conduct. The more serious Part I arrests (homicide, rape, robbery, aggravated assault, burglary, car theft) declined and made up 15 percent of the 2003–2007 total arrests. Bratton linked reduced crime, in part, to pedestrian stops. There were over a half million pedestrian and motorist stopped in 2002, and by 2007 there were an additional 288,000 stops, a 49 percent increase, bringing the total to over 875,000 police stops. While some officers argued the consent decree discouraged them from stopping citizens, these statistics argued otherwise. In 2002, only 15 percent of police stops ended in arrest, and by 2007 these numbers doubled to 30 percent of police stops that ended in arrest. Researchers concluded that the quantity and quality of police work improved with the LAPD. Borrowing from the Boston and New York neighborhood policing model, officers were frequently removed from responding to routine calls-for-service and consequently, improved strategic relationships with community leaders and activists. However, the more aggressive style of police stops, as was the case in NYC, led to racial disparity questions. In 2008, African-Americans accounted for 9 percent of the city's general population, but 23 percent of officer stops. Latinos were the exception as they accounted for 48 percent of the stops, and that percentage roughly matched their representation in the general population.

More than two-thirds of Black and Hispanic residents thought the job the LAPD was doing was good or excellent, indicating a rise (from 71 to 83 percent) in public satisfaction with the police. However, about 10 percent of Black residents reported almost none of the LAPD officers they encountered treated them with respect. Bratton faced the same problem as most national chiefs in recruiting Blacks to become police officers, and their numbers declined amongst new officer hires. However, nearly three-fourths of Black officers agreed or strongly agreed that the LAPD was better than before Bratton's appointment. The higher Black officer perceptions of improvement contrasted with the lower 62 percent of white officers who agreed the department improved.[96]

The Harvard researchers sought to determine if the consent decree placed on the LAPD hindered their police work. Their findings concluded that the practice of broken windows policing could effectively reduce crime simultaneous with reform efforts. While the department aggressively responded to crime and disorder with increased stops, they also scrutinized the police stops and required officers to file reports for each incident. These reports allowed for timely assessments and determining if the officers properly exercised their police authority. An unbiased computerized software program assessed the police stops.

The LAPD fulfilled Section II of the consent decree when they contracted with Sierra Systems Group to develop an internal mechanism that would serve as an early intervention or warning system for specific officers. The system is called the Training Evaluation and Management System II (TEAMS II). The Christopher Commission recommended the original TEAMS system in the wake of the Rodney King beating in 1991 but never implemented the program. TEAM II became operational on March 12, 2007, through the Information Technology Division on the LAPD Administration Building's Eighth floor. The system tracks officers' stops, pursuits, traffic accidents, civilian complaints, use of force investigations, and any

96 Through the assistance of Lt. Fred Booker, a trusted Black officer, Bratton was introduced to members of LA's Black community. Booker vouched for his chief and encouraged his constant presence in South and East LA. Through arranged meetings at barbershops, such as Tolliver's in South Central LA, and Black churches, Bratton earned their respect. In what he called his highest compliment, "Sweet" Alice Harris, a popular Black neighborhood activist, said Chief Bratton really sees us. Along with the assistance of Rice, Bratton was able to form partnerships between the police and the Black community that had not previously existed.

internal discipline. The system statistically matches officers with peer groups who are doing similar jobs and then compares them to determine when officers fall outside of the standard deviation. Once an officer falls outside a threshold, the system creates an action item and notifies the officer and their supervisor. Supervisors then review the report and meet with the officer to determine if there's a pattern of conduct and what disposition would be most effective. Building on the culture of transparency, each officer has access to their TEAMS report, and the Inspector General's Office is supposed to review the system regularly. The use of serious force has dropped each year since 2004. In addition to reduced crime during Bratton's leadership, the TEAMS II system has enhanced police integrity and helped build police legitimacy and public trust.

2007 Rampart Reconsidered

In 2003, Bratton requested the Police Commission conduct an after-action analysis of the Rampart CRASH crisis. The request created the fifth report on the scandal. The report's goal was to sustain long-term cultural shifts and policy implementation to avoid future large-scale corruption. Challenges related to LAPD supervisors signing off on search warrants that lacked probable cause and questionable supervision over gang units. A blue-ribbon commission panel was formed and tasked with conducting a post-scandal analysis to understand the Rampart Scandal's causes and identify threats that may cause corruption to reoccur. Over the next four years, the panel interviewed over 200 individuals in the LAPD and throughout the city's criminal justice system and reviewed past investigation reports related to Rampart.

The final 101-page report, released in 2007 to the Police Commission, was titled *Rampart Reconsidered*.[97] The panel concluded their report with seven recommendations aimed at prosecutorial agencies positioned to prevent or respond to the next corruption crisis:

1. Conduct an analysis of the LA County Criminal Justice System's integrity to study how wrongful convictions occur.
2. Develop more robust checks and interventions with prosecutors that target police perjury and misconduct. Be transparent about the police corruption cases that are prosecuted.
3. Improve prosecutorial inter-agency coordination at the federal and local level and not impair investigations.
4. Create a standing task force with the federal and local authorities to coordinate investigations of police corruption cases and improve effective communication.
5. Improve training within prosecutorial agencies to understand and handle police corruption cases.
6. Prepare Federal prosecutors to handle local police misconduct cases without being overly reliant on the DOJ that may slow their investigations.
7. Improve information disclosure processes between the LAPD and the City Attorney's Office to expedite the release of relevant materials.

Conclusions from the report stated that the federal court was able to provide the independence and authority to push the LAPD to sustain its focus on reform. The report recommended that the consent decree be extended and suggested that the inspector general should have increased independence from the department to conduct investigations on police misconduct. Bratton highlighted another conclusion of the report, which was the need for additional

97 See www.lapdonline.org/search_results/content_basic_view/32828.

police officers, and this led to Mayor Villaraigosa's authorization for the hiring of 1,000 additional officers.[98]

The primary author of the 2007 *Rampart Revisited* report was civil rights attorney Connie Rice,[99] who served as the chair of the blue ribbon Rampart review panel. Bratton conducted lengthy interviews with Rice prior to becoming chief as part of his consultant assistance with the consent decree. As chief, he frequently met with Rice and John Mack,[100] the past President of the LA Urban League chapter (1969–2005) and the member of the LA Board of Police Commissioners, to continually learn about concerns from minority leaders. He provided Rice with her own parking spot at police headquarters and won her admiration and support. Rice went from being the main antagonist who consistently sued the LAPD to become one of its chief allies, starting with Bratton and subsequent chiefs. The police union also supported Rice's study on *Rampart Revisited* to alleviate the police's negative perceptions.

In 2009, Bratton resigned. That same year, Rice started a gang-intervention academy taught by former gang members, academics, and other stakeholders. The academy, still in effect, lasts 15 weeks and treats gang activity like a disease that needs to be treated, managed, and ultimately defeated. Rice convinced Bratton to discontinue certain police practices, such as having suspects be put into prone positions or kneel during stop-and-frisk situations. Expectations are for captains to respond in person to every homicide and treat victims with respect. Bratton also showed up at many homicide scenes and continually consulted with minority leaders, which allowed him to win their praise.

Leaving LA in Good Hands

On October 25, 2007, Chief Bratton started his second five-year term with the LAPD. That year he received *Governing* magazine's "Public Official of the Year" award. By August 2009, half-way through his second term, Bratton announced he was leaving the LAPD after learning the *LA Times* prepared a story that he decided to take a position in the private sector. In 2009 Bratton was also the President of the Major Cities Chiefs Association. As evidence of real leadership success, Bratton's role in reforming the LAPD could be seen in his equally qualified three internal candidates who lined up to be his successor.

Bratton left the LAPD with his goals met: significant crime reduction with 54 percent less violent crime, reduced civilian complaints, the consent decree lifted, and improved officer morale. He helped transform the department and the divided city from decades of dysfunction and racial division. The prior dysfunction was apparent in the 1992 riots, the O.J. Simpson verdict's aftermath, and the Rampart Scandal. The transformation was evident when 83 percent of the city's residents rated the department's performance as good or excellent. In November 2009, Mayor Villaraigosa replaced the interim chief. He appointed Charlie Beck[101] to be Bratton's successor as chief, a position he had aspired to since being hired to the department in 1977, where his father also served as a deputy chief. Under Beck's full two-term

98 On July 1, 2020, the LA City Council voted to cut police funding as part of the national "defunding movement," and the number of officers went below 10,000 (Zahniser, Smith, & Reyes, 2020), matching numbers before the 2007 *Rampart Revisited* study.

99 Rice is the daughter of an Air Force colonel and received her law degree from Harvard University. She is also the second cousin to former Secretary of State Condoleezza Rice. See Rice (2014).

100 Mack died in 2018 of cancer at the age of 81.

101 Beck served as LAPD chief from November 2009 until June 2018. In December 2019, as a testament to his leadership success, Chicago Mayor Lori Lightfoot asked for his assistance as interim chief for the Chicago Police Department after she terminated Eddie Johnson. Beck served as interim CPD chief until April 15, 2020, and was succeeded by David Brown. Beck's successor at the LAPD was Michel Moore.

leadership, crime fell an additional 26 percent. The LAPD added over 2,000 officers from 1992 to 2012 but had two-thirds fewer arrests, choosing instead to deal with offenses through more creative alternatives, especially for juvenile offenders.

England – Consulting

On September 11, 2009, Bratton was bestowed the title Commander of the Most Excellent Order of the British Empire (CBE) by United Kingdom Ambassador to the United States Sir Nigel Sheinwald while he was still LA chief. Queen Elizabeth II conferred the CBE on the advice of the Foreign Commonwealth Secretary. The ceremony took place at Sheinwald's residence to recognize Bratton's work to promote intelligence sharing and best practices in policing between the two countries. Britain's admiration for Bratton reoccurred in the summer of 2011 with a media frenzy that followed the shooting death of mixed race Mark Duggan by the British police. Thousands rioted and looted across London for the next seven days. Prime Minister David Cameron[102] contacted Bratton to assist with the response and hired him as a consultant. Cameron also tried to hire Bratton as London's police chief, but the job required British citizenship.

Bratton's time in the private sector continued to be lucrative. He joined Altegrity Risk International and was named chairman of Kroll Advisory Solutions, a global risk mitigation and response firm, where he served as chairman from 2009 to 2012. In 2010 Altegrity and Kroll integrated. Bratton worked for both while running his own consulting company and serving on several boards, including Rite Aid and Motorola. In 2011 he worked with senior researcher Zach Tumin from the Kennedy School of Government at Harvard University on a management leadership book titled *Collaborate or Perish: Reaching Across Boundaries in a Networked World* (Bratton & Tumin, 2012). However, Bratton reported that nothing compared to leading a police force. In his mid-60s, he let the 2013 New York mayoral candidates, who would be replacing three-term Mayor Michael Bloomberg, know that he was available to come back as their police commissioner. His announcement came when the NYPD experienced numerous critical reports for its overuse of stop-and-frisk strategies.

New York City Police Department – Commissioner (2014–2016)

In December 2013, Mayor-elect Bill de Blasio[103] announced he would appoint Bratton as the 42nd Police Commissioner of the NYPD, 18 years after he held the leadership position as the 38th commissioner. Ironically, Bratton succeeded Ray Kelly both times. Kelly was the 37th and 41st NYPD Police commissioner and served as commissioner for 14 years, longer than his predecessors. The selection of Bratton came in the aftermath of a mayoral campaign that promised to fix controversial policies of stop-and-frisk on the heels of a historic federal court ruling.

Bratton has consistently contended that all officers should understand two concepts and integrate them into their police operations: "apologize" and "explain" (Bratton & Knobler, 1998). He suggested that officers are far less likely to face criticism if they take action in the aftermath of controversial behavior, whether it was lawful or not. Historically, as previously outlined, the professional policing model downplayed the notion that officers should explain their actions to citizens or apologize for any perceived errors they made. Bratton saw this traditionalist approach as detrimental to police legitimacy and the well-being of

102 At age 43, Cameron was the youngest prime minister in two centuries (Hough, 2010).

103 De Blasio was the 109th Mayor of NYC and stands 6 foot 5 inches, the tallest mayor in the city's history.

police-community relations, particularly in urban settings (Schafer, 2013). The need to apologize certainly came about toward the end of the summer of 2013, when a federal judge ruled the use of stop-and-frisk by the NYPD was unconstitutional. Bratton needed to reform the nation's largest police agency, once again.

Stop-and-Frisk Ruled Unconstitutional – Summer 2013

In 2012, the Center for Constitutional Rights (CCR) brought a federal class-action lawsuit, *Floyd et al. v. City of New York et al.*, which challenged stop-and-frisk as racially biased inherently unconstitutional. Plaintiffs included David Floyd,[104] David Ourlicht, Lalit Clarkson, and Deon Dennis. These named plaintiffs represented thousands of Black and Latinos who alleged unconstitutional stop-and-frisk. Under Commissioner Kelly and billionaire Mayor Michael Bloomberg,[105] the number of stop-and-frisk incidents rose every year and reached record numbers – over 685,000 in 2011. The NYPD made the stop-and-frisk data transparent and provided demographics broken down by precinct, age, and race on its website. Quarterly reports, released to the New York Civil Liberty Union (NYCLU), showed a peak in 2011. Seventy of the 76 precincts indicated that African-Americans and Latinos accounted for more than half of the police stops. Moreover, 90+ percent of the police stops were in 33 precincts. Critics further contended there was no correlation between stop-and-frisk and crime; yet African-Americans and Latinos were more likely to be frisked than whites and were less likely to be found with a weapon. Lastly, 90 percent of people stopped received no punishment, and less than 2 percent had a weapon in their possession.

On August 12, 2013, following a nine-week trial, Judge Shira Scheindlin denied appeals from the police union and ruled the NYPD resorted to policies that equated to racial profiling. In a 195-page decision, the court determined that the NYPD increasingly used stops during periods of crime decline without regard to the Fourth Amendment (protection from unreasonable searches and seizures) or the Fourteenth Amendment (equal protection clause). The court used reports from the NYCLU to justify its opinion. Between 2004 and 2012, African-Americans and Hispanics made up about 83 percent of those stopped by the police while representing slightly more than half of the city's residents. The NYPD justified the disparity by stating the stops occurred more frequently in high-crime neighborhoods where young minority men disproportionately committed crime. Judge Scheindlin countered with data that the police released 90 percent of those stopped without an arrest or summons.

The legal framework for the NYPD stop-and-frisk tactics comes from the 1968 Supreme Court ruling *Terry v. Ohio*. In that decision, the Court held that stop-and-frisk was constitutional under certain conditions centered on officers having reasonable suspicion that the person had committed or was about to commit a crime. For officers' protection, the court allowed the police to perform a quick pat-down of a person's outer clothing for weapons if they had reasonable suspicion that the person stopped was armed. Justifying reasonable suspicion would need to be specific and articulated in subsequent written reports and not based upon officers' hunches.

104 On February 27, 2008, Floyd claimed that he attempted to help a basement tenant enter his apartment in a building owned by his godmother. The tenant and Floyd were in the process of finding the correct key when three NYPD officers stopped to question them on burglary suspicion. Officers indicated on their report that Floyd was not searched, and they were unaware of any quota expectations from their supervisors.

105 Bloomberg is ranked as the 9th richest person in the United States and 14th wealthiest individual in the world, with an estimated net worth of $58 billion. He held the NYC mayor position for three consecutive terms. In November 2019, Bloomberg apologized for his previous stop-and-frisk support, noting his administration's misguided policy inspired anti-police movements (Kenny, 2020).

Judge Scheindlin ruled the practice of stop-and-frisk by the NYPD was unconstitutional, and they went far beyond the intent of *Terry v. Ohio*. She ordered the precincts to develop a pilot program for body-worn cameras with the most stop-and-frisk incidents and the development of an independent monitor to ensure reform efforts. Following a national trend, prosecutors also announced they would no longer take minor marijuana cases. This reversal came from data that 70 percent of people arrested for marijuana had no prior convictions. Moreover, whites and minorities did not differ in marijuana use; yet more than 85 percent of New Yorkers arrested for marijuana were African-American or Hispanic.

On January 30, 2014, Mayor de Blasio, without consulting Bratton,[106] announced he would drop an appeal, filed by Mayor Bloomberg's corporate counsel, on Judge Scheindlin's federal court ruling that the NYPD's use of stop-and-frisk policies was unconstitutional. Bratton disagreed with dropping the appeal but was not consulted by Mayor de Blasio (Bratton & Knobler, 2021, pp. 15). Additionally, the federal court assigned an independent monitor and issued a 2016 report from the Inspector General's Office. That report found a lack of empirical evidence to demonstrate a link between increased summons and misdemeanor arrests with drops in felony crime. Nonetheless, broken windows policing remained a primary strategy for the NYPD.

Bratton's Redemptive Leadership

Under de Blasio, the city chose not to appeal Judge Scheindlin's ruling, and a joint remedial process to meet court recommendations was undertaken through Bratton. Bratton wanted to see the NYPD redeemed in the wake of the federal court ruling. Since the last time he was Commissioner, crime had declined 80 percent; yet some residents perceived officers acted like racist occupiers. While the reduction of stop-and-frisk incidents was a goal for both the mayor and the commissioner, Bratton was also quick to defend the operation of stop, question, and frisk. He asserted that every stop did not end with a frisk, and officers' ability to question people on the street was critical to their discretionary effectiveness. Stop and possibly frisk is the opposite of passive, reactive law enforcement that existed during the American crime waves from the 1960s to 1980s under the professionalization reform era when police leaders more tightly controlled discretion.

Bratton worked to maintain a good relationship with Mayor de Blasio, an earlier lesson from his first stint as NYPD Commissioner under Mayor Giuliani. However, unlike Giuliani, de Blasio was a liberal mayor who centered his campaign on ending what he perceived as discriminatory practices from the NYPD. De Blasio ran a campaign ad with his racially mixed son Dante declaring his dad would end stop-and-frisk. This stance did not endear him to the police rank and file. Bratton provided the mayor with support in lowering stop-and-frisk incidents so he could meet his campaign promises. In doing so, Bratton provided an analogy that the city was like cancer patients who are no longer sick. If New York had less crime (or cancer), the NYPD should no longer be pushing officers to provide high numbers of stop-and-frisk (or chemotherapy).

NYC in 1994 was utterly different from NYC in 2000. However, assertive tactics of broken windows policing, practiced through stop-and-frisk, continued to increase under Kelly's leadership rather than adjusted according to the significantly lower crime. Bratton connected with the new liberal mayor, noting that decreased crime was not necessarily associated with increased stop-and-frisk or arrests. If NYC was now one of the safest cities in the country, it should be policed as such and not with the same broken windows aggressive style of the 1990s

106 Author's interview with Bratton on November 4, 2020.

policing. A testament to Bratton's leadership was his recognition that crime is complex, and successful policing strategies can change.

As the new commissioner, in January 2014, Bratton again brought in Kelling as a consultant. They argued that, fundamentally, broken windows policing worked. As such, the theory should not be abandoned nor equated exclusively to zero-tolerance policing or stop-and-frisk (this argument is described in greater detail in the appendix under George Kelling). Kelling argued that broken windows policing is misunderstood by critics and supporters and, worse yet, misapplied by law enforcement leaders who attempted to replicate Bratton's success. Before his death in May 2019, Kelling lamented that police leaders should not utilize broken windows policing as a high-arrest and high-incarceration program. If done correctly, as pointed out in 1829 by Sir Robert Peel, the police should see their effectiveness through the absence of crime and disorder, not through more visible arrests and street harassment.

A 2013 report by the Brennan Center for Justice, through the Vera Institute of Justice, determined that broken windows policing reduced incarceration (Austin, Jacobson & Chettiar, 2013). More police should not equate to increased incarceration and if we want to impact crime, we should look towards hiring more police (see Cook & Ludwig, 2011), rather than being the only country that spends more on prisons than on the police (Cook & Ludwig, 2011). Under Bratton, the NYPD reduced contact through stop-and-frisk, and reduced incarceration even further. According to Kelling, broken windows policing should focus on illegal behavior, not just suspicious behavior, meaning the use of stop-and-frisk under Commissioner Kelly had run amuck. It went beyond the original intent of the broken windows theory (Kelling & Wilson, 1982). The new model required a precision-based balance between liberty interests, community concerns, and public order.

Critics of broken windows policing have argued that the strategy encourages officers to impose a rigid morality structure onto diverse populations. And affluent communities do not receive equal enforcement of this morality. In this vein, zero-tolerance policing has been linked to broken windows policing. Bratton and Kelling took issue with this linkage, arguing that broken windows policing encourages highly discretionary police activity that must be appropriately managed and supervised by police leaders. They saw zero-tolerance policing as part of the O.W. Wilson reform era that attempted to limit discretionary decision-making, while order-maintenance policing could only be done effectively through partnerships and the consent of those guarded by well-trained officers. Kelling links the proper use of order-maintenance policing with both community and POP but admits that some police leaders have not created the necessary linkage (Kelling, 2015a). As crime plummeted in NY and LA, there was less of a need for order-maintenance policing seen through stop-and-frisk. Consequently, Bratton was appointed for a second term as the NYPD police commissioner to redeem his beloved department and reduce stop-and-frisk incidents while still advocating that broken windows policing is an effective policing strategy.

Traditional criminologists and progressive politicians continue to target stop-and-frisk methods as racist. This criticism remains bonded to President Johnson's Great Society Program that asserts the root cause of crime is linked to societal racism and poverty. Consequently, the police can have little impact on crime other than reactive patrol tactics and attempting to clear cases. Kelling and Bratton asserted the opposite, believing their leadership demonstrated that the police do matter. If the police operate under constitutional guidelines, a democratic government's basic premise should be to protect public order and respect for the law. Bratton's second attempt at leading the NYPD was to succeed in both.

With the assistance of Kelling, Bratton replayed his past leadership success by distributing confidential surveys to the department and setting up close to 100 committees with middle-ranked officers instead of only top brass. The committees allowed him to more quickly identify leadership talent within the NYPD, while at the same time, he created important collaborative decision-making mechanisms. In addition to stop-and-frisk, Bratton knew the importance of terrorism prevention in all cities, especially in NY. Building on the counter-terrorism initiatives in LA, Bratton brought back John Miller, who was a deputy commissioner the first time Bratton led the NYPD and was his bureau chief with the LAPD.

John Miller

Bratton hired John Miller, age 55, to be his Deputy Commissioner of Intelligence and Counterterrorism. Showing his respect for Miller, Bratton stated he might not have accepted the position to lead the NYPD once again if Miller had not agreed to be his deputy commissioner. Miller was previously Bratton's DCPI during his first stint as NYPD Commissioner (1994–1995). He then became an *ABC News* correspondent in 1995 and became famous for interviewing Osama bin Laden in Afghanistan in 1998. Miller reported on the events of September 11, 2001 in NYC and became a co-anchor with Barbara Walters for *ABC News 20/20*. In January 2003, Bratton convinced Miller to leave his media position and become Bureau Chief of Counterterrorism and Criminal Intelligence with the LAPD. He also managed the department's Major Crimes Division, bomb squad, and hazardous materials unit. Based on his lessons as a journalist covering the causes of the 9/11 terrorist attacks, Miller led the LA Joint Regional Intelligence Center (JRIC) design that became a fusion center to combine intelligence gathered by the LAPD LA Sheriff's Office and the FBI. The organizational structure also allowed the department to conduct its first counterterrorism operations. In August 2005, Miller left the LAPD and became the Assistant Director of Public Affairs for FBI Director Robert Mueller, becoming the first non-agent to head up their public affairs office.

In December 2008, *Security* magazine published its third annual Top 25 Most Influential People in the Security Industry and listed Bill Bratton as number 6, thanks in no small part to John Miller and one of the most comprehensive counter-terrorism operations in the country. Bratton and Miller developed critical infrastructure advancements and communication with the private security industry through an operation called "Archangel" to defend and prevent terrorist attacks against likely targets. The operation created agency cooperation and coordination to effectively manage and apply strategic resources to prevent, deter, mitigate, and respond to critical incidents. In October 2011, Miller returned to the media and became a senior correspondent for *CBS News*, and two years later, he would be back working for the NYPD and Bratton. After Bratton retired from the NYPD, Miller remained as chief of intelligence and counter-terrorism. Despite his public views on calling President-elect Trump unfit for office, Bratton remained the Vice-Chair of the Homeland Security Advisory Council from 2011 to 2020. In August 2020, he was named chair, replacing William Webster.[107] During the 2020 protests, Bratton did not support President Trump's call for using the military against the demonstrators (Sozzi, 2020).

"Hands up- Don't Shoot" and "I Can't Breathe" – Brown, Garner, Floyd

NYPD Police officers murdered – Wenjian Liu and Rafael Ramos

Bratton compared the NYPD and CompStat to the engine of a car. Like any other engine, systems need to be tuned in order to operate efficiently. In this manner, the court challenge that questioned the constitutionality of stop-and-frisk operations demonstrated that the

107 Webster is the only person to direct both the FBI (1978–1987) and the CIA (1987–1991).

engine was not in tune with community expectations. CompStat accountability meetings changed in response, and precinct commanders trained rank and file officers to have quality stops over quota systems. Officers should have reasonable suspicion that can be articulated with evidence more substantial than just furtive movements. This retraining demonstrated Bratton's leadership to re-engineer existing police strategies instead of reinventing a new style of policing. Bratton and Kelling's re-engineering process quoted Sir Robert Peel's[108] principle of police effectiveness as measured by the absence of crime and disorder, not the police presence in dealing with it.

Only months into the retraining, a citizen police encounter rocked the NYPD and grabbed international headlines. At 3:30 in the afternoon on July 17, 2014, NYPD officers on Staten Island confronted Eric Garner, a 43-year-old Black man, in front of a convenience store at 202 Bay Street in Tompkinsville. Based on previous encounters, officers suspected Garner was selling untaxed individual cigarettes from packs.[109] Garner, who had been arrested more than thirty times, was part of a group that travelled to Virginia to buy cigarettes in mass quantity and then resell them so consumers could avoid the $5.85 tax Mayor Bloomberg had levied on New Yorkers. A pack of cigarettes for $11 was far more than what the men and women frequenting Tompkins Square were willing to pay. Garner told the police he was tired of being harassed, and he pulled away as they attempted to arrest him. Plainclothes Officer Daniel Pantaleo approached Garner from the back and put his arms around his neck, bringing him to the ground in what the NYPD would later say was a chokehold that went against departmental policy. Garner repeated the words "I can't breathe" 11 times as he laid face down on the sidewalk and then lost consciousness.[110] Officers then laid Garner on his side and called the ambulance, which took seven minutes to arrive. He was pronounced dead at the hospital an hour later. Bratton suspended Officer Pantaleo while the internal investigation commenced, which was a custom of the NYPD process while any criminal proceedings were adjudicated.

A few weeks later, on August 9, 2014, Michael Brown, an 18-year-old Black man, was fatally shot six times by white police officer Darren Wilson in Ferguson, Missouri. A Grand Jury refused to indict Officer Darren Wilson on November 24, 2014, and citizens protested, rioted, and looted the city for the next several days. Protests also erupted in NYC, and Bratton walked to Times Square to survey the demonstrations. On the evening of November 24, 2014, demonstrators splattered Bratton's suit with fake blood as New Yorkers protested Garner and Brown. Unlike Brown's shooting death, the Garner incident, July 17, 2014, was filmed on a cell phone by Garner's friend, Ramsey Orta,[111] who was present during the encounter. Orta also worked for *Copwatch* in the city and frequently tried to film encounters with residents and the NYPD. The medical examiner reported that Garner's death was a homicide caused by compression to the neck, asthma, heart disease, and obesity. Homicide is not a criminal charge the same way murder is and only states the cause of death came from others' intentional actions. Almost five months after the incident, and only weeks after the Grand Jury refused to indict Officer Wilson, a Grand Jury also declined to indict Officer Pantaleo. These failed

108 Peel is considered the father of modern British policing, ushering in the Metropolitan Police Act in 1829 and the reason British Police officers are called "bobbies." He served twice as the Home Secretary (1822–1827; 1828–1830) and twice as the Prime Minister (1834–1835; 1841–1846).

109 Officer Justin Damico admitted to inflating posthumously arrest papers that charged Garner with a felony tax charge and two misdemeanors for selling untaxed cigarettes and resisting arrest (Sisak, 2019).

110 The "I can't breathe" symbolism of what some members of the community have considered misuse of force was symbolically discussed in the Penny Harrington chapter when Marine Corp Vietnam Veteran Tony Stevenson died from a police chokehold on April 20, 1985 and in Minneapolis when George Floyd died from an officer's knee to the back of his neck on May 25, 2020.

111 In 2016, Orta was sentenced to four years in prison for weapons and drug charges.

indictments caused many demonstrations throughout the country that carried the "I can't breathe" logos for the Garner incident and "Hands up, don't shoot" for the Brown incident.

In December 2014, five days before Christmas, Ismaaiyl Abdullah Brinsley shot and seriously wounded his ex-girlfriend Shaneka Thompson in Baltimore. He telephoned family members, claiming the shooting was an accident and Thompson had attempted to stop him from committing suicide. Brinsley had been arrested twenty times prior (Bratton & Knobler, 2021) and knowing he would be arrested yet again, he chose a different path. He boarded a bus to NYC and posted on his Instagram page, "I'm putting Wings on Pigs Today … They Take 1 of Ours … Lets Take 2 of Theirs" (Clarke & French, 2017). Brinsley also called Thompson's mother to apologize for shooting her daughter and she subsequently contacted the Baltimore County Police about his Instagram post (Bratton & Knobler, 2021). The Baltimore County Police contacted the NYPD to alert them minutes before Brinsley fired four shots through a police car window at NYPD officers Rafael Ramos and Wenijian Liu[112] in Brooklyn's Bedford-Stuyvesant neighborhood.[113] Both later died at Woodhull Hospital. Brinsley then fled to a subway and committed suicide. The killings were ostensibly committed in protest of Garner and Brown.

The timing of Ramos and Liu's murders could not have been worse for Mayor de Blasio. He was locked in a contract dispute with the police union for better pay. New York is one of the only large cities that pays police officers the same wages as firefighters and street sanitation workers. Officers were also still reeling from Mayor Bloomberg's decision to move the power to prosecute civilian complaint cases away from internal NYPD attorneys to the Civilian Complaint Review Board and his decision to drop an appeal against the federal court ruling that ruled the NYPD's use of SQF was unconstitutional. Along with the national social justice protests over the deaths of Brown and Garner, the deaths of Ramos and Liu ignited a firestorm of officer emotions. On the evening the officers were fatally shot, the mayor held a press conference and the police union organized officers to turn their backs on de Blasio when he spoke. Union police leader Patrick Lynch denied it was an organized demonstration against the Mayor's perceived anti-police rhetoric, but Bratton thought otherwise. Although he refused to penalize the officers who protested the mayor, Bratton perceived their protest was disrespectful and not helpful. Many NYPD officers were further infuriated when, in July 2015, the city announced a settlement of close to $6 million with the Garner family (Taibbi, 2017). Officers would continue to turn their backs on Mayor de Blasio when he spoke at future funerals of slain officers.

Bratton responded to Garner's death by announcing an end to his predecessor's practice of sending officers right out of the academy to the hot spots for crime. Instead, new police officers received more extended training and gradual transition with varied shifts. Additionally, all officers received training on speaking politely to the public and using at least three officers to takedown suspects who resist arrest. In July 2019, four and half years later, Attorney

112 After presenting a eulogy at the funeral for Officer Ramos in Queens, Vice President Joe Biden and his wife Jill made an unplanned visit to meet Officer Liu's parents. Officer Liu's wife helped translate Biden's conversation with her in-laws. Biden made a connection with Wei Tang, Officer Liu's father, sharing his pain about losing a loved one. Biden's first wife, Neilia and his infant daughter Naomi were killed in a car accident on December 18, 1972, shortly after his election to Congress. A few months after Liu's murder, Biden lost his son Beau to brain cancer and was touched when Officer Liu's father arrived at the wake, as reflected upon in Biden's book *Promise Me, Dad* (Biden, 2017). Two and half years after Liu's murder, his wife gave birth to their daughter after being artificially inseminated (Celona, 2017).

113 A similar unprovoked incident occurred on September 12, 2020. Provoked by George Floyd's in-custody death in May 2020 in Minneapolis, 36-year-old Deonte Murray ambushed 31-year-old LA County Deputy Claudia Apolinar and her 24-year-old male partner. Both survived after being shot in the face and head as they sat in their police vehicle in Compton. Murray was arrested three days after the ambush on an earlier carjacking case.

General William Barr announced the DOJ would not bring charges against any of the officers involved in the Garner case. A month later, after an NYPD internal investigation concluded, Commissioner James "Jimmy" O'Neil terminated Pantaleo. Pantaleo filed a subsequent lawsuit against the NYPD, alleging his dismissal was arbitrary and capacious. In March 2021, he lost his lawsuit to get his job back. Ultimately, Bratton does not believe that Officer Pantaleo intended to kill Garner but within the struggle to apprehend him, did apply a chokehold that was against departmental policy. His perception of George Floyd, however, was that he was murdered.

On May 25, 2020, George Floyd, a Black man, died at the age of 46 in Minneapolis while in handcuffs lying face down on a city street while Officer Derek Chauvin, a white man, pushed his left knee on to the right side of Floyd's neck for nearly nine minutes. During the last three minutes, Floyd was unresponsive and citizens, with their cell phone cameras recording, pleaded for officer Chauvin and three other officers to get him medical assistance. Like Garner six years prior, an independent autopsy report ruled Floyd's death was a homicide brought on by asphyxiation. However, unlike Floyd, in the Garner case the Grand Jury deliberated for two months and chose not to indict. In the Floyd case, Chief Medaria Arradondo, Minneapolis's first Black chief, terminated all four officers. The chief had Chauvin arrested, and prosecutors charged him with murder. Over the next several months, mass protests and riots broke out in all 50 states and internationally. In about half the states and Washington, DC, Governors activated their state National Guard to quell mass police protests for the first time since the 1992 riots in LA. During the 2020 protests, Bratton served as a senior law enforcement analyst for MNBC. He perceived the symbolism of police solidarity with the demonstrators as helpful in changing perceptions of legitimacy. However, he warned that New York officers laying down their arms and taking a knee in memory of Floyd was potentially misguided in the face of agitators and anarchists who were purposely looting and inciting violent encounters with the police.[114]

On April 20, 2021, a jury deliberated for ten hours and found Chauvin guilty on all three counts of murder. This was the first time a white officer was found guilty of murdering a Black citizen in Minnesota. A month prior, the Minneapolis City Council unanimously approved a $27 million wrongful death lawsuit settlement with George Floyd's family, the largest pretrial civil rights settlement in US history, subsequently signed by Mayor Jacob Frey (Hauck, Hayes, & Yancey-Bragg, 2021).

Leaving the NYPD Again

At the end of 2015, several private companies recruited Bratton. On March 3, 2016, his father passed away, and he began to feel the need to provide more financial assistance to his family. In May 2016, Bratton took a trip to Italy, and by June, he had decided to resign. On September 16, 2016, Bratton officially resigned a second time as the commissioner of the NYPD and was replaced by insider O'Neil, an officer with the NYPD since 1983 with the transit police. A week later, Bratton received the Woodrow Wilson Award for Public Service and fulfilled his promise by significantly reducing stop-and-frisk from 600,000+ incidents in 2011 to only 12,000 in 2016,[115] a 98 percent drop. Crime still declined. The New York City Civil Liberties Union (NYCLU) publishes this data annually. While Mayor

114 In October 2020, an op-ed in *City & State* called for Bill Bratton's return to help lower surging crime and police brutality in New York amid the pandemic and mass protests (Allon, 2020). In May 2019, an op-ed from the *Boston Herald* asked for Bratton to return to lead the BPD (Lucas, 2019).

115 See www.nyclu.org/en/stop-and-frisk-data.

de Blasio and the NYPD remained supportive of broken windows policing, they significantly reduced misdemeanor arrests. With lowered residential confrontations and reduced crime, strategies shifted to improving quality interactions and increased de-escalation training. O'Neil continued to emphasize Bratton's NY version of precision policing, which included neighborhood policing that incentivized officers to first make people safe and then community relations would improve as an outgrowth. On November 4, 2019, O'Neil also resigned to take advantage of offers from the private sector. Dermot Shea, chief of detectives, became the 44th NYPD Commissioner in December 2019, to the consternation of many Black leaders in NYC who wanted to see Deputy Commissioner Benjamin Tucker appointed. Note: Two African-American Police Commissioners have led the NYPD in the past: Ben Ward (1984–1989) and Lee Brown (1990–1992).

Final Lessons – Raise the Expectations for Police Departments

Throughout his 50-year career in law enforcement, Bratton's leadership style defied the belief held by many police leaders and criminologists that the police don't impact crime. Like other police leaders discussed in this book, at his core, Bratton is a criminology student, but as a police leader, he subscribed to the belief that crime and corruption is a management problem, not a sociological problem. Sociological explanations have traditionally argued that the causes of crime are linked to demographic shifts, economic conditions, and various social trends, all beyond police managers' purview. Bratton takes issue with these conclusions, arguing that most street-level crime is very disorganized and opportunistic. He argues that the police have a discreet advantage over most criminals due to advanced equipment, training, and strategic planning.

While past studies have failed to link increases in police resources to reductions in crime, Bratton takes issue with the assumption that all police work is done with the same intensity level or agreed upon evidence-based practices. Criminologists have often based their research on traditional reactive models of police leadership. Bratton argues that his contemporary leadership style has broken the mold of the professionalization reform era.

The traditional reactive policing models stemmed from early reform police leaders' work described earlier with Teddy Roosevelt and O.W. Wilson. Their reform leadership was further institutionalized in the aftermath of the 1967 Presidential Commission, *The Challenge of Crime in a Free Society* and the 1968 Kerner Commission Report, discussed more fully in the proceeding appendix. The commission's central assumption was that crime stemmed from macro-level structural causes such as poverty and racism. Consequently, they recommended resources to prepare youth for employment, improve schools and housing, eliminate employment and housing discrimination, and provide minimal family incomes. The problem was that both reports did not include the police in the solutions and concluding perspectives were that the police did not really impact crime.

Since the justice system cannot impact these macro-level societal causes of crime, they are forced to only reactively process offenders without long-term prevention considerations. Conservative politics too often argued the country needed to restore family values through a crime control model and further pushed a reactive law and order approach. The aftermath has been a five-decade era of massive criminal justice expansion and the largest prison population the world has ever seen. Within this structure, communities stuck in high-crime neighborhoods expect the police to patrol, but in a way that's not overly intrusive or confrontational. The primary responsibility is to respond to serious crime quickly. Minor offenses are essentially decriminalized or seen as a second priority. In the 2021 defunding and decriminalization movement, Bratton argued we are making a mistake by repeating history during a time period when violent crime increased. New York City experienced a 44 percent increase in murders in 2020 compared to 2019 and a 53 percent increase in shootings. There were nearly 2,000 more murders in the United States in 2020 (8,077) compared to 2019 (6,087). Bratton sees the defunding movement as contradictory and foolish given these increases (Campanile, 2021). This version of the reform movement also demonstrates a lack of understanding what was accomplished when Bratton's leadership team focused on partnerships, problem-solving, and place-based criminology (the three p's of policing) that diverted strategies away from traditional reactive law enforcement.

Under the reactive professional model, when the police intervene in reaction to a call for service, dispatch considers patrol "out of service." Police are considered "in service" when providing random and, as assumed, preventative patrol. As Kelling (2019) points out, most departments still operate within the archaic "professionalization" structure. This narrowed view sees the police simplistically as the front end of a mechanism that feeds the rest of the criminal justice system, often through discriminatory practices.

Early police reform leaders were able to confront police corruption problems that plagued policing nationally. However, later research challenged assumptions that the narrowed role of patrol engaged in random preventative patrol impacted crime (see Kansas City Preventative Patrol Experiment, Kelling, Pate, Dieckman, & Brown, 1974, discussed in the proceeding appendix). Wilson (1978) drew a different conclusion, arguing *what* the police did was more important than the amount of patrol rubber on the road. Indeed, research on hot spot policing (Braga, 2002; Eck, 2002; Weisburd & Eck, 2004) has indicated that patrol focused on particular individuals and locations can impact crime. Consequently, giving officers analytical data about spatial and temporal crime trends is much more important than how fast they arrive at a call for service and more in line with Peel's nine principles for effective policing. Bratton sees defunding police budgets, and moving resources towards other government services, as misguided, dangerous, and not understanding of the prevention principles of the Peelian policing mission.

Bratton's leadership focused on reform-minded lessons of accountability driven by Teddy Roosevelt and O.W. Wilson to confront serious urban crime problems and the largest corruption scandals in our country's history. He also created a paradigm shift with lessons from research that challenged reactive law enforcement's realities and encouraged focused discretionary decision-making. In doing so, expectations shifted from random patrol duties to tactical directives that included both enforcement strategies and preventative tactics. In this modern era of police leadership, Bratton argues that officers should have timely and accurate data in addition to certain levels of freedom in deciding how to respond to the data. The challenge for Bratton was to remove past constraints placed on officers that impeded their creative problem-solving capabilities while at the same time not losing the necessary discipline to manage improper behavior. While having a critical mass of police officers available to do the job will always be important, decisions on officers' deployment and the information they receive for their deployment are crucial. Lastly, officers' understanding of their role expectations is most important. Ambitious expectations for that role, according to Bratton, will always be the engine for reform leading to significant crime/disorder reduction.

In the aftermath of the federal court ruling that challenged zero-tolerance interpretations of broken windows policing, Bratton's ambitions with reforming the NYPD refocused on the importance of police legitimacy. According to the National Research Council's Committee to Review Research on Police Policy and Practices, police practice evaluations should measure the impact on crime control and police legitimacy perceptions (Skogan & Frydl, 2004). As a result, the NYPD reduced its use of stop-and-frisk and refocused its efforts on public trust and confidence in police services. A shift toward precision policing[116] was a valuable way to manage procedural justice (see Tyler & Wakslak, 2004), noting that public perception of fairness impacts the police. In doing so, Bratton and the NYPD reduced future lawsuits to refocus on developing and repairing partnerships.

Tipping Point Leadership

Bratton is a transformational leader. He successfully re-engineered police departments seven times. Kim and Mauborgne[117] (2004) described Bratton's style as tipping point leadership and identified four strategies he took:

1 Bratton **broke through the cognitive hurdle** by creating stakeholders with his command staff through CompStat accountability meetings, but he also required his management team to spend time in the field. For example, once command staff from the transit police rode the subway, they saw first-hand the problems with turnstile jumpers, youth gangs, and aggressive panhandlers. These experiences allowed the team to embrace creative problem-solving equally.
2 Bratton **sidestepped the status quo resource hurdle**. Past leaders reduced their ambitions due to naysayers, dooming their agency to mediocrity, or they spent a considerable amount of time fighting for more resources. Each of these approaches takes the leader's attention away from real problems. For most police leaders, problems can be found with prolific offenders and hot spot locations. Bratton followed the research through CompStat and "putting cops on the dots" to focus on his resources. This strategy was referred to as precision-policing during his time as Police Commissioner (Bratton & Murad, 2018).
3 Bratton **jumped the motivational hurdle** by focusing on vital influential people to become key change agents. As the leader of very large organizations, Bratton recognized he wouldn't reform everyone and everything. However, he could be persuasive with the kingpins, and they would become the tipping point. Tipping point leadership indicated that if the right leaders were persuaded to become change agent champions, you could tip them, and they would, in turn, topple all the other pins. For Bratton, his kingpins were key commanders in charge of precincts held accountable through the CompStat meetings. Once the creation of high-performance expectations impacts the culture, change agents are empowered, and reform trickles down through the ranks.
4 Bratton **knocked over political hurdles** that inevitably resisted change. Often naysayers are silenced after they are put on respected teams or committees and given some additional responsibility. For example, John Timoney was Bratton's main competition to lead both the NYC and LA police departments. As commissioner, Bratton named Timoney as his number two since he knew several of the most charismatic managers in both

116 Precision policing was a response to overmedicating cities with too many stop-question-frisk (SQF) incidents. The new mission was to improve quality over quantity. This approach is not systematized like CompStat or theoretical like broken windows, or operationalized like community-policing strategies. Instead, precision policing seeks out shared responsibilities between the police and community leaders to identify the small percentage of violent offenders doing the most damage (See Bratton & Murad, 2018).

117 The Kim and Mauborgne (2004) article on "tipping point leadership" came after Renee Mauborgne randomly met Bratton at the airport and he had a copy of the book *Turnaround: How America's Top Cop Reversed the Crime Epidemic* (1998) – author's interview with Bratton on November 3, 2020. Their book *Blue Ocean Strategy* (2004) has become one of the most sold leadership books globally (see Kim & Mauborgne, 2004; 2013; 2017).

departments and could assist Bratton in navigating those who would attempt to sabotage transformation efforts.

Bratton took a public health approach to policing and saw analogies to treating a traumatized patient. Medical treatment choices will almost always have side effects and may be painful, but eventually, the pain subsides, and the patient improves. Unlike his predecessors, Bratton recognized the need to withdraw the medicine at a certain point. In this way, Bratton believes that his style of utilizing broken windows policing matches with Sir Robert Peel's nine principles of policing:

1 To prevent crime and disorder, as an alternative to their repression by military force and severity of legal punishment.
2 To recognize always that the power of the police to fulfill their functions and duties is dependent on public approval of their existence, actions and behavior, and on their ability to secure and maintain public respect.
3 To recognize always that to secure and maintain the respect and approval of the public means also the securing of the willing cooperation of the public in the task of securing observance of laws.
4 To recognize always that the extent to which the cooperation of the public can be secured diminishes proportionately the necessity of the use of physical force and compulsion for achieving police objectives.
5 To seek and preserve public favor, not by pandering to public opinion, but by constantly demonstrating absolute impartial service to law, in complete independence of policy, and without regard to the justice or injustice of the substance of individual laws, by ready offering of individual service and friendship to all the members of the public without regard to their wealth or social standing, by ready exercise of courtesy and friendly good humor, and by ready offering of individual sacrifice in protecting and preserving life.
6 To use physical force only when the exercise of persuasion, advice, and warning is found to be insufficient to obtain public cooperation to an extent necessary to secure observance of law or to restore order, and to use only the minimum degree of physical force which is necessary on any particular occasion for achieving a police objective.
7 To maintain at all times a relationship with the public that gives reality to the historic tradition that the police are the public and that the public are the police, the police being only the members of the public who are paid to give full-time attention to duties which are incumbent on every citizen in the interests of community welfare and existence.
8 To recognize always the need for strict adherence to police-executive functions, refrain from even seeming to usurp the powers of the judiciary of avenging individuals or the State, and authoritatively judging guilt and punishing the guilty.
9 To recognize always that the test of police efficiency is the absence of crime and disorder and not the visible evidence of police action in dealing with them.

NOTE: In actuality, Peel did not directly write these nine principles for modern policing, and he was wrongfully quoted throughout several textbooks. Indeed, Peel would not have objected to the more expansive interpretations, but the actual nine principles were traced to a 1948 book on British policing (Reith, 1948). The nine principles served as an expansion to the original 1829 "Instructions to Police Officers" written collaboratively by Peel with his first police commissioners: Charles Rowan and Richard Mayne (Peel, Rowan, & Mayne, 1829). They initially provided five main principles:

1 Prevention of crime: "The principal object to be attained is 'the prevention of Crime.' To this great end, every effort of the Police is to be directed [rather] than by the detection and punishment of the offender, after he has succeeded in committing the crime … When in any Division offenses are frequently committed, there must be reason to suspect that the Police are not in the Division properly conducted. The absence of crime will be considered the best proof of the complete efficiency of the Police."
2 Know your beat: "It is indispensably necessary, that he should make himself perfectly acquainted with all the parts of his beat or section, with the streets, thoroughfares, courts, and houses. He will be expected to possess such a knowledge of the inhabitants of each house, as will enable him to recognize their persons … He should be able to see every part of his beat, at least once in ten minutes or a quarter of an hour; and this he will be expected to do."
3 Maintain order: "In watching the conduct of loose and disorderly persons, and of all persons whose behavior is such as to excite just suspicion, he will keep in mind that the prevention of crime, one great object of all their exertions, will be best attained by making it evident, that they are known and strictly watched, and that certain detection will follow any attempt to commit a crime."
4 Use common sense and discretion: "The following General Instructions … are not to be understood as containing rules of conduct applicable to every variety of circumstances that may occur in the performance of their duty; something must necessarily be left to the intelligence and discretion of individuals."
5 Be polite and control your temper: "He will be civil and attentive to all persons, of every rank and class; insolence or incivility will not be passed over … There is no qualification more indispensable to a Police Officer than a perfect command of temper, never suffering himself to be moved in the slightest degree, by any language or threats that may be used; if he does his Duty in a quiet and determined manner, such conduct will probably induce well-disposed by-standers to assist him, should he require it."

These foundational principles, regardless of the origination, have served Bratton well throughout his career. His tenure within a multitude of small and large agencies provided Bratton with a unique lens for the practice of transitional leadership in policing. His impact on the field has been more extensive than any other.

A listing of past and current leaders in the BPD, NYPD, and LAPD is provided in Tables 5.1–5.3, respectively.

Table 5.1 Boston Police Department Commissioners

Years	*Name*
1878–1880	Henry Russell[i]
1894–1899	Augustus Martin[ii]
1906–1918	Stephen O'Meara[iii]
1918–1922	Edwin Curtis[iv]
1922–1930	Herbert Wilson

i Russell was also the first commissioner of the Boston Fire Department.
ii Martin was elected 30th Mayor of Boston (1884–1885) before becoming police commissioner.
iii O'Meara was the first commissioner also to be an editor for *The Boston Journal*.
iv Curtis was elected 34th Mayor of Boston (1895–1896) before becoming police commissioner. As commissioner, he refused to recognize the police union and provoked the 1919 Boston Police Strike (Russell, 2005).

Table 5.1 Cont.

Years	*Name*
1930–1934	Eugene Hultman
1934–1935	Joseph Leonard[v]
1935–1936	Eugene McSweeney
1936–1943	Joseph Timilty[vi]
1943–1957	Thomas Sullivan
1957–1962	Leo Sullivan[vii]
1962–1972	Edmund McNamara[viii]
1972–1976	Robert di Grazia
1976–1985	Joseph Jordan
1985–1993	Francis Roache[ix]
1993–1994	**Bill Bratton**
1994–2003	Paul Evans[x]
2004–2006	Kathleen O'Toole[xi]
2006–2013	Ed Davis[xii]
2014–2018	Bill Evans[xiii]
2018–2021	Bill Gross[xiv]
2021–	Dennis White[xv]

Table 5.2 represents the modern era NYC police commissioners not listed at the end of the chapter on Roosevelt.

v Leonard was BPD Police commissioner for only a couple of months, the shortest tenure in BPD history. He was appointed by Governor Joseph Ely, who chaired the Boston Finance Commission, but was challenged by his predecessor, Frank Goodwin. Leonard resigned rather than deal with the pending court battle.

vi Timilty was chief during the November 28, 1942, Cocoanut nightclub fire, killing 492 individuals, the second deadliest in American history. Timilty resigned in the aftermath of indictments, which a judge quashed, related to allowing gambling establishments.

vii Sullivan was a state senator from 1941 to 1947. He resigned as police commissioner after Governor John Volpe brought him up on corruption charges.

viii McNamara was drafted into the NFL, but his football career was cut short by his service with the Navy in WWII. He was an FBI agent before he joined the BPD.

ix Roache served on the Boston City Council for several years after he retired. He died in 2018 at the age of 82.

x Evans joined the BPD in 1970 with the same starting class as Bratton. From 2003 to 2007 he worked in Britain's Home Office Police Standards Unit to help assess British police departments' performance.

xi O'Toole became the first female BPD Police Commissioner. She left the BPD and moved to Ireland to become the Chief Inspector of the Garda Inspectorate. O'Toole returned to the United States and was the Seattle Police Chief from 2014 to 2017.

xii Davis went through the Lowell Police Department ranks (1978–2006) before taking over the BPD. He was Commissioner during the Boston Marathon Bombing on April 15, 2013, before his resignation.

xiii Evans was instrumental in being the command officer that led to the capture of Dzhokhar Tsarnaev, who committed the Boston Marathon bombing with his brother Tamerian Tsarnaev. As a firefight erupted, Evans ordered his officers to hold their fire so they could take Tsarnaev alive through the FBI negotiation team (McPhee, 2017). Evans left the BPD and became chief of police at Boston College in 2018.

xiv Gross became the first Black Commissioner of the BPD. He announced his retirement in January 2021 after Boston Mayor Marty Walsh was nominated to be President Biden's labor secretary.

xv White became the second Black Commissioner of the BPD on February 1, 2021. Two days later, he was placed on leave pending a city investigation into a 1999 domestic violence incident. His daughter called her mother's, White's ex-wife, allegations concerning domestic violence a lie (Carraggle, 2021). The National Organization of Black Law Enforcement Executives (NOBLE) called for White's reinstatement. In June, 2021, acting mayor Kim Janey, Boston's first female and first Black mayor, terminated White.

Table 5.2 New York City Police Commissioners 1966–2020

Years	*Name*
1966–1970	Howard Leary
1970–1973	Patrick Murphy[i]
1974–1978	Michael Codd
1978–1983	Robert McGuire
1984–1989	Benjamin Ward[ii]
1990–1992	Lee Brown[iii]
1992–1994 & 2002–2014	Ray Kelly[iv]
1994–1996 & 2014–2016	**Bill Bratton**
1996–2000	Howard Safir
2000–2002	Bernie Kerik
2016–2019	James O'Neil
2019–	Dermot Shea

Table 5.3 lists LAPD police chiefs. Since 1969, there have been only six chiefs, compared to a six-year span in the 1920s when the LAPD went through eight chiefs, with an average of less than one year in office. Several footnotes attempt to draw in the history of the LAPD and chiefs, including August Vollmer's one-year experiment (1923–1924) and Bill Bratton's more extended seven-year commitment as a genuine reform chief (2002–2009).

Table 5.3 Los Angeles Police Department Chiefs

Years	*Name*
1865–1870	William Warren[i]
1876–1877	Jacob Gerkens[ii]

i Murphy (no known relation to the prior two Murphys who led the NYPD in 1901 and 1950) led the following police agencies: NYPD, Detroit, Washington DC, and Syracuse. He helped create the PERF in 1975 and was the President of the Police Foundation, which pushed for reform in the use of deadly force and more efficient use of police resources, including the hiring/promotion of women and minorities. Murphy is also mentioned in the appendix to the Wilson chapter under Goldstein.

ii Ward became the first Black Commissioner of the NYPD.

iii Brown was also discussed in the chapter on Harrington. He began his policing career in San Jose, California, in 1960 while he completed his bachelor's degree in criminology from Fresno State University. Ten years later, he earned his master's and Ph.D. degrees from the University of California, Berkeley, and became a professor at Portland State University, where he met Penny Harrington. In 1974, Brown became Sheriff of Multnomah County, Oregon. From 1982 to 1990, he was the first Black Chief of the Houston PD before becoming NYPD Commissioner. Although Brown did not reveal it at the time, he resigned as NYPD Commissioner and returned to Houston to be with his wife, Yvonne, who was dying of cancer. From 1993 to 1996, he was President Clinton's drug czar, and from 1998 to 2004, he was Houston's first Black mayor. Brown was also one of the founders of the NOBLE. See https://noblenational.org/.

iv Kelly was the first deputy commissioner when Brown resigned as NYPD Commissioner. Kelly served out the five-year term and became the longest-serving commissioner and the only individual to rise from NYPD police cadet to become commissioner twice. He served as the 37th and 41st Police Commissioner of the NYPD (Kelly, 2016).

i Warren was elected town marshal in 1865 and informally given the title Police Chief in 1869 as the leader of his six-man department. He also served as the town's dog catcher and collected a percentage of any taxes collected. Officer Joseph Dye killed Warren after a lengthy feud escalated to a fatal gun battle between the two men. Warren is the only LAPD marshal/chief to be killed on duty (Bultema, 2013).

ii Gerkens was a member of the city council and the first officially paid chief. He designed uniforms for his 13-man department, spent one year as chief, two years as assistant chief, and then retired.

Table 5.3 Cont.

Years	*Name*
1876–1877	Emil Harris[iii]
1878–1880 & 1881–1883	Henry King
1880–1881	George Gard[iv]
1883–1885 and 1888	Thomas Cuddy[v]
1885–1885	John Horner
1885–1886	James Davis
1886–1887	John Skinner
1887–1888	P.M. Darcy
1888–1888	Lester Grant (L.G.) Loomis[vi]
1888–1889	Hubert Benedict
1889–1889	Terrence Cooney
1889–1900	John Glass[vii]
1900–1904	Charles Elton
1904–1905	William Hammell
1905–1906	Walter Auble[viii]
1906–1909	Edward Kern[ix]
1909–1909	Thomas Broadhead
1909–1910	Edward Dishman
1910–1910	Alexander Galloway
1911–1915	Charles Sebastian[x]
1915–1916	Clarence Snively[xi]

iii Harris was one of the original six officers and the only Jewish police chief for the LAPD.

iv Gard, along with Hammel (1904–1905), served as police chief and LA County Sheriff.

v Cuddy was forced to resign on bribery charges and also served a six-month sentence on a contempt of court charge.

vi Loomis was wrongly labeled as chief for 25 days. He was not actually the chief. In 1887, six months after he became patrolman, Loomis was promoted, with another officer, to become LAPD's first sergeants. In 1888, he received another promotion to be a captain since lieutenant positions did not exist. As stated in the previous footnote, Cuddy resigned as chief, and Mayor Henry Workman subsequently instructed Captain Loomis to carry on the daily operations. However, he never "officially" made him chief. Workman then appointed Benedict as the new chief. However, newly elected Mayor John Bryson appointed his chief, Cooney, who lasted three months. In December 1888, Loomis was demoted back to patrol. Bryson's tenure as mayor would be even shorter than Cooney, 2 ½ months, because of a city charter change. However, Bryson did manage to appoint six of his sons to the 80-man LAPD force. The new mayor, Henry Hazard, appointed James Burns to replace Cooney, but the city council voted against his selection. Hazard then appointed Glass. Through the confusion, both Burns and Glass reported for a few days as LAPD chiefs (Taylor, 2017). Glass eventually provided a momentous change, stability, and professionalism throughout his decade as chief.

vii Glass hired Robert Stewart, LA's first Black patrol officer.

viii Auble was fatally shot in the line of duty by a burglary suspect two years after he was chief while he was a captain. He was the third LAPD officer killed while on duty.

ix In 1908, Kern served as the President of the IACP and brought the international conference to the West Coast in LA. In April 1912, after several battles with alcoholism, Kern committed suicide with his firearm.

x Sebastian became the first patrol officer to become police chief and then Mayor of LA (30th Mayor 1915–1916) due to his popularity in fighting vice crimes. As chief, he saw drunkenness as a disease, not a crime, and he deferred homeless drunks to a Municipal Farm rather than a jail. Crops were grown at the farm to help feed jail inmates. He was the first to use a patrol wagon as an ambulance and facilitate the state to pass laws to relegate speeding and automobile registration to track ownership. Unfortunately, while he was mayor, his professional reputation was tainted when his wife shared letters he wrote to his mistress with the press, who published his affair's details. He died in 1929 at the age of 56 from a previous stroke while living with his mistress in Venice (Bultema, 2013).

xi Snively, a newspaper reporter without law enforcement experience, created an anti-cigarette campaign ordering his officers not to smoke and set a good example for juveniles. At the time, Snively believed cigarette smoking caused weak bodies, weak intellect and created delinquency.

Table 5.3 Cont.

Years	*Name*
1916–1919	John Butler[xii]
1919–1920	George Home
1920–1920	Alexander Murray[xiii]
1920–1921	Lyle Pendegast[xiv]
1921–1922	Charles Jones[xv]
1922–1922	James Everington[xvi]
1922–1923	Louis Oaks[xvii]
1923–1924	**August Vollmer**[xviii]
1924–1926	R. Lee Heath
1926–1929 & 1933–1938	James Davis[xix]
1929–1933	Roy Steckel
1938–1939	David Davidson
1939–1941	Arthur Hohmann
1941–1949	Clemence Horrall
1949–1950	William Worton
1950–1966	Bill Parker
1966–1967	Thad Brown
1967–1969	Tom Reddin
1969–1978	Ed Davis
1978–1992	Daryl Gates[xx]
1992–1997	Willie Williams

xii Butler was the first to recruit civilians to help manage administrative functions actively. By 1958, 25 percent of LAPD employees were civilians. More than 2,600 civilians support the LAPD today.

xiii Murray was chief for the month of October 1920.

xiv Pendegast was a city prosecutor before being appointed chief. He attempted to create a merit hiring/promotion system and reform the department. Eight months later, with Mayor George Cryer's election, whom political boss Kent Parrot controlled, he was replaced.

xv Jones was a detective sergeant when he was named chief. Putting a lower-ranked officer in charge of the department was advantageous for newly elected mayors. It meant the new chief did not owe anyone for past promotions and the new chief could be loyal to the mayor alone (Bultema, 2013). However, after six months of frustration, Jones resigned.

xvi Everington was a retired army colonel with no law enforcement experience. As one of three chiefs in 1922, he famously stated an honest man could not be LAPD chief. After four months of intense attempts at reform, he was fired, and the department would avoid civilian chief appointments for the next 25 years.

xvii Mayor Cryer appointed detective Oaks at the age of 40. He is mentioned in the Vollmer chapter.

xviii Vollmer produced monumental reform in the LAPD in just one year. He convinced city hall to fund the hiring of 250 additional officers, instituted a 90-training program that would evolve into the LAPD Police Academy, and received hefty raises for officer salaries. Vollmer also hired a crime analyzer and initiated an intelligence test to remove incompetent officers and only hire those with certain levels of intellect. Officers who scored highest were put into a specialized unit, known as the "crime crushers" and sent to hot spot locations based upon his analyzer. When Vollmer's reform year was up, a billboard in the city announced the return of political corruption and vice with the proclamation "THE FIRST OF SEPTEMBER WILL BE THE LAST OF AUGUST" (Bultema, 2013).

xix Davis discharged 245 officers for misconduct, one-fifth of the force during the Prohibition Era. He received Vollmer's written support but was demoted with Mayor John Porter's election, who had links to the Ku Klux Klan (Bultema, 2013). Mayor Frank Shaw brought Davis back as chief but would be linked to significant corruption and became the first mayor of a major city recalled by voters. During this period of the Great Depression, employment and promotions were all for sale. Thousands of citizens carried symbolic badges that allowed them a free pass as an award for Mayor Shaw's supporters. Davis's Lieutenant William Parker (future long-term chief) helped amend a city charter to insulate the chief's job from the mayor's political wills so the chief could not be arbitrarily removed without a full commission hearing. The charter change would substantially impact the LAPD's future, so the mayor's office would not completely control future chiefs.

xx See Gates (1992).

Table 5.3 Cont.

Years	*Name*
1997–2002	Bernard Parks
2002–2009	**Bill Bratton**
2009–2018	Charlie Beck
2018–	Michael Moore

Appendix – George Kelling

George Lee Kelling was born on August 21, 1935, in Milwaukee[118] to George and Mathilda (Benn) Kelling. He grew up on the Northwest side in a predominant tight-knit German neighborhood with what sociologists would call high collective efficacy.[119] Kelling's father was a firefighter, and his mother worked in a factory. Residents walked to neighborhood stores, taverns, and restaurants while they formed relationships with one another. His family then moved further north into a neighborhood zoned for single-family housing, making it more difficult for families to walk to local businesses. As the populous used their vehicles more frequently, out of necessity, neighborhood closeness waned. The causes of community detachment became important lessons for Kelling as he entered his post-secondary education and subsequent work as an academic.

Kelling attended Saint Olaf College[120] in Northfield, Minnesota, where he earned his bachelor's degree in philosophy in 1956. He then attended Northwestern Lutheran Theological Seminary in Saint Paul, MN, for two years. From 1956 to 1965, Kelling worked as a child-care counselor and Hennepin County probation officer (before the *In re Gault*[121] decision), as an assistant superintendent of county detention services in Milwaukee, and headed a residential treatment center for disturbed youth in Lino Lakes, Minnesota. In 1962 he received a Master's degree in Social Work at the University of Wisconsin-Milwaukee, where he subsequently taught in the School of Social Welfare from 1965 to 1970. He completed a Ph.D. in social welfare at the University of Wisconsin-Madison in 1973.

During this period, Kelling was married to Sally Jean Mosiman, and they had two children, George and Kristin. They divorced in 1974, and he married Catherine Coles in 1982, an urban anthropologist and Africanist, and a lawyer. Coles taught at Dartmouth College and later was a research associate at the Kennedy School of Government at Harvard University. Kelling lived in Hanover, New Hampshire, and died at 83 years of age on May 15, 2019, of congestive heart failure and melanoma.

118 Kelling published *Policing in Milwaukee: A Strategic History* (2015) as part of the Urban Life Series (Kelling, 2015b).

119 Sociologists have used the term *collective efficacy* to explain how crime is less likely to occur in urban neighborhoods when community members share values, trust one another, know one another on a first name basis, and are willing to intervene to prevent violence and crime (Sampson, Raudenbush, & Earls, 1997). As detailed later, the collective efficacy hypothesis also challenges the broken windows hypothesis, from which Kelling is most known.

120 On April 15, 2014, Kelling spoke to students at his alma mater, St. Olaf College, and a chapter for Black Lives Matter protested before his evening speech. Rather than being dismayed, Kelling was energized by the students and insisted on meeting with the chair of the student group for breakfast the next day.

121 The 1967 U.S. Supreme Court decision, *In re Gault*, provided the Fourteenth Amendment Due Process Clause applied to juvenile defendants giving them specific rights such as timely notification of charges; attorney representation; the right to confront witnesses; and the right against self-incrimination. Kelling's role as an early juvenile probation officer frequently put him in an informal role of recommending sentencing to a judge without interference from prosecutors or defense attorneys. He was allotted discretionary problem-solving capabilities without legal restrictions that would come after *In re Gault*, which ultimately encouraged prosecutorial involvement and increased their power (see Coles & Kelling, 2002).

Police Foundation

Kelling, through the encouragement of Herman Goldstein and Frank Remington, began his career in research with the Police Foundation,[122] where he worked from 1971 to 1980 directing projects to improve American policing. He was engaged in conducting large-scale experiments on policing strategies, with two of the most well-known being the Kansas City Preventative Patrol Experiment and the Newark Foot Patrol Experiment.

Kansas City Preventative Patrol Experiment (1972–1973)

The Kansas City Preventative Patrol Experiment occurred between 1972 and 1973 in Kansas City, Missouri. The research design centered on matching police beats and evaluating the dependent variable differences (e.g. crime, response times, calls for service) based on the following independent variables: removal of routine patrol, regular patrol, and doubling/tripling patrol. In addition, researchers used a pre and post-test design to evaluate the following: if residents noticed the changes in patrol; if different levels of patrol impacted crime; if varying levels of patrol impacted citizen fear or perceptions of crime; and if satisfaction of police services changed based upon levels of patrol. The experiment's initial start proved difficult as officers tainted the results to believe that their absence of patrol endangered citizens. The experiment showed that citizens were not aware of patrol changes and increasing or decreasing patrol had no impact on crime. Further, neither satisfaction with police services nor their likelihood of reporting crime changed according to patrol levels (Kelling et al., 1974).

A few years later, another experiment took place in Kansas City entitled "Police Response Time: Its Determinants and Effects" to determine if response time impacted clearance rates and solvability (Pate, Ferrara, Bowers, & Lorence, 1976). The study also looked at links between response time and citizen satisfaction with the police. Research findings indicated that response time did not affect clearing serious crime or satisfaction. Spelman and Brown (1984) reported that police managers were jolted by the research findings and were skeptical. However, their skepticism was negated when the PERF confirmed the earlier findings (Spelman & Brown, 1981) that citizen-reporting time and community cooperation has the most impact on the possibility of arrest, not police response time.

Therefore, reformists such as O.W. Wilson pushed the guiding strategies that indicated routine preventative patrol and response time were effective police management strategies. Despite the Police Foundation's research challenges, routine preventive patrol and fast response time continued to be a core reactive strategy for many contemporary police managers.

Newark Foot Patrol Experiment (1980–1981)

The Newark Foot Patrol Experiment report was published in 1981 through sponsorship from the NIJ and when Patrick Murphy served as the president of the Police Foundation. New

122 The Police Foundation is headquartered in Washington, DC, as an independent, non-partisan, and non-membership organization dedicated to improving policing through innovation and science. The Ford Foundation founded the Police Foundation in 1970 with a $30 million grant. This grant came from the insistence of former Philadelphia Assistant Public Defender Charles Rogovin, who served as a commissioner to the newly developed Law Enforcement Education Program (LEEP) through the Department of Justice. Rogovin was frustrated that federal LEEP funds being spent on police equipment and not on educating police officers (Bratton & Knobler, 2021). The Police Foundation is the oldest organization working toward improving policing through scientific research and works with numerous government agency partners and the private sector to encourage evidence-based approaches to improve policing and the alignment of recommendations that are found to be effective. See www.policefoundation.org/.

Jersey Police Chief Hubert Williams succeeded Murphy and was appointed the president of the Police Foundation in 1985, in the aftermath of the study. He would serve as President for the next 27 years, until 2012, as the foundation's longest-serving president.

The purpose of the foot patrol experiment in Newark was to evaluate the effectiveness of an initiative that came in the aftermath of New Jersey's "Safe and Clean Neighborhoods Program." Chief Williams was part of an initiative in which 28 cities had budgeted tax revenue to incentivize officers to walk their beat assignments. The politicians were enthusiastic about the prospects of reducing crime. Simultaneously, chiefs and officers were skeptical, noting that past reformers, such as Wilson in Chicago, had discredited foot patrol since it reduced police mobility and response time. Pragmatically, officers disliked the hard work of walking and being in the direct environment of the cold and rain. Moreover, many saw foot patrol as a demotion or linked to disciplinary procedures.

The Police Foundation study utilized three research designs: (1) attitudinal comparisons of foot patrol with mobile patrol; (2) comparisons of reported crime in Elizabeth, New Jersey differentiated by the use of foot patrol or lack of foot patrol; (3) beats that were matched samples to compare reported crime, arrests, victimization, fear, and satisfaction comparing foot patrol or lack of foot patrol. As part of this research design, Kelling was a participant-observant and accompanied officers walking foot beats. He documented how they enforced local norms of order and how they dealt with social behaviors around bus shelters, noisy youth, and loiters. Research supported foot patrol in terms of fear of crime and community satisfaction with police services. Kelling concluded that since foot patrol officers were more likely to deal with minor disorder problems, police could more effectively utilize their discretion to provide behavior standards. For example, they might allow public drinking, but not on the main streets. The police would negotiate with panhandlers and tell them they could only ask for money from people moving, not standing still. These negotiated behavioral expectations with the community, and those who live on the streets, established informal rules that people generally followed.

Moreover, police services were appreciated by those most connected to the disorder problems. While the foot patrol intervention failed to demonstrate a significant impact on crime, arrest, or victimization, it increased citizens' perception of safety and gave researchers more questions than answers. As detailed in the chapter on Chuck Ramsey, later foot patrol experiments in Philadelphia demonstrated significant violent crime reductions within treatment locations (Ratcliffe, Taniguchi, Groff, & Wood, 2011).

The Police Foundation's landmark research created the spark to shift toward community-oriented policing (Police Foundation, 1981). This philosophical shift promoted organizational strategies centered on partnerships, problem-solving, and crime prevention. For Kelling, the strategy of recognizing officer discretion and allowing them to negotiate neighborhood consensus by encouraging partnerships would become the central perspective for his life's work.

James Q. Wilson

James Quinn Wilson was born on May 27, 1931, and passed away on March 2, 2012, in Boston, after battling leukemia. From 1961 to 1987, he was the Shattuck Professor of Government as a political scientist at Harvard University. From 1987 to 1997, he was at the UCLA Anderson School of Management, and from 1998 to 2009, he was at Pepperdine University's School of Public Policy. From 1985 to 1990, Wilson served on the President's Foreign Intelligence Advisory Board, and in 2003, George W. Bush awarded him with the Presidential Medal of Freedom. In 2012, after Wilson passed, Kelling wrote a reflection for *Subject to Debate*, the

PERF newsletter (Kelling, 2012). Wilson was a longtime supporter of PERF and received its Leadership Award, its highest honor, in 2009.

Kelling and Wilson had been acquaintances throughout the 1970s when Wilson served on the Board of Directors for the Police Foundation. Wilson began serving in this capacity in 1970 and was the chairman of the board from 1984 to 1993. His first intervention came when Kelling challenged a sociologist reviewer who did not want to publish the Kansas City Preventative Patrol Experiment results. Wilson intervened and urged the publication. Their next contact came in late 1981 when Wilson provided questions and praise for the Newark Foot Patrol Experiment. Kelling's work on the Newark Foot Patrol Experiment impressed Wilson, and he requested his assistance with a pending *Atlantic Monthly* paper (Kelling, 2015a). Kelling responded to Wilson's co-author request stating that he could cite the Newark study in his paper. Wilson became more insistent that Kelling be his co-author on an article, but with a warning. Wilson told Kelling that he would be linked to political conservatism in criminology's predominantly liberal field if he did the paper. Kelling explained that he was used to the partisan criticism, having experienced this from both criminologists and the police following the Kansas City Preventative Patrol Experiment (Kelling, 2012).

A Ten-Page Magazine Article That Would Change the Face of Policing – Atlantic Monthly (1982)

Upon Wilson's insistence, Kelling provided his notes for the article, and Wilson quickly returned a draft for Kelling's review before sending it off to the editors for *Atlantic Monthly*.[123] Wilson came up with the metaphor of the broken window on his own, stating that as a broken window is left untended, it is a sign that no one cares and leads to additional broken windows. The broken window metaphor was transferred to disorderly behavior and argued that if that behavior was not challenged, it demonstrates the same level of apathy, which will lead to additional fear of crime, more serious predatory crime, and overall urban decay. While the literature widely supported the link between disorder and fear of crime, namely the Newark Foot Patrol Experiment, the connection between disorder and serious crime was more controversial and provided the most discussion between Kelling and Wilson and subsequent critics.

In addition to the Newark experiment, Jane Jacobs, Philip Zimbardo, and Oscar Newman influenced research before the 1982 broken windows article. Each is described below.

1 Jane Jacobs,[124] a journalist, author, and activist, wrote *The Life and Death and Life American Cities* in 1961. With limited college education and no training in urban planning, Jacobs became an icon with her withering attacks on the male-dominated real estate industry. She criticized urban planning that led to zoning regulations for single-family housing; created large public housing units for the minority poor that was infested with crime; and allowed for housing discrimination. She opposed large-scale urban renewal projects that drove freeways through inner-cities[125] and tore the social fabric out of main street America (Jacobs, 1961). President Johnson's 1967 Commission Report, *The Challenge of*

123 The *Atlantic Monthly* is a literary and cultural commentary magazine that was founded in 1857 in Boston. Historical writers for the magazine have included Ralph Waldo Emerson, Oliver Wendell Holmes, and Henry Wadsworth Longfellow.

124 Jacobs died in 2006 at the age of 86. She lived in the NYC Greenwich Village Apartments at 555 Hudson Street between West 11th and Perry Street. A street sign at that location is symbolically named Jane Jacobs Way.

125 Examples of these urban renewal strategies can be seen in the novel *Motherless Brooklyn* (Letham, 1999) and the 2019 film directed by Edward Norton starring Alec Baldwin.

Crime in a Free Society, recommended the police should formally participate in community planning in all cities.

2 Phil Zimbardo, a social psychology professor from Stanford University, arranged for an automobile to be parked in a Bronx, NYC neighborhood with no license plates and its hood up and a second identical vehicle parked in a Palo Alto, California neighborhood. The Bronx vehicle was vandalized and stripped for parts 23 times over three days. The Palo Alto vehicle parked near Stanford University was untouched for a week. Zimbardo attempted to provide signs it was abandoned by leaving the hood up, but someone closed it during a rainstorm. Then Zimbardo sent his male students to smash the car with a sledgehammer. They hesitated at first, but after the first blow and permission from their professor, they loudly encouraged each other to strike the vehicle repeatedly. The year was 1969, and Zimbardo determined both communities were apathetic to the abandoned cars that gave off signals that no one cared (Zimbardo, 1973).

3 Oscar Newman[126] was an architect professor at Columbia University in NYC when he published Creating Defensible Space in 1973 through the U.S. Department of Housing & Urban Development (HUD). The principles behind Newman's work was geared toward crime prevention and community stabilization planning for cities throughout the United States that built on concepts of repairing broken windows and creating territoriality through community partnerships (Newman, 1973).

Kelling was surprised that their broken windows article became the cover story of the March 1982 edition of the *Atlantic Monthly* magazine. Two decades after the publication, he was reflective on Wilson's warning that the article would cause criticism from criminologists and that they would be called racist or worse (Bratton, Wilson, Kelling, Rivers, & Cove, 2004). Too often, residents of urban America were negatively impacted by open prostitution, graffiti, abandoned vehicles, public intoxication, rowdy youth, and aggressive panhandling. While the police acknowledged these problems, they reported they were too overloaded with patrol duties and responding to calls for service that dealt with serious crime and doubted they had the resources to respond to low-level disorder (i.e. the broken windows). Wilson and Kelling proposed that police strategies change. Instead of focusing on major crimes, the police should focus on maintaining social order (e.g. rowdy youth, people smoking pot or drinking in public, and subway fare beaters). This argument came at an opportune time during rising crime throughout the 1980s and eventually bipartisan support for more police and high incarceration rates. The 1982 article finally gained traction with law enforcement once they realized that perceptions of being overburdened by calls for service should not circumvent the need to conduct quality-of-life policing. Mainstream academics provided little attention to the article. However, decades later, Kelling was told by editors from the *Atlantic Monthly* that their 1982 article was reproduced more than any other (Kelling, 2012).

Wilson vs. Wilson (and Kelling)

O.W. Wilson ushered in the reform era of policing in the 1960s that introduced quasi-militaristic law enforcement with goals set to rapid response and deterrent mobile patrol. This shift was partly due to the political corruption issues that plagued policing and untested

126 Newman died in 2004 in Albany, New York. His theories on defensible space and urban design was re-popularized in the 2015 HBO mini-series *Show Me a Hero* based on a non-fiction book that detailed white middle-class Yonkers, New York and their resistance to federally mandated public housing development in the 1980s (Belkin, 2015).

assumptions regarding preventative patrol and the effectiveness of rapid response on clearance rates. Kelling and Wilson encouraged police leaders to shift back to foot patrol strategies arguing this style of policing should not be seen as a relic of the past but instead an integral part of effective crime prevention. Under the broken window approach, officers were also encouraged to utilize their discretion and intervene in low-level offending such as public drinking, overt drug use, and prostitution.

For Kelling, the lessons of problem-solving low-level offending came from being a graduate student influenced by Herman Goldstein when their paths converged in the early 1970s at the University of Wisconsin-Madison. Goldstein was O.W. Wilson's executive assistant at the Chicago Police Department from 1960 to 1964 before becoming a law professor at UW-Madison. (Goldstein's work is detailed in the appendix to the chapter on O.W. Wilson). Goldstein developed POP from those early reform lessons, which became part of the broken windows concept.

Kelling reported that communication with his co-author was irregular after their 1982 publication in the *Atlantic Monthly* (Kelling, 2012). He suspected that Wilson referred inquiries he received about their paper to him directly. In 1984, an early test of broken windows came when the New York MTA began cleaning graffiti off the subway train cars. The MTA continued to clean other damaged cars immediately so that vandals would be denied satisfaction from their transgressions (Kelling & Bratton, 2015). By 1989, the subway system had very little graffiti, ridership increased, and the MTA publicly claimed victory.

The big breakthrough for Kelling's career as a police consultant under the "father of broken windows" persona came in 1989 when New York Transportation Authority Chairman Bob Kiley contacted him to help with homelessness in the subway system. Kelling determined the larger problem was general lawlessness throughout the transit system that included robberies and fare evasion. He assisted in hiring Bratton as transit chief in 1990, and together, they began to build strategies to test the broken windows hypothesis. Bratton was the first police leader to try Wilson and Kelling's concepts and return to a police management model that encouraged officer discretion and negotiated order maintenance. This strategic change drifted from O.W. Wilson's standard concepts of reactive law enforcement that limited officer discretion with numerous rules and regulations. Alternatively, Bratton and Kelling applied concepts of community policing with a focus on order maintenance. The hypothesis theorized that as the police took care of small disorder problems, citizens are empowered, reclaim public spaces, and prevent future criminality.

However, Bratton and Knobler (2021) make an important distinction that perceptions of general safety must come before community policing can be successful. The analogy was sending the Red Cross to the battlefield ahead of the infantry. The community must have some sense of cohesion and social organization prior to effectively implementing community policing. One effective collaborative precision strategy for impacting safety came from David Kennedy's call-in initiatives and the National Network for Safe Communities out of John Jay College (see https://nnscommunities.org/). That initiative focused on the select few offenders who were causing most of the problems in a given neighborhood, calling those individuals into a community meeting where they are met with law enforcement, prosecutors, employment providers, social workers, and community advocates. One group offers a stick and the other a carrot. Most offenders take an honorable way out of their criminal lifestyles. The underlying lesson is that effective call-ins, and perhaps broken windows policing, should occur prior to shifts towards community policing can be effectively implemented.

Bratton's use of Kelling's broken windows policing approach began with strategies directed to crime prevention and fear reduction in the city subway. They looked toward collaborative policing and the development of partnerships that would be necessary in times when the police inevitably make mistakes. They also strategized that fixing broken windows required high levels of transparency and vested stakeholders. Bratton intentionally invited his command staff to ride the subway system, along with his officers, and meet with passengers. Loudspeakers announced that transit officers would be boarding trains so passengers knew they would be checking for disorder issues. Transit officers referred to the "crackerjack box" effect noting that one in seven fare evaders had an open warrant for their arrest. One out of 21 was carrying an illegal weapon (Kelling, 2019). To speed up arrests, they deployed buses that would serve as mobile processing centers so transit officers would not have to waste time and resources traveling to downtown headquarters for processing. These tactics all signaled to the public that transit police would routinely challenge low-level offending, and legitimate users of the transit system could use public spaces with less fear of victimization. Further, the broken windows strategies provided signals to the legitimate transit users that their concerns mattered and the police would take their safety seriously.

Bratton and Kelling recognized that as public satisfaction with police services improved, the drops in crime were an inevitable by-product. They also found measuring that satisfaction was an improved way to rate police efficiency rather than response time and crime statistics. As crime rates plummeted, the transit officers understood the critical link between disorder and crime. A 2001 report by Kelling and William Sousa further solidified the assessment and links between misdemeanor arrests and less violence. Sousa was one of Kelling's graduate students at Rutgers University. Their research found, on average, every arrest for a misdemeanor was associated with 0.036 fewer violent crimes (Kelling & Sousa, 2001).

Critics of Broken Windows

Decades have passed since the *Atlantic Monthly* published Wilson and Kelling's paper, and both authors have since passed away. Yet, it continues to be one of the most influential works in policing and the most controversial, with numerous attacks directed toward their public-order advocacy. These attacks have come from criminologists, law professors, civil rights protesters, and politicians. The critics view broken windows policing as an intended strategy for the oppression of minority populations. They point to the disparity involved with policing high-crime minority-dominated neighborhoods through stop-and-frisk tactics. Others argued that the link between disorder and crime, especially without proper community policing supplements, is faulty and counterproductive (Gau & Pratt, 2008).

Columbia law professor Bernard Harcourt has vehemently argued that order-maintenance policing is racist (Harcourt, 1998) and headlined cases like Eric Garner's death in 2014 as a catalyst to abolish broken windows style policing. Harcourt received his law degree and a Ph.D. in political science from Harvard University. He represented clients on death row and those serving life in prison before his academic work. In *Illusions of Order: The False Promise of Broken Windows Policing*, Harcourt challenged the evidence supporting broken windows and provided further challenges to data used by Kelling and Sousa (2001) and Skogan (1990). Specifically, Harcourt determined that the correlation between robbery and disorder is insignificant when race is held constant, and Newark neighborhoods were left out of Skogan's multicity analysis (Harcourt, 2001).

Harcourt furthered his criticism of broken windows policing with economist Jans Ludwig (2006), from the University of Chicago, to measure the impact of a 1994 program called *Moving to Opportunity* (*MTO*) that was used in several large urban cities. The social experiment allowed a unique opportunity to test the broken windows hypothesis empirically. Approximately 4,600 low-income families in high-crime public housing communities randomly received vouchers to move to less disorderly and disadvantaged communities. The researchers found that arrest rates did not significantly change in neighborhoods with lower social disorder and concluded that broken windows policing is not the most optimal use of scarce law enforcement resources (Harcourt & Ludwig, 2006).

This economist perspective fell in line with the top-selling book *Freakonomics* written by journalist Stephen Dubner and economist Steven Levitt in 2005. *Freakonomics: A Rogue Economist Explores the Hidden Side of Everything* had a chapter that looked at the crime drop across the nation and argued the 1973 *Roe v. Wade* decision is the primary correlate for the decline in crime. The economists argued that legalized abortion significantly reduced the number of at-risk youth that would have been in their crime-prone age during the 1990s (Levitt & Dubner, 2005). They further argued that some cities experienced drops in crime without practicing broken windows policing. Kelling and Coles (1996) argued that the extent of reductions seen in NYC far exceeded the national decline. Another economist (Reyes, 2007) argued that 56 percent of the national drop in violent crime could be attributed to removing lead from gasoline and paint in buildings, previously linked to cognitive and behavioral problems.

Other prominent researchers challenged the connection between disorder and crime. Eck and Macguire (2000) contributed to Alfred Blumstein's book, *The Crime Drop in America* with a chapter that concluded there were many variables linked to the drop in crime throughout the 1990s other than broken windows policing. They argued the evidence on broken windows policing was mixed and raised questions with the improbable nature of aggressively policing perceived disorder while maintaining police-community relations. Hinkle and Weisburd (2008) found that saturated patrol in high-crime neighborhoods produced more fear with residents than social/physical disorder. Their research also questioned how broken windows policing might negatively impact community policing and incite more fear if not correctly implemented. O'Brien, Farrell, and Welsh (2019) conducted a meta-analysis on 96 studies that looked at the effects of disorder on aggressive behavior and fear of crime. They failed to find significant links between disorder and fear of crime or aggressive behavior and levied criticisms toward weak research designs that support broken windows policing. Manning (2001) argued the crime drop in the 1990s in NYC mimicked crime declines across the nation. He further argued that Giuliani, Bratton, Kelling, and others legitimized quality of life policing and CompStat tactics through their marketing campaigns (referred to as dramaturgy) with the media. According to Manning (2001), the crime drop's spectacle was manufactured with the change in aggressive-style police tactics. However, officers received little training on how to properly police quality of life initiatives or how to build better relationships with the community.

Sampson and Raudenbush (2001) further acknowledged the importance of police-community relations and argued that serious crime increased when neighborhoods lacked collective efficacy. They contend that policing disorder is only moderately correlated to reductions in crime. In their analysis, if collective efficacy increases (i.e. when people have more significant ties to their neighborhood and familiarity with one other), serious crime is reduced through increased informal social control mechanisms. The structural characteristics of neighborhoods and neighborhood cohesion, not levels of disorder, impact most crime (Sampson & Raudenbush, 2001). Other factors such as religion may also enhance collective efficacy and buffer crime and illicit drug use (Jang & Johnson, 2001). Therefore, resources should be directed toward enhancing collective efficacy and less focus on policing disorder. Sampson and Raudenbush (2004) extended the debate by questioning what makes disorder a problem is arbitrary. Disorder is often a social construct created by political and police leadership rather than in close consultation with residents.

Dickinson (2008) agreed and uses a culture of poverty theory to argue against saturated patterns of policing lower-class communities simply because upper-class leaders have defined their expectations of what constitutes orderly behavior. Other scholars became even more critical, referring to Wilson and Kelling as "aversive racists" (Stewart, 1998) and that their main policy recommendation to the police is "kick-ass" (Bowling, 1999). Kelling begrudgingly left the "kick-ass" term in the original article, despite Wilson's warning, to capture what occurred in the post-O.W. Wilson Chicago era (Kelling, 2012). However, like Kelling, Bratton argues that broken windows policing is neither racist nor zero-tolerance, but an effective tool, one of many, to police specific locations where normative behaviors have run amuck (Bratton, 2021).

In a more scathing attack, historian Hinton (2016) described the 1965 Moynihan[127] Report as a ruse to push a national misconception that linked poverty and crime to Black communities' innate features. According to Hinton, this report laid the foundation for broken windows policing, CompStat, and predictive policing. Consequently, the government divested from community welfare initiatives and invested heavily in crime control and punishment, resulting in a ratio of one in every 31 American adults and one in 11 Black men under some restriction of the criminal justice system. Hinton (2016) reported Moynihan collaborated with Wilson and Kelling.

Answering the Critics

Five Big Ideas: ABF and POP, Pulling-Levers, CompStat, Broken Windows, Hot Spots

Kelling challenged academic critics by arguing that five big ideas have had the most significant influence on policing, and these ideas have, for the most part, fallen outside of the scope of traditional criminology (Kelling, 2019). These five big ideas, described below, included: the American Bar Foundation (ABF)[128] study, POP, pulling-levers or focused deterrence, CompStat, and broken windows policing.

Kelling suggested that community policing had its origins in the ABF research (Ohlin & Remington, 1993), POP (Goldstein, 1990), and situational crime prevention (Clarke, 1995). This research stemmed from law professors and a social psychologist. David Kennedy, a public policy scholar, influenced police leaders through the Boston Gun Project and the National Network for Safe Communities with pulling-levers strategies and targeted deterrence (Braga & Weisburd, 2012; Kennedy, 1997). Similar to Goldstein, Kennedy achieved academic and consulting success without a Ph.D. degree or a criminology label. CompStat swept through international police leadership as a by-product of the private sector and the entrepreneurial spirit of Bratton and Maple (Weisburd et al., 2003). Broken windows policing evolved from political scientist Wilson and social worker Kelling (Kelling & Wilson, 1982). Hot spot policing research may be the only exception within the five big ideas derived from criminologists (see Pierce, Spaar, & Briggs, 1988; Sherman, Gartin, & Buerger, 1989; Weisburd, Maher, & Sherman, 1992).

Kelling further argued that each of these five big ideas fell beyond the scope of traditional criminology that historically sought to answer *why* people commit crimes. For Kelling and many police leaders, analytical questions related to *how* and *when* were more critical than *why* offenders commit crime (Kelling, 2001). This focus co-opted much of what criminal justice

127 Daniel Patrick Moynihan was a sociologist and Assistant Secretary of Labor under President Johnson. In 1965, his Moynihan Report was titled "The Negro Family: A Case for National Action," arguing that the rise in Black single-mother families was caused by a destructive ghetto culture, not by a lack of employment opportunities.

128 Goldstein's initiation into funded research came via the ABF study and the Ford Foundation. (The ABF research is discussed more fully in the appendix of the O.W. Wilson chapter on Goldstein.)

higher education taught and drove significant policy and public discourse. As such, much of this policy was directed toward crime control and not toward institutionalizing strategies that could focus on prevention, as advocated throughout the five big ideas of policing. Within this approach, Bratton has called on a strategic focus of the three "P's" of policing: partnerships, problems, and prevention (Bratton & Knobler, 2021).

Kelling's Academic Career

Kelling's academic career took him from the Police Foundation to Harvard University, then to Northeastern University in Boston, and finally to Rutgers University in Newark, where he became a professor emeritus. Kelling was also a fellow at the Manhattan Institute. In addition to *Fixing Broken Windows* (1996), he worked with his wife Catherine Coles on the concept of community prosecution. In this work, Kelling and Coles studied how prosecutors can become more strategic through tighter partnerships with the police, church leaders, and vested community stakeholders. Wilson and Kelling (1982) encouraged collaborative police discretion and creative community problem-solving. Kelling and Coles (1999) encouraged collaborative prosecutorial partnership strategies, which were especially critical to counter youth violence and disorder. Community prosecution seeks shifts toward crime prevention that fit restorative justice models and community-justice courts. Examples include drug rehabilitation court, domestic violence diversion, and veteran's court. These alternative problem-solving courts also took place in NYC during the 1990s crime drop (see Berman & Feinblatt, 2005).

Kelling's Last Plea – Research Support for Broken Windows Community Policing

Kelling (2019) was adamant that broken windows policing should be done through neighborhood-level negotiations with the community to help establish normative behavior. These neighborhood-level connections are far different from zero-tolerance policing, where the police alone define what is considered orderly or disorderly conduct. These negotiations will reach different conclusions depending on what part of the community is being policed and better defines the democratic principles of decentralized police strategies. The distinction between negotiated and zero-tolerance policing has been the most misunderstood aspect of broken windows strategies. Even so, Kelling (2019) points to the success of the strategy in a multi-decade pre and post comparison. In 1990, NYC peaked at 2,262 murders and over 100,000 robberies. By 2017, the city had 292 murders and less than 14,000 robberies.

Braga and Bond (2008) analyzed broken windows policing and crime reduction in Lowell, Massachusetts. Their methodology included systematic observational research, and their unit of analysis was 911 calls. They argued that calls for service are not biased the way traditional dependent variable police data is since it has nothing to do with officer discretion. Their research generally supported broken windows policing to reduce calls for service, especially when officers were given preventative strategies in hot spot locations.

Other agencies began to use different versions of broken windows policing, and researchers found alternative assessments. One evaluation came from Fort Worth, Texas and researchers concluded more aggressive policing of disorder offenses played a significant role in reducing property crimes, but not violent crimes (Hyunseok, Hoover, & Hee-Jong, 2010). The Fort Worth version of CompStat accountability meetings was more cordial, meaning line-staff supervisors were not ridiculed by command staff in the same way as early CompStat meetings.

Queensland (northeast Australia) used a problem-oriented intervention model to police disorder, which led to significant reductions in the total number of reported crime (Mazerolle, Rombouts, & McBroom, 2007). The use of POP to target disorder was supported by Wilson and Kelling in another paper for the *Atlantic Monthly* titled "Making Neighborhoods Safe" (Wilson & Kelling, 1989). While the paper did not garner as much traction as their 1982 article, they recognized the need to differentiate the art of negotiated broken windows policing from zero-tolerance policing tactics that rely too heavily on stop-and-frisk.

The last article Kelling wrote was titled "Community Policing, Rightly Understood" as part of being a fellow with the Manhattan Institute for Policy Research, a New York conservative think tank. The Winter 2019 edition of the quarterly *City Journal* published Kelling's last article. In his writing, Kelling laments that community policing and order-maintenance efforts are not at odds but part of a larger style of negotiated policing (Kelling, 2019). Kelling has advocated for negotiated orderly street behavior through community partnerships since his work with the Police Foundation in the 1970s. The conflict over order-maintenance policing has drawn critics who have linked zero-tolerance tactics with racially biased stop-and-frisk statistics. For Kelling, residents in all communities want disorder policed, but officers need to be especially sensitive with formulating partnerships with residents living in high-crime neighborhoods. Lastly, as he concluded in his 2015 paper for *Politico*, "Don't blame my 'broken windows' theory for poor policing,"[129] citizens must also be lead to accept their critical role in demanding adequate police leadership and governing disorder in their neighborhoods (Kelling, 2015a). For Kelling, the broken windows policing approach is a powerful tool that can be misused and morphed into oppression if it excludes community policing. If the broken windows community policing style is understood and supported by the appropriate leaders, crime reduction will occur, and police legitimacy will improve. Bratton's attempts to avoid the perversion of broken windows policing by including the community and encouraging officer discretion occurred throughout his career, especially within his second stint as the 42nd Police Commissioner with the NYPD.

In 2015, the Manhattan Institute awarded George Kelling with the Alexander Hamilton Award. The award honors individuals who have fostered a revitalization of cities' commerce and civic life. Bill Bratton spoke at the award dinner and also became the 2017 recipient of the same award. Both Bratton and Kelling accepted these awards as the Black Lives Matter rallies swept the nation, not knowing the more considerable impact in 2020. They both provided warnings about the need for community policing reflections within the broader broken windows approach. They both also understood from their long experiences in policing that while Black communities are rightfully concerned about misuse of police authority, they are more concerned with the lack of effective policing and other social service applications that fail to impact quality of life throughout their communities.

Kelling's posthumous warning against zero-tolerance policing, as connected toward broken windows policing, is demonstrative in 2020 mass protests and riots that followed George Floyd's death in Minneapolis. Kelling spent years on the defense from the far right and the far left from what he determined was a misinterpretation of broken windows policing, which he argued should include dosages of negotiation, social work, and community policing. Kelling often stated that good intentions do not always result in an acceptable policy. While the broken windows theory was considered divisive by many, Kelling's academic approach to the complexities of policing was not. He was open-minded to criticism, continually insisted on

129 Kelling did not provide this title for his paper and disliked what *Politico Magazine* editors came up with (author's interview with Catherine Coles on November 11, 2020). The subtitle was labeled "The co-author of an influential approach to police tactics argues it's been misunderstood."

nuances, and emphasized the need for collaborative policing that engages disorder in a manner that involved the majority of the community in problem-solving.

Kelling understood that the metaphor of the broken window had, at times, taken on a life of its own. He also understood that he needed to connect back to his roots as a social worker. Unfortunately, we will never know what Kelling's views on the 2020 riots would have been. However, as demonstrated by McPhail, Schweingruber, and McCarthy (1998), riots of the 1960s were noted for extreme violence and connected to the police use of escalated force, while policing protests of the 1980s and 1990s were led by *negotiated management*, which falls in line with Kelling's pleas. These pleas mimic O.W. Wilson's leadership in Chicago and his treatment of protesters led by Martin Luther King, Jr. and the unfortunate issues that evolved, after Wilson retired, during the 1968 Democratic Convention. Kelling's emphasis on community policing, through enhanced legitimacy at the neighborhood level in the months and years before the 2020 social justice protests, is critical. An investment in neighborhood relations has emphasized throughout this book, especially within the chapters on Harrington, Ramsey, and Magnus's leadership.

It is short-sighted to find friends amid mass protests, especially if previous long-term trust-building has not been part of the overall police strategy. Failed police legitimacy may be one of the most critical lessons from Kelling in the aftermath of the 2020 mass protests and riots. Kelling emphasized that these relationships develop when the police routinely negotiate street-level justice and properly manage disorder in a palpable manner by the larger community. Ironically, Kelling's link back to social work, without an overreliance on the formal criminal court system, has its roots in Minneapolis, 70 years before George Floyd's death when he attended the Northwestern Lutheran Theological Seminary. Floyd's death at the hands of the police sparked the unprecedented 2020 mass protest and riots that erupted throughout the country and internationally. Kelling would have likely encouraged a reinvestment toward negotiated community policing as a wise and transformational investment for the coming decade.

In July 2020, Brian Anderson interviewed Bill Bratton for the *City Journal* to express his take on the mass protests that erupted after Floyd's in-custody death. In a concluding reflection on the late George Kelling, Bratton expressed his opinion on what his academic colleague would have said about the current affairs of policing (Bratton & Anderson, 2020):

> *I know exactly what he would say. I spent quite a bit of time with George in his final months in terms of on the phone or going up to visit him several times up in Hanover. And he was very concerned that his legacy, and it was extraordinary legacy, the whole concept of what he was about, that was being misconstrued, mislabeled, misinterpreted, and attacked. And what I'm talking about is his focus on community policing, his focus on an element of community policing, broken windows. The idea of Sir Robert Peel's initial nine philosophies, that basic mission, to police, is to prevent crime and disorder. George and Wilson clearly understood in the '70s and '80s, we gave up on doing anything about the disorder and that increasing disorder, basically, it provided fertile ground for the growth of violent crime.*
>
> *And for that message, we would develop police enforcement of minor crimes against minority communities. George was attacked very vehemently by some of these aggressive reform components that are out there now leading the charge. It was such a misinterpretation, if you will. A conscious misinterpretation with George was all about.*
>
> *George really felt that quality of life policing was an essential component of community policing. Because if you want a partnership with the community, you have to focus on what they're concerned about. And if you look at the 311 calls or 911 calls around the country, not just in New York, the bulk of the calls coming from the poor, minority communities are about quality of life. Guys played dice on my doorstep, a prostitute using my hallway, the smoking of drugs in the hallways of public*

housing developments. Just because you're poor or a minority doesn't mean you don't want the same thing everybody else wants. You want a safe environment. You want to have a night's sleep. You want to be able to go into your home without being accosted by people drinking on your doorstep or shooting drugs or dealing drugs.

And to deal with the violent crime, you need the police. Communities cannot deal with violent crime by themselves. And police cannot deal with it by themselves either. They need the participation of the community. And that's what the very essence of George was all about. This idea of police, community, partnering together to identify the problems that needed to be addressed, whether it's violent crime or broken windows. And what was the goal? Prevention. The idea of preventing. And it worked very well in the '90s. Were there excesses? Unfortunately. Maybe over-incarceration in some instances, over-policing in others, but minority communities want the police. And as an example of a deterioration of a city, you see that happening right now in New York City.

In the Wall Street Journal, it was reported the city is now going to give up, as part of its funding crises, any effort other than on public buildings. Do you do anything about graffiti? Well, graffiti is one of those broken windows that's extraordinarily visible in making a city look out of control. And what is the thing that you see so many of these demonstrations, what they attempt to do, is show that they're in control. They mark everything up with graffiti. It's like in the wilderness, the idea of marking your territory. And graffiti used by gangs and even used by many of these demonstrators is intended to spread fear, spread concern, spread a message. And a lot of these messages are not about Black Lives Matter or about justice for all. It's about the "F" the police, kill the police, kill the pigs. I'm sorry. That's not appropriate when you're no longer going to remove that type of graffiti.

And so that's just another broken window in what was the grand mosaic of a city that was working. Unfortunately, a lot of those windows in that grand mosaic, as David Dinkins, the mayor back in the '90s used to describe it, well, that grand mosaic is breaking down very dramatically in New York City and indeed, around the country.

In May 2020, PERF reflected on the loss of George Kelling, Herman Goldstein, and David Bayley.[130] A couple of reflections are worth noting – the first from Ed Flynn, who retired as the chief of the Milwaukee Police Department in February 2018, and the second from Bill Bratton (Photo 5.4).

Ed Flynn, former Police Chief in Milwaukee, Wisconsin; Arlington, Virginia; Springfield and Chelsea, Massachusetts:

George was my mentor and guide long before I actually met him. As I worked my way up the chain of command in Jersey City, his eloquent, inspirational and empathetic prose gave me an invaluable framework to understand my work. As importantly, his rigorous research on police methods and tactics (the Kansas City Patrol Experiment, the Newark Foot Patrol Experiment) challenged conventional wisdom in important ways.

When I did finally get to know him, I was chief in Chelsea, MA: the poorest city in the state with the highest violent crime rate. With a new Community Policing grant, I hired IACP to do community-oriented policing training for the entire department, and I insisted that George be the keynote speaker. He agreed.

And he was just what the cops needed to hear. He was a missionary (as befitted his divinity school training) for the inherent worth of policing and of community connection, and he clearly understood and valued police officers' work. The department turnaround started with that speech.

But afterwards, George confided something in me. He said, "I'm not sure I'm going to cash this check from the IACP." When I asked, "Why not?" he replied, "The IACP viewed me as an

130 See https://perf.memberclicks.net/trendingmay23.

apostate, as a heretic, as a danger to law enforcement after the Kansas City study. I think I might frame this check in recognition that my heresy became doctrine!" I think it was the Lutheran in him.

Bill Bratton (Police Executive Research Forum, 2020)

My first exposure to George Kelling was reading the Atlantic Monthly article on "broken windows," which resonated with me, because that's what I had found in the 70s. I was living what he was writing about.

George loved being out in the field and walking around with the cops. That's why that report was so influential. He was not writing about someone else's experiences; he was writing about his own. He wasn't an academic; he was a field researcher. He didn't just write about what others thought. He wrote about his own experiences.

Kelling understood cops because he spent a lot of time with them. That's why I enjoyed him so much. We had that shared respect and empathy for what cops were trying to deal with. The transit initiative was the one where we really bonded. People were giving up on New York, and certainly giving up on the subway. But we really believed that the community policing model, as we understood it, could work in the subways, the streets, and foreign countries.

Later when I was chief in Los Angeles, I took him down to skid row. He loved every moment of those several days, walking around skid row, because he looked at it from the perspective of how to fix it. Everywhere he looked, it was about "How can I make this better?" George also wrote in a way that allowed you to understand his experiences, and how he passionately believed that we could make things better by practicing what he was writing about.

Photo 5.4 Left to right: Bill Bratton and George Kelling.
Photo credit: New York Daily News.

References

Allon, Tom (2020). Bring back Bill Bratton to fight crime and police brutality. *City and State*. August 27.

Anderson, Jake (2020). *Gone at midnight: The tragic story behind the unsolved internet sensation*. Toronto, ON: Citadel Press.

Armstrong, Michael (2012). *They wished they were honest: The Knapp Commission and New York City Police Corruption*. New York, NY: Columbia University Press.

Austin, James, Michael Jacobson, and Inimar Chettiar (2013). How New York City reduced mass incarceration: A model for change? New York, NY: Brennan Center for Justice at NYU Law and the Vera Institute.

Belkin, Lisa (2015). *Show me a hero: A tale of murder, suicide, race and redemption*. New York, NY: Back Bay Books.

Bennett, William J., John J. DiIulio, Jr. and John Walters (1996). *Body count: Moral poverty and how to win America's war on crime and drugs*. New York, NY: Simon and Schuster.

Berman, Greg and John Feinblatt (2005). *Good courts*. New York, NY: The New Press.

Biden, Joe (2017). *Promise me, Dad: A year of hope, hardship, and promise*. New York, NY: Random House.

Bittner, Egon (1970). *The functions of the police in modern society: A review of the background factors, current practices, and possible role models*. Chevy Chase, MD: National Institute of Mental Health.

Bond, Richard and Michael Carlin (2014). *Tupac 187: The red knight*. United Kingdom: Martin Productions.

Bowling, Benjamin (1999). The rise and fall of New York murder: Zero tolerance or crack's decline? *British Journal of Criminology, 39*(4): 531–554.

Bradley, Bill (2021). Rudy Giuliani says 'Trial by Combat' was reference to 'Documentary' 'Game of Thrones'. *Huffington Post*. January 14.

Braga, Anthony. (2002). Problem-oriented policing and crime prevention. Monsey, NY: Criminal Justice Press.

Braga, Anthony. (2005). Hot spots policing and crime prevention: A systematic review of randomized controlled trials. *Journal of Experimental Criminology 1*: 317–342.

Braga, Anthony A., and Brenda J. Bond (2008). Policing crime and disorder hot spots: A randomized controlled trial. *Criminology 46*: 77–607.

Braga, Anthony and David Weisburd (2012). The effects of 'pulling-levers' focused deterrence strategies in crime. *Campbell Systematic Reviews. 6*: 1–91.

Bratton, William (1997). Crime is down in New York City: Blame the police. In Norman Dennis (Ed.), *Zero tolerance: Policing a free society. 35*: 29–42. London: The IEA Health and Welfare Unit Choice in Welfare.

Bratton, William (1999). Great expectations: How higher expectations for police departments can lead to a decrease in crime. In Robert Langworth (Ed.), *Measuring what matters: Proceedings from the Policing Research Institute Meetings: National Institute of Justice and Office of Community-Oriented Policing Services* (pp. 11–26).

Bratton, William and Jon Murad (2018). William Bratton on "Precision Policing: Data, discretion, and community outreach can ensure a new era of public safety" *City Journal*. August 1.

Bratton, William and Brian Anderson (2020). Police on the brink: A conversation with William Bratton. *City Journal*. July 22.

Bratton, William and Peter Knobler (1998). *Turnaround: How America's top cop reversed the crime epidemic*. New York, NY: Penguin Random House.

Bratton, William and Peter Knobler (2021). *The profession: A memoir of community, race, and the arc of policing America*. New York, NY: Penguin Random House.

Brattton, William (2021). Opinion: As a longtime police chief, I believe we have to reestablish trust. *The Washington Post*. June 4.

Bratton, William and Zachary Tumin (2012). *Collaborate or perish*. New York, NY: Random House.

Bratton, William, James Q. Wilson, George Kelling, Rev. Eugene Rivers, and Peter Cove (2004). This works: Crime prevention and the future of broken windows policing. *Center for Civic Innovation: At the Manhattan Institute. 36*. April.

Brown, Elizabeth and George Barganier (2018). *Race and crime: Geographies of justice*. Oakland, CA: University of California Press.

Bultema, James (2013). *Guardians of Angels: A history of the Los Angeles Police Department*. West Conshohocken, PA: Infinity Publishing.

Burnham, David (1970). Graft paid to police here said to run into millions. *New York Times*. April 25.

Burnham, David (1971). Murphy promotes an inspector for fighting police corruption. *New York Times*. August 28.

Burns, Sarah (2012). *The Central Park Five: The untold story behind one of New York City's most infamous crimes*. New York, NY: First Vintage Books.

Buntin, John (2009). *L.A. noir: The struggle for the soul of America's most seductive city*. New York, NY: Harmony Books.

Campanile, Carli (2021). Ex-top cop Bratton: NY went too far to aid criminals, long summer ahead. June 10.

Cannon, Lou (1999). *Official negligence: How Rodney King and the riots changed Los Angeles and the LAPD*. Boulder, CO: Westview Press.

Carlin, Michael and Russell Poole (2016). *Chaos merchants: Murders of Tupac Shakur and notorious BIG*. Los Gatos, CA: Smashwords.

Carraggle, Mike (2021). Police commissioner's daughter says abuse allegations are a lie: Tiffany White told GBH the 1999 allegations levied by her mother against Dennis White are false. *GBH News*. February 16.

Celona, Larry (2017). NYPD cop's daughter is born three years after his death. *New York Post*. July 25.

Churchill, Ward and Jim Vander Wall (2002). *Agents of repression: The FBI's secret wars against the Black Panther Party and the American Indian Movement* (2nd ed.). Cambridge, MA: South End Press.

Clarke, Ronald V. (1995). Building a safer society: Strategic approaches to crime prevention. *Crime and Justice 19*: 91–150.

Clarke, David Jr. and Nancy French (2017). *Cop under fire: Moving beyond hashtags of race, crime, and politics for a better America*. Franklin, TN: Worthy Books.

Coles, Catherine and George Kelling (2002). "New trends in prosecutors' approaches to youthful offenders." In Gary Katzmann (Ed.), *Security our children's future: New approaches to juvenile justice and youth violence*. Washington, DC: The Brookings Institution.

Cook, Philip and Jens Ludwig (2011). More prisoners versus more crime is the wrong question. Washington, DC: Brookings Institution, Policy Brief No. 185.

Cooper, Kenneth (1981). The public service career of Barry M. Locke. *Boston Globe*. July 18.

Cutner, Max (2015). 30 years after Bernhard Goetz, a subway shooting evokes comparisons. *Newsweek*. March 13.

Davis, Duane 'Keefe D' and Yusuf Jah (2019). *Compton street legend: Notorious Keffe D's street-level accounts of Tupac and Biggie Murders, Death Row Origins, Suge Knight, Puffy Combs, and Crooked Cops*. Santa Monica, CA: KingDoMedia.

Davis, Robert C., Pedro Mateu-Gelabert, and Joel Miller (1999). Can effective policing also be respectful? Two examples in the South Bronx. *Police Quarterly 8*(2): 229–247.

De Pario, Maria (2017). Evaluation of needlestick injuries and other exposure to bloodborne pathogens among officers in a city police department. U.S. Department of Health and Human Services, Centers for Disease Control and Prevention. National Institute for Occupational Safety and Health.

Dickinson, Maggie (2008). The making of space, race and place: New York City's war on graffiti, 1970–the present. Critique of Anthropology 28: 27–45.

Domanick, Joseph (2015). *Blue: The LAPD and the battle to redeem American Policing*. New York, NY: Simon & Schuster.

Donovan, John (2005). I have no use for this fellow Parker: William H. Parker of the LAPD and his feud with J. Edgar Hoover and the FBI. *Southern California Quarterly 87*(2): 171–198.

Eck, John and Edward Maguire (2000). Have changes in policing reduced violent crime? An assessment of the evidence. In Alfred Blumstein and Joel Wallman (Eds.), *The crime drop in America 207*: 228. New York, NY: Cambridge University Press.

Eck, John. (2002). Preventing crime at places. In L. Sherman, D. Farrington, B. Welsh & D. L. MacKenzie (Eds.), Evidence-based crime prevention (pp. 241–294). New York, NY: Routledge.

Eterno, John and Eli Silverman (2010). The NYPD's Compstat: Compare statistics or compose statistics? *International Journal of Police Science & Management 12*(3): 426–449

Fletcher, George P. (1988). *A crime of self-defense: Bernhard Goetz and the law on trial.* Chicago, IL: The University of Chicago Press Books.

Gascon, Luis and Aaron Rousell (2019). *The limits of community policing: Civilian power and police accountability in Black and Brown Los Angeles.* New York, NY: New York University Press.

Gates, Daryl (1992). *Chief: My life in the L.A.P.D.* New York, NY: Random House Publishing.

Gau, Jacinta M. and Travis C. Pratt (2008). Broken windows or window dressing? Citizens' (in)ability to tell the difference between disorder and crime. *Criminology & Public Policy* 7: 163–194.

Gilbert, Mike (2008). *How I helped OJ get away with murder.* Washington, DC: Regnery Publishing, Inc.

Gladwell, Malcom (2000). *The tipping point: How little things can make a big difference.* New York, NY: Little, Brown and Company.

Goldstein, Herman (1979). Improving policing: A problem-oriented approach. *Crime & Delinquency 25*(2): 236–258.

Goldstein, Herman (1990). *Problem-oriented policing.* New York, NY: McGraw-Hill Publishing.

Haas, Jeffery (2011). *The assassination of Fred Hampton: How the FBI and the Chicago police murdered a black panther.* Chicago, IL: Chicago Review Press.

Harcourt, Bernard. (1998). Reflecting on the subject: A critique of the social influence conception of deterrence, the broken windows theory, and order-maintenance policing. *Michigan Law* Review *97*: 291–389.

Harcourt, Bernard (2001). *Illusion of order: The false promise of broken windows policing.* Cambridge: Harvard University Press.

Harcourt, Bernard and Jens Ludwig (2006). Broken windows: New evidence from New York City and a Five-City social experiment. *University of Chicago Law Review 73*(271): 271–321.

Harris, David (2005). *Good cops: The case for preventative policing.* New York, NY: The New Press.

Hauck, Gracy, Christal Hayes, and N'dea Yancey-Bragg (2021). Derek Chauvin trial live: 7 jurors now seated as Minneapolis announces $27M settlement with George Floyd's family. *USA Today.* March 12.

Hinkle, Joshua and David Weisburd (2008). The irony of broken windows policing: A micro-place study of the relationship between disorder, focused police crackdowns and fear of crime. *Journal of Criminal Justice 36*: 503–512.

Hinton, Elizabeth (2016). *From the war on poverty to the war on crime: The making of mass incarceration in America.* Cambridge: Harvard University Press.

Hough, Andrew (2010). David Cameron becomes youngest Prime Minister in almost 200 years. *The Daily Telegraph, London.* May 11.

Hyunseok, Jang, Larry Hoover, and Hee-Jong Joo (2010). An evaluation of Compstat's effect on crime: The Fort Worth experience. *Police Quarterly 13*(4): 387–412.

Jacobs, Jane (1961). *The death and life of the great American cities.* New York, NY: Vintage Books.

Jang, Sung and Johnson, Byron (2001). Neighborhood disorder, individual religiosity, and adolescent use of illicit drugs: A test of multilevel hypotheses. *Criminology 39*(1): 109–144.

Johnson, Terrance and Raymond Cox III (2004). Police ethics: Organizational implications. *Public Integrity* 7(1): 67–79.

Kading, Greg (2011). *Murder rap: The untold story of the Biggie Smalls & Tupac Shakur murder investigations by the detective who solved both cases.* (self-published): One-Time Publishing.

Kelling, George L. (2001). Broken windows and the culture wars: A response to selected critiques. In R. Matthews and J. Pitts (Eds.), *Crime, disorder, and community safety.* London, UK: Routledge.

Kelling, George L. (2012). Reflection on James Q. Wilson. *PERF subject to debate 26*(2): 1–2. March/April.

Kelling, George L. (2015a). Don't blame my 'broken windows' theory for poor policing. *Politico.* August 11.

Kelling, George L. (2015b). *Policing in Milwaukee: A strategic history. Urban Life Series (Book 8).* Marquette, WI: Marquette University Press.

Kelling, George L. (2019). Community policing, rightly understood. *City Journal, Winter.*

Kelling, George L. and Catherine M. Coles. (1996). *Fixing broken windows.* Glencoe, IL: Free Press.

Kelling, George L. and Catherine M. Coles (1999). Prevention through community prosecution. *The Public Interest 136*: 69–70.

Kelling, George L. and James Q. Wilson (1982). Broken windows: The police and neighborhood safety. *Atlantic Monthly 249*(3): 29–38.

Kelling, George L. and William Bratton (2015). Why we need broken windows policing. *City Journal, Winter.*

Kelling, George L. and William Sousa (2001). Do police matter? An analysis of the impact of New York City's police reforms. *Manhattan Institute for Policy Research: Center for Civic Innovation.* December 1.

Kelling, George L., Tony Pate, Duane Dieckman, and Charles Brown (1974). The Kansas city preventative patrol experiment: A technical report.

Kelly, Raymond (2016). *Vigilance: My life serving America and protecting its Empire City.* New York, NY: Hachette Book.

Kennedy, David (1997). Pulling levers: Chronic offenders, high-crime settings, and a theory of prevention. *Valparaiso University Law Review 31*(2).

Kenny, Caroline (2020). Bloomberg apologizes for stop-and-frisk policy for the first time on the campaign trail following release of a 2015 tape. *CNN.* February 13.

Kim, W. Chan and Renee Mauborgne (2004). *Blue ocean strategy: How to create uncontested market space and make the competition irrelevant.* Brighton, MA: Harvard Business Review Press.

Kim, W. Chan and Renee Mauborgne (2013). Tipping point leadership. *Harvard Business Review.* April.

Kim, W. Chan and Renee Mauborgne (2017). *Blue ocean shift: Beyond competition.* New York, NY: Hachette Books.

King, Rodney and Lawrence Spagnola (2012) The riot within: My journey from rebellion to redemption. New York, NY: HarperCollins Publishers.

Klieman, Rikki and Peter Knobler (2004). *Fairy tales can come true: How a driven woman changed her destiny.* New York, NY: Harper Paperbacks.

Koon, Stacey and Robert Deitz (1992). *Koon presumed guilty: The tragedy of the Rodney King affair.* Washington, DC: Regnery Gateway.

Kutner, Max (2015). 30 years after Bernhard Goetz, a subway shooting evokes comparisons. New York, NY: *Newsweek*, June 7.

Levitt, Stephen and Steven Dubner (2005). *Freakonomics: A rogue economist explores the hidden side of everything.* New York, NY: William Morrow & Co.

Levitt, Leonard (2009). NYPD *confidential: Power and corruption in the country's greatest police force.* New York, NY: Thomas Dunne Books.

Lucas, Peter (2019). Paging Bill Bratton-You're needed in Boston. *Boston Herald.* May 25.

Lynch, R.G. (1978). *Police manager – Professional leadership Skills* (2nd ed.). Rockleigh, NJ: Allyn and Bacon, Inc.

Manning, Peter (2001). Theorizing policing: The drama and myth of crime control in the NYPD. *Theoretical Criminology 5*: 315–344.

Moore, Mark (2021). Ex-NYPD Commissioner Bill Bratton calls for 09/11-like panel to probe Capitol riots. *New York Post.* January 10.

Letham, Jonathan (1999). *Motherless Brooklyn.* New York, NY: Vintage Books.

Lowry, Brian (2020). 'Trial 4' tell another story of police misconduct and systematic injustice. *CNN.* November 11.

Maas, Peter (1973). *Serpico: The cop who defied the system.* New York, NY: Viking Press.

Maple, Jack and Chris Mitchell (1999). *The crime fighter: Putting the bad guys out of business.* New York, NY: Broadway Books.

Mazerolle, Lorraine, Sacha Rombouts, and James McBroom (2007). The impact of Compstat on reported crime in Queensland. *Policing: An International Journal 30*(2): 237–256.

McPhail, Clark, David Schweingruber, and John McCarthy (1998). Policing protest: The control of mass demonstrations in Western Democracies (pp. 49–69). In Donatella della Porta and Herbert Reiter (Eds.), *Social movements, protest, and contention (Vol 6).* Minneapolis, MN: University of Minnesota Press.

McPhee, Michelle (2017). *Maximum harm: The Tsarnaev Brothers, the FBI, and the road to the marathon bombing.* Lebanon, NH: University Press of New England.

Meili, Trisha (2003). *I am the Central Park jogger: A story of hope and possibility*. New York, NY: Scribner.
Moore, Tina and Craig McCarthy (2020). NYPD captains' union calls for end of CompStat program. *New York Post*. June 24.
Newman, Oscar (1973). *Defensible space through urban design*. New York, NY: Collier Books.
Nicolaou, Elena (2019). Where is Trisha Meili, the "Central Park Jogger," now? *Refinery29*. May 29.
O'Brien, Daniel, Chelsea Farrell, and Brandon Welsh (2019). Looking through broken windows: The impact of neighborhood disorder on aggression and fear of crime is an artifact of research design. *Annual Review of Criminology 2*: 53–71.
Ohlin, Lloyd and Frank Remington (1993). *Discretion in criminal justice: The tension between individualization and uniformity*. Albany, NY: SUNY Press.
Pate, Tony, Amy Ferrara, Robert Bowers, and Jon Lorence (1976). *Police response time: Its determinants and effects*. Washington, DC: Police Foundation.
Peel, Robert, Charles Rowan, and Richard Mayne (1829). Sanction of establishment of police. *No. 8 Augmentation*. London, UK: Home Office.
Pierce, Glenn, Susan Spaar, and LeBaron Briggs (1988). *The character of police work: Strategic and tactical implications*. Boston, MA: Center for Applied Social Research, Northeastern University.
Police Executive Research Forum (2020). PERF trending: People, ideas, and events: Remembering 3 giants in the field of policing. May 23rd. www.policeforum.org/trendingmay23
Police Foundation (1981). *The Newark foot patrol experiment*. Washington, D.C.: 1909 K St., N.W., Washington 20006: Police Foundation.
Ratcliffe, Jerry, Travis Taniguchi, Elizabeth Groff, and Jennifer Wood (2011). The Philadelphia foot patrol experiment: A randomized controlled trial of police patrol effectiveness in violent hotspot. *Criminology 49*(3): 795–831.
Reese, Renford (2005). *Leadership in the LAPD: Walking the tightrope*. Durham, NC: Carolina Academic Press.
Reith, Charles (1948). Principles of British policing. *A short history of the British police*. Oxford, UK: Oxford University Press.
Reyes, Jessica W. (2007). Environmental policy as social policy? The impact of childhood lead exposure on crime. *The B.E. Journal of Economic Analysis & Policy Contributions* 7: 1–41.
Rice, Connie (2014). *Power concedes nothing: The unfinished fight for social justice in America*. New York, NY: Scribner.
Roberts, Sam (2019). Jay Kriegel, a 'New York City Patriot' is dead at 79. *New York Times*. December 5.
Rosenfeld, Richard, Michael Deckard, and Emily Blackburn (2014). The effects of directed patrol and self-initiated enforcement on firearm violence: A randomized controlled study of hot spot policing. *Criminology, 52*(3): 428–449.
Russell, Francis (2005). *A city in terror: Calvin Coolidge and the 1919 Boston police strike*. Boston, MA: Beacon Press.
Sampson, Robert and Stephen Raudenbush (2001). Disorder in urban neighborhoods-Does it lead to crime? National Institute of Justice, U.S. Department of Justice.
Sampson, Robert and Stephen Raudenbush (2004). Seeing disorder: Neighborhood stigma and the social construction of "Broken Windows". *Social Psychology Quarterly 67*: 319–342.
Sampson, Robert, Stephen Raudenbush, and Felton Earls. (1997) Neighborhoods and violent crime: A multilevel study of collective efficacy. *Science 277*(5328): 918–924.
Schafer, Joseph A. (2013). *Effective leadership in policing: Successful traits and habits*. Durham, NC: Carolina Academic Press.
Serena, Katie (2018). The story of Bernhard Goetz-The mugging victim turned New York's "Subway Vigilante". *All That's Interesting (ATI)*. March 15.
Shapiro, Edward (2006). *Crown Heights: Blacks, Jews, and the 1991 Brooklyn riot*. Waltham, MA: Brandeis University Press.
Sheth, Sonam (2021). Rudy Giuliani admits Biden is president hours after being sued for $1.3 billion by voting-machine company. *Yahoo!news*. January 25.
Sherman, Lawrence, Patrick Gartin and Michael Buerger (1989). Hot spots of predatory crime: Routine activities and the criminology of place. *Criminology 27*: 27–56.
Sisak, Michael (2019). NYPD officer says he inflated charge against Eric Garner. *AP News*. May 21.

Skogan, Wesley (1990). *Disorder and decline: Crime and the spiral decay in American neighborhoods.* Berkeley. CA: University of California Press.

Skogran, Wesley and Kathleen Frydl (2004). *Fairness and effectiveness in policing: The evidence.* Washington, DC: The National Academies Press.

Sozzi, Brian (2020). Former NYPD police commissioner Bill Bratton: I don't support Trump's use of military for law and order in the streets. *Yahoo!finance.* June 16.

Spelman, William and Dale Brown (1981). *Calling the police: Citizen reporting of serious crime.* Washington, DC: National Institute of Justice.

Stewart, Gary (1998). Black codes and broken windows: The legacy of racial hegemony in anti-gang civil injunctions. *Yale Law Journal 107*(7): 2249–2279.

Stone, Christopher, Todd Foglesong, and Christine Cole (2009). "Policing Los Angeles under a consent decree: The dynamics of change at the LAPD." Program in Criminal Justice Policy and Management Working Paper Series, Harvard Kennedy School. May.

Sullivan, Randall (2002). *Labyrinth: A detective investigates the murders of Tupac Shakur and Notorious B.I.G., the implication of Death Row Records' Suge Knight, and the origins of the Los Angeles police scandal.* New York, NY: Atlantic Monthly Press.

Sullivan, Randall (2019). *Dead wrong: The continuing story of the city of lies, corruption, and cover-up in the notorious BIG murder investigation.* New York, NY: Atlantic Monthly Press.

Taibbi, Matt (2017). *I can't breathe: A killing on Bay Street.* New York, NY: Spiegel & Grau.

Taylor, Robert (2017). Lester Grant Loomis: The chief who never was. *The hot sheet: Publication of the Los Angeles Police Museum* (No. 77).

Timoney, John (2010). *Beat cop to top cop: A tale of three cities.* Philadelphia, PA: University of Pennsylvania Press.

Trojanowicz, Robert and David Carter (1998). *Philosophy and role of community policing.* Rockville, MD: U.S. Department of Justice, Office of Justice Programs, The National Institute of Justice.

Tyler, Tom and Cheryl Wakslak (2004). Profiling and police legitimacy: Procedural justice, attributions of motive, and acceptance of police authority. *Criminology 42*(2): 253–282.

Weisburd, David and Eck, John (2004). What can police do to reduce crime, disorder, and fear? *Annals of the American Academy of Political and Social Science 593*: 42–65.

Weisburd, David, Lisa Maher, and Lawrence Sherman (1992). Contrasting crime general and crime specific theory: The case of hot spots of crime. *Advances in Criminological Theory*, *4*: 45–69.

Weisburd, David and Lorraine Green (1995). Policing drug hot spots: The Jersey City drug market analysis experiment, *Justice Quarterly 12*(4): 711–735.

Weisburd, David, Stephen Mastrofski, Ann Marie McNally, Rosann Greenspan, and James Willis (2003). Reforming to preserve: Compstat and strategic problem solving in American policing. *Criminology & Public Policy 2*(3): 421–456.

Williams, Juan (2016). *We the people: The modern-day figures who have reshaped and affirmed the founding fathers' vision of America.* New York, NY: Crown Publishers.

Wilson, Carlene and Neil Brewer (1992). One- and two-person patrols: A review. *Journal of Criminal Justice 20*(5): 443–453.

Wilson, James Q. and George L. Kelling (1989). Making neighborhoods safe. *Atlantic Monthly 263*(2): 46–52.

Wilson, James Q. (1978). *Varieties of police behavior: The management of law and order in eight communities.* Cambridge, MA: Harvard University Press.

Woldoff, Rachael (2011). *White flight/Black flight: The dynamics of racial change in an American neighborhood.* Ithaca, NY: Cornell University Press.

Zahniser, David, Dakota Smith, and Emily Reyes (2020). Los Angeles cuts LAPD spending, taking police staffing to its lowest level in 12 years. *LA Times.* July 1.

Zimbardo, Phil (1973). A field experiment in auto shaping. In C. Ward (Ed.), *Vandalism.* London, UK: The Architectural Press.

Chapter 6

Chuck Ramsey – Chicago CAPs Program, Chief of Washington, DC Metropolitan Police and Commissioner of the Philadelphia Police

The Rise of Black Police Leaders

Charles "Chuck" Herbert Ramsey was born on March 23, 1950, in Chicago, Illinois, at Provident Hospital and grew up on the South Side in the Englewood neighborhood. He grew up at 6616 South May Street, near Ogden Park, and then at 7354 South Union Street near Hamilton Park. His mother, Katherine L. Ramsey, worked as a licensed practical nurse at Provident Hospital, where she gave birth to her son. His father, Charles L. Ramsey, was a bus driver for the Chicago Transit Authority (CTA) hired shortly after World War II as some of the first African-American drivers. Ramsey's older sister, Sharon, worked as a dean's executive assistant at the University of Illinois at Chicago. His younger brother, Howell "Butch" Ramsey, worked for the post office.

In 1968, Ramsey enrolled in the Chicago Police Department (CPD) cadet program at the age of 18, a year after he graduated from Francis Parker High School, while he was a freshman at the University of Illinois at Chicago. He became a sworn officer in February 1971. A few years later, Ramsey tested for a rare sergeant exam.[1] He chose to try for promotion after watching an older officer, Walter Miller, carry an obese body from a third-floor building. Ramsey decided he did not want to be doing that type of work when he became a senior officer. In 1977, Ramsey was 27 years old and promoted to sergeant, one of the youngest to make that rank.

In 1981, he attended the Drug Enforcement Administration (DEA) Narcotics Supervisors School. A few years later, in 1984, he was promoted to lieutenant. In 1986, Ramsey attended the FBI National Academy and began his degree program with Lewis University. That same year he was promoted to become Commander of the Area 1 Detective Division in the Bureau of Investigative Services. In 1988, he served as the Commander of the Patrol Division in the 11th District with the Bureau of Operational Services. In April that same year, he married Sylvia Randall, and their son Charles[2] was born the following December. In 1990, he earned his bachelor's degree, followed by a master's degree a year later. In 1992, he created a basic operational model for the department's Chicago Alternative Policing Strategy (CAPS), described

1 Ramsey reflected that he tested to become a sergeant in 1973 and felt fortunate to do so before female officers were added to the competitive lists (author's interview on August 20, 2020).

2 In the summer of 2014, at the age of 27, Charles Ramsey, Jr. was sworn by his father into the PPD as one of 47 recruits. He graduated from Penn State University and worked in the city's juvenile probation department (McCrone, 2014). Ramsey said this was the proudest day of his police career, and he surprised himself when he teared up after he swore his son in as a PPD officer (author's interview, August 20, 2020). His son later resigned from the PPD and became a federal agent with the Bureau of Alcohol, Tobacco, Firearms and Explosives (BATF).

DOI: 10.4324/9780429272226-7

more fully later. He concluded his career with the CPD serving as the Deputy Superintendent in the Bureau of Staff Services from 1994 to 1998 before he left to become the first external chief for the Metropolitan Police Department (MPD) in Washington, DC.

Ramsey was the chief of the MPD for eight years, retired, and then came out of retirement to serve as the Commissioner for the Philadelphia Police Department (PPD) from 2007 to 2016. In November 2014, Ramsey was asked by President Barack Obama[3] to co-chair a task force that would make recommendations on how the country's police forces could improve community relations in the wake of riots that stemmed from the fatal shooting of Michael Brown in Ferguson, Missouri. The *Task Force on 21st Century Policing* report was reassessed in several cities across the country after the spring/summer 2020 mass police protests. After nearly 50 years of serving three policing departments, Ramsey retired again in 2016 but continued to contribute a calming voice for ongoing police reform efforts. His decades of law enforcement experience are a testament to African-American police leadership and all police leadership. The historical roots of Black officers, including the city departments Ramsey led (Chicago, Washington, DC, and Philadelphia), are further detailed.

First Uses of Policing African-Americans and Hiring African-American Police Officers

African-Americans have always been policed (Dulaney, 1996). The first American police forces carried a dual purpose. In the northern states, labor conflict caused the need for the police through the industrialization movement, and African revolts caused the need for slave patrol in the South. Northern states attempted to follow the "British model" of policing, while southern states created their brand of slave patrols. While slavery did not bound northern police development, they still targeted protests and uprisings in segregated Black communities. Frequently, clashes occurred between Black and white populations in the north that evolved out of competition for employment. Policing in southern states was rooted in slave patrols, which involved volunteer white vigilantes who enforced slavery laws. In the early 1700s, the first slave patrols appeared in South Carolina (Hadden, 2001). These volunteer patrols returned escaped slaves to their owners and often violently put down insurrections. They also made sure both the slaves and slave owners followed plantation rules. In this vain, the conception of American policing was to target a dangerous underclass, which often consisted of poor immigrants and African-American slaves.

America's First Black Police Officers

There is no documentation on who was the first Black police officer(s) in the United States, but we know they came from "freed slaves" on the New Orleans city guard. In 1805, the city council passed an ordinance that allowed freed Blacks to serve on the early militaristic policing models as long as they had white supervisors. The Black city guard had the precarious paid responsibility of catching slaves who attempted to escape in addition to thwarting insurrections. This conflict came to historical fruition in January 1811 when an estimated 500

3 Ramsey had never met President Obama when Obama was a Senator in Illinois and was surprised when he received the phone call asking him to co-chair the task force (author's interview with Ramsey in August 2020). Ramsey met President Joe Biden several times, when he was Vice President, and expressed how generous he was with his time and how he befriended his wife Sylvia on a train ride to Wilmington from Washington, DC. Ramsey previously met with President Obama at the White House on April 19, 2011, for a listening session on immigration with Bill Bratton, Reverend Al Sharpton, and LA City Council President Eric Garcetti.

Africans in New Orleans organized the largest slave revolt in American history known as the German Coast Uprising. After putting down the insurrection, slave owners decapitated 100 slaves and put their heads on stakes for 40 miles along River Road from a plantation to the heart of the French Quarter (Rasmussen, 2012). The paradoxical process of using Blacks to police Blacks was short-lived, and by 1822, the council directed the city labor manager to only employ white males in the city guard.

The first "official" opportunity for Black police officers occurred in April 1839, as Black and white mobs clashed in Pittsburgh. Leaders from Black neighborhoods approached Mayor Jonas McClintock[4] and argued they would need to defend themselves since the night watch police officers were unwilling to protect Black citizens. Mayor McClintock opted to deputize several Black citizens as special police officers temporarily, and an interracial force was able to disarm and desist the white mob. This action represented the first example of interracial policing in American history (Ullman & Delaney, 1971). However, the progress was slow, and the Fugitive Slave Act of 1850[5] caused northern and southern police agencies to arrest and incarcerate Blacks disproportionately and furthered their vigilantism against Black populations.

Policing Black America after the Civil War

After the Civil War and President Abraham Lincoln's assassination in April 1865, Vice President Andrew Johnson[6] became President. Johnson was a Democratic Senator and Governor from Tennessee and was part of Lincoln's reelection a year before his assassination. The decision to replace his former Vice President, Hannibal Hamlin, from Maine, with southern sympathizer Johnson changed history. President Johnson pardoned Jefferson Davis[7] from treason charges, attempted to end Reconstruction,[8] and by the end of 1865 appointed governors in the South sympathetic to Southern culture. Johnson vetoed the Civil Rights Act of 1865 and provided a message to the South that Black lives did not matter. In April 1866, Congress overrode Johnson's veto, and the Civil Rights Act became law without a Presidential signature.

4 McClintock was a medical doctor who garnered local fame by treating local residents during the cholera epidemic in the 1830s. He was elected mayor at the age of 28 and organized the first 18-man police department.

5 The Fugitive Slave Act of 1850 was a pivotal lead up to the Civil War as it pressured citizens to take sides on slavery.

6 Johnson grew up poor, was against succession, and blamed affluent Southerners for the destructive Civil War. He used his new power as President to require Southerners to appeal to him directly for pardons from their war crimes. Once pardoned, these Southern leaders were given back land that the Freedmen's Bureau otherwise held as part of Southern Reconstruction. Johnson essentially helped redistribute land back to Southern whites and fought any legislation that attempted to aid freed slaves.

7 Davis, the youngest of nine siblings, served as the president of the Confederate states from 1861 to 1865. Before the Civil War, he represented Mississippi as a Democratic Senator and in the House of Representatives. He also served as the Secretary of War from 1853 to 1857 with President Franklin Pierce. Davis received a pardon from President Johnson on Christmas Day 1868 along with other Southern Confederates who personally requested a pardon (Hattaway & Beringer, 2002).

8 Reconstruction began in December 1863 and included the organization of military districts to supervise Southern politics. Reconstruction ended with the Presidential Compromise of 1877. Rutherford B. Hayes lost the popular election, but three southern states were disputed for their electoral votes. Northern Republicans agreed to withdraw Union troops from the South if Southern Democrats agreed to support Hayes's election. In doing so, Hayes's election effectively ended the Reconstruction monitoring of southern politics, and southern Blacks would again be disenfranchised. Note: Examples of other Presidents elected without the popular vote include John Quincy Adams, Abraham Lincoln, James Garfield, Benjamin Harrison, Woodrow Wilson, Harry Truman, John F. Kennedy, Richard Nixon, Bill Clinton, George W. Bush, and Donald Trump.

While southern slave patrols disappeared in the aftermath of the Civil War, they switched to Black Codes, forcing African-Americans to work for low wages. Moreover, the Black Codes caused massive arrests of Blacks for minor vagrancy infractions and forced them to become part of a convict lease system (Blackmon, 2008). Southern whites also took Black children for "apprenticeships" from indentured poor Black parents to teach them labor skills. The Federal Government challenged policing African-Americans with the passage of the Civil Rights Act in 1868 and the Fourteenth Amendment, which was supposed to provide Blacks with equal protection through constitutional guarantees of due process. Southern states and local communities responded a decade later, formalized Jim Crow[9] laws, and further subjugated Black citizens for the next century.

New Orleans Riots and Rise of Black Police Officers

Several race riots erupted throughout the country following President Lincoln's assassination, most notably the New Orleans Massacre on July 30, 1866. White Democrats, who included many police and firemen, attacked Republican protesters, many of them Black freedmen, outside of the Mechanics Institute in New Orleans. The protesters had called for a Constitutional Convention due to the state legislature's refusal to let Blacks vote and their enactment of Black Codes. The result was a confrontation leading to 48 deaths, mainly Black protesters, and more than 200 wounded (Hollandsworth, 2001). The 1866 New Orleans riots were an extension of the Civil War and Southern unrest. National outrage allowed Republicans to gain the majority of Congress three months later and catalyzed support for the passage of the Fourteenth Amendment.[10]

Following the race riots of 1866, several cities began to demand an integrated police force. In May 1867, New Orleans Union Military Governor General Philip Sheridan[11] removed Mayor John Monroe and appointed Edward Heath, originally from Maine, to be the city's new mayor. Mayor Heath received an order to hire ex-Union soldiers for at least half its police force. Heath responded by putting in place an all-white police force, including many aggressors of the New Orleans riots that targeted Black protesters (Nystrom, 2010). The nation's first African-American newspaper, the *New Orleans Tribune*, retorted and argued that the city should allow Negroes to police its city populous. Specifically, Dr. Louis Charles Roundanez, editor and founder of the newspaper, encouraged the new mayor, through his newspaper on May 11, 1867, to appoint colored police officers. New Orleans had more Black citizens than any other city during Reconstruction with 50,456, followed by Baltimore with 39,558 and Washington, DC with 35,455 (Rousey, 1987, pp. 223–224).

On May 28, 1867, Louisiana Governor James Madison Wells appointed Charles Courcelle, an ex-slave, to be a commissioner on the New Orleans police board (Flores-Robert, 2011).

9 There is no agreement on the origin of who Jim Crow was, but it likely was a name used by slaves to describe plantation owners. In the 1820s, white actor Tom Rice did a racist depiction of Black culture by portraying a trickster by Jim Crow's name. Eventually, Jim Crow became a symbolic name to describe state and local southern laws that allowed segregation. The roots of Jim Crow laws began in 1877 with Supreme Court rulings that permitted states to segregate, and in 1883, the Court challenged the Civil Rights Act of 1875 and confirmed "separate but equal" was possible. Jim Crow laws were officially upheld in 1896 through *Plessey v. Ferguson*.

10 The Fourteenth Amendment, officially adopted on July 9, 1868, gave citizenship to slaves and was opposed by President Johnson. A few months prior, on March 2–3, 1868, Johnson became the first President to be impeached by the House of Representatives for violating the Tenure of Office Act. Johnson sought to replace Secretary of War Edwin Staton without Congressional approval. The act was later repealed and found unconstitutional.

11 Sheridan was a popular General and close ally to Grant. He served as the military governor of the Fifth Military District (Texas and New Orleans) and removed several politicians from office for being impediments to Reconstruction efforts. Sheridan was terminated by President Johnson and later brought back by President Grant to continue Reconstruction efforts.

New Orleans City Council also responded to Roundanenz's plea and hired more than a dozen Black police officers, including Octave Rey, who became the nation's first Black police captain (Rousey, 1987). However, these Black officers could only arrest other Blacks and were expected to enforce Jim Crow segregation.

New Orleans appointed more Black officers than any other southern city during Reconstruction. By 1870, New Orleans had hired 182 Black officers, with a total force of 647 officers (Rousey, 1987, p. 224), and three of the five Police Board members were Black.[12] Several other southern cities followed the New Orleans model and hired Black officers to protect the Black populous from endemic white mob violence. On April 12, 1870, Deputy William Johnson, in Jacksonville, Florida, became the first recognized Black police officer killed in the line of duty two days after being injured by an intoxicated suspect.

History of the First Black Officers in Ramsey's cities – Chicago, Washington, DC, Philadelphia

Ramsey led in three police departments that historically achieved more Black appointments and promotions than any other northern city. Reform movements led by Roosevelt, Vollmer, and Wilson drove police professionalism, and the reform measures both assisted and hindered Blacks in becoming officers. The 1930s represented a second wave of police reform.[13] New standards included mandatory high school diplomas and intelligence tests. In some respects, progressive chiefs sought out Black police officers, but civil service exams also caused the exclusion of Black applicants. However, patronage remained, and Blacks continued to be hired based upon their political connections. Despite the increase of Black officers employed during the reform era, the color line and embedded racism continued to prevent these officers from attaining promotions or being assigned to enforce laws against white citizens.

Chicago

In 1871, a decade after Washington, DC hired Black officers, Chicago hired James Shelton, the city's first Black officer, and the first Black to be hired to any branch of Chicago government (McCall, 1987, pp. 97). However, he was not allowed to wear a traditional police uniform for the first decade he was hired, he could not arrest white suspects, and the CPD assigned Shelton to work plainclothes in Black neighborhoods. On October 19, 1912, William Childs, a college graduate, was appointed by Mayor Carter Harrison, Jr.[14] to be the nation's first Black

12 Yvonne Bechet was hired as the first Black female officer for the New Orleans Police Department in 1968. She served until 1990 and retired as a Deputy Superintendent. She died in July 2020 at the age of 83.

13 The first police reform took place in 1890–1930. It included Roosevelt's reform efforts in New York City, Vollmer's leadership in Berkeley, and Wilson's efforts in Wichita. This reform era also included Progressive efforts that attempted to accomplish the following: rid the police from politics; create hiring and promotion standards through civil service exams; centralize police administration; and professionalize the police through the creation of quasi-militaristic bureaucratic structure. The timing of these reform efforts converged with the entry of Black officers into American law enforcement. However, white-dominated departments frequently negated hiring Black officers and claimed they did not pass the civil service exams required for entry. In this vain, the first wave of police reform did not dramatically impact police policies for hiring Black officers and those same departments were frequently involved in race riots. For example, in Atlanta, Washington, DC, Chicago, and St. Louis, white officers were found to actively beat, disarm, and shoot Black protesters.

14 Carter Henry Harrison IV, like his father, was elected five times as Chicago's mayor (1897–1905 and 1911–1915). In 1904, Harrison attempted to receive the Democratic nomination to be President but lost to Alton Parker, whom Theodore Roosevelt easily defeated. Harrison was the first Chicago-born native to be elected mayor (see Harrison, 1944).

police lieutenant. Ironically, Mayor Harrison's father[15] appointed Shelton to be the city's first Black police officer. Upon his promotion, Childs was relegated to the Bureau of Identification and worked a desk job for the next ten years instead of being put in charge of white officers. In 1922, he bitterly resigned and reported his resentment to the *Chicago Defender*,[16] the same newspaper that reported his promotion.

On March 28, 1918, Grace Wilson became the first Black female officer in Chicago and, according to a 1918 article in *Chicago Defender*, was the first Black female officer in U.S. history.[17] In 1916, when three of the 27 women who had passed the exam for the police force were African-American, only Grace Wilson found her way onto the force, where she served until her retirement 25 years later. However, it would not be until 1974 when female officers were allowed to do patrol duties and wear the same uniforms as male officers. Before this change, female officer uniforms included skirts for their specialized assignments. Ramsey reflected on this change by stating how officers were upset when the 10th District converted a new locker room and restroom for the newly hired women patrol officers.[18]

John Scott came from Houston, Texas, and joined the CPD in 1940. He ascended to the level of captain. Scott received support from the Chicago ward politicians and was the first Black officer to serve a command rank until his retirement. Other Black captains followed, and the CPD led the country with such promotions. It would not be until the 1960s when other cities would replicate promoting Black officers. Despite the CPD's efforts to diversify, mass protests and riots against the police have long existed. Cities across the country rioted the weekend after the Thursday, April 4, 1968 assassination of Martin Luther King, Jr. in Memphis. Ramsey was a senior in high school and witnessed his city experience one of the worst riots in the country, which left nine dead and the west side destroyed by numerous fires. Mayor Daly became infamous when he told reporters that his order to the CPD was "to shoot to kill any arsonist or anyone with a Molotov cocktail in his hand and to shoot to maim or cripple anyone looting any stores in our city" (Cohen & Taylor, 2000, p. 624).

Protests and riots continued into the following year, from October 8 to 11, 1969, during the "Days of Rage." Rioters in the downtown Chicago Loop threw rocks and injured 23 police officers, which led to over 100 arrests (Burrough, 2016). Ramsey reflected that he joined the police cadet program in 1968 and wanted to stay away from downtown so nothing would happen that might impact his future police application.[19] The ongoing demonstrations in 1969 grew out of protests at the 1968 Democratic National Convention. The Weatherman faction with the Students for a Democratic Society organized the demonstrations. The group pushed for direct action in the streets to push political agendas to end the Vietnam War, police brutality, and move the American culture toward racial equality.

15 Mayor Carter Harrison, Sr. was elected Mayor of Chicago for five two-year terms (1879–1887). However, he was assassinated before completing his fifth term at his home by Patrick Prendergast, a disgruntled political supporter who thought he would get a government appointment from Harrison. Prendergast was found guilty and hung a year later, the only client to receive capital punishment that was represented by fame defense attorney Clarence Darrow (Radeska 2017).

16 The *Chicago Defender* started in 1905 and targeted its reporting to African-American readers (Michaeli, 2016).

17 As described in the Harrington chapter, it is historically debated on what city hired the first female officer and what city hired the first Black female officer. The LAPD also claims to have hired the first Black female officer, Georgia Ann Robinson, when she volunteered in 1916 and was officially paid in 1919 as a jail matron and juvenile crime prevention. Robinson's 12-year career was cut short when she permanently lost her eyesight after being injured by a prisoner. However, she continued working as a community activist in public campaigns to desegregate schools and beaches (Corsianos, 2009).

18 Author's interview with Ramsey on August 20, 2020.

19 Author's interview with Ramsey on August 20, 2020.

Washington, DC

African-Americans have been a significant part of Washington, DC since the city was first declared the national capital in 1791 (McQuirter, 2003). In 1800, Blacks represented 25 percent of the city's total population, brought mainly for slavery purposes. In 1861, Washington, DC was one of the first northern cities to hire Black police officers, although no records exist of these officers' names (Dulaney, 1996). On April 16, 1862, Congress passed the District of Columbia Emancipation Act, making their slaves the first to be officially freed in the nation before President Lincoln's Emancipation Proclamation. In July 1862, Lincoln mulled over a draft of his Emancipation speech with his cabinet. As a military strategy, the address served to free slaves in southern states so they would not assist in the rebellion against the union. In January 1863, he officially signed the formal proclamation, and by January 1865, he successfully lobbied both houses of Congress to pass the Thirteenth Amendment.

During the Reconstruction Era after 1865, more than 25,000 African-Americans moved to the nation's capital. In 1868, Washington, DC citizens elected the first Black municipal officeholder. The year prior, Howard University[20] was founded and soon became a magnet for Black professors and students. In 1870, the Preparatory School for Colored Youth became the city's first public high school, later renamed Dunbar High School, and attracted many college-bound and advanced degreed teachers. By the turn of the twentieth century, Washington, DC had the largest percentage of African-Americans in the nation. While "Jim Crow" was not formally structured in Washington, DC, segregation still existed in public schools and recreation facilities.

There is a unique history of Black officers and chiefs in the nation's capital city. Black officer William West arrested President Ulysses Grant in 1872, the only President ever to be arrested. West was one of two Black, former slave police officers working in Washington, DC during the Reconstruction Era, appointed on August 1, 1871. According to a September 27, 1908 edition of the *Washington Evening Star*, West arrested President Grant on the corner of 13th and M Street for driving a team of horses and his carriage too fast in dangerous places (Rosenwald, 2018). West had stopped Grant the previous day and issued a warning, and there had also been prior warnings. During a second incident, he decided to arrest him and bring him to the police station. Reportedly, officers at the station were unsure if they could charge a sitting president without an impeachment. The result was Grant paid a $20 bond and walked back to the White House after the police confiscated his horse and carriage. The city prosecutor then dropped the case. Twenty years later, the MPD hired Henry Lacey, the nation's first Black detective, and sergeant.

The city police department was led for 17 years by Richard Sylvester, Jr. from July 1898 to April 1915. Sylvester coined the term "third degree" to describe police interrogation. He described arrests as the first degree, transportation to jail as the second degree, and interrogations as the third degree. Superintendent Sylvester was a proponent for professionalizing the police through a paramilitaristic structure, and from 1901 to 1915 he served as the President of the International Association of Chiefs of Police (IACP). Sylvester retired as chief in the aftermath of charges filed against him after failing to protect protesters who marched in Washington, DC

20 Howard University has a number of famous graduates, several listed throughout this book. Examples include Thurgood Marshall (first Black Supreme Court Justice 1967–1991), Benjamin Davis, Sr. (first Black General in the Army), Sean "Puff Daddy" Combs (musician who attended Howard in 1989 and 1990), Walter Washington (Washington, DC's first elected mayor 1975–1979), Adrian Fenty (Washington, DC Mayor 2007–2011), and Kamala Harris (second Black female US Senator from 2017 to 2021 and first Black Vice President beginning in 2021).

for Women's Suffrage in 1913, the day before Woodrow Wilson's inauguration. Both the police and male residents physically harassed the women protesters (Roberts, 2017).

After Wilson took the Presidency (1913–1921), his administration instituted segregation in several Federal Government agencies. Throughout the U.S. Treasury, Post Office, and Interior Departments, bathroom facilities and lunchrooms were segregated. Moreover, outright dismissals of Black federal employees became common. Wilson[21] terminated 15 out of 17 Black federal supervisors and replaced them with white workers (O'Toole, 2018). The head of the Internal Revenue division in Georgia fired all his Black employees, reportedly stating, "There are no government positions for Negroes in the South. A Negro's place is in the fields" (Gossett, 1997, p. 279). In 1914, the government required photographs on all federal job applications. On November 12, 1914, Wilson met with civil rights leader William Monroe Trotter about segregation concerns (Matthews, 2015). Wilson attempted to argue with Trotter and his Black delegation that his administration was not putting Negro employees at a disadvantage but instead was preventing friction with the white employees. When Trotter retorted, Wilson's staff escorted him out of the oval office (Lehr, 2015).

By July 1919, race riots occurred in the nation's capital (Krugler, 2014). In the 1930s, President Franklin Roosevelt worked to end segregation in the Federal Government. Campaigns by Black leaders called for African-Americans to boycott a white-owned business that operated in predominantly minority neighborhoods but refused to hire Black employees. These leaders also organized protests against police brutality and unfair housing restrictions. By 1948, the protests caused the Supreme Court to declare that racially restrictive housing covenants were unconstitutional (see *Hurd v. Hodge*). In 1951, law professor James Nabrit, Jr.,[22] from Howard University, filed an appeal for desegregating a junior high school in Washington, DC in *Bolling v. Sharpe*. This ruling became a precursor for the national landmark *Brown v. Board of Education* ruling, which declared that separate education was unconstitutional. By 1957, Washington, DC, became the first city in the nation, with more than half of its residents being African-American. Throughout the 1960s, the city became the epicenter for the civil rights movement, culminating in the 1963 march for Jobs and Freedom, which brought more than 250,000 people to the Lincoln Memorial.

In 1965, Owen Davis[23] became the first Black captain of the MPD to lead a precinct, and in 1969 he was named the deputy chief to Chief John Layton. A few years later, President Lyndon Johnson[24] appointed Walter Washington to be the Mayor-Commissioner of the District. By 1970, Black officers made up 35 percent of the MPD force, the highest in the country. Gail Cobb became the nation's first Black female officer to be killed in the line of duty and only the second female to be killed nation-wide while on foot patrol on September 20, 1974.[25]

21 In June 2020, Princeton University announced they would remove Wilson's name from their public policy school and its residential college. The move came four years after the university decided to keep his name and reject student protests (Pietsch, 2020). Wilson was the president of Princeton University from 1902 to 1910 before he was the Governor of New Jersey from 1911 to 1913 and then two-term President from 1913 to 1921.

22 Nabrit was the president of Howard University from 1960 to 1965. From 1965 to 1967, he served as the first African-American Deputy U.S. Ambassador to the United Nations and then returned to Howard University as the president from 1968 to 1969. Nabrit died in 1997 at the age of 97.

23 Davis retired in 1973 and passed away in 2007 at the age of 91.

24 In 1967, President Johnson replaced the three-commissioner government organized to run the District since 1871 with a government structure headed by a single commissioner, assistant commissioner, and a nine-member city council. Washington became the first Black mayor of a major American city, followed by Carl Stokes's elections in Cleveland and Richard Hatcher in Gary, Indiana, the same year.

25 Martha Shanaman was the first female officer killed in the line of duty in 1971 during an escape attempt while working in a Detroit women's detention facility. A jury convicted John Bryant of second-degree murder of Officer Cobb in 1975 along with eight other individuals who were implicated in a bank robbery scheme to create a Black mafia that would fund legitimate Black businesses. After serving 18 years in prison, Bryant was

That year, Congress also passed a law giving the District home rule, which allowed for a mayoral election[26] and increased self-governance. Washington became the first mayor to be elected in Washington, DC, and served in that capacity from 1975 to 1979. By the time of the new mayor's election, Blacks politically and culturally led the city with more than 70 percent of the general population. The District became the first city in the nation to employ a majority of Black officers. Eighty-five years after Lacey became the first promoted MPD Black officer, Mayor Washington appointed Burtell Jefferson to be the MPD's first Black chief in 1978 as his term was ending. Jefferson led the MPD a decade after Black citizens became the majority of the District's local population. He would be the last major city Black chief to be appointed in the 1970s.

As discussed more fully in a later section, Marion Barry proceeded Walter Washington as the second Black mayor in 1979 and served until 1991. Barry earned his eagle scout as a youth and was pursuing his Ph.D. degree in chemistry when he opted to enter the civil rights movement. He was re-elected for a fourth term and served 1995–1999. Barry also served on the District city council from 1975 to 1979, and in 1966, as a civil rights activist, he called the majority-white MPD an "occupying army." As mayor, Barry encouraged his Black chiefs to recruit Black citizens. After only three years as chief, Jefferson feuded with newly elected Mayor Barry and eventually resigned. Other Black chiefs followed Jefferson: Maurice Turner, Jr. in 1981; Isaac Fulwood in 1989; Fred Thomas in 1992; and finally Chuck Ramsey in 1998. When Ramsey became chief in 1998, the MPD force was 67 percent Black.[27]

Philadelphia

In 1881, Democratic Mayor Samuel King,[28] who served from 1881 to 1884, appointed the first Black officers to the PPD: Charles Draper, Alexander Davis, Louis Carroll, and Richard Cardwell. White citizens and other officers continually harassed these first Black PPD officers. Many Philadelphia residents would not accept Black policemen's authority, and some white cops quit their jobs rather than work alongside the first Black officers. On his first day on the force, in 1881, Charles Draper was followed by a mob of whites yelling racial slurs. Draper was a Navy veteran from the Civil War almost two decades earlier and had helped to intercept slave ships from West Africa. Alexander Davis was a former slave who remarkably overcame his nightmarish past to earn a degree from Howard University Law School. Despite his academic achievement, the city did not permit Davis to practice law because of his skin color, so he took a job with the PPD instead.

Like Chicago, the city's political patronage system controlled police appointments. Particularly in Philadelphia, political connections to the Republican Party machine were

paroled in 1992 but rearrested by the MPD in 1993 for possession of crack cocaine. After years of trial delay, that case was thrown out after a judge ruled that the police lacked probable cause to search Bryant's vehicle before his arrest (Wilbanks, 2000). Cobb's son Damon was four years old when his mom was killed. He is currently serving a life sentence after being convicted of first-degree murder in 1993 (Root, 1994).

26 In addition to home rule change, the House of Representatives voted to approve Washington, DC as the 51st state on June 26, 2020, with a vote of 232-180 (Duehren, 2020). The Republican-led Senate voted that bill down. The District's population is more than 700,000, which is more populous than Vermont or Wyoming. However, the residents of the District are not represented in Congress even though they pay federal taxes. If the District were to become a state, the bill calls for the new state to be named Washington Douglas Commonwealth, after Frederick Douglas, and they would be represented by two senators (likely Democrats) and one representative.

27 In 2016, the MPD police force was 55 percent Black and falling with predictions that white officers would eventually become the majority (Jaffe, 2016). According to the 2019 Census Bureau, Blacks are now slightly under the majority for the first time in 50 years in the general population. However, in 2021, this perdiction turned out not to be true as Blacks represent 60 percent of the MPD and whites represent 31 percent of the 3,819 total number of officers.

28 King was the last Democratic mayor of Philadelphia until 1952 (McCaffery, 1993).

necessary to receive employment in the PPD. While more Blacks received police jobs in Philadelphia than in Chicago due to the patronage system, the vast majority of the police force remained white into the 1970s and preyed on African-American communities. By 1905, the PPD had nearly 100 Black officers assigned exclusively to Black neighborhoods. These racial strides ended in 1912 when James Robinson became the chief of the PPD and served until 1920. Like Vollmer, Robinson was a veteran of the Spanish-American War. He began to create a militarized department under the guise of professionalism. He connected the rise of Black populations with criminality and disorder, and arrests dramatically increased in African-American neighborhoods during his tenure. From 1917 to 1918, due to rising police brutality against Black residents, the Association for the Protection of Colored People was formed. Members carried cards to indicate that they would have backing from the association's well-funded legal team if the police attacked them. In 1911, African-Americans made up about 11 percent of all arrests. By the 1920s, through Robinson's militaristic leadership, Blacks made up almost a quarter of all arrests even though they represented less than 8 percent of the total population (Adams, 2015).

In the aftermath of Robinson's leadership, the city undertook a comprehensive study of race and crime. It confirmed that Blacks were disproportionally arrested for low-level offenses and were easy prey (Thompson, 1926, p. 254). A survey in 1952 indicated a similar pattern of police misconduct as found in the 1920s. Police harassment of Black residents or any mixed-race social gathering was common (Fyfe & Kane, 2006). These reports also indicated the need for hiring additional Black officers. In 1925, after 12 years working as a patrol officer, Robert Forgy became the first Black officer to be promoted. However, a few short years later, the PPD removed the corporal position and demoted Forgy to patrol. The following year, the department symbolically promoted Forgy to the rank of sergeant. However, he was not permitted to wear stripes on his uniform and instead was assigned to work plainclothes homicide. Hypocritically, the PPD ordered Forgy to wear his uniform during parades or when civic organizations toured the department. It was not until 1943 that the PPD would promote another Black officer, James Anderson, who became a sergeant in charge of a specialized squad of Black detectives. In 1952, Forgy officially wore his uniform while on duty as a desk sergeant for the 23rd District (Dulaney, 1996). He died a year later (Reaves, 1991). In 1953, the PPD numbered 4,224 men with 149 Black officers, none of which were ranked higher than patrol (Kephart, 1954, p. 326).

In 1957, the police utilized shotgun squads to drive through African-American neighborhoods to demonstrate a show of force. They conducted these same tactics in the 1920s. In the same year, a study confirmed that most white officers in the PPD believed Blacks are predisposed to crime and should be treated more strictly than white violators (Kephart, 1957). A 1963 study on police shootings showed that the PPD fatally shot 32 men during the prior decade, 1950–1960. Almost 90 percent of the 32 men were Black, although Blacks constituted 22 percent of the general population (Robin, 1963, pp. 226–227). Only two of the 32 fatalities led to criminal charges filed against officers. Subsequent juries returned not guilty verdicts for both officers.

Race riots in 1967 in North Philadelphia instigated Frank Rizzo's rise. (The appendix of the O.W. Wilson chapter, under Herman Goldstein, also discusses Rizzo). Rizzo became an icon in Philadelphia and represented a complex dichotomy of political leadership when it came to race. He was the police commissioner from 1967 to 1971 and the mayor from 1972 to 1980. As police commissioner, in 1968, Blacks constituted 20 percent of the total officers, more than any other city. However, by 1970, Black officer hiring declined from 27 percent in 1966 to 8 percent in 1970, according to a class-action lawsuit against the city in *Commonwealth of Pennsylvania v O'Neill*. In 1978, *Philadelphia Inquirer* journalists William Marimow and Jon Neuman won a Pulitzer Prize for documenting the long pattern of police brutality under Rizzo's leadership (Neumann & Marimow, 2009).

Black Police Officers in the Modern Era

In the late 1960s and into the early 1970s, there were a series of efforts to bring in a participatory management style to policing. The belief was that if officers were intellectually and collectively involved in deciding how to structure their work, they would feel less alienated and become more effective. The participatory managerial style fit with democratic values and practices that were espoused by academics. Efforts were scattered throughout policing, met with some success, and positively impacted the recruitment of minority officers. In 1970, Blacks made up about six percent of police officers. However, leaders abandoned participatory management by the mid-1970s.

Today, approximately 58,000 African-American police officers work across the country representing close to 13 percent of all sworn officers, which matches the number of female officers and represents the percentage of the total Black American citizens. In cities with populations over 250,000, 20 percent of the police officers are Black, and 14 percent are Hispanic. In Chicago, about 30 percent of the general population are Black, and 50 percent are white. The CPD has half white officers, 25 percent Hispanic, and 21 percent Black officers. In Washington, DC, about 47 percent of the population are Black and 45 percent are white. The MPD has the highest rate of Black officers making up more than half of the force, with 31 percent of MPD officers being white and 7 percent Hispanic. In Philadelphia, about 44 percent of the general population are Black, but 57 percent of the 6,500 PPD officers are white, and the number of Black officers has dropped since 2000 (Dean, 2017). Black police recruits blame the Philadelphia's hiring system (Vargas, 2020).

African-American Police Administrators

Breaking through the brass ceiling in policing has been more difficult for minority officers than getting hired into entry patrol. Before the 1950s, only two Black officers in the entire country reached command positions: Octave Rey of New Orleans (1868–1877) and John Scott in Chicago (1940–1946). Both became captains. However, as New Orleans Democrats gained back their political power, Rey's career was cut short and a period of Redemption replaced the Republican-led Reconstruction. Progress made for southern Blacks during Reconstruction was quickly swept away during Redemption and Jim Crow.

In the late 1950s, towns with a small number of Black residents had Black chiefs ascend to their departments' highest position, not through appointments but to take over as "interim chief" for white chiefs who were unable to complete their duties. There was no threat from the limited number of Black chiefs in these communities due to the small African-American populations and lack of formal appointments. In other instances, appointing Black police chiefs became political publicity stunts. The stunts frequently involved mayoral and city council conflict. Aurora, Illinois (the city where the author is a professor at Aurora University) represents one example of a political publicity stunt.

> On October 14, 1958, Aurora Mayor Paul Egan (two-term mayor in office from 1954–1962) called a public meeting at city council chambers and encouraged attendees to "bear arms." Mayor Egan was subsequently arrested by Aurora Police Department (APD) Chief

Donald Curran for a breach-of-the-peace statute and jailed for four hours. Egan then filed a federal lawsuit in district court for $5 million in damages, but a judge dismissed the case, and a subsequent appeal also dismissed.[29]

Egan was notorious in the national media, who claimed he was the worst mayor in the country (Asbell, 1956). He sought the $8,000 a year job as Aurora mayor due to financial problems supporting his wife and five children on $27 a week in unemployment compensation. The second-largest city in Illinois had a population of 57,000 in 1959, and Egan repeatedly tried to replace what he described as a corrupt and politically connected police force. The four city council members consistently outvoted the mayor on several issues, including his constant nominations to replace his police chief, which reportedly included a 100-year-old parrot named Senor Carr (Ormond, 2019). The city council concurred with Egan when he appointed a popular Black Baptist Minister, Bob Wesby, to become police chief. Although symbolic, this may have represented the nation's first Black chief in a community with a population of over 50,000 (Dulaney, 1996, p. 83). However, no evidence exists to indicate the city council approval made this appointment official. Wesby was a prominent civil rights leader in the Midwest, marched with Martin Luther King, Jr., and was colleagues with Jesse Jackson. In 1961, he was arrested in Jackson, Mississippi, as part of the "freedom riders."[30] In the summer of 1988, at the age of 61, Wesby traveled to Atlanta, Georgia, to be part of the Democratic National Convention.

On July 22, 1988, only hours after returning to Aurora, street preacher Calvin Green, age 29, entered Wesby's Progressive Baptist Church and killed him with an ax near the church altar. Shortly afterward, Wesby's body was found by a maintenance worker who testified against Green after he unknowingly ran into the murderer and directed him to an exit. Green received a life sentence in a bench trial (Sjostrom, 1989) and resides at the Pontiac Correctional Center.

In 1890, African-American Alfred C. Lucas began a 16-year career as a transport wagon driver for the APD transporting the sick, the dead, arrestees, and prisoners. On October 5, 1964, Aurora hired Clinton Mayes as its first Black police officer. In 1969, five years after Mayes's hire, he was promoted to be a sergeant but resigned a few months later and stated that neither the police department nor the community was ready for a Black police supervisor. In 2021, Aurora's first Black mayor, Richard Irvin, nominated Keith Cross to be the city's second Black police chief, after the retirement of Kristen Ziman, the city's first female police chief.

The aftermath of the civil rights movement in the 1960s provided some gains notable for policing. For example, the National Black Police Association (NBPA)[31] began in 1972, and the National Organization of Black Law Enforcement Executives (NOBLE)[32] began in 1976. Before the founding of these organizations, Cleveland, Ohio, became the first big city to appoint

29 See https://law.justia.com/cases/federal/appellate-courts/F2/275/377/215878/

30 The "freedom riders" were civil rights activists who intentionally rode mixed-race interstate buses in 1961 into the segregated South to challenge the non-enforcement of the U.S. Supreme Court decision *Boyton v. Virginia* (1960), which ruled that segregated buses were unconstitutional. While most southern states continued to ignore the federal ruling, the activists incited their own arrests to bring attention to the issue, which also included racial segregation in restaurants and public transportation waiting rooms. The Freedom Riders openly challenged the Southern Jim Crow segregation status quo restrictions and brought credibility to the civil rights movement while putting themselves in harm's way through arrest. Moreover, officers often allowed white mobs to attack the freedom riders before they were arrested.

31 The NBPA is a non-profit corporation that operates out of Washington, DC, with regional associations that serve as advocate forums for minority police officers and a network for professional development with an annual conference. See www.blackpolice.org/

32 NOBLE has nearly 60 chapters and represents over 3,000 members worldwide, including command executives from all government levels of law enforcement. See https://noblenational.org/

a Black police leader. Although Blacks did not represent a majority of the Cleveland population, they still elected their first Black mayor, Carl Stokes, in 1967. Stokes was the first Black mayor for a major U.S. city. In his first few years in office, he went through two white police chiefs before appointing Benjamin Davis, Jr.[33] as their first Black public safety director. This selection, initially thought to be safe, turned out to be disastrous. Davis was a West Point graduate and the first Black General in the Air Force (Davis, 1991; Earl, 2010). His father, Benjamin Davis, Sr., was the first Black Brigadier General in the Army, which occurred in 1940 (Fletcher, 1989). Davis took a law and order managerial approach, without a municipal law enforcement background, that frequently conflicted with Stokes's more liberal mayoral goals. After six months, Davis resigned, citing differences with the mayor on handling Black militants and enemies of law enforcement.

A similar story occurred in Newark, New Jersey. In 1970, the city elected Kenneth Gibson, its first Black mayor and the country's second Black big-city mayor (Holmes, 2020). Gibson opted to appoint a white police administrator, John Redden, a protégé of New York City Police Commissioner Patrick Murphy (1970–1973). (Murphy is also discussed in the chapter on Bill Bratton and the O.W. Wilson chapter appendix with Herman Goldstein.) Redden ran into conflicts with Mayor Gibson and most Black city council members before resigning a couple of years later. In January 1973, Gibson selected Black Lieutenant Edward Kerr as interim chief for $25,000 annually. However, the three Black councilmen could not gain enough support from their six white counterparts to approve the mayor's appointment (Johnson, 1973). After six months, Kerr was officially approved and became Newark's first Black police director. He lasted a year. After Gibson's reelection, Lieutenant Hubert Williams replaced Kerr, became Newark's second Black police director, and successfully served in that role from 1974 to 1985.

In 1974, Maynard Jackson became the country's third big-city Black mayor in Atlanta. Court battles ensued when Jackson attempted to fire his white police chief, John Inman. After the courts upheld Inman's contract as chief, Jackson did an end-around. He created a public safety commissioner position to be in charge of police, fire, and civil defense operations.[34] In late summer 1974, he appointed his Black college friend, Reginald Eaves, to this position, despite his lack of police administration experience. Eaves represented the first Black to be in charge of a large-city southern police department.

After four years, Atlanta brought in Lee Brown to be the second Black public safety commissioner, where he served until 1982 before leaving to become the chief in Houston. George Napper[35] became the first Black chief, who served under Lee Brown, during his tenure in Atlanta from 1978 to 1982. The chief title symbolically remained in Atlanta. After he left, Brown became Houston's first Black police chief in 1982 and the first external Houston chief appointed in 40 years. Before Brown's position as chief, in the 110-year history of the Houston Police Department (HPD), only one Black officer had achieved a promotion above Sergeant's rank. Lieutenant Jerry Jones received his lieutenant promotion 14 days before Brown's arrival (Dulaney, 1996, p. 93). Brown successfully reformed the HPD over the next seven years before becoming the second Black commissioner for the NYPD in 1990. This request came from New York City's first Black mayor, David Dinkins, and Brown replaced Benjamin Ward, who served as the first Black commissioner for the NYPD. Brown left New York in 1992 and returned to Houston.

33 Davis also became famous as the World War II Tuskegee Airmen commander, as shown in the 1995 movie *The Tuskegee Airmen*, which starred Laurence Fishburne and Cuban Gooding Jr. Davis is played by Andre Braugher. He died in 2002 at the age of 89. Amid the 2020 mass police protests, President Trump appointed the first African-American chief of staff for the Air Force, General Charles Q. Brown. Brown was the second Black commander to be on the Joint Chiefs of Staff, the first being General Colin Powell. Powell was the 12th Chair of the Joint Chiefs of Staff, and the youngest to hold that position, from 1989 to 1993. He also served as President Bush's Secretary of State from 2001–2005.

34 By 1990, the Department of Public Safety was abolished and individual departments for police, fire, and corrections were reinstated with Eldrin Bell appointed as chief.

35 Napper died on October 2, 2020 at his Atlanta home at the age of 81.

Although not exhaustive, Table 6.1 lists Black police leaders in urban departments with Black female police leaders listed in italics.

Table 6.1 African-American Police Leaders in Large Cities (Female Police Leaders in Italics)

Name	*City*	*Position*	*Years*
Benjamin Davis, Jr.[i]	Cleveland	Public Safety Director	1970–1970
Boston Daniels[ii]	Kansas City, KS	Chief	1970–1971
Edward Kerr	Newark	Police Director	1973–1974
Hubert Williams[iii]	Newark	Police Director	1974–1985
A. Reginald Eaves[iv]	Atlanta	Public Safety Commissioner	1974–1978
George Austin[v]	Newport News, VA	Chief	1975–1983
William "Bill" Hart[vi]	Detroit	Chief	1976–1991
Odell Sylvester[vii]	Berkeley	Chief	1977–1980
Lee Brown[viii]	Atlanta	Public Safety Commissioner	1978–1982
	Houston	Chief	1982–1990
	New York	Commissioner	1990–1992
George Napper[ix]	Atlanta	Director of Police Services	1978–1982
Burtell Jefferson[x]	Washington, DC	Chief	1978–1981
Maurice Turner, Jr.[xi]	Washington, DC	Chief	1981–1989
Ronald Nelson	Berkeley	Chief	1982–1990
Reuben Greenberg	Charleston	Chief	1982–2005
Estella Patterson	Raleigh	Chief	2021–
Fred Rice, Jr.	Chicago	Superintendent[xii]	1983–1987
Tyree Broomfield, Jr.	Dayton	Chief	1983–1987
Benjamin Ward	New York	Commissioner	1984–1989

i Davis died in 2002 at the age of 89.

ii Daniels died in 1995 at the age of 90.

iii Williams died on March 10, 2020. He was the first Black President of the National Police Foundation. The Police Foundation is discussed more fully under George Kelling in the appendix to the chapter on Bill Bratton. The mission of the Police Foundation is to advance policing through innovation and science. It is the oldest non-partisan national organization dedicated to improving American policing.

iv Eaves did not have any police experience when he was appointed to be Public Safety Commissioner in Atlanta from 1974 to 1978. He was appointed by his college friend, Maynard Jackson, who was elected as the country's third big city Black mayor. Eaves's position as Public Safety Commissioner was different than police chief, but still worth noting. Eaves was proceeded by Lee Brown, discussed more fully in the chapter on Harrington, and they both represent the first Black leaders in Southern law enforcement. Eaves later served federal prison time for extortion. He died in 2015 at the age of 81.

v Austin died in January 2008 at the age of 86.

vi In 1974, Coleman Young was elected as Detroit's first Black mayor (a position he held for five terms and 20 years) and appointed Hart to be the city's first Black chief. Dr. Hart received a Ph.D. in educational sociology from Wayne State University and became the nation's longest-serving Black chief with 14 years as Detroit chief. However, his reputation was marred with a federal embezzlement conviction in May 1992 after he was accused of stealing $2.6 million of taxpayer funds intended for undercover drug operations. Hart received a ten-year federal sentence. By 1998, nearly 61 percent of Detroit's police force was Black, second to Washington, DC.

vii Sylvester became Berkeley's first African-American police chief 78 years after August Vollmer hired the city's first Black officer, Walter Gordon.

viii In 1997, Brown was elected the first Black mayor of Houston. See Brown, 2012.

ix Dr. Napper received his Ph.D. in criminology from the University of California at Berkeley and served as the President of the NOBLE in 1986. Napper died in October 2020 at the age of 81.

x See Williams and Kellough (2006). Jefferson died on March 19, 2021, at the age of 96.

xi The Metropolitan Police Academy is named in the honor of Turner.

xii Sam Nolan, another African-American, was Acting CPD Superintendent for several weeks in 1979 before Chicago's first Black mayor, Harold Washington, appointed Rice, on August 27, 1983. Rice became the city's 55th head of the CPD and the first permanent Black police superintendent.

Table 6.1 Cont.

Name	*City*	*Position*	*Years*
Bishop Robinson	Baltimore	Commissioner	1984–1987
Clarence Dickson	Miami	Chief	1985–1989
Warren Woodfork	New Orleans	Chief	1985–1991
William "Mugsy" Moore	Pittsburgh	Chief	1986–1987
Robert Johnson	MI	Chief	1986–1994
Robert Johnson	MS	Chief	1994–1997
Robert Johnson	MI	Chief	1997–2000
LeRoy Martin	Chicago	Superintendent	1987–1992
Sylvester Daughtry	Greensboro	Chief	1987–1998
Walter Adams[xiii]	Jersey City, NJ	Chief	1988-1989
James Ivy	Memphis	Director	1988–1991
Willie Williams[xiv]	Philadelphia	Commissioner	1988–1992
	Los Angeles	Chief	1992–1997
Floyd Powell	Wichita	Chief	1989–1989
Edward Woods	Baltimore	Commissioner	1989–1993
Isaac Fulwood	Washington, DC	Chief	1989–1992
Ralph Cothran[xv]	Chattanooga	Chief	1989–1995
Eldrin Bell	Atlanta	Chief	1990–1994
Dashiel Butler	Berkeley	Chief	1990–2002
David Walker	Jackson, MS	Chief	1991–1991
Stanley Knox	Detroit	Chief	1991–1994
Jerry Oliver	Pasadena	Chief	1991–1995
	Richmond, VA	Chief	1995–2002
	Detroit	Chief	2002–2003
Johnnie Johnson, Jr.[xvi]	Birmingham	Chief	1991–1998
Jimmy Wilson	Jackson, MS	Chief	1992–1994
Joseph Samuels	Oakland	Chief	1994–1999
	Richmond, CA	Chief	1999–2003
Richard Neal	Philadelphia	Commissioner	1992–1998
Fred Thomas[xvii]	Washington, DC	Chief	1992–1995
Joseph Samuels	Oakland	Chief	1994–1999
	Richmond, CA	Chief	1999–2003
Richard Williams	Madison, WI	Chief	1993–2004
Charles Moose[xviii]	Portland	Chief	1993–1999
	Montgomery County	Chief	1999–2003
Patrick Oliver	Cleveland, OH	Chief	1994–1994
Ike McKinnon[xix]	Detroit	Chief	1994–1998
Arnold Gibbs	Cape Coral, FL	Chief	1994–2002

xiii Adams died in September 2020 at the age of 85. He was preceded by Chief John Fritz who committed suicide in February 1988 by firearm at his police desk.

xiv Williams was the first Black to lead the PPD and then the LAPD. He is also discussed in the chapter on Bill Bratton. See Williams and Henderson (1996). Williams died in April 2016 at the age of 72.

xv See Patton (1997).

xvi Johnston was Birmingham's second Black police officer.

xvii Thomas had a police cruiser marked "Chief of Police" and regularly responded to calls for service and stopped suspects. He was inside police headquarters on November 22, 1994, when a gunman killed a police sergeant and two FBI agents inside the Cold Case Squad offices. Chief Thomas helped assist a fifth victim to a medical helicopter. The author of this book was across the street from MPD headquarters, working as an investigator for the Public Defender Service on the day of the shooting.

xviii See Moose and Fleming (2004).

xix McKinnon served as Detroit's Deputy Mayor from 2013 to 2016.

Table 6.1 Cont.

Name	*City*	*Position*	*Years*
Richard Pennington	New Orleans	Superintendent	1994–2002
	Atlanta	Chief	2002–2010
Beverley Harvard[xx]	Atlanta	Chief	1994–2002
Ronald Lowe	Dayton	Chief	1995–2000
Emmett Turner	Nashville	Chief	1996–2003
Bernard Parks	Los Angeles	Chief	1997–2002
Benny Napoleon[xxi]	Detroit	Chief	1998–2001
Jerry Demings	Orlando	Chief	1998–2002
Robert "RC" White[xxii]	Greensboro	Chief	1998–2003
	Louisville	Chief	2003–2011
	Denver	Chief	2012–2018
Harold Hurtt	Phoenix	Chief	1998–2004
Terry Hillard[xxiii]	Chicago	Superintendent	1998–2003
Charles Ramsey	**Washington, DC**	**Chief**	***1998–2007***
	Philadelphia	**Commissioner**	**2008–2016**
Terrell Bolton	Dallas	Chief	1999–2003
Ronald Daniel[xxiv]	Baltimore	Commissioner	2000–2000
Norman Williams	Witchita	Chief	2000–2015
Mary Bounds	Cleveland	Chief	2001–2002
Dennis Duval	Syracuse	Chief	2001–2004
Anthany Beatty	Lexington	Chief	2001–2007
Rodney Monroe[xxv]	Macon, GA	Chief`	2001–2005
	Richmond, VA	Chief	2005–2008
	Charlotte-Mecklenburg, NC	Chief	2008–2015
Prentice "Earl" Sanders[xxvi]	San Francisco	Chief	2002–2003
Andre Parker	Richmond, VA	Chief	2002–2004
Robert Moore	Jackson, MS	Chief	2002–2005
Eddie Compass	New Orleans	Chief	2002–2005
Sylvester Johnson	Philadelphia	Commissioner	2002–2008
Richard Pennington	Atlanta	Chief	2002–2010
Thomas Warren	Omaha	Chief	2003–2008
Ella Bully-Cummings	Detroit	Chief	2003–2008
Annetta Watts Nunn	Birmingham	Chief	2003–2008
Kevin Clark[xxvii]	Baltimore	Commissioner	2003–2004
Leonard Hamm[xxviii]	Baltimore	Commissioner	2004–2007

xx Harvard was the first Black woman and only the third female to lead a major police department.

xxi Napoleon was elected Sheriff of Wayne County in 2009. He died in December 2020 from COVID-19 complications at the age of 65.

xxii White began his career in 1972 with the Washington, DC Metropolitan Department. He was an assistant chief before becoming the Director of the Columbia Housing Authority Office of Public Safety in 1995. In 2003 he became the chief of the newly formed Louisville Metro Police Department. In 2011, PERF assisted Denver with a national search that led to White becoming the police chief. In 2015, White was named a member of PERF's Board of Directors. In 2019 White served a few months as interim chief for the Asheville Police Department.

xxiii See Hillard and Jurkanin (2006).

xxiv A few months into the commissioner position, Daniel resigned after refusing to back Mayor Martin O'Malley's crime-fighting strategies.

xxv Monroe rose through the ranks of the Washington, DC MPD starting in 1979 before he left to become a chief.

xxvi Sanders died in January 2021 at the age of 83.

xxvii Clark was an NYPD Commander. After 21 months as Commissioner in Baltimore, he was fired over domestic abuse allegations.

xxviii Mayor Sheila Dixon fired Hamm during a 2007 crime wave. See Hamm (2019).

Table 6.1 Cont.

Name	*City*	*Position*	*Years*
Noble Wray	Madison, WI	Chief	2004–2013
Shirlene Anderson	Jackson, MS	Chief	2002–2005
William Powell	Aurora, IL	Chief	2005–2008
H. McCarthy Gipson	Buffalo	Commissioner	2006–2009
Tim Bellamy	Greensboro	Chief	2006–2010
Val Demings[xxix]	Orlando	Chief	2007–2011
Roy Minter, Jr.	Denton, TX	Chief	2007-2011
	Peoria, AZ	Chief	2011-2018
	Savanaah, GA	Chief	2018-
Darryl Boykins[xxx]	South Bend	Chief	2007–2012
A.C. Roper[xxxi]	Birmingham	Chief	2007–2018
Daniel Isom	St. Louis	Commissioner	2008–2013
Brian Norwood	Richmond, VA	Chief	2008–2013
Frank Adderley	Fort Lauderdale	Chief	2008–2019
James Barren	Detroit	Chief	2009–2009
Warren Evans[xxxii]	Detroit	Chief	2009–2010
Anthony Batts	Oakland	Chief	2009–2011
Alex Hayes	Omaha	Chief	2009–2012
Rebecca Coleman	Jackson, MS	Chief	2009–2013
Earl Cook	Alexandria, VA	Chief	2009–2016
Joel Fitzgerald[xxxiii]	Missouri City, TX	Chief	2009–2013
	Allenton, PA	Chief	2013–2015
	Fort Worth, TX	Chief	2015–2019
	Waterloo, IA	Chief	2021-
Ralph Godbee[xxxiv]	Detroit	Chief	2010–2012
George Turner	Atlanta	Chief	2010–2016
Charles McClelland	Houston	Chief	2010–2016
Frank Fowler	Syracuse	Chief	2010–2018
Jeri Williams	Oxnard, CA	Chief	2010–2016
	Phoenix	Chief	2016-
Al Thomas[xxxv]	Lexington	Chief	2010–2016
	Charlottesville		2016–2017

xxix Demings was elected to the U.S. House of Representatives in 2016 and was on a shortlist to become President Biden's Vice President. Deming's husband, Jerry, is also a former Orlando police chief and was elected Sheriff and Mayor of Orange County.

xxx Boykins was demoted by 30-year-old Mayor Pete Buttigieg (Boykins then resigned) after four white officers were illegally recorded and making racist remarks. Boykins and the officers sued, and the case settled for $800,000. Buttigieg later campaigned as a Democratic candidate for President. In 2021, he was confirmed as President Biden's Secretary of Transportation and became the first openly gay Cabinet member in U.S. history.

xxxi In May 2021, Roper became the nation's first Black U.S. Army Reserve lieutenant general.

xxxii Evans was also Wayne County Sheriff from 2003 to 2009.

xxxiii Fitzgerald rose through the ranks of the PPD. He earned a Ph.D. degree in Business Administration from Northcentral University.

xxxiv Both Detroit chiefs Evans and Godbee were forced to resign with links to sexual affairs with subordinate Internal Affairs Officer Angelica Robinson (Ng, 2012). These resignations were on the heels of Mayor Kwame Kilpatrick resigning in 2008 after he was charged with perjury and obstruction of justice. After serving seven years in prison, President Trump commuted Kilpatrick's sentence on January 20, 2021. He could have served an additional 20 years in prison with convictions linked to corruption, misuse of funds, mail fraud, and tax evasion.

xxxv Thomas resigned in the aftermath of the August 12, 2017 "Unite the Right" rally that brought hundreds of white supremacists together from throughout the country leading to one death when a car plowed into a group of protesters. Thomas was criticized for being too passive before declaring an unlawful assembly.

Table 6.1 Cont.

Name	*City*	*Position*	*Years*
David Brown[xxxvi]	Dallas	Chief	2010–2016
	Chicago	Superintendent	2020-
Howard Jordan	Oakland	Chief	2011–2013
Sheilah Coley	Newark	Chief	2011–2014
Derrick Diggs	Toledo	Chief	2011–2014
	Fort Myers	Chief	2016-
Keith Humphrey	Norman	Chief	2011–2019
	Little Rock, AK	Chief	2019-
Darryl Forte	Kansas City, MO	Chief	2011–2017
Anthony Bates[xxxvii]	Baltimore	Commissioner	2012–2015
Floyd Simpson[xxxviii]	Corpus Christi	Chief	2012–2015
Rick Hite	Indianapolis	Chief	2012–2014
Carl Charles	Downey, CA	Chief	2012–2016
Lindsey Horton	Jackson, MS	Chief	2013–2014
Carmen Best[xxxix]	Seattle	Chief	2013–2020
Cassandra Deck-Brown	Raleigh	Chief	2013–2021
James Craig[xl]	Cincinnati	Chief	2011–2013
	Detroit	Chief	2013–2021
Kenton Buckner[xli]	Little Rock, AK	Chief	2014–2018
	Syracuse	Chief	2014–2018
Calvin Williams	Cleveland	Chief	2014-
Alfred Dunham	Richmond, VA	Chief	2015–2018
Kerr Putney	Charlotte-Mecklenburg	Chief	2015–2020
Delrish Moss[xlii]	Ferguson, MO	Chief	2015–2018
Eliot Isaac	Cincinnati	Chief	2016-
Mike Rawlings	Memphis	Director	2016–2021
Eddie Johnson	Chicago	Superintendent	2016–2019
Darnell Henry	Newark	Chief	2016–2020
Richard Ross, Jr.[xliii]	Philadelphia	Commissioner	2016–2019
Cerelyn "C.J." Davis	Durham	Chief	2016–2021
	Memphis	Chief	2021-

xxxvi Brown is the fifth African-American to lead the CPD. In the summer of 2020, the top three commanders of the CPD were Black for the first time in the department's history. Eric Carter and Barbara West were both promoted to Deputies of Superintendent Brown. West also became the highest-ranking Black female in the history of the CPD.

xxxvii Mayor Stephanie Rawlings-Blake terminated Bates as 2015 homicides spiked in Baltimore.

xxxviii Simpson was killed in a motorcycle accident on May 3, 2015, at the age of 51. He previously retired as Assistant Chief in Dallas.

xxxix Best, Seattle's first Black police chief, resigned in September 2020 after the city council approved a $4 million budget cut and possibly 100 police officers. At one point, the council considered cutting the police budget in half. Best joined Ramsey's company, 21 CPSolutions. See www.21cpsolutions.com/

xl Craig also served as chief in Portland, Maine from 2009 to 2011, the city where intern Herman Goldstein first met O.W. Wilson in 1954, as described in the appendix to the Wilson chapter.

xli Buckner served as the chief of Syracuse in a civilian capacity because he was unable to pass their stringent physical fitness exam. The physical standards for a male recruit (age 40–49) were a mile and half run in 13 minutes 50 seconds, 18 push-ups, and 29 sit-ups. Buckner could still carry a firearm with a state permit.

xlii Although Ferguson, Missouri only has a population slightly higher than 20,000 (and other chiefs listed in this table are for populations over 100,000) Moss is still worth noting as he took over the Ferguson Police Department in the aftermath of the Michael Brown fatal shooting and the riots of 2015. Moss was preceded by Chief Tom Jackson and two interim chiefs. Moss came to Ferguson from the Miami Police Department where he served for 32 years. Jason Armstrong was hired as the second Black chief of Ferguson in 2019.

xliii Ross was a recipient of the prestigious Gary Hayes Award from PERF, as were Ramsey and Bratton. He resigned in the summer of 2019 after two lawsuits filed by minority female officers alleged ongoing sexual harassment and the commissioner's failure to adequately intervene.

Table 6.1 Cont.

Name	*City*	*Position*	*Years*
Gina Hawkins	Fayetteville	Chief	2017-
Delma Noel-Pratt	Miami Gardens	Chief	2017-
Daniel Hahn[xliv]	Sacramento	Chief	2017-
William Scott	San Francisco	Chief	2017-
Renee Hall[xlv]	Dallas	Chief	2017–2020
Catrina Thompson[xlvi]	Winston-Salem	Chief	2017-
Danielle Outlaw[xlvii]	Portland	Chief	2017–2019
	Philadelphia	Commissioner	2019-
Anthony Campbell	New Haven	Chief	2017–2019
Medaria Arradondo[xlviii]	Minneapolis	Chief	2017-
Darryl Sousa[xlix]	Baltimore	Commissioner	2018–2018
Lawrence Weathers	Lexington	Chief	2018-
Murphy Paul	Baton Rouge	Chief	2018-
James Davis	Jackson, MS	Chief	2018-
Frank Dixon	Denton, TX	Chief	2018-
Patrick Smith	Birmingham	Chief	2018-
John Hayden, Jr.	St. Louis	Commissioner	2018-
Reginald Burgess[l]	North Charleston, SC	Chief	2018-
RaShall Brackney	Charlottesville	Chief	2018-
William Gross [li]	Boston	Commissioner	2018–2021
La'Ron D. Singletary[lii]	Rochester, NY	Chief	2019–2020
Daryl Green	Lansing, MI	Chief	2019–2021
Michael Harrison	Baltimore	Commissioner	2019-

xliv Hahn was adopted and raised in a white family that had two biological children before his adoption.

xlv In 1971, when Hall was six months old, her father was a 27-year-old Detroit police officer and was murdered while investigating a gambling and prostitution crime ring. Hall also joined the Detroit PD and worked her way up to become deputy chief before moving to Dallas to become their first female chief. She resigned in September 2020 amid the mass protests.

xlvi Thompson's husband, Alonzo, is the former Assistant Chief of the Winston-Salem Police Department. He then became chief for the Spartanburg Police Department in South Carolina.

xlvii Outlaw was the successor to Ross after Deputy Chief Christine Coulter served as an interim. Outlaw received the prestigious Gary Hayes Award from the PERF in 2015 when she was a deputy chief in Oakland.

xlviii Arradondo was appointed as the first Black chief of Minneapolis after Janee Harteau's resignation, the first female Minneapolis chief. Arradondo led the department through the 2020 mass police protests that followed George Floyd's death and four officers' termination: Derek Chauvin, Tou Thao, J Alexander Kueng, and Thomas Lane. Their trials were held separately, with Chauvin beginning in March 2021 and the other three in August 2021. Before Chavin's trial began, the Minneapolis City Council unanimously agreed to a $27 million wrongful death settlement with Floyd's family. Chief Arradondo testified for the prosecution against Chauvin stating he violated departmental use of force policy. On April 20, 2021, a jury found Chauvin guilty of murder in the second-degree, third-degree, and manslaughter. On June 25, 2021, Judge Peter Cahill sentenced Chauvin to 22 ½ years in prison.

xlix Sousa resigned after being charged with three misdemeanors for failure to file federal income tax returns.

l Burgess was hired nearly three years after the fatal shooting of Walter Scott as he ran away from Officer Michael Slager. Slager was convicted of second-degree murder and obstruction of justice and received a 20-year prison sentence.

li Gross became Boston's first Black Commissioner, 140 years after the city hired Sgt. Horatio Homer as it's first Black officer (Neal, 2016).

lii Singletary, and his deputy chief, resigned in September 2020 following mass protests in Rochester over the March death and investigation of Chicago-native Daniel Prude. The Prude family released the body camera footage from the arrest. Officers placed a spit hood over Prude's head during what appeared to be a mental health breakdown (PCP was later found in his system), causing his death seven days later. In the aftermath of the video release, Mayor Lovely Warren suspended the seven officers involved in Prude's arrest, leading to Chief Singletary's resignation. In February 2021, the grand jury failed to indict the officers. However, Attorney General Letitia James supported an unusual judicial ruling to disclose the grand jury records.

Table 6.1 Cont.

Name	*City*	*Position*	*Years*
Shaun Ferguson	New Orleans	Superintendent	2019-
Eric Payne	Grand Rapids	Chief	2019-
Shawny Williams	Vallejo, CA	Chief	2019-
Chuck Lovell	Portland	Chief	2020-
Jeff Glover	Tempe	Chief	2020-
Wendell Franklin	Tulsa	Chief	2020-
Randal Taylor	Indianapolis	Chief	2020-
Ed Drain	Plano, TX	Chief	2020-
Johnny Jennings	Charlotte-Mecklenburg	Chief	2020-
Brian James	Greensboro	Chief	2020-
Jody Blackwell[liii]	Richmond, VA	Interim Chief	2020–2020
Cynthia Herriott-Sullivan	Rochester	Interim Chief	2020-
Gerald Smith	Richmond, VA	Chief	2020-
Yevette Gentry[liv]	Louisville	Interim Chief	2020-2021
Bisa French	Richmond, CA	Chief	2020-
John Drake	Nashville	Chief	2020-
Thomas Glover	Lafayette, LA	Chief	2020-
Brian Peete	Montpelier, VT	Chief	2020-
Donny Williams	Wilmington, NC	Chief	2020-
Robert Contee, III	Washington, DC	Chief	2021-
Shon Barnes[lv]	Madison, WI	Chief	2021-
Sheryl Victorian	Waco, TX	Chief	2021-
Dennis White	Boston	Chief	2021-2021
LeRonne Armstrong	Oakland	Chief	2021-
Rodney Bryant	Atlanta	Chief	2021-
Karl Oakman	Kansas City, MO	Chief	2021-
Tawana Moody[lvi]	Jersey City, NJ	Chief	2021-
Marcus Dudley, Jr.	Abilene, TX	Chief	2021-
Kenneth McCoy	Anchorage, AK	Chief	2021-
Mark Talbot	Hampton, VA	Chief	2021-
Troy Finner	Houston, TX	Chief	2021-
Elaine Bryant	Columbus, OH	Chief	2021-
Keith Cross	Aurora, IL	Chief	2021-

Englewood to the Chicago Police Department (CPD) 1968–1998

Ramsey grew up on Chicago's South Side in the Englewood neighborhood, one of three children born to a practical nurse and a bus driver with the CTA. In 1965, when he was 15 years

liii Blackwell was interim chief of the Richmond, Virginia Police Department for ten days before he stepped down.

liv Gentry became the first Black woman to lead the Louisville Metro Police Department after the fallout of the Breonna Taylor shooting on March 13, 2020. A $12 million settlement with the Taylor family was one of the largest for a Black female victim of a fatal police shooting (Chavez & Carrega, 2020).

lv Barnes served in the Marine Corps and received a Ph.D. degree in Leadership Studies from North Carolina Agriculture and Technical State University. His dissertation research focused on racial disparities in traffic stops. Barnes started his law enforcement career with the Greensboro Police Department. Before taking the Madison Chief position, Barnes was a Deputy Chief in Salisbury, North Carolina. He then served as the Director of Training and Professional Development in Chicago through the newly created Civilian Office of Police Accountability (COPA). COPA replaced the Independent Police Review Authority (IPRA) in 2016 after the Laquan McDonald fatal shooting, discussed earlier in this chapter. The IPRA was created in 2007 as a replacement to the Office of Professional Standards (OPS). The OPS was created in 1974 amid police brutality cases.

lvi Moody is also the first non-sworn civilian to lead the Jersey City Police Department.

old, his brother Butch's best friend and next-door neighbor, Tony Brown,[36] was fatally stabbed in front of his home by a local gang. Brown had spent his last day hanging out with Ramsey and his brother at their home.[37]

On June 19, 1970, CPD Officer Kenneth Kaner parked in his squad car near the front of Ramsey's home, the exact location Tony Brown was killed, on the NW corner of 74th and Union Street. Five individuals approached Kaner's police vehicle as he wrote a missing person report and fatally shot him on the right side of his face with a 12-gauge sawed-off shotgun. Ramsey had just returned home from an evening cadet shift when he heard the loud boom from the fatal shot, which awoke his father, who then called the police. The perpetrators were stopped minutes later for a traffic violation, and Officer Kaner's service weapon was in their vehicle along with the shotgun. Ramsey went to high school with one of the perpetrators, Bradley Green, and his sister went to school with another one of the individuals with the last name Redwine.[38] Kaner's son became a member of the CPD Marine Unit, and they named a boat the "Kenneth Kaner" in memory of his father.

These events triggered Ramsey's interest in helping to prevent violent crime. Three tactical police officers from the Englewood District also influenced his decision to consider a law enforcement career. The officers befriended Ramsey when they visited the Super Foods Center grocery store at 75th and Harvard, where he worked. They would often arrive at the store in the evenings because one of the officers had a sister who worked as a cashier, and he wanted to make sure the employees left the store safely. The officers enticed Ramsey to enroll in the Chicago Police cadet program and get his education paid for to attend the University of Illinois at Chicago as a pre-med student. Ramsey was reluctant since the police had such a bad reputation throughout his neighborhood, and his goal was to become a doctor. However, after several days of reflection, Ramsey decided to take a bus with his father to CPD headquarters and take the cadet program's rigorous admission tests.

Ramsey's law enforcement career began in the summer of 1968 when he joined the CPD as an 18-year-old police cadet. That cadet program was started in 1962 by O.W. Wilson before any court actions related to affirmative action forced increased hiring of minorities. The cadet program enabled young men between the ages of 17 and 20 to attend a training program and learn about police procedures while cadets assisted with various clerical duties. At the age of 21, cadets became eligible to take the CPD exam. In the early 1970s, budget issues led to eliminating the cadet program, despite several attempts to bring it back in the mid-1980s (McNally, 1986) (Photo 6.1). By 2005, the city brought back the cadet program for college students between the ages of 18-21.

Four years after becoming a police cadet, Ramsey graduated from the Chicago Police Academy and was quickly promoted relative to other minority officers. He became Chicago's youngest African-American sergeant in 1977 at the age of 27, then its youngest African-American lieutenant in 1984.[39] In 1988 Ramsey became the youngest African-American to be promoted to

36 Ramsey described how Brown's bedroom window was directly across their bedroom window and how they would spend their evenings talking to one another (author's interview with Ramsey on August 20, 2020).

37 Ramsey explained that his father found Brown gasping for air after he was fatally stabbed outside their home. This was only the second time he ever saw his father cry, the first occurring after his Grandmother's death (author's interview with Ramsey on August 20, 2020).

38 Author's interview with Ramsey on August 20, 2020.

39 In an August 20, 2020 interview with the author, Ramsey pointed out that despite his success in getting promoted in the CPD, he considered himself very lucky to avoid what he saw as systemic racism. He reflected on the exact scores of his initial performance evaluation. Ramsey explained that performance evaluations counted for 30 percent of the officer's grade, and the districts were expected to have an 85 percent on their officers' evaluations. As a young officer, Ramsey discovered his white partner received a 91 percent, while he was given an 83 percent on his evaluation. When he questioned his lieutenant, whom he worked with daily, Ramsey was told he was young and not to worry about his low ranking. However, Ramsey also discovered that he had the second-highest test score in the Tenth District. However, his overall rating put him at 483 on the promotion

Photo 6.1 Chuck Ramsey with the Chicago Police Department.
Photo provided to the author by Chuck Ramsey.

the rank of captain. In 1989, Ramsey's precinct was ranked first in Chicago for crime reduction and felony arrests. By his late 40s, Ramsey had risen to the rank of deputy superintendent.

Chicago Police History

In 1830, Chicago had its first version of policing with an elected police constable, Orsemus Morrison. Initially, two police assistants helped Morrison protect the town's population of approximately 3,200 (Mitrani, 2013). By 1835, the State of Illinois officially authorized a police force for Chicago, and in 1842, the city elected Marshall Orson Smith. Cyrus Bradley became Chicago's first police chief on May 26, 1855, and he created the first Detective Division with a Departmental motto: "At danger's call, we'll promptly fly; and bravely do or bravely die." Officers began to wear official uniforms under Bradley. In 1860,[40] the common council stripped newly elected Mayor John Wentworth of political control over the CPD. Instead, they gave management authority to three police commissioners who selected a police superintendent to lead the department. In 1861, the commissioners kept Bradley as the CPD Superintendent. By 1875, Springfield legislatures determined the CPD commissioners could not control rampant corruption and returned power to the mayor. Subsequently, Chicago mayors were allowed to appoint a single police commissioner with the city council's consent.

Haymarket Square Riot – May 4, 1886, with Reflections on the 2020 Riots

Starting May 1, 1886, residents and commuters to industrialized Chicago witnessed an unusual clear skyline as the shops and factories were shut down by strikers who, in solidarity,

list because of the arbitrary performance evaluation. Ramsey found that most Black officers were in their 50s before they got promoted to sergeant.

40 In the 1860 Chicago mayoral election, Democrat Wentworth defeated Republican Walter Gurnee. Both Wentworth and Gurnee served as mayor before this election, and both served under opposite party affiliation. Gurnee was elected as a Democrat in 1851. Wentworth was elected in 1852 as a Republican and was re-elected in 1857.

protested for eight-hour workdays. This strike was organized nation-wide by the Federation of Organized Trades and Labor Unions. Ominous of the 2020 riots, Chicago was crippled by days of protests. However, the McCormick Reaper Works, a factory that produced new farm equipment and was a couple of miles outside of downtown Chicago, remained an anomaly as strikebreakers kept the factory running through protection from CPD officers. On May 3, the police opened fire on a crowd of striking protesters,[41] killing two outside the McCormick factory. The shooting resulted in a much larger protest the following day. As was the case nearly 135 years later, following the May 25, 2020 death of George Floyd in Minneapolis, a large crowd angered over the perceived misuse of police force was easily motivated on May 4, 1886.

Additionally, as was the case in the 2020 protests, some radical anarchists took advantage of the gathering and incited riots as a means for dismantling American capitalism, arguing that business owners exploited workers with low wages and dangerous working conditions. Many of the radicals in 1886 included German immigrants and anarchists. Other protesters came to denounce the police actions from the previous day. An estimated 2,000 protesters arrived on Desplaines Street, near Randolph Street, in an area known as Haymarket, where the streets widened, and farmers sold daily produce. Chicago Mayor Carter Harrison[42] came to observe the rally.

After several pro-labor speeches, the crowd lessened to a few hundred as it began to drizzle rain. Several hours into the rally, as speakers warned of future police brutality, 176 CPD officers arrived in formation to disperse the remaining crowd (Green, 2007, p. 6). According to *Chicago Tribune* reporters, a small rocket shot into the air, and when it landed amongst the police, a bomb went off. That bomb killed seven officers, an additional officer died two years later from his injuries, and injured approximately 70 others as chaotic gunfire from both sides erupted (Green, 2007). Only one of the officers who died had more than two years of law enforcement experience (Lindberg, 1991).

The Chicago riots set off national xenophobia as police agencies across the country arrested numerous foreign-born radicals and labor organizers. In August 1886, a jury convicted eight men, in a controversial jury trial, with links to the Haymarket bombing. On November 11, 1887, the city hung four of these men. One individual committed suicide on the eve of his execution by detonating a dynamite cap in his mouth. Two others subsequently had their death sentences commuted to life in prison by the governor. In 1893, Governor John Peter Altgeld pardoned the last three activists and faced enormous political backlash (Sampson, 1993).

The labor movement saw the men convicted of the Haymarket riots as martyrs. A monument to the men, unveiled in 1893, is located in Forest Park at the cemetery where they are buried. A nine-foot statue of a Chicago policeman was unveiled and dedicated to the CPD officers who perished at the McCormick site a few years after the riots. The monument was the first statute in the nation erected in dedication to the police, and it would be moved seven times as a result of being targeted by subsequent protesters. On the exact day of the riots, 41 years later, a streetcar driver intentionally jumped the tracks and crashed into the monument. A year later, the statue was restored and moved to Union Park. In 1956, the statue moved back to its original location and overlooked the newly built Kennedy Expressway. On the 82nd anniversary of the riots, in 1968, protesters vandalized the statue with black paint. On October 6, 1969, a bomb was detonated between the statue's legs and scattered pieces onto

41 In addition to the Haymarket conflict, on Memorial Day, 1937, the CPD fatally shot ten strikers from the Steel Workers Organizing Committee (SWOC) and wounded 40 others by gunfire. The police also beat over 100 additional strikers with their clubs (Hogan, 2014).

42 Harrison was the first mayor to appoint a Black CPD officer before he was assassinated in his home during his fifth mayoral term.

the Kennedy Expressway. The statue was rebuilt and unveiled on May 4, 1970, but again blown up by a bomb on October 6, 1970. Mayor Richard J. Daley had the statue rebuilt and posted a 24-hour police guard, which cost thousands of dollars in police overtime before the statute was relocated to the CPD headquarters' lobby in 1972.

In 1976, the department enclosed the statue in a courtyard inside the Chicago Police Academy. For nearly 30 years, the graffiti-marked pedestal, where the police statue once stood, remained at the run-down Haymarket square and became a landmark for protesters and anarchists. On June 1, 2007, the statue was rededicated at police headquarters with a new pedestal and unveiled by Officer Mathias Degan's (the first officer to be killed by shrapnel from the bomb) great-granddaughter. Symbolic statutes would become the target of mass protests in 2020, many including relics from the Confederacy. For example, Former Philadelphia Police Commissioner and Mayor Frank Rizzo's statue, discussed later in this chapter was removed in the summer of 2020.

1918–1919 Pandemic and the Race Riots

In 1917, extra officers were temporarily hired as part of the Chicago Police Reserves and used to assist full-time officers with crowd control. These reserved officers were instrumental in enforcing strict public health regulations when the misnomer Spanish flu (otherwise known as the H1N1 avian virus) pandemic hit in 1918. In 1918–1919, the pandemic became the deadliest flu outbreak in modern history, killing an estimated 50–100 million people worldwide and 675,000 Americans while infecting an estimated 500 million people worldwide, or one-third of the world's population. (The 1918–1919 pandemic era is also discussed in the chapter on Vollmer, and details provided on how Berkeley, California reacted.)

As was the case in many cities, the pandemic caught Chicagoans off guard. In September 1918, Chicago's health commissioner, Dr. John Dill Robertson,[43] stated there was no cause for alarm in initial reports (Robertson & Koehler, 1918). He was considered utterly unqualified by the city's medical establishment (Nichols, 2020). Over the next two months, over 8,500 Chicagoans died of pneumonia. The hardest hit were people between the ages of 20 and 40. Robertson then encouraged citizens to wear sterilized gauze masks to prevent germs from spreading, and the newspapers printed directions on how readers could make homemade masks. Stingy landlords were pressured to heat their properties so tenants could avoid catching a cold and spreading the flu.

The media and politicians urged Chicagoans to place "no kissing" signs in their homes. The mayor ordered the police to arrest individuals who spit on sidewalks or sneezed without covering their faces. Public dancing was outlawed, sporting events canceled, and public meetings were banned. Residents were encouraged to burn used tissues, and soiled handkerchiefs were to be boiled in water and soaked in disinfectant (Fornek, 2005). Police General Superintendent John Garrity refused to order his officers to arrest people who sneezed without covering up. However, he did ask officers to use courtesy and explain to citizens why they needed to cover their sneeze. He also had signs posted throughout public spaces and warned that spitting would lead to arrest and prosecution. Smoking was banned on all streetcars to cut down on spitting and to purify the air. The CPD broke up any public gatherings that grew too large. Saloons and billiard halls remained open, as did churches on the grounds that religion

43 Robertson was a surgeon at Cook County Hospital and a professor at the American College of Medicine and Surgery. In December 1903, he presented a research paper that claimed bathing was an unhealthy habit that encouraged infectious disease because washing overheated the body and left internal organs without nourishment (Nichols, 2020).

was essential for community morale. Public schools remained open, as did their windows to allow fresh air into the buildings, and children were encouraged to wear wraps around their faces. By the end of the pandemic in 1919, an estimated 10,000 people in Chicago had perished. By 1920, the Chicago Police Reserves disbanded due to a lack of support from the city council.

Ironically, as connected to the Covid-19 pandemic and the 2020 mass social justice protests and riots,[44] Chicago experienced one of its bloodiest race riots in the summer of 1919 within the pandemic. This friction came when Chicago's Black population more than doubled in 1910–1920, going from 44,000 to over 109,000 as thousands moved north to escape Southern racism and violence. Moreover, when the Great War broke out, Blacks were granted industrial jobs but were not allowed to keep those jobs when the war ended.[45]

Racial tension within the city came to a boiling point on Sunday, July 27, 1919, when Eugene Williams, an African-American 17-year-old, drifted into a white segregated swimming beach near 29th Street; Blacks were supposed to stay on their beach near 25th Street. Williams drowned after rocks were thrown at him, which caused an ensuing conflict between Blacks and whites at the beach. Black witnesses specifically pointed to George Stauber as one individual who threw rocks at Williams, and they flagged down Officer Daniel Callahan (Lindberg, 1991). They demanded Officer Callahan arrest Stauber, but the officer refused and arrested a Black man instead (Barrett, 2020). Callahan then left but was pursued by the Black witnesses, which quickly led to protests and riots throughout the city that lasted into the first few days of August 1919. Although not segregated by law, 90 percent of Chicago's Black population lived in neighborhoods on the South Side that ran between 12th and 39th Streets and between Wentworth Avenue and Lake Michigan. The CPD dispatched 2,800 of its 3,500 officer force to African-American communities and violently put down the protesters (Krinitsky, 2017, pp. 99–100). The police saturation in Black neighborhoods left very few officers to patrol downtown, where white residents clashed with Black residents, leading to numerous beatings.

Superintendent Garrity was only months on the job (appointed on November 25, 1918) when he faced the pandemic and the summer 1919 riots.[46] Garrity ordered all establishments where men congregate, other than for religious purposes, to be closed as a means for trying to end the riots. Mayor William "Big Bill" Thompson[47] refused to ask Illinois Governor Frank Lowden[48] for assistance from the Illinois National Guard, despite Garrity's

44 On May 31st, Mayor Lori Lighfoot requested the assistance of the Illinois National Guard from Govenor J.B. Pritzker. This was the first time such a request occurred since the 1968 riots. Clashes between protesters and the CPD continued to occur throughout the summer of 2020 but climaxed on July 17th at Grant Park. Officers guarded Christopher Columbus's statute (erected in 1933 during the World's Fair) and were pelted by projectiles and incendiary devices, leading to 49 officer injuries and 18 hospitalized (Rosenberg-Douglas, Gorner, Anderson, & Pratt, 2020). Only 12 arrests were made with charges of mob action, injury to police officers, and property destruction. Officers struck protesters with clubs causing injuries. In the early morning hours of July 24th, in an effort to avoid future clashes, Mayor Lightfoot had the city remove Columbus statues in Grant and Arrigo Parks.

45 In the chapter on Magnus, this same time period after World War I is discussed. As white soldiers returned home from the war, they demanded their jobs in the factories back, and Black unemployment rose causing racial tension.

46 Ironically, Superintendent David Brown was also only a month on the job (he assumed office on April 15, 2020) when the social justice protests erupted in May 2020.

47 Thompson was ranked as one of the most unethical mayors in the country due to his corrupt links with Al Capone. He served as Chicago's mayor from 1915 to 1923 and from 1927 to 1931 (Wendt & Kogan, 2005).

48 After the riots ended, Governor Lowden called for a Chicago Commission on Race Relations to investigate solutions to racial tensions. Conclusions from the commission were published three years later by the University of Chicago under the title *The Negro in Chicago: A Study of Race Relations and a Race Riot.* This report led to

long experience as a Colonel, a rank he earned in 1907, in the guard. Thirteen days later, as the riots persisted, Governor Lowden sent 6,000 members of the guard to end the conflict. In the end, 38 residents, which included both Blacks and whites, were dead, several hundred injured, and over a thousand lost their homes (Sandburg, Buhle, & Lippmann, 2013). State's Attorney MacLay Hoyne presented 17 indictments, all against Black men, which helped exonerate the almost all-white CPD and helped formulate the story for the media and historians that Blacks started the riots and had guns and ammunition warehoused in their social clubs. The Black protesters replaced the German anarchists from the Haymarket Riots 33 years prior. In the aftermath, Black Chicagoans retreated and would not be heard from in this manner again for another 45 years.

In response to ongoing racial tension, the CPD created a Human Relations Section in 1942, the first in the country, that evolved into the Civil Rights Unit. This unit primarily investigated hate crimes. Despite efforts to counteract racial strife, the CPD remained heavily segregated until the early 1960s and the hiring of civilian O.W. Wilson as Superintendent. (A previous chapter covers Wilson's reform efforts in the CPD.)

The Chicago Outfit: Al Capone

Al Capone was born in 1899 in Brooklyn, New York, to Italian immigrants and worked many legitimate and illegitimate jobs,[49] including a few years in semi-pro baseball. In 1919,[50] the mob summoned Capone to Chicago to work for his mentor, Johnny Torrio,[51] who would eventually head the criminal syndicate that became the Chicago Outfit. At that time, there were an estimated 1,313 gangs in Chicago (Thrasher, 1927).[52] The Irish contentiously controlled organized crime on the North Side, and the Italians had control on the South Side. The Italian faction, led by Torrio and Capone, clashed with the Irish mob, controlled by Dion O'Banion. In the beginning years of Prohibition, Torrio brokered an uneasy truce with O'Banion so both the Italians and the Irish could profit. Torrio bootlegged beer into Chicago daily from his West Hammond, Indiana brewery, which became well-received because of its high quality.

Capone and Torrio ran into problems after a series of brewery crackdowns ordered by reform Mayor William Evett Dever. Dever succeeded corrupt Mayor Bill Thompson from 1923 to 1927 as Chicago's 42nd mayor. To avoid future crackdowns by the CPD and Mayor Dever, Capone moved their bootlegging operations to Cicero, Chicago's west suburb, and became a national celebrity, frequently doing interviews with the media and flamboyantly

President Wilson and Congress passing legislation, which attempted to decrease racial strife through further segregation.

49 Capone got the nickname "Scarface" after a bar fight that occurred after Al insulted a woman and her brother, Frank Gallucio, slashed his face in retaliation.

50 The Chicago White Sox were also scandalized this same year, 1919, when it was determined that players had been paid by gamblers to intentionally lose the World Series and their team became infamously known as the "Black Sox." Chicago Police Superintendent John Garrity called the Grand Jury investigation into the 1919 White Sox a joke, as many politically influenced police leaders saw gambling as expected and should not be an indictable offense (Cook, 2015).

51 Torrio took over after his uncle, Jim Colosimo, was assassinated on May 11, 1920, inside his cabaret's vestibule located at 2126 South Wabash Avenue. Torrio and Capone ordered the hit on Colosimo because of his apprehension to get involved with bootlegging during Prohibition. The Catholic Church refused to participate in Colosimo's funeral, and the Chicago archdiocese decreed he could not be buried in consecrated ground.

52 Thrasher (1927) identified gangs in the North, West, and South Sides of Chicago based upon immigration and tribal identity.

flashing his jewelry, custom suits, cigars, and gourmet food. While in Cicero, Capone bribed local officers and politicians while maintaining control over the town council elections.

In 1924, Frank Capone, Al's brother,[53] was in charge of making sure Republican Cicero Village President Joseph Klenha[54] was elected mayor since he was on their payroll. The Democratic challenger was town clerk William Pflaum, who had his campaign offices ransacked. Ralph Capone, Al's other brother, beat up Robert St. John[55] in front of his wife after St. John wrote newspaper stories about Cicero's political corruption. St. John founded the *Cicero Tribune* the year prior, at the age of 21, and became the nation's youngest newspaper editor and publisher. St. John published articles about the corruption that had permutated Cicero politics from the Capone gang. Cicero Police Captain Theodore Svoboda attempted to arrange a meeting between St. John and Al Capone at the police station so he could apologize for his brother and pay for medical expenses. St. John refused the meeting and the money. Capone then bought out the *Cicero Tribune,* and St. John left town.

Concerned Cicero citizens requested Cook County Judge Edmund Jareki assist in stopping voter intimidation. Jareki deputized 70 plainclothes CPD officers and sent them to Cicero on the election afternoon. On April 1, 1924, the plainclothes CPD officers confronted Frank Capone at one of Cicero's polling stations located at 2219 South Chicago Avenue. A gunfight erupted, leading to the death of Capone. Capone likely thought the officers were rival gang members and allegedly fired his gun first. Chicago news outlets praised and condemned the CPD for killing Al Capone's brother, later ruled justifiable. The lavished funeral procession that followed included $20,000 worth of flowers purchased from the North Side Schofield flower shop, operated by O'Banion.

The truce between the Italians and the Irish ended when O'Banion set Torrio up to be arrested in May 1924 by the CPD during the Sieben Brewery raid (Klerks, 2006), located at 1464 North Larrabee, which is now the Near North Career Metro High School. On November 10, 1924, the Italians got their revenge, and 32-year-old O'Banion was fatally shot by six bullets inside the Schofield[56] flower shop in downtown Chicago, near the corner of West Chicago Avenue and East Superior Street (Keefe, 2003). Torrio and Capone attended his funeral, infuriating O'Banion's partners, Hymie Weiss and Bugs Moran.

After a funeral procession that rivaled Frank Capone's, two of the largest in Chicago's history, Weiss, born in Poland, took over the Irish gang and attempted to avenge his mentor's loss. Weiss and Moran unleashed a mob *Beer War* that led to over 300 people murdered over the next few years (English, 2005). A few months after O'Banion's murder, on January 24, 1925, Weiss and Moran ambushed Torrio after he returned to his South Shore home, at 7011 S. Clyde Avenue, with his wife, Ann. As he was carrying packages into his house, Torrio was shot numerous times but miraculously survived. He was then locked up at the Lake County Jail in Waukegan, Illinois, and served nine months for the Sieben Brewery bust that O'Banion had set up with the CPD. After his sentence, Torrio gave up his operations to 26-year-old Capone, departed to Italy, and resided there for several years before returning to New York City after Italian Dictator Benito Mussolini put political pressure on the mafia. Torrio never set foot in Chicago again.

53 Al Capone had six brothers and two sisters. One of his brothers, Vincenzo, changed his name to James Hart and became a Prohibition agent that investigated liquor sales to Indian tribes.

54 Klenha and Cicero Chief of Police Theodore Svoboda were later found guilty of violating the Volstead Act but avoided jail time through appeals.

55 St. John lived until he was 100 years old, died in 2003, and wrote numerous books based on his international news media correspondence.

56 The Schofield flower shop was torn down on August 13, 1960. In 2021, a new commercial building opened where the flower shop once stood.

Weiss and Moran continued to threaten Capone. On September 20, 1926, they fired over 2,000 rounds from Thompson submachine guns into Capone's Hawthorne Inn headquarters located at 4833 W. 22nd Street. A few weeks later, on October 11, 1926, Weiss was fatally gunned down outside the same Schofield flower shop where his mentor O'Banion was murdered, across from the Holy Name Cathedral.[57] Capone called a press conference to deny he had anything to do with Weiss's murder. He then began to work on reclaiming political control of Chicago.

Capone convinced former corrupt Mayor Big Bill Thompson to run against Deaver. After Capone got Thompson back as mayor, he moved his operations out of Cicero. In July 1928, he moved into the Lexington Hotel,[58] again holding a press conference to show off his new residence at 2135 S. Michigan Avenue. Speakeasies (illegal drinking establishments) continued to grow during this period and numbered over 10,000 in the Chicagoland area, far more than licensed bars in Chicago today.

On February 14, 1929, Capone targeted his last rival of O'Banion's gang, Bugs Moran. On Valentine's Day, uniformed Chicago Police Officers, who were actually disguised hitmen[59] working for Capone, ordered seven Moran gang members to line up along a wall and then fatally fired over 70 rounds of ammunition into their victims. The massacre occurred inside a garage for the SMC Cartage warehouse located at 2122 North Clark Street[60] in the Lincoln Park Neighborhood. Moran,[61] the hit's primary target, was alive only because he ran late for the gang's meeting. Capone preplanned his alibi by taking a vacation in Miami. Because the hitmen dressed in CPD uniforms, rumors persisted that the police may have played a role in the murders to get revenge for the killing of a police officer's son (Helmer & Bilek, 2006).

The St. Valentine's Day Massacre facilitated the creation of the country's first crime laboratory at Northwestern University, as described in the Vollmer chapter. The massacre caused the public and the media to turn against Capone and he became the target of federal law enforcement. On October 11, 1931, Capone was sentenced to federal prison on three counts of tax evasion. Capone served seven years of an 11-year sentence, one of the longest sentences ever given for tax evasion. Capone spent four-and-a-half years of his federal prison sentence at Alcatraz. While he was in prison, Congress ratified the Eighteenth Amendment on December 5, 1933, and prohibition ended. In 1938, the CPD purchased the Northwestern crime lab, which marked the end of the deadliest eras for the CPD. From 1920 to 1939, more than 40 percent of all CPD officers were killed in the line of duty. Capone was paroled in November 1939, suffering from prolonged syphilis and dementia. He died inside his mansion,

57 Holy Name Cathedral is located at 730 N Wabash Avenue and still has remnants of bullet holes from the Weiss shooting.

58 After the St. Valentine's massacre, the Lexington Hotel was referred to as "Capone's Castle." The hotel was closed in 1980. On April 21, 1986, a live television program hosted by Geraldo Rivera looked into locked vaults in the hotel, which were empty. The building was demolished in 1995. It is now the location of a residential high rise called "The Lex."

59 Three prime suspects in the St. Valentine's Day massacre were John Scalise, Albert Anselmi, and John Guinta. Mobster lore was that the assassins bragged about the hit and planned to betray Capone, leading Capone to beat all three with a baseball bat at a dinner party. On May 8, 1929, all three suspects were found in Hammond, Indiana beaten and shot to death (Helmer & Bilek, 2006).

60 The building where the St. Valentine's Day massacre occurred was demolished in 1967 and is now a grassy area. Tar marks from the parking garage/warehouse roof can still be seen on the original attached building's brick wall.

61 Moran was arrested in Kentucky by FBI agents on July 6, 1946, for bank robberies. On February 25, 1957, at the age of 63, Moran died while serving federal time in Leavenworth Prison.

located at 93 Palm Avenue[62] in Palm Island, Florida, on January 25, 1947, from complications of a stroke and subsequent heart attack. He was 48 years old.

CPD Brutality and the Legacy of Jon Burge

The CPD has a long history of officers' criminal activity, brutality, and corruption. Since 1960, there have been 295 officers convicted of serious crimes that included drug dealing, police brutality, destroying evidence, theft, murder, and protecting organized crime (Hagedorn et al., 2013). The case against Lt. Jon Burge,[63] Commander of the Area 2 Detective Division (1981-1986), exemplifies the depths of how the CPD subculture protected itself through a blue wall of silence in which officers are taught not to testify or whistleblow against fellow officers. In 1988, he became Area 3 (Brighton Park) Detective Commander. Burge, and at least 64 other officers, tortured more than 100 Black suspects throughout the 1970s and 1980s. Methods included electric shocks to victims' genitals, suffocation with typewriter covers, threats with loaded guns, and radiator burns. Dozens of officers knew about the torture but failed to report it. The Cook County State's Attorney was unable to prosecute a single officer for crimes related to torture. Moreover, the CPD did not publicly discipline any officer for failing to reveal unethical police practices.

Burge's CPD career began in 1970. Nearly two decades later, in 1989, he was acquitted in a hung jury in a civil trial that alleged police torture and a subsequent cover-up. In 1991, he was suspended from the department, and in 1993 he was terminated from the CPD. After his termination, the Fraternal Order of Police (FOP) unsuccessfully attempted to enter a float in the South Side Irish parade honoring Burge. In 2003, Governor George Ryan pardoned four individuals linked to Burge's coerced confessions from death row.[64] Only after federal prosecutors stepped in did Burge get criminally prosecuted. In 2008, U.S. Attorney Patrick Fitzgerald charged Burge with obstruction of justice and perjury related to his 1989 civil lawsuit testimony. He was convicted on all counts on June 28, 2010, and spent nearly four years in federal prison. The city paid an estimated $57 million in settlements to Burge's victims (Schroedter, 2014). On April 14, 2015, Mayor Rahm Emanuel announced he was creating a $5.5 million budget line to fund individuals victimized by Burge. Chicago became the first city to approve reparations to compensate victims, or family members, of police torture. The following month, Emanuel formally apologized to those victims on behalf of the city (Dardick & Byrne, 2013). Burge died at the age of 70 in September 2018 at his home in Apollo Beach, Florida.

62 Capone purchased his 6,077 square-foot mansion in South Beach Miami in 1928 for $40,000. He reportedly spent $200,000 (equivalent to $2.85 million today) on renovations and enhanced security that consisted of a guardhouse, seven-foot-high wall surrounding the property, searchlights, and a coral rock grotto. His wife Mae sold the property in 1952. In 2018, Capone's mansion was listed at $14.9 million, and by the spring of 2020, it was still unsold and listed at $12.9 million.

63 Ramsey reflected on knowing Burge. He was not too surprised to hear about his unethical investigative tactics of arrestees based upon Burge's stories about being involved with Vietnamese POWs' torture (author's interview with Ramsey on August 20, 2020). Ramsey worked as a detective in Area 1 Detective Division at 51st and Wentworth, north of where Burge's activities occurred.

64 The Burge torture incidents led to Governor Ryan putting a moratorium on Illinois's executions in 1999, and by 2003, he commuted more than 160 death sentences to life sentences. The executive moratorium eventually led the state legislature to abolish capital punishment in 2011 under Governor Pat Quinn (see Ryan & Possley, 2020). Ryan served five years in federal prison after being convicted of corruption. He was released in 2013.

Ramsey CPD Career – A Record of Police Reform

Ramsey rose through the CPD ranks serving six years as a patrol officer, seven years as a sergeant, four years as a lieutenant, one year as a captain, four years as Commander of the Narcotics Section, two years as Deputy Chief of the Patrol Division, and four years as Deputy Superintendent. Along the way, many members of the CPD influenced his desire to reform the department's reputation. One particular reflective story was shared on February 12, 2016, when the National Law Enforcement Officer Memorial Foundation interviewed Ramsey. He discussed Officer Paris Patton, who worked for him. Patton was very skillful at de-escalation in the aftermath of narcotics raids. He can be considered the antithesis of Burge. Patton's view was that everyone starts their life as a perfect ten, but lost three points if they are born poor, lost three points if they are born a minority, and lost three points if their family is dysfunctional without role models. The perfect ten is now down to one, and the one is their dignity and self-respect. These individuals will fight to hold onto their dignity and self-respect if challenged, meaning officers should always give individuals their dignity and self-respect, even if the have to arrest, which establishes police legitimacy.

Chicago Alternative Policing Strategy (CAPS)

The CAPS was experimentally run in April 1993 in five police districts. By May 1995, the strategy was operational throughout each police district, with Ramsey, as Deputy Superintendent, in charge. (The CAPS initiative came through the Mayor Richard M. Daley administration, 33 years after his father asked Wilson to reform the CPD as detailed in a previous chapter.) An essential component of the CAPS was to develop closer working relationships between the police and residents in each beat (Skogan et al., 2000). This outreach was seen as a key to long-term crime reduction and counter the horrific history of corruption and brutality from the Burge era. Ramsey and Barbara McDonald,[65] the civilian Director of the Research and Development, created five critical features for the CAPS.

1 A problem-solving[66] model became the core component of the CAPS strategy. Problem-solving meant expectations that officers engaged in proactive crime prevention by prioritizing neighborhood problems, analyzing the causes of those problems, coming up with creative responses based upon data they gathered through their analysis, and assessing the results from the chosen responses.
2 Officers were to receive stable beat assignments in order to have enough time to develop an understanding of community needs and develop trust with the residents so they could collaboratively meet those needs.
3 Officers would be involved in frequent beat meetings with residents to better advise district commanders about the needs of the community.

65 In June 2000, McDonald became the CPDs first civilian employee to be named a deputy superintendent to the Bureau of Administrative Services, in charge of the department's personnel, finance, data systems, and research and development units (Wilson, 2000).

66 When Ramsey was directed to take over the CAPS initiative, he heard of Herman Goldstein and POP and decided to randomly call him, not knowing about Herman's connection to Chicago and the O.W. Wilson era. To his surprise, Herman was very gracious with his time through multiple phone calls. He arranged to meet with Ramsey and other officers in Chicago to encourage their efforts with the CAPS initiative. Ramsey said Herman gave them the confidence to move forward with their strategies (author's interview with Ramsey on August 20, 2020).

4 Officers were expected to have a broader role in mobilizing other stakeholders and city services to solve various problems related to abandoned cars, graffiti, loitering youth, and inoperable street lights.
5 Increased use of crime mapping software and analysis to properly identify crime patterns and hotspots.

Evaluative CAPS research was continually completed by the Institute for Policy Research and led by Wes Skogan from Northwestern University. Evaluation funding also came from the National Institute of Justice (NIJ), the Illinois Criminal Justice Information Authority (ICJIA), and the John D. and Catherine T. MacArthur Foundation. Research determined that familiarity and participation in the CAPS program continued to grow each year of the evaluation. In 1996, a little more than half of the Chicago residents surveyed knew about CAPS, but by 1999, 80 percent knew about the initiative. Citizen involvement took place through district advisory committees, and participation involved planning and strategizing based on local problems and priorities. Each of Chicago's 279 beat locations held meetings that were open to all residents. On average, seven police officers and 26 residents attended each meeting (Skogan et al., 2000), and attendance rates were highest in poor, high-crime communities, where public safety was the most significant concern.

Positive and negative results came out of subsequent research evaluation. On the success side, community involvement increased, and surveys indicated that the CAPS successfully addressed many neighborhood problems. As a testament to Ramsey's command of the CAPS initiative, he received the "Gary Hayes" Police Executive Research Forum (PERF) award.[67] However, research also indicated that officers might be unable to develop long-term relationships in an authentic way because they had to respond to 911 calls continually. Moreover, evaluations demonstrated that the CAPS was not successful with youth involvement or the integration of Hispanic residents who may have been mistrustful of the police due to immigration issues.

Perhaps one of the more significant issues dealt with the combined confusion with problem-solving models and continuous beat meetings with residents. As detailed in the Goldstein appendix to the Wilson chapter, there are differences between problem-oriented policing (POP) and community policing. While good problem-solving often involves the community, it does always have to. In most instances, problems can be proactively addressed by targeting specific stakeholders who have a vested interest in seeing a particular problem solved. The CAPS meetings likely had attendees with little vested interest in helping solve neighborhood problems that did not specifically impact their families. Officers probably had little interest in genuinely becoming proactive analyzers of problems, and the community would be unable to impact serious crime without their law enforcement input.

By the late 2000s, after Ramsey had already left the CPD, the department cut CAPS funding considerably, and attendance within beat meetings dropped significantly. In January 2013, Mayor Emanuel issued a press release and attempted to revitalize the CAPS by decentralizing funding resources, but the overall budget for CAPS remained the same. Public confidence in the CAPS initiative remained low. Ramsey brought these lessons to his new leadership positions with a recognition that community-policing plans will never be self-sustaining within the traditional law enforcement bureaucratic structure. For community-oriented, or POP to be successful, it has to be thoroughly incorporated into the organizational structure at

67 Hayes is mentioned in the chapter on Bill Bratton, who received the 2nd PERF Gary Hayes Award in 1987. Ramsey received the Gary Hayes Award in 1994. Ramsey is also a past President of the PERF. Hayes was a student of Herman Goldstein, was the founding member of the PERF, died at the age of 40 of cancer, as discussed in the appendix to the chapter on Wilson.

all levels and continually rejuvenated through both funding and leaders who provide passionate support for the underlying philosophical shift that these alternatives espouse.

CPD to Metropolitan Police Chief (1998–2006)

In 1998, Ramsey was a finalist to be the next superintendent of the CPD, to replace Matt Rodriguez,[68] but lost out to Terry Hillard, who served from 1998 to 2003. The day after the city announced Hillard as the CPD Superintendent, Ramsey was contacted by a search firm asking him to apply for the vacant MPD chief position. After a four-month process and more than 50 candidates, Ramsey was named the chief, a position he would hold for the next eight years. Until Ramsey, the MPD had never appointed an external chief, and the reforms he accomplished were monumental.

Ramsey oversaw a multi-million-dollar upgrade to the MPD district stations during his tenure, which included implementing new communications and information technology, and a 3-1-1 non-emergency system. He expanded training programs for both police recruits and veteran officers to enhance the quality of their service. Ramsey redefined the Department's mission to focus on crime prevention and community policing strategies that encompassed neighborhood-based partnerships and problem-solving. A training initiative called Partnerships for Problem Solving combined with a Senior Citizen Police Academy. These combined initiatives resulted in crime being at its lowest levels since reporting statistics first developed, in Washington, DC, in the late 1960s. Opinion surveys also indicated that public confidence in the MPD increased annually during Ramsey's tenure as chief.

Metropolitan Police History

In 1790, Maryland and Virginia agreed to give up some of their land to establish the nation's capital city. For the next decade, Maryland and Virginia appointed constables to police the Federal City until a charter was approved to establish Washington, DC, officially. The District was then able to protect itself through an auxiliary night watch with one captain and 15 policemen paid through the federal treasury. By the 1860s, because of the Civil War and the Confederacy threat, military camps surrounded the District. Thousands of troops poured into the city, and along the outskirts, and one of the largest brothels attracted crooks, gamblers, pickpockets, prostitutes, and thugs. Amongst the chaotic influx of the mixed population, President Lincoln recognized that the auxiliary night watch was inadequate. Consequently, he became personally interested in establishing a local police department to help patrol the District.

On August 6, 1861, Lincoln convinced Congress to pass a bill that established the Washington, DC MPD for its relatively small 75,000 residents that continued to grow with numerous outsiders. In comparison, New York City had 800,000 residents, and Philadelphia's population was a half-million. A week after the MPD establishment, Lincoln sent the Board of Metropolitan Police to New York City to learn how their police agency attempted to replicate Sir Robert Peel's modern police force in London, which evolved out of their Parliament's 1829 Metropolitan Police Act. By September 1861, the MPD appointed attorney William Webb as their first superintendent. The MPD also received Congressional approval for an authorized strength of up to ten sergeants and a patrol force not to exceed 150 officers for

68 Rodriguez announced his retirement in November 1997, in the aftermath of reports that he was close friends with Frank Milito, a convicted felon who owned a gas station and failed to pay income taxes. Associations with known felons went against CPD policy. Early that year, Mayor Daley had initiated a commission to investigate police corruption after seven CPD officers were indicted on federal drug conspiracy charges (Belluck, 1997).

ten precincts. Webb received $1,500 annually, the sergeants made $600 a year, and patrolmen were paid $480. Officers worked 12-hour shifts, seven days a week, no days off, and no time allotted for vacations.

Lincoln's Assassination and the Failure of the MPD

On April 14, 1865, Good Friday, the MPD assigned 26-year-old Officer William Crook as President Lincoln's bodyguard throughout the day. He was supposed to be relieved at 4:00 PM by Officer John Frederick Parker, but he was predictably late. Crook volunteered to stay late, but Lincoln persuaded him to go home. Around the same time, witnesses reported seeing 26-year-old John Wilkes Booth[69] riding a new fast rented horse down Pennsylvania Avenue. Booth made a brief stop at Grover's Theatre to verify that Mrs. Lincoln had declined an offer to attend the play *Aladdin! The Wonderful Lamp* and Lincoln's young son Tad would be attending instead. He also verified that President Lincoln and his wife Mary Lincoln, along with Mr. and Mrs. Ulysses Grant, would attend Ford's Theatre to see *Our American Cousin*. Booth was a star actor throughout the District and an open sympathizer to the Confederacy. He last acted at Ford's Theatre in March 1865 and was well acquainted with his fellow actors and the theatre layout, which allowed him to come and go as he pleased.

The fateful date of April 14, 1865, was only five days after General Grant's appearance at the Appomattox Court House in Virginia to accept the surrender of Confederate troops[70] from General Robert E. Lee, a significant event to help push for an end to the four-year Civil War. That war resulted in approximately 623,000 troops killed (not including civilian casualties), the deadliest conflict in American military history. Grant and his wife Julia had checked into the Willard the evening prior, Washington's most luxurious hotel. Around 11 AM, the morning of April 14th, Lincoln began his cabinet meeting with General Grant in attendance. Around the same time, a telegram was delivered to Grant's wife at the Willard Hotel, supposedly from Lincoln, instructing her and her husband to be their guests that evening at Ford's Theatre. Booth had plans to assassinate both Grant and Lincoln at Ford's Theatre, while other co-conspirators killed Vice President Johnson and Secretary of State William Seward. While the Lincolns anticipated their guests for the evening play would be the Grants, the President did not send any message directly to the Willard Hotel. Grant's wife had already asked her husband if they could leave for New Jersey on a train later that day to visit their family. After their cabinet meeting, Grant met privately with Lincoln, apologized, and stated he would not attend the theatre that evening. Also, Mrs. Grant sent a separate message to the White House that begged her husband to cancel their evening plans with the Lincolns again, partly because she did not get along with Mrs. Lincoln and partly because the message she received at her hotel room spooked her. While she had breakfast in the hotel's lobby, Mrs. Grant saw the man who delivered the telegram to her room with another individual, she later said resembled Booth[71] (Hutchinson, 2020). Grant would obsess the rest of

69 Booth had a romantic relationship, possibly a secret engagement, with Lucy Lambert Hale, New Hampshire Senator John Parker Hale's daughter. Lucy was also romantically involved with Lincoln's son Robert. A photo of Lucy was found on Booth after he was killed by Union soldiers (described more fully later) on April 26, 1865, 12 days after he assassinated President Lincoln.

70 On the day of the President's assassination, Booth was likely incensed to see 440 shackled Confederate soldiers and eight generals marched through downtown DC as thousands of residents lined the streets to watch (Hutchinson, 2020, p. 100). It was only a few years earlier, on April 16, 1862, nine months before the *Emancipation Proclamation*, that Washington, DC abolished slavery in the District and freed 3,100 Black men and women while they reimbursed those who legally owned the slaves.

71 Julia Grant's revelations from the day Lincoln was assassinated came about in her memoirs written years after April 14, 1865. Her memoir was written for her children and grandchildren. She died of kidney and heart

his life, wondering if he could have prevented Lincoln's assassination had he been present at Ford's theatre that evening.

In November 1864, five months prior to the assassination, the MPD created a permanent detail of four officers to protect Lincoln, including John Parker, one of the first 150 officers who started the DC Police Department.

> Ward Hill Lamon, a U.S. Marshal stationed in DC and a close Illinois friend of Lincoln, requested the presidential security detail from the MPD. Lamon was also Lincoln's self-proclaimed bodyguard who famously argued with Allan Pinkerton over his security. Before the Presidential election, Lamon lived in Danville and then Bloomington, Illinois, and worked the legal circuit as a law partner with Lincoln before moving to DC for his presidency. The fateful Easter weekend of 1865 began with Lincoln's request for his friend to go to Richmond to observe the Confederacy surrender issues. In *Recollections of Abraham Lincoln*, Lamon (1994) stated that he implored the president not to leave the White House at night, particularly to the theatre before he departed. This was not the first time Lamon played a role in trying to thwart an assassination. Along with Pinkerton and Kate Warne,[72] Lamon accompanied Lincoln on his train ride in February 1861 to his inauguration. The President-elect's travel plans and his attire were switched, through the advice of Pinkerton, to thwart an alleged assassination attempt in Baltimore. After Booth's horrific success, Lamon would again accompany his friend by train in his funeral procession back to Springfield, Illinois. Lamon even purchased the train that led Lincoln to his final resting place.

Parker was four hours late to take his shift as Lincoln's police bodyguard on April 14, 1865. He was a terrible choice to guard the President's box at Ford's Theatre. Parker was previously charged for dereliction of duty for being drunk on duty and frequently visited some of the 400 brothels that existed throughout the District, distracting him from his law enforcement duties. The Lincolns arrived late to Ford's Theatre, about a half-hour after the play had begun, and because of the irresponsible Parker, unaccompanied by any security. A doorman at Ford's Theatre, and Parker, greeted the Lincolns. Before this greeting, Parker arrived late at the White House, and the staff instructed him to proceed to the theatre to meet the President, who had left without any security.[73] Noting the President's arrival, the actors on stage paused, and the orchestra played "Hail to the Chief" as the house lights went up and the crowd issued a standing ovation.

Parker was initially seated outside Lincoln's box, in the passageway by the door, which would have been a perfect position to stop Booth's assassination. However, he could not see the stage from his security seat, so after the Lincolns settled into their box with their guests, Parker moved to the first gallery to enjoy the play. To make matters worse, during the second and final intermission, Parker left the theatre and went next door to the Star Saloon to share

failure on December 14, 1902, and her memoir was not published until 1975 (Simon, 1975), leading some historians to question the authenticity of her recollections.

72 Warne was employed with Pinkerton's Detective Agency in 1856 and became known as the nation's first female detective (Enss, 2017).

73 After the assassination, John Ford attempted to reopen his theatre for performances on July 10, 1865. But Secretary of War Stanton dispatched troops to stop the show and eventually used federal funds to buy the theatre for $100,000 so it would not be used for entertainment. On June 9, 1893, during Edwin Booth's (John Booth's brother) funeral in New York, Ford's old theatre's interior walls collapsed and killed 22 workers inside. (Shortly before his father's assassination, Robert Lincoln reported that Edwin Booth saved him from serious injury or death when he grabbed him from a New Jersey train platform after he fell.) In 1968, Ford's Theatre was reopened to the public as a national historic site that produces live performances and an interactive museum.

drinks with Charles Forbes, Lincoln's assistant, and his carriage driver Francis "Ned" Burke. Booth also had drinks at the Star Saloon during that time, as he had done throughout the day. Only Charles Forbes returned to the theatre to stand outside the Presidential box for the play's third and final act and unsuspectedly allowed Booth to enter the box.

As the last act resumed, Booth had already talked his way into the hallway that led to Lincoln's box. The assassin nudged open a door with a broken lock and shot the President in the back of the head with a small .44-caliber single-shot derringer, made by Henry Derringer from Philadelphia. Lincoln was seated next to his wife. Major Henry Rathbone[74] and his fiancée Clara Harris were in the same box and were the Grant's replacement guests. Rathbone fought with Booth after he shot Lincoln and Booth slashed him with a dagger before making his escape by leaping to the stage and then ran out of the theatre to his awaiting horse. It was well past midnight when Parker arrived at the MPD station with Lizzie Williams, a prostitute he arrested (allegedly for not granting him free favors), that he learned the fate of President Lincoln.[75] Officer Crook, who protected Lincoln earlier in the day, held Parker directly responsible for Lincoln's death. Crook wrote about this view in his book that detailed his time working in the White House and protecting five presidents (Crook, 1910). However, at least a dozen other occasions previously occurred when Lincoln visited theatres with little to no presidential security protection.

MPD Chief A.C. Richards[76] ordered his entire force to be put on duty to assist the Union Army with the investigation to locate Booth and other conspirators[77] following the assassination. The following month, Richards also charged Parker with dereliction of duty, but transcripts of any discipline are missing, and charges later dismissed. The MPD kept Parker as an officer. Ironically, the department reassigned him to protect Lincoln's wife, who dismissed him, despite his pleas for her forgiveness. Weeks before the assassination, Mrs. Lincoln wrote a letter on Parker's behalf to exempt him from the Civil War draft, and some historians believe she was related to him on her mother's side (Martin, 2010). Parker remained employed with the MPD for the next few years. However, on August 13, 1868, he was fired for sleeping on duty. He died in 1890 and was buried in an unmarked grave with his wife and three children in Washington, DC (Martin, 2010). No known photographs exist of Parker.

On April 15th at 4:00 AM, only hours before Lincoln was pronounced dead, Booth and 23-year-old co-conspirator David Herold[78] escaped Washington, DC. They arrived at the

74 Rathbone suffered from mental illness later in life. On December 23, 1883, he attacked his children and then fatally shot and stabbed Clara, his wife, while she attempted to protect their children. Rathbone attempted suicide by stabbing himself five times in the chest. He then blamed his wife's murder on an intruder but was convicted and sent to an asylum for the criminally insane in Germany for the rest of his life. He died on August 14, 1911, at 74 years of age.

75 About nine hours after Booth shot him, Lincoln died in a home across the street from Ford's Theatre. After an elaborate funeral in Washington, DC, a special train transported his body to Springfield, Illinois, making several stops along the way. Lincoln's Secretary of War, Edwin Stanton, ordered that no photographs of Lincoln's body could be taken and the coffin remained closed. However, on April 24th, one photographer was able to take a photo from the distance of the open casket, and the image remained a secret for 90 years, until 1952 when a 14-year-old boy accidentally discovered it while on a visit to the Lincoln home in Springfield (Hutchinson, 2020, p. 214).

76 Richards was chief (Major and Superintendent) for 14 years. Previous to becoming chief, he was a teacher, and afterward, he became a lawyer, practicing law in Washington, DC, before he retired in Florida.

77 The other conspirators consisted of Lewis Powell (attempted to assassinate the Secretary of State Seward in his home by stabbing him multiple times), George Atzerodt (was supposed to assassinate Vice President Johnson but got drunk instead), and Mary Surratt (ran a boarding house and allegedly helped Booth).

78 On July 7, 1865, Herold, George Atzerodt, and Mary Surratt were executed by hanging in Washington, DC. Surratt became the first woman executed by the Federal Government. The film, *The Conspirator*, was released in April 2011, on the 146th anniversary of Lincoln's assassination, and alluded to doubts over Surratt's guilt. Since

Maryland home of Dr. Samuel Mudd,[79] a Confederate sympathizer and slave owner, who treated Booth for a fractured leg he injured when he shimmied down the second-floor box and fell on the stage of Ford's Theatre after he shot Lincoln. Twelve days after Lincoln's assassination, soldiers located Booth and Herold held up in a barn near Port Royal, Virginia, 60 miles south of the capital. Herold surrendered, but Booth refused. The barn was set on fire by Union soldiers, and Sergeant Thomas "Boston" Corbett[80] fatally shot Booth in the neck in what he alleged was self-defense. Booth lived, paralyzed, for a few hours before dying on the front porch of the farmhouse. Initially, Corbett was arrested for not following the Secretary of War Stanton's orders to take Booth alive to stand trial. Corbett was later declared a patriot, but he spent the rest of his life defending his actions. A couple of decades after he killed Booth, Corbett was declared insane and sent to an asylum[81] in Kanas, where he later escaped and is believed to have died in a Minnesota fire.

Garfield's Assassination

In 1878, the Federal Government officially abolished the Metropolitan Police Board, and a new board of commissioners appointed by Congress took over governance duties. On July 2, 1881, the MPD investigated President James Garfield's assassination, its second presidential assassination in 16 years.[82] Before his assassination, which took place at a railroad station in Washington, DC on the southwest corner of Sixth Street and Constitution Avenue NW, the local newspapers reported the President was leaving the city with his family for summer vacation. Garfield was elected only four months before his assassination. It was common for Presidents to travel without security details, although Lincoln did utilize armed guards due to the Civil War and numerous threats against him. MPD Officer Patrick Kearney responded to the sound of two shots inside the train depot's reception area, which struck Garfield. Kearney took Charles Guiteau into custody as he attempted to board his horse and carriage to escape.

1976, the Federal Government executed 16 individuals. Ten executions occurred in 2020, and three more in President Trump's last days in office in 2021. In January 2021, Lisa Montgomery was executed in federal prison by lethal injection. The last woman executed by the Federal Government was 67 years prior.

79 The phrase "your name is Mudd," meaning you are not very popular, has been said to stem from Dr. Mudd treating Booth's injured leg on April 15, 1865. A military commission later found Dr. Mudd guilty of aiding and conspiring with Booth and he was sentenced to life. His death penalty was denied by a single vote. In 1869, he was released from prison after President Johnson pardoned him. In actuality, the phrase "your name is mud" appeared in print decades prior to the Lincoln assassination and was used to reference "a stupid twaddling fellow."

80 Corbett was a profoundly religious street preacher. In July 1858, he propositioned two prostitutes while he walked home from a church meeting and was so disturbed by his behavior that he castrated himself with scissors and attended a prayer meeting before seeking medical treatment. The fervent Christian and Union soldier who spent time in a Confederate POW camp believed God ordered him to kill Booth on April 26, 1865 (Jenson, 2015).

81 Mary Lincoln was also ordered to an asylum in Batavia, Illinois, on May 20, 1875, by a judge after her estranged relationship with her son Robert Todd Lincoln and a possible suicide attempt. A few months later, she was released to the custody of her sister in Springfield. On July 15, 1882, exactly 11 years after her youngest son's death, Mrs. Lincoln had a stroke and died at the age of 63.

82 President Lincoln's son Robert became Garfield's Secretary of War. Lincoln came to the train station on July 2, 1881, apologized for not taking the trip with the Garfield, and returned to his office where he was informed by an aide that Garfield had been shot in what would become the second Presidential assassination. Twenty years later, President William McKinley invited Robert Lincoln to the Pan American Exposition in Buffalo, and Lincoln was present for the nation's third Presidential assassination in September 1901 (Emerson, 2012). Political anarchist Leon Czolgosz assassinated McKinley. The only other president to be assassinated after McKinley was John F. Kennedy on November 22, 1963, described in the Goldstein appendix to the chapter on O.W. Wilson.

Garfield died 79 days later, at age 49, due to infection and doctors' inability to find the bullet lodged near his spleen in addition to the unsterilized procedures used at the time (Millard, 2012). Guiteau's motivation stemmed from being disgruntled that he could not get a job in the Garfield White House, despite several attempts to do so. His case represented the first attempt to use an insanity-defense in a high-profile criminal case (Kingsbury, 2002). Guiteau was hung in the nation's capital on June 30, 1882, almost one year after he shot Garfield. Reportedly, he danced his way to the gallows, waved to the audience, shook hands with the executioner, and recited a poem he had written called "I am Going to the Lordy" (Millard, 2012).

Perils of Policing Mass Protests – 1932, 1968, 2020

History continued to put officers of the MPD in peril. During Prohibition 25 officers were killed, mainly by gunfire, while pursuing those involved in illegal liquor sales (Peck, 2011). In addition to the perils of policing Prohibition, MPD officers had to challenge protesting veterans in the summer of 1932 during the Great Depression. An estimated 43,000 protesters, which included 15,000 World War I soldiers known as the "Bonus Army," began to arrive in Washington, DC, in May 1932, demanding payment for past military service (Dickson & Allen, 2020). Veterans and their families came to the nation's capital to collect on a 1924 "bonus" payment promised by the Government to those who served in the Great War. In that year, Congress overrode President Coolidge's veto and ordered that veterans receive $1 a day for domestic services and $1.25 a day for overseas services (Dickson & Allen, 2003). However, Congress deferred this compensation until 1945 based on budgetary concerns as the Depression set in.

During the Great Depression period, the three commissioners managed the District rather than a mayor. The President appointed the commissioners, and they were in charge of the MPD. Throughout the early summer of 1932, MPD Chief Pelham Glassford arrived on his blue motorcycle to meet with the protesters and their families, and he utilized the Marine Corps to help anyone who was sick. Glassford was a former brigadier general and World War I veteran. The local community sympathized with the protesters and their families and often brought them food and other supplies. During this time, Jim Crow flourished in Washington, DC, and other southern cities, but protesting families in the encampments became fully integrated without any significant issues. The Justice Department's Director of the Bureau of Investigation (later becoming the FBI) was 37-year-old J. Edgar Hoover. Hoover attempted to gather evidence that the protesting Bonus Army began with Communist organizers, but his allegations were not substantiated.

After a couple of months, Attorney General (AG) William Mitchell curtailed MPD Chief Glassford's servant leadership and ordered him to remove the protesters on the morning of July 28, 1932. Glassford arrived with approximately 100 of his officers to follow his orders. The removal was to target an encampment in Anacostia Park on the District's southeast side and several occupied dilapidated buildings in downtown Washington, DC. That afternoon, a conflict arose, and MPD officers fatally shot two veterans, and a few officers were also injured. The deadly conflict led President Hoover to order in 8,000 military troops, under General Douglas MacArthur's command, to disperse the protesting veterans. For the first time in our country's history, tanks rolled through the capital streets targeting protesting citizens along with 200 cavalry troops led by General George Patton.

Initially, the protesting veterans and their families cheered the cavalry and the troops sensing they were there to march in solidarity. This admiration quickly turned ominous when the troops were seen with masks and hurdling tear-gas grenades to disperse the mass protest, which set off fires amongst the shelters protesting families had built. After the protesters dispersed the downtown area, Hoover ordered MacArthur to stop their pursuit (Dickson & Allen, 2003), but MacArthur ignored this command[83] believing the protesters were still a threat. MacArthur and his troops proceeded to Anacostia Park and torched the protesters' encampment (Tuccille, 2018). Dwight Eisenhower was one of MacArthur's junior aides and would later comment that he told MacArthur[84] not to be publicly involved with the raid.[85] This raid was the most extensive use of the military[86] on national soil since the Civil War.

The Trump Administration repeated the history of using National Guard troops in response to Black Lives Matter protesters in the nation's capital in June 2020. Protesters besieged the District in the aftermath of George Floyd's in-custody police death on May 25, 2020, in Minneapolis during the COVID-19 pandemic. The District's National Guard was called out again, with multiple municipal police agencies, on January 6, 2021, after Trump supporters broke windows and converged into the US Capitol to protest the presidential election. President Trump's aides convinced him to order in the National Guard to protect the Capitol after he incited his supporters that morning during a speech outside the White House. Critics contend that the law enforcement response was different for the Capitol insurrection than the Black Lives Matter protesters six months prior. DC Mayor Muriel Bowser[87] swore in MPD Chief Robert Contee III[88] as acting chief only four days before the Capitol attack. Capitol Police Officer Brian Sicknick,[89] age 42, died the day after the Capitol's attack from injuries sustained from the rioters. Four other Trump protesters also died. Injuries were sustained by 58 MPD officers and 81 Capitol officers (Speare-Cole, 2021). Capitol Police Chief Steve Sund resigned a couple of days after the attack. Ramsey perceived a double-standard existed when it came to the large police

83 History would repeat itself nearly two decades later, and President Truman relieved MacArthur of his Command on April 11, 1951. During this period, North Korea had crossed the 38th parallel to bring communism to South Korea. General MacArthur successfully drove the Koreans back north and disagreed with Truman that a ceasefire was warranted. He broke rank with his commander and chief and wanted to bomb Chinese cities for supporting North Korea and wanted to push troops north of the 38th parallel, and liberate North Korea from communist control. Truman feared these aggressive actions would be a catalyst for another world war as the country was still recovering from WWII (Brands, 2016). MacArthur died in 1964 in Washington, DC, at the age of 84, about four months after President Kennedy's assassination. Before his assassination, Kennedy had already authorized a state funeral for MacArthur.

84 Eisenhower was more candid of his opinion on MacArthur's raid on the Bonus Army with historian Stephen Ambrose when he said "I told that dumb son-of-a-bitch he had no business going down there" (Ambrose, 1985), referring to Anacostia Park.

85 Eisenhower's stance against top generals being publicly involved in military action against U.S. protesters was similar to General Mark Milley's (the nation's highest ranking military officer and chair of the Joint Chiefs of Staff) apology on June 11, 2020. Milley apologized for being present in Lafayette Square with President Trump during a photo op on June 1st at St. John's Church, which occurred after peaceful protesters were beaten and cleared with tear gas by MPD officers. The protesters were part of the 2020 international demonstrations against police misuse of force following the death of George Floyd in Minneapolis. General Milley apologized for the appearance that the military was involved in domestic politics (Lubold & Youssef, 2020).

86 By 1944, President Franklin Roosevelt signed into law the "G.I. Bill" to readjust and guarantee proper payment and education for veterans. In this same year, the Generals' embarrassment over putting down the Bonus Army uprising was put in the past as Eisenhower liberated Europe, Patton led troops into Seine, France, and MacArthur planned the liberation of the Philippines.

87 Bowser was the eighth mayor to serve the District, assuming office in 2015, and the second female mayor after Sharon Pratt served from 1991 to 1995. She is the first Washington, DC African-American female mayor.

88 Contee is the sixth African-American chief to lead the MPD and the first since Ramsey left in 2007.

89 Sicknick's cremated remains were laid in the Capitol Rotunda on February 2–3, 2021. This was the 39th remembrance honored in the Capitol and the first without a coffin. Sicknick was buried at Arlington National Cemetery.

presence to address the Black Lives Matter protesters, and the Capitol invasion lacked preparedness. In the aftermath, Ramsey cautioned the long-term implication on our democracy, the divided America we have become, and that the divide runs much deeper than the Presidency (Augenstein, 2021). The Capitol's last attack took place 207 years prior, on August 24, 1814, when the British burned government and military buildings in Washington, DC, as part of the War of 1812.

At the end of 1951, Robert Murray started his tenure as the longest-lasting leader of the MPD. For 13 years, Murray became the Vollmer of the MPD and was named Major/Superintendent and then Chief in 1953 once Congress passed the District Government Reorganization Act. He brought much-needed reform to a demoralized force by instituting an internal affairs division, successfully getting pay raises for officers, fully integrating assignments without racial bias, and drastically improving departmental infrastructure.

By 1963, violent crime surged, and the District led the nation in the number of murders per capita. John Layton, chief from 1964 to 1969, followed the lead of O.W. Wilson and began the first Police Cadet Program and attempted to improve police training and the community relations unit. In 1968, following the April 4th assassination of Martin Luther King, Jr. over 20,000 rioters overwhelmed the MPD. After four days of riots, there were 13 dead, and over 1,000 businesses were damaged and destroyed by fires and looting (Hansen, 2018). President Johnson dispatched approximately 13,600 federal troops, including the National Guard, to the District's streets to end the mass protests and riots. This amount of soldiers surpassed the number used by MacArthur and Patton to put down the Bonus Army uprising. The use of troops in the country's capital in 1968 became the largest occupation of an American city since the Civil War (Walker, 2018). The District sustained an estimated $27 million in damage or close to $200 million in 2020 dollars. Many businesses would never reopen. By 1969, the District was in such despair that President Richard Nixon took a personal interest in the MPD and helped increase the number of officers from 2,000 in 1969 to 5,100 in 1973 (Price, 1989).

Jerry Wilson was the chief from 1969 to 1974 and ushered in a reform agenda that saw a reduction in crime. He had a close relationship with President Nixon and became the only MPD chief to be put on *Time Magazine*'s cover. In 1968, Presidential candidate Nixon called DC a national disgrace because of surging violence. By 1972, crime was on the decline, and the President declared the city one of the safest in the country despite ongoing protests directed primarily at ending the Vietnam War.

Washington, DC became an epicenter for 2020 protests following the Minneapolis in-custody death of George Floyd on May 25, 2020. On May 29th, the Secret Service put the White House on lockdown and violently clashed with protesters. Consequently, President Trump was temporarily rushed to a bunker underneath the White House (Lemire & Miller, 2020). Protests continued through the next several weeks, and monuments along the National Mall were vandalized (Bowden, 2020). On June 5th, the DC Public Works Department painted the words "Black Lives Matter" with 35-foot yellow letters along 16th Street NW on the north side of Lafayette Square near the White House. Mayor Bowser officially posted a street sign and renamed the area Black Lives Matter plaza (Wu, 2020). Leaders of the movement added to the mural by painting "Defund the Police" (Tan, Mill, Chason, Schmidt, & Amenabar, 2020).

Maurice Cullinane was the MPD chief from 1974 to 1979 and led the department during a harrowing experience on March 9, 1977, when hostages were taken during an armed takeover by the Hanafi Muslim Sect at the City Council Building. Marion Barry was hit by a ricocheted shotgun pellet when the Hanafi Muslims took over the District's city hall building. His wound was superficial, but he was hospitalized. A two-day siege, which included hostages, came to an end through FBI negotiators and Muslim ambassadors.

Mayor Marion Barry (1979–1991, 1995–1999)

Barry was the Mayor of Washington, DC, from 1979 to 1991 and again from 1995 to 1999. He also served three terms on the DC City Council. Two of Barry's deputy mayors went to prison for corruption. On January 18, 1990, the FBI arrested Barry with his former girlfriend, Hazel Diane "Rasheeda" Moore, in a joint sting operation with the MPD. Barry, videoed inside a hotel room, smoked crack cocaine.[90] Unbeknownst to Mayor Barry, Moore was set up to work as a government informant and told him he should freebase before they had sex, which led to his arrest (Agronsky, 1991). Barry served six months in prison, 1991–1992, and then made his political comeback and was re-elected to a fourth term as the District's mayor. In 2004 he was elected to the city council but later pleaded guilty to not paying taxes and tested positive for cocaine in a court-mandated drug test. In 2008, Barry was again re-elected to the city council. Barry died on November 23, 2014, of a heart attack, at the age of 78.

When Barry was elected mayor in 1979, the MPD had 4,073 officers. By 1988, there were 3,782 officers. Over that time, adjusting for inflation, the police department budget also shrank by $50 million (Harriston & Flaherty, 1994). A rise in violent crime in the late 1980s caused a 20-month hiring binge in the MPD throughout 1989 and 1990. From 1987 to 1990, murders in the District increased four straight years: 225, 369, 434, 483 (Escobar, 1991). As the violence increased, the MPD faced the retirements of 60 percent of its force and pressure from Congress to withhold federal funds if they did not quickly hire replacement officers. In a haste to meet the congressional deadline or risk losing $430 million, the MPD hired 1,471 officers. Police reformers Vollmer and Wilson fought their entire careers to rid the police profession from political influence. The MPD binge-hiring in response to the politicians attests to the importance of this conflict.

The Consequences of MPD's Hiring Binge[91]

Investigative reporters from the *Washington Post* (Harriston & Flaherty, 1994) found that police academy graduates from 1989 to 1990 accounted for-

- More than 50 percent of the 201 MPD officers arrested occurred between 1989 to 1994. These officers were charged with everything from shoplifting to murder, and some had multiple arrests.
- More than 50 percent of departmental disciplinary proceedings included making false statements, failing to obey orders, and neglecting duty. Disciplinary procedures doubled for the MPD after the hiring binge.
- One in every 14 officers had a previous criminal arrest since background investigations were cut short.
- One in 20 applicants were rejected by the psychological services unit. Traditionally (before the hiring binge), one in five candidates were rejected in psychological screenings.

90 Barry's son, Marion Christopher Barry, from his third wife Effi Slaughter, died of a drug overdose at the age of 36 on August 14, 2016.

91 In 1994–1995, the author of this book worked as a criminal investigator for the Washington, DC Public Defender Service when the District was riddled with high crime. It was also well known that the police were embattled with numerous misconduct cases, obsolete technology, and a shortage of qualified officers (see Forman, 2017).

- An average of 1,000 individuals took the police exam each month, and 60 percent passed with an additional 1,500 a month who signed up for the police cadet program. The department took about 25 percent of the applicants, which greatly exceeded past hiring by the MPD; one in 12 and a national average of one in ten.

The friction over the MPD and the District residents erupted in 1991 when rookie officer Angela Jewell attempted to arrest Salvadoran Daniel Enrique Gomez for disorderly conduct during Cinco de Mayo celebrations. Allegations were made that Gomez came at Officer Jewell with a hunting knife, but witnesses disputed this after Jewel shot him in the chest. Approximately 400 spontaneous protesters began to attack the police while Gomez was handcuffed. The protest led to riots and looting, mainly in the Mount Pleasant neighborhoods in the District's Northwest territory. For several hours protests spread and Mayor Sharon Pratt ordered that the police resist making arrests in fear that it would antagonize more violence (Pratt, 2011). Over the next two nights, rioting and looting continued, a state of emergency was declared and a curfew imposed. In the end, over 60 police vehicles were damaged or destroyed, and around 30 businesses were looted or otherwise damaged. Four years later, a jury dismissed Gomez's civil lawsuit for $4 million. Two years prior to the civil ruling, criminal charges against Gomez ended in a hung jury and the prosecution refused to retry the case (Miller, 1995).

In 1993, the MPD led the nation in officers getting arrested. That year, prosecutors filed criminal charges against 79 officers in the MPD. With a force of 4,220, criminal charges equated to a rate of 19 per 1,000 officers. In comparison cities that same year: the NYPD arrested 90 officers (a force of 30,000 and a rate of three per 1,000); Detroit arrested 69 officers (a force of 4,000 officers and a rate of 17 per 1,000, but all were not officers), and; St. Louis arrested 20 officers (a force of 1,500 and a rate of 13 per 1,000). Based on a sharp increase in police corruption tips, the FBI launched Operation Broken Faith, culminating in the December 1993 arrests of "The Dirty Dozen" officers charged with taking bribes to protect cocaine dealers (Dugan, 1995). Five of the 12 officers charged in the FBI drug conspiracy came to the MPD through their cadet program (York & Castaneda, 1993).

Washington, DC, Police Shootings: Failed Investigations

In the 1970s, the Use of Service Weapon Review Board, which included civilian reviewers, was established to investigate officer uses of force (Milton, Wahl, Lardner, & Abrecht, 1977). Homicide detectives investigated fatal shootings, which were supposed to be reviewed by the district command. This review system changed in the 1980s and 1990s as investigations were often incomplete, sporadically done at the district level, and at times reviewed through immediate supervisors and not district command. Moreover, in 1997, an estimated 60 percent of officers never requalified at shooting ranges (Leen, Craven, Jackson, & Horwitz, 1998). More troubling, the lapses in requalification included 75 percent of officers involved in shootings.[92] There was no budgetary reason for the lack of requalification, just mismanagement to ensure officers' training.

Lapses in firearm training converged with MPD officers issued new Austrian-made Glock 17 firearms (this occurred in 1989) to confront increased violence connected to the crack cocaine epidemic. The Glock handguns are known for the lack of external manual safety allowing the weapon to be fired more quickly with a more effortless trigger squeeze. The pistol carries a magazine of 17 bullets and one in the chamber, which tripled officers' firepower. In

92 Some researchers have questioned the practicality of past and present firearm qualification measures, but mainly as it involves the officers' ability to accurately shoot when under stressful situations (Morrison & Vila, 1998).

1989, before the full effect of the newly issued Glock handguns and the new officer hires could be felt, the MPD shot and killed four people; by 1995, the number had climbed to 16. No other large city experienced a similar increase in officer shootings during that period. In 1988 MPD officers discharged their weapons 76 times, but in 1995 (seven years after Glock firearms were issued and in the aftermath of the hiring binge), they discharged their weapons 154 times (Leen et al., 1998, p. A01). From 1987 to 1997 there were more than 120 accidental discharges (Leen & Horwitz, 1998), far exceeding other cities.

Investigative reporters from the *Washington Post* determined the MPD became the nation's deadliest police force throughout the 1990s (Leen et al., 1998). Their investigative reporting won them a Pulitzer Prize and determined the District led the country in both murders and officer shootings. The reporters found that MPD officers fired their weapons twice as much as officers in New York, Los Angeles, Chicago, and Miami, which cost the District millions in court settlements. From 1994 to 1998, MPD officers shot and killed 57 people, three more than Chicago, which has three times the police force and five times the population.[93] During this same period, MPD officers were involved in 640 shooting incidents, 40 more than Los Angeles with double the officers and six times the population. From 1975 to 1983, New York averaged 1.36 fatal shootings annually by police per 1,000 officers, and Washington's rate was nearly identical at 1.44, according to a study by the IACP. By 1995, New York's rate had dropped below one, and Washington's had risen to nearly four.

The lack of accountable investigations and false reporting was apparent throughout the 1990s. MPD policies indicated that a district commander should investigate officer-involved shootings (OIS) and homicide detectives investigate fatal shootings. Once the internal investigation is complete, federal prosecutors are supposed to review the case and consider criminal law violations. The last level of oversight in the MPD was the three-member "Use of Service Weapon Review Board" to determine if violations of departmental policies occurred and if internal disciplinary actions were needed. However, investigations did not occur with numerous OIS cases, and when investigations did occur, they often involved immediate supervisors rather than commanders, U.S. Attorneys, or the Review Board. In four-and-a-half years (January 1994–May 1998), 422 documented police shootings were justified 87 percent of the time. Fifty-three of the shootings were ruled improper, and 33 of those were considered accidental. The remaining 20 unjustified shootings included domestic altercations, suicides, and shots fired at animals. Only two of the shootings resulted in criminal charges against officers. One officer spent 15 days in jail, and the other received probation.

In one ten-month stretch, 1992–1993, the *Washington Post* (Jackson, 1998) reported that Officer Lawrence Walker[94] was involved in five shootings. In three of these shootings, Walker shot suspects in the back with two fatalities and one severely injured. The internal investigations, led by Walker's supervisor Sgt. Donald Gossage, declared all of these shootings justified. Supervisors skipped other oversight measures. In March 1993, Walker fatally shot a 19-year-old drug suspect and was placed on routine administrative leave.

However, Walker and his partner, Officer Dwayne Mitchell, were allowed to keep their police firearms for protection. On May 18, 1993, Mitchell and Walker reported they had one beer apiece at Walker's apartment and went to buy more beer around midnight. They confronted Nathaniel "Bud" Mitchell (same last name as Officer Mitchell but no relation), a

93 To make matters worse, it was discovered from 1994 to 1997, the MPD stated there were 29 fatal police shootings. However, reporters determined there were 43 fatal shootings, with seven mislabeled as nonfatal. Moreover, seven were strangely missing (Jackson, 1998).

94 Walker was assigned to a 12-member rapid deployment squad who averaged more than 300 drug and gun arrests a year.

38-year-old panhandler carrying a toy gun that the officers said they saw him using to threaten his drinking partner. Mitchell ran from officers Walker and Mitchell. The officers reported the suspect aimed the toy gun at them as they pursued. Walker and Mitchell fired 23 rounds at "Bud" Mitchell and struck him four times, but only once in the front right shoulder and three times in the back. The media determined that investigators did not check the officers' blood alcohol levels after the shooting. Moreover, Mitchell and Walker later changed their reports to indicate that "Bud" Mitchell pointed his gun at them while the officers were still in their vehicle. Since that incident, Walker became involved in four other shootings or a total of ten shootings throughout the 1990s (Jackson, 1998). Families filed five separate lawsuits against Officer Walker.

Other examples include the following:

- December 1994, Officer Julius Dancy claimed Michael Rutledge grabbed his gun after a foot pursuit. Rutledge said the officer shot him in the back after he ran. Rutledge was unarmed and not charged with any crime. The city settled for $750,000 while a jury deliberated on a $10 million civil suit (Miller, 1999).
- February 1995, Officer Kristopher Payne fatally shot Antonio Williams seven times after he claimed Williams pointed a gun at him during a foot chase. An eyewitness stated that Payne stood over Williams and shot him in the head. Five months after the incident, a muzzle-to-garment test showed the shot that struck Williams in the head was fired from a couple of feet away, despite police investigators ruling the shooting was justified (Jackson, 1998).
- May 1995, Officer Michelle Bullard requalified her Glock pistol at the range, her first in four years. While off-duty, Bullard took her teenage daughter to fish in Rock Creek, near the Watergate Hotel. She got into an argument with Jamaican-born Rudyard Bradshaw, who was also fishing. Bullard stated that Bradshaw was continually belligerent, and she flagged down a U.S. Park Police officer to have him removed. After some time, their fishing lines crossed, and another argument ensued, leading Bullard to display her Glock, which caused Bradshaw to reach toward his waistband, but he was not armed. Bullard admitted to shooting Bradshaw twice, in the stomach and buttocks, but a third bullet hit his neck, just below his left ear. A final report on the incident was written a month later by Bullard's supervisor, Lt. Beverly Medlock, who admitted that she did not have access to medical reports and did not interview Officer Bullard. The MPD arrested Bradshaw for making felonious threats, but prosecutors dropped their case by August 1995 (Jackson, 1998).
- May 1995, Officer Vernell Tanner shot and killed a 16-year old in a car wanted for reckless driving and running a stoplight.[95] A witness claimed the officer was never in danger (Castaneda, 1995).
- August 1995, an off-duty officer walking his dog fired his weapon 11 times to stop an unarmed motorist who hit a utility pole and left the accident scene. The same month, another officer ended a police chase of a truck driver who had rammed several cars by firing his weapon 38 times, killing the unarmed driver (Leen, 1998).
- June 1996, an officer shot and killed 18-year-old unarmed Eric Anderson, accidentally, during a traffic stop, initially claiming he feared Anderson was getting ready to run him over.

95 During a five-year analysis (1994–1998), MPD officers reported that they shot at 54 vehicles, killing nine people and wounded 19 others. None of these vehicular suspects had firearms in their possession but were accused of "vehicular attacks" (Leen et al., 1998).

MPD OIS cases peaked in 1995, and 36 percent of those shootings occurred with off-duty officers, considerably more than the national average of 17–22 percent in other large cities. Additionally, more than half of MPD's fatal shootings in 1995 occurred with off-duty officers, compared to national averages of 9–16 percent (Leen et al., 1998). Off-duty shootings are problematic since the officers involved are not readily identifiable. They are often under the influence when these incidents occur and are usually acting alone without backup officers. These circumstances increasingly opened the MPD up to lawsuits.

MPD Officers Killed

In addition to the increase in police shooting citizens, the hiring binge's mishap appeared to impact officer safety. In five years, 1993–1998, the MPD lost nine MPD officers, eight by gunfire,[96] and in three years, fellow officers fatally shot three police officers. In all three instances, white police officers shot Black officers in civilian clothes, mistaking them for being criminals, including one pregnant female officer. The last officer killed in the 1990s occurred on July 18, 1998, Thomas Hamlette, Jr., a Black officer with a year and a half on the MPD force. Hamlette was off-duty standing in front of a family owned nightclub when he got into an argument with another man and brandished his service weapon. Off-duty officer William Hyatt, Jr., approached the scene and ordered Hamlette to drop his gun, not knowing he was an MPD officer, and fired several rounds, fatally striking Hamlette and wounding two others. Hamlette was the first officer killed after Ramsey became the chief in April 1998, and his family believed he was killed because he was Black. The other eight officers killed in the 1990s (five that were Black) occurred before Ramsey's arrival. They include the following:

1. Jason White, shot five times by a drug dealer, was the first MPD officer killed since 1987 (12/03/93).
2. Hank Daly, shot inside police headquarters by Bennie Lawson, who also killed FBI Agents Martha Dixon Martinez and Michael Miller (11/22/94). Lawson was proving he was not a snitch to fellow gang members and used Martinez's gun to kill himself.
3. James McGee, Jr., shot while off-duty by an MPD officer who mistook him for a gunman (02/07/95).
4. Scot Lewis, ambushed by a gunman, whom his partner killed (10/06/95).
5. Anthony Simms, struck by a pickup truck during a traffic stop (05/25/96).
6. Brian Gibson, ambushed and shot in his patrol car (02/05/97).
7. Oliver Wendell Smith, Jr., shot outside his home while off-duty during a robbery (02/26/97).
8. Robert Johnson, Jr., ambushed by a gunman (04/26/97).

Financial mismanagement plagued the District in the early 1990s. A June 1994 audit indicated that the District was on the verge of bankruptcy, and the deficit was on track to hit $1 billion by 2000 (Jost, 1996). President Bill Clinton established a five-member Federal Control Board[97] to problem-solve the existing half of billion-dollar debt through the 1995 District of Columbia Financial Responsibility and Management Assistance Act. Clinton provided the control board the authority to override bad decision-making from the mayor and city

96 During Ramsey's nearly ten-year tenure as chief (1998–2006), only one MPD officer, after Hamlette, Jr., was killed by gunfire, Sgt. Clifton Rife, shot while off-duty during a robbery in which he also shot the suspect (06/02/04).

97 By September 2001, the board was disbanded after a fourth consecutive balanced budget cycle.

council. They also concluded a reformer was needed to lead the MPD. In November 1996, the board took over managing the MPD from Mayor Barry and brought in the consulting group Booz, Allen Hamilton.[98] The consultants conducted a series of management studies on the MPD. A leak caused their confidential reports to become headline news with the *Washington Post* (Thompson, 1997). These reports demonstrated the management ineptness of cardboard boxes filled with drugs and cash, police vehicles unaccounted for, unguarded warehouses with firearms and other equipment, low clearance rates on homicide cases, and lost evidence. Worse yet, these were problems that the department was aware of for years (Joyce, 2007).

On top of the corruption, use of force, and inventory issues that plagued the MPD in the aftermath of its hiring binge, Chief Larry Soulsby[99] resigned in November 1997 amid allegations of impropriety. Soulsby shared a luxury apartment with Lt. Jeff Stowe. Their landlord dramatically reduced their rent based upon their claims that undercover drug investigations occurred through the use of the apartment. The rent, $650 a month, should have been a going rate of $3,000 a month (Locy, 1998). Stowe pleaded guilty[100] for embezzling $55,000 from the MPD and two counts of extortion linked to payoffs he demanded from two married men in return for not revealing his knowledge that they visited a gay club in Southeast Washington (Collins, 1998). Soulsby was not implicated in any wrongdoing and indicated that he was not aware of any improprieties before resigning after leading the MPD for 28 months (Struck & Powell, 1997).

Bill Bratton, detailed in a previous chapter, commented through the title of his first memoir (Bratton & Knobler, 1998) that the MPD was in "a classic *turnaround* situation" for an outside reformer since "an insider has baggage, and it's a hell of a lot harder to reform a police department that way" (Powell, 1997). Ultimately, President Clinton's control board served as the search engine that contacted Ramsey, flew out to Chicago, and met with him at the O'Hare Hilton to encourage his candidacy (Photo 6.2).

Ramsey the Reform Chief (1998–2006)

Ramsey was 48 years old when he became the chief of the MPD's 3,600-member force in April 1998. He beat out Interim Chief Sonya Proctor and 50 other candidates to secure a five-year contract for $150,000 annually, a $40,000 raise over his deputy superintendent position in Chicago. Over the prior two decades, the MPD had gone through five police chiefs. Ramsey was the fifth African-American (all males) to lead the force, the 28th chief since its inception in 1861, the first external chief, and the longest-serving chief since the District home rule went into effect.[101]

98 Booz Allen Hamilton is a multi-billion dollar publicly traded information technology consulting firm headquartered in McLean, Virginia, with 80 offices worldwide. The company was founded in 1914 in Evanston, Illinois, by Edwin Booz after he graduated from Northwestern University. The company has several intelligence officers, including at one time Edwin Snowden, on its staff and is known as the world's most profitable spy organization (see Kleiner, 2004).

99 Chief Soulsby was featured on *60 Minutes* after a secret pact he made with Captain William "Lou" Hennessy was leaked. Hennessy was angry at Soulsby for a transfer he received, and the chief promised him choice assignments in return for his silence (Struck & Powell, 1997). This type of negative publicity on the nation's capital and its police department continued to be problematic.

100 Six years after his guilty plea, the federal investigation into MPD's impropriety was ruled closed, and Stowe was sentenced to 23 months (Santana, 2003). His sentence was delayed and reduced based upon information he provided to U.S. Attorneys on corruption with the Ironworkers' former president Jake West who was convicted of stealing union money (Lengel, 2003). West frequently dined and golfed with Chief Soulsby and Stowe.

101 Kathy Lanier proceeded Ramsey as the District's first female chief and served from 2007 to 2016.

Photo 6.2 Chuck Ramsey with President Bill Clinton.
Photo provided to the author by Chuck Ramsey.

Similar to Wilson's start as a reformer of the CPD in the 1960s, Ramsey concluded the MPD needed a complete overhaul.[102] Like Wilson, he attempted to centralize management and organized seven police districts into three regional operational commands led by assistant chiefs. However, Ramsey also decentralized command control and made all seven police districts full-service with patrol and detective functions.

New recruitment mechanisms targeted military bases and college campuses to find more qualified officers. By 2000, two years of college education, or prior military/police experience, had become a mandatory requirement for being hired into the MPD. In line with the professionalization era that stemmed from Vollmer and Wilson, higher education levels for officers and military backgrounds were perceived as critical to demonstrate the social skills to interact with the dynamic communities that were increasingly diversified by culture, language, and perceptions of mistrust in police services. The new recruitment strategies also meant that new police recruits might be less likely to be Black or native to the District, which was upsetting to some of the DC Black Police Caucus members. Lastly, to expand recruitment efforts

102 In an August 2020 interview with the author, Ramsey stated that MPD officers had to bring their own toilet paper to work with them because of how dysfunctional the city of Washington, DC had become. He commented that police vehicles were over ten years old, and the department was purchasing used tires from the US Park Police.

geographically, the MPD utilized national online advertising along with allowing lateral-transfers[103] in which officers could potentially keep their prior rank and salaries.

Like previous reform leaders, Ramsey also hired many civilians to take on roles previously monopolized by sworn officers, mainly through administrative positions, which increased the number of officers available for patrol. He reduced the number of officers assigned to protect the mayor and budgeted more training funds to enhance police accountability. This reallocation of top departmental officials provided expectations for teams of officers and civilian employees to create community alliances and improve community policing efforts. Kevin Morison became one of Ramsey's leading reform advocates. Before moving to Washington, DC in June 1998 to assist Ramsey, Morison spent nine years with the ICJIA as their assistant director of public information. Within his capacity at the MPD, he helped build the department's online communication and community outreach capacities before he moved on to become a staff member for the National Law Enforcement Officers Memorial Fund. Morison continued to work with Ramsey after becoming PERF's Chief Program Officer and directed research related to reduced use of force and ingratiation of community policing strategies.

Nola Joyce[104] also became instrumental in assisting Ramsey's leadership reform. In Chicago, she worked six years as the Deputy Director of the Research and Development Division for the CPD and the CAPS initiative, as previously detailed. She arrived in Washington, DC in June 1998 at the same time as Morison to assist Ramsey again and became the Chief Administrative Officer for the MPD. Joyce was instrumental in helping Ramsey expand community policing throughout the District and aligning a performance-based budget with strategic organizational structural changes. In September 2007, she completed her thesis for her Master's Degree at the Naval Postgraduate School in Monterey, California. Her thesis title was "Can you lead me now? Leading in the complex world of Homeland Security" and was mainly based upon her observations and interviews with Ramsey (Joyce, 2007).

A month after Morison and Joyce's arrival, on July 24, 1998, Russell Weston, Jr.[105] entered the nation's Capitol and fatally shot two Capitol police officers and wounded a third. By law, the MPD is responsible for all murder investigations in the District. Because of this event's high-profile nature, there was a heated debate between Ramsey, the FBI, and the Capitol Police. However, Ramsey quickly established his leadership, even though he was only on the job for a few months, and the MPD took over the investigation. The imagery of the MPD leading the investigation was critical for Ramsey's future reform efforts.

Community Policing

A couple of months after Morison and Joyce arrived, and during the first summer he became chief, Ramsey took his command staff back to Chicago with him where he spoke at the August 11–14, 1998, Office of Community-Oriented Policing conference in Chicago that was titled "Beyond the Rhetoric: Facing the Challenges of Community Policing" so they could better understand his reform approach. Ramsey referred to his community policing initiatives as "policing for prevention." The strategy involved neighborhood-based partnerships that were similar to his endeavors with the CAPs program in Chicago. The strategy also

103 See https://joinmpd.dc.gov/career-position-2020/lateral-officer

104 Joyce assisted Ramsey in Philadelphia as Deputy Commissioner and Chief Administrative Officer. She was also appointed to the National Academy of Science's panel on Modernizing the nation's crime statistics and a national policing expert that provided testimony for President Obama's Task Force on 21st Century Policing.

105 Weston, Jr. had a long history of paranoid schizophrenia when he fatally shot Officer Jacob Chestnut and Detective John Gibson and wounded Officer Douglas McMillan. He remains at a federal correctional center in Butner, North Carolina, indefinitely, and a judge ruled he could be forced medicated (Feinberg, 2002).

called for problem-solving along with systematic prevention efforts. In addition to providing training for officers and supervisors with links to community policing, there was also community training through an initiative called Partnerships for Problem Solving. This initiative established a Senior Citizen Police Academy and liaison units for minority citizens, gay/lesbian residents, and community members with hearing issues. Strategic assessments found that crime plummeted to the lowest levels on record and opinion surveys indicated a significant increase in public confidence.

Getting back the public confidence in the MPD did not come easy, and Ramsey helped define a unique vision of community policing without necessarily using the buzz words. Instead, Ramsey described how the police should be seen as part of the community's tapestry and interwoven into that tapestry as a means for helping to define the community. With this metaphor planted, Ramsey attempted to demonstrate a vision that everyone could understand rather than supplying a strict definition for community policing. Ramsey recognized the importance of linking the image of the chief's identity to the broader organizational identity. Within this public image building, Ramsey intentionally took on the role of the Public Information Officer (PIO) his first couple of years as chief to mold a new image for the MPD around broad concepts of community policing, accountability, and transparency. Once he sensed a public image change for the MPD, he could begin to back off his numerous press conferences and focus on other strategic planning dimensions such as use of force.

Use of Force Solutions

Ramsey was disturbed that the MPD did not have a central repository for information on police shootings and declared that the use of deadly force was now perceived as one of the most critical police officers' actions to track. (Ramsey was involved in fatally shooting a suspect during a Chicago drug bust, which was ruled justified.) He made the bi-annual recertification of firearm training mandatory. Also, Ramsey instituted a team of hand-selected elite officers, known as the Force Investigations Team (FIT), to be dispatched to the location of any serious or fatal use of force. Lastly, to avoid future vehicular shootings, officers were instructed not to put themselves in front of any vehicles and were increasingly trained on nonfatal uses of force.

Ramsey went a step further to create accountability and new training when he asked for the Department of Justice (DOJ) to review the MPD's use of force policies and entered into a memorandum of agreement to reform the department. The DOJ, under AG Janet Reno[106] and Assistant AG Eric Holder, helped assist the MPD before collaborative reform was popularized.[107] Traditionally, Federal oversight is pushed upon departments through consent decrees in the aftermath of high-profile protests, riots, and police shootings. Ramsey demonstrated new insight as a leader when he was invited in a DOJ review, noting departments generally improve in the aftermath of such reviews.

Additionally, Ramsey tasked Josh Ederheimer,[108] an MPD police captain, with the job of creating a new use of force policy and a "tactical village" to train officers on various scenarios. After a two-year investigation, the DOJ determined the MPD made an effective program under Ramsey's leadership. In 1998 there were 11 citizens killed through officer use of force,

106 Reno was the first female AG and the second longest serving AG, served 1993–2001, after William Wirt who served from 1817 to 1829. Reno passed away from Parkinson's disease in 2016.

107 Collaborative Reform agreements would be formalized under President Obama's administration and AG Eric Holder.

108 Ederheimer became Assistant Chief with the MPD and then acting Director for the DOJ Office of Community-Oriented Policing. When Ramsey was the Commissioner of the PPD, he voluntarily agreed to a DOJ Collaborative Reform Agreement. Ederheimer helped conduct a review of the PPD's OIS.

covering the first nine months of being chief. In 1999, there were four citizen fatalities and two in 2000. In the spring of 2002, an independent monitoring team was put into place to continually assess MPD's progress in meeting requirements for proper training and use-of-force investigations. That same year, the MPD developed a comprehensive reporting policy that required officers to document and detail all uses of force, leading to a culture of declining use of force. In 2001, there were 28 intentional firearm discharges by officers, but by 2010 there were only seven. By 2008, the MPD complied with their memorandum of agreement, and Ramsey was credited with successfully reforming the MPD. In 2015, another audit took place with an independent monitor and reported the MPD was in compliance and policed the district in a fair and unbiased manner that defined constitutional[109] policing as a model for the nation.

Education and Training

Shortly after Ramsey became the chief of the MPD, he toured the U.S. Holocaust Museum with David Friedman, Regional Director of the Anti-Defamation League, and survivor Irene Weiss. He spoke of this experience in subsequent interviews and a *Ted Talk* he did on June 15, 2011, in Philadelphia when he was police commissioner. Ramsey recognized the horrific role the German police played in the Holocaust and how law enforcement institutions, which were once Democratic, followed Nazi orders and violated their oath. For Ramsey, the lesson was seeing how powerful stereotypes and bias could be on large groups of individuals over a short ten-year period in Germany and how it can change Democratic nations. The police have not always stood on the right side of the law, and there's a need to confront inherent biases that are woven into police subcultures. In response, Ramsey and his command staff put together a curriculum for recruits, which included a museum tour, so officers could more deeply understand the importance of their oath and constitutional policing.

Before Ramsey arrived in 1998, in-service training was practically nonexistent beyond officer recruit training. This new training became even more vital after 9/11 and various national issues that dealt with biased policing. The Holocaust education program provided officers with an understanding of why populations are suspicious of the police. The training program started in 1999 under the title "Law Enforcement and Society: Lessons from the Holocaust." By October 26, 2005, more than 20,000 police officers and 4,000 FBI agents had completed the program (Joyce, 2007, p. 46). In appreciation for his Holocaust training program, Ramsey received the Sigmund Livingston[110] Award in 2001. Previous recipients have included Justice Thurgood Marshall and AG Holder. Ramsey also received the 2005 Civic Leadership Award from the U.S. Holocaust Memorial Museum.

Chandra Levy and September 11, 2001

On May 6, 2001, the parents of Chandra Levy[111] reported her missing to the MPD. They resided in Modesto, California, and their daughter served as an intern at the Federal Bureau of

109 In 2002, Ramsey was also awarded by the Parents Family and Friends of Lesbian & Gays (PFLAG) for his efforts toward improving constitutional policing.

110 Livingston was a Jewish attorney who settled in Bloomington, Illinois with a degree from Illinois Wesleyan University. He moved to Illinois and founded the Anti-Defamation League in 1913 and spoke out against anti-Semitism while he challenged Jewish stereotypes.

111 Levy's skeletal remains were found a year after her disappearance in Rock Creek Park in Northwest Washington, DC. Five-term California Congressman Gary Condit's alibi was solid but he was wrongfully targeted through an ongoing MPD investigation into Levy's disappearance (Peace & Condit, 2016). Immigrant Ingmar Guandique

Prison in Washington, DC. Levy's father also confided in the MPD that his daughter was having an affair with U.S. Congressman Gary Condit. The MPD appeared to botch the high-profile case, and the Levy family began to hold vigils to bring home Chandra that attracted national media attention (Higham & Horwitz, 2010). Ramsey knew the case could impact the MPD image the same way the 1996 murder of JonBenet Ramsey[112] affected the Boulder, Colorado police. Boulder replaced Police Chief Tom Coby the same year Ramsey became MPD chief. Four months later, the country and the media became distracted from the Levy story.

On the morning of September 11, 2001,[113] Ramsey was in a meeting when two planes hit the New York City World Trade Center about one hour and 40 minutes apart. He activated a newly built Joint Operations Command Center (JOCC), which officially opened the morning of 09/11/01. MPD officers responded to assist at the Pentagon following the third intentional plane crash, even though it was located in neighboring Arlington County, Virginia. MPD officers also helped the U.S. Park Police lock down all Federal buildings along the National Mall and established a perimeter around the White House. Ramsey was among several other law enforcement leaders who predicted there would be additional attacks after a fourth hijacked plane crashed in a field in Pennsylvania, 230 miles west of Philadelphia. The Special Operations Division (SOD) was the only unit Ramsey had to assign the new function of homeland security that was not tied to calls for service. However, the SOD was already handling Presidential and dignitary functions. The MPD needed new change leadership, given the scope of the challenges. Consequently, Cathy Lanier took command of the Office of Homeland Security and Counter-Terrorism (OHSCT) and launched the Terrorist Incident Prevention Program (TIPP). For his efforts, in 2006, Ramsey received the FBI's Leadership in Counter Terrorism Award (Photo 6.3).[114]

International Monetary Fund/World Bank Protests – April 2000 and September 2002

In April 2000, protests were planned in Washington, DC, against the International Monetary Fund (IMF)[115] on the heels of the November 1999 World Trade Organization (WTO) riots in

was already arrested for attacking women in Rock Creek Park and had apparently confessed to another inmate that he attacked Levy. The MPD failed to follow up until March 3, 2009, when they arrested him while he was in prison for the previous attacks. He was eventually convicted by a jury of Levy's murder but a retrial and appeal led to prosecutors dropping charges in 2016 because of unrelated witness perjury. Guandique was deported back to El Salvador on May 5, 2017.

112 Ramsey (no relation to Chuck Ramsey), a six-year-old girl who had won numerous beauty competitions, was found murdered in her basement from strangulation and a broken skull hours after her wealthy parents, John and Patsy, reported her missing the day after Christmas in 1996. A mysterious ransom note was also left in their home. Responding officers contaminated the crime scene by removing the body. Two days after the murder, Ramsey's parents hired defense attorneys and initially refused to cooperate with the police investigators believing they were incompetent. The police felt the Ramsey's covered up the crime but failed to get a Grand Jury indictment (Schiller, 1999; Wecht & Bosworth, 2016). In 2006, Patsy died from ovarian cancer. In 2008, the Boulder District Attorney officially exonerated the Ramsey's for the murder of their daughter. John struggled financially, lost his wealth, and remarried in 2011 (Ramsey, 2012).

113 On 09/11/01, four coordinated terrorist attacks were led by 19 members of Al-Qaeda. Their attack resulted in nearly 3,000 fatalities and over 25,000 injuries, mainly from the New York City World Trade Center buildings' collapse. These fatalities included the loss of 343 firefighters and 72 police officers and represented the deadliest terrorist attack in history with an estimated $10 billion in damage.

114 In 2008, Ramsey also received the John Penrith Leadership Award from the FBI and the Major Cities Chiefs executive institute. (Bratton received the same award in 2009.) In addition, from 2013 to 2017, Ramsey was part of the federal Homeland Security Advisory Council (NIAC).

115 Washington, DC also serves as the headquarters for the IMF.

Photo 6.3 **President George W. Bush, Chuck Ramsey and his wife Sylvia.**
Photo provided to the author by Chuck Ramsey.

Seattle that overwhelmed the police and led to the resignation of Chief Norm Stamper. Ramsey was determined not to share the same fate. Executive Deputy Chief Terrance Gainer was in charge of the SOD and drew up plans to police the protests. Ramsey redid the plans and reached out to suburban departments for assistance (Joyce, 2007). Arlington Police Chief Ed Flynn was particularly impressed with Ramsey's leadership and willingness to partner in a cooperative regional policing strategy (Davis, 2000). Officers at the ground level received assistance from CCTV and communication from their command center. Ramsey spent time on the front lines meeting with both his riot geared officers and the protesters. Arrangements were made to escort protest leaders through the police line and conduct symbolic arrests of several hundred demonstrators so they could save face with other protesters. Ramsey saw the handling of the protests as a turning point in how officers and the community viewed the MPD, reestablishing community pride and officer morale. However, not everyone shared this view. In June 2010, a federal judge approved a settlement of a class-action lawsuit for $13.7 million for wrongful arrests from the April 2000 protests (Glod, 2010). This event also sparked a 2004 city procedural law that set out policies for the MPD to follow in policing future protests that prohibited encircling protesters without probable cause to arrest demonstrators.

On September 27, 2002, another sizeable anti-capitalist protest occurred in the District's Pershing Park, on the east corner outside gates of the White House. Protesters, again, targeted meetings of the World Bank and the IMF.[116] Those meetings took place on September 29, 2002. Protesters equipped themselves with rocks and smoke bombs as they clashed with the MPD officers and tried to block intersections and sidewalk paths throughout the District downtown. In a crowd control strategy, the MPD enclosed the protesters and arrested 647 people without any orders to disperse (Franken, Hung, & Ahler, 2002). Others were taken into custody but not formally charged. During the arrests, the MPD used batons and struck several protesters. Worse yet, several of those arrested were journalists or pedestrians that were not there to protest. The aggressive police strategy was due to protest plans to shut down the city. Three and a half years later, the DC Court of Appeals ruled the arrests violated the Fourth Amendment, and the following summer, the city agreed, once again, to pay $8.25 million in damages (Hsu, 2016). Ramsey apologized for the arrests (Mitchell, 2004).

Recognition to Resignation

Ramsey became the chief of the MPD on April 21, 1998. An annual report to District citizens had not been publicly completed since 1993 but was completed every year that Ramsey was chief and put on the MPD website for transparency. On the website, Ramsey outlined his top priorities as the new chief was to reorganize the department to improve its ability to fight crime, fix essential infrastructure, and restore the public's confidence in the MPD. During that first year, crime in the District plummeted to 1972 levels, and this included a 16 percent drop in violent crime.[117] Five-year trends in annual homicides are indicative of changes in the District's violent crime levels. From 1991 to 1995, the city averaged 428 homicides annually, but this five-year trend was reduced to 247 annual homicides from 1998 to 2002, under Ramsey's leadership. From 2003 to 2007, the annual homicides were reduced further to 198. Within the Uniform Crime Report (UCR) Part I Index crime rate comparisons, in 1997, the District rate was 9,860 offenses per 100,000 residents, and by 2006, the crime rate was cut by 57 percent to 5,666 per 100,000 (Joyce, 2007, p. 39).

Ramsey faced some criticism in the early months of 2003 as there appeared to be a surge in violent crime. He declared a state of crisis and implemented several emergency policies that included suspending contract rules on how officers' scheduled time off and use of sick leave. Homicides numbered 248 in 2003 and were 262 the previous year leading the city council to extend his contract with a narrow 7-–6 vote. However, clearance rates on homicides began to improve as community policing strategies began to take hold. The clearance rates for homicide in 2001 were 49 percent and increased to 64 percent in 2006, the highest rate of comparable benchmark cities. By 2005, the District's crime rate was lower than any year since 1965, and there were fewer than 200 homicides for two consecutive years, 2004 (198) and 2005 (196). In contrast, a decade earlier, in 1994 alone, the District had 399 homicides.

The year before Ramsey became the chief of the MPD, the District had 301 murders, and a decade later, the year he retired, they had 169 murders. In a 1997–2006 comparison with other benchmark cities, Washington, DC outperformed all other major cities for reductions in homicides (Joyce, 2007, p. 39). Overall, crime rates declined by 40 percent during Ramsey's eight-year tenure as MPD chief. He institutionalized a community policing philosophy into

116 The IMF and World Bank meetings take place in the fall after the summer "G-7" meetings. The "G" refers to "group" for the leading finance ministers of major industrial countries that control half of the world's wealth. The G-7 countries consist of Canada, Japan, France, the United Kingdom, Italy, Germany, and the United States. Other countries have joined and been dismissed year-to-year, including Russia. Russia was removed in 2014, and President Trump advocated for their return. The demonstrators perceived that the policies of the World Bank only benefit wealthy countries and not developing nations.

117 See MPD annual reports https://mpdc.dc.gov/page/mpd-annual-reports

the MPD culture and significantly improved recruiting, hiring, and infrastructure through a $100 million Congressional appropriation.

Ramsey officially resigned as police chief on January 2, 2007, on the day Adrian Fentry was elected as the new DC mayor. Before becoming mayor, Fentry was one of the six city council members who had voted not to extend Ramsey's contract. Ramsey had served longer than any chief over the past three decades since home rule took effect (Klein & Nakamura, 2006). He then became a security consultant to the United States Senate Sergeant of Arms and the Washington, DC Convention Center. During that year, he served on the Independent Commission on Security Forces of Iraq, leading a prominent group of law enforcement professionals into Baghdad to review policy and train Iraqi Police Forces.[118] The report they generated was submitted to the United States Congress and garnered international attention and praise. In February 2008, Ramsey also completed an Executive Leadership Program at the Naval Postgraduate School, Center for Homeland Defense and Security.

During the aftermath of his retirement from the MPD, Ramsey also applied to be the commissioner of the Baltimore Police Department (BPD), but they hired internal candidate Fred Bealefeld III instead. From 1989 to 2019, Baltimore went through ten police commissioners. In mid-March, Chicago Mayor-elect Emanuel encouraged Ramsey to apply to be the Superintendent of the CPD. However, Philadelphia Mayor-elect Michael Nutter[119] also contacted Ramsey and offered a competitive $60,000 raise to become the Commissioner of the PPD. Ramsey accepted an annual salary of $255,000 in 2008.

Philadelphia Police History

In 1681, William Penn, a Quaker, was given a charter from King Charles II for Pennsylvania, which included a 35-acre tract that became Philadelphia. The King chartered the land to repay a debt he owed to Penn's father. Policing Philadelphia informally began when colonial authorities appointed English constables to regulate the working-class leisure activities. Penn also appointed a sheriff to regulate the growing population. By 1700, the Common Council established a volunteer night watch from property owners who were expected to carry a bell and alert the constable if they witnessed criminal activity within their assigned post.

A 1751 ordinance better defined the night watch's job and duties for the constables, who supervised the watch. The watch system became the first paid law enforcement officers, but this pay came from a fee system based upon warrants they served.[120] The system was not very effective as those serving watch were frequently asleep or intoxicated during their service, and those with wealth corrupted the system. In 1833, a communal private prosecution system kept aldermen and the mayor very busy. Steinberg (1989) provided a glimpse at Philadelphia before the government-run police department when citizens had constant contact with the legal system. The historical research was done through various court documents and notes from alderman and demonstrated how the police slowly eroded the involvement of the immigrant and laboring poor in the court system. The private prosecution system made the justice system less accessible and increased political corruption (Steinberg, 1989).

118 In 2011, Ramsey, as the Commissioner of the police in Philadelphia, received the Patriotic Employer Award from the Secretary of Defense.

119 Nutter served as the 98th Mayor of Philadelphia for two terms from 2008 to 2016 (see Nutter, 2018).

120 Superintendent Hilary Baker created the first paid, uniformed watch through an Act of Assembly on May 22, 1797. He appointed 20 watchmen for day patrol and 15 for night patrol to protect Philadelphia from vandalism and looting. Baker died at the age of 52 from contracting yellow fever during an outbreak in the city as citizens fled, and Baker stayed to assist his watchmen. He was a veteran of the Revolutionary War and served the PPD for less than one and a half years.

In addition to experiments on justice, Philadelphians were conflicted about slavery. On May 14, 1838, Pennsylvania Hall, located at Haines and 6th Street, became the first building in the nation constructed for American abolitionists. However, an angry white mob of an estimated 10,000 city residents burned the hall to the ground four days after construction was complete, along with the Shelter for Colored Orphans. Firefighters protected surrounding buildings, but they refused to protect Pennsylvania Hall. The police did not make any arrests. A couple weeks later, the abolitionist Board of Directors sued the police for failure to protect them against the white mob. City officials responded with claims that the abolitionists provoked the riot because of the promiscuous intermingling indoors and outdoors of Blacks and whites. In 1941, the state Supreme Court settled the case and ordered the city to pay the board $28,000 (Runcie, 1972).

In 1841, the PPD formalized, and the government was entirely in charge of the justice system. However, numerous boroughs, townships, and districts fractured the system, and continued growth in immigrants meant increased riots. On May 3, 1850, the Marshal Act established a Philadelphia Police District in reaction to the riots. An elected county police marshal led the newly hired officers, set at one officer per 150 taxable residents. This arrangement provided tax revenue for a centralized paid quasi-militaristic police force. The 1850 legislation also granted the police marshal the ability to declare a state of emergency, which was repeated during the 2020 mass police protests that included curfew restrictions put in place. Mayors across the country used legislation from the nineteenth century to impose curfews during mass protests and ordered their police to arrest those in violation.

Creation and Evolution of the Philadelphia Police Department

In 1854, the Consolidation Act was passed as politicians linked working-class protests and riots to deficiencies in decentralized government structures. This legislation formalized the PPD and consolidated the city and county government. The consolidation and the establishment of the PPD were done to prevent riots, maintain order, and apprehend criminals. This was the first time the public saw the policemen wearing uniforms to signify the difference between the government and citizens. These government agents were expected to discipline the growing industrial immigrant working class, but in contradiction, the departments also served as a soup kitchen for the hungry and homeless.

The police jurisdiction covered a wider area of close to a half-million residents policed by approximately 820 patrolmen. The new officers were given tiered salaries according to their rank. The mayor was provided the power to appoint one lieutenant and two sergeants for each district and could give them direct orders. Alderman, established by the city council, served as magistrates allowing for criminal arrests to be adjudicated at the district station houses. After 1857, a police chief headed the centralized department and was appointed by the mayor.

Philadelphia was an example of a northern city that attempted to replicate the London modern police department that came out of the 1829 Metropolitan Policing Act led by Sir Robert Peel. All the northern police departments were based upon the following premise: tax revenue support for full-time police employees; bureaucratically organized; fixed rules and procedures to govern work performance; and officer accountability through governmental authority (Lundman, 1980). As described earlier, this was vastly different from southern police departments formed under the auspice of slave patrol.

Policing through America's Racial Divide

Regardless, both northern and southern police agencies were challenged by America's racial divide. The five years after the Civil War ended slavery, three consequential Amendments were passed: 13th abolished slavery (December 1865); 14th gave equal protection under the law (July 1868), and the 15th gave Black men voting rights (February 1870). These Constitutional Amendments dramatically impacted future encounters between the police, politicians, and citizens. Consequently, Black men would face future police arrest and white intimidation at the polling stations. An example from Philadelphia occurred on October 11, 1870, when a scuffle between the police and Black voters[121] ensued at Fifth and Lombard Street. Federal investigators charged 23 men with violating the 15th Amendment, and four of these individuals were police officers, including one lieutenant (Saint, McCoy, Rowan, & Russ, 2020).

Two critical events impacted the close of the nineteenth century. On May 18, 1896, *Plessy v. Ferguson* ruled that Jim Crow racial segregation was constitutional, and this would remain until the Court reversed its decision in 1954. The second event concerned the publication from W.E.B. Du Bois's *The Philadelphia Negro* showing that before the Civil War, African-Americans made up 5 percent of the city's population but made up nearly 33 percent of the jail population. The disparities in arresting Blacks in Philadelphia came as officers patrolled the city on horses and wood-rimmed bicycles. Horse-drawn wagons transported criminals to police boats that headed north on the Delaware River to Holmesburg prison. The route is one of the uses for the phrase "up the river" to express prison time,[122] and those who received time were frequently minorities or otherwise not politically connected. In 1903, Muckraker journalist Lincoln Steffens referred to Philadelphia as the nation's most corrupt city (McCaffery, 1993).

Philadelphia's Mayoral Republican Dominance (1858–1952) and Police Corruption

Philadelphia began a long string of Republican Party mayoral domination from 1858 to 1952.[123] Ward leaders sponsored police applicants, and officers were expected to reward their sponsors by collecting protection money from vice operators that included gambling and prostitution. One exception came in 1911–1915, when the Progressive "Keystone"[124] Party was able to get Rudolph Blankenburg elected, with the help of Democrats, in an attempt to reform the PPD with professional standards (Vickers, 2019). Police professionalism was being developed on the opposite side of the country through August Vollmer in Berkeley, California and several cities attempted to replicate his reform efforts. New policies barred the police from participating in politics while on duty, provided expectations for patrol, and attempted to be accountable to the public by publishing crime data reports.

However, machine politics returned in 1915, and any reform efforts were quickly forgotten. During the September 19, 1917 primary, the "bloody fifth" ward became infamous when a New York gang beat mayoral candidate James Carey by McCall Public School and fatally shot police officer George Eppley who attempted to protect Carey (Stern, 2016). Blame for these events fell on existing Mayor Thomas Smith, who utilized the police to harass Carey's supporters during his reelection bid. An investigation resulted in the arrest of Mayor Smith and

121 Octavious Catto was a Black political organizer who was assassinated on election day during 1870 in the melee of police attacks on Black voters. Despite numerous witnesses, a jury found the assassin not guilty. Almost 150 years later, in 2017, a statue of Catto became the first public monument in Philadelphia to honor an African-American.

122 "Up the river" also stemmed from Sing-Sing Prison in New York, which is located north of the city along the Hudson River.

123 The only exceptions to the (1858–1952) Republican mayoral dominance were Daniel Fox (1869–1872), Samuel King (1881–1884), and Rudolph Blankenburg (1911–1916) discussed above, all one-term mayors.

124 Pennsylvania is known as the "keystone" state. A keystone is a wedge in the center of an arch that locks all other pieces of the arch in place. These parts are dependent on the keystone.

the head of the Republican Party. An outraged public demanded accountability, and Mayor Smith was indicted on conspiracy charges to commit murder and impeding fair elections. However, the mayor was later acquitted (McCaffery, 1993).

While the city did pass another charter for political reform that required civil service requirements on all government employee hiring, politicians co-opted any funds to enforce these reforms and maintained the patronage status quo. Ridding the police of corruption was made all the more difficult, if not impossible, throughout the Prohibition Era. In August 1928, a grand jury focused on bootlegging found hundreds of officers involved with collecting graft to protect bootleggers. Max "Boo Boo" Hoff, king of the Philadelphia bootleggers, was known to have openly sent turkeys and Christmas cards to the homes of officers in gratitude for their services in protecting organized crime.

In 1924, Philadelphia elected Republican Mayor W. Freeland Kendrick. He sought to clean up municipal government corruption. Kendrick turned to his friend President Calvin Coolidge to lend Marine Corps General Smedley Butler to his city as the director of public safety in charge of the police and fire department from 1924 to 1925 (Short, 1977). Butler could not officially terminate corrupt officers, so he moved them around to undermine their contacts and profits with local politicians and criminal rackets. Under his leadership, hundreds of speakeasies were raided and destroyed, at times using active Marines in his raids. He encouraged police officers to kill bandits and created military-style checkpoints throughout the cities to search citizens. Eventually, his aggressive tactics weighed on the city, and although successful in reducing crime, Mayor Kendrick asked for his resignation, and he returned to the Marine Corps.

During Prohibition, an investigation of the PPB found 138 officers unfit to serve and 63 arrested. However, almost all were eventually acquitted (Haller, 1985). A 1937 grand jury investigated the city's government corruption and indicted 348 people, including 52 policemen, various city officials, Mayor Davis, and many gambling operators (Myrsiades, 2008). Virtually all of them were later acquitted. Finally, a grand jury convened from 1948 to 1951, leading to numerous indictments, several suicides, and eventually, in 1951, the election of Joseph Clark, Jr. as a one-term Democratic Mayor. Since that election, Philadelphia has always elected a Democratic mayor ending the nearly century-long reign of Republican control.

In 1951, voters also ratified a Home Rule Charter, which served as the city's constitution, allowed for greater municipal self-governance, and separated the police from politics. In actuality, this was the third attempt to separate politics from the PPD. The first attempt at a civil service system was adopted in 1885 when officers were supposed to be selected based upon merit instead of political connections. The 1951 home rule charter was most pertinent because it gave greater union protections for the FOP and established collective bargaining. Consequently, decades of mayoral Republican domination ended.

Democratic Mayor Clark, Jr. selected Tom Gibbons as police commissioner to reform the PPD. Under Gibbons, the home rule era began with a "broken windows" style crackdown on small-level street disorder in coordination with federal agents who enforced new anti-narcotics laws. Wealthy investors that backed the home rule campaign were motivated to renew the downtown and have the police wage an aggressive campaign against low-level disorder, homeless individuals, and frequently minorities. In January 1958, Black residents testified before the city council and reported numerous illegal street searches, racial harassment, and unlawful home raids. By October of that year, Mayor Richardson Dilworth created the nation's first civilian review board. However, because of various court petitions, it was difficult to hold meetings. In 1966, after filing several lawsuits, the FOP won a legal battle that caused the civilian complaint review board to disband. At the end of 1969, Mayor James Tate abolished the Police Advisory Board, which was tasked to handle civilian complaints against the police. Tate announced this order at a meeting with commanding PPD officers and received a one-minute standing ovation (Clancy, 1969).

The Rise of Police Commissioner and Mayor Frank Rizzo[125]

The 1964 Philadelphia race riot, also referred to as the Columbia Avenue riot, occurred in the predominantly African-American north side of the city on August 28–30. The *Philadelphia Tribune*, akin to the *Chicago Defender*, catered to Black readers and ran several articles about police brutality against Black residents and officers not being held accountable. Additionally, riots occurred a month prior in Harlem and Rochester. On the evening of August 28, 1964, Odessa Bradford got into an argument with a Black and white officer for not moving her vehicle that was blocking an intersection on 23rd Street and Columbia Avenue. Bradford's street argument with the police eventually led to a physical confrontation, and arrests were made. Rumors circulated that a pregnant Black woman had been beaten and perhaps killed by white officers. This bogus rumor motivated angry mobs to fill the streets, which lead to looting and burning white-owned businesses in North Philadelphia along Columbia Avenue.

Deputy Chief Frank Rizzo,[126] who was in charge of the uniformed division, wanted to stop the rioters with a full-frontal attack. Police Commissioner Howard Leary opted to hold back, and Rizzo referred to him as a "gutless bastard" (Donner, 1992, p. 207). Leary later published a detailed account of how the police managed the riots (Leary, 1966) in which 225 stores were damaged or destroyed at an estimated cost of $3 million. However, there was no loss of life directly linked to the riots, but a few hundred individuals were injured, and 774 arrests were made (Berson, 1966). The riots also involved confrontations between Black Muslims and Black Baptist Ministers[127] who had different views on strategies surrounding civil rights protests.

Throughout most of 1965, Girard College[128] became the center for several protests, led by NAACP President Cecil Moore, and clashes with Rizzo's uniformed police division. Much of the protest dealt with conflicts over racial integration at the college.

> Rizzo started as a beat cop in 1943, where he participated in raids at coffee houses known to attract hippies and homosexuals throughout the 1950s into the 1960s. He became police commissioner following several protests and riots from 1967–1971. The riots and racial conflicts facilitated Rizzo's political rise,[129] and his popularity grew as he loudly spoke about the need for a law and order approach to crime control. With the law and

125 Rizzo's statue was erected across from the Philadelphia City Hall on December 30, 1998, but it caused controversy even before it was unveiled. The city initially agreed to remove the statue by 2021. However, after being vandalized by mass protesters, the statue was removed on June 3, 2020. Mayor Pratt used a legal loophole to quickly remove the statue based upon perceived risk to public health and safety (Crimmins, 2020).

126 A full review of Rizzo's life can be found in *Rizzo: The Last Big Man in Big City* America, written by *Philadelphia Inquirer* reporter Sal Paolantonio (1993). In 2016, playwright Bruce Graham brought *Rizzo* to the stage at the Philadelphia Theatre Company.

127 This civil rights protest divide occurred on the national stage between Martin Luther King, Jr. and Malcolm X.

128 Girard College was opened in 1848 through donations from banker Stephen Girard who specified scholarship money was to be used exclusively for "poor male white orphan children." By 1968, the U.S. Supreme Court ruled Girard had violated the Fourteenth Amendment, and the college began to accept minority students.

129 Rizzo is also discussed in the appendix of the O.W. Wilson chapter under Herman Goldstein. Goldstein observed the aggressive police managerial style of Captain Rizzo while conducting field experiences in Philadelphia as a graduate student in the early 1950s.

> order verbiage, Rizzo left policing and was elected mayor of Philadelphia, as a Democrat, for two terms from 1972–1980.[130]

In addition to the 1964 riots and the 1965 clashes with demonstrators at Girard College, Rizzo's leadership as the commissioner was tested on November 17, 1967, when a student-run organization, the Central Coordinating Committee (CCC), launched a planned demonstration in front of various Philadelphia schools and the Board of Education. The protests were done to demand increased hiring of Black school administrators, better conditions for public schools, and Black studies' inclusion into the curriculum (Birger, 1996). Approximately 3,500 students, although organizers disputed this number, avoided going to class and chose to be part of the demonstrations.[131] By midday, two busloads of roughly 400 police officers arrived in riot gear, and Rizzo ordered the officers to "get their black asses" (Dyson, 2014, p. 67), which led to the attack of the protesters, 22 injuries, including five officers and a priest, and 57 arrests. Rizzo was blamed for the brutal response against unarmed student protesters, but he also received support from other Philadelphians. Comparisons were also made with the 1966 Kensington Riots, which involved white student protesters who demonstrated against integration. Although they made arrests, the police did not break up the demonstration in the same way they did with African-American protests.

Rizzo's Attack on the Black Panthers

As the new police commissioner, Rizzo also became nationally infamous for a raid on three offices of the Black Panther Party (BPP) on Monday, August 31, 1970, after four officers were shot the weekend prior (Janson, 1970), one fatally.[132] The BPP publicly declared war on police officers.[133]

> The Philadelphia raids occurred the day after what would have been the 22nd birthdate of Fred Hampton had he not been fatally shot nine months prior while in his Chicago apartment located at 2337 West Monroe Street. Hampton was killed while lying in his bed in a predawn raid by a tactical unit within the Cook County State's Attorney's Office in collaboration with the CPD and the FBI (Haas, 2011). On December 4, 1969, the Chicago BPP raid occurred as officers executed a warrant to search for illegal firearms. Hampton was supposed to be the spokesman for the national BPP and was a founder of the Rainbow Coalition, along with chairing the Illinois BPP chapter. Four other BPP

130 After being a two-term mayor, Rizzo became a radio host and attempted to become a third term mayor after he switched his party affiliation from Democrat to Republican in 1986. He won the Republican nomination in 1991 but died of a heart attack on July 16th prior to the general election.

131 A student walk-out of this scale would not occur for another 50 years, on April 20, 2018, following the student protests against gun violence in remembrance of the 17 students fatally shot at Marjory Stoneman Douglas High School in Parkland, Florida on February 14, 2018.

132 Forty-three-year old Sgt. Frank Von Colin was in the Cobbs Creek guardhouse at 63rd and Catherine Street when he was fatally ambushed on August 29, 1970, by a radical group known as the Revolutionaries. Five individuals were implicated and received life sentences for first-degree murder.

133 The day before the raid on the BPP, Tom Gibbons was a 25-year-old officer who was hit by three bullets that nearly killed him during a traffic stop of a stolen car. His father, Tom Gibbons Sr., mentioned earlier, was appointed Police Commissioner by Mayor Clarke, Jr., the first Democratic Mayor since Sam King in 1881, and attempted to reform the PPD from 1952 to 1960. After being shot, his son was forced to retire in the summer of 1972 and became an investigative journalist for the *Philadelphia Inquirer*. He wrote a front-page article for the *Philadelphia Inquirer* following the Dallas shootings in 2016 and the use of the improvised explosive that killed the police assassin. Ironically, Gibbon's shooting would lead the PPD to be the first to use improvised explosives against civilians, as described in the preceding paragraphs.

> members were wounded, and one was killed (Mark Clark) inside Hampton's apartment.[134] Two officers were also injured by a shotgun blast believed to have been fired by Clark after he was shot by a barrage of over 90 shots by the police. A $47 million civil lawsuit filed by relatives of Hampton and Clark was settled for $1.85 million, 12 years after the raid took place. In February 2021, the movie *Judas and the Black Messiah* was released based on a plea deal the FBI made with William O'Neil, who subsequently infiltrated the Chicago-based BPP and gathered intelligence on Hampton prior to the deadly raid.

Nine months after the Chicago BPP raid, Philadelphia officers arrested members of the Black Panthers and strip-searched them in front of the news cameras. Media photos went international and showed BPP members stripped to their underwear outside of their home and held at police gunpoint before they were placed into a police wagon and formally arrested. Rizzo referenced the BPP with the following quote: "They should be strung up. I mean within the law. This is actual warfare" (Pearlstein, 2010, p. 521). All charges against BPP members from the August 31, 1970 raids were later dropped.

The Attacks on the MOVE

A couple of years after the BPP raids, Rizzo was elected mayor and publicly opposed desegregating city schools and new public housing projects in majority-white neighborhoods. To further his law and order image, Rizzo lashed out at anti-police protesters, referenced his 1975 reelection bid, and stated, "Just wait after November, you'll have a front-row seat because I'm going to make Attila the Hun look like a faggot" (Skolnick & Fyfe, 2010, p. 139). This quote became a reality in 1976 and 1978 when Mayor Rizzo became infamous during confrontations with MOVE (short for "The Movement"). This liberation group began in 1972 in Philadelphia by John Africa.[135] The MOVE group lived as a primitive "back to nature" communal family and disdained modern technology, materialism, and the government establishment. They advocated for animal rights and racial equality. The communal group of 12 adults and 11 children lived at a home located at 309 North 33rd Street, and they later acquired the adjoining house at 307 North 33rd Street in Powelton Village of West Philadelphia. Eventually, in response to Rizzo, they became more militant, and members all changed their last names to "Africa" after their founder and leader John.[136]

MOVE Attack I (1976)

The initial confrontation between the police and MOVE occurred on March 28, 1976, when PPD officers came to their home with approximately ten police cars after a disturbing the peace call. MOVE members told the police to leave, and a confrontation occurred with several thrown to the ground and beaten by the police. Janine Phillips Africa alleged her three-week-old baby was caught in the conflict, and the baby's skull was fatally fractured. However, a birth

134 Haas (2011) reports that the police fired 90–99 rounds inside the apartment. BPP member Mark Clark allegedly fired a shotgun, but this likely went off as he was going down after being fatally shot. Deborah Johnson was eight months pregnant with Hampton's son and was uninjured as she laid in bed with Hampton during the raid. Johnson claimed she was ordered out of the bedroom, and Hampton was then fatally shot.

135 John Africa's birth name was Vincent Leaphart. Between 1972 and 1978, the PPD made 193 arrests of his MOVE members resulting in 93 subsequent court cases (Boyette & Boyette, 2013).

136 In September 2020, *HBO* released the documentary *40 Years a Prisoner* that chronicles the events surrounding the 1978 raid on MOVE. The documentary centered on Mike Africa, Jr.'s quest to free his parents, who were imprisoned for the death of Officer Ramp. Mike was born in prison and saw his parents freed in 2018 during the documentary filming.

certificate did not exist since the baby, named Life Africa, was born in the MOVE compound. MOVE members held their own press conference a few days later and showed reporters the baby's body. No charges were filed against the police, and the cases against the arrested MOVE members for assault on the police officers were dropped.

MOVE Attack 2 (1978)

The next confrontation occurred in 1978 after several city inspectors were not allowed to access the MOVE home based upon noise and sanitation complaints. The tabloid *Philadelphia Daily News* instigated a subsequent raid after running several stories that detailed the overtime police cost (estimated at $1.2 million) in surveilling the MOVE house and their members. Rizzo received a court order to force their eviction and, along with Commissioner Joseph O'Neill,[137] opted to surround the home with snipers, several hundred police officers, and a blockade of the street and home denying any entry of food and water. MOVE members and their children were not allowed to pass the blockade without proper identification and proof of residence. Eventually, some food was provided for the children inside the home with no assurance that they would get the food.

When Rizzo inevitably gave the order on August 8, 1978, to forcefully evict the MOVE members with fire hoses and tear gas, gunfire erupted. One officer, James Ramp, was killed, and 16 others, including two firefighters, were injured. As members were flushed from their home, the media captured video and photos of Delbert Africa[138] (AKA Delbert Orr) being beaten by three officers. The beating of Delbert led to mass protests throughout Philadelphia. The three officers (Joseph Zagame, Terrance Mulvihill, and Charles Geist) were arrested and charged with assault. On August 6, 1979, a couple of thousand officers protested their arrest with chants of "I wear blue, take me too." During the trial, Judge Stanley Kubacki circumvented the case, issued a directed verdict, and stated the officers should never have been charged. This unusual ruling did not allow the case to go to the jury.

At the subsequent bench trial for the murder of Officer Ramp, MOVE members, who became known as the MOVE 9, defended themselves with court-mandated backup counsel. The defendants claimed Officer Ramp was fatally shot in the back of the head by friendly fire from his fellow officers. The case was prosecuted by District Attorney Ed Rendell,[139] a case he later said he regretted. After a 19-week trial, the most expensive trial in Philadelphia history, each of nine was convicted of third-degree murder and conspiracy to murder 52-year-old Officer Ramp and received sentences ranging from 30 to 100 years from Judge Edward Malmed (Williams, 2012). Seven individuals were paroled, starting in June 2018–February 2020, after each served more than 40 years in prison. The remaining two previously died while in prison. Three members were paroled with the supportive assistance of District Attorney Lawrence Krasner's letters to Leo Dunn, Chairman of the Pennsylvania Board of Probation and Parole.

MOVE Attack 3 (1985)

Both groups, the PPD and the MOVE members, felt degraded from the 1978 encounter. The original MOVE home was demolished immediately after the 1978 raid, destroying all evidence, and they relocated to 6221 Osage Avenue, a home owned by John Africa's sister. The second,

137 O'Neill died in May 2019 at the age of 94. He was the first PPD Commissioner with a college degree.

138 Delbert was released from prison in January 2020 after serving 41 years. He died in June 2020 at the age of 73.

139 Rendell became the Democratic nominee against Rizzo in the 1991 general mayoral election, but Rizzo died of a massive heart attack prior to election day. Rendell became a two-term mayor (1992–2000) and a two-term Pennsylvania Governor (2003–2011). See *A Nation of Wusses* (Rendell, 2012).

almost inevitable, police confrontation with MOVE occurred on Mother's Day weekend, May 1985, when they attempted to, once again, evict and serve a search warrant.[140] Mayor Woodrow Wilson Goode, Sr. (Philadelphia's first Black mayor)[141] issued the eviction notice. The eviction notice came after several neighborhood complaints stemmed from composting that attracted rats in violation of city sanitation codes. Other complaints included neglect, and blaring Black liberation messages and obscenities from loudspeakers attached to the house and the roof.

MOVE members, once again, heavily fortified their residence. Windows and doors were boarded up and a bunker built on top of the roof. On May 12, 1985, the neighborhood surrounding the MOVE home was evacuated, and Commissioner Gregore Sambor ordered members out of the house, but they did not comply. Sambor also perceived the bunker on the roof as a tactical advantage for MOVE members, who were believed to be armed and barricaded. The house was doused with a water barrage from firehouses. Later, CS gas was used, but MOVE members still did not leave. After a long standoff, a 90-minute gun battle ensued with the police using over 10,000 rounds of ammunition. Several members of the media and residents who did not evacuate were seen on live television taking cover during the sporadic shooting, all seemingly coming from the police. Four weapons in the MOVE home were later recovered but found to be inoperable.

After MOVE members still failed to exit the home, a decision was made to drop a bag of C4 improvised explosive gel, generally used in underwater mining, onto the roof of the home. The gas was dropped from a Pennsylvania State Police helicopter in the hopes that the cubicle bunker on top of the roof could be penetrated, and gas dropped directly into the home to flush out the occupants. However, this "entry device" strategy went terribly wrong. The bomb ignited a gasoline-powered generator that was on the roof. Sambor conferred with Fire Commissioner William Richmond to determine if they let the fire burn,[142] could they put it out in time after MOVE members exited the home. Richmond agreed with this strategy, but the results were catastrophic, and the fire spread quickly to the surrounding row houses. Based on the 1978 confrontation, there was fear that MOVE members might shoot the firefighters, so they were held back. The fire led to the death of six adults and five children inside the home, destroyed 53 surrounding homes, and left 250 evacuees homeless (Boyette & Boyette, 2013). During proceeding testimony, Mayor Goode alleged he ordered Sambor to put out the fire, and Sambor stated he gave that order to Fire Commissioner Richmond. However, Richmond denied he received the police order.

Only Ramona Africa and Michael Ward (13 years of age) survived. Officer James Berghaier rescued Ward as he stumbled out of the burning home and then collapsed. Berghaier ran toward Ward to rescue him but was warned by other officers not to do so because it was probably a setup. "Nigger lover" was later written on Berghaier's police locker. In the aftermath, he became the first PPD officer to be granted disability from post-traumatic stress disorder when he left his job as an officer two years later (Wooley, 1995).

Ward lost his mother and MOVE founder John Africa in the fire that started from the bomb that was dropped on his home (Norward, 2019). He was raised by his father, joined the

140 District Attorney Rendell convinced Mayor Goode that a search warrant and eviction notice should be executed on the MOVE house. Judge Lynne Abraham signed the warrant. Abraham became the first female District Attorney in Philadelphia and served four terms from 1991 to 2010.

141 Wilson served as mayor from 1984 to 1992. In 1988, Wilson was re-elected and defeated Rizzo (who had switched to the Republican Party). Thirty years after the 1978 raid, Wilson apologized and believed Officer Ramp was killed by friendly fire. In 1988, Wilson appointed Willie Williams as the first Black PPD Commissioner.

142 A 2013 documentary, *Let the Fire Burn*, was directed and produced by Jason Osder. Also see Boyette and Boyette (2013). July 7, 2016, marked the second time the police denoted a C4 explosive to end a standoff when the Dallas Police used a robot to kill Micah Johnson, who fatally shot five officers and injured nine others.

military, and died in a hot tub of acute alcohol intoxication in 2013 while on a cruise ship. Following the bombing, two grand jury investigations occurred, but no charges were brought, and a commission report cited city officials for being reckless (Norwad, 2019). Commissioner Sambor resigned in November 1985, believing he was being made a scapegoat for Mayor Goode. Ramona Africa was convicted on conspiracy and rioting charges from arrest warrants issued before the bombing and served seven years in prison. She remains a spokesperson for MOVE and the sole adult survivor and only living individual from the 1985 bombing.[143] The city settled a lawsuit for $1.5 million in 1996 with MOVE members. A $12.8 million in a jury verdict was paid to other residents who had their homes destroyed (Evans, 2020). In May 2021, Mayor Jim Kenney asked for the resignation of Philadelphia Health Commissioner Thomas Farley after he admitted that he arranged, in 2017 through the medical examiner's office, for the cremation and disposal of bone fragment remains of bombing victims without the notification of family members. Farley's resignation came on the 36th anniversary of the MOVE bombing.

Philadelphia Police Corruption – Philadelphia Police Misuse of Force

Jonathan Rubinstein's (1973) research,[144] advocated for greater accountability within the PPD. As an inside researcher, he went through the Philadelphia Police Academy but was precluded from being a sworn officer. Rubinstein found the academy training to be too brief and unrealistic for what the officers faced. He found little guidance or supervision in the field where "bribery is everywhere" (Rubinstein, 1973, p. 404). The 1974 Pennsylvania Crime Commission found corruption to be "ongoing, widespread, systematic and occurring at all levels of the Police Department" (Pennsylvania Crime Commission, p. 96).

PPB officer's misuse of force was also prevalent with corruption. A Public Interest Law Center study of the PPD found that almost half of all police shootings violated the state law throughout the previous decade (Fyfe, 1982). The report stated that 75 people shot by the police were never charged with a violent crime. The reason for the lack of charges was because these individuals were retreating and unarmed during their police encounters. In 1978, two-thirds of people fatally shot by the police were Black or Hispanic, and disciplinary actions against offending officers were rare. In August 1979, the DOJ unsuccessfully tried to file a civil rights lawsuit against Rizzo and the PPD. The lawsuit marked the first time the Federal Government attempted to go after a municipal police department rather than an individual for brutality. A couple of months after the suit was filed, a federal judge dismissed most of it. During this same period, the PPD reached its peak size with approximately 8,500 officers.

In 1980, Mayor William Green imposed new limitations on when officers are allowed to use deadly force, leading to a two-thirds decrease in police shootings from 1979 to 1982 (Saint et al., 2020). However, subsequent research demonstrated the alternative uses of force besides shooting were just as problematic. A 1984 investigation from *The Philadelphia Inquirer* revealed that K-9 units conducted dog attacks on more than 350 people over 33 months, which lead to the removal of a dozen officers. However, no criminal charges got passed a grand jury (Marimow, 2009).

Throughout the 1980s and into the 1990s, PPD narcotics officers were accused of systematically beating, robbing, and framing suspects in their drug investigations. The corruption was especially prevalent in the 39th District, and ten of those officers receive prison sentences. As was the case with the LAPD Rampart Scandal (described in the Bratton chapter), the brutality

143 Ramona received treatment for lymphoma cancer that she believes was caused by the chemicals in the C-4 explosive dropped on her home in 1985 (Shaw, 2018).

144 Rubenstein's research was supervised by the famed sociologist Erving Goffman.

and corruption from the 39th District officers became public after it spilled across city jurisdiction. The noted ringleader was Officer Jack Baird,[145] who enticed other officers to rob and beat suspected drug dealers and plant evidence (Fazlollah, 1996; Kramer, 1997). One investigating FBI official noted that the history of these scandals is for the police to continually repeat their corrupt activities due to their political pressure to produce results (McDougall, 1997).

The culmination of repeated incidents of the excessive use of force and corruption in the PPD was on display on September 4, 1996. Attorneys from the American Civil Liberties Union (ACLU), the NAACP, and the Police-Barrio Relations Project filed a federal lawsuit in the Eastern District of Pennsylvania against the city of Philadelphia alleging systematic corruption and misconduct in the PPD. There was also a simultaneous settlement agreement for a task force to be created to ensure reform and improve internal affairs operations. Mayor Rendell, footnoted earlier as the DA who prosecuted the MOVE 9, responded by setting up another task force to investigate corruption in addition to creating the Integrity and Accountability Office. Additionally, the city overturned more than 500 drug convictions and paid more than $4 million as part of a settlement.

In 1998, the internal affairs units within the PPD consolidated under one inspector, and Mayor Rendell appointed John Timoney as an external police commissioner to bring further reform. (Timoney, mentioned in the Bratton chapter, was second in command at the NYPD.) In one of his first major acts as police commissioner, Timoney restructured the PPD's Internal Affairs unit, bought in strategies related to stop-and-frisk following the broken-windows style of policing he learned in New York, and implemented CompStat. Throughout his tenure (1998–2002) and his successor Sylvester Johnson (2002–2008), tens of thousands of drug arrests were made as the PPD attempted to retake neighborhoods infested with overt dealing.

Within these drug arrests, stories of police corruption also continued to rip the headlines. The extent of the PPD corruption found its way to investigative reporters Wendy Ruderman and Barbara Laker from the *Philadelphia Daily News*. Their 2010 ten-month investigative series, title *Tainted Justice*, earned them a Pulitzer Prize, and they published a book in 2014 titled, *Busted: A Tale of Corruption and Betrayal in the City of Brotherly Love*. The story came from Ventura "Benny" Martinez. Martinez became a confidential informant (CI) for a PPD narcotics squad and helped make nearly 200 arrests of dealers from 2003 to 2010. When he feared for his life, Martinez walked into Ruderman and Laker's press offices and asked for his story to be told. This story included routine police corruption, fabricated evidence, officers who committed sexual assaults, and officers who looted immigrant-owned small businesses. Inside these immigrant stores, officers destroyed video surveillance equipment so they could steal cash, knowing they were not likely to report the crimes. Benny's status as a CI was revealed when a wealthy drug dealer, with legal representation, hired a private investigator and found that he was paid by members of the narcotics squad, mainly Officer Jeffrey Cujdik (Ruderman & Laker, 2014). Martinez also rented a home from Cujdik and paid his rent through cash he received as his CI, which violated departmental policy.

At the time, the community and the police were especially sensitive to Ruderman and Laker's "anti-police" reporting because of officers recently killed in the line of duty. None of the officers killed appeared to be linked to corruption. Before 2006, the PPD did not lose any officers from gunfire for a decade. However, starting in 2006–2015, the PPD lost 11 officers,[146]

145 Baird can be compared with NYPD Detective Michael Dowd, described in the Bratton chapter. Dowd was the subject of 20 or more misconduct allegations in the seven years leading to his arrest, and Baird was the subject of 26 or more complaints before his arrest (Fyfe & Kane, 2006). Yet, these officers routinely received near-perfect job ratings (Collins, 1998).

146 Eight of the 11 officers killed in the line of duty were during Ramsey's tenure as commissioner (2008–2015). His leadership and empathy for these officers, and their families, were noted when he spoke at their funerals.

seven killed by gunfire, three vehicular assaults, and one training accident.[147] In the aftermath of their investigative reports on police corruption, a police blog was established and revealed both Ruderman and Laker's home addresses. Comments on that blog were made wishing the reporters would be raped or killed, and they were nicknamed the "Slime Sisters." The reporters received numerous threatening emails and phone calls. In July 2014, John McNesby, President of the PPB FOP, held a press conference and stated the Pulitzer Prize should be revoked because the reporters bribed some of their investigative sources by paying their utility bills and providing them with diapers for their children.

As was the case following the civil lawsuit in 1996, investigative journalism caused hundreds of drug cases to be re-examined and several thrown out. In 2009, Ramsey ordered that a task force be created with the PPD internal affairs and requested assistance from the FBI and the city's Inspector General's Office (Clark, 2014). The city paid out $2 million to immigrant shop owners and two women whom a PPD officer sexually assaulted. None of the officers received criminal charges, but two received internal discipline, and one was terminated (Newall & Whelan, 2014). Ramsey terminated Officer Cujdik, but the powerful FOP and an arbitrator got him reinstated[148] (Whelan & Newall, 2014).

In addition to persistent corruption, Philadelphia experienced 406 murders in 2006, the highest amount since 1997 when there were 409 murders. In that same year, the PPD fatally shot 22 people, the highest amount in 32 years. In 2007, mayoral candidate Michael Nutter won the Democratic primary, and a friend recommended that he meet Ramsey. At the time, Nutter admitted he never heard of Ramsey, and based on the persistent recommendation, Nutter traveled to Washington, DC, to meet with him. On November 15, 2007, mayor-elect Nutter announced he would nominate Ramsey as his next police commissioner when he took office on January 7, 2008. That same year the mayor declared a crime emergency for Philadelphia.

Philadelphia Police Commissioner (2008–2015)

Ramsey came out of retirement to officially start leading the PPD on January 7, 2008, the same day as Nutter's inauguration. Twenty-four days into his swearing-in, Ramsey released his 2008 strategic plan that included the following ten performance goals, many that focused on violent crime and matched what Bratton had done in New York and Los Angeles:

1 Geographic concentration (hot spots[149]) of violent crime
2 Geographic accountability for command staff

Ramsey also kept in contact with the families and hung photos of the fallen officers in his office. He posthumously promoted one officer, Patrick McDonald, to sergeant while speaking at his funeral.

147 A 12th officer could be included in the list from 2006 to 2015. Officer Walter Barclay died of complications from a gunshot wound he sustained 40 years' prior from a burglary suspect. In addition, Officer John Dewitt's training accident death resulted from complications from shoulder surgery that stemmed from an injury he received while on duty from a car accident in 1984. Two of the vehicular assaults occurred from drunk drivers and one from a stolen vehicle, which struck Officer Isabel Santiago-Nazario.

148 From 2011 to 2019, an analysis showed the FOP successfully overturned or reduced officer discipline about 70 percent of the time. In 170 cases analyzed for a nine-year study, the city paid 26 officers at least $1.2 million in back pay (Bender & Gambacorta, 2019).

149 Hot spots are not always easy to define (Taylor, 2010). Generally, hot spots are conceived of small street segments where reported crime is known to concentrate according to various software (e.g. ArcGIS through ESRI) that assists police departments in analyzing their data. In the case of the PPD, the data analysis included official incident crime recorded by the police and their arrest data (Haberman, 2016).

3 Strategic deployment of patrol and specialized units to target violent crime through gun possession arrests, warrant enforcement, and stop-and-frisk tactics
4 Prevention of retaliatory violence
5 Aggressive traffic enforcement
6 Quality of life enforcement to reestablish normative public behavior
7 Collaborative strategies with city residents
8 Collaborative strategies with city officials external to the PPD to help with the removal of abandoned vehicles, graffiti removal, improved street lighting, and securing abandoned property
9 Collaboration with law enforcement agencies
10 Assessment of PPD's crime prevention efforts

Ramsey led the fourth largest[150] municipal department in the country with more than 6,600 sworn and 850 civilian employees. He started as the commissioner of the PPD during the recession, which lasted throughout 2008 and into 2009. A two-year hiring freeze created the loss of nearly 400 sworn positions. Despite these challenges, within five years, the total crime returned to levels Philadelphia had not seen since the 1950s. Violent crime was lower than any time since 1985, and homicides were down 40 percent in the city's nine most dangerous districts. Those nine districts previously accounted for 65 percent of homicides and 75 percent of all shootings. From 2006 to 2007, before Ramsey's arrival, Philadelphia averaged almost 400 murders annually.

In comparison, in the last couple of years Ramsey was commissioner, the city averaged 268 murders annually. In 2015, for the first time since 1969, there were fewer than 300 murders in Philadelphia for three consecutive years. In his last months as commissioner, the PPD received state accreditation from the Pennsylvania Law Enforcement Accreditation Commission, a process built around Ramsey's eight years of reform. Ramsey's reform began in earnest within the first few months he became commissioner with the ten goals previously listed.

Ramsey also sent the message that officers would no longer be protected if they misused force. On May 7, 2008, only four months into his new position, PPD officers were videoed beating and kicking three men after a high-speed pursuit ended. Ominous of Rodney King in LA, the video was broadcasted nationwide. The following morning Ramsey stated in an interview that he was troubled by the incident and it was under review. He also indicated that the officers might have been influenced by the fatal shooting of Sergeant Stephen Liczbinski by bank robbers five days prior. On May 19, 2008, Ramsey announced that after a thorough review, the four officers would be terminated, and four other officers would be disciplined for failure to intervene. Ramsey's prompt and transparent actions sent a message to the public and his officers that accountability would occur within the PPD.

Trust the Criminologists

During the recession, police administrators around the country were determined to do more with less. Like Vollmer and Wilson, Ramsey has long been inspired by evidence-based practices that came from criminological research. In 2010, he was nominated by Jerry Ratcliffe[151]

150 The larger departments in 2008 included NYPD (over 36,000); Chicago (over 13,000); LAPD (over 9,700); LA County Police (over 9,400); and California Highway Patrol (over 7,000) (Reaves, 2011).

151 Ratcliffe is a criminal justice professor at Temple University. He consults with police agencies throughout the world and focuses on intelligence-led policing strategies. Before becoming an academic, Ratcliffe was a police officer with the London MPD. See Ratcliffe (2016, 2019) and Ratcliffe and Sorg (2017).

(Temple University) and Wes Skogan (Northwestern University) and inducted into the Center for Evidence-Based Crime Policy Hall of Fame. Two testimonials speak to Ramsey's commitment to evidence-based crime policy.

I have worked with Charles H. Ramsey for almost twenty years, first in Chicago, then in the District of Columbia, and now in Philadelphia. I first worked with him on the Chicago Alternative Policing Strategy. I was fairly young and certainly a naive civilian research practitioner. Charles Ramsey was appointed as the Co-Project Director of CAPS and he immediately understood that the success of such a major change initiative rested on receiving valid, real-time assessments of the implementation efforts. Today he talks about the need to discover the right 'dosage' of police intervention and understanding what works and why. He encourages the Philadelphia Police Department to work with researchers to better test our long-held beliefs. Today there are conversations between Philadelphia Police Deputy Commissioners and Temple University researchers about how to implement a randomized, experimental designed study to test which methodology – problem-solving, foot patrol, or offender-focused approaches – is most effective in combating violent crime. He is promoting evidence-based policing by his actions and mentoring the next generation of police executives.

Nola M. Joyce, Chief Administrative Officer, PPD

I have had the pleasure of working with Commissioner Ramsey during his tenure in both Washington, DC, and Philadelphia. In both cases, he came in ready for a challenge – murder and shooting rates that were spiraling out of control. I have been astounded to see the success that he has achieved in reducing these terrifying figures in each city. In Washington, his impact was seen in the push toward community policing, increase in hiring standards, and the Regional Operations Command. In Philadelphia, his PPD2020 plan is in the process of bringing similar measures to his new home – and the results are already evident.

Dr. Camille Barnett, former Managing Director for the City of Philadelphia and former City Manager for Washington, DC

When Ramsey arrived in Philadelphia, he partnered with Ratcliffe and Temple University to conduct one of the largest quasi-experiments on foot patrol since George Kelling did so in Newark, as discussed in the Bratton chapter appendix. Results from the Police Foundation's Newark foot patrol experiment (Police Foundation, 1981) sparked a philosophical shift toward community policing even though the research results were anticlimactic since it did not indicate a reduction in crime. Foot patrol did become the emergent cornerstone of community policing since the Newark experiment showed that community perceptions of the police improved, and fear of crime was lowered.

In the summer of 2009,[152] Temple University partnered with Ramsey and the PPD to analyze close to 250-foot patrol officers that were randomly distributed across 60 violent crime hotspots. Putting foot patrol officers in statistical hotspots was the novel part of advancing the experiment. It followed earlier hotspot policing research that indicated directed patrol techniques into neighborhoods with the most concentrated calls for service reduced crime problems (Sherman & Weisburd, 1995). Ramsey believed that foot patrol officers become a more entrenched part of the community's fabric and offer a sense of familiarity, safety, and

152 The year 2009 was also when Ramsey, a devout Catholic, received the Keys & Sword Award at the Cathedral Basilica of Saint Peter and Paul. The award was taken from the symbols of the saints and acknowledged actions that reflect Gospel values of faith, selfless service, personal sacrifice, respect, and valor. Ramsey and his wife Sylvia attended regular Mass at the Cathedral.

pride in a given neighborhood. After 12 weeks, a linear regression model determined that violent crime was significantly reduced in the treatment locations (Ratcliffe, Taniguchi, Groff, & Wood, 2011), and the three decades of doubts regarding foot patrol were erased.[153]

Specifically, 240 police academy graduates did foot patrols about 16 hours a day for five days a week over the summer of 2009 and successfully reduced violence by 23 percent across 60 targeted hot spots compared to 60 control areas. As a result, Ramsey continued to have all new academy graduates begin their policing careers on foot patrol in the most troubled neighborhoods, giving the officers an appreciation for the residents not causing disorder in those neighborhoods. The lesson was that most residents, even in high-crime areas, are decent people whom foot patrol officers should respect. Enhancing foot patrol was part of Ramsey's commitment to community policing and his attempt to be data-driven through CompStat, but doing so without sacrificing police legitimacy. The Philadelphia experiment demonstrated that small, high-crime hotspots for violence could be cooled statistically by well-placed foot patrol officers dedicated to a community policing philosophy. The research also exemplified the crucial connections between police leaders and academic evaluators (see Joyce, Ramsey, Stewart, 2013).

In addition to evaluating the impact of foot patrol, Ramsey agreed to assess generalized hot spot policing (Groff et al., 2015). These locations were critical to study as criminologists have long argued that hot spot policing is an effective strategy (Braga & Weisburd, 2010; Braga, Papachristos, & Hureau, 2012). Ignoring these problem places will lead to further negative social attributes, based on routine activities, that destabilize normative behavior (Taylor, 1997).

Researchers from Temple University implemented a randomized controlled field experiment to test the differential impact of foot patrol, POP, and offender-focused policing on 81 hot spot locations. Within these locations, 27 were randomly selected, with 20 receiving treatment and seven served as control sites. The researchers determined that offender-focused treatment sites experienced a 42-percent reduction in violent crime compared to control locations (Groff et al., 2015). Moreover, community perception of enhanced police practices in hot spot locations was not significantly different (in neither a positive nor a negative way) from control sites (Ratcliffe, Groff, Sorg, & Haberman, 2015). Lastly, POP and foot patrol treatment sites did not experience significant violent crime reduction. However, researchers detailed several difficulties related to an authentic implementation of POP principles that mainly had to do with the expectations that officers were supposed to be analytical during their downtime and between other duties. Therefore, the dosage of POP activities became difficult to determine. Many sites did not implement any POP strategies that should have targeted violent crime.

A fundamental research question that stems from a focus on hot spots is what type of policing is needed when directing resources to the most problematic places. The lesson for Ramsey and other similar police leaders, such as Bratton during his second leadership experience with the NYPD, relates to the quality of arrests in hot spot locations rather than focusing on quantity. This can only be accomplished through more intensive analysis to determine the who and when to direct resources to hot spot locations, which can be captured through

153 During Rizzo's tenure as commissioner, approximately 100 of the 7,000 officers conducted foot patrol. Rizzo argued "We've got more foot beat men than we had before now. Let's be practical. You put a policeman in a residential area and he walks around and says hello and shakes hands-and what good does he do? This is not policing" (Ratcliffe & Sorg, 2017, p. 22). Rizzo also believed that foot patrol officers displaced crime to other locations where they were not present, and stated "The day of preventing crime is over. We have to have the ability to apprehend and this is what we do in Philadelphia" (Grimes, 1971, p. 3; Rattcliffe & Sorg, 2017, pp. 22).

Goldstein's POP concepts (Goldstein, 1979, 1990) and more comprehensive community collaboration philosophy.

Stop-Question-and-Frisk

When Ramsey came to the PPD, he continued the strategies of his predecessors, Timoney and Johnson, with aggressive stop-and-frisk tactics that were detailed in the chapter on Bratton and in the appendix with Kelling. These strategies occurred in predominantly African-American districts with the highest crime and calls for service. Ramsey continued to defend stop-and-frisk and called the tactic legal and an effective use of police strategy to lower violent crime as long as it's exercised within the constitution.

As was the case with the NYPD, federal civil rights lawsuits were filed that alleged citizens in Philadelphia were being stopped and frisked without adequate or reasonable suspicion and that minorities, Black and Latino, were disproportionately targeted. In the 2010 ruling *Bailey v. Philadelphia*, the court used data from 2009 and found over 250,000 stops consisted of 72 percent African-American citizens, even though they made up 44 percent of the general city population. Less than 9 percent of those individuals were arrested after the stop. However, these stops are based upon theories linked to crime prevention rather than arrest. The case was settled in 2011, led to a consent decree, and again like the NYPD, stops declined dramatically. However, in the fall of 2018, three years after Ramsey retired from the PPD, another class-action suit was filed utilizing six months of 2018 data alleging that 16 percent of stops, which accounted for more than 6,000 citizens, were done without justification. Moreover, 80 percent of these stops and 87 percent of the frisks were Blacks and Latinos. The lawsuit indicated that officers needed more than re-training, and police executives should be able to discipline officers without being circumvented by union protection. Ramsey continually provided support for stop-and-frisk strategies but stated just because an officer stops someone does not mean they should frisk them.

> *Most of the complaints we get are not about the stop, they're about the way the person was treated during the stop. We're focusing our training on how to have positive interactions under intense circumstances. The art of conversation is something we're beginning to lose*
>
> (La Vigne, Lachman, Rao, & Matthews, 2014, p. 31).

Trust the Feds – It's Not Consent Decrees but Collaborative Reform Agreements

While crime dropped, increased OIS continued to perplex PPD leadership. In 2012, the police shot 52 citizens and were involved in 59 OIS, the highest number since 1979. Fifteen of these shootings were fatal. The 2012 increase compared to 2011 numbers when the PPD shot 35 people (Wood, 2013). Consequently, in May 2013, Ramsey repeated his MPD experiment and asked for technical assistance from the DOJ. That assistance came from the Office of Community Oriented Policing Services (COPS) as part of their collaborative reform agreements that were linked to AG Eric Holder's priority on civil rights. These collaborative reform agreements were markedly different from consent decrees in which the DOJ's civil rights division was forced upon municipal departments based upon high-profile problems. While departments technically volunteer for a consent decree, it usually comes from a court order in the aftermath of civil rights lawsuits based upon the improper use of force and constitutional violations. President Clinton's Violent Crime Control and Law Enforcement Act of 1994 initiated consent decrees. The first one was done in 1997 with the Pittsburgh Police

Department until the agreement was lifted too early (Davis, Henderson, Mandelstam, Ortiz, & Miller, 2005). During President Obama's administration, the Federal Government launched several investigations on local police agencies related to constitutional policing challenges and forged various reform agreements and formalized consent decrees. However, consent decrees became nonexistent from 2016 to 2020 with the Trump administration. In 2021, President Biden is likely to hit restart on several of the consent decree reform standards (Coleman, 2020).

In addition to consent decrees, Obama's administration began collaborative reform agreements through the COPS Office and a continuance for exercising best practices linked to community and constitutional policing strategies, which serve as a roadmap for reform measures. Notably, the collaborative reform agreements are free, unlike the consent decrees, which can cost a city nearly $1 million a year for several years they are under the decree. The point of the collaborative reform agreements through the COPS Office is to prevent court orders that would bring in the expensive DOJ civil rights division to clean up significant problems.

The COPS Office piloted their collaborative reform agreements in 2011 with the Las Vegas Police Department. Ramsey read their evaluative report and thought they could do the same for Philadelphia. The COPS Office partnered with the CNA Institute for Public Research to provide technical assistance to departments that asked for help, showed indications they could implement change, and had the type of leadership willing to accept reform. The focus was on improving police-community relations through procedural justice and constitutional policing principles, as reflected earlier in the aftermath of Ramsey's tour of the Washington, DC Holocaust Museum. The collaborative reform agreements sought organizational transformation through policy, practice, training, and the tactics that historically jeopardized an agency's legitimacy with its community. The ultimate goal was to create long-term and sustainable strategies that impact public trust, rather than short-term charters or grand jury hearings done in the past.

The DOJ review on PPD OIS included a year-long investigative process by an interdisciplinary team of researchers who conducted multiple site visits. The review team went through training modules, use of force review board hearings, interviews with various community stakeholders, and wrote a final report with recommendations. In total, the researchers interviewed 150 individuals throughout the PPD. Before the final report was complete, Ramsey and the PPD launched a website that significantly increased OIS transparency.[154] That website detailed the dates and locations of OIS, showed if the offender was wounded, killed, arrested, and what the review board determined in addition to any action taken from the District Attorney. The website also includes links to geographical maps for every gun crime and OIS shooting. Not surprisingly, these maps are closely linked together, meaning most OIS shootings occur near locations where past gun crimes are concentrated within hotspots for crime.

Ramsey also wanted to publicly reveal the names of officers involved in shootings within 72 hours while it was being investigated. The FOP vehemently protested this type of transparency and backed a city council bill to prevent officers' names from being released while investigations on the OIS took place. The FOP argued that assassins would hunt these officers. In the fall of 2017, a judge denied the FOP's motion for injunctive relief to prohibit the city from continuing to release the names of officers involved in on-duty shooting incidents. The judicial decision led to "Back the Blue" rallies that often ran counter to the "#Black Lives Matter" demonstrations, discussed more fully later.

154 In addition to increased transparency, on December 19, 2013, Ramsey announced police reforms would include mandatory videos taken for homicide interrogations (years after most cities had already done so), limitations to how long suspects could be held, and new rules on how photo lineups would be presented to victims and witnesses (Gambarcorta, 2013).

From 2007 to 2016, there were more than 430 OIS. Eighty percent of citizens shot by the PPD from 2007 to 2014 were Black, and 45 percent were considered unarmed. In almost every case, prosecution of the officers is avoided. Two high-profile case examples come from 2014 and 2017.

> During the COPS Office review of PPD's OIS, on April 22, 2014, two plainclothes officers shot 20-year-old pizza deliveryman Philippe Holland, a college student working two jobs, by firing 14 shots into his vehicle, leaving him with a permanent seizure disorder. The officers had less than two years of experience and responded to a shots fired call for service. There were competing accounts of where witnesses thought a suspect was walking. However, witnesses did give statements that the responding officers did not wear badges nor announce they were the police when they approached Holland's car. Three bullets struck Holland, two in his leg and one in his face. Three years later, a lawsuit was settled for the largest payment in city history- $4.4 million, just as jury selection was about to start. The officers were put on paid administrative leave, were not prosecuted, and were later suspended but kept their jobs. Ramsey went to the hospital to apologize to the victim and his mother.
>
> (Dean, 2017)

For the past 50 years, only one PPD officer, Ryan Pownall, was indicted for killing 30-year-old David Jones on June 8, 2017. (In October 2020, terminated officer Eric Ruch Jr. was indicted for the fatal shooting of 25-year-old Dennis Plowden Jr. following a high-speed pursuit that occurred on the evening of December 27, 2017). Pownall stopped Jones for riding a dirt bike on a city street leading to a scuffle. Jones dropped his gun and attempted to run away, leading Pownall to shoot him twice in the back. Surveillance video footage showed Pownall shoot Jones in the back twice as he ran away unarmed. The Grand Jury indicted Pownall for reckless endangerment and murder. The judge downgraded his charges to third-degree manslaughter. Ramsey's predecessor, Commissioner Richard Ross, terminated Pownall (Palmer, 2017). It may have been the second time Pownall shot a citizen for running away (Gambacorta, 2020). On July 27, 2010, Pownall believed he shot Carnell Williams-Carney, who had recently been released from prison, had an illegal firearm and attempted to run from officers. The officers fired ten shots at him, believing he was a deadly threat. It's impossible to know if Pownall shot Carney because the round that hit him in the back is still lodged on his spine, causing paralysis. Carney's shooting was deemed justified. In the second shooting, the city provided Jones's family with $1 million to avoid a future civil lawsuit.

On March 23, 2015, the DOJ held a press conference with U.S. Attorney Zane Memeger, Director Office of COPS Ron Davis, Mayor Nutter, and Ramsey to discuss their findings and recommendations. Their 188-page report, titled "Collaborative Reform Initiative: An Assessment of Deadly Force in the PPD," listed 48 deficiencies with training, policies, and supervision along with 91 recommendations for best practices (Fachner & Carter, 2015). Within the proposals, there were four broad objectives:

1 Enhanced training related to officer and public safety in deadly force situations
2 Improved quality and transparency of deadly force investigations
3 Strengthened use of force review process
4 Institutionalized organizational learning processes and practices related to deadly force incidents

Table 6.2 indicates the progress made in the aftermath of the COPS Office collaborative reform initiative with comparison four-year averages. The table also connects OIS, violent crime, and officer safety, all showing declines.

Table 6.2 Four-Year Averages of Murders, Shooting Victims, OIS, Citizens, and Officers Killed

Category	*2007–2010 Annual Average*	*2011–2014 Annual Average*
Murders	333	288
Shooting victims citywide	1,497	1,215
Officer-involved shootings (OIS)	54	44
Rate per 100,000 for OIS	1.8	1.28
Citizens killed by the police	13	11
Officers killed by weapon	1.25	0.2

In 2015, Ramsey's last year as commissioner, the PPD had 23 officer shootings, half of the 2011–2014 average. This number was nearly matched, 24 OIS, in 2016. However, in 2017 OIS incidents were down to 14, 12 in 2018, and nine in 2019. No citizens were killed by OIS in 2019. This total marked the lowest number of OIS in 50 years. Notably, the reductions demonstrated the importance of Ramsey's legacy, evidence-based community policing strategies linked to foot patrol, and federal collaborative reform initiatives. Lastly, Philadelphia has not had an officer killed by gunfire since March 5, 2015.[155]

#BlackLivesMatter

While the investigative DOJ visits to the PPD began in 2013 and lasted until the spring of 2015, it also occurred in the backdrop of 2014 and 2015 in Ferguson, Missouri. In the aftermath of the Michael Brown shooting, many consider the riots in Ferguson a culmination of the #Black Lives Matter Movement, that is, until the spring/summer 2020 mass protests. The movement revealed the depth of conflict between communities of color and their police agencies. Ramsey has argued that the Black Lives Matter movement may be missing an opportunity to drive national conversations toward protecting those lives from all violence, some of which include unethical policing. However, much of it involves inner-city violence between citizens. A historical summary of the movement is further detailed.

The Black Lives Matter movement has its roots in July 2013 after George Zimmerman, captain of a neighborhood watch program in Sanford, Florida, was acquitted of murder and manslaughter after he fatally shot unarmed 17-year-old Trayvon Martin on February 26, 2012. The hashtag #BlackLivesMatter[156] was posted on various modes of social media following Zimmerman's acquittal and became nationally recognized in 2014 during demonstrations following the fatal shooting of Michael Brown. Sanford[157] is 25 miles north of Orlando, with approximately 53,000 residents and a police force of 140 officers. In May 2012, Rick Myers[158] was asked to take over the department intermittently by the city manager based on

155 An exception occurred on March 13, 2020. Sergeant James O'Connor, IV was killed by gunfire during a SWAT raid.

156 Originators of the hashtag (Alicia Garza, Patrisse Khan-Cullors, and Opal Tometi) helped establish a national network and various local chapters throughout the country. Also, see Garza (2020) and Khan-Cullors and Bandele (2017).

157 Sanford is also noted for driving Jackie Robinson out of its city during spring training for the Brooklyn Dodgers in 1946 (Lamb & Long, 2017).

158 Myers is a 2009 member of the Michigan State University School of Criminal Justice Hall of Fame and a mentee of Herman Goldstein. He served as a police chief in five different states, including Newport News, Virginia; Colorado Springs, Colorado; Appleton, Wisconsin; Lisle, Illinois; and Plymouth, Michigan. In 2017, he was named Executive Director for the Major Cities Chiefs Association, and President of the national police accreditation body – CALEA (Commission on Accreditation for Law Enforcement Agencies, Inc.).

a no-confidence vote directed toward Chief Bill Lee. In April 2013, Elgin, Illinois Deputy Chief Cecil Smith was appointed Sanford Chief, the city's fifth chief over the prior seven years. Smith was the city's second Black[159] chief and the first in central Florida to implement body cameras for his officers.

On July 17, 2014, Eric Garner was killed at the age of 43 in New York City after an NYPD officer put him in a chokehold. (This incident is detailed in the chapter on Bratton.) Garner's said the words "I can't breathe"[160] 11 times to the officer before he died. This phrase became a further mantra for the Black Lives Matter movement. On August 9, 2014, 18-year-old Michael Brown was fatally shot six times in Ferguson, Missouri. Five weeks later, on September 16–17, Ramsey, who was the President of the PERF,[161] convened a critical issues summit in Chicago with 180 police executives to discuss Ferguson's implications. Ramsey addressed the difference between warrior and guardian mindsets and asked which one of these we want our police to be. A few months later, protests and riots erupted in Ferguson and across the country, when a Grand Jury failed to indict Officer Darren Wilson in Brown's fatal shooting. In the first half of the following year, violent crime spiked in select cities, and perceptions were made that a "Ferguson effect" was causing the increase based on the police being hesitant to enforce the law in fear of being labeled a racist.

In a subsequent study of the 2015 crime increase, 56 cities were analyzed, and 40 experienced increased homicides (Rosenfeld, 2016). This marked the biggest homicide increase in 25 years, although the 2014 murder rate was the lowest since 1957. Another analysis indicated a national 10 percent murder rate increase in 2015 (Donohue, 2017). Like most increases or decreases in crime, academics could not agree on the cause. Ferguson's events revealed there was still a great deal of mistrust between the police and communities of color, and this revelation would explode five years later in the spring/summer of 2020.

FBI Director Comey on 2015 Policing – Michael Brown, Freddie Gray, Laquan McDonald

In 2015, FBI Director James Comey spoke out about the racial tension and hinted about future threats. Comey was the seventh director of the FBI and served from 2013 to 2017, under President Obama and President Trump, before his May 9, 2017 termination.[162] He drew headlines in 2015 for his open and frank conversations about rising urban crime rates and dismissing those who felt it was just a "blip" and not a trend toward future problems. Comey cautioned against conclusive statements on the causes of increased crime and any significant reforms that police leaders or politicians would attempt. He indicated that middle-size cities continued to show decreases in violent and property offenses, but something was also happening in America's race relations that should be given proper attention.

In 2015, public-opinion polls by Pew Research demonstrated that American's negative views toward race-relations were close to those in 1992 following the Los Angeles riots after

159 Sanford's first Black chief was Joe Dillard in 1998–1999.

160 In Minneapolis, transcripts showed George Floyd muttered these same words more than 20 times before his death on May 25, 2020 (Oppel & Barker, 2020).

161 Ramsey is the only police executive to simultaneously hold the prominent positions of being President of both PERF and the Major Cities Chiefs Association. He also served on the IACP Executive Committee and is the only police leader to receive a leadership award from the three major law enforcement organizations – the FBI National Executive Institute, PERF, and the Major Cities Chiefs Association.

162 Comey became the second director of the FBI to be terminated. President Clinton terminated William Sessions in 1993 in the aftermath of a 161-page internal report from the DOJ that cited numerous ethical failures of Sessions, who improperly billed the FBI for vacation travel and personal home construction.

officers were acquitted for the beating of Rodney King. Moreover, the presidential campaign was divisive and targeted race and immigration as hot bottom issues for voters. In effect, Comey's comments about increased violent crime concerns helped shape candidate Trump's law and order campaign. On February 12, 2015, Comey surprised many law enforcement leaders when he encouraged an open discussion about race in America to a packed auditorium at Georgetown University. He did so again on October 23, 2015, at the University of Chicago Law School when he spoke about an increase of violence, empowered minority communities, and officers' hesitation to enforce the law. FBI Directors have traditionally not made public forum speeches, leaving the political discussion to elected officials. Comey took his chances and spoke about Americans being at the crossroads of race relations and encouraged the populous to play an active role in understanding one another better.

On May 25, 2016, Comey was asked to speak at the iconic Sixteenth Street Baptist Church in Birmingham, Alabama, on the last day of the 2016 annual conference on civil rights and law enforcement. The church was iconic since it experienced the September 15, 1963 bombing that killed four young Black girls and injured 22 other parishioners. Although the FBI concluded that the bombing was linked to specific members of the Ku Klux Klan, it was nearly 15 years later before one individual was tried and convicted of first-degree murder. Comey continued to warn the public to engage in improvements with race relations before more unrest spread.

On April 12, 2015, 25-year-old Freddie Gray was arrested by the BPD for possessing a knife. He was left unrestrained in a police van during his transportation to booking. He later fell into a coma due to injuries sustained to his spinal cord during his arrest and transport. Gray died from these injuries a week after his arrest, and the medical examiner classified his death a homicide. Two years later, a consent decree was agreed to after the DOJ determined the BPD engaged in a pattern and conduct of practice that violated constitutional rights.

On October 20, 2014, 17-year-old Laquan McDonald was fatally shot by Chicago Police officer Jason Van Dyke. On April 15, 2015, two days before Gray's death, a $5 million settlement was made with the McDonald family before they filed a wrongful death lawsuit. This agreement also occurred a day after Rahm Emanuel won a run-off election for his second mayoral term. The agreement stipulated that the fatal shooting dashcam video could not be released until the investigation was completed. On November 25, 2015, the Cook County Court circumvented the agreement and ordered the CPD to release the shooting video. Van Dyke was then charged with first-degree murder, and Mayor Rahm Emanuel[163] terminated Police Commissioner Garry McCarthy.[164]

Before hiring McCarthy in 2011, newly elected Mayor Emanuel attempted to entice Ramsey to become his CPD commissioner, but that deal did not materialize. Ramsey did assist Emanuel six years later as a consultant to the CPD as federal civil rights investigations occurred in the McDonald shooting aftermath (Cournoyer, 2016). However, this arrangement only lasted a few months (Spielman, 2016). Cook County State's Attorney Anita Alvarez lost her reelection in 2016. On September 4, 2018, Mayor Emanuel announced he would not run for a third mayoral term, a year after making the opposite announcement. The removal of the police commissioner, county prosecutor, and the mayor were all linked to perceived

163 Emanuel was President Obama's White House Chief of Staff in 2008, but he later resigned and was elected Chicago's mayor in 2011, succeeding Richard M. Daley's five-term 22-year incumbency (1989–2011). Daley's father, Richard J. Daley, served 21 years (1955–1976).

164 McCarthy spent 19 years in the NYPD (1981–2006) and six years as the chief of the Newark Police Department (2006–2011) under mayor Corey Booker's leadership. After Emanuel terminated him, McCarthy attempted to run against him for mayor of Chicago, but his campaign fizzled after Emanuel announced he would not seek a third term.

problems with the CPD handling of the McDonald shooting and ongoing issues with the misuse of force. On October 5, 2018, Van Dyke was found guilty of second-degree murder and 16 counts of aggravated battery with a firearm. The lead prosecutor was Joe McMahon, who came from Kane County rather than Cook County. Four months later, Van Dyke was sentenced to almost seven years in prison. Three CPD officers were found not guilty for writing police reports that allegedly attempted to cover up Van Dyke's fatal shooting of McDonald. A month after McDonald's fatal shooting in Chicago, 12-year-old Tamir Rice was shot and killed by the Cleveland Police while on a playground with a toy gun tucked in his waistband. The Cleveland officers were not indicted. On December 29, 2020, six years after Rice was killed, the DOJ announced they were closing their case and declining to prosecute the Cleveland officers.

President's Task Force on the 21st Century Policing

A month after Rice was killed, and in response to the increased protests from Black Lives Matter, President Obama signed an executive order to create a Task Force on 21st Century Policing. He asked Ramsey and Laurie Robinson[165] to co-chair the task force[166] to rebuild community trust, enhance institutional transparency, and promote crime reduction. The task force members, each listed in the preceding footnote, were intentionally diverse and included members of the police union, lawyers, academics, civil rights activists, and police executives. At the time of his appointment, Ramsey was also the president of the Major Chief's Police Association and PERF, the only police leader to hold both positions simultaneously. The task force was given 70 days to come up with a report and recommendations (Photo 6.4).

The task force met on seven occasions in January and February 2015. Listening sessions took place in Washington, DC, Phoenix, and Cincinnati. More than 100 individuals were called upon by the task force to provide input in listening sessions[167] and written testimony. The task force's final report was issued in May 2015 and outlined several suggestions for improving policing to make it more safe, effective, and constitutional. Fifty-nine recommendations involved several action items organized around six main topics that the task force referred to at pillars. These pillars were as follows:

1 **Building Trust and Legitimacy** – based on research indicating people follow the rules when they feel the police are acting legitimately
2 **Policy Oversight** – that reflect community values
3 **Technology and Social Media** – that helps enhance transparency and trust
4 **Community Policing and Crime Reduction** – that emphasized a police culture that respects dignity for all

165 Robinson is a professor in the George Mason University Criminology, Law and Society department. See Robinson (2020).

166 Nine other members of the task force included Cedric Alexander, Deputy Chief Operating Officer for Public Safety in DeKalb County, Georgia; Jose Lopez, Lead Organizer for Make the Road New York; Tracey Meares, Yale Law Professor; Brittany Packnett, Executive Director with Teach for America; Susan Lee Rahr, Executive Director for Washington State Criminal Justice Training Commission; Connie Rice, Co-director for the Advancement Project (and discussed in the Bratton chapter); Sean Smoot, Director and Chief Counsel for the Police Benevolent & Protective Association; Bryan Stevenson, Executive Director of the Equal Justice Initiative; and Roberto Villaseñor, Chief of Tucson Police Department.

167 Listening sessions from January 13, 2015 can be seen at www.youtube.com/watch?v=FmjVrED_9dc

Photo 6.4 Chuck Ramsey with President Barack Obama.
Photo provided to the author by Chuck Ramsey.

5 **Officer Training and Education** – federal support for national training standards and mandatory crisis intervention training (CIT)
6 **Officer Safety and Wellness** – encouraging departments to understand problems with shift lengths and collect data to understand officer injuries and death better

Two overarching recommendations were provided to President Obama. The first stated that a National Commission should be created to examine all areas of the justice system, as was done in 1967 under the President's Commission on Law Enforcement and Administration of Justice and in 1931 under the Wickersham Commission. (The LBJ Crime Commission is discussed in the Herman Goldstein appendix of the Wilson chapter, and the 1931–1932 Wickersham Commission is discussed in the chapter on Vollmer.) The second recommendation President Obama received was to take a comprehensive and inclusive look at community-based initiatives that seek to address issues connected to poverty, education, and health and safety.

On June 4, 2020, during the international mass police protests, Ramsey and other past members of the task force wrote an op-ed for the *New York Times* titled "There is a Playbook for Police Reform: We Helped Write It" (Ramsey, Davis, Villasenor, & Smoot, 2020). In the op-ed, the writers implored police agency leaders to step in and provide clear and precise guidance for officers' use of force. They purported that such policies and direction would have prevented George Floyd's death on May 25, 2020, in Minneapolis. The task force's work in 2015 also led to the creation of the consulting group 21CPSolutions, LLC,[168] located in Chicago. Ramsey was the founder and is one of seven consultants, with four additional senior advisors and 13 associate consultants.

National Constitution Center

When Ramsey became the commissioner of the PPD, he drove past the National Constitution Center (NCC) located on the Independence Mall several times, wondering what went on inside. Eventually, he was introduced to Jeffrey Rosen, President and CEO of the NCC. Reflective of his MPD observations of Holocaust Museum, Ramsey helped create a four-hour program called "Policing in a More Perfect Union." The program was designed to help police recruits understand how their role as officers is to defend the Constitution as defined by the Bill of Rights and additional Amendments. The training course immerses the police recruits into a historical understanding of police legitimacy, community discussions to understand various views on justice and fairness, and tours of the NCC museum to understand the relationship between the police, civil rights and influential Supreme Court decisions. As a consequence of this experience, Ramsey had his role call command staff read through the First Amendment of the Constitution at every shift to remind his officers of their role in upholding due process rights.

Ramsey became one of many invited speakers to the NCC. On October 13, 2015, he began to speak about Constitutional policing at a town hall. However, minutes into his talk, several protesters stood up from the audience and disrupted his interview with Jeff Rosen. PPD officers allowed their protest and yelling to go on for a few minutes before escorting them outside so the town hall could continue. Ramsey's response to the multiple interruptions during his discussion speaks to his demeanor and leadership. He talked about some understanding of why the protests were occurring. A month earlier, on September 1st, protesters also interrupted Ramsey's speech at the Eastern State Penitentiary. This protest lasted longer, and Ramsey left without speaking about his strategies for improving police-community relations in the wake of Michael Brown's death in Ferguson and Eric Garner's death in New York City. On March 31, 2016, Ramsey returned to the NCC and spoke about policing in a democratic society with Barry Friedman and Tracey Meares. On July 27, 2016, Ramsey spoke at the Democratic National Convention in Philadelphia in support of Presidential Candidate Hillary Clinton. On June 30, 2020, Ramsey again spoke at the NCC symposium with Dr. Tracey Meares to discuss police legitimacy and the battle for the Constitution within the pandemic and mass police protests.

Ramsey's Retirement

Ramsey announced his retirement from the PPD on October 14, 2015, which was also the end of Nutter's second mayoral term.

President Obama responded to Ramsey's retirement with the following statement:

> *I want to offer my heartfelt gratitude to Commissioner Charles 'Chuck' Ramsey for his nearly five decades of leadership and service with some of this nation's largest law enforcement agencies. From Chicago to DC to Philadelphia, Commissioner Ramsey has always supported our women and men in uniform and the communities they bravely serve and protect each and every day. While I've known about his outstanding work over the years, it was when I appointed Chuck as a co-chair of my Task*

168 21CP Solutions is short for 21st Century Policing Solutions. See www.21cpsolutions.com/

Force on 21st Century Policing that I was able to rely on his counsel and leadership. For several months earlier this year, he played a vital role in bringing together leaders from across the country to create a clear and concise report including key recommendations for building stronger trust between communities and the law enforcement agencies that protect them. I am extraordinarily grateful for Chuck's service and wish him an enjoyable and restful retirement.

Ramsey retired as the highest-paid city employee in Philadelphia with a $270,000 a year salary.[169] Only a few weeks into his retirement, in January 2016, he became a public safety consultant in Wilmington, Delaware (Pizzi, 2016). The goal was to implement recommendations from the 21st Century Policing Task Force under President Obama. In 2017, he became a law enforcement analyst for CNN. He was also appointed by Tom Wolfe, Governor of Pennsylvania, to chair a commission on crime and delinquency and joined a committee on school safety. In 2019, Ramsey's PPD predecessor, Commissioner Richard Ross, Jr., resigned amid sexual harassment claims filed against his officers. Seventy-two officers were also taken off of street duty over racist Facebook posts. Additionally, in August 2019, six officers were shot and injured while serving a drug warrant in North Philadelphia after an eight-hour standoff.

Similar to Vollmer and Wilson, Ramsey spent the spring of 2020 in the classroom as Distinguished Policy Fellow at the Leo Model Foundation[170] Government and Public Affairs Initiative at the University of Pennsylvania, teaching a seminar law course with John Hollway, Associate Dean and Executive Director of the Quattrone Center. Policing topics discussed and debated included the use of force, policing errors, technological advances in policing, community responsibility, how prison sentencing impacts the police, and the 21st Century Policing Task Force recommendations. In addition to Penn Law, Ramsey served as an inaugural Distinguished Visiting Fellow at Drexel University's Lindy Institute for Urban Innovation from 2016 to 2018. In this capacity, he helped develop a multi-disciplinary master's degree in urban strategy and served as an advisor for the Criminology and Justice Studies Department.

Epilogue – Ramsey and PERF Reflections on the Use of Force post-2020 Mass Protests

On June 18 and 30, 2020, the PERF held virtual town hall meetings in reaction to the COVID-19 pandemic and the international mass police protests that erupted after George Floyd died in Minneapolis the previous month. The discussions dealt with training from an outdated use of force continuum. Within the continuum training, officers learn to increase their force based on the suspect's resistance level.

The continuum essentially looks like a staircase within the following:

1 Verbal, nonverbal noncompliance (Officer presence and verbal direction)
2 Passive resistance (Officer touch control)
3 Active resistance (Officer empty-hand tactics, chemical agents utilized)

169 By way of comparison, the average big-city police chief earned over $200,000 in 2017 in total compensation (Jeffrey, 2018). In 2017, James O'Neill earned $226,000 as NYPD Commissioner. LAPD Chief Charlie Beck made $350,000 in total compensation. Danielle Outlaw started as Philadelphia Commissioner in 2020 at $285,000. In Chicago, Jody Weis resigned as the Superintendent of the CPD in 2011 with a $310,000 salary. When Eddie Johnson was fired as CPD Superintendent, he earned $260,000 compared to Emmanuel, who made $216,000 as mayor but reported $554,000 in total income (Ruthhart, 2018).

170 The Leo Model Foundation Government and Public Affairs Initiative invites visiting government officials, like Ramsey, to share their real-world experiences with students and faculty through seminars, guest lectures, and student career conversations.

4 Active aggression (Officer use of a taser and other impact weapons)
5 Aggravated aggression (Officer use of deadly force)

Since 2005, the PERF raised questions concerning the training and linear thought process that supported use of force continuums (Ederheimer & Fridell, 2005) and argued that it does not accurately reflect violent police encounters' dynamic nature. Ramsey's concern was directed at the continuum's assumption that conflict is resolved by taking another step upward toward the higher levels of force until the incident is over as if there were a simplistic approach to a complex problem. Moving up the use of force staircase is easy, but ratcheting it back down through de-escalation techniques is not part of mainstream policing. In 2012, the PERF expanded their concern and offered an integrated approach to minimize the use of force, including de-escalation strategies and a Critical Decision-Making Model (CDM). In 2015, the PERF argued for developing a CDM linked to use of force considerations. The CDM allows officers to assess dozens of factors in dynamic situations to determine the best way to resolve a problem, which may not require any use of force.

Moreover, timely past data analysis should be provided to the officer related to the call's given location. It's critical to know the history of previous calls, who the individual is that made the call, an indication of mental health concerns, and any weapons available at the scene. If there is a track history of dealing with the place location or the caller, other individuals (e.g. social workers) should also be called into the scene to assist the police response. Better yet, mental health providers should be called in after previous calls were made. In 2016, the PERF issued 30 guiding principles for departments to rethink and retrain strategies to defuse critical incidents. In 2019, the PERF issued a training guide connected to suicide by cop to equip officers better to peacefully resolve incidents in which suspects attempt to force officers to end their life.

Ramsey added to the discussion by talking about the importance of policies he had implemented with the MPD and PPD, including banning chokeholds, banning shooting at vehicles, and providing officers with a duty to intervene. Just as doctors and researchers are provided with a Hippocratic oath of first do no harm and protect the sanctuary of life, police officers also need to be committed to not making the incident worse through their actions.

As past president, Ramsey has stayed active with the PERF and Director Chuck Wexler,[171] especially with issues dealing with the use of force and events that have transpired since George Floyd's in-custody police death. Leaders within the PERF are now pushing to "go upstream," which means instead of studying use of force incidents afterward, police executives should consider how the incidents could have been prevented by understanding why it occurred in the first place. If officers understood how opportunities to de-escalate the use of force were missed rather than justified, new forms of training could emerge. The following represents the examples of new training possibilities-

- Tactics matter and should be directed toward disengaging low-level confrontations and not putting officers in positions where they have to use deadly force
- De-escalation skills are critical, and officers need to be taught and allowed to step back, call for assistance, and plan different safe actions
- Respect is at the center of all conflict, and through the lessons of the late CPD Detective Paris Patton, if one is left with only their self-dignity, they will fight any threats to take it.

171 Wexler has been the Executive Director of the PERF since 1993. In February 2021, the *Washingtonian* named him as one of the most influential individuals in civil rights and criminal justice.

- Learning from use of force incidents is not second-guessing and should be done to prevent future incidents
- Increased training should be directed toward effectively policing the mentally ill through vested stakeholders that can assist with adequate housing, drug/alcohol treatment, and long-term support
- Integrated training to replicate how events unfold in real-world events
- Diversified police agencies that better represent the communities they serve

Tables 6.3–6.7 represent police leaders from Washington, DC, and Philadelphia.

Table 6.3 includes all the MPD chiefs.

Table 6.3 Washington, DC Police Chiefs

Years	*Name*
1861–1864	William Webb[i]
1864–1878	Almarin C. Richards[ii]
1878–1879	Thomas Morgan
1879–1883	William Brock
1883–1886	William Dye[iii]
1886–1886	Samuel Walker (six months)
1886–1898	William Moore[iv]
1898–1915	Richard Sylvester
1915–1920	Raymond Pullman[v]
1920–1921	Harry Gessford
1922–1925	Daniel Sullivan
1925–1929	Edwin Hesse
1929–1931	Henry Pratt
1931–1932	Pelham Glassford[vi]
1932–1941	Ernest Brown
1941–1946	Edward Kelly
1946–1947	Harvey Callahan[vii]
1947–1951	Robert Barrett[viii]
1951–1964	Robert Murray
1964–1969	John Layton
1969–1974	Jerry Wilson
1974–1978	Maurice Cullinane

i Webb was selected by President Cleveland to the prestigious position as the President of the Washington, DC Board of Commissioners, where he served from 1886 to 1889.

ii Richards was a vocal Republican and present in Ford's Theatre the night of President Lincoln's assassination.

iii Before becoming police chief, Dye was a Union War Veteran and served in the army from 1853 to 1870 and then in the Egyptian Army from 1873 to 1878. After he was police chief, he became a military advisor to the King of Korea.

iv Moore helped modernize the MPD over his 12 years as chief. In 1893, the city made over 27,000 arrests, far exceeding contemporary numbers. In July 1898, Moore died of illness while he was chief.

v Pullman created the Traffic Division and the Woman's Bureau, which became a national standard for other departments across the nation. In February 1920, Pullman died of illness while he was chief.

vi Glassford was a West Point graduate and a World War I brigadier general war veteran. He resigned as MPD chief in protest over actions taken on the Bonus Army, discussed in this chapter. He later briefly served as Phoenix Police Chief and then returned to active duty for two years during World War II.

vii Callahan died of illness while he was chief.

viii Barrett's tenure as chief was marred by corruption allegations throughout the detective bureau and bribery scandals. In 1957, Barrett was indicted for federal income tax evasion.

Table 6.3 Cont.

Years	*Name*
1978–1981	Burtell Jefferson
1981–1989	Maurice Turner
1989–1992	Issac Fulwood
1992–1995	Fred Thomas
1995–1997	Larry Soulsby
1997–1998	Sonya Proctor (interim six months)
1998–2006	**Charles Ramsey**
2007–2016	Cathy Lanier
2016–2020	Peter Newsham
2021-	Robert Contee, III

Philadelphia went from Police Marshals (1850–1855) to Chiefs (1855–1892) to Superintendents (1892–1952) to Commissioners (1952–present). These are listed in Tables 6.4–6.7, respectively.

Table 6.4 Philadelphia Police Marshalls

Years	*Names*
1850–1853	John Keyser
1853–1855	John Murphy

Table 6.5 Philadelphia Police Chiefs

Years	*Names*
1855–1867	Sam Ruggles
1867–1872	St. Clair Mulholland[i]
1872–1879	Kennard Jones
1879–1884	Samuel Given
1884–1887	James Stewart
1887–1889	James Lamon

Table 6.6 Philadelphia Superintendents

Years	*Names*
1890–1881	James Lamon[i]
1892–1899	Robert Linden[ii]
1899–1904	Harry Quirk
1904–1912	John Taylor
1912–1920	James Robinson
1920–1931	William Mills
1931–1936	Joseph LeStrange

i Mulholland was a Colonel in the Union Army during the Civil War. He also became a United States Pension Agent under Presidents Cleveland, McKinley, and Teddy Roosevelt.

i In 1890, Lamon was paid $3,000 annually.

ii Linden also worked for the Pinkerton Detective Agency (Churchill, 2004).

Table 6.6 Cont.

Years	*Names*
1936–1937	James "Shooey" Malone
1937–1940	Edward Hubbs
1941–1952	Howard Sutton[iii]

Table 6.7 Philadelphia Police Commissioners

Years	*Name*
1952–1960	Thomas Gibbons
1960–1962	Albert Brown
1962–1965	Howard Leary
1966–1967	Edward Bell
1967–1971	Frank Rizzo[i]
1971–1980	Joseph O'Neill[ii]
1980–1984	Morton Solomon[iii]
1984–1985	Gregore Sambor
1985–1986	Robert Armstrong (interim)
1986–1988	Kevin Tucker[iv]
1988–1992	Willie Williams[v]
1992–1998	Richard Neal
1998–2002	John Timoney[vi]
2002–2008	Sylvester Johnson
2008–2015	**Charles Ramsey**
2016–2019	Richard Ross, Jr.
2019–2020	Christine Coulter (interim)
2020-	Danielle Outlaw[vii]

iii Sutton helped initiate the Police Athletic League (PAL) as a nonprofit in 1947. The PAL was created to improve police relationships with children while providing them opportunities for growth.

i Rizzo was the first Italian-American Commissioner and later Mayor of Philadelphia.

ii O'Neill passed away on May 22, 2019, at 94 years of age. Allegations of police brutality during his tenure led to the first time the Department of Justice filed a federal lawsuit against a municipal department alleging that officers routinely used excessive force. O'Neill was also in charge of the first 1978 raid on MOVE occupants, discussed in this chapter. He was the first individual with a college degree to be police commissioner.

iii Solomon was the first Jewish officer to lead the PPD. He was a reformist who reduced police involved shootings. Supporters argue that if Solomon had not been replaced by Sambor, the MOVE bombing would have never occurred.

iv Tucker was a retired Secret Service agent when he came in as the first outsider since the 1920s to reform the PPD following the MOVE scandal, Sambor's resignation, and several corruption cases. Before he retired from the secret service, Tucker was assigned to protect Jacqueline Kennedy and her children following JFK's assassination. Tucker reintroduced several community policing reform strategies that included mini-police stations in high-crime neighborhoods.

v Williams was the first African-American PPD Commissioner before he became LAPD chief.

vi Timoney is also discussed in the Bratton chapter. He emigrated from Dublin, Ireland, with his family when he was in middle school. Timoney worked in the NYPD from 1967 to 1996 and became Bratton's Chief of the Department and First Deputy Commissioner. After he was chief for the PPD, he was chief in Miami from 2003 to 2010. Despite being an avid long-distance runner, Timoney died of lung cancer on August 16, 2016, at 68 years of age.

vii Outlaw was the first Black female PPD commissioner and first permanent PPD female commissioner.

References

Adams, James (2015). *Urban Reform and Sexual Vice in Progressive-Era Philadelphia: The Faithful and the Fallen*. Lanham, MD: Lexington Books.

Agronsky, Jonathan (1991). *Marion Barry: The politics of race*. Latham, NY: British American Publishing.

Ambrose, Stephen (1985). *Eisenhower volume I: Soldier, general of the army, president-elect, 1890–1952*. New York, NY: Simon and Schuster.

Asbell, Bernard. (1956). The worst mayor in America: [Paul Egan of Aurora, Ill.]. *Chicago, 3*(3): 24–29. January 1.

Augenstein, Neil (2021). 'They failed the country': Ex-DC chief cites 'double standard' in Capitol, Black Lives Matter preparedness. *wtopnews*. January 7.

Barrett, Claire (2020). The Chicago race riot of 1919: How the death of Eugene Williams shook America. *Historynet*. June 2.

Belluck, Pam (1997). Top Chicago police official will retire over disclosure. *New York Times*. November 15.

Bender, William and David Gambacorta (2019). Fired, then rehired. *The Philadelphia Inquirer*. September 12.

Berson, Lenora (1966). *Case study of a riot: The Philadelphia story*. New York, NY: Institute of Human Relations Press, American Jewish Committee.

Birger, Jon (1996). Race, reaction, and reform: The three Rs of the Philadelphia School politics, 1965–1971. *The Pennsylvania Magazine of History and Biography, 120*(3): 163–216.

Blackmon, Douglas (2008). *Slavery by another name: The re-enslavement of Black Americans from the civil war to World War II*. New York, NY: Anchor Books.

Bowden, John (2020). Iconic Washington, DC, monuments defaced in night of protests. *The Hill*. June 1.

Boyette, Michael and Randi Boyette (2013). *Let it burn: MOVE, the Philadelphia Police Department, and the confrontation that changed a city*. San Diego, CA: Endpapers Press.

Braga, Anthony, Andrew Papachristos, and David Hureau (2012). The effects of hot spots policing on crime: An updated systematic review and meta-analysis. *Justice Quarterly, 31*(4): 633–663.

Braga, Anthony and David Weisburd (2010). *Policing problem places: Crime hot spots and effective prevention*. New York, NY: Oxford University Press.

Brands, H.W. (2016). *The general vs. the president: MacArthur and Truman at the brink of the nuclear war*. New York, NY: Doubleday.

Bratton, William and Peter Knobler (1998). *Turnaround: How America's top cop reversed the crime epidemic*. New York, NY: Random House.

Brown, Lee (2012). *Policing in the 21st century: Community policing*. Bloomington, IN: AuthorHouse.

Buntin, John (2015). Charles Ramsey: The man supposed to fix America's relationship with cops. *Governing: The Future of States and Localities*. November.

Burford, Michelle and David Brown (2017). *Called to rise: A life in faithful service to the community that made me*. New York, NY: Ballantine Books.

Burrough, Bryan (2016). *Days of rage: America's radical underground, the FBI, and the forgotten age of revolutionary violence*. London, England: Penguin Books.

Castaneda, Ruben (1995). Officer wasn't in danger, witness to slaying says. *Washington Post*. May 17.

Chavez, Nicole and Christina Carrega (2020). Breonna Taylor settlement is among largest payouts to a police shooting. *CNN*. September 16.

Churchill, Ward (2004). From the Pinkertons to the PATRIOT Act. *CR: The New Centennial Review, 4*(1): 1–72.

Clancy, John (1969). Tate kills advisory board, terms action gift to police. *The Philadelphia Inquirer*. December 23.

Clark, Anna (2014). Busted is a tale of police corruption – and of a newspaper on edge: Philadelphia Daily News reporters turn Pulitzer-winning series into a book. *Columbia Journalism Review*. March 31.

Cohen, Adam and Elizabeth Taylor (2000). *American pharaoh: Mayor Richard J. Daley – His battle for Chicago and the nation*. New York, NY: Little, Brown and Company.

Coleman, Emma (2020). Federal intervention in police departments to return under Biden. *Route Fifty*. November 17.

Collins, Allyson (1998). *Shielded from justice: Police brutality and accountability in the United States*. New York, NY: Human Rights Watch.
Cook, William (2015). *Bibb Falk: The man who replaced Shoeless Joe*. Jefferson, NC: McFarland & Company, Inc. Publishers.
Corsianos, Marilyn (2009). *Policing and gendered justice: Examining the possibilities*. Toronto, Canada: University of Toronto Press.
Cournoyer, Caroline (2016). Chicago police hire Charles Ramsey to reform the system. *Governing: The Future of States and Localities*. January 25.
Crimmins, Peter (2010). How Kenney was able to remove the Rizzo statue without additional approval. *WHYY: PBS, National Public Radio*. June 10.
Crook, William (1910). *Through five administrations*. New York, NY: Harper and Brothers.
Dardick, Hal and John Byrne (2013). Mayor: 'Sorry' for Burge torture era. *Chicago Tribune*. September 11.
Davis, Benjamin, Jr. (1991). *Benjamin O. Davis, Jr.: An autobiography*. Washington, DC: Smithsonian Institution Scholarly Press.
Davis, Robert, Nicole Henderson, Janet Mandelstam, Christopher Ortiz, and Joel Miller (2005). *Federal intervention in local policing: Pittsburgh's experience with a consent decree*. U.S. Department of Justice: Office of Justice Programs.
Davis, Patricia (2000). Police pact suits D.C. suburbs. *Washington Post*. May 4.
Dean, Mensah (2017). Amid questions, officers cleared of shooting innocent deliveryman. *The Philadelphia Inquirer*. April 24.
Dickson, Paul and Thomas Allen (2003). World War I: 100 years later. *Smithsonian Magazine*. February.
Dickson, Paul and Thomas Allen (2020). *The bonus army: An American epic*. Mineola, NY: Dover Publications.
Donner, Frank (1992). *Protectors of privilege: Red squads and police repression in urban America*. Berkeley, CA: University of California Press.
Donohue, John (2017). Comey, Trump, and the puzzling pattern of crime in 2015 and beyond. *Columbia Law Review, 117*(5).
Duehren, Andrew (2020). How Washington, D.C., would become a state. *The Wall Street Journal*. June 26.
Dugan, Paul (1995). Anatomy of a sting. *Sun Sentinel*. October 22.
Dulaney, Marvin (1996). *Black police in America*. Bloomington, IN: Indiana University Press.
Dyson, Omari (2014). *The Black Panther Party and transformative pedagogy: Place-based education in Philadelphia*. New York, NY: Lexington Books.
Earl, Sari (2010). *Benjamin O. Davis Jr.: Air Force general and Tuskegee Airmen leader (military heroes)*. Edina, MN: ABDO Publishing Company.
Ederheimer, Joshua and Lorie Fridell (2005). *Chief concerns: Exploring the challenges of police use of force*. Washington, DC: Police Executive Research Forum.
Emerson, Jason (2012). *Giant in the shadows: The life of Robert T. Lincoln*. Carbondale, IL: Southern Illinois University Press.
English, T.J. (2005). *Paddy whacked: The untold story of the Irish American gangster*. New York, NY: HarperCollins Books.
Enss, Chris (2017). *The pinks: The first women detectives, operatives, and spies with the Pinkerton National Detective Agency*. Guilford, CT: TwoDot Books.
Escobar, Gabriel (1991). Washington area's 703 homicides in 1990 set a record. *The Washington Post*. January 2.
Evans, Richard Kent (2020). *MOVE: An American religion*. New York, NY: Oxford University Press.
Fachner, George and Steven Carter (2015). *An assessment of deadly force in the Philadelphia police department, collaborative reform initiative*. Washington, DC: Office of Community Oriented Policing Services. See www.phillypolice.com/assets/directives/cops-w0753-pub.pdf
Fazlollah, Mark (1996). From prison, ex-cops call offenses routine. *The Philadelphia Inquirer*. May 12.
Feinberg, Aimee (2002). Forcible medication of mentally ill criminal defendants: The case of Russell Eugene Weston, Jr. *Stanford Law Review, 54*(4): 769–791.
Fletcher, Marvin (1989). *America's first Black general: Benjamin O. Davis, Sr., 1880–1970*. Lawrence, KS: University Press of Kansas.

Flores-Robert, Vanessa (2011). *Black policemen in Jim Crow New Orleans* (Master's Thesis). New Oreans, LA: University of New Orleans.

Forman, James, Jr. (2017). *Locking up our own: Crime and punishment in Black America*. New York, NY: Farrar, Straus, and Giroux.

Fornek, Scott (2005). Coronavirus' impact on Chicago recalls the Spanish flu pandemic of 1918–19. *Chicago Sun-Times*. October 16.

Franken, Bob, Shirley Hung, and Mike Ahler (2002). Hundreds arrests at IMF protests: 'G-24' finance ministers are meeting. *CNN*. September 27.

Fyfe, James and Robert Kane (2006). *Bad cops: A study of career-ending misconduct among New York City police officers*. Washington, DC: National Institute of Justice.

Fyfe, James (1982). *Readings on Police Use of Deadly Force*. Washington, DC: Police Foundation.

Gambacorta, David (2020). Three years after a fatal police shooting in Philadelphia, glimpses of change. *The Philadelphia Inquirer*. June 8.

Gambacorta, David (2013). Philly police to adopt sweeping interrogation reforms come Jan. 1. *The Philadelphia Inquirer*. December 19.

Garza, Alicia (2020). *The purpose of power: How we come together when we fall apart*. New York, NY: Penguin Random House.

Glod, Maria (2010). D.C. agrees to $13.7 million settlement in 2000 mass arrest. *Washington Post*. July 1.

Green, James (2007). *Death in the Haymarket: A story of Chicago, the first labor movement and the bombing that divided gilded age America*. New York, NY: First Anchor Books.

Grimes, S. (1971). Foot patrolmen losing out to red cars. Philadelphia, PA: *Philadelphia Bulletin*. Feburary 4.

Groff, Lizz, Jerry Ratcliffe, Cory Haberman, Evan Sorg, Nola Joyce, and Ralph Taylor (2015). Does what police do at hot spots matter? Philadelphia policing tactics experiment. *Criminology, 53*(1): 23–53.

Golding, Bruce (2018). Unindicted co-conspirators named in the NYPD corruption case. *New York Post*. April 29.

Goldstein, Herman (1979). Improving policing: A problem-oriented approach. *Crime & Delinquency, 25*(2): 236–258.

Goldstein, Herman (1990). *Problem-oriented policing*. Philadelphia, PA: Temple University Press.

Gossett, Thomas (1997). *Race: The history of an idea in America*. New York, NY: Oxford University Press.

Haas, Jeffery (2011). *The assassination of Fred Hampton: How the FBI and the Chicago police murdered a Black Panther*. Chicago, IL: Chicago Review Press.

Haberman, Cory (2016). *COPS on dots doing what? The differential effects of police enforcement actions in hot spots* (PhD Dissertation). Philadelphia, PA: Temple University.

Hadden, Sally (2001). *Slave patrols: Law and violence in Virginia and the Carolinas*. Cambridge, MA: Harvard University Press.

Hagedorn, John, Bart Kmiecik, Dick Simpson, Thomas Gradel, Melissa Zmuda, David Sterrett, Ivana Savic, Justin Escamilla, Magdalena Waluszko, Dalibor Jurisic, Tricia Chebat (2013). Crime, Corruption, and Cover-ups in the Chicago Police Department. Chicago, IL: University of Illinois at Chicago Department of Political Science. Anti-corruption Report 7. See- https://pols.uic.edu/wp-content/uploads/sites/273/2018/10/ac_policecorruptionb6e6.pdf

Haller, Mark (1985). Philadelphia bootlegging and the report of the special August grand jury. *Pennsylvania Magazine of History and Biography, 109*(2): 215–233.

Hamm, Leonard (2019). *The Hamm rules on relationships, leadership, community, and love*. Pittsburgh, PA: Dorrance Publishing Company.

Hansen, Drew (2018). Then and now: D.C.'s riot-ravaged blocks 50 years later. *Washington Business Journal*. March 30.

Hattaway, Herman and Richard Beringer (2002). *Jefferson Davis, Confederate President*. Lawrence, KS: University Press of Kansas.

Harrison, Carter (1944). *Growing up with Chicago*. Chicago, IL: Ralph Fletcher Seymour Publishers.

Harriston, Keith and Mary Flaherty (1994). D.C. police paying for hiring binge. *Washington Post*. August 28.

Helmer, William and Arthur Bilek (2006). *The St. Valentine's Day Massacre: The untold story of the gangland bloodbath that brought down Al Capone*. Nashville, TN: Cumberland House.

Higham, Scott and Sari Horwitz (2010). *Finding Chandra: A true Washington murder mystery*. New York, NY: Scribner.
Hillard, Terry and Thomas Jurkanin (2006). *Chicago police: An inside view: The story of superintendent Terry G. Hillard*. Springfield, IL: Thomas Publisher.
Hogan, John (2014). *The 1937 Chicago steel strike: Blood on the Prairie*. Mount Pleasant, SC: The History Press, Arcadia Publishing.
Hollandsworth, James, Jr. (2001). *The New Orleans race riot of July 30, 1866*. Baton Rouge, LA: Louisiana State University Press.
Holmes, Robert (Ed.). (2020). *A mayor for all the people: Kenneth Gibson's Newark (1970–1986)*. Newark, NJ: Rutgers University Press.
Hsu, Spencer (2016). U.S., District settle in last mass-arrest lawsuit in 2002 World Bank protests. *Washington Post*. April 13.
Hutchinson, Robert (2020). *The Lincoln assassination: What really happened*. Washington, DC: Regnery Publishing.
Jackson, David (1998). Holes in the files: Investigations of police shootings often leave questions unanswered. *Washington Post*. November 17.
Jaffe, Harry (2016). DC's police force may soon be majority white. *Washingtonian*. May 26.
Janson, Donald (1970). Policeman slain, 3 shot, in Philadelphia. *The New York Times*. August 31.
Jeffrey, Jeff (2018). Fighting crime pays: The best-paid police chiefs in America. *The Business Journals*. November 27.
Jenson, Bill (2015). The insane story of the guy who killed the guy who killed Lincoln. *Washingtonian*. July 12.
Johnson, John (1973). Newark council oks black police director. *Jet: A Johnson Publication*. Volume XLIV, No. 18: July 26.
Jost, Kenneth (1996). Governing Washington, DC. *CQ Researcher, 6*(44): 8.
Joyce, Nola (2007). *Can you lead me now? Leading in the complex world of homeland security* (Master's Thesis). Monterey, CA: Naval Postgraduate School.
Joyce, Nola, Charles Ramsey, and James Stewart (2013)Commentary on smart policing. *Police Quarterly, 16*(3): 358–368.
Keefe, Rose (2003). *Guns and roses: The untold story of Dean O'Banion, Chicago's big shot before Al Capone*. Toronto, Canada: Cumberland House Publishing.
Kephart, William (1954). The integration of Negroes into the urban police force. *Journal of Criminal Law and Criminology, 45*(3): 325–333.
Kephart, William (1957). *Racial factors and urban law enforcement*. Philadelphia, PA: University of Pennsylvania Press.
Khan-Cullors, Patrisse and Asha Bandele (2017). *When they call you a terrorist: A black lives matter memoir*. New York, NY: St. Martins Publishing Group.
Kingsbury, Robert (2002). *The assassination of James A. Garfield*. New York, NY: Rosen Publishing Group.
Krinitsky, Nora (2017). *The politics of crime control: Race, policing, and reform in Twentieth-Century Chicago* (PhD Dissertation). Ann Arbor, MI: University of Michigan.
Klein, Allison and David Nadamura (2006). Chief Ramsey to step down, sources say. *Washington Post*. November 18.
Kleiner, Art (2004). *Booz Allen Hamilton: Helping clients envision the future*. Greenwich, CT: Greenwich Publishing Group.
Klerks, Cat (2006). *Johnny Torrio: Mastermind of the Chicago underworld*. Toronto, Canada: Altitude Publishing.
Kramer, Michael (1997). How cops go bad. *Time*. December 15.
Krugler, David (2014). *1919, the year of racial violence: How African Americans fought back*. New York, NY: Cambridge University Press.
Lamon, Ward Hill (1994). *Recollections of Abraham Lincoln: 1847–1865*. Lincoln, NE: The University of Nebraska Press.
La Vigne, Nancy, Pamela Lachman, Shebani Rao, and Andrea Matthews (2014). *Stop and frisk: Balancing crime control with community relations*. Washington, DC: Office of Community Oriented Policing Services.

Leary, Howard (1965). Role of the police in riotous demonstrations. *Notre Dame Law Review, 40*(5): 499–507.
Leen, Jeff (1998). Moving targets: Despite department rules, officers often have used gunfire to stop drivers. *Washington Post.* November 16.
Leen, Jeff and Sari Horwitz (1998). Armed and unready: City pays for failure to train officers with sophisticated weapon. *Washington Post.* November 18.
Leen, Jeff, Jo Craven, David Jackson, and Sari Horwitz (1998). District police lead nation in shootings: Lack of training, supervision implicated as key factors. *Washington Post.* November 15.
Lehr, Dick (2015). The racist legacy of Woodrow Wilson. *The Atlantic.* November 27.
Lemire, Jonathan and Zeke Miller (2020). Trump took shelter in White House bunker as protests raged. *U.S. News & World Report.* June 1.
Lengel, Allan (2003). After 6 years of doubt, a nod of vindication. *Washington Post.* October 20.
Lindberg, Richard (1991). *To serve and collect: Chicago politics and police corruption from the Lager Beer riot to the Summerdale scandal.* New York, NY: Praeger.
Locy, Tony (1998). Luxury unit allegedly for Soulsby: Former police chief's friend enters guilty pleas. *Washington Post.* January 27.
Long, Michael and Chris Lamb (2017). *Jackie Robinson: A spiritual biography: The faith of a boundary-breaking hero.* Louisville, KY: Westminster John Knox Press.
Lubold, Gordon and Nancy Youssef (2020). Top General apologizes for being at Trump church photo shoot: 'My presence in that moment and in that environment created a perception of the military involved in domestic politics'. *The Wall Street Journal.* June 11.
Lundman, Robert (1980). *Police and policing: An introduction.* New York, NY: Holt, Rinehart and Winston.
Marimow, William (2009). Part 1: Roughing up Philadelphia: The police K-9 cases. The *Philadelphia Inquirer.* June 4.
Martin, Paul (2010). The assassination of Abraham Lincoln: Lincoln's missing bodyguard. *Smithsonian Magazine.* April 7.
Matthews, Dylan (2015). Woodrow Wilson was extremely racist- even by the standards of his time. *VOX.* November 20.
McCaffery, Peter (1993). *When bosses ruled Philadelphia.* University Park, PA: Pennsylvania State University Press.McCrone, Brian (2014). Police commissioner Ramsey's son joins department ranks. *Philly.com.* June 5.
McDougall, Christopher (1997). Law and disorder. *Philadelphia Weekly.* (June 18).
McNally, Susan (1986). Bring back police cadet program. *Chicago Tribune.* August 17.
McQuirter, Marya (2003). *African-American heritage trail.* Washington, DC: Cultural Tourism DC.
Michaeli, Ethan (2016). *The defender: How the legendary black newspaper changed America.* Geneva, IL: Houghton Mifflin Harcourt Publishers.
Millard, Candice (2012). *Destiny of the republic: A tale of madness, medicine, and the murder of a president.* New York, NY: First Anchor Books.
Miller, Bill (1995). Jury rejects suit in police shooting. *Washington Post.* May 19.
Miller, Bill (1999). D.C. to pay $750,000 to man shot while fleeing police. *Washington Post.* April 21.
Milton, Catherine, Jeanne Wahl, James Lardner, and Gary Abrecht (1977). *Police use of force.* Washington, DC: Police Foundation.
Mitchell, Zoe (2005). D.C. settles with Pershing Park protesters. *Dcist.* January 24.
Mitrani, Sam (2013). *The rise of the Chicago police department: Class and conflict, 1850–1894.* Urbana, IL: University of Illinois Press.
Moose, Charles and Charles Fleming (2004). *Three weeks in October: The manhunt for the serial sniper.* New York, NY: New American Library.
Morrison, Gregory and Bryan Vila (1998). Police handgun qualification: Practical measure or aimless activity. *Policing: An International Journal of Police Strategies & Management, 21*(3): 510–533.
Myrsiades, Linda (2008). Grand juries, legal machines, and the common man jury. *College Literature, 35*(3): 158–178.
Neal, Anthony (2016). Sergeant Horatio J. Homer: Boston's first black police officer. *The Bay State Banner.* February 4.

Neumann, Jonathan and William Marimow (2009). Beatings by police 'widespread' in city, study finds. *The Philadelphia Inquirer.* May 28.

Newall, Mike and Aubrey Whelan (2014). No criminal charges for four Philly officers in 'Tainted Justice' cases. *The Philadelphia Inquirer.* April 24.

Ng, Christina (2012). Detroit police chief suspended amid six scandal allegation: This is the second time Godbee has been linked to a sex scandal in two-year tenure. *ABC News.* October 3.

Nichols, Jeff (2020). The maverick at the center of Chicago's 1918 flu response. *Reader: City Life.* May 12.

Norward, Lindsey (2019). The day Philadelphia bombed its own people: A oral history of a 1985 police bombing that changed the city forever. *VOX.* August 15.

Nutter, Michael (2018). *Mayor: The best job in politics.* Philadelphia, PA: University of Pennsylvania Press.

Nystrom, Justin (2010). *New Orleans after the civil war: Race, politics, and a new birth of freedom.* Baltimore, MD: John Hopkins University Press.

Oppel, Richard Jr., and Kim Barker (2020). New transcript detail last moments for George Floyd. *New York Times.* July 18.

Ormond, Mary (2019). Paul Egan, unvarnished: "A bunch of lousy gangsters." *That was Paul Egan's view of politicians. How he became.* Aurora, IL: Aurora Historical Society.

O'Toole, Patricia (2018). *Woodrow Wilson and the world he made.* New York, NY: Simon & Schuster.

Palmer, Chris (2017). Philly officer who fatally shot fleeing man in back will be fired. *The Philadelphia Inquirer.* September 7.

Paolantonio, Sal (1993). *Frank Rizzo: The last big man in big city America.* Philadelphia, PA: Camino Books.

Patton, Carl (1997). *Big Ralph: Reflections of a Black police chief.* Blue Ridge Summit, PA: Psyche Books.

Peace, Brenton and Gary Condit (2016). *Actual malice: A true crime political thriller.* Los Angeles, CA: Ghost Mountain Books.

Pearlstein, Rick (2010). *Nixonland: The rise of a president and the fracturing of America.* New York, NY: Scribner.

Peck, Garrett (2011). *Prohibition in Washington, D.C.: How dry we weren't.* Charlestown, SC: The History Press.

Pennsylvania Crime Commission (1974). *Report on police corruption and the quality of law enforcement in Philadelphia.* Saint Davids, PA: Commonwealth of Pennsylvania, Office of Attorney General. Available from www.ncjrs.gov/pdffiles1/Digitization/17888NCJRS.pdf

Pietsch, Bryan (2020). Princeton will remove Woodrow Wilson's name from school. *New York Times.* June 27.

Pizzi, Jenna (2016). Wilmington hires ex-Philly top cop as public safety consultant. *Delaware Online-The News Journal.* January 11.

Police Foundation (1981). *The Newark foot patrol experiment.* Washington, D.C.: Police Foundation.

Powell, Michael (1997). D.C. police changes should start at top, specialists say. *Washington Post.* October 21.

Pratt, Sharon (2011). Lessons from a D.C. riot. *Washington Post.* August 12.

Price, Debbie (1989). 'Murder Capital' label has long stalked D.C. *Washington Post.* April 4.

Radeska, Tijana (2017). Famous lawyer Clarence Darrow, opposed to the death penalty, lost only one client to execution. *The Vintage News.* July 30.

Ramsey, Charles, Ronald Davis, Roberto Villasenor, and Sean Smoot (2020). There is a playbook for police reform: We helped write it. *New York Times.* June 4.

Ramsey, John (2012). *The other side of suffering: The father of JonBenet Ramsey tells the story of his journey from grief to grace.* New York, NY: Hachette Book Group.

Rasmussen, Daniel (2012). *American uprising: The untold story of America's largest slave revolt.* New York, NY: HarperCollins Publishers.

Ratcliffe, Jerry, Elizabeth Groff, Evan Sorg, and Cory Haberman (2015). Citizens' reactions to hot spots policing: Impact on perceptions of crime, disorder, safety and police. *Journal of Experimental Criminology, 11*: 393–417.

Ratcliffe, Jerry, Travis Taniguchi, Elizabeth Groff, and Jennifer Wood (2011). The Philadelphia foot patrol experiment: A randomized controlled trial of police patrol effectiveness in violent hotspot. *Criminology, 49*(3): 795–831.

Ratcliffe, Jerry (2019) *Reducing crime: A companion for police leaders.* New York, NY: Routledge.
Ratcliffe, Jerry and Evan Sorg (2017) *Foot patrol: Rethinking the cornerstone of policing.* New York, NY: Springer Publishing.
Ratcliffe, Jerry (2016) *Intelligence-led policing* (2nd ed.). London, UK: Routledge.
Reaves, James (1991). *Black cops.* Philadelphia, PA: Quantum Leap Publishers.
Reaves, Brian (2011). Census of state and local law enforcement agencies, 2008. Washington, DC: US Department of Justice, Office of Justice Programs, Bureau of Justice Statistics.
Rendell, Ed (2012). *A nation of wusses: How America's leaders lost the guts to make us great.* DeKalb, IL: John Wiley & Sons.
Roberts, Rebecca Boggs (2017). *Suffragists in Washington, DC: The 1913 parade and the fight for the vote.* Charlestown, SC: The History Press.
Robertson, John Dill and Gottfried Koehler (1918). Preliminary report on the influenza epidemic in Chicago. *The American Journal of Public Health, 8*(11): 848–856.
Robin, Gerald (1963). Justifiable homicide by police officers. *Journal of Criminal Law and Criminology, 54*(2): 225–231.
Robinson, Laurie (2020). Five years after Ferguson: Reflecting on police reform and what's ahead. *The Annals of the American Academy of Political and Social Science, 687*(1): 228–239.
Root, Douglas (1994). Blood relations. *Washington Post.* June 5.
Rosenberg-Douglas, Katherine, Jeremy Gorner, Jovonte Anderson, and Gregory Pratt (2020). Police say attacks on officers in Grant Park protest appeared organized as more than 20 complaints filed against cops. *Chicago Tribune.* July 20.
Rosenfeld, Richard (2016). *Documenting and explaining the 2015 homicide rise: Research directions.* Washington, DC: National Institute of Justice.
Rosenwald, Michael (2018). The police officer who arrested a US President – could it happen again? *The Sydney Morning Herald.* December 16.
Rousey, Dennis (1987). Black policemen in New Orleans during Reconstruction. *The Historian, 49*(2): 223–243.
Rubinstein, Jonathan (1973). *City police.* New York, NY: Farrar, Straus, and Giroux.
Ruderman, Wendy and Barbara Laker (2014). *Busted: A tale of corruption and betrayal in the city of brotherly love.* New York, NY: HarperCollins Publishers.
Runcie, John (1972). Hunting the Nigs' in Philadelphia: The race riot of August, 1834. *Pennsylvania History, 39*(2): 187–218.
Ruthhart, Bill (2018). Rahm Emanuel made $554K last year, his highest income as mayor. *Chicago Tribune.* December 24.
Ryan, George and Maurice Possley (2020). *Until I could be sure: How I stopped the death penalty in Illinois.* Lanham, MD: Rowman & Littlefield Publishers.
Sandburg, Carl, Paul Buhle, and Walter Lippmann (2013). *The Chicago race riots: July, 1919.* New York, NY: Dover Publications.
Saint, Dain, Craig McCoy, Tommy Rowan, and Valerie Russ (2020). Black and blue. *The Philadelphia Inquirer.* July 15.
Sampson, Robert (1993). Governor John Peter Altgeld pardons the Haymarket prisoners. *Illinois Times.* July 22–28.
Santana, Arthur (2003). Ex-D.C. officer gets 23 months for extortion, theft, fraud. *Washington Post.* October 25.
Schiller, Lawrence (1999). *Perfect murder, perfect town: The uncensored story of the JonBenet murder and the grand jury's search for the final truth.* New York, NY: HarperCollins Publisher.
Schroedter, Andrew (2014). Beyond Burge. *Better Government Association.* April 3.
Shaw, Colt (2018). MOVE members say 1985 bomb gave Ramona Africa cancer. *Philadelphia City Life.* August 23.
Sherman, Lawrence and David Weisburd (1995). General deterrent effects of police patrol in crime "hot-spots": A randomized controlled trial. *Justice Quarterly, 12*(4): 625–648.
Short, John (1977). The Philadelphia connection. *Marine Corps Gazette* (Vol. 61–62). November.
Simon, John (1975). *Memoirs of Julia Dent Grant.* Carbondale, IL: Southern Illinois University Press.

Sjostrom, Joseph (1989). Killer of Aurora minister is sentenced to life term. *Chicago Tribune.* September 6.

Skogan, Wesley, Susan Hartnett, Jill DuBois, Jennifer Comey, Karla Twedt-Ball, and Erik Gudell (2000). *Public involvement: Community policing in Chicago.* Washington, DC: Institute for Policy Research, National Institute of Justice.

Skolnick, Jerome and James Fyfe (2010). *Above the law: Police and the excessive use of force.* Glencoe, IL: Free Press.

Speare-Cole, Rebecca (2021). 134 police officers assaulted in Capitol riots, Justice Department says. *Newsweek.* January 25.

Spielman, Fran (2016). Ramsey bows out as paid adviser to Chicago Police Department. *Chicago Sun-Times.* April 22.

Steinberg, Allen (1989). *The Transformation of Criminal Justice: Philadelphia, 1800-1880.* Chapel Hill, NC: The University of North Carolina Press.

Stern, Bennett L.C. (2016). *Bosses and blackjacks: A tale of the bloody fifth in Philadelphia.* Scotts Valley, CA: CreateSpace Independent Publishing.

Struck, Doug and Michael Powell (1997). Soulsby brought himself down. *Washington Post.* November 26.

Tan, Rebecca, Michael Mill, Rachel Chason, Samantha Schmidt, and Teddy Amenabar (2020). Protesters paint 'Defund the police' right next to D.C.'s 'Black Lives Matter' mural. *Washington Post.* June 7.

Taylor, Ralph (1997). Order and disorder of streetblocks and neighborhoods: Ecology, microecology and the systematic model of social organization. *Journal of Research in Crime and Delinquency, 34*(1): 113–155.

Taylor, Ralph (2010). Hot spots do not exist, and four other fundamental concerns about hot spot policing. In N. Frost, D. Freilich, & T. Clear (Eds.), *Contemporary issues in criminal justice policy* (pp. 271–278). Belmont, CA: Wadsworth, Cengage Learning.

Thompson, Anna (1926). A survey of crime among Negroes in Philadelphia. *Opportunity, 4*: 217–286.

Thompson, Cheryl (1997). Detailing failings on D.C. police department. *Washington Post.* April 9.

Thrasher, Frederic (1927). *The gang.* Chicago, IL: University of Chicago Press.

Tuccille, Jerome (2018). *The war against the Vets: The World War I bonus army during the great depression.* Lincoln, NE: Potomac Books.

Ullman, Victor and Martin Delany (1971). *The beginnings of Black nationalism.* Boston, MA: Beacon Press.

Vargas, Claudia (2020). 'It's because I'm Black': Rejected police recruits say system is racist. *nbc10 Investigates.* August 6.

Vickers, George (2019). *The fall of bossism.* Sacramento, CA: Creative Media Partners, LLC.

Walker, J. Samuel (2018). *Most of 14th Street is gone: The Washington, DC riots of 1968.* New York, NY: Oxford University Press.

Wecht, Cyril and Charles Bosworth, Jr. (2016). *Who killed JonBenet Ramsey?* New York, NY: Graymalkin.

Wendt, Lloyd and Herman Kogan (2005). *Big Bill of Chicago.* Evanston, IL: Northwestern University Press.

Whelan, Aubrey and Mike Newall (2014). Fired narcotics officer to return to force. *The Philadelphia Inquirer.* November 20.

Wilbanks, William (2000). *True heroines: Police women killed in the line of duty throughout the United States from 1916–1999.* Paducah, KT: Turner Publishing Company.

Williams, Damon (2012). After 34 years, MOVE 9 still in prison. *Philadelphia Tribune.* August 12.

Williams, Brian and J. Edward Kellough (2006). Leadership with an enduring impact: The legacy of Chief Burtell Jefferson of the Metropolitan Police Department of Washington, D.C. *Public Administration Review 66*(6): 813–822.

Williams, Willie and Bruce Henderson (1996). *Take back our streets: Fighting crime in America.* New York, NY: Scribner Book Company.

Wilson, Reid (2020). Philadelphia removes statue of ex-mayor seen as 'deplorable monument to racism, bigotry, and police brutality. *The Hill.* June 3.

Wilson, Terry (2000). Promotions give new face to police brass. *Chicago Tribune*. June 24.
Wood, Sam (2013). Exclusive: Shooting by Philly police soar as violent crime plummets. *Philadelphia Inquirer*. May 14.
Wooley, Wayne (1995). For one heroic police office, the 1985 siege still sears his thoughts. *Los Angeles Times*. June 4.
Wu, Nicholas (2020). 'Black lives matter' painted in 50-foot yellow letters near White House to honor George Floyd protesters. *USA Today*. June 5.
York, Michael and Ruben Castaneda (1993). 12 on D.C. force arrested in corruption probe. *Washington Post*. December 15.

Chapter 7

Chris Magnus – Chief of Fargo, Richmond, California, and Tucson, Arizona

The Authentic Community Policing Chief

Christopher Jens Magnus was born on October 26, 1960, in Easton, Pennsylvania, but raised in Lansing, Michigan. He is the youngest of four children, with two older sisters, Beth Magnus and Carol Cole, and an older brother, Gerhard Magnus. His father, Gerhard, was an Art History professor at Michigan State University (MSU) and his mother, Louise, was a piano teacher. Magnus did not have any family involved in policing, but he was self-motivated to be engaged in community organizing. In 1976, at the age of 15, he worked with peers to set up a statewide youth-led juvenile justice advocacy organization called the Three O'clock Lobby while attending East Lansing High School (McKenzie, 2017). The Michigan advocacy group evolved from the Office of Juvenile Justice Services (OJJS). In January 1977, Magnus became the director and incorporated the Three O'clock Lobby. The group ran a toll-free telephone line to help youth with questions about their rights and further assisted with referrals. By 1979, the group folded due to a lack of funding (New Designs for Youth Development, 1980).

Magnus's community organizing advocacy grew out of his admiration for Cesar Chavez[1] and the United Farm Workers (UFW) (see Bardacke, 2012). This early reflection on Chavez's tenacity helped Magnus survive future challenges directed toward his police leadership. He became involved in organizing primary and secondary boycotts of grapes, lettuce, and Gallo wine as part of a protest. As a result, his family had a brick thrown through the window of their home. They suspected that it came from an employee of a store that picketers targeted.[2]

Lansing, Michigan Police Department

Magnus began his career in policing in 1979 as a dispatcher for the Lansing Police Department (LPD). He graduated with an Associate's Degree in business and received his paramedic training through Lansing Community College. This background led Magnus to employment as an EMS provider working on an ambulance and in the emergency room at Hayes Green Beach Hospital in Charlotte, Michigan. Upon completing the Mid-Michigan Police Academy at Lansing Community College, he worked two part-time police jobs, one with the Ingham County Sheriff's Department as a seasonal parks police deputy, and the other with the Vermontville Township Police Department. The Livingston County Sheriff's Department also hired him as a deputy sheriff.

1 Chavez was born in 1927 and died at the age of 66. He was an American labor leader and civil rights activist for Latino Americans, and he co-founded the National Farm Workers Association, later renamed the United Farm Workers (UFW) union.

2 Author's interview with Magnus on March 28, 2020.

DOI: 10.4324/9780429272226-8

In 1985, Magnus was hired back to the LPD as a patrol officer while he finished his bachelor's degree in criminal justice from MSU, where he graduated in 1986. Magnus was an LPD officer during the 1980s crack epidemic and described his work as "incredibly backwards and exactly the kind of policing that people are pissed about today" (Chaffin, 2020). Magnus credited professors and criminal justice coursework from MSU for his evolved thinking. Over the next 15 years, he rose to captain's rank in Administrative Services with the LPD. During this period, Magnus returned to MSU and completed his master's degree in Labor and Industrial relations in 1990.

Magnus returned to MSU during the leadership of Professor Robert "Bob" Trojanowicz,[3] who provided academic support for community-oriented policing (COP) through the School of Criminal Justice. Trojanowicz described COP as a philosophy of full-service, personalized policing. This philosophy seeks to decentralize police strategy and give officers permanent beat assignments with expectations that they work proactively with citizens to identify and solve problems (see Trojanowicz & Carter, 1988). Community policing became fundamental in Magnus's future reform efforts.

As a police captain, Magnus worked with professors from the MSU School of Criminal Justice to improve police traffic encounters. In March 1999, the LPD mailed surveys to citizens who received a traffic citation to determine officers' professionalism. The survey also served as a pretest baseline to measure future surveys. After Magnus left the department to become the Fargo Police Department chief, Chief Mark Alley took the research a step further. He hired Professor David Carter and Andra Katz-Bannister as consultants to assist the LPD in addressing racial profiling concerns. Researchers and the police conducted focus groups and community meetings, which led to new data collection forms that tracked demographic information on all traffic stops. The newly acquired demographic data evolved into an early warning system that assisted police supervisors in targeted training directed toward officers who may inappropriately be engaging in racial profiling (Reisig, 2001).

Leadership Is Dangerous

In 1999, Magnus left Michigan to become the chief of the Fargo, North Dakota Police Department. He successfully facilitated the country's first two-state shared dispatch service and a refugee liaison program. In 2006, Magnus became the chief of the Richmond, California Police Department and vastly improved police-community relations at a time of dramatic declines in murders and violent crime. He also advocated against police misuse of force. In 2015, he became the chief in Tucson, Arizona, and led the department through a significant budget shortfall and community policing policies that challenged federal immigration views.

Leadership is dangerous (Heifetz & Linsky, 2017), and as a change agent, Chief Magnus faced his share of leadership danger. Change agents provide transformational leadership through guidance and support for stakeholders to the change. In the world of police leadership, internal and external changes impact both the police and the community they serve. Moreover, change agents serve as a liaison between police leadership and those who sponsor the change. For example, in Richmond, the direct sponsors of Magnus's change were the city manager and the city council and, indirectly, young male minorities who were frequent victims and offenders of violent crime. Magnus represents change agents who consistently explain why change is taking place, advocates for the change, disseminates information, anticipates disruptions, develops strategies to counteract disputes, pushes for improved analysis,

3 Trojanowicz was a leading academic researcher who influenced community policing. On February 11, 1994, he passed away from a heart attack at the age of 52, but community policing advocates continued his work.

and encourages innovative responses that evolve from improved analysis (Heifetz & Linsky, 2017). Change agent leaders are not timid about assessing their initiatives' effectiveness to measure if their police agency has become more efficient in crime reduction without compromising police legitimacy. Magnus demonstrates authentic leadership to assess police legitimacy through open and frequent dialogue with the communities he serves.

Leaders become dangerous when they question conventional values, beliefs, and organizational habits. Magnus demonstrated leadership that challenged the professionalization models that Roosevelt and Wilson advocated through the reform eras. He also understood the perversion of broken windows policing that left out the community when the strategy was morphed into zero-tolerance policing. Police leaders in the twenty-first century face many perils related to adaptive change. These changes are not amenable to authoritative expertise or standard operating procedures (Heifetz & Linskey, 2017) that historically defined police professionalization. Magnus is a contemporary police reform leader because he challenged misuse of force during the initial Black Lives Matter movement and did so in a way that many criticized as going beyond his authority. Magnus's dramatic stand with the Black Lives Matter movement (in part by holding a sign at a peaceful protest in Richmond that stated "Black Lives Matter") came in the wake of a six-year civil lawsuit, ultimately resolved in his favor. That lawsuit came from a group of Black commanders in the Richmond Police Department who alleged that he created discriminatory promotional practices and a racially hostile work environment. These events are described in detail later in the chapter (Photo 7.1).

Leadership requires disturbing people with a rate they can absorb (Heifetz & Linsky, 2017). Magnus disrupted departmental and community views on immigrants during his leadership in Fargo and Tucson. His challenge was to avoid the marginalization of immigrants and to

Photo 7.1 On December 9, 2014, Chris Magnus stood in solidarity with demonstrators along Macdonald Avenue in Richmond, California, to protest Michael Brown and Eric Garner deaths.

Photo credit AP/Bay Area News Group, Kristopher Skinner.

create local connections, regardless of their citizenship status, as a way to police more effectively. This type of leadership was described in the chapter under O.W. Wilson when, as the Superintendent of the Chicago Police Department, he ordered his officers to protect civil rights protesters engaged in civil disobedience. Magnus provided the same leadership when it came to policing concentrated minority neighborhoods that had experienced high rates of violence. Because of his successful leadership with immigrants and improving minority relations, President Obama's Task Force on 21st Century Policing requested his testimony. Additionally, a Senate committee during the Trump Administration invited his testimony on border security and transnational drug cartels. His leadership challenges, lessons, and successes are detailed below.

Fargo, North Dakota (Chief 1999–2005)

Magnus became the 29th chief of Fargo, North Dakota, in 1999 and served through 2005. Fargo was Magnus's first experience as a police chief. In Fargo, he facilitated the nation's first two-state regional dispatch system, a forensic children's interview center, and a refugee liaison program.

Brief History of Fargo Law Enforcement

Fargo was founded in 1871 and developed along the westward railroad lines. The city was named after William G. Fargo, the Northern Pacific Railroad director and co-founder of the Wells Fargo Express Company (Holzkamm, 2001). John E. Haggart was elected the sheriff of Cass County in 1874 and became the Fargo Town Marshal in April 1875, following the incorporation of the 600-resident city in January 1875. In 1881, George Holes became the first police chief with one sergeant and eight patrol officers. In 1875, the city rented a jail for $15 per month, and by 1876 they built a wood plank jail. In 1881, the town required day-shift officers to ensure that street lamps had enough oil and night-shift officers to light and extinguish them. In 1882, officers received uniforms and provided the chief $100 a month, while patrolmen earned $75 monthly.

In 1890, North Dakota Agriculture College, which became North Dakota State University in 1960, was founded through the first appropriation senate bill introduced into the North Dakota State Legislature. Senator Haggart,[4] Fargo's first law enforcement official and the state's first senator, introduced Senate bill #1 to appropriate the college. The governor approved the bill on March 8, 1890. On January 3, 1892, the first term began with 123 students enrolled. In 1898, Martin Flanigan became Fargo's first detective, and approximately ten officers were issued bicycles for patrol and assistance with traffic. In 1913, Erma Irwin was hired as the first policewoman, a few years after Los Angeles hired Alice Wells. In 1915, the city purchased squad cars for officer patrol.

Regional Dispatch

Because of Magnus's early career in law enforcement as an emergency dispatcher and EMS, he recognized the need for effective dispatch services. In 2001, as a chief, he helped initiate a Joint

4 Haggart was elected to the state's first senate in 1889 and served for a decade before he resigned to take a position as a deputy with the U.S. Marshals Service. He died in 1905 at 59 years of age while he was a U.S. Marshal (North Dakota State University archives). See https://library.ndsu.edu/fargo-history/

Powers Agreement between Cass County in North Dakota and Clay County in Minnesota. These counties cover the city of Fargo and the city of Moorhead, respectively. Fargo created the Red River Regional Dispatch Center as the first in the nation to cross state lines to jointly manage dispatch operations for police, fire, and medical response. The shared dispatch between the two counties in North Dakota and Minnesota services were about 210,000 residents.

Refugee Liaison Program

While Magnus was the chief in Fargo, the city, like many communities around the country, experienced an influx of refugees. Since 1997, there have been approximately 4,000 refugees in Fargo, mainly from Bosnia, Liberia, Iraq, and Bhutan. The city also serves a diverse population of Native Americans. Unique challenges occur when the children are quickly assimilated into the school system and supported with English as a second language (ESL) programs while the parents are left behind. Frequently, the parents work odd jobs as cleaners or laborers and are not able to learn a new language confidently. The harsh winters in Fargo further isolate families that are less likely to have vehicles than the general population. It became critical for law enforcement to connect with refugee families to create familiarity and explain police resources. Often, the police connected with second-generation children who had better language skills. These connections allowed the police to counter the public perception that refugees were harmful to the city economy, engaged in more crime than the general population, and created a tax burden for Fargo residents.

The cost of accepting refugees is an ongoing concern for many cities, and the need to assess those costs is critical (see Blau & Mackie, 2017). The Fargo City Commission initiated the Human Relations Commission to study the costs and benefits of refugee resettlement in Fargo. Although these efforts occurred after Magnus left to become the chief in Richmond, California, the assessment nevertheless provides insight for police and other community leaders to decide if they should support refugee liaison programs. In 2014, the working group determined that foreign-born residents contributed approximately $543 million to the city's GDP, far outpacing resettlement costs. The National Academies of Science backed this finding and demonstrated how accepting first-generation refugees provided fiscally positive results for North Dakota. National data has further determined that second- and third-generation immigrants provided a return on investment (ROI), while first-generation incurred a cost. The uniqueness of North Dakota first-generation immigrants, estimated at a favorable cost of approximately $3,250 a person, is one of the highest in the country (National Academies of Sciences, 2016).

Fargo's creation of a police liaison program to initiate meetings with new refugees was a critical step within its community policing philosophy under Magnus. The program worked with social service providers to ensure that basic needs are met and educated refugees on proper police interaction. Fargo officers also educated refugees on how American laws define domestic violence and state laws defined alcohol use, age of sexual consent, and driving privileges. Noting that many of these new residents are fearful of the police, these contacts are critical for formulating effective social control mechanisms.

Research indicated that immigrants were beneficial to the economy and police outreach to new immigrants became critical for inclusion. Despite this research, Burleigh County, which includes the capital city Bismark, held a vote to ban refugees in December 2019. They became the first county to do so on the heels of President Trump's September 2019 executive order requiring states and local governments to provide written consent before resettling refugees. Ultimately, residents overwhelmed the Burleigh County Commission chambers and pressured the commission to keep welcoming refugees.

Police Scandals – Los Angeles, Oakland, Richmond

At the turn of the twenty-first century, the Los Angeles Police Department (LAPD), Oakland Police Department (OPD), and Richmond Police Department (RPD) were all involved in numerous scandals that led to leadership changes and various external oversights.

Los Angeles Police Department (LAPD)

The LAPD was under a consent decree in 2000 in the aftermath of the Rampart Scandal. Rick Caruso,[5] President of the Police Commission, recommended the replacement of Chief Bernard Parks. Bill Bratton was hired as a consultant to assist in making recommendations to fulfill the consent decree. By 2002, he was brought in as the chief to complete the recommendations as detailed in a previous chapter.

Oakland Police Department (OPD)

During the same period as the LAPD Rampart Scandal, Oakland police detectives known as the "Riders" allegedly made false arrests, used excessive force, planted evidence, and falsified police reports. Frank Vazquez, the alleged ringleader, fled to Mexico after being indicted. A jury acquitted three other officers, and the city settled with one officer for $1.5 million for wrongful termination. A subsequent federal civil rights case ended with the city paying out nearly $11 million to 119 individuals for police brutality, leading to a 2003 federal court monitor (Bay Area News Group, 2012). Oakland Chief Richard Word resigned in 2004. Subsequently, twelve other chiefs led the department, including five interim chiefs and a city administrator, Sabrina Landreth, who took over the department as a civilian from June 2016 to January 2017. Landreth resigned as a city administrator in March 2020 and LeRonne Armstrong became chief in February 2021.

The 2015–2016 period of time was captured in a documentary film by Pete Nicks when he was given unprecedented access to the OPD and embedded with the department to highlight the reform efforts of Chief Sean Whent during the Black Lives Matter national protests. *The Force* premiered in January 2018 (BondGraham, 2017). A sex scandal involving Oakland and Richmond officers, detailed later in this chapter, brought an end to Whent's career in Oakland, although he was not involved directly. Further problems arose when the Oakland Inspector General's Office reported that the OPD under-reported use of force in more than one-third of instances assessed in 2018 involving non-white suspects.

Richmond Police Department (RPD)

The RPD was involved in several scandals dealing with sexual offenses and misuse of force, leading to the retirement of 54-year-old Chief Joseph Samuels, Jr. in 2003. At the time of his forced retirement, Samuels was the President of the 19,000-member International Association of Chiefs of Police (IACP). He received a "no-confidence" vote from the Richmond Police Officers Association (RPOA) that followed questionable promotions. His support from Mayor Irma Anderson[6] also diminished when Commander Armand Mulder, Samuels's top advisor, retired after being accused of sexual harassment. Other problems persisted. Civilian complaints tripled during Samuel's time as a chief; officers arrested an off-duty detective for driving while

5 Caruso is a billionaire businessman, developer, and founder of a real estate company.

6 Anderson was the first Black woman to serve on the Richmond City Council (1993–2000) and the first African-American woman elected mayor.

intoxicated after he broke through a toll gate and tried to evade California Highway Patrol; and an officer received a 16-year prison sentence after pleading guilty to molesting his 10-year-old son (Johnson, 2003). Samuels, an Oakland church Deacon at the Allen Temple, was previously the first Black Oakland Police Chief from 1993 to 1999 before being forced out by Mayor Jerry Brown.[7]

Samuel's Richmond predecessor was Chief William Lansdowne[8] (1994–1998). Lansdowne was credited with cutting Richmond murders in half through the nationally funded Comprehensive Homicide Initiative, discussed below, and, given the period of the 1990s, embraced assigning some of his officers to practice community policing. (Magnus would go beyond Lansdowne's version of community policing units and attempt to institutionalize the philosophy throughout the entire police force.) Mayor Anderson announced a nationwide search to replace Samuels and bring a reform-minded chief with similar leadership as Lansdowne. During the search process, the department utilized two interim chiefs; only the second and third times the department had to do so. Charles Bennett was interim from August 2003 to December 2004, and Terry Hudson was interim from January 2005 to January 2006. In the summer of 2006, four city council members called for a state of emergency in Richmond, asked for $2 million to fight a surge of violence, and compared their city to war-torn Iraq (Zamora, 2005). The city council declaration occurred just months into Magnus's role as the new chief in Richmond.

Richmond, California

Richmond, California, is located on the west side of Contra Costa County and spans 32 miles of shoreline. San Francisco is 18 miles southwest of Richmond on the opposite side of the bay. In December 1849, California's first legislature met in San Jose, and Edmond Randolph represented San Francisco. Randolph was from Richmond, Virginia, and persuaded the land surveyors to label the area northeast of the San Francisco Bay, the city he represented, "Point Richmond." Richmond's population has experienced growth in most decades, moving from 6,800 in 1910 to an estimated 110,000 in 2018. From 1950 to 1960, there was a 28 percent decline in population as World War II shipyard workers were no longer needed. In the 1970s, the Hilltop Mall was developed in the northern portion of Richmond, causing a further decline in downtown commercial investment. From 1970 to 1980, the city experienced its second population decline, albeit a smaller 6 percent. The modern 110,000 population contains a majority-minority population with 31% white, 27% African-American, and 40% Latino.

History of Richmond Police Department (RPD)

In 2009, the RPD celebrated its 100th anniversary. Captain Allwyn Brown,[9] who replaced Magnus as the chief in January 2016, researched the department's history in anticipation

7 Brown was Oakland Mayor from 1999 to 2007. From 2007 to 2011, he was Governor Arnold Schwarzenegger's Attorney General and he was the 34th (1975–1983) and 39th (2011–2019) Governor of California.

8 Lansdowne joined the San Jose Police Department in 1966 and was hired as the Richmond Chief in 1994. In 1998, he returned as the chief of San Jose (1998–2004), and the city was recognized as the safest in America. In 2004, he became the chief of San Diego PD (2004–2014) and served for the next ten years before he decided to retire amid inappropriate sexual contact between officers and female suspects. In 2014, Major Cities Chiefs Association (MCCA) President Charles Ramsey presented Lansdowne with its MCCA Leadership Award.

9 Brown resigned in September 2019 amid allegations that work expenses were improperly approved by his wife Belinda Brown, who served as Richmond's finance director with fiduciary responsibilities for the city.

of the century mark. The department's early history involved San Pablo Township ranchers electing Frank Moitoza to serve as a constable in 1901. On August 7, 1905, Richmond was incorporated and hired Harry Stevens to serve as a night watch. He also became the city's first police officer. The city charter became effective and ratified by the state in 1909, and James Arnold became the official first police chief under the charter. During the 1940s, the shipyards produced wartime employment but also created a surge in crime. In 1943, RPD Chief Emmett Jones secured federal funding to hire an additional 75 officers to complement the existing 54 policemen. During the 1930s and 1940s, the RPD arrested 2,149 individuals annually.[10] In 1944, with the increase in officers and a narrowed crime-fighting professionalization role, arrests surged to 43,754, targeting Blacks recruited by the Kaiser shipyards with federal wartime funds.[11]

History of Richmond's Race Relations

Richmond has a blue-collar tradition as an adjunct city to a larger, more prosperous San Francisco and other outlying suburbs. It is a smaller city in the same vein as Newark to New York, Gary to Chicago, and Camden to Philadelphia (Fyfe, Goldkamp, & White, 1997). Each of these adjunct cities has higher concentrations of minority and disadvantaged populations with a history of racial tensions linked to law enforcement.

Ku Klux Klan (KKK)

From 1914 to 1925, the KKK was active in Richmond. On July 4, 1924, an estimated 750 Klansmen openly marched in the downtown parade with their white robes and hoods (Cocoltchos, 1979). The original intent was to march in the nearby Oakland parade, but the city denied their permit. Richmond did not approve or deny the Klan's subsequent permit and allowed them to march. Klan members were a direct outgrowth of Southern whites who came to the Bay Area seeking employment and were often actively recruited by California's municipal law enforcement agencies. The low number of minorities in Richmond during the 1920s allowed the city to avoid the race riots that plagued other American towns post-World War I (Moore, 2001).

Kaiser's Shipbuilding

During the buildup for World War II, California received massive federal funding allowing for the mass hiring of minorities who moved to the west coast for employment. Henry Kaiser[12] owned steel companies and hired thousands of workers with the slogan, "We can build ships faster than the enemy could sink them." As Richmond's male white population experienced the military draft, Kaiser's recruitment teams faced a labor shortage in Richmond and recruited young African-Americans from the Midwest and South. They were eager to escape post-depression hardship and Jim Crow laws. In doing so, Kaiser challenged Richmond's largest employer, Chevron Oil, and their dismal record of hiring minorities. By the end of the war, the shipyards employed over 100,000, and 20 percent were African-American (Moore,

10 See http://ca-richmond2.civicplus.com/1848/A-Century-of-Service

11 See www.ci.richmond.ca.us/1848/A-Century-of-Service

12 Kaiser was known as the father of American shipbuilding during World War II. His lessons from the Ford assembly plant led to welding instead of riveting ships. Welding could be taught to thousands of unskilled employees, many of them women, and allowed the construction process to be completed more quickly.

2001). Despite this, Black children were not allowed to be enrolled in Kaiser's child development center, a forerunner of Project Head Start,[13] and most Blacks lived in segregated public housing torn down after the war. If public housing residents could afford private housing after the war, they often faced discriminatory lending practices along with confrontational white neighbors.

1960s Civil Rights Movement-North Richmond and the Iron Triangle

In March 1966, a school fight at Richmond High School[14] between white and Black students spilled outside the school. Students threw rocks, and property destruction ensued. RPD Chief Charlie Brown issued an order to shoot all looters. Much of the white community supported the chief's order. Like much of the country, additional protests and riots occurred in 1968. National Guard troops were dispatched to Richmond following three days of protests after a white officer wounded an unarmed 15-year-old Black youth.

The Chevron Richmond Refinery plant responded to the racial conflicts by investing in real estate and building a self-contained community next to its plant, away from downtown Richmond. The aftermath has been a community plagued with violence that the Contra Costa Sheriff's Department merely reacts to without community policing investment. When Magnus began his tenure as Richmond chief, Sheriff Warren Rupf told him, "Richmond's a hell hole. Always has been—always will be."[15] In 2017, North Richmond had a declining population of 3,700 people, made up of a diverse 33% African-American, 50% Hispanic or other race, and 17% white.[16] The goal of creating a refuge from downtown Richmond did not come to pass as North Richmond experienced a 30% poverty rate. In an April 24, 2013 email to the Richmond City Council and residents, Magnus mentions the issues with policing North Richmond:

> *Although the media often refer to many crimes in our immediate area as having been "committed in Richmond," a great deal of our retaliatory gang violence involves young men who live or hang out in unincorporated North Richmond — which is not part of the City. Because of this, a significant number of gun crimes associated with our larger community are the responsibility of the Contra Costa County Sheriff's Department.*
>
> *This means it's essential that RPD work closely with the Sheriff's Department. When a shooting occurs, it's not uncommon for the perpetrators to flee from Richmond into North Richmond or vice versa. This complicates our ability to make arrests and close cases, but despite this reality, our officers and detectives communicate on an ongoing basis with CCSO deputies and investigators. We also work regularly with investigators from the DA's Office.*

In central Richmond, the "Iron Triangle" refers to a residential area that includes the downtown business district. Ironically, this was a term used during the Vietnam War after an area in South Vietnam on the Cambodian border that the communists continually destabilized from

13 Head Start began as part of President Lyndon Johnson's War on Poverty and the Economic Opportunity Act of 1964 that focused on helping children from low-income and disadvantaged families with preschool children to meet their emotional, social, psychological, and nutritional needs.

14 The 2005 award-winning film *Coach Carter*, starring Samuel Jackson, was inspired by Richmond High School Black basketball coach Ken Carter, who famously locked out his undefeated team for not honoring their academic and behavioral contracts. Initially, the Richmond community was outraged but eventually gave Coach Carter their support. Every one of the players he coached from 1997 to 2002 graduated.

15 Author's interview with Magnus on March 28, 2020.

16 See https://datausa.io/profile/geo/north-richmond-ca/

French and American troops. In Richmond, the "Iron Triangle" takes its name from three railroad tracks that enclose the downtown neighborhoods and have been notorious for high-crime and concentrated violence. In 2019, Richmond had approximately 110,000 residents, with 20,000 living in the "Iron Triangle," 66 percent minority. Minority concentration in the "Iron Triangle" grew as affluent housing and commercial investment in the north competed with downtown businesses.

The Cowboys vs. The Guardians of Justice

In the 1980s, *60 Minutes* host Mike Wallace covered a story about two white RPD police officers that shot and killed Black residents Johnny Roman, age 25, and Michael Guillory, age 22, in two separate occurrences. In January 1982, RPD officers Clinton Mitchell and Samuel Dudkiewicz shot Roman four times after attempting to arrest him for a harassment claim. Officer Mitchell reported that he thought Roman reached for a shotgun. Officer Dudkiewicz shot Guillory through his bedroom window and said he thought he was reaching for a weapon – but the police did not recover any guns.

The federal lawsuits, *Roman vs. City of Richmond* and *Guillory vs. City of Richmond*, were filed by the National Association for the Advancement of Colored People (NAACP) against the RPD, police chief Leo Garfield, and deputy chief Ernest Clements. The trial began in December 1982 but halted six weeks later when the city reportedly settled. However, in an attempt to defend the reputation of the RPD, the five white members of the Richmond City Council voted to reject a $760,000 settlement agreed to by family members of Roman and Guillory. The city council also rejected a second settlement offer of $260,000. As the trial continued, it was revealed that the jury members heard that a settlement had been reached and then denied. This revelation led Federal District Judge Robert Aguilar to declare a mistrial. On February 1, 1983, a new trial began with a new jury.

During the trial, Richmond's general population was 48 percent African-American and 40 percent white. The 161-member RPD was 20 percent African-American, and the trial showed the divisiveness between the white and Black officers. The civil suit alleged that the defendants all failed to address a pattern of misconduct and reckless unprofessionalism by a deviant subculture of white police officers on the swing shift who referred to themselves as "cowboys" because of the Western-style boots they wore. Attorneys entered into evidence a photograph of the officers on horseback holding a confederate flag. Several Black officers broke rank and testified at the trial against officers Mitchell and Dudkiewicz. They claimed that an unwritten code of conduct condoned the rogue cowboy violence that led to Roman and Guillory's deaths. The Black officers represented a group they referred to as the "Guardians of Justice." They felt compelled to testify against a pattern of misconduct they felt police leaders and city officials condoned.

Although officers Mitchell and Dudkiewicz were not found guilty in a criminal proceeding, Roman and Guillory's families did receive $3 million from the civil jury, a much larger amount than the original settlement agreement. The civil suit sent a strong message to the RPD to change its racially biased culture. The lawsuit resulted in the most significant judgment for racially motivated wrongful death in the U.S. history at that time.[17] The different reactions of Black and white viewers of the *60 Minutes* coverage of the federal verdict on the Richmond case served as a national precursor to the not guilty verdicts of the officers involved with the Rodney King beating and the murder case against OJ Simpson, as detailed in the chapter on Bratton.

17 The calls to reform the RPD in the aftermath of the jury verdict were in sharp contrast to the "kick-ass" approach that came from Wilson and Kelling's broken windows (1982) policing article the year prior (Louis, 1983).

Cinco de Mayo Celebration 2002

As demographics in Richmond shifted, a more heterogeneous population caused increased friction. On May 5, 2002, officers in charge of crowd-control at the city's Cinco de Mayo celebrations arrested approximately two dozen people around 23rd Street and Lowell Avenue. Witnesses alleged that the officers pepper-sprayed the crowd and beat them with clubs and flashlights after handcuffing several party-goers. They further claimed that officers denied them medical care after detaining them at police headquarters. Among the arrestees were local political activist Andres Soto and his two sons, Che and Alejandro. In the aftermath, the community protested, later won a settlement, and voters elected a coalition of progressive politicians to change Richmond. The police commission investigation concluded that the RPD used excessive force and racially abusive behavior toward the Latino group. A separate federal lawsuit resulted in a 2004 out-of-court settlement with a dozen plaintiffs for approximately $175,000 (Rogers, 2012).

The Cinco de Mayo incident called into question the leadership of Chief Samuels and the larger divide between the city council and the growing Latino community. That community called for stronger civilian police oversight and progressive political leadership across the board. Soto ran unsuccessfully for the city council and did not receive support from the police and fire unions. However, the Richmond Progressive Alliance emerged as a powerful political coalition, which helped usher in reform-minded leaders, including a new city manager, police chief, and ultimately a Green Party mayor.

The Rodney King and OJ Simpson cases and the LAPD Rampart Scandal served as historical tipping points for state-wide demands for police reform in the 1990s. In Richmond, the Cowboy case and the court-ordered reforms that followed did not appear sufficient, as demonstrated by the 2002 Cinco de Mayo riot. These scandals eventually led to Chief Magnus's external hire to usher in a new era of racial healing without the baggage of being tied to the previous culture. However, a year after his employment, senior-ranked Black officers sued Magnus and the city for biased promotions and racial harassment. After a long-drawn-out court battle, a jury unanimously sided with the city and Magnus.

Officers' Lawsuit on Promotional Discrimination (2007–2012)

Richmond Confidential,[18] an online news service produced by the University of California Berkeley Graduate School of Journalism, actively reported the discrimination lawsuit that began in March 2007 and lasted until April 2012. The $18 million lawsuit started when seven African-American police officers sued Richmond, Magnus, and Deputy Chief Lori Ritter for discriminatory promotional practices and created a hostile work environment. Ritter was married to a former member of the 1980s "cowboys" officers highlighted by *60 Minutes*. The plaintiffs included Captain Eugene McBride, Lieutenants Johan Simon, Cleveland Brown,[19] Shawn Pickett, Michael Booker, Arnold Threets,[20] and Sergeant James Jenkins.

18 See https://richmondconfidential.org/?s=magnus+lawsuit

19 Plaintiff Cleveland Brown was second in command when Magnus was hired. He took a year's paid leave on a compensation claim for a knee injury he suffered when he jumped out of his chair while watching a televised sporting event. The city accused Brown of fraud and wanted to terminate his employment. In 2010, he was demoted to a lieutenant and eventually dropped his lawsuit with an agreement that he would receive his full pension and retire with his captain rank. The city also agreed to relieve Brown of his portion of the $439,000 in legal costs ordered by the judge for the lawsuit.

20 Threets served as the union president of the Richmond Police Managers Association (RPMA) and was the lawsuit's ringleader. Moreover, Threets is a Christian fundamentalist who has strong views against homosexuality and was disgruntled that a gay man was selected as his new chief (Author's interview with Magnus – March 28, 2020). In 2018, he retired as an RPD Captain, and in June 2019, Threets was named the Assistant Chief of Inspectors for the Contra Costa District Attorney's Office.

The defense, provided by the city at an estimated cost that exceeded $4.5 million (Waldholz, 2012), demonstrated that promotions under the new chief were mainly non-white. These promotions included the first Latino deputy chief Ed Medina, and Allwyn Brown, a Black sergeant who skipped becoming a lieutenant and received a captain promotion. Magnus also named Ritter the first female to serve as the deputy chief and second in command for the RPD, making the plaintiffs subordinates. When Magnus was appointed the chief in 2006, he promoted more minorities than the previous Black police chiefs. He ushered in a massive reorganization of the department, emphasized improved police legitimacy, provided greater accountability, and instituted a community policing philosophy throughout the departmental ranks. Magnus also followed geographic hot spot policing research (see Weisburd, Telep, Hinkle, & Eck, 2010) to restructure patrol allocation as a means for replacing violence suppression units (VSU), which consisted of roving mobile patrols that did not focus on forming neighborhood relationships. These tactical shifts were another rationale for the lawsuit from the change resistors that the plaintiffs represented.

A key defense witness, Captain Mark Gagan,[21] testified that plaintiff Lieutenant Shawn Pickett threatened him on several occasions and had schemed with attorneys to orchestrate encounters with the new chief they could later use in court. Pickett was in charge of the Investigative Service Division (ISD) when Magnus changed how officers could be promoted to that division. Pickett and other Black officers boycotted the process and claimed that Magnus was trying to keep Black officers out of the ISD. African-American Captain Anthony Williams also testified in support of Magnus and Ritter. He praised their leadership while rejecting claims that they were racists. The civil case lasted five years, and the trial lasted over three months. In the last month of the trial, labor economist Mark Cohen testified that officers would have taken pay cuts if they were promoted to be deputy chiefs due to overtime and other perks enjoyed by officers. The lower pay from the promotions came from differentiating the command staff base salary and inability to earn overtime. Phillip Allman, another economist, refuted Cohen and argued that the plaintiffs suffered financially by not being promoted. As a chief, Magnus's track record showed that by 2014, 60 percent of the 182 active officers in Richmond were African-American, Latino, Asian, or Native American (Early, 2014).

Richmond Police Chief (2006–2015)

City Manager Bill Lindsay was recruited to Richmond in 2005 following the Cinco de Mayo plaintiffs' out-of-court settlement. He was previously the city manager in Orinda, a city of fewer than 20,000 residents located 9 miles east of Berkeley and 17 miles southeast of Richmond. Upon Lindsay's arrival, Richmond faced a $35 million budget crisis, laid off 300 city employees, and closed several libraries and city centers due to incompetent government leadership. The unemployment rate of Black men between the ages of 16 and 24 was at 36 percent, the city had been mismanaged amid the financial recession, and violent crime had surged along with police scandals linked to Chief Samuels. In the summer of 2005, four city council members called for a state emergency and a $2 million increase in police expenditures.

21 Captain Gagan was terminated on November 22, 2017, under Magnus's replacement, Chief Allwyn Brown. Brown alleged that Gagan shared an internal police report with the media related to an investigation on Councilman Eduardo Martinez, who was suspected of driving a city vehicle while under the influence of alcohol. Martinez claimed that he was a robbery victim, his cell phone was lost, and he used the city vehicle to drive to a hotel to report his victimization. City Manager Lindsay reinstated the popular Gagan in May 2018, ruling that there was no justification for his termination. See www.sfgate.com/news/article/Fired-Richmond-police-captain-wins-his-job-back-12888371.php

Additionally, in response to surging violence, they asked for assistance from the California Highway Patrol and the Contra County Sherriff's Department (Lum & Fischer, 2005).

In 2018, Lindsay retired at 62 years old and left Richmond with a budget surplus and historically low unemployment rates. In 2014, Richmond had 11 murders, the lowest since 1971. The leadership shift for Richmond took place over a decade. From 2005 to 2009, the city experienced 203 murders, and over the next five years, 2010–2014, there were 92 murders. The 111-murder decrease over five years was a testament to the city's reforms, creative outreach directed at those most prone to violence, and a change in police leadership. Lindsay reported that one of his most significant contributions to Richmond was the hiring of Fargo Chief Magnus.

On November 28, 2005, Lindsay announced that Magnus had accepted his offer to become Richmond's 18th police chief. Lindsay brought Magnus to one of the most dangerous cities in the country, a sharp contrast from Fargo, a city ranked as one of the safest cities in America with an average of two murders a year. City leaders knew that their new chief was unusual right away when Magnus bought a home near downtown and commuted to work on his bicycle. Most RPD officers chose to live outside the city and not near the crime. Magnus reported his frustration with hearing shots fired late at night and members of a neighborhood association knocking on his door to report crimes. Eventually, the city developed a program to offer officers free rent if they would live in public housing, but very few officers took advantage of this opportunity. The new chief consistently encouraged his officers to conduct bike patrols, hand out business cards, and share their email and cell phone numbers with residents. Noting the previous success of Lansdowne in cutting Richmond murders in half through some use of community policing and federal support, Magnus took this vision a step further. While chiefs throughout the nation have created community policing units, Magnus believes that every officer should be doing community policing and that this philosophy should be inculcated throughout the department.[22] As previously noted, the philosophical belief in community policing's transformative nature throughout a police organization was the original vision of Trojanowicz and the creation of the National Center for Community Policing through the School of Criminal Justice at MSU (Trojanowicz & Bucquerous, 1991).

As an external reform chief, Magnus conducted a massive reorganization of the RPD, emphasizing community policing that impacted all 150 officers. Officers received longer beat patrol assignments in neighborhoods with concentrated crime, which created greater accountability. Officers were encouraged to develop first-name relationships with residents and a sense of problem-solving ownership throughout their beats. Magnus saw a dual benefit from the community policing shift. First, the community worked more collaboratively with the police resulting in reduced crime. Second, officers had higher morale and became more productive over their careers since they were not stuck in the cycle of arresting the same offenders and repeatedly going to the same calls for service locations. Under Magnus's leadership plan, RPD officers saw that their work was meaningful and that they could make a difference in the community they policed.

Eventually, Magnus did move out of Richmond downtown to a more suburban neighborhood in Richmond after marrying Terrance Cheung on May 10, 2014, in nearby Berkeley, California. Cheung had been the chief of staff for Contra Costa Supervisor John Gioia, who performed their ceremony and then became the chief of staff for Richmond Mayor Thomas Butt.[23] Magnus became the first openly gay male police chief to marry while he was the chief.

22 Author's interview with Magnus on March 28, 2020.
23 Butt was elected the Mayor in 2015 and served the prior two decades within city council.

During his nearly decade-long tenure as the chief of the RPD, he implemented several reforms. His long-term commitment to residential trust with police services was at the heart of transforming Richmond's reputation for gun violence. His success in doing so connected to his understanding of the long history of violence reduction strategies in Richmond and the support of many initiatives that fell outside of traditional law enforcement. These initiatives are described below, followed by a more detailed look at the leadership of Magnus.

Richmond's Violence Reduction Initiatives

Richmond has been a petri dish for several grant-supported violence reduction strategies. One of the first occurred through Chief Lansdowne's leadership and President Clinton's Attorney General Janet Reno's encouragement. Other violence reduction initiatives included programs that operated external to the RPD but were nonetheless collaborative. In the following section, a brief history of violence in America is discussed along with contemporary reduction strategies implemented in Richmond – namely the Comprehensive Homicide Initiative, Operation Peacemaker, and Ceasefire.

Historical National Trends in Murder and the Richmond Story

Researchers and practitioners have long believed that social and economic variables link to violence and that the police have little control over these sociological factors. (Details of the sociological causes of crime appear in previous chapters on Wilson and Bratton, reflective of evolving challenges that underlined the assumptions made by President Johnson's 1967 Crime Commission Report that supported the *Great Society Program*.)[24] For example, southern states consistently suffer higher violence rates than northern states. Researchers have linked the violence to the historical maintenance of slavery, class distinction, an honor code, and the weather (see Cohen & Nisbett, 1994). However, none of these explanations for violence are under the purview of the police. Other researchers have conflicted findings that link the availability of firearms and murder rates (Hemenway, 1997; Kleck, 2015; Yu, Lee, & Pizzaro, 2020).

Murder rates during the twentieth century follow a U-shaped trend (Zahn & McCall, 1999), with high rates in the early 1930s and then steep drops that followed the end of prohibition. Downward trends in murders occurred throughout most of the 1930s through the 1950s and then spiked in the 1960s. Historians attribute the 1960s increased violence to frustration linked to shifts in employment and consumption as the country moved into a postindustrial era with fewer manufacturing jobs and a greater emphasis on education (Lane, 1997). Towns like Richmond fit the profile of postindustrial cities faced with high unemployment, especially with minority residents, and the significant increase in 1960s postwar baby-boom males who reached their crime-prone age. Television also allowed the country to repeatedly replay images of violence, highlighted with Kennedy and King's assassinations and clashes between the police and protesters.

By the late 1980s and into the 1990s, murders spiked again. Even with declines in the 2000s, nationwide racial disparity in gun homicide is apparent. In 2010, Black males between the ages of 15 and 19 were 30 times more likely than white males and more than three times as likely as Hispanic males within the same age cohort to be killed by firearms. In 2012, the

24 Johnson's domestic agenda was labeled "The Great Society," with the goal of eliminating poverty and racial injustice. The initiatives focused on the causes of crime and violence with federal funding directed toward education, poverty, transportation, and racial inequality. Much of this funding competed with war efforts in Vietnam.

firearm homicide rate of Black men between 20 and 29 years of age was about 89 per 100,000. In Honduras, the country with the highest homicide rate, there were 90.4 intentional murders per 100,000 that same year (Reeves & Holmes, 2015).

Richmond set a new record in 1991 with 62 murders, 52 of which were gun-related within a population of 98,000, a rate seven times higher than the national average (White, Fyfe, Campbell, & Goldkamp, 2003). Murders decreased by over 40% in the latter 1990s. However, throughout the mid-2000s, murders were back up to an annual average of over 40. Two Richmond initiatives for addressing gun violence include the 1995–1998 Comprehensive Homicide Initiative and the 2010–2015 Operation Peacemaker.

Comprehensive Homicide Initiative (1995–1998)

In January 1993, at the direction of Attorney General Janet Reno, 20 members of the International Chiefs of Police (IACP) held a "Murder Summit" to produce federal and state policymakers' comprehensive strategies to reduce urban violence. Their report, *Violent Crime in America: Recommendations of the IACP Summit on Violent Crime*, was issued in April 1993. In November 1994, a second summit included 55 academics and practitioners, chaired by IACP Fourth Vice President Darrell Sanders, Chief of the Frankfort, Illinois Police Department. These summits culminated with 39 recommendations that emphasized community-wide strategies involving multi-dimensional and multi-disciplinary collaboration between law enforcement and various stakeholders.

Interestingly, murder increased nationally, evolved with increased stranger incidents, and random outdoor violence was different from the past. The first quote from the summit report came from the FBI: "The typical assumptions associated with homicides throughout this century must be reevaluated in view of the unprecedented shift in national homicide patterns as evidenced in the 1990s. Every American now has a realistic chance of murder victimization in view of the random nature the crime has assumed" (IACP, 1995). The Comprehensive Homicide Initiative asked, "Can the lessons and methods of problem and community-oriented policing be applied to homicide investigations, a specialization that has, in effect, remained aloof from all but technological change? Can traditional police homicide work be recast to include a strong preventative component?" (White, Fyfe, Goldkamp, & Campbell, 2000, p. vi).

Richmond, California, became a test site for the IACP recommendations under the leadership of Lansdowne (Richmond chief 1994–1998). In 1995, the Bureau of Justice Assistance (BJA), housed in the federal Department of Justice, funded the Richmond Comprehensive Homicide Initiative. The test site's goal was to develop critical information to make homicide prevention strategies more effective across the country. At the time of the implementation, census demographics indicated that Richmond's population was 44% African-American, 36% white, 12% Asian, and 8% other. Most homicides in Richmond resulted from firearms. In the year the BJA funding started, Richmond experienced 34 homicides, and 32 of these occurred by firearm. Researchers also determined that the circumstances of homicide changed. In the 1980s, about half of the homicides occurred outdoors, but in the 1990s, more than two-thirds occurred outdoors, indicating gangs and drive-by shootings. The federal initiative challenged Richmond to change its conventional wisdom and see homicides as a more significant problem with community violence. This perspective followed recommendations that came out of the IACP murder summit. After a year of planning, the RPD developed a series of strategies that included both enforcement (e.g. improved investigations) and non-enforcement initiatives (e.g. enhanced partnerships and prevention).

In March 1996, the RPD hosted a community violence summit and invited various government officials and members of the public. At the meeting, they developed a survey that the RPD subsequently administered, primarily in the Iron Triangle neighborhoods, soliciting support and asking for improvement suggestions. Encouragingly, 70 percent of respondents reported a willingness to participate in violence reduction strategies (Office of Juvenile Justice and Delinquency Prevention, 1996). The RPD prevention efforts were also directed toward an improved partnership with the West Contra Costa Unified School District and returning truants to school rather than implementing punishments that forced youth out of class (Fyfe, Goldkamp, & White, 1997).

The Comprehensive Homicide Initiative's evaluation included an interrupted time-series analysis and an autoregressive integrated moving average (ARIMA) to determine if the strategies impacted homicides. The time-series analysis explained monthly levels of homicide fluctuation (i.e. the main dependent variable). Data taken from RPD homicide reports compared three eras: 1985–1989 (stability); 1990–1994 (increased homicide); and 1995–1998 (post-treatment). The evaluation determined that the Comprehensive Homicide Initiative essentially turned back the clock to the early 1980s numbers. From 1985 to 1989, Richmond averaged an annual 27 homicides. Over the next five years, 1990–1994, homicides nearly doubled and averaged an annual 50 homicides. Throughout the Comprehensive Homicide Initiative, 1995–1998, the numbers returned to an annual average of 27 homicides (White et al., 2003).

The Comprehensive Homicide Initiative demonstrated the benefits of an approach that combined offender and place-oriented responses. It was a problem-oriented policing project that called for the collaboration of multiple stakeholders. The subsequent evaluation determined that outdoor murders dropped 37 percent, drive-by shootings dropped 64 percent, gun-related murder dropped 43 percent, and drug-related murder dropped 59 percent (White et al., 2000, ix). Critical themes from the Comprehensive Homicide Initiative arose. First, measurable police/community relationships are vital to murder clearance and prevention purposes. Second, future strategies should also attempt to be multi-disciplinary and multi-faceted, building partnerships between the RPD and community stakeholders. Third, and what the researchers (White et al., 2000) called the most compelling, the initiative provided a problem-oriented approach that challenged past use of traditional law enforcement homicide units that were previously exclusive to only follow-up investigative detectives.

Operation Peacemaker

After steady declines in violence during the latter 1990s, firearm assaults and murder escalated again, leading Richmond to look for new solutions. In 2001, the city experienced a low of 18 homicides. However, between 2005 and 2009, Richmond experienced an annual average of 41 homicides, 47 in both 2007 and 2009, creeping up to the numbers experienced in the early 1990s.

Office of Violence Prevention – Office of Neighborhood Safety

In reaction to the spike in homicide, the city council created the Office of Violence Prevention (OVP) and hired consultants from The Mentoring Center, an Oakland-based nonprofit agency dedicated to mentoring young minority males. The OVP investigated Richmond gun violence before the hiring of Magnus. They provided a commissioned report in 2007 on violent crime in 2005–2006 (Spiker, Williams, Diggs, Heiser, & Aultson, 2007). The report indicated that Richmond followed national trends of decreased violent crime since the late 1980s. However, the rate of violent crime (2,399 per 100,000) was significantly different from California's average violent crime rate (534 per 100,000). The report was ominous for Magnus's first year as the chief, showing that 2006 homicides increased to 42, and firearm assaults represented a 13-year high. Most violent crime victims were Black males between the ages of 18 and 24 and occurred in the "Iron Triangle" predominantly between 8 PM and midnight.

In the summer of 2006, there was a competitive process with several consulting groups bidding to assist Richmond in efforts to reduce gun violence. Deputy City Manager Leslie Knight encouraged the Mentoring Center Team to apply for the city contract, and they were awarded that contract in August 2006. By the end of the year, Richmond's murder rate was nine times the national average. The Office of Violence Prevention Development Team (OVPDT), later referred to as the Office of Neighborhood Safety (ONS), replaced the OVP. Devonne Boggan, discussed more fully below, was the Policy Director at Safe Passages and a consultant with OVPDT and was tapped by City Manager Lindsay to lead Richmond's ONS. Magnus was supportive of creating the ONS, the first for any U.S. city,[25] but also continued to work with a range of community groups to implement a Chicago-based model of Operation Ceasefire, described more fully below. City Manager Lindsay gave office space to Boggan in city hall, and Magnus was in his second year as the chief of the RPD when murders hit a 13-year high, with a rate of nearly 46 per 100,000 compared to 4.7 per 100,000 in similar-sized California cities (Huguet, Servat, & Stofer, 2016; Matthay et al., 2019). In July 2007, the mayor's office and the city council unanimously voted to ratify the ONS. The non-law enforcement initiative, within Lindsay's office, officially opened its doors for business on October 23, 2007.[26]

In the summer of 2010, the ONS launched a fellowship program marketed as "Operation Peacemaker" that targeted African-American males between the ages of 16 and 24 who were most susceptible to both perpetrating and being victims of gun violence. The ONS focused on violence reduction through both community and individual interventions. The community-level intervention included a street outreach strategy that focused on the environmental context of behavior (see Sallis, Owen, & Fisher, 2008). The individual intervention provided an evidence-based, comprehensive strategy through conflict mediation (Decker et al., 2008). Both interventions looked to prevent future offenders from shooting and victims from being shot. Pragmatically, the street-level intervention came from ONS staff who made contact with identified high-risk youth and young adults. Their goal was to mediate conflict and refer them to appropriate services while also providing stipends to incentivize their participation and celebrate behavior change. Intervention contacts were frequently offered, quietly, to the ONS by the RPD's updated lists on active shooters.[27]

Operation Peacemaker garnered national attention when the ONS announced that they would pay participants up to $1,000 a month in stipends for a period of nine months of the 18-month fellowship (Huguet, Servat, & Stofer, 2016). They advocated that this nominal cost provided a savings benefit to the city with a ROI in crime reduction. Funds for the stipends and other fellowship program costs (e.g. life skills training, cognitive behavioral therapy (CBT), travel, and subsidized internship/employment) came from private donations, which comprised roughly $1.5 million of the ONS $2.7 million budget. The other $1.2 million came from city funds. The ONS spent approximately $25,000 on each fellow every year, which they argued was a cheaper alternative to having the young men engage in gun violence and significantly less expensive than paying for incarceration. Moreover, stipends

25 Chief Magnus's support of the ONS was verified directly by the author through Boggan and Magnus's interviews. Both saw the potential of positive influence from the ONS. There are now more than 20 offices similar to the ONS around the country, and Boggan takes great pride in influencing the creation of these city offices.

26 Author's interview with Boggan on May 2, 2020.

27 Author's interview with Magnus on March 28, 2020.

have helped validate trust and reinforce positive identities, especially with minority youth (Spencer, Noll, & Cassidy, 2005).

The notion of paying offenders not to commit gun violence was nationally controversial and had critics on the Richmond City Council. However, by 2013, the murder rate had plummeted to 11 per 100,000. This rate was far lower than comparable cities such as Oakland, 23 per 100,000, and Detroit, 47 per 100,000 the same year. By the end of 2014, the homicide rate dropped 76 percent to a 40-year low with a rate of 13 per 100,000. In-depth evaluations of the ONS Operation Peacemaker were completed by the National Council on Crime and Delinquency (NCCD), the Sol Price School of Public Policy at the University of Southern California (USC), and the Center for Health and Community out of the University of California, San Francisco, each summarized below.

National Council on Crime and Delinquency (NCCD)[28]

Richmond City Council commissioned the NCCD and the California Wellness Foundation to conduct a process evaluation on ONS and the fellowship initiative from Operation Peacemaker. By March 2015, the ONS had four cohorts of 94 targeted fellows. From 2010 to 2013, ONS staff averaged 2,994 outreach contacts annually (Wolf, Lippman, Glesmann, & Castro, 2015, p. 26), and by 2013 homicides reached an all-time per-capita low. Over five years after the launch of Operation Peacemaker and other violence prevention strategies, murder decreased 53 percent from an average of 38 annually to 18 annually in the post-intervention five years. Several factors were cited for the drop in crime, including policing efforts under Magnus's leadership and improved economic conditions. Qualitative interviews with Richmond clergy credited the ONS as being a significant influencer in firearm violence. The NCCD determined that 94 percent of the targeted youth were still alive, 84 percent avoided injury by firearm, and 79 percent avoided offender firearm-related activity. However, the study's limitations included a lack of a randomized control sample and difficulty teasing out the spurious effect of multiple competing independent variables.

University of Southern California (USC) Price School[29] of Public Policy

Researchers from USC worked with the ONS and Richmond city to conduct a cost-benefit analysis (CBA) of the fellowship program through Operation Peacemaker (Huguet et al., 2016). Data from 2010 to 2014 provided five years of post-intervention variables. The analysis showed that homicides decreased by an average of 55 percent. Additional analysis looked at four categories of costs and seven categories of benefits.[30] Researchers determined that the ONS produced a net present value (NPV) of over $500 million during the five years of analysis due

28 The NCCD was established in 1907 as a nonprofit research/policy advocacy organization that sought to standardize the new juvenile justice system following the first juvenile court in Cook County, Illinois, in 1899. Fourteen probation officers in Minneapolis created the NCCD. Today, the council has offices in Madison, Wisconsin, and Oakland. The council's research center is focused on criminal justice, child welfare, adult protective services, and education. See www.nccdglobal.org/

29 In November 2011, the Price family set up a $50 million endowment with the USC School of Public Policy to honor Sol Price, the Price Club founder, which would later merge with Costco. The goal of Price Philanthropies is to help transform low-income neighborhoods in urban settings, and the research of the USC School of Public Policy matched this mission.

30 Cost variables: budget, volunteers, internal/external audits. Benefit variables: internships/employment, GED productivity, reduced recidivism from GED, college, re-entry programs, cognitive behavioral therapy, and homicide reduction.

to the prevention of shootings and murders and the reduced recidivism that came from the prosocial aspects of the fellowships. While several limitations of the study exist, the research indicates that the ONS fellowships' costs are nominal compared to the potential benefits.

Center for Health and Community

Ellicott Matthay, through the Center for Health and Community at the University of California San Francisco, was the lead researcher in the most current evaluation and only quasi-experiment of Operation Peacemaker (Matthay et al., 2019). Matthay et al. analyzed homicide and assaults from 2005 to 2016 and determined that reduced firearm violence in Richmond resulted in 55 percent fewer deaths and hospital visits and 43 percent fewer crimes. However, non-firearm violence increased, with 16 percent more deaths/hospital visits and 3 percent more crime. The researchers discussed the difficulties in disentangling the causes of firearm injury/death declines and non-firearm injury/death increases. Similar conclusions from the NCCD research indicated that competing variables included the leadership of Chief Magnus, the reorganization of departmental deputy chiefs, and the special investigations units that focused on gun crimes during the decade of analysis. Other competing variables included the Rising Youth and Social Equity Center (RYSE) that provided a safe place for youth who experienced city violence. Call-in initiatives, replicating the traditional Ceasefire, also began in 2012. However, from June 2010 until 2012, the Operation Peacemaker fellows' intensity cannot be underestimated and is discussed more fully below under the ONS director DeVone Boggan.

DeVone Boggan

Boggan attended Lansing Eastern High School in Lansing, Michigan, but did not know Magnus until they met in Richmond.[31] Lindsay and Magnus wanted to bring Chicago's version of Ceasefire/Cure Violence (see Braga, Kennedy, Waring, & Piehl, 2001; Braga & Winship, 2005) to Richmond, and they tapped Boggan to facilitate the grant applications to fund it. Boggan has a law degree from Golden State University and extensive experience mentoring at-risk youth. His motivation to succeed in his new role was heightened in August 2008 when he lost his youngest brother, Dhanthan after he was fatally shot in Lansing, Mchigan at 32 years of age.[32] His older brother, Dan was the head football coach at Lansing's Sexton High School mentoring youth and the family vowed not to seek revenge for the murder. His shared experience with the fellows hired as outreach workers allowed for a grounded and authentic resolve to end the impact of gun violence on Richmond minority populations. Numerous local and national media outlets, including ABC *Nightline*, *The New York Times*, *The Washington Post*, NPR, and *Mother Jones*, covered Boggan's work in Richmond.

Funding – California Gang Reduction Intervention and Prevention (CalGRIP)

In 2008, Boggan began applying for California Gang Reduction Intervention and Prevention (CalGRIP)[33] grants to bring Ceasefire to Richmond but was denied in March 2009. CalGRIP competitive grants came from Governor Arnold Schwarzenegger's[34] $9.2 million in funds for

31 Author's interview with Magnus, January 5, 2020.

32 Author's interview with Boggan, May 2, 2020.

33 The CalGRIP provides grant funding to cities who commit to utilizing collaborative strategies to support comprehensive suppression, intervention, and prevention efforts.

34 Schwarzenegger was the 38th Governor of California, in office November 2003–January 2011.

local assistance directed toward violence prevention. Boggan opted to start his own initiative, referred to as a "ghetto Ceasefire," that later became the Operation Peacemaker Fellowship and then Advance Peace.[35] By 2010, Boggan demonstrated new partnerships, including the City of San Pablo, to prepare the grant application and secured $382,689 over two years to assist their outreach efforts. The initiative was titled "Beloved Community: West Contra Costa Partnership for Youth," with the ONS as the lead agency in partnership with the Richmond Police Activities League (RPAL).[36] The CalGRIP grants continued into the current era. On April 19, 2018, the California Board of State and Community Corrections announced that 20 applicants would receive additional CalGRIP grant funds, including Richmond. Richmond was awarded $500,000 for its initiative "Beloved Community-Next Level," which seeks to continue to serve at-risk youth.

Cure Violence – Ceasefire

Boggan's self-start program came in the aftermath of reading about Gary Slutkin's Cure Violence (see Skogan, Harnett, Bump, & DuBois, 2009; Picard-Fritsche & Cerniglia, 2013) work in Chicago that viewed gun violence through a public health lens. Slutkin got his start in San Francisco as an epidemiologist and physician in the 1980s. He then worked for a decade in Africa to reduce tuberculosis and noticed the effect of public health on disease. Slutkin returned to his hometown in Chicago to work on the causes of homicide and its links to learned behavior and lifestyles. As he saw with infectious diseases, an analogy for creative inoculation is helpful to prevent violent crime.

Slutkin's Chicago organization was called Ceasefire and later CureViolence. The model declared that violence begets violence and is spread the same way disease in African villages is spread. Moreover, disease becomes acceptable rather than routinely challenged by healthcare providers, the same way Chicago residents in low-income neighborhoods become desensitized after continual exposure to violence and accept it as normal behavior. From a public health perspective, gun violence was seen as comparable to diabetes, meaning that there was no cure, but the disease can be managed. Therefore, the ONS identified Richmond youth whom they believed were diseased with violence, and their inoculation evolved from being exposed to the "peacemaker" fellowship program. Convincing youth to participate in the inoculation fellowship is comparable to convincing people to get immunized against Covid-19 and the Delta variant in 2021.

Boggan's vision for the ONS[37] also stemmed from his understanding of Teny Gross's work in Providence, Rhode Island. In 2000, Gross started the Institute for the Study and Practice of Nonviolence using the principles of Dr. Martin Luther King, Jr., in addition to the work of David Kennedy,[38] through the Boston Gun Project (Kennedy, 1997; 1998). In 2015, Gross

35 See www.advancepeace.org/

36 CalGRIP evaluative reports can be seen at www.bscc.ca.gov/s_calgrip/.

37 Boggan was frustrated with the city's inability to fund and organize a Ceasefire program to his liking, so he implemented his own program. Ceasefire was ultimately implemented involving the PD and other community groups, but Boggan had moved on to do his own fellowship program. Both Ceasefire and the fellowship program coexisted during much of Magnus's time in Richmond. Lindsey concluded that since neither effort could be conclusively correlated with lower gun violence levels, he believed that both should be supported and sustained (Author's interview with Magnus on March 28, 2020).

38 David Kennedy has been a professor of criminal justice at John Jay College in New York City since 2005. His work is mentioned in the chapter on Bratton, and he developed *Operation Ceasefire*, a group violence intervention initiative in Boston during the 1990s. He is also the High Point Model architect on drug market intervention (Kennedy & Wong, 2009) and domestic violence (Kennedy, 2020). In 2009, he founded the National Network for Safe Communities (see https://nnscommunities.org/) with President Clinton's former NIJ Director Jeremy Travis. Travis also served as the fourth President of John Jay College from 2004 to 2016.

moved to Chicago to create a second non-violence institute. Richmond's version of Ceasefire remained in question (Shanafelt, 2012).

ONS – Precision Outreach

In 2009, Magnus and the RPD publicly stated that they estimated that 17–30 individuals committed 70 percent of violent crimes (Wolf et al., 2015). In response to those statements, Boggan's initiative, along with Ceasefire, offered a precision alternative to police sweeps and mass incarceration that has plagued traditional law enforcement responses to gun violence.[39] Instead of extensive crackdowns, the ONS offered an alternative to mentor those most prone to violence exclusively. These individuals were frequently among the youth most resistant to change and chronically unresponsive to help.

The ONS was launched in October 2007 and initially trained four individuals, each with their own offending backgrounds, to work as neighborhood change agents and conduct outreach specific to the Iron Triangle neighborhoods. Boggan joked that "this is possibly the only job around that requires you to have a criminal background" (Childers, 2015). It was critical for targeted participants to believe that Boggan's change agents were not working to investigate their past offending behaviors and were genuinely invested in being a positive influence in their lives. Magnus and City Manager Lindsay formed a partnership with Boggan. The RPD worked in the background to help identify those responsible or at-risk in Richmond's gun violence culture.[40] Although the change agents do not readily share information with the RPD, they share a common preventative goal, which came at some RPD officers' consternation.

As city employees, change agents responded to locations where there was gunfire and listened to police scanners for reports of shots fired. Like the police, they interviewed people surrounding the shooting incidents, careful not to impede police investigations. In the aftermath of a shooting, they attempted to seek out those connected to the shooting and offer alternative ways out of retaliatory violence. Suppose we comprehensively address what drives gun violence. In that case, the fellowship's premise is to achieve change that is impossible by relying on the standard model of investigation and law enforcement arrest. Outreach workers get to know the offenders personally and intensely mentor them toward positive self-esteem and conventional success opportunities. In doing so, they work to transform the lives of the city's most lethal young men.

Breaking the cycle of violence is challenging, noting that most young men who engage in illegal gunfire have been exposed to significant trauma and never learn how to deal with conflict other than through retaliatory violence. As with most traumas, other variables that put these individuals at risk include substance abuse, poor education, inadequate housing arrangements, and a lack of perceived opportunities for change. As change agents form relationships with the targeted population, they also direct them to community services to assist in housing options,

39 The author was engaged in similar research with the Aurora, Illinois Police Department in a project that was titled "Finding Typhoid Mary: Ganging up on Offenders who Facilitate Violence." The project was nominated for the Herman Goldstein Award at the 2013 international problem-oriented policing conference in Dayton, Ohio. In the city of Aurora, population 200,000, Boggan's contemporary was Clayton Muhammad, who initiated a mentoring group known as Boys II Men and was recognized by the Obama Administration's initiative "My Brother's Keeper." Like Boggan, Muhammad, who works in the mayor's office, heard from the police that a very small group of offenders were the cause of the vast majority of gun violence. Over five years, shootings were cut in half, and murder was reduced 78 percent through a comprehensive gang strategy (see Kooi, Thomas, Muhammad, & Cervantes, 2013; Kooi, 2020).

40 Author's interview with Magnus on January 5, 2020.

anger management, and substance abuse treatment. These interventions all contribute to skill-building through CBT to help targeted youth identify the thoughts and emotions that influence their behavior. Research supports the intensity of outreach and may depend on where targeted individuals are in their life-course (Roman, Decker, & Pyrooz, 2017).

The fellowship program was scheduled for 18 months and consisted of seven focused touch-points that participants must accomplish (Wolf et al., 2015):

1 Engage in multiple daily contacts with change agents from the ONS.
2 Develop a "LifeMAP" (Life Management Action Plan) and take measurable steps to progress toward those goals.
3 Participate in civic, educational, and social horizon-building interactions and excursions outside of Richmond, some of which would include interactions with fellows from rival gangs and neighborhoods.
4 Engage in internship opportunities.
5 Learn to navigate social service support mechanisms (e.g. addiction counseling and anger management where their change agent accompanies them).
6 Participate in an intergenerational mentoring elders circle.
7 Receive a monetary stipend of up to $1,000 a month for LifeMap goal achievement. (Fellows become eligible for stipend opportunities after six months of program participation. Stipends are awarded based on a Participation Level and LifeMAP achievement quotient.)

Fellows are assigned to two categories: Junior fellows (aged 14–17) and senior fellows (aged 18–25+). Most (97 percent) are African-American, nearly half (45 percent) are fathers, and about one in five (21 percent) have been victims of previous gun violence (Wolf et al., 2015, p. 13). Besides the intensive mentoring, the fellowship also organized trips for its participants/fellows outside of Richmond. As an opportunity, fellows could travel outside of California or the United States. The catch was that participants had to agree to travel with a rival fellow and learn to interact along the trip instead of committing retaliatory violence. Trips included tours of college campuses, South Africa, Mexico City, New York, and Washington, DC, where youth met with public leaders and participated in community service projects. For the participants, these retreats away from Richmond demonstrated that there is life outside of street violence, and fellows can make amends with those who have committed violence toward them, their families, or close friends.

ONS Controversies

The ONS approach attempts to circumvent retaliatory violence without input from the criminal justice system. This approach differs from David Kennedy's version of Ceasefire (see Kennedy, Piehl, & Braga, 1996; Kennedy, Braga, & Piehl, 1997; Kennedy & Braga, 1998) and created tension with many RPD officers. Outreach workers know that the program is often seen as a "hug a thug" initiative that coddles criminals and rewards them for harmful behavior. On October 14, 2011, the conflicting perceptions culminated at city hall in the ONS offices when fellowship street rivals started a fistfight. A subsequent police report indicated that ONS staff were non-cooperative and refused to implicate anyone involved. Once the story leaked to the press, Magnus sensed that the controversy was problematic for both the ONS and the RPD and the strides were made for reducing violence in Richmond. He issued the following open letter of apology (reproduced in its entirety below). While traditional police managers seldom apologize, Magnus's open leadership style demonstrates honest transparency regarding the given incident, subsequent police report, and what the RPD was doing to improve. In doing so, his open letter salvaged the promising violence reduction work that came from both the ONS and the RPD.

October 26, 2011

Dear City Manager Lindsay, Richmond City Council Members, Director Boggan, and Members of the Ceasefire Working Group:

Recent events involving the Richmond Police Department (RPD) and the Office of Neighborhood Safety (ONS) have raised important questions and undermined the confidence of some community residents have in our ability to work together effectively within the City to reduce violence. I am deeply frustrated by this because I believe both RPD and ONS have made significant strides over the past several years to engage the community successfully in violence-reduction efforts. Both the Police Department and ONS have highly committed, active, and hard-working employees, who have been doing their best to diminish gun violence in our city, albeit through different methods and sometimes with different resources. The common resource we both rely on, however, is the confidence and trust of the community. When this trust is compromised, our shared mission becomes more difficult to achieve and we lose the public's support.

On Friday, October 14th, a fight between individuals from two rival neighborhood groups took place at City Hall in the Office of Neighborhood Safety when some of these individuals inadvertently came in contact with one another. When officers responded to the scene, they discovered broken items, overturned furniture, and a large amount of blood suggesting a more serious assault might have taken place. In addition, it was clear that multiple individuals involved in the incident had left the scene prior to the officers' arrival. The responding officers, including a supervisor, began questioning the staff and others from ONS who were still present.

A little history may be helpful at this point. Several years ago when the position of "Neighborhood Change Agent" (NCA) was created within the ONS, RPD played a key role in establishing a set of protocols to address how NCAs and the Police Department could interact when necessary and avoid situations where the safety of the NCAs would be compromised. This involved establishing one or more liaisons from the PD who could be contacted as needed by the ONS Director or other ONS personnel should situations arise when it was necessary or appropriate to exchange information. Typically, this communication involved general concerns about when the streets were "heating up" rumors about things going on at the neighborhood level, or specific concerns about safety. NCAs are justifiably concerned about being perceived as agents of the police (and for the record, once again, they have no connection with the PD)—so the hope was that this "liaison" process could address these concerns. For the most part, the liaison process and the existing protocols between RPD and ONS have worked well, however the incident on Friday the 14th was somewhat different than what these protocols had previously been used to deal with. First, the responding patrol officers were not well versed in the protocol process, since the primary liaison with ONS in the past was a lieutenant assigned to the Police Department's Special Investigations Section (SIS). Most of the interactions between ONS and the liaison were confidential, so it would be unusual for patrol personnel to be aware of them. Secondly, the Police Department hadn't envisioned the protocols would apply to situations involving a crime that had just occurred in the City Hall offices of the ONS, where there was the possibility of serious injuries and there was one or more perpetrators outstanding. The responding officers expected full access to all ONS personnel and others present at the scene for immediate interviews, so they were surprised and unhappy when the individuals present were unwilling to speak with them—instead referring them to the ONS Director (who was not present or immediately available). Their reports clearly reflect these frustrations.

I believe a series of mistakes and miscommunications, directly and peripherally related to this incident, took place involving Police Department personnel. I would like to extend my apologies and accept full responsibility for these mistakes, which include the following:

- *In response to media inquiries, spokespersons for the Police Department incorrectly stated that the Department was not receiving any cooperation from the ONS. In fact, the protocols as they currently exist were largely followed. This misstatement of information was not intentional or malicious, but rather was the result of a breakdown in communication within the Police Department. To the degree that this has harmed the credibility or reputation of the ONS Director, I am deeply sorry. I believe this communication breakdown highlights the importance of reevaluating if the existing protocols best meet the needs of all parties involved for situations of this kind.*
- *A reporter obtained a copy of the police report associated with this incident before the Department should have officially allowed it to be released. Regrettably, leaks concerning salacious or high profile events/crimes are not uncommon within police agencies, but the timing of the press gaining access to this report made a difficult situation worse.(It should be noted, however, that this report would have become a public record once the police investigation was closed.)*
- *The initial police report indicated that there was "a chorus of 'I ain't seen nothin'" from ONS personnel who were present at the scene. While this may have been the gist of what the officers heard from one or more persons, phrasing it in this way was unnecessarily provocative and unprofessional.*
- *Administrative personnel within the Department, including me, should have done a better job reaching out to Director Boggan earlier during the period following this incident. Deputy Chief Brown left a message with Director Boggan on Friday, but when the two of them were unsuccessful in reaching each other, I should have made follow-up calls to Director Boggan early that following week. I believe if Director Boggan and I had spoken with each other sooner, we could have helped resolve some of the confusion and fallout that stemmed from this incident.*
- *The process of rotating police personnel through different assignments in the Police Department is both contractually addressed and administratively mandated for a wide range of reasons. Regrettably, two personnel (including one who had been assigned as a liaison to ONS for several years) were both rotated into new assignments at approximately the same time—and shortly before this incident took place.The detective assigned to work with the Ceasefire program had also made a specific request to return to a Patrol assignment, which the Department accommodated. In retrospect, I can appreciate why some of our community partners in the Ceasefire program might be alarmed about the Department's commitment to this endeavor based on this detective's reassignment. For this reason, I will maintain his assignment to the Ceasefire program for one additional year. I will also take steps to ensure we do a better job communicating with the ONS about RPD personnel transfers that impact that ONS activities. The relationship between a police department and city entity such as the Office of Neighborhood Safety is a complicated one. Both are focused and heavily committed to reducing crime and violence, yet both need to approach this goal somewhat differently. In many ways, the incident at City Hall highlighted issues we needed to deal with eventually because of the inevitable challenges associated with the populations we serve, the work we do, and the legal constraints we have. I have very strong confidence that moving forward, the Police Department will take all necessary steps to fortify its relationship with ONS, work more effectively with our community partners to implement the Ceasefire project, and address the ONS-RPD protocol concerns that need to be resolved.*

Having said all of that, I want to acknowledge once again that real harm has been done, and I believe it is the community that has suffered the most as a result of the miscommunications, poor decision-making, and unnecessary tensions associated with this incident. For this, I am very sorry. It is my job to effectively address interdepartmental issues of this kind before they reflect unfavorably on the City. I sincerely regret that in this case, I failed to meet this expectation. In addition, I believe important relationships based on trust between members of the Ceasefire Working Group and the Police Department have suffered. I am committed to repairing these relationships and helping us achieve our mutual goals. I look forward to meeting with the Working Group to discuss all these and other issues in the near future.

Sincerely yours,
Chris Magnus
Chief of Police

According to Boggan, the most significant aspect of the altercation was a fight that ended with a bloody nose and a few bumps rather than with gunfire. Magnus's letter demonstrated a collaborative spirit between the ONS and the RPD. In writing it, he risked further alienating his officers, who often discredited Boggan's work and jeopardized his push toward community policing. However, Magnus provided the type of transparent leadership that is too often unique in law enforcement and gained a level of legitimacy that would prove critical for his ongoing success.

Chief Magnus Leadership

During the time of ONS, Richmond was able to add 40 additional officers, bringing the sworn total in the police department to 195. Other departments, such as Oakland, could not add officers because of high salaries and pensions from high-ranking officers. In Richmond, officers pay into their pensions and have been doing so since a financial crisis in the 1990s. Oakland officers began pension contributions in 2011. Consequently, Magnus was able to hire more officers. Like Bratton, Magnus also facilitated the inclusion of CompStat[41] crime-mapping technology that allowed them to become more geographically directed in patrol strategies. As was the case in New York City, CompStat allowed Magnus to decentralize the chain of command and give more responsibility to middle management. If a violent crime occurred in the middle of the night, the notification went out to the district captain responsible for coordinating officers and community members in the impacted area. Magnus and the captains frequently responded to the scene as well. Before this level of direct accountability, police managers were often notified about high-level crimes the morning after.

The ONS initiatives followed place-based criminology that allocates resources toward a small number of offenders, victims, and places producing the most significant amount of harm. The "power of few" (see Sherman, 2007) advocates that resources should be allocated toward a reduction of harm through precision-style policing. Social network analysis provides examples of how resources can be more effectively targeted toward preventing retaliatory violence (Papachristos, 2009).

Richmond was divided into districts and, more importantly, beat assignments. Officers were given longer-term beat assignments and held accountable for crime and disorder in their beats. Long-term geographic deployment in hot spot locations, as driven by CompStat, allowed the department to become more targeted in crime prevention and community relations (see Braga & Weisburd, 2010). Expectations were for beat officers to attend neighborhood council meetings and conduct foot patrol while claiming ownership of their neighborhoods' problems. Officers enhanced communication through relationship building and de-escalation skills, making batons, pepper spray, and firearms less necessary.

41 The roots of the CompStat approach are detailed in the chapter on Bratton and the work of Jack Maple.

Magnus also opted to budget for two Contra Costa County prosecutors to work out of the police department and focus exclusively on gangs and cases dealing with firearms. While gang suppression was an important consideration, lessons from the 1990s' Comprehensive Homicide Initiative emphasized strengthening neighborhood bonds with officers through community collaboration. Magnus shared the responsibility of lowering gun violence with multiple entities in the city, as discussed more fully below.

Magnus led when Richmond became a city that reinvented itself and demonstrated the power of grassroots politics and municipal government as sources of innovation through community collaboration. This collaboration fits with the community policing philosophy that Magnus brought to the west coast from his Midwest Michigan education. Ironically, this transformation occurred just seven miles up the coast from the police professionalization movement's birthplace and Chief Vollmer's revolutionary work in Berkeley at the turn of the twentieth century. Magnus's success in transforming the departmental philosophy to community policing served as an example for chiefs across the country. He also enjoyed the support of Mayor Gayle McLaughlin.

Mayor Gayle McLaughlin (2006–2014)

In 2006, Green Party candidate Gayle McLaughlin defeated incumbent Irma Anderson as the mayor of Richmond and became a two-term mayor in 2010. McLaughlin relocated to Richmond from Chicago only a few years before being elected to the city council and then mayor. Richmond became the largest city in the country with a Green Party mayor (McLaughlin, 2018). In 2014, after serving her mayoral two-term limit, McLaughlin was re-elected to the city council. Her progressive policies included a minimum wage increase, defeat of a casino development, challenge to lending practices that led to bank evictions and foreclosures, using eminent domain to seize underwater homes, and fairer taxation of Richmond's largest employer, Chevron Corporation (Early, 2017). Richmond was also one of the country's first cities to attempt to get a soda tax, but the voters rejected it.

Holding Property Owners and Banks Accountable – Removing Abandoned Vehicles

In 2008, the Richmond City Council passed an ordinance that allowed banks to be fined if foreclosed properties were neglected and not maintained. Foreclosed homes and dilapidated properties become crime facilitators and targets for scrap metal theft (Kooi, 2010). The ordinance allows for banks that own properties with code violations to receive fines up to $1,000 a day. In the first year, the ordinance brought $780,000, mainly from properties in wealthier neighborhoods (Harless, 2011). The money collected from these fines went to job programs for at-risk youth and community land trusts. Several properties, especially those in less affluent neighborhoods, were owned by mortgage companies that deliberately obscured their ownership as a means to avoid financial penalties from the city ordinance. McLaughlin and Magnus provided public support to the Alliance of Californians for Community Empowerment (ACCE), who sought to hold property owners accountable for letting their properties become dilapidated. The response toward run-down properties in Richmond resulted from the subprime loan crisis when nearly 1.3 million homes became foreclosed throughout 2007, and banks lost an estimated $391 billion (Bernanke, 2008).

In response to the 2007 subprime loan crisis, Magnus practiced "third party" policing, which seeks to persuade, and at times coerce, stakeholders into taking responsibility for the reduction and prevention of crime (see Buerger & Mazerolle, 1998; Mazerolle & Ransley,

2005; Mazerolle, Higginson & Eggins, 2016). In one of Herman Goldstein's last publications, he identified the need for police departments to increasingly shift and share responsibility for public safety problems (Goldstein & Scott, 2011). Parents, landlords, business owners, and other local government regulators become co-producers of police services once responsibility is shifted and shared. These proactive strategies come from leaders within problem-oriented policing departments who facilitate stakeholder guardianship. At times, the public may be cooperative with these initiatives. However, when cooperation fails, the police may have to be more coercive, such as advocating for ordinance violations and fines. Through the support of Mayor McLaughlin, Magnus targeted third-party property owners as the cause of facilitating crime if they abandoned their responsibilities.

By holding property owners responsible, the use of third-party policing served to legitimize Magnus and the RPD. Magnus furthered his credibility when he met with neighborhood groups to discuss their priorities. While there was an assumption that violent crime would be the community's primary concern, when asked, members overwhelmingly expressed complaints related to abandoned cars. In addition to dilapidated buildings, abandoned vehicles provided a daily sense that no one cared about Richmond's working-class neighborhoods' plight. While this priority was somewhat shocking, Magnus consolidated city code enforcement and abatement divisions into the RPD to facilitate quicker responses and cooperation. This "broken windows" style of policing addressed physical attributes of crime and challenged property owners while removing thousands of abandoned vehicles. Civil abatement procedures used to clean up the abandoned vehicles provided the chief with credibility. Richmond's dramatic reduction in homicide connects with the RPD's foundational commitment to community concerns through third-party policing techniques.

Community and Broken Windows Policing

On March 29, 2007, the Office of COP held a regional roundtable discussion in Richmond. The purpose of the discussion was to focus on the challenges of advancing community policing, emphasizing the type of leadership necessary for full implementation and departmental institutionalization. Notably, the roundtable stressed partnerships being cultivated in good times and not just in crises. Magnus met this challenge, and the core mission of the RPD was shifted to an all-encompassing community policing philosophy. Expectations are for every one of the 195 officers to engage in community policing with no distinctions. Magnus looked for empathetic officers who carried high emotional intelligence traits with an understanding of the importance of building community relationships and treating everyone respectfully, even suspected offenders. They were also encouraged to attend festivals and have fun with the residents. A new performance evaluation system rewarded officers for building relationships with residents, community leaders, and neighborhood associations.

Within the COP Office's roundtable discussion in the spring of 2007, enforcement efforts were essential. RPD strategy avoided aggressive style stop-and-frisk since the community did not support it. However, Magnus and the COPs Office knew that officers would respect community policing strategies if enforcing orderly behavior was also encouraged. In this context, Magnus made it known to the media and his officers that he supported broken windows policing but not sacrificing community relations. In this manner (see the Appendix to the chapter on Bratton), Magnus supported George Kelling's broken windows policing theory that emphasized negotiated policing and community collaboration.

Taylor (2001) suggested that effective incivility reduction is rooted in a policing tradition of stable relationships with residents and responsiveness to local concerns. If police leaders are solely committed to increasing misdemeanor arrests to demonstrate officer productivity, such strategies will undermine relationships in low-income neighborhoods (Skogan & Frydl, 2004). These neighborhoods are likely to have concentrated minority populations with a history of mistrust. In this vein, Magnus recognized that aggressive order maintenance policing, or zero-tolerance policing, does not have to be tied to broken windows policing. Zero-tolerance policing is a strategy that consists of stopping, questioning, and frisking any pedestrian or driver that acts suspicious, with the goal of arrest whenever possible. The underlining assumption is that any successfully perpetrated low-level offenses will lead to more serious crimes at the given location. However, Braga, Welsh, and Schnell (2015) failed to demonstrate significant crime reduction through zero-tolerance interventions. Moreover, these crackdowns may be counterproductive (Maher & Dixon, 2001). Magnus understood the full nature of precision policing within the broken windows context and how alternative strategies implemented in place of zero tolerance would allow for significant residential support.

Police managers misinterpret Kelling and Wilson (1982) when they look to crack down on anything perceived as disorderly. The essence of broken windows policing called for short-term negotiated policing tactics directed to specific behaviors that generated fear while enhancing police legitimacy in hot spots (Brown & Wycoff, 1987). Examples include police challenging disorderly drunks, aggressive panhandling, and juveniles who openly intimidate pedestrians. However, within the problem-oriented policing guide on crackdowns, Scott (2003) demonstrated the short-term benefits and long-term drawbacks of zero-tolerance police strategies that crack down on offenders. Magnus followed the recommendations that crackdowns should be directed toward specific offenses rather than on entire neighborhoods. Once there are reductions of disorder in particular locations, the strategy should end or evolve, so police legitimacy is not challenged (see Braga, Welsh, & Schnell, 2015). In this context, the analogy of fishing with a spear rather than a net makes sense.

As Richmond continued to be impacted by the transformational leadership within their police department, it was critical for Magnus to share the intent of his community policing and broken windows strategies. Open sharing was vital when violence inevitably increased, but not in a manner that impacted overall trends. On August 24, 2013, Magnus wrote the following email to the city council and partly to the Richmond community to explain the challenges and strategies for homicide. The email described the number of personnel working in the RPD, a description of the technology utilized, and their use of Ceasefire.

Dear City Council and other Richmond Community Members:

We have recently seen an increase in gun violence in Richmond – much of it associated with gang activity, some of it simply a result of "personal beefs" between individuals. Unfortunately, gun violence frequently occurs in clusters – in many cases because incidents of retaliation follow the initial shooting – and are very difficult to prevent.

I am often asked how the Police Department investigates these gun violence cases, especially homicides, and why they are difficult to prevent and solve. Here are some of the strategies and tools we use, as well as some of the challenges we face:

Resources: Almost every police agency believes it needs more resources to solve (and of course, prevent) homicides and other serious gun crimes. The plain truth, however, is that the need for additional resources (especially personnel) is much greater in Richmond than many other communities, simply because of the amount of gang violence and the overall challenges of crime in the city.

When I ask members of the public how many sworn police officers we have in Richmond, I get answers like "1,000", or "500." We actually have 195 sworn personnel, which includes everyone from the newest recruit (who may still need to go through a Basic Police Academy or be partnered up with a training officer for on-the-job training) all the way up to me — the Chief. About 90 of our personnel are patrol officers (about another 20 are supervisors: patrol sergeants and lieutenants) — and about 15–30 of these personnel are on duty at any given time patrolling the entire city. The remainder of our sworn staff are detectives, officers assigned to special details like the Regulatory Unit or Recruiting and Training, as well as Administrative personnel. In addition, most people do not realize that we always have personnel on leave days, vacation, going through mandatory training, recovering from injuries or on long-term disability, and otherwise away from the job for a myriad of reasons.

There are approximately a dozen investigators available to handle homicides, although about half of them are primarily assigned to work robberies. Homicides tend to come in groups, so the reality is that these personnel can be spread very thin. Homicide investigators may be called out day or night, 7 days a week, and then work long, long hours to follow-up on a murder or serious shooting in that key period following the crime(s).

Thanks to the support of the City Council and the City Manager, RPD has been fortunate that our overall staffing levels have increased over the past 7 years. Despite these increases, however, we are still staffed below what a city with our level of crime ideally needs.

Our department utilizes a variety of technologies to assist us with the investigation of violent crime, including Crime Lab services (which come with a hefty price tag through the Sheriff's Department), Closed Circuit TV (also expensive and complicated to operate, maintain, and monitor), ShotSpotter (which triangulates gunfire to provide the location and type of gun being fired — but it can't help with the fact that shooters generally don't stick around for the police!), and license plate readers (LPRs). Residents often assume these technologies are available and functioning throughout the entire city, but because of cost, they are mostly limited to neighborhoods with higher levels of violent crime. This is frustrating to many members of the public and police officers alike, who wish there was a camera or a gunshot sensor available and operating in every area where crimes occur.

The Department also relies on our crime analysis resources, including our ability to track field contacts, provide timely crime data to our personnel, and conduct meaningful analysis of crime trends. We have one Crime Analyst who works behind the scenes with our officers and detectives to track serious crimes, including gang activity. This has to be done carefully and accurately to protect people's rights and to be most effective

Thanks to recent action by the City Council, the Department is contracting for a service known as "Predictive Policing," which is being successfully used in other cities, such as Los Angeles and New York City, to utilize complex algorithms in predicting where future crimes are likely to occur so greater resources can be placed in these locations. It sounds like science fiction, but this process has a track record of proven positive results.

Ceasefire: The Richmond Police Department is part of the Ceasefire — Lifelines to Healing working group and overall effort. The Ceasefire program cannot prevent all homicides, but it is recognized as a "best practice" around the country to reduce shootings. The Ceasefire program involves police detectives and other key individuals identifying persons involved in, or at high risk for committing, gun violence. These individuals are then "called in" to participate in a discussion about the law enforcement consequences (greater police attention, enhanced prosecution efforts, etc.) for continuing to commit shootings. They also hear an important message from the community, which is that people care about them and that a support system exists to help them turn their lives around. This effort involves community groups, service providers, the faith community, formerly incarcerated individuals, and many others.

There are no instant or magical outcomes associated with the Ceasefire program, but real prevention and long-term successes are hard to measure and difficult to achieve. This program requires the persistent dedication and commitment of many people and groups. It also requires sufficient funding and resources to provide effective interventions. To provide sustainable interventions, shooters who want to make major life changes often need life-skills training, employment, mental health and substance abuse services, anger management and conflict resolution skills, education, and other assistance.

Few of these services are available to the degree they are needed in our community, despite the best efforts of many groups and people.

No Giving Up: Here's one especially important thing I'd like people to know about our homicide investigations: We don't give up. Homicide cases are never closed. Even when evidence is very limited and no witnesses have come forward; even when we have exhausted all leads — unsolved homicide cases remain open in case information or evidence is developed later (sometimes years later) that helps us solve a case and charge a suspect.

A good example of this is a 2009 homicide case that our investigators just made an arrest on. We know how important this kind of closure is to victims' families and friends. It's also important to our personnel, who have often spent several thousand hours investigating a case. Our personnel are invested in these cases.

Another important thing to keep in mind: The Department offers a standing $10,000 reward for information leading to the arrest and conviction of the person or persons who committed any homicide — even a homicide many years ago. Lesser rewards may be available for critical information that helps us with other serious shooting cases.

I hope this information has helped explain the ongoing work and challenges faced by the police (and others) in addressing the problem of gun violence in our community. This work is difficult and there are many obstacles to achieving success. We are fortunate to have considerable support, and an ongoing commitment for this work, from our City Council and other regional elected leaders. We also have a caring group of residents who are highly invested in this effort. That said, nothing is easy — and our needs remain considerable. I appreciate your time in learning more about these issues and your willingness to partner with us as we move forward.

Chris Magnus
Chief of Police

From Magnus's transformational leadership, Richmond in 2014 was vastly different from ten years prior. In 2004, the city had 38 homicides, and there were only 11 in 2014. Violent crimes numbered 1,078 in 2004, and ten years later, the number decreased to 833 violent crimes. Lastly, there were 7,090 property crimes in 2004 and 2,808 fewer property crimes ten years later. While these numbers were significantly less than the prior decade, Magnus reported to the city council that the RPD responded to 122,159 calls for service in 2014. Nearly 3,000 of these calls, or 2 percent, resulted in an arrest and the 357 guns confiscated. Notably, only 6 percent of the 3,000 arrests required the use of force. Out of those cases, officers used a Taser about 25 percent of the time. During 2014, there were 182 suspects forcibly arrested, and about 39 percent of the suspects were injured, along with 22 officers (Early, 2017). The fact that the RPD and Magnus had these exact statistics to track forcible arrests is a testament to the leadership and analytics that forced accountability onto the RPD. While Magnus maintained a focus on reducing officer misuse of force and violent crime in 2014, the rest of the country was on the verge of experiencing increases not seen in decades.

Ferguson, Missouri – The Shooting Death of Michael Brown

One year after the August 2013 Magnus email, Ferguson, Missouri, became the national centerpiece for America's racial tension and a resurgence to the Black Lives Matter movement. On August 9, 2014, shortly after the noon hour, 28-year-old Ferguson, Missouri police officer Darren Wilson[42] fatally shot 18-year-old resident Michael Brown. Witness accounts about

42 Wilson resigned from the Ferguson PD after the Grand Jury declined to indict him because he would jeopardize other officers. Wilson reportedly bought a $500,000 home, making sure his name was not on the deed,

what occurred that day varied. Brown's friend, Dorian Johnson,[43] claimed that Officer Wilson questioned them both about walking in the middle of Canfield Drive and told them to get on the sidewalk. Wilson later claimed that he overheard a radio call related to a robbery minutes earlier at the *Ferguson Market & Liquor* store, and Brown and Johnson matched the suspects' description. However, Chief Thomas Jackson stated that Wilson did not know about the robbery call when he confronted Brown and Johnson for walking in the middle of the street.

In March 2017, the documentary film *Stranger Fruit*[44] was released and showed two non-audio surveillance videos from security cameras inside the store. The first video took place a little after 1 AM on August 9, 2014, showing Michael Brown giving a bag of marijuana to store clerks and the clerks bagging a cigarillos box to give to Brown as a consensual exchange. In the documentary, Johnson stated that this type of bartering is common. However, Brown hands back the cigarillos bag, and according to the documentary filmmaker Jason Pollock, he returned 11 hours later to retrieve his item. Upon his return, Brown was challenged by store owner Andy Patel, causing a confrontation that the police would later describe as a strong-armed robbery. In the second video, Brown hands a box of Swisher Sweet cigars to Johnson and shoves owner Patel on his way out of the store without paying for the product. The police released the film to the media as a justification for the confrontation and fatal shooting. The store owner did not call the police and did not want to release the surveillance video. (The police received the call from a customer.) He had two additional stores in the area, and all three stores were burned and looted during the subsequent Ferguson riots (Smith, 2017). After the documentary film release, an attorney for the store owner held a press conference challenging Polluck's conclusions from the video surveillance and indicated that Brown originally left the store because the clerks asked him to return the unpaid merchandise.

Minutes after Brown and Johnson left the store, Wilson confronted them from his SUV Chevy Tahoe police vehicle and told them to get on the sidewalk. A heated conversation ensued, and Johnson claimed that he saw Officer Wilson grab Brown by the neck through his police vehicle window. Wilson claimed that Brown attacked him through his window and tried to grab his firearm. During the melee of the altercation, Wilson fired two shots, grazing Brown's right hand. Johnson and Brown both fled on foot. Witness accounts then vary. Wilson exited his police SUV, and a foot pursuit ended quickly. Johnson claimed that Brown turned to face Wilson and put his hands up, while Wilson claimed that Brown charged him. Wilson fired ten additional shots, and six of those hit Brown, all in the front of his body, during the second altercation.

A forensic specialist, Dr. Michael Baden, argued that the last shot fired was fatal and was in a downward trajectory into Brown's head as he fell to the ground (Curry & Ghebremedhin, 2014). The blood should have pooled underneath Brown, but due to the slight slope of Canfield Drive, the blood flowed for several feet. For about ten minutes, Brown's body lay uncovered as area residents videoed from their cell phones. For the next four hours, Brown's body, partially covered with a tarp, laid on Canfield Drive as the investigation ensued and

on the outskirts of St. Louis with help from donations he received from supporters (Engel, 2015) and keeps a low profile. He lives with his wife, Barb, a former Ferguson police officer (Halpern, 2015).

43 Johnson had only met Brown a few weeks before the shooting. He was new to the neighborhood and had just recently moved in with his girlfriend and daughter. In November 2019, the U.S. Supreme Court declined to hear an appeal from Johnson, who filed a lawsuit alleging that his civil rights were violated when Brown was fatally shot, and they both ran from Officer Wilson.

44 *Strange Fruit* was a song recorded by Billie Holiday in 1939 to protest the lynching of African-Americans comparing these atrocities to fruit hanging from trees. The song was perceived as a declaration of war, led to an intensive investigation from the FBI with allegations of inciting a mob, and created the start of the civil rights movement (Smith, 1944). In February 2021, *Hulu* also released the film *The United States v. Billie Holiday*.

the summer temperature rose to over 90 degrees. Chief Jackson later wrote that this type of protocol needed to be changed (Jackson, 2017). After the fatal shooting, Wilson returned to the department unescorted, washed the blood off his hands before investigators could take photographs, and submitted his firearm into evidence. Questions about unorthodox forensic protocols surfaced after detectives photographed his facial injuries at the Fraternal Order of Police union building rather than at Ferguson Police headquarters (Hamburger & Marton, 2014).

On November 24, 2014, a Grand Jury failed to indict Wilson.[45] On March 4, 2015, a separate investigation by the FBI and attorneys from the Department of Justice Civil Rights Division cleared Wilson of any wrongdoing. They stated that the evidence indicated he acted in self-defense. However, a separate report concluded that the Ferguson police routinely violated residents' constitutional rights, especially African-Americans, in a pattern of unlawful conduct. A week later, Ferguson Police Chief Jackson resigned.

The Ferguson riots, or what has been called an uprising, initially lasted throughout August 2014. Other protests or uprisings occurred the following summer. The protests led to the destruction and looting of numerous businesses and physical encounters with the police that included police use of tear gas and rubber bullets. Media coverage reported the full tactical and militarized police response that converged onto Ferguson. The protests, linked to others around the country, caused a resurgence of the Black Lives Matter movement, which began in Sanford, Florida, following the fatal shooting of Trayvon Martin by George Zimmerman. Ferguson demonstrators carried the slogan "Hands up, don't shoot," which followed some witness accounts that Brown, unarmed, had his hands up when Wilson used lethal force.

Magnus's ability to think empathetically about his impact on the community he serves won him high praise from communities both inside and outside of Richmond. Magnus became a national expert in the wake of protests linked to Ferguson. In September 2014, he came to Ferguson as one of two law enforcement experts tapped by the DOJ to review Ferguson's police practices. He helped prepare a federal report that was heavily critical of the Ferguson Police Department leadership and the discriminatory traffic stops that were the primary source of friction between the local Black community and the police. For Magnus, this lesson had its roots in Lansing, Michigan and the analysis of traffic stops from criminal justice researchers from MSU. Magnus also accompanied DOJ attorneys to St. Louis County on several occasions to assist with interviews, ride-alongs with Ferguson officers, and attendance at community meetings. In writing a final report about Ferguson's events, Magnus's role created a national platform broadcasting his successes in Richmond. That success included significant reductions in violent crime coupled with a decrease in the police use of force.

On December 9, 2014, Richmond mimicked other American cities protesting the death of Brown in Ferguson. Through social media, protesters across the country were encouraged to stand in solidarity for four and a half hours as a symbol of the time Brown's corpse laid in the street while the police conducted their investigation. As O.W. Wilson did in Chicago when he met with Martin Luther King, Jr. and promised him police protection during their demonstrations, Magnus and his command staff met with the protesters and had pizzas delivered to feed the demonstrators. Approximately, 100 people were part of the protest, and one female protester asked Magnus if he would hold up a hand-painted sign with the words "Black Lives Matter" toward passing traffic. It should not be surprising that Magnus, likely

45 In August 2018, St. Louis County elected a Black prosecutor, 43-year-old Wesley Bell. Bell replaced 67-year-old Robert McCulloch, who held the position for more than 25 years. The new reform-minded prosecuting attorney spent several months secretly reviewing the Wilson-Brown shooting case, but in July 2020, he announced that he could not ethically bring new charges.

reflective of his Michigan days working for the youth advocacy Three O'clock Lobby, decided to hold up the protester's sign.

Magnus's photo holding the controversial sign went viral throughout the traditional mass media and on social media. The image provided a sharp contrast to the clashes between protesters and the police in Oakland, Berkeley, New York, and Ferguson. The RPOA, or the union, criticized their chief for violating departmental policy and participating in political activities while in uniform. Alison Wilkinson, an attorney for the RPD Union, commented that the chief has a First Amendment right to free speech, but the state law explicitly bars him from sending a message while in uniform (Zernike, 2007). Magnus saw the sign as innocuous, and his decision to hold it up was a meaningful gesture of goodwill, believing that Black lives and all lives matter. Magnus further commented that he would make the same decision if he had it to do over, but he would also be better prepared for the fallout. Five and half years later, several police leaders around the country would take a knee in solidarity with massive protests against the police in a manner that few would have ever predicted during the time Magnus held onto a Black Lives Matter sign.

After reporters photographed Magnus holding the #BlackLivesMatter[46] sign, his story as a reform-minded chief went viral and stirred a national response.[47] During this time, the national media reported on his community policing success and the fact that he was an openly gay white male in charge of policing a predominantly minority city. These discussions carried interest in contrast to the racial conflict seen throughout other cities following high-profile deaths of minority men by white police officers.

The Anti-Ferguson (Reducing Officer Use of Force)

On September 6, 2014, *The Contra Costa Times* headlined a story titled "Use of Deadly Force by Police Disappears on Richmond Streets." A week later, in a twist of fate, on September 14, 2014, Richmond experienced its first fatal officer-involved shooting since 2007. In the early morning hours, foot patrol officer Wallace Jensen followed up on a loitering complaint and confronted an intoxicated Richard Perez II outside of a liquor store. A physical fight ensued, and Perez attempted to take Jensen's gun, leading to the fatality.

In the aftermath of the civilian fatality, the RPD and the city provided enormous transparency in their investigations. Magnus reached out to the community via Facebook to explain the incident and explain the procedures of two separate investigations. The Perez family

46 The #BLM movement started after July 13, 2013, not guilty verdict of George Zimmerman for the shooting death of Trayvon Martin in Sanford, Florida. In December 2019, Zimmerman filed a $100 million lawsuit (Siemaszko, 2019) against Martin's family, attorney Benjamin Crump and publisher HarperCollins (see Crump, 2019). In February 2020, Zimmerman filed a $265 million lawsuit against Pete Buttigieg (former mayor of South Bend, IN and President Biden's Secretary of Transportation) and Elizabeth Warren (Massachusetts Senator) for defamatory tweets from their Twitter accounts regarding the fatal shooting of Trayvon (Peters, 2020).

47 In the 2020 mass protests, several police agencies chose to walk in solidarity with protesters. Some examples include – Officers in Coral Gables, Florida, took a knee in response to the death of George Floyd; Genesse County Sheriff Chris Swanson in Flint, Michigan, said that he wanted a parade, not a protest and joined the march; Camden, New Jersey officers helped carry a protest sign that read "Standing in Solidarity"; Santa Cruz, California Chief Andy Mills (proponent of Goldstein, POP and 2000 recipient of PERF's Gary Hayes Award) took a knee with protesters, and his department tweeted, "in memory of George Floyd and bringing attention to police violence against Black people"; Black and white officers in Kansas City holding a sign that read "END Police Brutality!"; Fargo officer holding hands with protesters with a sign that read "We are one race...The HUMAN race"; and Ferguson officers took a knee for nine and a half minutes in memory of George Floyd as crowds cheered. However, much of the collaborative protests ended after the first couple of weeks of June, and police protest participation did not continue.

responded and invited Magnus to Perez's memorial services. He accepted the family's invitation and attended the service with Deputy Chief Allwyn Brown in their civilian attire.

Richmond could have been Ferguson in 2015. However, Magnus's transformational leadership set the city on a different path, which provided the social fabric to buffer the city from the damage of national protests that continued throughout 2015. Richmond was no longer a powder keg waiting to erupt since Magnus spent nearly a decade instituting community policing that helped ease the tension between the police and the Black and Latino communities. While chiefs historically spent only a few years in charge of RPD, Magnus was able to accomplish more through his longer tenure. The reduction in police use of force and reduced violent crime served to effectively address community concerns in the wake of the Ferguson-induced protests and riots.

Magnus also joined a panel of policing experts after the April 19, 2015, death of Freddie Gray in a Baltimore Police Department (BPD) custody wagon. The panel investigated if there was a pattern of misconduct that contributed to the death of Gray. Ultimately, the DOJ independent investigation determined insufficient evidence to support any civil rights charges against the BPD.

President Obama's Task Force on 21st Century Policing

In December 2014, President Obama created the President's Task Force on 21st Century Policing through an executive order. The executive order stated that the task force's purpose was to identify the best means to provide effective partnerships between the police and local communities to reduce crime and increase trust. On May 18, 2015, the task force issued a final report[48] on recommendations and an implementation guide[49] to improve American policing. Conclusions from the report recommended that police agencies develop a Serious Incident Review Board that included both community and sworn police staff to review officer-involved shootings. Further, communities should decide on what form of civilian oversight was needed to meet their needs.

The task force was co-chaired by Charles Ramsey, detailed in the previous chapter. At the time, Ramsey was the Philadelphia Police Commissioner, PERF President, and President of the Major Cities Chiefs Association (MCCPA). Another task force member included Tucson Chief Roberto Villasenor, whom Magnus would replace at the end of 2015. On February 13, 2015, Magnus testified from Phoenix at a listening session with President Obama's task force. He recommended the need for stronger community policing throughout entire departments and not just within specialized units. This emphasis on community-wide policing throughout the department is rooted in Magnus's education at MSU and the work of Professor Robert Trojanowicz. The School of Criminal Justice at MSU started the National Center for Community Policing in 1983, during the period Magnus attended the university. The following excerpt is from Magnus's recommendations to President Obama's task force:

> *Richmond has struggled with historically high rates of crime and has often been among the nation's most violent cities, even when crime has decreased nationally. Public safety and a longstanding distrust of the police have been top concerns of residents for many years. In response to these concerns, the Richmond community committed to addressing violent crime as a public health crisis. Like most public safety agencies, a number of years ago (and even now), Richmond PD believed it was practicing*

48 See https://cops.usdoj.gov/pdf/taskforce/TaskForce_FinalReport.pdf

49 See https://noblenational.org/wp-content/uploads/2017/02/President-Barack-Obama-Task-Force-on-21st-Century-Policing-Implementation-Guide.pdf

"community policing," although quality relationships between most residents (especially residents of color) and police officers were largely non-existent or strained at best. Community policing was synonymous with "public relations," and a small, select group of officers did the majority of the department's community outreach. Since 2006, the department has made a number of changes to address these issues and build a more effective partnership with residents.... Common threads woven throughout these changes have included a commitment to accountability (e.g., a more accessible/rigorous complaint process, and follow-through on commitments and projects), approachability (e.g., getting cops out of cars, engaged at community events, being friendly, and recognizing the importance of demonstrating empathy), as well as transparency (e.g., providing access to the media, advocacy groups, and others to policy development, crime-fighting strategies).[50]

In addition to pushing for a department-wide community policing philosophy, as discussed with President Obama's task force, Magnus was also able to eliminate officers who were not supportive of transformational community policing changes. By 2015, only about a dozen RPD officers had a longer tenure than Magnus. In his nine years as chief, Magnus demoted and fired more officers than two decades of previous chiefs combined. Magnus also used new technology to ensure community policing remained the core mission and encouraged officers to be accountable for their behavior. This accountability came through body cameras, vehicle monitoring, and the IAPro "blue team" system for tracking citizen complaints. These real-time uses of technology allowed watch commanders to monitor beat officers. For example, they could observe how fast officers were driving and how often they interacted with residents. These systems allowed the department to be transparent and proactive with how officers behave.

Through higher levels of officer accountability, community policing became a cornerstone of the departmental mission. Magnus's Richmond office photos exemplified the cornerstone by showing his officers at a community barbeque and dancing at a block party. Making connections with neighborhood leaders was the key to success, challenging officers on biases they often unknowingly carried into the job.

In February 2015, in the wake of *#BlackLivesMatter*, Magnus called upon Dr. Lori Fridell[51] and her team of experts from Fair and Impartial Policing, LLC.[52] The academic team held several training sessions with the RPD to help reduce and counter implicit bias (see Fridell, 2017a). For Fridell, the training was a homecoming of sorts; her father Leo was a longtime public school teacher in Richmond who had written his own guide on local politics, including the RPD, for his social studies class. Officers have been adversarial toward Fridell's training on bias. However, work in Richmond was more fruitful, given the cultural foundation on community policing Magnus provided before Ferguson and the arrival of Fridell's training.

That same month, February 2015, Magnus was star-struck with the appearance of news reporter Katie Couric who spent 90 minutes questioning him on his policing strategies (Marshland, 2015) (Photo 7.2).

In further recognition of his leadership, the White House asked Magnus to send one of his officers to meet with President Obama and Vice President Biden to discuss why their community policing efforts were successful. Magnus selected RPD officer Erik Oliver to attend the February 24, 2015, White House meeting and discuss in his own words why he felt that the

50 See www.policeforum.org/assets/docs/Subject_to_Debate/Debate2015/debate_2015_marmay.pdf

51 Fridell is a criminology professor at the University of South Florida. Prior to this position, she was the Director of Research at the Police Executive Research Forum (PERF). See Fridell (2017b).

52 See https://fipolicing.com/

Photo 7.2 Photo of Katie Couric and Chris Magnus January 30, 2015.
Photo courtesy of the Richmond Police Department.

department was having success. The White House also sent Attorney General Loretta Lynch to Richmond on a fact-finding mission to understand what made Richmond unique.

The year 2015 was marked by national recognition for Magnus and the RPD. Within his thriving community policing transformation, Magnus improved police accountability by changing how the RPD investigated the use of force. To reduce police misuse of force and ensure fair investigations, Magnus moved the RPD internal affairs function to a newly created Office of Professional Accountability (OPA) located in city hall, outside of police headquarters. The belief was that the OPA would serve as a future model for other agencies and communities who distrust their police. One of the first investigations the OPA dealt with was police misconduct with a teenage prostitute exploited by officers from numerous police agencies, including Richmond. The subsequent recommendation from the OPA was for the termination of one officer and the suspension or demotion of ten other officers. However, the city council later reversed its decision and opted not to terminate the Richmond officer. By this time, Magnus was already on his way to become the chief in Tucson.

Richmond and Oakland Sex Scandal 2015

The year 2015 was the final year Magnus was the chief in Richmond and the year Oakland became marred with a police sex scandal leading to a lawsuit the would involve the RPD and Magnus, a year and a half after he left and became the chief in Tucson. The plaintiffs ultimately withdrew their lawsuit against Magnus and the RPD.

Richmond native Jasmine Abuslin, initially known by the pseudonym Celeste Guap, sued both the OPD and RPD, alleging that police leaders ignored her exploitation with officers in 2015 when she was a minor. The sexual encounters occurred with on-duty and off-duty officers from Oakland, Richmond, Livermore, San Francisco, and sheriff's deputies in Alameda and Contra Costa Counties. Abuslin also claimed that officers provided her with information about planned uncover prostitution stings and promised her immunity from arrest in exchange for sex.

The sexual exploitations were revealed in September 2015 when 30-year-old Oakland Officer Brendan O'Brien committed suicide and left a note that stated Abuslin blackmailed him. At that time, Abuslin messaged O'Brien and said that she was in Puerto Rico celebrating her 18th birthday. Frustrated with O'Brien's perceived uncaring response, Abuslin contacted his supervising officer, revealing the underage sexual encounters. According to Abuslin, seven months before his suicide, she ran to O'Brien's squad car while she was running to escape her pimp. O'Brien helped protect her but did not create an incident report. A couple of weeks later, they saw each other again and exchanged phone numbers. This contact led to several sexual encounters. O'Brien then introduced her to other officers who repeated the same sexual behavior with Abuslin.

Additionally, in June 2014, approximately eight months before he met Abuslin, O'Brien was suspected of killing his wife, Huerta Lopez. Lopez, his wife, was found dead from a gunshot wound in O'Brien's apartment. The fatal gunshot came from O'Brien's firearm. The death was initially ruled a suicide, but several officers were suspicious at the time. Specifically, Oakland Sergeant Mike Gantt wanted O'Brien to be investigated but felt that his superiors pushed him off the case. Gantt later sued the OPD for retaliating against him when he tried to investigate O'Brien. Additionally, Abuslin came to Robert Warshaw's attention, a federal compliance director assigned to provide federal oversight of the OPD as part of a decade-long court order. During Warshaw's investigation of the suicides, he discovered that OPD internal investigations were going on for months, but he was not informed, which violated the oversight requirements.

Abuslin claimed that she had sex with over 30 officers from seven different agencies throughout 2015 and 2016, including the school resource officer from her alma mater high school. Multi-agency investigations into the Abuslin sex scandal led to charges against several police officers and the resignation of Oakland Police Chief Sean Whent. Media sources indicated that Whent and his wife Julie knew about O'Brien's liaisons with Abuslin. They ordered officers investigating the sexual misconduct to report to OPD Deputy Chief John Lois rather directly to Whent (BondGraham & Winston, 2016).[53] Oakland settled the case by paying Abuslin nearly $1 million in response to her lawsuit. The Abuslin settlement followed an earlier 2008 Oakland settlement for $2 million given to 16 Asian women who alleged that they were groped, harassed, and victimized by Oakland Officer Richard Valerga. Valerga received a six-month jail sentence. For Richmond, the sex scandal was far from over but became a problem for their new chief.

In April 2016, Allwyn Brown, an Oakland native, was officially sworn in as the 16th chief of the RPD (Cases, 2016). Brown was the deputy chief for Magnus, as described earlier, and had more than 30 years of experience in the RPD. He was also the first chief in 23 years to be appointed internally, a testament to Magnus's transformational leadership. During the transition, Richmond had 186 officers, 60 staff members, and dispatchers. Brown would only last a few years as RPD chief.

On September 10, 2019, Brown resigned amid ethical questions related to his travel expenses approved by his wife, Belinda Brown, the Richmond finance manager. His resignation followed a no-confidence vote (117 that agreed out of 136 who voted) from the RPD union. Bisa French then became the interim chief. French, who has both African-American and Latina ethnicities, became the first woman to lead the RPD.

In the summer of 2017, Abuslin again made international news when she sued the RPD and specifically Chief Brown, Magnus, and internal affairs division head Lt. Brian Dickerson for supervisory liability. Abuslin alleged that, like Chief Whent, Richmond officials knew about the sexual exploitation but did not adequately intervene. Richmond chief Brown arranged

53 In 2017, BondGraham and Winston received the Society of Professional Journalists and the James Madison Freedom of Information Awards for their reporting on the Oakland Police Department.

for Abuslin's transportation to a drug rehabilitation center in Florida in the summer of 2017. Members of the media claimed that this trip was a ruse to keep her silent and that it qualified as tampering with a witness. Abuslin ran from the rehab center in Florida but was escorted back by armed security guards. By January 2018, she dropped her Richmond lawsuit, reportedly because Abuslin no longer wanted to testify. At the time of her lawsuit, Magnus had already been the chief in Tucson for a year and a half.

Tucson, Arizona (Chief 2016–Present)

Michael Ortega became the city manager of Tucson in March 2015 and, within the first few months, sought out Magnus to replace retiring Chief Roberto "Taz" Villasenor, who had a $200,000 salary. The Tucson Police Department (TPD) is five times the size of the RPD. Magnus was initially interviewed for Richmond's position by the police union's vice president and later by the Citizen Police Chief Appointment Advisory Committee. While the union was impressed by Richmond's reduced crime and increased police hiring/compensation, they also expressed concerns about his participation in the Black Lives Matter rally and his creation of the external OPA as a replacement for internal affairs. Consequently, the Tucson police union overwhelmingly supported Dallas Deputy Chief Malik Aziz instead of Magnus. However, the vast majority of the advisory committee preferred Magnus, and the final decision went to City Manager Michael Ortega, Mayor Jonathan Rothschild, and the city council.

Magnus became the 47th chief of the TPD in January 2016. The department had about 900 sworn officers and 300 civilian employees with a budget of $168 million. However, the city faced a $25.6 million deficit for fiscal 2017, and the city council forced the PPD to reorganize through an $11 million reduction. While the decision to make this cut came before Magnus's arrival, it certainly did not endear him to the already tenuous union relationship. Magnus navigated this initial hardship without eliminating officers, outside of normal attrition, and the department eventually returned to full capacity with over 900 sworn personnel.

Brief History of the Tucson Police Department

In 1871, Tucson incorporated, along with its police department. Over the first ten years, the city had 30 different marshals and chiefs of police. The voters elected the marshals and police chiefs until 1930. After 1930, the selection authority for police chiefs became decided by the city council. On January 25, 1934, the national media reported John Dillinger's arrest in Tucson. After his arrest, Lake County, Indiana, had Dillinger transferred to a jail in Crown Point. The transfer occurred because of a January 15, 1934 robbery at the First National Bank of East Chicago, which resulted in 43-year-old Officer William O'Malley's fatal shooting. On March 3, 1934, Dillinger escaped the Crown Point jail using a wooden gun. Four months later, law enforcement officers fatally shot Dillinger outside the Biograph Theater in Chicago on July 22, 1934 (Toland, 1995). Tucson commemorates their arrest by hosting a "Dillinger Days" festival that includes reenactments. Today, the population in Tucson's city is approximately 535,000, with the likelihood that there are many more uncounted residents who are undocumented.

Patrol Allocation

As he did in Richmond, Magnus focused on community policing and immediately overhauled the strategies for conducting street patrol in Tucson. He reconfigured downtown Tucson into its own district instead of a division. Officers reported to an Operations West Captain as other patrols shifted into neighborhoods with the most frequent calls for service. Magnus also moved several nonpatrol specialty units to patrol duties focused on hot spot locations and enhancing neighborhood relations (see Skogan & Frydl 2004; Weisburd & Eck 2004).

After geographically reallocating patrol, Magnus focused on all residents' satisfaction, including those undocumented, especially in high-crime areas. Lessons from the zero-tolerance era of policing taught police leaders that, while high-crime areas produce higher police response levels, residents still expect the police to be respectful and lawful in their crime control efforts (Meares & Skogan 2004; Tyler 2004). Police should proactively challenge disorder but avoid random stop-and-frisk. Studies of satisfaction with citizens indicate that fairness is the most critical following a police encounter (Tyler, 2001). Four dimensions of fair police-citizen interactions (Skogran & Frydl, 2004) certainly fit Magnus's community policing vision through patrol allocation. The first dimension encourages officers to ensure that citizens have meaningful participation in their interactions with the police. Second, citizens should perceive that their police are unbiased and neutral regarding their assessments of situations. Third, citizens should feel like they receive respect and dignity. Lastly, the police are considerate of citizens' needs and concerns in order to inspire trust. They can create this trust by explaining their decision-making to the citizens and accounting for their conduct.

Magnus recognized that hot spot policing would generate increased police-community contacts in very small areas regardless of its specific approach or tactics. Police behavior in these areas will significantly influence the amount of support and involvement from the affected community members. To maximize their ability to manage crime problems in these places, Magnus pushed officers to have fair interactions and develop strong partnerships with community members. While this work is sometimes difficult and time-consuming, long-term community engagement efforts pay dividends in improving the quality of police-community relationships and collaborative crime prevention efforts, as was shown in Richmond.

Fighting the NRA and Conceal Carry Federal Legislation

In the fall of 2017, Magnus became the voice for law enforcement leaders opposed to regressive gun-lobby-backed federal gun legislation. The legislation, influenced by the NRA, pushed to overrule various state laws that restricted some uses of concealing and carrying firearms. Tucson is especially sensitive to gun violence, given the shooting of U.S. Congresswoman Gabrielle Giffords on January 8, 2011, outside of a Safeway Store during a community event called "Congress on your Corner." That morning, a deranged 22-year-old named Jared Lee Loughner shot Giffords in the head with a Glock 19 semi-automatic handgun. Loughner also killed six other individuals, including Federal District Court Judge John Roll, Gabe Zimmerman (one of Gifford's staffers), and 9-year-old Christina-Taylor Green. Giffords survived the shooting and suffered permanent brain damage. She is married to Mark Kelly,[54] former astronaut and U.S. Navy Captain.

Magnus spoke out against the "Concealed Carry Reciprocity Act" that forces all states to recognize conceal carry laws from other states rather than allowing states to decide on their firearm legislation. Magnus argued that federal legislation creates more danger for police officers, who were increasingly ambushed and targeted for gun violence in 2016. On July 7,

54 In November 2020, Kelly became the fourth NASA astronaut to be elected to Congress when he unseated Republican Martha McSally, a former Air Force combat pilot. This Senate election was held for Senator John McCain's seat, who died in 2018 at 81 years of age, and Republican Arizona Governor Doug Ducey had temporarily appointed McSally.

2016, Micah Johnson killed five officers and injured nine others in Dallas. Johnson claimed that the shootings were in retaliation for the police killings of Alton Sterling in Louisiana and Philando Castile in Minnesota. In the early morning hours of July 8, 2016, a remote-controlled robot detonated a bomb and killed Johnson, a first for the U.S. law enforcement.

Magnus also spoke out against Congressional consideration to deregulate the Federal Government from monitoring the purchase of silencers. In both cases, Magnus argued that more officers would be assaulted and killed by gunfire. Despite Magnus's plea, the Concealed Carry Reciprocity Act passed and went into effect in 2019. The law allows qualified individuals to carry their handguns into any state, much like a driver's license, without fear of arrest from different legal restrictions. In July 2019, the U.S. Supreme Court left the federal law intact, requiring firearm silencers to be registered federally.

Immigration

On March 3, 2017, Border Patrol in Tucson reported the description of a man who escaped their custody after being admitted to Banner University Medical Center for evaluation. His prior arrest was for illegal entry. The TPD assisted the Border Patrol in a fruitless search for two hours and then denied the agents access to set up a command post in their Operations West Parking Lot, perceiving that the efforts would be a waste of resources. The friction between the two agencies garnered national attention.

In December 2017, Magnus wrote an op-ed for *The New York Times* (Magnus, 2017). He expressed his concern with the Trump Administration's campaign against "sanctuary cities" and their attempts to link Byrne grant funding to only those communities who were not self-identified as "Sanctuary Cities." In retaliation for not working closely with ICE and the Border Patrol on civil immigration enforcement, the Federal Government withheld funding previously directed to crime prevention, drug treatment, and mental health programs. Federal courts ruled against the presidential executive order that withheld money from sanctuary cities. However, that decision was overturned in February 2020 by a federal appellate court (Correal, 2020). More importantly, Magnus worried that increased federal crackdowns on immigrants would undo any progress attempted with increased police legitimacy in hot spot locations. Magnus (2017) wrote:

> *The message from Washington is that cities need to refocus on "law and order." Yet the harsh anti-immigrant rhetoric and Mr. Session's reckless policies ignore the basic reality known by most good cops and prosecutors: If people are afraid of the police, if they fear they may become separated from their families or harshly interrogated based on their immigration status, they won't report crimes or come forward as witnesses.*
>
> *When crime victims and witnesses are unwilling to testify because they're afraid an Immigration and Customs Enforcement agent will be waiting to arrest them at the courtroom doors, real criminals go unpunished. It means drug dealers and people who commit domestic and sexual violence are free to exploit a voiceless class of victims; such criminals become a threat to us all.*

Magnus further pointed out the hypocrisy of Attorney General Sessions. The AG previously spoke out against consent decrees and other initiatives that sought to challenge "local control" of police agencies. However, Sessions dictated immigration policies to local police agencies under the guidance of the Trump Administration. He contended that the Federal Government should not punish cities for rejecting demands to crack down on immigrants to the peril of community relations and clearance rates. The irony is that the federal call for law and order directly impacted the interest of safety and justice.

Arizona SB1070

On April 23, 2010, Governor Jan Brewer signed into law Arizona Senate Bill 1070 to target illegal immigration in the country's strictest anti-immigration law. The law required local police to enforce federal immigration laws when they have a suspicion that a suspect is in the country illegally. In subsequent court battles, the Department of Justice (under the Obama Administration) challenged federal supremacy. Magnus reported that TPD cases referred to Border Patrol are few in number and have to be very specific in nature. Under his leadership, civil immigration enforcement does not go beyond what is required explicitly by SB1070. In 2016, the Supreme Court weighed in on that law stating that officers should not have prolonged stops or detentions based solely on verifying immigration status. Magnus referred to this interpretation as an essential tipping point. Concerns from the police were two-fold: Arizona officers filed lawsuits that claimed SB1070 created increased safety liability; police chiefs worried that immigrant families would be less likely to report a crime or be cooperative with investigations.

Use of Force

Legal standards that govern if the police are justified in using force often hang on *Graham v. Connor*. This 1989 U.S. Supreme Court decision dealt with a physical confrontation between the Charlotte-Mecklenburg Police and Dethorne Graham. On November 12, 1984, Graham suffered a diabetic insulin reaction and had his friend William Berry drive him to a convenience store to buy orange juice to regulate his low blood sugar. A long line of customers deterred his purchase, and Graham ran back outside to Berry's car to find another location for his juice. An officer outside the store subsequently pulled Berry's car over to inquire why Graham ran out of the store. Upon questioning Graham, and due to his odd behavior, officers called for backup officers. Several officers arrived on the scene and put Graham in handcuffs with the belief that he was intoxicated. Graham suffered a broken foot, bruised forehead, injured shoulder, and cuts on his wrists during his encounter with the police. Later, Graham filed a lawsuit in federal District Court claiming that Officer Connor and other officers used excessive force and violated his Fourteenth Amendment rights. The District Court and the Court of Appeals ruled in favor of the officers. The U.S. Supreme Court kicked the case back to the District Court for retrial, where Graham lost again. However, in doing so, the Court rewrote what "reasonableness" means and set a new standard for the use of force based upon the officer's perspective on the scene and not on the burden that required a plaintiff to prove that the police acted with malicious intent. The new standard requires officers to individualize the facts of each encounter and determine the seriousness of the suspected crime, whether the suspect poses an imminent threat to safety, and whether the suspect is trying to resist arrest.

Schmidt (2017) reported that Tucson officers were seldom disciplined after use of force investigations. From January 1, 2010, through July 8, 2016, the TPD had 186 civilian complaints related to use of force allegations. Only seven complaints were found to be "justified," with five officers suspended and the other two receiving counseling. These findings mimic the national narrative and build upon the public's mistrust that the police fail to hold themselves accountable. That narrative provides unique challenges for contemporary police leaders and incited much of the 2020 mass police protests. However, reform leaders like Magnus have challenged the traditional narrative.

Before Magnus, use of force incidents with the TPD were reviewed by a board of inquiry (BOI) any time police actions caused death, serious injury, or a discharged firearm. Three voting members on the BOI included two lieutenants and one member who was considered a peer and the same rank as the officer being investigated. Participating reviewers also included the city attorney's office, a city council member who represented the ward where the use of force occurred, and a representative from the Independent Police Auditor's Office. The participating reviewers were involved in all aspects of the investigation but were not voting members. The three voting members of the BOI did not have legal subpoena power, but they could talk to anyone they wanted to complete their investigation. In the aftermath of an investigation, officers involved in a shooting would be notified of a hearing date and receive a union representative. The BOI was required to produce one of the following findings from their hearing: justified, within the departmental policy; justified, with policy violation(s); tactical/training improvement opportunity; or not justified, not within departmental policy. In the aftermath of the board's decision, the TPD chief has the opportunity to concur, not concur, or send the report back for additional action. The board was not given any authority related to discipline, and any use of force deemed not justified was sent to the officer's chain of command for corrective actions (Brenckenridge, 2018).

Magnus made substantial changes in the use of force review board for the TPD. He created a critical incident review board (CIRB), referred to as a Sentinel Event Review Board, that followed transparency guidelines outlined by the President's Task Force on 21st Century Policing.[55] The adaptive change in the TPD use of force policy was also published on their departmental website[56] and covered by the media. One of Magnus's significant changes was including community representatives on the CIRB and a member of the Citizen Police Advisory Review Board. An independent police auditor helps select community members to serve on the CIRB, keeping the police out of the selection process (Brenckenridge, 2018).

The timing of investigations following use of force also changed and allowed for administrative investigations and criminal proceedings to occur simultaneously and independently. This change means that the much slower criminal proceedings do not delay the CIRB decision. Additionally, the change authorized the CIRB to independently issue a report to the chief that indicates if the officer was compliant or not compliant with policies. Unlike other police agencies, Tucson officers can be compelled to be interviewed by the CIRB, and dissenting board members can submit a memorandum to the chief documenting concerns. The CIRB was structured to improve community-police relations, and all investigative reports are published on the departmental website, demonstrating a much higher degree of transparency than many police agencies. Like other police leaders discussed throughout this book, Magnus's reform efforts attracted national attention.

On January 16, 2017, Magnus was one of six chiefs invited to Wisconsin to meet with Speaker of the House Paul Ryan as part of a delegation from the Police Executive Research Forum (PERF) to discuss what type of training and policies could reduce police use of force. Magnus discussed the TPD strategies regarding the reporting mechanism and de-escalation techniques that officers are increasingly trained to utilize.

Finally, in response to the 2020 mass police protests, Magnus demonstrated that the TPD was one of the nation's first departments to implement the "8 can't wait project"[57] in conjunction with Campaign Zero.[58] The eight policies the TPD implemented, before the summer of 2020, to reduce use of force include:

55 See www.themarshallproject.org/documents/2082979-final-report-of-the-presidents-task-force-on
56 See www.tucsonaz.gov/police/general-orders
57 See https://8cantwait.org/
58 Campaign Zero was launched online in August 2015 and provided ten proposals to reduce officer-involved shootings and misuse of force. See www.joincampaignzero.org/

1 A ban on chokeholds
2 Requirements for de-escalation
3 Requirements for warnings to be given before shooting
4 Requirements to exhaust alternatives before shooting
5 Requirements for officers to intervene if fellow officers are using excessive force
6 A ban on shooting at moving vehicles
7 Establishing a force continuum (see PERF solutions in the Ramsey chapter)
8 Requirements for comprehensive reporting of use of force incidents

In the summer of 2020, only San Francisco was rated comparable to the TPD in the full implementation of the "8 can't wait" initiative.[59] Other police agencies throughout the country only partially implemented the given eight policies.

In-Custody Deaths

In the spring/summer of 2020, Magnus and the TPD were the center of scrutiny after they experienced an in-custody death on April 21st but did not publicize the incident until June 23rd. The added scrutiny came because the death occurred a month before George Floyd in Minneapolis. Magnus forced the resignation of the three officers involved in the in-custody death due to multiple policies being violated. He also took personal responsibility for his delay in reviewing the officers' body-worn cameras and offered his resignation to Mayor Regina Romero (Photo 7.3).[60]

However, Mayor Romero declined his offer to resign. On June 30, 2020, the mayor approved a new TPD policy, which reduced any delays in details released to the public related to in-custody deaths. Unfortunately, the new policy was put into immediate use from an incident on August 4, 2020, when 29-year-old Jesus Gutierrez died of an overdose after being handcuffed in the backyard of a Tucson man who called to report a trespasser (Jess, 2020). In this incident,

Photo 7.3 Tucson Chief Chris Magnus on May 23, 2018.
Photo from Mamta Popat/Arizona Daily Star.

59 See https://8cantwait.org/compare/
60 Romero was elected the first Latina woman Mayor of Tucson in November 2019 and the only Latina Mayor in the 50 largest U.S. cities.

the publicly released body-worn camera footage showed officers turning Gutierrez on his side, administering Narcan, which all TPD officers carry, removing handcuffs, and administering CPR. Magnus complimented the officers' actions in this incident and released the body-worn camera video, not because of a violation of internal policies but to be transparent.

Officer actions in the August in-custody death differ from the April 21st flashpoint incident dealt with the death of 27-year-old Carlos Ingram-Lopez after his grandmother called 911 and reported that he was naked and acting erratically. Body-worn cameras showed officers restrained Lopez in a garage and placed him face down while he screamed, groaned, and then died. A subsequent autopsy determined that Lopez died of cardiac arrest caused by a high amount of cocaine and a preexisting heart condition. As he has done in the past, Magnus met with the Lopez family to express his condolences and called the event a "terrible tragedy." In August 2020, the family filed a civil suit against Tucson for $10 million. However, the Pima County State's Attorney's office issued a 14-page memorandum that explained their decision to decline the criminal prosecution of the three officers who resigned.

On July 9th, Magnus demonstrated further transparency by writing an article for the *Arizona Daily Star* to explain the TPD process, ongoing reform efforts, and to answer his critics. Magnus (2020) writes:

> *The practice of making public notifications about such deaths varies greatly among police agencies around the country. To the best of our knowledge, for at least the last decade, TPD has not previously provided automatic public notifications about in-custody deaths unless requested (these investigations become public records at the conclusion of the criminal and administrative inquiries and any associated disciplinary appeal rights). In-custody deaths are rare and require further investigation to understand what happened. In addition, it has been our practice to defer to the wishes of the family for privacy.*
>
> *Going forward, in order to meet the public's need for immediate transparency, if there is an in-custody death we will release information about these deaths even though it may be preliminary and incomplete. Barring exceptional circumstances involving constitutional rights, statutory prohibitions, or other legal requirements, we will also release body-worn camera footage within 72 hours.*
>
> *This new approach is not without possible negative consequences. Releasing information before an investigation is complete can compromise both criminal and administrative investigations, potentially invalidating disciplinary actions and improperly influencing criminal charging decisions by prosecuting authorities.*

In addition to notifying the community about the policy changes regarding in-custody deaths, Magnus released four reports and videos of other in-custody deaths that occurred with TPD officers during the past ten years. He showed that the events are rare, complicated, and tragic when the police have to use force within departmental policy.

Lastly, Magnus did not stop simply because the prosecution declined to file charges against the officers involved. He called for a Sentinel Event Review to bring together 15 diverse individuals to review the TPD policies. The review board intentionally included various leaders who were medical professionals, mental health providers, civic leaders, police union representatives, police critics, and academics. Leaders of the review board included John Hollway and Michael Scott. Hollway, associate dean from the University of Pennsylvania law school, also served as the executive director of the Quattrone Center for the Fair Administration of Justice. Scott, director of the Center for Problem-Oriented Policing at Arizona State University, is also discussed in the Appendix to the chapter on O.W. Wilson. The group eventually came up with 53 recommendations and an 80-page report to improve the TPD. The final report called for improved training for both officers and dispatch providers, tracking arrests with particular emphasis on minority populations, and monitoring new restraint techniques to limit the misuse of force (Alaimo, 2020). Both Hollway and Scott commented that the review process brought about by Magnus was groundbreaking and could be compared to what occurs through the aviation community when a commercial aircraft crashes. The Sentinel Event Review Board offered Tucson what Minneapolis failed to provide in the aftermath of George Floyd's in-custody death, a comprehensive and a painful, transparent effort to understand what went wrong and what could be done to avoid future in-custody deaths (Doyle, 2020). This process moves beyond merely looking for the racist cop to blame for the incident and looks at how the whole process, from dispatch to custody situations, puts both officers and citizens at-risk.

Conclusions

Chris Magnus provides an example of a twenty-first-century police leader who understands police reform lessons from all the former police leaders detailed in this book: Roosevelt, Vollmer, Wilson, Bratton, Harrington, and Ramsey. He is also the only active chief of the seven written about during the publication of this book. The following represents examples of police reform that Magnus shares with each of the police leaders detailed in this book. These reforms measures and leadership approaches can be helpful as it relates to the 2020 mass police protests.

1 Roosevelt was an outside police reformer, as was Magnus. Roosevelt's midnight rambles allowed him to understand poverty and immigration at the ground level while also looking to hold his officers accountable. For many years, Magnus lived in inner-city Richmond and commuted to work on his bike. He stressed the importance of forming relationships with the lower-class and immigrant populations while staying focused on corruption and misuse of force. This outreach was evident in his refuge liaison program in Fargo, his community policing success in Richmond, and his policy changes regarding Tucson's use of force.
2 Vollmer would undoubtedly have been intrigued and likely supportive, as was Magnus, of Boggan's creative outreach work through the ONS. This social work outreach perspective, directed at the specific problem of youth gun violence, fits into Vollmer's focus on a primary police mission directed toward crime prevention. Sir Robert Peel established this same mission in London with the 1829 Metropolitan Police Act. Vollmer was also supportive of using the newest advances and technology in policing, as Magnus demonstrated through his use of CompStat, Shot-Spotter®, and other predictive policing capabilities.
3 Wilson was a reform leader who stressed the importance of getting politics out of police and knew that politicians will always have some role in how laws get enforced. Magnus understood Wilson's lessons regarding political influence on policing and the need to communicate effectively with political leaders. Like Wilson, Magnus has been seen as a national leader in law enforcement and asked to address Congress during both the Obama and Trump Administrations. Police chiefs have always maintained a tenuous balance between their leadership roles and local political leaders' whims. Both Wilson and Magnus were fortunate to have the support of critical political leaders. However, as change agents, they both also faced their share of critics. These critics' power was evident with Wilson's departures from Fullerton and Wichita and academic challenges at the UC-Berkeley. For Magnus, his critics came through unsuccessful lawsuits filed against him that alleged he had created a hostile work environment. Magnus is also a follower of Herman Goldstein and the history of how problem-oriented policing evolved out of Wilson's reform efforts. He encourages officers to find solutions to identified problems while

understanding the long-term need for analysis and responses linked to the most relevant community stakeholders.

4 Bratton and Kelling's version of broken windows policing has historically been misused. Magnus is supportive of the more precise use of this approach. Broken windows policing does not call for a generalized crackdown on any behavior that is perceived as disorder. Instead, twenty-first-century police leaders recognize that crackdowns are temporary. Instead, stop, question, and possible frisk strategies should be used within precision policing as directed toward specific behaviors that generate fear or perceptions of crime. Examples from Bratton and Kelling include crackdowns specifically on aggressive panhandling, turnstile jumpers, and citizen behavior that equate to intimidation. For Magnus, broken windows policing has to be connected to community policing and the importance of talking to the community to determine their perceptions of disorder. After persuading the community to become vested stakeholders in the *turnaround*, the title of Bratton's biography, the social/physical environment can be changed to make it less hospitable to crime and disorder.

5 Harrington was an insider to the Portland Police Bureau when she was named the chief, but in a way, she was the largest outsider that the historically masculine field of policing had in 1985. As the first openly gay male chief to be married, Magnus also challenged the stereotype of policing in America. Harrington shut down the drug unit when she determined that they were not accountable. Magnus shut down the RPD "street teams" and the "cowboy" image of undercover officers that would routinely roust anybody walking around in high-crime neighborhoods in the hopes that they might have a weapon, drugs, or outstanding warrant. These were the types of failed zero-tolerance policing strategies that both Harrington and Magnus sought to avoid.

6 Ramsey has been on the national stage for police reform during the past couple of decades, and Magnus has frequently been called to that same national stage. Both have served on numerous federal task forces and pushed for full implementation of community policing throughout the departments they have led. They continue to contribute to the PERF and develop evidence-based practices for improving police behavior well into the twenty-first century.

7 Magnus stands alone as the only active chief of the seven selected for this book. His external Sentinel Event Review Board has helped the police answer its contemporary critics and suggest reform to prevent future in-custody death. This review process offered the Tucson community far more than most other departments provided in the aftermath of in-custody deaths. Importantly, Magnus's leadership allowed changes to occur based on external feedback, so the department enhanced its accountability.

Tables 7.1–7.3 depict lists of police leaders from Fargo, Richmond, and Tucson.

Table 7.1 Fargo, North Dakota Police Marshals

Years	*Name*
1875–1876	John Haggart
1876–1877	Henry O'Neil
1877–1878	Patrick Devitt
1878–1879	Joe Moran
1879–1880	C.S. Foster

Table 7.2 Fargo, North Dakota Police Chiefs

Years	*Name*
1881–1882	George Holes (Marshal/Chief)
1882–1883	John Bartley
1883–1887	Tim Garvey
1888–1891	Richard Fields
1892–1893	Gabriel Grant
1894–1896	Patrick Barnes
1896–1898	William Best
1898–1902	Fred Bowers
1902–1903	Frank Regan
1903–1906	Samuel Gowland
1906–1907	Cleveland Waide
1908–1909	Gabriel Grant
1910–1911	George Bowers
1912–1913	Conrad Keefe
1913–1915	James Bingham
1915–1917	Chauncey Troyer
1917–1929	Louis Dahlgren
1929–1931	Edward Madison
1931–1946	Charles Albright
1946–1946	Oscar Peterson
1946–1949	Loyd Jester
1949–1953	Edward Nelson
1953–1963	J. Walter Olson
1963–1966	J. Dwight Woodley
1966–1986	Edwin Anderson
1986–1989	W. Douglas Franks
1989–1999	Ronald Raftevold
1999–2006	**Chris Magnus**
2006–2015	Keith Ternes
2015–2020	David Todd
2020–	David Zibolski

Table 7.3 Richmond, California Police Chiefs

Years	*Names*
1909–1914	James Arnold
1914–1919	Charles Walker
1919–1924	W.H. Wood
1924–1933	Dan Cox
1933–1947	Lewis Jones
1948–1949	Wymann Vernon[i]
1949–1955	Ernest Phipps
1955–1968	Charles Brown
1968–1971	Robert Murphy

i Vernon graduated from the University of California and was a reform chief for the Oakland PD following several corruption scandals. He spent one year on leave helping to reform the RPD. He led the Oakland PD until 1959 pushing out much of the corruption.

Table 7.3 Cont.

Years	*Names*
1971–1974	Lourn Phelps
1974–1983	Leo Garfield
1983–1993	Earnest Clements
1994–1998	William Lansdowne
1998–1999	Edward Duncan
1999–2003	Joseph Samuels, Jr.
2003–2004	Charles Bennett (interim)
2005–2006	Terry Hudson (interim)
2006–2016	**Chris Magnus**
2016–2019	Allwyn Brown
2019–	Bisa French[ii]

Tables 7.4 and 7.5 represent police leaders from Tucson, Arizona.

Table 7.4 Tucson, Arizona Police Marshals

Years	*Name*
1871–1871	William Morgan[i]
1871–1873	John Miller
1871–1873	Francis Hodges
1873–1873	John Thayer[ii]
1873–1875	Francisco Esparza

Table 7.5 Tucson, Arizona Police Chiefs

Years	*Name*
1876–1879 & 1881–1885	Adolph Buttner[i]
1877–1877 & 1879–1881	Isaac Brokaw
1884–1884	Matthew Johnson
1885–1893	William Roache
1893–1893	Lucas Estrella
1894–1894	John Zimmerman
1894–1896	Robert Paul[ii]
15 additional chiefs	*elected positions until 1930
1925–1933	John Dyer[iii]

ii French is the first African-American female chief, her mother being Puerto-Rican, for the RPD and became the youngest captain in the department's history in 2013 at the age of 37. French also served as the public spokeswoman for RPD. At the age of 18, she became a single mother and fought to achieve her life goals. Her husband is an Oakland Police officer. She considered Magnus a mentor and was a vocal advocate for community policing and the Family Justice Center's expansion, an innovative resource center for domestic violence victims.

i Morgan was the first town marshal. He served for only two months before leaving Tucson (Morgan, 1962).

ii Thayer was also a probate judge. He only spent two months as town marshal.

i Buttner, Tucson's first chief, was believed to have died of alcohol consumption on November 7, 1885.

ii See Miller (1956) for details on Chief Paul's encounters with Arizona outlaws.

iii Dryer was the last elected chief. In 1930, the chief position became part of civil service and no longer attached to political elections. During Dryer's tenure, officers were on duty for 12-hour shifts and received $150 a month in pay.

Table 7.5 Cont.

Years	*Name*
1933–1938	Christopher Wollard[iv]
1938–1939	Henry Hilles[v]
1939–1940 & 1945–1957	Don Hays[vi]
1940–1944	Harold Wheeler
1945–1945	Jesse Ingle
1956–1957	Paul Bohart
1957–1969	Bernard Garmire[vii]
1969–1981	William Gilkinson[viii]
1981–1992	Peter Ronstadt[ix]
1992–1993	Elaine Hedke[x]
1994–1998	Douglas Smith[xi]
1998–2008	Richard Miranda[xii]
2008–2009	Kermit Miller (acting chief)
2009–2015	Roberto Villaseñor[xiii]
2016–	**Chris Magnus**

References

Alaimo, Carol Ann (2020). Candid assessment propels Tucson police reform effort into national spotlight, experts say. *Tucson.com*. October 5.

Bardacke, Frank (2012). *Trampling out the vintage Cesar Chavez and the two souls of the United Farm Workers*. New York, NY: Verso.

Bay Area News Group (2012). Oakland: Where "the Riders" are today. *East Bay Times*. December 12.

iv John Dillinger was captured in Tucson on January 25, 1935, during Chief Wollard's tenure. Dillinger was brought to a jail in Crown Point, Indiana, for a bank robbery that he committed in East Chicago, Indiana, ten days prior. On March 3, 1935, he escaped from the Crown Point jail and continued to commit additional robberies.

v Hilles served concurrently as Tucson Fire Chief.

vi Hays received a salary of $275 a month as police chief.

vii Garmire died in 2011 at the age of 96. His law enforcement career began in the Indiana State Police and he then reached the assistant chief rank in Fort Wayne, Indiana. From 1950 to 1957, he was the chief in Eau Claire, Wisconsin. Like Vollmer, he was instrumental in facilitating a Police Campus at the University of Arizona that provided Tucson officer opportunities to earn their college degree. After Tucson, Garmire became the chief of the Miami Police Department from 1969 from 1975. He also taught for a number of universities and the FBI Academy.

viii Gilkinson died on January 2, 2020, at the age of 94. In addition to his 30-year police career, with 12 years as chief, he was a veteran of World War II and Korea.

ix Peter Ronstadt's sister is Linda Ronstadt. She became a famous solo recording artist in 1968 with backup musicians that included several members of the Eagles, who formed their band in the 1970s. Peter also sang backup on some of her recordings. Linda was romantically involved with California Governor Jerry Brown and filmmaker George Lucas. In 2014, she was inducted into the Rock and Roll Hall of Fame.

x Hedke became the first female chief in Tucson. After 20 months, the police union had a no-confidence vote, and she resigned and took a leadership position to assist with the annexation program.

xi Smith came to Tucson with 26 years of experience in the Minneapolis Police Department and three years as the chief of the Ann Arbor, Michigan Police Department. After he resigned as Tucson chief, he became a director to the state's High Intensity Drug Trafficking Area group. In 2004, Smith took a position with Dyncorp to help build police agencies in Afghanistan.

xii Miranda retired and became the Tucson city manager until 2014. The pension system allowed him to become one of the highest-paid individuals in Tucson.

xiii Villaseñor is also footnoted in the Ramsey chapter for serving on President Obama's Task Force for 21st Century Policing.

Blau, Francine D. and Christopher Mackie (2017). The economic and fiscal consequences of immigration. National Academies of Sciences, Engineering, and Medicine. National Academies of Sciences, Engineering, and Medicine. *The Economic and Fiscal Consequences of Immigration*. Washington, DC: The National Academies Press.

Bernanke, Ben (2008). The economic outlook. Report for the House of Representatives. Washington, DC: Government Printing Office.

BondGraham, Darwin and Ali Winston (2016). The real reason why Oakland's Police Chief was fired. *East Bay Express*. June 10.

BondGraham, Darwin (2017). The Force fails to tell the real story about OPD. *East Bay Express*. September 13.

Braga, Anthony A., David M. Kennedy, Elin J. Waring, and Anne M. Piehl (2001). Problem-oriented policing, deterrence, and youth violence: An evaluation of Boston's Operation Ceasefire. *Journal of Research in Crime and Delinquency 38*(3): 195–225.

Braga, Anthony and Christopher Winship (2005). Creating an effective foundation to prevent youth violence: Lessons learned from Boston in the 1990s. Boston, MA: Rappaport Institute Policy Brief PB-2005-5, September 26.

Braga, Anthony and David Weisburd (2010). *Policing problem places: Crime hot spots and effective prevention*. New York, NY: Oxford University Press.

Braga, Anthony, Brandon Welsh, and Corey Schnell (2015). Can policing disorder reduce crime? A systematic review and meta-analysis. *Journal of Research in Crime and Delinquency, 52*(4): 567–588.

Brenckenridge, John H. (2018). Civilians on police use-of-force review boards: A delphi study involving six police departments. Masters of Arts thesis in security studies (Homeland Security and Defense) from the Naval Postgraduate School.

Brown, Lee and MaryAnn Wycoff (1987). Policing Houston: Reducing fear and improving service. *Crime and Delinquency 33*: 71–89.

Buerger, Michael E. and Lorraine G. Mazerolle (1998). Third-party policing: A theoretical analysis of an emerging trend. *Justice Quarterly 15*(2): 301–327.

Cases, Angelica (2016). Allwyn Brown sworn in as Richmond's new police chief. *Richmond Confidential*. April 21.

Chaffin, Joshua (2020). Unorthodox Arizona police chief insists reform can work: Tucson's Christopher Magnus supports Black Lives Matter- and opposes calls to 'defund' the police. *Financial Times*. June 23.

Childers, Linda (2015). Richmond anti-violence program recognized as a national model. *California Health Report*. December 28.

Cocoltchos, Christopher (1979). *Invisible government and the viable community: The Ku Klux Klan in Orange Country, California, during the 1920s*. Los Angeles, CA: UCLA.

Cohen, Dov and Richard E. Nisbett (1994). Self-protection and the culture of honor: Explaining southern violence. *Society for Personality and Social Psychology 20*(5): 551–567.

Correal, Annie (2020). Trump can withhold millions from 'sanctuary' states, court rules. *The New York Times*. February 26.

Crump, Ben (2019). *Open season: Legalized genocide of colored people*. New York, NY: HarperCollins Publishers.

Curry, Colleen and Sabina Ghebremedhin (2014). Michael Brown could have survived first 5 shots, last shot killed him, autopsy says. *ABC News*. August 18.

Decker, Scott, Tim Bynum, Jack McDevitt, Amy Farrell and Sean Varano (2008). *Street outreach workers: Best practices and lessons learned*. [Innovative practices from the Charles E. Shannon Jr. community safety initiative series]. Boston, MA: Northeastern University, Institute on Race and Justice Publications, Paper 17.

Doyle, James (2020). Tackling racism in courts and police: Start with the system. *The Crime Report*. September 24.

Early, Steven (2014). California police chief connects cops to the community. *YES! Magazine*. December 1.

Early, Steve (2017). *Refinery town: Big oil, big money, and the remaking of an American city*. Boston, MA: Beacon Press.

Engel, Pamela (2015). The ex-cop who shot Michael Brown a year ago opens up about his life as both an outcast and a hero. *Business Insider.* August 3.

Fridell, Lorie (2017a). Explaining disparity in results across studies assessing racial disparity in police use of force: A research note. *American Journal of Criminal Justice 42*: 502–513.

Fridell, Lorie (2017b). *Producing bias-free policing: A science-based approach.* New York, NY: Springer Publishing.

Fyfe, James, John Goldkamp, Michael White (1997). Strategies for reducing homicide: The comprehensive homicide initiative in Richmond, California. Bureau of Justice Assistance. Washington, DC: U.S. Department of Justice, Office of Justice Programs.

Goldstein, Herman and Michael Scott (2011). Shifting and sharing responsibility for public safety problems. Problem-oriented guides for police, response guide series no. 3, Center for Problem-Oriented Policing: U.S. Department of Justice; University of Wisconsin Legal Studies Research Paper No. 1340.

Halpern, Jake (2015). The cop. *The New Yorker.* August 3.

Hamburger, Tom and Jerry Markon (2014). Ferguson testimony shows inconsistencies, unorthodox forensic practices. *Washington Post.* November 26.

Harless, William (2011). Mayor, police chief pledge tougher stance on blight and banks. *Richmond Confidential.* September 7.

Heifetz, Ronald A. and Marty Linsky (2017). *Leadership on the line: Staying alive through the dangers of leading.* Boston, MA: Harvard Business Review Press.

Hemenway, David (1997). Survey research and self-defense gun use: An explanation of extreme overestimates. *Journal of Criminal Law and Criminology 87*(4): 1430–1445.

Holzkamm, Tim E. (2001). *The history and growth of the city of Fargo: Historic context study.* Fargo, ND: Fargo Historic Preservation Commission.

Huguet, Rachel, Janet Li, Caroline Servat, and Katharine Stofer (2016). Cost benefit analysis: Operation peacemaker. USC Price School of Public Policy. Unpublished Report.

International Association of Chiefs of Police (1995). Murder in America: Recommendations from the IACP Murder Summit. Washington, DC: U.S. Department of Justice – National Institute of Justice.

Jackson, Thomas (2017). *Policing Ferguson, policing America: What really happened – and what the country can learn from it.* New York, NY: Skyhorse Publishing.

Jess, Steve (2020). Tucson man dies in police custody. *Arizona Public Media.* August 4.

Johnson, Chip (2003). A Pandora's box opens in Richmond/Police force depleted by several scandals. *SF Gate.* May 26.

Kelling, George L. and James Q. Wilson (1982). Broken windows: The police and neighborhood safety. *Atlantic Monthly 249*(3): 29–38.

Kennedy, David, Anne Piehl, and Anthony Braga (1996). Youth violence in Boston: Gun markets, serious youth offenders, and a use-reduction strategy. *Law and Contemporary Problems. 59*: 147–196.

Kennedy, David (1997). Pulling levers: Chronic offenders, high-crime settings, and a theory of prevention. *Valparaiso University Law Review 31*: 449–484.

Kennedy, David, Anthony Braga and Anne Piehl (1997). The (un)known universe: Mapping gangs and gang violence in Boston. In David Weisburd and Thomas McEwen (Eds.), *Crime mapping and crime prevention.* New York, NY: Criminal Justice Press.

Kennedy, David (1998). Pulling levers: Getting deterrence right. *National Institute of Justice Journal. 236*: 2–8.

Kennedy, David and Anthony Braga (1998). Homicide in Minneapolis: Research for problem solving. *Homicide Studies 2*(3): 263–290.

Kennedy, David and Sue-Lin Wong (2009). The High Point drug market intervention strategy. Washington, DC: U.S. Department of Justice and Office of Community-Oriented Policing.

Kennedy, David (2020). Domestic violence in High Point, North Carolina. In Michael Scott & Ronald Clarke (Eds.), *Problem-oriented policing: Successful case studies (1st Edition).* New York, NY: Routledge.

Kleck, Gary (2015). The impact of gun ownership rates on crime rates: A methodological review of the evidence. *Journal of Criminal Justice, 43*: 40–48.

Kooi, Brandon R. (2010). Theft of scrap metal. Problem-oriented guides for police. Problem-specific guides series (Guide no. 58). Washington, DC: Office of Community-Oriented Policing.

Kooi, Brandon R., Greg Thomas, Clayton Muhammad, and Ignacio Cervantes (2013). Finding Typhoid Mary: Ganging up on offenders who facilitate violence. Presented at the International Problem Oriented Policing Conference as a finalist for the Herman Goldstein Award. October 7, 2013. See https://popcenter.asu.edu/sites/default/files/13-34_aurora_il.pdf

Kooi, Brandon R. (2020). Gang violence in Aurora, Illinois. In Michael Scott & Ronald Clarke (Eds.), *Problem-oriented policing: Successful case studies*. New York, NY: Routledge.

Lane, Roger (1997). Murder in America: A history. Columbus, OH: Ohio State University Press.

Louis, Errol (1983). When the tough get going. *The Harvard Crimson*. October 5.

Lum, Rebecca R. and Karl Fischer (2005). Richmond leaders declare 'emergency' over killings. *Contra Costa Times*. June 17, 2005.

Magnus, Chris (2017). Tucson's police chief: Session's anti-immigrant policies will make cities more dangerous. *The New York Times* (op-ed). December 6.

Magnus, Chris (2020). Changing how we handle deaths in custody: TPD remains a progressive, community-based police force. *The Arizona Daily Star*. July 9.

Maher, Lisa and David Dixon (2001). The cost of crackdowns: Policing Cabramatta's heroin market. *Current Issues in Criminal Justice 13*(1): 5–22.

Marshland, Brad (2015). Richmond police chief: 'All lives matter. That's really what community policing should be about.' *Yahoo! News*. March 22.

Matthay, Ellicott, Kriszta Farkas, Kara Rudolph, Scott Zimmerman, Melissa Barragan, Dana Goin, and Jennifer Ahem (2019). Firearm and nonfirearm violence after Operation Peacemaker fellowship in Richmond, California, 1996–2016. *American Journal of Public Health 109*(11): 1605–1611.

Mazerolle, Lorraine, Angela Higginson, and Elizabeth Eggins. 2016. *Protocol: Third party policing for reducing crime and disorder: A systematic review*. The Campbell Collaboration Library of Systematic Reviews 9. Oslo, Norway: The Campbell Collaboration.

Mazerolle, Lorraine, and Janet Ransley (2005). *Third party policing*. Cambridge, UK: Cambridge University Press.

McKenzie, Lesley (2017). Chris Magnus. *Citizens of Humanity*. June 20.

McLaughlin, Gayle (2018). *Winning Richmond: How a progressive alliance won City Hall*. Brooklyn, NY: Hard Ball Press.

Meares, Tracey and Wesley Skogan (2004). Lawful policing. Faculty Scholarship Series. Paper 521. Yale Law School.

Miller, Joseph (1956). *Arizona: The last frontier*. New York, NY: Hastings House.

Moore, Shirley (2001). *To place our deeds: The African-American community in Richmond, California, 1910–1963*. Berkeley, CA: University of California Press.

Morgan, William (1962). William Morgan: First village marshal of Tucson. *Arizoniana 3*(3): 47–50.

National Academies of Sciences, Engineering and Medicine (2016). The economic and fiscal consequences of immigration. Washington, DC: The National Academies Press.

New Designs for Youth Development (1980). The three o'clock lobby of Michigan: A new designs interview with Chris Magnus. May/June: 14–19.

Office of Juvenile Justice and Delinquency Prevention (1996). Reducing youth gun violence: An overview of programs and initiatives. Program summary. Washington, DC: U.S. Department of Justice, Office of Justice Programs.

Papachristos, Andrew (2009). Murder by structure: Dominance relations and the social structure of gang homicide. *American Journal of Sociology 115*(1): 74–128.

Peters, Jay (2020). George Zimmerman sues Warren and Buttigieg for $265 million over 'defamatory' Travyon Martin tweets. *The Verge*. February 19.

Picard-Fritsche, Sarah and Lenore Cerniglia (2013). *Testing a public health approach to gun violence: An evaluation of Crown Heights Save Our Streets, a replication of the Cure Violence Model*. New York, NY: Center for Court Innovation.

Reeves, Richard and Sarah Holmes (2015). *Guns and Race: The different worlds of black and white Americans*. Washington, DC: The Brookings Institution.

Reisig, Michael (2001). Results from the 2001 traffic enforcement citizen survey. Report submitted to Lansing, Michigan Police Chief Mark Alley. See https://lansingmi.gov/DocumentCenter/View/1033

Rogers, Robert (2012). Ten years after the controversial Cinco de Mayo arrests, Richmond and its police have changed. *The Mercury News*. May 13.

Roman, Catherina, Scott H. Decker, and David C. Pyrooz (2017). Leveraging the pushes and pulls of gang disengagement to improve gang intervention: Findings from three multi-site studies and a review of relevant gang programs. *Journal of Crime and Justice 40*(3): 316–336.

Sallis, James, Neville Owen, and Edwin Fisher (2008). Ecological models of health behavior (pp. 465–486). In Karen Glanz, Barbara Rimer, and Kasisomayajula Viswanath (Eds.), *Health behavior and health education. Theory, research and practice* (4th Edition). San Francisco, CA: Jossey-Bass.

Schmidt, Caitlin (2017). Tucson police officers rarely disciplined for using excessive force. *Tucson.com*. September 22.

Scott, Michael (2003). *The benefits and consequences of police crackdowns. Problem-oriented guides for police*, Response Guide No. 1. Washington, DC: U.S. Department of Justice, Office of Community Oriented Policing Services.

Shanafelt, Callie (2012). Can ceasefire work in Richmond? *California Health Report*. September 24.

Sherman, Lawrence (2007). The power few: Experimental criminology and the reduction of harm. *Journal of Experimental Criminology 3*(4): 299–321.

Siemaszko, Corky (2019). George Zimmerman sues Trayvon Martin's family for $100 million in damages. *NBC News Digital*. December 4.

Skogan, Wesley, Susan Harnett, Natalie Bump, and Jill DuBois (2009). *Evaluation of CeaseFire-Chicago*. Chicago: Northwestern University Institute for Policy Research.

Skogan, Wesley and Kathleen Frydl (2004). *Fairness and effectiveness in policing: The evidence*. Washington, DC: The National Academies Press.

Smith, Lillian (1944). *Strange fruit*. New York, NY: Reynal and Hitchcock.

Smith, Mitch (2017). New Ferguson video adds wrinkle to Michael Brown case. *The New York Times*. March 12.

Spencer, Margaret B., Liz Noll, and Elaine Cassidy (2005). Monetary incentives in support of academic achievement: Results of a randomized field trial involving high-achieving, low-resource, ethnically diverse urban adolescents. *Evaluation Review, 29*(3): 199–222.

Spiker, Steve, Junious Williams, Rachel Diggs, Bill Heiser, Nic J. Aultson (2007). An analysis of violent crime in Richmond, California from January 1, 2005 to December 31, 2006. *Urban Strategies Council*. February 7.

Taylor, Ralph (2001). *Breaking away from broken windows: Evidence from Baltimore neighborhoods and the nationwide fight against crime, grime, fear and decline*. Washington, DC: The National Institute of Justice.

Toland, John (1995). *The Dillinger days*. Lebanon, IN: Hachette Books.

Trojanowicz, Robert and David Carter (1998). *Philosophy and role of community policing*. Rockville, MD: U.S. Department of Justice, Office of Justice Programs, The National Institute of Justice.

Trojanowicz, Robert and Bonnie Bucqueroux (1991). Community policing and the challenge of diversity. National Center for Community Policing – School of Criminal Justice at Michigan State University. National Criminal Justice Reference Service (NCJRS).

Tyler, Tom (2001). Public trust and confidence in legal authorities: What do majority and minority groups members want from the law and legal institutions? *Behavioral Sciences and the Law 19*:215–235.

Tyler, Tom (2004). Enhancing police legitimacy. *Annals of the American Academy of Political and Social Science 593*:84–99.

Waldhotz, Rachel (2012). City has spent $4.5 million defending against discrimination lawsuit. *Richmond Confidential*. April 13.

Weisburd, David L., Cody W. Telep, Joshua C. Hinkle, and John E. Eck (2010). Is problem-oriented policing effective in reducing crime and disorder? Findings from a Campbell systematic review. *Criminology & Public Policy 9*(1): 139–172.

Weisburd, David and John Eck (2004). What can police do to reduce crime, disorder, and fear? *Annals of the American Academy of Political and Social Science 593*: 42–65.

White, Michael, James Fyfe, John Goldkamp, Suzanne Campbell (2000). *Re-defining the police response to homicide: Assessing the Richmond, California comprehensive homicide initiative*. Philadelphia, PA: *Crime and Justice Research Institute*.

White, Michael, James Fyfe, Suzanne Campbell, and John Goldkamp (2003). The police role in preventing homicide: Considering the impact of problem-oriented policing on the prevalence of murder. *Journal of Research in Crime and Delinquency 40*(2): 194–225.

Wolf, Angela, Del Prado Lippman, C. Glesmann, and E. Castro (2015). *Process evaluation for the Office of Neighborhood Safety*. Oakland, CA: National Council on Crime and Delinquency.

Yu, Sung-suk, Daiwon Lee, and Jesenia Pizarro (2020). Illegal firearm availability and violence: Neighborhood-level analysis. *Journal of Interpersonal Violence 35*(19–20): 3986–4012.

Zahn, Margaret and Patricia McCall (1999). Trends and patterns of homicide in the 20th century United States (pp. 9–23). In M. Dwayne Smith and Margaret Zahn (Eds.), Homicide: A sourcebook of social research. Thousands Oaks, CA: Sage Publishing.

Zamora, Jim H. (2005). 4 on council call for a state of emergency: The idea is to raise $2 million to fight violent crime wave. *San Francisco Gate*. June 17.

Zernike, Kate. (2007). Violent crime in cities show sharp surge. *The New York Times*. March 9.

Index

For Product Safety Concerns and Information please contact our EU
representative GPSR@taylorandfrancis.com
Taylor & Francis Verlag GmbH, Kaufingerstraße 24, 80331 München, Germany

www.ingramcontent.com/pod-product-compliance
Ingram Content Group UK Ltd.
Pitfield, Milton Keynes, MK11 3LW, UK
UKHW052217190926
475702UK00006B/1071
* 9 7 8 1 4 9 8 7 6 8 9 2 4 *